W9-AFN-757

THE AMERICAN CITY

The American City

Historical Studies

JAMES F. RICHARDSON **University of Akron**

Xerox College Publishing

Waltham, Massachusetts / Toronto

To my mother, Grace M. Richardson

CONSULTING EDITOR   Irwin Unger, *New York University*

ACKNOWLEDGMENTS

JOSEPH BOSKIN, "The Revolt of the Urban Ghettos, 1964–1967" from *The Annals of the American Academy of Political and Social Science* 382, March 1969: 1–14. Reprinted by permission of The American Academy of Political and Social Science and Joseph Boskin.

ROBERT D. CROSS, Introduction from *The Church and the City, 1865–1910,* edited by Robert D. Cross, copyright © 1967, by The Bobbs-Merrill Company, Inc., reprinted by permission of the publisher.

SCOTT DONALDSON, "City and Country: Marriage Proposals" from *American Quarterly* 20, Fall 1968: 547–566. Copyright, 1968, Trustees of the University of Pennsylvania. Reprinted by permission of *American Quarterly* and Scott Donaldson.

ROBERT M. FOGELSON, "The Quest for Community." Reprinted by permission of the publishers from Robert M. Fogelson, *The Fragmented Metropolis: Los Angeles 1850–1930.* Cambridge, Mass.: Harvard University Press, Copyright, 1967, by the President and Fellows of Harvard College.

HERBERT J. GANS, "Urbanism and Suburbanism as Ways of Life: A Re-evaluation of Definitions" from *Human Behavior and Social Processes* edited by Arnold M. Rose. Copyright © 1962 by Houghton Mifflin Company. Reprinted by permission of Houghton Mifflin Company.

NATHAN GLAZER AND DANIEL P. MOYNIHAN, "How the Catholics Lost Out to the Jews in New York Politics." Reprinted from *Beyond the Melting Pot* by Nathan Glazer and Daniel P. Moynihan by permission of The M.I.T. Press, Cambridge, Massachusetts. Copyright © 1963, 1970 by the Joint Center for Urban Studies of the Massachusetts Institute of Technology and the President and Fellows of Harvard College. This material appeared as an article in *New York* 3, August 10, 1970: 39–49 and is reprinted as it appeared there with the exception of illustrations, captions, and editorial insertions.

OSCAR HANDLIN, "The Modern City as a Field of Historical Study." Reprinted from *The Historian and the City* edited by Oscar Handlin and John Burchard by permission of The M.I.T. Press, Cambridge, Massachusetts. Copyright © 1963 by the Massachusetts Institute of Technology and the President and Fellows of Harvard College.

JAMES A. HENRETTA, "Economic Development and Social Structure in Colonial Boston" from *The William and Mary Quarterly,* 3rd ser., 22, January 1965: 75–92. Reprinted by permission of James A. Henretta.

KENNETH T. JACKSON, "The Urban Klansman" from *The Ku Klux Klan in the City, 1915–1930* by Kenneth T. Jackson. Copyright © 1967 by Oxford University Press, Inc. Reprinted by permission.

RAYMOND L. KOCH, "Politics and Relief in Minneapolis During the 1930s" from *Minnesota History* 41, December 1968: 153–170. Reprinted by permission of *Minnesota History* and Raymond L. Koch.

ERIC L. MCKITRICK, "The Study of Corruption" from *Political Science Quarterly* 72, December 1957: 502–514. Reprinted by permission of Eric L. McKitrick.

ZANE L. MILLER, "Boss Cox's Cincinnati: A Study in Urbanization and Politics, 1880–

1914" from *The Journal of American History* 54, March 1968: 823–838. Reprinted by permission of the Organization of American Historians.

DAVID MONTGOMERY, "The Working Classes of the Pre-Industrial American City, 1780–1830" from *Labor History* 9, Winter 1968: 3–22. Reprinted by permission of *Labor History*.

HUMBERT S. NELLI, "Italians in Urban America." Unpublished paper. Reprinted by permission of Humbert S. Nelli.

GILBERT OSOFSKY, "Harlem Tragedy: An Emerging Slum" from *Harlem: The Making of a Ghetto* by Gilbert Osofsky. Copyright, 1963, 1965, 1966 by Gilbert Osofsky. Reprinted by permission of Harper & Row, Publishers, Inc.

JOHN W. PRATT, "Boss Tweed's Public Welfare Program" from *The New York Historical Society Quarterly* 45, October 1961: 396–411. Reprinted by permission of The New York Historical Society and John W. Pratt.

GIDEON SJOBERG, "The Preindustrial City" from *The American Journal of Sociology* 60, January 1955: 438–445. Copyright 1955, by the University of Chicago. Reprinted by permission of The University of Chicago Press and Gideon Sjoberg.

BAYRD STILL, "Patterns of Mid-Nineteenth Century Urbanization in the Middle West" from *The Mississippi Valley Historical Review* 28, September 1941: 187–206. Reprinted by permission of the Organization of American Historians.

GEORGE ROGERS TAYLOR, "The Beginnings of Mass Transportation in Urban America" from *The Smithsonian Journal of History* 1, Summer 1966: 35–50 and 1 (No. 3), 1966: 31–54. Reprinted by permission of *The Smithsonian Journal of History* and George Rogers Taylor.

RICHARD C. WADE, "Urban Life in Western America, 1790–1830" from *The American Historical Review* 64, October 1958: 14–30. Reprinted by permission of Richard C. Wade.

SAM BASS WARNER, JR., "If All the World Were Philadelphia: A Scaffolding for Urban History, 1774–1930" from *The American Historical Review* 74, October 1968: 26–43. Reprinted by permission of Sam Bass Warner, Jr.

JAMES WEINSTEIN, "The Small Businessman as Big Businessman: The City Commissioner and Management Movements" from *The Corporate Ideal in the Liberal State* by James Weinstein. Copyright © 1968 by James Weinstein. Reprinted by permission of Beacon Press and James Weinstein.

James Mingle, a graduate student at the University of Akron, gave the selections and the headnotes a close and perceptive reading. Arlene Lane and the secretarial staff of our Urban Studies department provided excellent service. My wife Marie gave the project her strong moral support and our children supplied their amused tolerance.

Contents

Introduction

In the last decade urban history has "arrived" in American colleges and universities, and increasingly in the nation's secondary schools. The growing academic interest reflects the impact of the census returns and the visual evidence available to any observer of American society. Both of these attest to the growing urbanization of the American people. As a group, urban historians seek to enrich our conception of the American past by raising questions and treating subjects too long neglected. They also hope to contribute to a more comprehensive view of our present situation and the probable and possible future. Historians believe that we cannot expect to understand where our cities are now, and where they are likely to go in the future, unless we have a clear sense of their past, of how things came to be what they are, and what urban trends are likely to prevail for at least the immediate future. If, as many Americans now seem to, we regard the urban present as intolerable and the probable future as horrendous, we should remind ourselves that action without thought is dangerous at best and that the disciplined and creative use of intellect is an indispensable ingredient for any program of positive change.

Despite the intrinsic interest of the subject and the long-standing importance of cities in American society, professional historians came slowly to the study of cities as institutions and of urbanization as a social process. Some early twentieth-century historians limited their view of history to the study of past politics; others devoted their scholarly lives to supporting or attacking Frederick Jackson Turner's famous thesis on the pivotal role of the frontier. The terms *urban* and *urbanization* may have smacked too much of the social sciences for those historians who thought of their discipline as an art or a humanity and who wanted to avoid any contamination from statistics, model-building, ideal types, or sociological jargon. Whatever the reasons, it is only in the last forty years that professional historians have tried to raise and answer the perplexing questions arising from urban growth and its consequences.

In that period a rich literature has developed, although one that does not lend itself readily to synthesis and generalization. Arthur Schlesinger, Sr.'s *The Rise of the City, 1878–1898,* published in 1933, a pioneering work of descriptive social history, gave a great fillip to systematic study of urban history. In its wake professional scholars began to produce comprehensive histories of particular cities, often called urban biographies. Among the more important of these are Bessie Pierce's three-volume study of Chicago; Blake McKelvey's four-volume history of Rochester, New York; Bayrd Still's *Milwaukee*; and Constance Green's two-volume history of Washington, D.C. Two of Schlesinger's students, Carl Bridenbaugh and Richard C.

Wade, produced important comparative histories of groups of cities. Bridenbaugh's two volumes, *Cities in the Wilderness* and *Cities in Revolt,* provided a sweeping survey of the five major colonial seaports from their founding to the onset of the American Revolution. Wade's first book, *The Urban Frontier,* depicted the early history of the trans-Appalachian cities, Pittsburgh, Lexington, Louisville, Cincinnati, and St. Louis. His second book, *Slavery in the Cities: The South, 1820–1860,* not only told the story of the rise and fall of this "peculiar institution" in the urban perimeter of the pre–Civil War South, but supplied considerable information and insight into the general patterns of southern urbanism. A third Schlesinger student, Oscar Handlin, published a model social history in his *Boston's Immigrants,* which examined the confrontation between the Irish and the Yankees in Boston from 1790 to 1865. A second edition extended the terminal date to 1880. In his years at Harvard, Handlin has trained a number of students who have given us some of our best work on urban and social history. Among them are Sam Bass Warner, Jr., whose *Streetcar Suburbs: The Process of Growth in Boston, 1870–1900* blazed new trails in the study of the interaction between popular values, economic and social change, and technology; and Stephan Thernstrom, whose *Poverty and Progress* restructured the question of social mobility in the nineteenth century. Bayrd Still at New York University and Richard C. Wade at the University of Chicago have also directed the work of a number of students who have made significant contributions to the corpus of urban scholarship.

A few brave scholars have attempted overviews of American urban history. In addition to his study of Rochester, Blake McKelvey has written two tightly packed general works, *The Urbanization of America, 1860–1915,* and *The Emergence of Metropolitan America, 1915–1966.* The latter is unfortunately titled, since McKelvey's theme is the relationship between the federal government and the major cities. Constance Green's *American Cities in the Growth of the Nation* provides a number of gracefully written sketches which attempt to relate major themes in American history to the stories of particular cities. The most successful urban history synthesis so far published is *A History of Urban America* by Charles Glaab and A. Theodore Brown.

These few attempts aside, most of the scholarship produced to date can be classified as case studies, histories of individual cities, or, more narrowly, examinations of particular facets of single cities. There are two major problems associated with case studies: how representative is the city or portion thereof being studied, and how do we achieve comparability and make valid generalizations from a number of separate cases? Unless we know the history of all or most cities, we are hard put to determine the representativeness of the subject. With some notable exceptions, until the last few years, scholars associated with major urban universities have done most of the writing. This fact has tended to focus their attention on a few select urban centers.

Thus, there are many valuable works on the history of Boston, Chicago, and New York, but there is little published on such important places as Cleveland, St. Louis, or Atlanta; to say nothing of a host of medium and smaller cities, though taken together these contain a majority of the urban population. Until we know more about the Akrons and the Omahas, our conceptualization of urban history will be one-sided and incomplete.

A further difficulty is that urban historians do not agree on the content or methodology of their specialty. As Charles Glaab has put it, "Is urban history the history of cities, the history of urbanization as a process, or the history of anything that takes place in an urban setting? The question has not yet been answered."[1] A number of scholars have suggested definitions and procedures in theoretical writings, but these do not yet seem to have influenced the practice of their colleagues.

The selection and construction of this anthology reflect these considerations. I have put this book together with the undergraduate student of American urban and social history in mind and have therefore avoided bibliographical and theoretical pieces of interest primarily to professors and graduate students. Those interested in such works can, and by all means should, look them up in the library. Since it would be impossible to cover adequately all facets of urban history in a volume of reasonable length, I have concentrated on the social history of cities. The reader will find in the pages that follow considerable material on racial and ethnic groups, social class, residential mobility, and social structure. In urban studies the lines between disciplines are imprecise and often meaningless, so I have included the work of sociologists as well as historians. Taken together, I hope the essays provide a coherent view of the developing social patterns in urban America, and that they give the reader a sense of the range, scope, and quality of recent scholarship.

■ ■ ■ ■ **Notes**

1 Charles N. Glaab, "The Historian and the American Urban Tradition," *Wisconsin Magazine of History* 46 (Autumn 1963): 13–25.

■ ■ ■ ■ **For Further Reading**

Bridenbaugh, Carl. *Cities in Revolt*. New York: Alfred A. Knopf, 1955.

———. *Cities in the Wilderness*. New York: Ronald Press, 1938.

Davis, Allen F. "The American Historian vs. The City." *The Social Studies* 56 (March 1965): 91–96; (April 1965): 127–135.

Glaab, Charles N. "The Historian and the American Urban Tradition." *Wisconsin Magazine of History* 46 (Autumn 1963): 13–25.

Glaab, Charles N., and A. Theodore Brown. *A History of Urban America*. New York: The Macmillan Co., 1967.

Green, Constance M. *American Cities in the Growth of the Nation*. Tuckahoe, N. Y.: John De Graff, 1957.

———. *Washington*. 2 vols. Princeton: Princeton University Press, 1962–1963.

Handlin, Oscar. *Boston's Immigrants*. Cambridge, Mass.: Harvard University Press, 1941. The second edition was published in 1959.

Hoover, Dwight W. "The Diverging Paths of American Urban History." *American Quarterly* 20 (Summer 1968): 296–317.

Lubove, Roy. "The Urbanization Process: An Approach to Historical Research." *Journal of the American Institute of Planners* 33 (January 1967): 33–39.

McKelvey, Blake. *The Emergence of Metropolitan America: 1915–1966*. New Brunswick, N. J.: Rutgers University Press, 1968.

———. *Rochester*. 4 vols. The first three volumes were published by Harvard University Press, 1945–1956, and the fourth by Christopher Press, 1961.

———. *The Urbanization of America*. New Brunswick, N. J.: Rutgers University Press, 1963.

Miller, Zane L. *Boss Cox's Cincinnati: Urban Politics in the Progressive Era*. New York: Oxford University Press, 1968.

Pierce, Bessie L. *A History of Chicago*. 3 vols. New York: Alfred A. Knopf, 1937–1957.

Richardson, James F. *The New York Police: Colonial Times to 1901*. New York: Oxford University Press, 1970.

Scheiner, Seth M. *Negro Mecca: A History of the Negro in New York City, 1865–1920*. New York: New York University Press, 1965.

Still, Bayrd. *Milwaukee: The History of a City*. Madison: State Historical Society of Wisconsin, 1948. Revised edition 1967.

Thernstrom, Stephan. *Poverty and Progress: Social Mobility in a Nineteenth-Century City*. Cambridge, Mass.: Harvard University Press, 1964.

Wade, Richard C. *Slavery in the Cities*. New York: Oxford University Press, 1964.

———. *The Urban Frontier*. Cambridge, Mass.: Harvard University Press, 1959.

Warner, Sam B., Jr. *Streetcar Suburbs: The Process of Growth in Boston, 1870–1900*. Cambridge, Mass.: M.I.T. Press and Harvard University Press, 1962.

———. *The Private City: Philadelphia in Three Periods of Its Growth*. Philadelphia: University of Pennsylvania Press, 1968.

1
The Preindustrial City

GIDEON SJOBERG

Gideon Sjoberg's essay on the preindustrial city may seem out of place in a collection on American urban history. Yet the picture he paints of cities in India and other nonindustrial societies helps to point up the special features of the modern or industrial city in the United States and Europe. Thus, while all cities have certain characteristics in common, there are distinct differences among them deriving from the level of technology and the economic and social organization. In differentiating among his urban types, Sjoberg lays heavy emphasis on the source of power, whether animate or inanimate, used to perform work in the city. The development of inanimate sources of power, he notes, helped bring about changes in land use, social structure, and the spread of mass education.

In some ways a more useful term than preindustrial *might be* premodern, *especially in contrasting Sjoberg's model with the American city of the eighteenth and early nineteenth centuries. Colonial Boston did not employ steam power, yet literacy and secularism, in the sense of the separation of religion from other areas of life, were considerably more widespread than in Sjoberg's traditional cities. The considerable transformation of European society from the fifteenth century onward formed the legacy of eighteenth-century Boston. Movable type, the Newtonian revolution in physics, and the development of sophisticated instruments of trade all impinged upon the American town and made it quite different in cultural patterns and social structure from Benares or Peiping.*

■ ■ ■ ■ For Further Reading

Gideon Sjoberg, *The Preindustrial City* (New York: The Free Press, 1960) is a book-length exposition of the ideas presented in this article. Lewis Mumford, *The City in History* (New York: Harcourt, Brace & World, 1961) is indispensable for anyone interested in cities in particular and civilization in general. You may not always agree with Mumford, but he is always stimulating and provocative and usually wise.

■ In the past few decades social scientists have been conducting field studies in a number of relatively non-Westernized cities. Their recently acquired knowledge of North Africa and various parts of Asia, combined with what was already learned, clearly indicates that these cities are not like typical cities of the United States and other highly industrialized areas but are much more like those of medieval Europe. Such communities are termed herein "preindustrial," for they have arisen without stimulus from that form of production which we associate with the European industrial revolution.

Recently Foster, in a most informative article, took cognizance of the preindustrial city.[1] His primary emphasis was upon the peasantry (which he calls "folk"); but he recognized this to be part of a broader social structure which includes the preindustrial city. He noted certain similarities between the peasantry and the city's lower class. Likewise the present author sought to analyze the total society of which the peasantry and the preindustrial city are integral parts.[2] For want of a better term this was called "feudal." Like Redfield's folk (or "primitive") society, the feudal order is highly stable and sacred; in contrast, however, it has a complex social organization. It is characterized by highly developed state and educational and/or religious institutions and by a rigid class structure.

Thus far no one has analyzed the preindustrial city per se, especially as it differs from the industrial-urban community, although Weber, Tönnies, and a few others perceived differences between the two. Yet such a survey is needed for the understanding of urban development in so-called underdeveloped countries and, for that matter, in parts of Europe. Such is the goal of this paper. The typological analysis should also serve as a guide to future research.

Ecological Organization

Preindustrial cities depend for their existence upon food and raw materials obtained from without; for this reason they are marketing centers. And they serve as centers for handicraft manufacturing. In addition, they fulfil important political, religious, and educational functions. Some cities have become specialized; for example, Benares in India and Karbala in Iraq are best known as religious communities, and Peiping in China as a locus for political and educational activities.

The proportion of urbanites relative to the peasant population is small, in some societies about 10 per cent, even though a few preindustrial cities have attained populations of 100,000 or more. Growth has been by slow accretion. These characteristics are due to the nonindustrial nature of the total social order. The amount of surplus food available to support an urban population has been limited by the unmechanized agriculture, transportation facilities utilizing primarily human or animal power, and inefficient methods of food preservation and storage.

The internal arrangement of the preindustrial city, in the nature of the case, is closely related to the city's economic and social structure.[3] Most streets are mere passageways for people and for animals used in transport. Buildings are low and crowded together. The congested conditions, combined with limited scientific knowledge, have fostered serious sanitation problems.

More significant is the rigid social segregation which typically has led to the formation of "quarters" or "wards." In some cities (e.g., Fez, Morocco, and Aleppo, Syria) these were sealed off from each other by walls, whose gates were locked at night. The quarters reflect the sharp local social divisions. Thus ethnic groups live in special sections. And the occupational groupings, some being at the same time ethnic in character, typically reside apart from one another. Often a special street or sector of the city is occupied almost exclusively by members of a particular trade; cities in such divergent cultures as medieval Europe and modern Afghanistan contain streets with names like "street of the goldsmiths." Lower-class and especially "outcaste" groups live on the city's periphery, at a distance from the primary centers of activity. Social segregation, the limited transportation facilities, the modicum of residential mobility, and the cramped living quarters have encouraged the development of well-defined neighborhoods which are almost primary groups.

Despite rigid segregation the evidence suggests no real specialization of land use such as is functionally necessary in industrial-urban communities. In medieval Europe and in other areas city dwellings often serve as workshops, and religious structures are used as schools or marketing centers.[4]

Finally, the "business district" does not hold the position of dominance that it enjoys in the industrial-urban community. Thus, in the Middle East the principal mosque, or in medieval Europe the cathedral, is usually the focal point of community life. The center of Peiping is the Forbidden City.

Economic Organization

The economy of the preindustrial city diverges sharply from that of the modern industrial center. The prime difference is the absence in the former of industrialism which may be defined as that system of production in which *inanimate* sources of power are used to multiply human effort. Preindustrial cities depend for the production of goods and services upon *animate* (human or animal) sources of energy—applied either directly or indirectly through such mechanical devices as hammers, pulleys, and wheels. The industrial-urban community, on the other hand, employs inanimate generators of power such as electricity and steam which greatly enhance the productive capacity of urbanites. This basically new form of energy production, one which requires for its development and survival a special kind of institutional complex, effects striking changes in the ecological, economic, and social organization of cities in which it has become dominant.

Other facets of the economy of the preindustrial city are associated with its particular system of production. There is little fragmentation or specialization of work. The handicraftsman participates in nearly every phase of the manufacture of an article, often carrying out the work in his own home or in a small shop near by and, within the limits of certain guild and community regulations, maintaining direct control over conditions of work and methods of production.

In industrial cities, on the other hand, the complex division of labor requires a specialized managerial group, often extra-community in character, whose primary function is to direct and control others. And for the supervision and co-ordination of the activities of workers, a "factory system" has been developed, something typically lacking in preindustrial cities. (Occasionally centralized production is found in preindustrial cities—e.g., where the state organized slaves for large-scale construction projects.) Most commercial activities, also, are conducted in preindustrial cities by individuals without a highly formalized organization; for example, the craftsman has frequently been responsible for the marketing of his own products. With a few exceptions, the preindustrial community cannot support a large group of middlemen.

The various occupations are organized into what have been termed "guilds."[5] These strive to encompass all, except the elite, who are gainfully employed in some economic activity. Guilds have existed for merchants and handicraft workers (e.g., goldsmiths and weavers) as well as for servants, entertainers, and even beggars and thieves. Typically the guilds operate only within the local community, and there are no large-scale economic organizations such as those in industrial cities which link their members to their fellows in other communities.

Guild membership and apprenticeship are prerequisites to the practice of almost any occupation, a circumstance obviously leading to monopolization. To a degree these organizations regulate the work of their members and the price of their products and services. And the guilds recruit workers into specific occupations, typically selecting them according to such particularistic criteria as kinship rather than universalistic standards.

The guilds are integrated with still other elements of the city's social structure. They perform certain religious functions; for example, in medieval European, Chinese, and Middle Eastern cities each guild had its "patron saint" and held periodic festivals in his honor. And, by assisting members in time of trouble, the guilds serve as social security agencies.

The economic structure of the preindustrial city functions with little rationality, judged by industrial-urban standards. This is shown in the general nonstandardization of manufacturing methods as well as in the products and is even more evident in marketing. In preindustrial cities throughout the world a fixed price is rare; buyer and seller settle their bargain by haggling. (Of course, there are limits above which customers will not buy and below which merchants will not sell.) Often business is conducted in a leisurely manner, money not being the only desired end.

Furthermore, the sorting of goods according to size, weight, and quality is not common. Typical is the adulteration and spoilage of produce. And weights and measures are not standardized: variations exist not only between one city and the next but also within communities, for often different guilds employ their own systems. Within a single city there may be different kinds of currency, which, with the poorly developed accounting and credit systems, signalize a modicum of rationality in the whole of economic action in preindustrial cities.[6]

Social Organization

The economic system of the preindustrial city, based as it has been upon animate sources of power, articulates with a characteristic class structure and family, religious, educational, and governmental systems.

Of the class structure, the most striking component is a literate elite controlling and depending for its existence upon the mass of the populace, even in the traditional cities of India with their caste system. The elite is composed of individuals holding positions in the governmental, religious, and/ or educational institutions of the larger society, although at times groups such as large absentee landlords have belonged to it. At the opposite pole are the masses, comprising such groups as handicraft workers whose goods and services are produced primarily for the elite's benefit.[7] Between the elite and the lower class is a rather sharp schism, but in both groups there are gradations in rank. The members of the elite belong to the "correct" families and enjoy power, property, and certain highly valued personal attributes. Their position, moreover, is legitimized by sacred writings.

Social mobility in this city is minimal; the only real threat to the elite comes from the outside—not from the city's lower classes. And a middle class—so typical of industrial-urban communities, where it can be considered the "dominant" class—is not known in the preindustrial city. The system of production in the larger society provides goods, including food, and services in sufficient amounts to support only a small group of leisured individuals; under these conditions an urban middle class, a semileisured group, cannot arise. Nor are a middle class and extensive social mobility essential to the maintenance of the economic system.

Significant is the role of the marginal or "outcaste" groups (e.g., the Eta of Japan), which are not an integral part of the dominant social system. Typically they rank lower than the urban lower class, performing tasks considered especially degrading, such as burying the dead. Slaves, beggars, and the like are outcastes in most preindustrial cities. Even such groups as professional entertainers and itinerant merchants are often viewed as outcastes, for their rovings expose them to "foreign" ideas from which the dominant social group seeks to isolate itself. Actually many outcaste groups, including some of those mentioned above, are ethnic groups, a fact which further intensifies their isolation. (A few, like the Jews in the predominantly Muslim cities of North Africa, have their own small literate religious elite which, however, enjoys no significant political power in the city as a whole.)

An assumption of many urban sociologists is that a small, unstable kinship group, notably the conjugal unit, is a necessary correlate of city life. But this premise does not hold for preindustrial cities.[8] At times sociologists and anthropologists, when generalizing about various traditional societies, have imputed to peasants typically urban kinship patterns. Actually, in these societies the ideal forms of kinship and family life are most closely approximated by members of the urban literate elite, who are best able to fulfil the exacting requirements of the sacred writings. Kinship and the ability to perpetuate one's lineage are accorded marked prestige in preindustrial cities. Children, especially sons, are highly valued, and polygamy or concubinage or adoption help to assure the attainment of large families. The pre-eminence of kinship is apparent even in those preindustrial cities where divorce is permitted. Thus, among the urban Muslims or urban Chinese divorce is not an index of disorganization; here, conjugal ties are loose and distinctly subordinate to the bonds of kinship, and each member of a dissolved conjugal unit typically is absorbed by his kin group. Marriage, a prerequisite to adult status in the preindustrial city, is entered upon at an early age and is arranged between families rather than romantically, by individuals.

The kinship and familial organization displays some rigid patterns of sex and age differentiation whose universality in preindustrial cities has generally been overlooked. A woman, especially of the upper class, ideally performs few significant functions outside the home. She is clearly subordinate to males, especially her father or husband. Recent evidence indicates that this is true even for such a city as Lhasa, Tibet, where women supposedly have had high status.[9] The isolation of women from public life has in some cases been extreme. In nineteenth-century Seoul, Korea, "respectable" women appeared on the streets only during certain hours of the night when men were supposed to stay at home.[10] Those women in preindustrial cities who evade some of the stricter requirements are members of certain marginal groups (e.g., entertainers) or of the lower class. The role of the urban lower-class woman typically resembles that of the peasant rather than the urban upper-class woman. Industrialization, by creating demands and opportunities for their employment outside the home, is causing significant changes in the status of women as well as in the whole of the kinship system in urban areas.

A formalized system of age grading is an effective mechanism of social control in preindustrial cities. Among siblings the eldest son is privileged. And children and youth are subordinate to parents and other adults. This, combined with early marriage, inhibits the development of a "youth culture." On the other hand, older persons hold considerable power and prestige, a fact contributing to the slow pace of change.

As noted above, kinship is functionally integrated with social class. It also reinforces and is reinforced by the economic organization: the occupations, through the guilds, select their members primarily on the basis of kinship, and much of the work is carried on in the home or immediate vicinity. Such conditions are not functional to the requirements of a highly industrialized society.

The kinship system in the preindustrial city also articulates with a special kind of religious system, whose formal organization reaches fullest development among members of the literate elite.[11] The city is the seat of the key religious functionaries whose actions set standards for the rest of society. The urban lower class, like the peasantry, does not possess the education or the means to maintain all the exacting norms prescribed by the sacred writings. Yet the religious system influences the city's entire social structure. (Typically, within the preindustrial city one religion is dominant; however, certain minority groups adhere to their own beliefs.) Unlike the situation in industrial cities, religious activity is not separate from other social action but permeates family, economic, governmental, and other activities. Daily life is pervaded with religious significance. Especially important are periodic public festivals and ceremonies like Ramadan in Muslim cities. Even distinctly ethnic outcaste groups can through their own religious festivals maintain solidarity.

Magic, too, is interwoven with economic, familial, and other social activities. Divination is commonly employed for determining the "correct" action on critical occasions; for example, in traditional Japanese and Chinese cities, the selection of marriage partners. And nonscientific procedures are widely employed to treat illness among all elements of the population of the preindustrial city.

Formal education typically is restricted to the male elite, its purpose being to train individuals for positions in the governmental, educational, or religious hierarchies. The economy of preindustrial cities does not require mass literacy, nor, in fact, does the system of production provide the leisure so necessary for the acquisition of formal education. Considerable time is needed merely to learn the written language, which often is quite different from that spoken. The teacher occupies a position of honor, primarily because of the prestige of all learning and especially of knowledge of the sacred literature, and learning is traditional and characteristically based upon sacred writings.[12] Students are expected to memorize rather than evaluate and initiate, even in institutions of higher learning.

Since preindustrial cities have no agencies of mass communication, they are relatively isolated from one another. Moreover, the masses within a city are isolated from the elite. The former must rely upon verbal communication, which is formalized in special groups such as storytellers or their counterparts. Through verse and song these transmit upper-class tradition to nonliterate individuals.

The formal government of the preindustrial city is the province of the elite and is closely integrated with the educational and religious systems. It performs two principal functions: exacting tribute from the city's masses to support the activities of the elite and maintaining law and order through a "police force" (at times a branch of the army) and a court system. The police force exists primarily for the control of "outsiders," and the courts support custom and the rule of the sacred literature, a code of enacted legislation typically being absent.

In actual practice little reliance is placed upon formal machinery for regulating social life.[13] Much more significant are the informal controls exerted by the kinship, guild, and religious systems, and here, of course, personal standing is decisive. Status distinctions are visibly correlated with personal attributes, chiefly speech, dress, and personal mannerisms which proclaim ethnic group, occupation, age, sex, and social class. In nineteenth-century Seoul, not only did the upper-class mode of dress differ considerably from that of the masses, but speech varied according to social class, the verb forms and pronouns depending upon whether the speaker ranked higher or lower or was the equal of the person being addressed.[14] Obviously, then, escape from one's role is difficult, even in the street crowds. The individual is ever conscious of his specific rights and duties. All these things conserve the social order in the preindustrial city despite its heterogeneity.

Conclusions

Throughout this paper there is the assumption that certain structural elements are universal for all urban centers. This study's hypothesis is that their form in the preindustrial city is fundamentally distinct from that in the industrial-urban community. A considerable body of data not only from medieval Europe, which is somewhat atypical,[15] but from a variety of cultures supports this point of view. Emphasis has been upon the static features of preindustrial city life. But even those preindustrial cities which have undergone considerable change approach the ideal type. For one thing, social change is of such a nature that it is not usually perceived by the general populace.

Most cities of the preindustrial type have been located in Europe or Asia. Even though Athens and Rome and the large commercial centers of Europe prior to the industrial revolution displayed certain unique features, they fit the preindustrial type quite well.[16] And many traditional Latin-American cities are quite like it, although deviations exist, for, excluding pre-Columbian cities, these were affected to some degree by the industrial revolution soon after their establishment.

It is postulated that industrialization is a key variable accounting for the distinctions between preindustrial and industrial cities. The type of social structure required to develop and maintain a form of production utilizing inanimate sources of power is quite unlike that in the preindustrial city.[17] At the very least, extensive industrialization requires a rational, centralized, extra-community economic organization in which recruitment is based more upon universalism than on particularism, a class system which stresses achievement rather than ascription, a small and flexible kinship system, a system of mass education which emphasizes universalistic rather than particularistic criteria, and mass communication. Modification in any one of these elements affects the others and induces changes in other systems such as those of religion and social control as well. Industrialization, moreover, not only requires a special kind of social structure within the urban community but provides the means necessary for its establishment.

Anthropologists and sociologists will in the future devote increased attention to the study of cities throughout the world. They must therefore recognize that the particular kind of social structure found in cities in the United States is not typical of all societies. Miner's recent study of Timbuctoo,[18] which contains much excellent data, points to the need for recognition of the preindustrial city. His emphasis upon the folk-urban continuum diverted him from an equally significant problem: How does Timbuctoo differ from modern industrial cities in its ecological, economic, and social structure? Society there seems even more sacred and organized than Miner admits.[19] For example, he used divorce as an index of disorganization, but in Muslim society divorce within certain rules is justified by the sacred literature. The studies of Hsu and Fried would have considerably more significance had the authors perceived the generality of their findings. And, once the general structure of the preindustrial city is understood, the specific cultural deviations become more meaningful.

Beals notes the importance of the city as a center of acculturation.[20] But an understanding of this process is impossible without some knowledge of the preindustrial city's social structure. Although industrialization is clearly advancing throughout most of the world, the social structure of preindustrial civilizations is conservative, often resisting the introduction of numerous industrial forms. Certainly many cities of Europe (e.g., in France or Spain) are not so fully industrialized as some presume; a number of preindustrial patterns remain. The persistence of preindustrial elements is also evident in cities of North Africa and many parts of Asia; for example, in India and Japan,[21] even though great social change is currently taking place. And the Latin-American city of Merida, which Redfield studied, had many preindustrial traits.[22] A conscious awareness of the ecological, economic, and social structure of the preindustrial city should do much to further the development of comparative urban community studies.

■ ■ ■ ■ **Notes**

1 George M. Foster, "What Is Folk Culture?" *American Anthropologist*, LV (1953), 159–73.
2 Gideon Sjoberg, "Folk and 'Feudal' Societies," *American Journal of Sociology*, LVIII (1952), 231–39.
3 Sociologists have devoted almost no attention to the ecology of preindustrial centers. However, works of other social scientists do provide some valuable preliminary data.

See, e.g., Marcel Clerget, *Le Caire: Étude de géographie urbaine et d'histoire écono-mique* (2 vols.; Cairo: E. & R. Schindler, 1934); Robert E. Dickinson, *The West European City* (London: Routledge & Kegan Paul, 1951); Roger Le Tourneau, *Fès: Avant le protectorat* (Casablanca: Société Marocaine de Librairie et d'Édition, 1949); Edward W. Lane, *Cairo Fifty Years Ago* (London: John Murray, 1896); J. Sauvaget, *Alep* (Paris: Librairie Orientaliste Paul Geuthner, 1941); J. Weulersse, "Antioche: Essai de géographie urbaine," *Bulletin d'études orientales,* IV (1934), 27–79; Jean Kennedy, *Here Is India* (New York: Charles Scribner's Sons, 1945); and relevant articles in American geographical journals.

4 Dickinson, p. 27; O. H. K. Spate, *India and Pakistan* (London: Methuen & Co., 1954), p. 183.

5 For a discussion of guilds and other facets of the preindustrial city's economy see, e.g., J. S. Burgess, *The Guilds of Peking* (New York: Columbia University Press, 1928); Edward T. Williams, *China, Yesterday and Today* (5th ed.; New York: Thomas Y. Crowell Co., 1932); T'ai-ch'u Liao, "The Apprentices in Chengtu during and after the War," *Yenching Journal of Social Studies,* IV (1948), 90–106; H. A. R. Gibb and Harold Bowen, *Islamic Society and the West* (London: Oxford University Press, 1950), Vol. I, Part I, chap. vi; Le Tourneau; Clerget; James W. Thompson and Edgar N. Johnson, *An Introduction to Medieval Europe* (New York: W. W. Norton Co., 1937), chap. xx; Sylvia L. Thrupp, "Medieval Gilds Reconsidered," *Journal of Economic History,* II (1942), 164–73.

6 For an extreme example of unstandardized currency cf. Robert Coltman, Jr., *The Chinese* (Philadelphia: F. A. Davis, 1891), p. 52. In some traditional societies (e.g., China) the state has sought to standardize economic action in the city by setting up standard systems of currency and/or weights and measures; these efforts, however, generally proved ineffective. Inconsistent policies in taxation, too, hinder the development of a "rational" economy.

7 The status of the true merchant in the preindustrial city, ideally, has been low; in medieval Europe and China many merchants were considered "outcastes." However, in some preindustrial cities a few wealthy merchants have acquired considerable power even though their role has not been highly valued. Even then most of their prestige has come through participation in religious, governmental, or educational activities, which have been highly valued (see, e.g., Ping-ti Ho, "The Salt Merchants of Yang-Chou: A Study of Commercial Capitalism in Eighteenth-Century China," *Harvard Journal of Asiatic Studies,* XVII [1954], 130–68).

8 For materials on the kinship system and age and sex differentiation see, e.g., Le Tourneau; Edward W. Lane, *The Manners and Customs of the Modern Egyptians* (3d ed.; New York: E. P. Dutton Co., 1923); C. Snouck Hurgronje, *Mekka in the Latter Part of the Nineteenth Century,* trans. J. H. Monahan (London: Luzac, 1931); Horace Miner, *The Primitive City of Timbuctoo* (Princeton: Princeton University Press, 1953); Alice M. Bacon, *Japanese Girls and Women* (rev. ed.; Boston: Houghton Mifflin Co., 1902); J. S. Burgess, "Community Organization in China," *Far Eastern Survey,* XIV (1945), 371–73; Morton H. Fried, *Fabric of Chinese Society* (New York: Frederick A. Praeger, 1953); Francis L. K. Hsu, *Under the Ancestors' Shadow* (New York: Columbia University Press, 1948); Cornelius Osgood, *The Koreans and Their Culture* (New York: Ronald Press, 1951), chap. viii; Jukichi Inouye, *Home Life in Tokyo* (2d ed.; Tokyo: Tokyo Printing Co., 1911).

9 Tsung-Lien Shen and Shen-Chi Liu, *Tibet and the Tibetans* (Stanford: Stanford University Press, 1953), pp. 143–44.

10 Osgood, p. 146.

11 For information on various aspects of religious behavior see, e.g., Le Tourneau; Miner; Lane; Hurgronje; André Chouraqui, *Les Juifs d'Afrique du Nord* (Paris: Presses Universitaires de France, 1952); Justus Doolittle, *Social Life of the*

Chinese (London: Sampson Low, 1868); John K. Shryock, *The Temples of Anking and Their Cults* (Paris: Privately printed, 1931); Derk Bodde (ed.), *Annual Customs and Festivals in Peking* (Peiping: Henri Veich, 1936); Edwin Benson, *Life in a Medieval City* (New York: Macmillan Co., 1920); Hsu.

12 Le Tourneau, Part VI; Lane, chap. ii; Charles Bell, *The People of Tibet* (Oxford: Clarendon Press, 1928), chap. xix; O. Olufsen, *The Emir of Bokhara and His Country* (London: William Heinemann, 1911), chap. ix; Doolittle.

13 Carleton Coon, *Caravan: The Story of the Middle East* (New York: Henry Holt & Co., 1951), p. 259; George W. Gilmore, *Korea from Its Capital* (Philadelphia: Presbyterian Board of Publication, 1892), pp. 51–52.

14 Osgood, chap. viii; Gilmore, chap. iv.

15 Henri Pirenne, in *Medieval Cities* (Princeton: Princeton University Press, 1925), and others have noted that European cities grew up in opposition to and were separate from the greater society. But this thesis has been overstated for medieval Europe. Most preindustrial cities are integral parts of broader social structures.

16 Some of these cities made extensive use of water power, which possibly fostered deviations from the type.

17 For a discussion of the institutional prerequisites of industrialization see, e.g., Bert F. Hoselitz, "Social Structure and Economic Growth," *Economia internazionale*, VI (1953), 52–77, and Marion J. Levy, "Some Sources of the Vulnerability of the Structures of Relatively Non-industrialized Societies to Those of Highly Industrialized Societies," in Bert F. Hoselitz (ed.), *The Progress of Underdeveloped Areas* (Chicago: University of Chicago Press, 1952), pp. 114 ff.

18 Miner.

19 This point seems to have been perceived also by Asael T. Hansen in his review of Horace Miner's "The Primitive City of Timbuctoo," *American Journal of Sociology*, LIX (1954), 501–2.

20 Ralph L. Beals, "Urbanism, Urbanization and Acculturation," *American Anthropologist*, LIII (1951), 1–10.

21 See, e.g., D. R. Gadgil, *Poona: A Socio-economic Survey* (Poona: Gokhale Institute of Politics and Economics, 1952), Part II; N. V. Sovani, *Social Survey of Kolhapur City* (Poona: Gokhale Institute of Politics and Economics, 1951), Vol. II; Noel P. Gist, "Caste Differentials in South India," *American Sociological Review*, XIX (1954), 126–37; John Campbell Pelzel, "Social Stratification in Japanese Urban Economic Life" (unpublished Ph.D. dissertation, Harvard University, Department of Social Relations, 1950).

22 Robert Redfield, *The Folk Culture of Yucatan* (Chicago: University of Chicago Press, 1941).

2
The Modern City as a Field of Historical Study

OSCAR HANDLIN

The preindustrial city described by Sjoberg secured its food supply from the surrounding countryside and in turn supplied that countryside with certain political and religious services. But city and country remained distinct entities with a limited range of contact; no one doubted where one left off and the other began. In the essay below, Oscar Handlin focuses on the changes responsible for and accompanying the destruction of the isolated city. The development of the national state, the rationalization of the economy, and the technological conquest of distance gave the city new functions. It now acted as the focal point for the exchange of goods and information which the new order required.

Internally the city had to adopt new conceptions of time and space and impose a personalized responsibility for the maintenance of order upon its individual citizens. Men had to govern their activities by the clock, endure the journey to work as space became specialized separating residence areas from work areas, and accept the discipline of the factory and the crowded public place. For many of its residents the new city proved overwhelming, and the isolated and normless individual, the "bum," became a familiar feature of urban life in many societies. The destruction of the traditional corporate society deprived men and women of the security and sense of belonging so important to personal identity. At the same time this breakdown liberated other individuals from the constraints of corporate society and expanded the range of choices and opportunities for the more fortunate. Thus, personal disintegration and greater personal freedom are both characteristics of the modern city.

Readers may well ponder Handlin's remarks on the impact of continuing urbanization upon the distinctive character of the modern city. If an Iowa farmer can now be regarded as "urban," as I think in many ways he can, is there any point in trying to distinguish between urban and nonurban in advanced societies? Have we reached a stage where many of the concepts and terms used to describe society, like urban and rural, have lost their meaning, necessitating the creation of new categories in order to understand patterns and processes?

▪ ▪ ▪ ▪ For Further Reading

Lewis Mumford, *The City in History* remains indispensable. Asa Briggs, *Victorian Cities* (New York: Harper & Row, 1965) is a comparative study of British cities in the nineteenth century. In an appendix to the American edition, Briggs makes some interesting comparisons with American cities of that time.

■ Seen from above, the modern city edges imperceptibly out of its setting. There are no clear boundaries. Just now the white trace of the superhighway passed through cultivated fields; now it is lost in an asphalt maze of streets and buildings. As one drives in from the airport or looks out from the train window, clumps of suburban housing, industrial complexes, and occasional green spaces flash by; it is hard to tell where city begins and country ends. Our difficulties with nomenclature reflect the indeterminacy of these limits; we reach for some vague concept of metropolis to describe the release of urban potential from its recognized ambit.

Contrast this visual image with that of the ancient or medieval city. It is still possible, coming up the Rhone, to see Sion in the Valais much as it looked four hundred years ago. From a long way off, one can make out its twin castles jutting into the sky. But the vineyards and orchards, the open fields and clumps of woodland, reach along the roadside to the edge of town. There, we cross a boundary to enter another universe, one which is whole and entire to itself. The record of sieges that lasted for months on end confirms the impression of self-containment. It is much so that Paris must once have been, and Athens.

The cities of the past were, of course, vulnerable to external assault and to disruptive changes that emanated from without. Wars, shifts in patterns of production and trade, and cultural innovations gathered force outside their walls and yet decisively altered their history. But even when they held agricultural lands and even when some residents tilled the soil, those earlier communities possessed an individual life of their own in a sense that their modern successors do not. The ancient world had been a world of cities, but each had been a world unto itself. The towns of the Middle Ages and the Renaissance, even those of the eighteenth century, were self-contained entities walled off from their surroundings, with which they had only precisely defined contacts. They provided a marketplace for the products of rural craftsmen and husbandmen; but the main lines of their trade ran to distant, often overseas, places. They were centers of administration. But the governmental and ecclesiastical functionaries existed apart in detachment. The distance between London and Westminster, between Paris and Versailles, even between Milan and the castle of the Sforzas, was more than symbolic; it measured the genuine isolation of the life of the bourgeois.[1]

On the map today London and Paris and Milan occupy the same sites as did the places which bore those names three hundred years ago; and subtle institutional and cultural ties run across the centuries. But it would be a mistake to regard the later communities as merely, or even primarily, the descendants of the earlier ones. The modern city is essentially different from its predecessors, and the core of the difference lies in the fact that its life is not that "of an organism, but of an organ." It has become "the heart, the brain, perhaps only the digestive system, of that great leviathan, the modern state." Its history cannot be understood apart from that of the more comprehensive communities of which it is a part.[2]

The distinctive feature of the great modern city is its unique pattern of relations to the world within which it is situated. Large enough to have a character of its own, the modern city is yet inextricably linked to, dependent upon, the society outside it; and growth in size has increased rather than diminished the force of that dependence. Out of that relationship spring the central problems of urban history—those of the organization of space within the city, of the creation of order among its people, and of the adjustment to its new conditions by the human personality.

It is, of course, perfectly possible to approach the history of these communities in a purely descriptive fashion—to prepare useful accounts of municipalities, markets and cultural centers on an empirical basis. But such efforts will certainly be more rewarding if they are related to large questions of a common and comparative nature. These introductory remarks aim to define some of those questions.

The forces that made the modern city what it is took form outside its own limits. Hence the increases were always unexpected and unanticipated. In the sixteenth and seventeenth centuries London, the first truly modern city, was repeatedly forbidden to grow; men who knew it as it was could not conceive what it would become. For the same reason, projections of future trends—whether prophetic or scientific—almost without fail fell far short of actuality, even in the most optimistic cultures. It was rare indeed that the facilities of a community anticipated its later needs, as those of Los Angeles did. The direction and rate of expansion were not foreseen because the generative impulses were not contained within the older urban society of merchants, artisans, and functionaries. They sprang from three profound and interrelated changes in the society external to them—the development of the centralized national state, the transformation of the economy from a traditional, household, to a rational, capital-using basis, and the technological destruction of distance.[3]

The political changes were first to show themselves; here the medieval cities were at their weakest. Few of them had ever disposed of substantial military force. Venice and Ragusa were unusual in this respect, perhaps because of their relation to the sea. Most other towns, at best, found protection from a stadtholder, or at worst, remained the victims of *condottieri* or feuding barons. Often they welcomed the security of monarchical authority, but they had no illusions about the extent to which that would increase their own power. In the face of any assertion of royal or national will, they could only acquiesce.[4]

That dependent situation has persisted to this day. Despite their wealth and their critical economic position, the great cities do not control themselves; indeed most of them remain underrepresented in their ability to influence state policy. Their subordination in the polity has decisively shaped many aspects of their development.

The economic metamorphosis from which the modern city emerged is conventionally referred to as industrialization—an inappropriate designation because factory production was only slowly, and late, incorporated into the urban economy and was, in any case, only one aspect of a more general development. The eye of the change occurred outside the city rather than within it. First in agriculture and then in industry, old household-oriented modes of production gave way to large-scale rationalized forms, ultimately mechanized, that immensely increased output. The need to distribute the products to territorially wide, rather than to local, markets directly implicated the city.

The influence of technological change upon communications needs little comment. The evidences are all about us; and the development that led from the early roads and canals to the railroad, the telephone, the wireless, and the airplane permitted the speedy concentration of goods, messages, and persons at the focal points of ever wider areas. The simultaneous acceleration in managerial skills that permitted the organized deployment of great numbers of men and materials was equally impressive. The pace of innovation was particularly rapid in the half century after 1875 when the character of the modern city was most precisely defined. Why there should have been so striking an outburst of creativity in those years is as elusive a question as why there should have been so striking a failure of creativity thereafter.

The centralized national state, the new productive system, and vastly improved communications created the modern city. Together they increased its population, they endowed it with novel economic functions, and they imposed upon its way of life a fresh conception of order.

The initial manifestation of the change was a rapid growth in urban population. The centralizing tendencies of the emerging states of the sixteenth and seventeenth centuries brought significant groups of newcomers to the capitals and to regional subcenters. Operations, formerly dispersed in particular units of administration, were now concentrated; and the steady growth of state power created many additional places. Numerous functionaries carried on the expanded volume of government business and brought with them their families and retainers. Moreover many noblemen found it necessary to live close to the focus of authority, either through choice to be near the source of favors as in Bourbon France, or through compulsion to be subject to control as in Tokugawa Japan. Ancillary educational and religious institutions gravitated in the same direction. All the people thus drawn to the city created a market for trade, crafts, and services which swelled the economy of their place of residence.[5]

These developments had subtle, long-term effects. Channels of communication with the rest of the country were established that deepened through use and that conditioned the routes of later railroad and telephone lines. In some places the extensive fiscal transactions of the central government laid a basis for subsequent banking developments. As important, the seat of power acquired a symbolic value that later acted as a magnet for other detached elements in the society; and national citizenship facilitated their free entry.

Urban population expanded preponderantly by immigration. Cataclysms of many types outside the city borders precipitously swelled the streams that flowed into it. A stroke of fortune such as the discovery of gold near San Francisco and Johannesburg, or population pressure in the hinterland, or a disaster such as the migrations into Bombay and Calcutta after partition quickly raised the number of residents. Colonial trade contributed to the same effect in London and Amsterdam. Most important of all, structural changes in agriculture and industry involved a total reorganization of the labor force and effectively displaced great numbers of human beings for whom the city was the only refuge.[6]

From these sources was derived the rapid increase in numbers characteristic of the metropolis. Through the nineteenth century the pace accelerated, with the very largest places growing more rapidly than the smaller ones. In 1800 the twenty-one European cities with a population of 100,000 or more held, in all, somewhat more than four and a half million souls, one thirty-fifth of the total. In 1900 there were 147 such places with a population of 40,000,000 or one-tenth of the total; and thirteen and one-fourth million lived within the narrowly defined political limits of the six largest cities. Were there means of estimating the true size of the urban districts involved, the number would be larger still. The same cities in 1960 had a population of about 24,000,000—again a gross underestimation of their genuine numbers. Meanwhile places of comparable dimension had appeared in America and Asia. In 1961 well over 85,000,000 persons lived in the world's twenty largest cities, each of which contained 2,500,000 or more residents. And the process was not yet over.[7]

Mere accretions of population, however, changed the fundamental character of the city but slightly. New people came in, but their presence in itself called for few radical accommodations on the part of the old residents who generally prospered from the increased demand for their services. The city spread through the addition of new areas to its living space. But the organization of life for some time remained much what it had been earlier. Growth to great size was a necessary precondition, but did not in itself bring the modern city into being. Edo (Tokyo) in 1868 is said to have had a population of about a million, London in 1660 held more than one-half million people; yet these places were but extended towns which functioned according to patterns set long before. Their nobility, mercantile pursuits, and artisans' handicrafts formed larger aggregates than before, but they were aggregates of units that were essentially unchanged. Characteristically, in such places the building trades occupied a large part of the total labor force, and they altered but little with the passage of time. Other pursuits remained much as they had been earlier. The number of smiths and tailors, of drapers and merchants grew; but the mere multiplication of stalls and shops did not change the character of the bazaar, of the lane or of the exchange.[8]

Nor did the new needs thrust upon the city by the transformation of agriculture and industry after the eighteenth century alone give it its modern identity. Viewed simply on the economic plane, there was nothing inherently novel in the relationship of the city to these changes. It had long been accustomed to receiving the placeless men who sought its shelter and it had always provided a market for the products of the countryside. What was new was the desire, and the ability, to impose a rational order upon the relations created by the new productive system. The evolution of that order not only brought the city into intimate dependence upon the surrounding society; it also entailed a thoroughgoing transformation in the urban way of life.

Earlier markets had been dominated by the characteristics of the fair; buyers and sellers had approached in the expectation that they might meet one another, but the actual encounters had been shot through with chance. Monopolies and other political controls, various systems of correspondence and intelligence, and numerous other devices had aimed to impart some regularity to these transactions, particularly in the exchange of the great staples—wine, wool, and later, spices, tea, tobacco, and sugar. But distance and the vagaries of household production had limited the utility of these efforts. In effect, the movement of goods came to a halt, started and stopped, within the city, and that discontinuity gave the entrepôt a considerable degree of autonomy.

That situation ceased to be tolerable after the eighteenth century. The new techniques resulted in a large and growing capacity for production far beyond local need; they involved heavy capital investments and considerable risk; and they entailed difficult administrative problems. The success of any enterprise hinged upon the ability to anticipate with some precision a favorable relationship between cost of production and selling price. It could only survive by planning, however primitive the means by later standards; and planning required dependability and predictability in access both to markets and to supplies.

The city supplied the essential mechanism: from it radiated the communications network—increasingly more extensive and more rapid—and within it were situated the facilities for transshipping, storing, and processing commodities on their way from producer to consumer. Here, too, was the apparatus of accounting and credit that made the movement of goods possible. The task of the city was that of speedy transmission. The more sensitive communications became, the more thoroughly the city was entangled in a mesh of relations that deprived it of autonomy and integrated it into a larger economic and social whole.[9]

The new role had profound consequences for the internal life of the city. Its effectiveness in the productive system of which it was a part depended upon its ability to create an appropriately functioning order within its own boundaries. The pressures toward doing so were critical in its development.

One can discover premature efforts to create such novel economic relationships in the role of Milan in Lombardy and in the experience of other Renaissance cities with their hinterlands. Such developments were abortive, not only because of their restricted territorial scope and because of technological limitations, but also because the corporate life inherited from the middle ages survived, indeed grew stronger; and that life significantly inhibited further changes. The seventeenth-century syndics who sat for Rembrandt's corporation portraits were custodians of communal organizations which resisted untoward changes. The destruction of their way of life was the necessary preliminary to the creation of a new urban order more in accord with the developing productive system.[10] Where that corporate life was weak or nonexistent to begin with, as in the United States, the process was all the faster.

Destruction of the older way of life was achieved through a convergence of political and economic forces. The national state eroded traditional elements of control and created new loci of power that dominated the city from outside it. The local aristocracy dwindled in importance; the old corporations were drained of influence; privileges were reshuffled; and new people rose to prominence. More generally, the national state undermined all traditional affiliations. It recognized only the indiscriminate relationship of citizenship. In its eyes there were only individuals, not members of clans, guilds, or even of households.

The changes in the productive system redistributed wealth to the advantage of men who could cast aside inherited modes of action to capitalize on fresh opportunities. The new economy encouraged the pursuit of individual profit rather than of status within a defined community; and the city housed a pack of people seeking after gain:

> Where every man is for himself
> And no man for all.[11]

The result was a new concept of orderly city life, one that no longer rested on a corporate organization of households, but instead depended upon a complex and impersonal arrangement of individuals. The process was already at work in the sixteenth century in England; it was immensely stimulated by the American and the French revolutions and was complete by the end of the nineteenth century.

We shall better be able to understand the character of the inner order of the modern city by regarding some of its specific manifestations.

An entirely new pattern for disposing of space appeared. The layout of the old city was altogether inappropriate. The population had already spread beyond the encircling walls and waters but it was inefficiently organized by a cumbersome and anachronistic plan. Churches, palaces, and other monumental structures occupied central places; squares and plazas pockmarked the limited area; and the streets ran but the short distances between nearby termini.

There was no reason why they should do more, for men had little need to travel since the household was both residence and place of work. Various districts were differentiated by occupational, class, or religious distinctions. But in each case, the basic unit was a self-contained familial entity that had a precisely defined place in the corporate life of the city. An increase in numbers was accommodated by multiplying the units, not by altering their character. In those unusual situations, as in the ghettoes, where space was constricted, the buildings rose upward and expansion was vertical. More frequently, where room was available, new clusters of settlement split off from the old and expansion was lateral. But until well into the nineteenth century growth in most places had simply multiplied the number of clusters; it had not altered their essential character.[12]

Reconstruction of the city plan depended upon the differentiation of living and working quarters. Such specialized use of space, reflecting the growing impersonality of business and its separation from the household, became prevalent everywhere except in professions like medicine, and in the service crafts where a personal relationship survived. Elsewhere, the dispersal of the population went hand in hand with the destruction of the household and was eased by the engulfment of suburb after suburb. The father and mother and children lived together but their life was detached from work. The categories of experience they shared in the home were unrelated to those of the job. Each individual left after breakfast to take up a separate task in the counting house or the shop or on the scaffold, to return in the evening to his residence some distance away, for each was an integer subject to a separate reckoning in the accounting of the productive system.[13]

The division of function was economical. Every productive or distributive operation became more efficient when it selected the individual employee according to his talents or cost apart from considerations of kin and clan, of family or ethnic grouping. Of course, no society fully realized the ideal of total fluidity that permitted its population to be sorted out in this manner; but the separation of work from residence encouraged an approach in that direction. The fact that single men and women always constituted a large proportion of the migrants into the city stimulated the trend as did related alterations in the behavior of settled families.

As a result space was released from all sorts of traditional expenses. The enterprise no longer had to bear the charge on land of high value, of wasteful drawing rooms and gardens. Precious urban acreage was withdrawn from farming. And the distribution of population by income levels permitted a rational valuation of space in terms of an abstract, calculated, rent. Speculation was the incidental by-product, rather than the cause, of this development.[14]

Specialization required and facilitated the construction of an entirely new urban plant, a good part of which was built with the aid of a remarkable burst of innovation that began shortly after 1820 and which reached its peak between 1875 and 1925. Space was reallocated with an eye toward its most profitable use; and buildings directed toward a single function—trade, industry, or residence—went up with ruthless efficiency. The process of differentiation created demands for services which theretofore had been unneeded or had been supplied within the household, for fresh foods, milk, water, waste disposal, light, transportation, and recreation. In the frenzy of construction, the city was entirely recast and its ties to the past obliterated. Even topography ceased to be an obstacle; hills were razed, marshes and lakes filled in, and shore lines extended to make way for the limitless grid. Goethe could still make out medieval Frankfurt in place names, markets, buildings, fairs, and topography. By 1870, hardly more than a few of these monuments and ceremonies survived.[15]

Now begins the time of travel, at first on foot. Dickens' characters still walk across London, and at about the same time a resident of Tokyo thinks nothing of tramping five miles to and five miles from his destination every day. Even in twentieth century Rio or Tokyo an inefficient transport system compels workers to spend six hours a day between home and job.[16] But in cost-conscious societies speed is an important consideration; in its interest new streets are driven through the city, straight and wide to carry an ever heavier stream of vehicles—at first horse drawn, later, motor propelled. The wheels roll above and below as well as on the ground and inconvenient rivers are bridged over and tunneled under. The critical breakthrough comes with the appearance of the common carrier. At the beginning of the nineteenth century, every conveyance still bears the appearance of the personal or family carriage or litter—even the long distance stages that take fare-paying passengers. It is not at all clear, when the first railroads are built, that they will follow a different line of development. But the carriages are thrown open for all to enter; mass travel becomes possible; and the meanest laborer moves on wheels.

The pace and ingenuity of this work were impressive by any standard. That the subways of London, Paris, New York, and Boston were built faster than those of Moscow, Stockholm, or Rome fifty years later must mean something, although it would be hazardous to try to make the meaning precise. Any such comparison is to some degree arbitrary and perhaps far-fetched. Yet the standard of achievement certainly was not lower a half-century ago than now, if we take into account the presumed improvement in technology since then. Travelers to New York today are aware that it will take seven years (1957–1964) to reconstruct La Guardia Airport and that Idlewild has been more than a decade in the building. Their predecessors fifty years ago were likely to reach the city through one of the largest buildings ever theretofore constructed at one time, one covering eight acres of ground, with exterior walls of one half a mile. They could enter through two tunnels under the Hudson River and four under the East River extending more than eighteen miles from Harrison, New Jersey, to Jamaica, Long Island. Work on this project began in June 1903; the Hudson tunnels were finished in three years, the East River tunnels in less than five and the Pennsylvania station in less than six. In September, 1910, the whole complex was in operation.[17]

The modern city demanded an immense number and variety of new buildings. Already in the eighteenth century architects like Claude-Nicholas Ledoux were compelled to devise new shapes for warehouses, for banks, for other commercial structures, and for dwellings appropriate to various classes of residents. Considerations of cost compelled them to adhere to the rule of geometry, and to stress functionalism and the rational organization of materials and space. In doing so they struggled against counter-pressures toward tradition and individualism, against counterpulls toward exoticism and a romanticized view of nature. By the second half of the nineteenth century, they had begun to work out the styles that accommodated the life of the modern city.[18]

Certainly the New York tenement block of 1900 was an unlovely object. Having dispensed with the old central court, it could pile its residents up in suffocating density. The reformers of the period were altogether right to attack overcrowding there and elsewhere and to complain that the cities had not adequately met their housing needs. Only, one must remember that overcrowding and need are relative concepts; and few later efforts have been notably more successful.[19] Comparison with the experience of Moscow in the 1930's, to say nothing of Calcutta in the 1950's, puts the achievements of a half-century ago in better perspective.[20]

The altered situation of the city called also for a new conception of time. In the rural past, years, months, days, and hours had been less meaningful than seasons, than the related succession of religious occasions, than the rising and setting of the sun. Small communities had their own flexible conceptions of chronology. Such habits had extended to the city as well. Each household had a large margin within which to set its own pace, for the tempo of all activities was leisurely. An analysis of the course of an eighteenth-century merchant's day, for instance, revealed long disposable intervals so that even when he was busy, it was upon terms he could shape for himself.[21]

The complex interrelationships of life in the modern city, however, called for unprecedented precision. The arrival of all those integers who worked together, from whatever part of the city they inhabited, had to be coordinated to the moment. There was no natural span for such labor; arbitrary beginnings and ends had to be set, made uniform and adhered to. The dictatorship of the clock and the schedule became absolute.[22]

No earlier human experience had made such demands. The army camp, plantation labor, and the ship's crew which came closest to it were coherent, closed societies, the members of which lived close together and in isolation from outsiders; the tasks involved had a rhythm of their own that regulated their budgets of time. But the modern city could not function except under the rule of a precise and arbitrary chronological order which alone could coordinate the activities of thousands of individuals whose necessary encounters with one another were totally impersonal. By the same token, literacy or some alternative code of signals was essential to the coexistence of people who did not know one another.

The new uses of space and time were indicative of what order meant in the modern city. Its complex life demanded myriad daily contacts of such sensitivity that it could not depend, as earlier, upon well-established and static connections among the stable households and the fixed corporate groups in which its population had been distributed. Instead it required its residents to behave individually and impersonally in terms of their function, and it assured regularity of contacts by rigid allocations of space and time.

That order made it possible to bring manufacturing, like other large-scale activities, into the cities. The planners of the early great factories thought of the only models of disciplined activity familiar to them, the barrack and the army camp; their sites—visionary or actual—were therefore invariably in the countryside, where the tolling bell from the clock tower of the mill replaced that of the village church. The similarity in design of factories and prisons was by no means coincidental.[23]

The urban factory was conceivable only well in the nineteenth century when it was possible to imagine that a labor force would come to work regularly and dependably. The process of transition in actuality took a number of forms. Some factory centers, like Manchester, grew into cities. In other cases, as in Pittsburgh or Zurich, a commercial center expanded to engulf nearby industrial communities. Elsewhere industry was drawn in by the attractions of superior transportation facilities, or by the presence of an abundant labor supply, as in Berlin, or Chicago; or the shift was a product of conscious government decisions as in Moscow after 1928. But whatever the immediate impulse, the necessary condition was the order that permitted the factory to function.[24]

The way of life of the modern city created grave social and personal problems. Any increase of size had always complicated the police of the community. But so long as the family, the clan, or the guild remained accountable for the behavior of its members, so long as the normal ambit of activities was restricted to a familiar quarter, the primary danger of deviant behavior came from strangers. When the decay of the household weakened the sense of collective security, the initial response was to control or exclude outsiders, to arrive at some accommodation with violent elements, and to maintain the isolation of the district within which its residents felt safe. At the end of the eighteenth century, as large a place as London had not moved beyond this point.

But these expedients were not long useful. The modern city was no *colluvies gentium*—a fortuitous accumulation of unfused populaces—as were ancient Rome, or Alexandria. Extended travel and promiscuous contacts were essential to it; and the frequent mingling of men unknown to each other generated the need for holding each individual responsible for his behavior. The ultimate goal was some sort of total index that would precisely identify and infallibly locate each person so that he could be called to account for his obligations and punished for his delinquencies. The steady development of governmental power, the contrivance of numerous devices for registration, and the appearance of a professional corps of administrators were steps toward an approximation of that goal.

More was involved than the containment of criminality. The urban resident had positive as well as negative responsibilities. He had not merely to refrain from such actions as were injurious to others; he was expected, in ways that were difficult to define explicitly, also to contribute to the total well-being of the community by civic actions. The collective tasks of the old household and guild could not be left in abeyance. Someone had to provide care for dependent persons, education for children, facilities for worship, media for cultural and sociable expression, and commemorative monuments and objects of awe and beauty. The police of a city thus included a wide range of functions connected with its health and security. The state assumed some of these obligations, but the scope of its activity varied widely from country to country. Although we cannot yet explain convincingly the differences in the depth of its involvement, it is clear that it nowhere preempted the field entirely. Much remained to be done through other forms.[25]

It was not possible, although men often longed to do so, to revive the old corporate institutions or the solidary rural communities from which so many residents had migrated. The modern city contained too many disparate elements, too often thrown together, and in too fluid a pattern of relations to permit such regressions. Instead, where abstinence by the state left a vacuum, the characteristic device of a voluntary association, directed toward the specific function, met the need. The rapid proliferation of such organizations drew together memberships united by common interests, common antecedents, or common points of view. The wide expanse of the city and the continuing migration which peopled it, shaped such groupings. In some places the effective modes of organization fell within territorial, neighborhood lines; the *quartier,* ward, *ku,* or *favela* was the matrix within which associations formed. Elsewhere cultural or ethnic affiliations supplied the determining limits of cooperative action.[26]

For a long time, the cost of this adjustment was recurrent, overt conflict. Leadership was effective only within limited circles, and there were few means of resolving the frequent crises that led easily into outbreaks of violence. Bread riots in the West and rice riots in the East expressed the desperation of the uncared-for elements in the community; and racial or social antipathies, smoldering beneath the surface, erupted at the least disturbance.[27]

By the end of the nineteenth century, the instruments for controlling such dangerous disorders were at least available, if not always effectively used. The reconstruction of the great cities permitted a strategic disposition of power to contain the mob. The maintenance of an armed police force deterred overt lawbreakers. Moreover, by then a complex of philanthropic, religious, educational, and cultural institutions had begun to elicit the acquiescence of the urban masses through persuasion. Thereafter conflicts took more negotiable forms, in the bargaining of labor unions and employers, and in politics which was less a partisan contest for power than an instrument of group accommodation. Disputes were increasingly subject to conciliable resolution through the mediating efforts of recognized leaders. However, the issues which could be confronted on the municipal level were limited and concrete; and the deeper economic and emotional grievances of the population were likely to be displaced into other channels.[28]

The life of the modern city created subtle personal problems. Here were distilled many of the general effects of change in the past two centuries: the break with tradition and the dissolution of inherited beliefs, the impact of science and technology, and the transformation of the family and of the productive system. In the city, as elsewhere, such decisive innovations were a source of both release and tension in the human spirit. Only, concentrated as they were in their urban form, these new impulses were far more volatile than elsewhere. Furthermore, the man of the city passed through experiences unique to his setting. The number and variety and speed of his contacts, the products of an original conception of space and time, the separation from nature, the impersonality and individuality of work all were novel to the human situation.

Evidence of the negative consequences was painfully abundant. On the Bowery or in Brigittenau drifted the uprooted masses who had lost personality, identity, and norms and who now were trapped in every form of disorder. The deterioration of man to bum was all to familiar in every modern city. Even the less desperate were heedless of the restraints of church and family; in London, Berlin, and New York of the third quarter of the nineteenth century, a majority of marriages and burials were unsolemnized by the clergy. The most prosperous tore at each other in vicious competition except when they indulged in fierce and expensive debauchery. High rates of mortality, suicide, alcoholism, insanity, and other forms of delinquency showed that men reared in one environment could not simply shift to another without substantial damage to themselves.[29]

At the high point of change, in the half-century after 1875, there were two distinct, although not contradictory, interpretations of the effects of the modern city upon the human personality. Those who focused their attention upon institutional developments, like Georg Simmel, Emile Durkheim, and, to some extent, Max Weber, took particular note of the decay of old forms which left the individual unsheltered, unprotected, and isolated, and therefore prone to deterioration. The later exaggerations of Spengler and Mumford distend these insights into a vision of imminent catastrophe.[30]

Exaggeration was easy because personal disorders were more visible in the city than in the country. But these observers were also limited by a fixed preference for what the city had been, a total systematic unit comprehending a defined order of institutions that no longer existed. It is significant that their views mirrored somber predictions, made long before. Rousseau and others had already warned of the inevitable results of urban detachment from nature before the process had even taken form. "Of all animals man is least capable of living in flocks. Penned up like sheep, men soon lose all. The breath of man is fatal to his fellows. . . . Cities are the burial pit of the human species."[31]

The personal hardships of adjustment to city life were genuine but they were distorted when examined in the perspective of the corporate, rural past. Other observers, whose gaze was fastened on the residents as human beings, made out a somewhat different pattern. "What can ever be more stately and admirable to me," asked Whitman, "than mast-hemm'd Manhattan?" Observing the curious procession of the ferry riders leaving work behind for their thousands of homes, he felt and expressed the wonder of their each being a person.[32] This was often the response of compassionate onlookers. At first regard, the city was totally inhuman; jungle, wilderness, hive, machine—these were the terms of the metaphors that sprang spontaneously to mind. But those sensitive enough to look more deeply found marvelous assertions of the human spirit even under these unpropitious circumstances. Here life was real and hard, and tested the human heart and mind so that emotions were deeper and reason more acute than elsewhere. Social scientists influenced by Darwinian conception of the survival of the fittest readily assumed that the city was the new environment within which a new, superior man would develop. And some who began half to understand the character of that life were tempted to idealize and romanticize even its least lovely aspects, the slums, the ruthless competition, and the grinding order.[33]

The two responses were not irreconcilable; indeed, in retrospect, they seem almost complementary, or perhaps, they were but different ways of describing the identical process. The decay of familiar institutions was another way of saying the release from traditional restraints; the unsheltered individual was also the liberated individual. The breakdown of the household and the attenuation of all the relationships formerly centered in it were the conditions of the liberation of modern man to all his painful tensions, all his creative opportunities. The hard stone of the city streets provided the stage for this drama; and it is the task of historical scholarship to explain its triumphs, its defeats, and its conflicts.

The modern city provided the scene for great outbursts of cultural creativity. Georgian London, Paris in the first decades of the Third Republic, Vienna toward the end of the reign of Franz Joseph, and Berlin of the 1920's were the settings of great achievements of the human spirit, in literature, in art, in music, and in science. Yet these were also, and at the same time, the scenes of bitter struggles for existence, of acute hardships suffered by hundreds of thousands of ill-prepared newcomers beaten down by insoluble problems. John Gay and William Hogarth, Anatole France and Honoré Daumier, Robert Musil and Berthold Brecht, and Charlie Chaplin and René Clair compiled a record of personal disasters, of moral disintegration, of human costs so high it could only be contemplated under the palliative gloss of humor. The laughter of their audiences did not conceal, it recognized the harsh truth. Yet the withering away of traditional guides to life, so debilitating in many ways, also set the individual free, left room for spontaneity and discovery, brought together selective new combinations of people, ideas, and forms, that permitted man to catch unsuspected glimpses of an unknown universe and an unfamiliar self.

Every aspect of the development of the modern city generated conflicts not resolvable within its own boundaries; that was a condition of its intimate relations with the society beyond its borders. The urban residents were divided among themselves, and they had to reckon with outsiders in their midst and beyond the walls, whose interests were intimately bound up with their own. Disputes of great importance were the result.

The city plan was therefore never simply the realization of an abstract design. Even in places created entirely afresh, as in Washington or St. Petersburg, it was the product of inescapable compromises. Within the city, the primary interest of the entrepreneurial groups and of the laboring population was to economize on the use of space. They wanted low rents, an efficient, functional allocation of the resources, and speedy interior transportation.

Such people met the determined, and sometimes effective, resistance of other elements, whose conceptions were still dominated by the static images of the rural landscape. The aristocracy—genuine and putative—wished to bring with them the commodious features of their landed estates. They expected the city to provide them with elegant squares to set off their homes, with picturesque monuments, and with parks and boulevards that would supply a back drop for the May Corso, for the Spring Parade, for the *ausflug* or Sunday excursion, for the gentleman on horseback and the lady in her carriage. Public transportation concerned them not at all.[34]

Immigrants who prospered to a lesser degree clung to the rural village as the model of home; they built wasteful villas in the sprawling suburbs and sought a restricted transport system that would take them conveniently to their desks and counters, yet prevent the city from engulfing them. Often their dogged struggles for autonomy hopelessly complicated any effort at urban reorganization, a problem as troublesome in Vienna, Leipzig, Manchester, and Liverpool in 1890 as in Boston and Nashville in 1960.[35]

The persistence of the rural model prevented these people from thinking of the city as a whole and as it was. From Robert Owen, Fourier, and the utopian socialists, to Ebenezer Howard, Frank Lloyd Wright, and Lewis Mumford, a good-hearted but illusory plea went forth for the rebuilding of urban life in garden cities or multiplied suburbs, where adults would not be tempted to squander their resources in the pub or music hall, nor children theirs in the sweetshop; and all would have access to the salubrious and moral air of the countryside.[36]

To such pressures were added those of agriculturists and industrialists in the hinterland concerned only with lowering the cost of transshipment, and of the state, increasingly preoccupied with security against insurrection or lesser threats to order. The great planners, like Baron Haussmann in Paris, found room for maneuver in the play of these forces against one another. But rarely did they find the city material they could mold into a unified and coherent whole.[37]

Urban elements were at a disadvantage in the determination of both municipal and national policies. The level of tariffs in the 1880's and 1890's, the routes of canals and railroads, and the character of the banking system vitally affected all cities. Yet their influence was perilously weak, underrepresented in the councils of state and divided, while the rural interests were monolithic and well entrenched. Paris, Rio, Rome did not govern themselves; and voices from the Platteland or Upstate were more likely to command than those from Johannesburg or New York. The political power of the country generally outweighed the economic power of the city.[38]

The clash of interests took its most subtle and most significant form in the contact of the diverse cultures that converged on the modern city. The folk traditions of the old bourgeois did not survive the disintegration of the corporate bodies in which it had been embedded; it was totally disrupted by the pressure from both above and below of alien elements.

The aristocracy surrendered its isolation and shifted some of its activities to the city. Still stabilized by its landed estates, it also drew support from new wealth and, in the nineteenth century, began the quest for a uniform, hierarchical culture at the peak of which it could stand. It wished more than indulgence in a lavish style of life; it wished also general acquiescence in its position. Indeed, to some extent it flouted the conventions of inferiors precisely in order to demonstrate its superiority. Legally recognized rank as in England and Prussia, the pretense of ancient lineage as in Austria and France, or arbitrary registers of inclusion as in the United States, asserted its claims to pre-eminence. In addition, it transformed the theater, the opera and the museum into institutions to display its dominance. The aristocracy turned music into classics, art into old masters, and literature into rare books, possessions symbolic of its status.[39]

The problems of other migrants into the city were of quite another order. The mass of displaced peasants were eager to transplant their inherited culture but the soil was inhospitable. Folk wisdom, inappropriate to the new conditions, took on the appearance of superstition; and folk art, detached from its communal setting, lost much of its authenticity. However these people fared, they were driven by anxiety—to retain the rewards of success, to avoid the penalties of failure. Some escaped through alcohol; others found moments of relief in the excitement of the yellow press, the music hall, and the popular theater.[40]

Above all, they needed to interpret their lives by seeing themselves as actors in a meaningful drama, and since it was inconceivable that they should be conquering heroes, they most readily visualized themselves as victims.

Of whom? Rarely of the aristocrat. Peasant and gentleman had a long history of accommodation; and their roles in city life engendered few direct conflicts. The lowly felt no compulsion to ape the high born, and gaped at the splendor of the carriages on the way to the opera without envy.

More often the villains were the capitalists, big business, whose wealth was abstract, was located in no communal context, and was attached to no responsibilities of position. Or sometimes, the enemy was the stranger—the Slav or the Jew or the Catholic or the Protestant Masons or the barbaric foreigner—who could be blamed for the ills of the city. Inhuman materialism, disregard of traditional faith, sensuality and obscenity were crimes against man; and for crimes, criminals were responsible; and they who came were guilty so that we who left home were but the innocent victims.[41]

The factory workers and craftsmen who held places in disciplined organizations found belief in socialism; the class struggle explained their present situation and offered them the hope of an acceptable future. But millions of placeless men could not so readily tear themselves away from the past. The shopkeepers and clerks, the casual laborers, the chaotic mass of men without function did not want the future; they wanted the security of the homes and families and blood communities they had never had or had lost in migration. That is, they wanted a miracle; and in their eagerness they became the gullible victims of nationalistic, racist, religious and quasi-religious fantasies of every sort. There is a particular interest, in Europe, in the ease with which these people allied themselves with some sectors of the aristocracy under the banner of a universal faith—Ultramontane Catholicism, pan-Germanism, pan-Slavism. Drumont and the royalist officer corps in France, Luëger and Prince Alois Liechtenstein in Austria, illustrated the attractiveness of tradition and authority for the demagogue and his mob. Perhaps analogous elements were involved in the revival of Shinto in Japan after 1868; they were certainly present in the history of fascism.[42]

The true miracle, however, was the emergence of a sense of civic consciousness connected with the old burgher traditions but responsive to the new character of the modern city. Its characteristics were tolerance to the point of latitudinarianism, rationalism, cosmopolitanism, pragmatism, and receptivity to change. It attracted the settled middle-class elements of the city, the leaders of organized labor and even demagogues suddenly charged with responsibility, as Luëger was in Vienna and La Guardia in New York; its essence was a creative reaction to the problems of the place; its achievement was the monumental building of the city to which I earlier referred.

Some decades ago—and I am deliberately vague about the date—a significant change appeared. The immediate local causes seemed to be the two wars, the depression, and new shifts in technology and population. However, these may be but manifestations of some larger turning in the history of the society of which the modern city is a part.

The differences between city and country have been attenuated almost to the vanishing point. The movement of people, goods, and messages has become so rapid and has extended over such a long period as to create a new situation. To put it bluntly, the urbanization of the whole society may be in the process of destroying the distinctive role of the modern city. It is symptomatic of this change that, in western societies, most migrations now originate, as well as terminate, in the modern metropolis.

This change may be related to a general slackening of urban spirit. The worldwide movement to the suburbs is not in itself new; this was always one of the ways in which the city expanded. What is new is the effective motivation—the insistence upon constructing small, uniform, coherent communities, and the surrender of the adventure of life in the larger units with all the hazards and opportunities of unpredictable contacts. Increasingly the men who now people the metropolis long for the security of isolation from the life about them. They strive to locate their families in space, with a minimum of connections to the hazards of the external world.[43]

Finally, there has been a perceptible decline in urban creativity. The regression to private transportation is indicative of what has been happening in other spheres as well. Despite other advances in technology and despite refinements in methods, the last thirty or forty years have witnessed no innovations to match those of the thirty or forty years earlier. We have done little more than elaborate upon the inherited plant; nowhere has there been an adequate response to the challenge of new conditions.

We console ourselves with the calculation that if the modern city has ceased to grow, the metropolitan region continues to expand. What difference that will make remains to be seen. In any case, it seems likely that we stand at the beginnings of a transformation as consequential as that which, two hundred years ago, brought the modern city into being.

Therein lies the historian's opportunity to throw light on the problems of those involved with today's city, either as practitioners or as participants. His task is not to predict, but to order the past from which the present grows in a comprehensible manner. He can illuminate the growth of the modern city from the eighteenth to the twentieth centuries to make clear what was permanent and what transient, what essential and what incidental, in its development.

Such an account as this essay has presented has perforce touched upon a few themes abstracted from a large number of cases. Yet the historian must deal with particulars, not with generalities. Certainly the stress, laid here upon the connections between the modern city and the surrounding society points to the decisive role of political, cultural, and economic variants, widely different from place to place.

Comparisons crowd immediately to mind. Did the differences between Washington and St. Petersburg in 1900, new capitals of expanding nations, emanate from the hundred-year disparity in their ages or from discernible differences between the United States and Russia? Did Shanghai and Singapore become what they did because they were perched on the edge of Oriental societies or because they were colonial enclaves? Did a tropical situation set the experiences of Rio and Havana apart from those of cities in the temperate zone; did their European population distinguish them from other tropical cities? Why did some cities fail to grow as others did, why were some more successful than others in resolving their problems?

No amount of theorizing about the nature of the city will answer questions such as these. We need fewer studies of the city in history than of the history of cities. However useful a general theory of the city may be, only the detailed tracing of an immense range of variables, in context, will illuminate the dynamics of the processes here outlined.[44] We can readily enough associate such gross phenomena as the growth of population and the rise of the centralized state, as technological change and the development of modern industry, as the disruption of the traditional household and the decline of corporate life. But *how* these developments unfolded, what was the causal nexus among them, we shall only learn when we make out the interplay among them by focusing upon *a* city specifically in all its uniqueness.

In the modern city, the contest between the human will and nature assumed a special form. Here man, crowded in upon himself and yet alone, discovered his potentialities for good and evil, for weakness and strength. Compelled to act within a framework of impersonal institutions, he was forced to probe the meaning of his own personality.

In the balance for two centuries now has lain the issue of whether he will master, or be mastered by, the awesome instruments he has created. The record of that issue deserves the best energies of the historian.

■ ■ ■ ■ **Notes**

1 Max Weber, *The City* (Translated and edited by Don Martindale and Gertrud Neuwirth; Glencoe, 1958), 70 ff.; Raffaele d'Ambrosio, *Alle Origini della città le prime esperienze urbane* (Napoli, 1956); A. Temple Patterson, *Radical Leicester* (Leicester, 1954), 3, 165.

2 George Unwin, *Studies in Economic History* (London, 1927), 49.

3 Norman G. Brett-James, *Growth of Stuart London* (London, 1935), 67 ff., 105 ff., 296 ff.; Walter Besant, *London in the Time of the Tudors* (London, 1904), 83; Boyle Workman, *The City that Grew* (Caroline Walker, ed., Los Angeles, 1935), 266 ff.

4 William A. Robson, *Great Cities of the World Their Government, Politics and Planning* (New York, 1955), 78 ff.; Société Jean Bodin, *Receuils*, VI (1954), 265 ff., 367 ff., 434 ff., 541 ff., 612.

5 See, e.g., Franklin L. Ford, *Strasbourg in Transition 1648–1789* (Cambridge, 1958), 159 ff.; Lewis Mumford, *The City in History. Its Origins, Its Transformations, and Its Prospects* (New York, 1961), 386 ff.; *Golden Ages of the Great Cities* (London, 1952), 192.

6 Adna F. Weber, *The Growth of Cities in the Nineteenth Century* (New York, 1899), 230 ff.; Besant, 226 ff.; Walter Besant, *London in the Eighteenth Century* (London, 1903), 213 ff.; Percy E. Schramm, ed., *Kaufleute zu Haus und über See Hamburgische Zeugnisse des 17., 18., und 19. Jahrhunderts* (Hamburg, 1949), pt. II; Emile Vandervelde, *L'Exode rural et le retour aux champs* (Paris, 1903), 39 ff.; Robson, 112 ff., 141, 683.

7 *Information Please Almanac, 1961,* 658; Edmund J. James, "The Growth of Great Cities," *Annals of the American Academy of Political and Social Science,* XII (1899), 1 ff.; Weber, *Growth of Cities,* 20 ff., gives extensive nineteenth-century statistics. See also for more recent data, International Urban Research, *The World's Metropolitan Areas* (Berkeley, 1959); Kingsley Davis, "The Origin and Growth of Urbanization in the World," *American Journal of Sociology,* LX (1955), 429 ff.; Norton S. Ginsburg, "The Great City in Southeast Asia," *Journal of Sociology,* LX, 455 ff.; Robert I. Crane, "Urbanism in India," *Journal of Sociology,* LX, 463 ff.; Donald J. Bogue, "Urbanism in the United States, 1950," *Journal of Sociology,* LX, 471 ff.; Irene B. Taeuber, *Population of Japan* (Princeton, 1958), 25 ff., 45 ff., 96 ff., 126 ff., 148 ff.; Kingsley Davis, *Population of India and Pakistan* (Princeton, 1951), 127 ff.; Vandervelde, 16 ff.; Edmond Nicolaï, *La Dépopulation des campagnes et l'accroissement de la population des villes* (Bruxelles, 1903); R. Price-Williams, "The Population of London, 1801–81," *Journal of the Statistical Society,* XLVIII (1885), 349 ff.

8 For the population of earlier European cities, see Roger Mols, *Introduction à la démographie historique des villes d'Europe* (Louvain, 1955), II, 502 ff. See also M. Dorothy George, *London Life in the XVIIIth Century* (London, 1925), 155 ff.

9 Robert M. Fisher, ed., *The Metropolis in Modern Life* (Garden City, 1955), 85 ff.; Weber, *Growth of Cities,* 170 ff. For earlier market relations see, "La Foire," Société Jean Bodin, *Receuils,* V (1953), *passim.*

10 See Douglas F. Dowd, "Economic Expansion of Lombardy," *Journal of Economic History,* XXI (1961), 143 ff.; *Storia di Milano* (Milan, 1957–1960), VIII, 337 ff., XIV, 835 ff.; Jakob Rosenberg, *Rembrandt* (Cambridge, 1948), I, 70 ff.; Weber, *The City,* 91 ff.; Mumford, 269 ff., 281 ff.; Société Jean Bodin, *Receuils,* VII (1955), 567 ff.; Schramm, *Kaufleute,* 185 ff.

11 Robert Crowley, quoted in Mumford, 343.

12 Gideon Sjoberg, *The Preindustrial City Past and Present* (Glencoe, 1960), 100 ff.; Martin S. Briggs, "Town-Planning," Charles Singer, *et al.,* eds., *History of Technology* (New York, 1957), III, 269 ff.; *Golden Ages,* 31–34, 67, 230; Mumford, 299 ff.

13 See Otis D. and Beverly Duncan, "Residential Distribution and Occupational Stratification," *American Journal of Sociology,* LX (1955), 493 ff.; R. P. Dore, *City Life in Japan. A Study of a Tokyo Ward* (Berkeley, 1958), 91 ff.

14 Mumford, 421 ff.; Fisher, 125 ff.; Weber, *Growth of Cities,* 322 ff.

15 *The Auto-Biography of Goethe. Truth and Poetry: From My Own Life* (John Oxenford, transl., London, 1948), 3, 4, 7–10, 12 ff.

16 Fukuzawa Yukichi, *Autobiography* (transl. by Eiichi Kiyooka, Tokyo, 1948); Robson, 510; Brett-James, 420 ff.

17 Pennsylvania Railroad Company, *The New York Improvement and Tunnel Extension of the Pennsylvania Railroad* (Philadelphia, 1910).

18 Emil Kaufmann, "Three Revolutionary Architects," *Transactions of the American Philosophical Society,* XLII (1952), 494 ff.; Helen Rosenau, *The Ideal City in Its Architectural Evolution* (London, 1959), 79 ff.

19 Mumford, 465 ff.; Dore, 40 ff.; Reinhard E. Petermann, *Wien im Zeitalter Kaiser Franz Joseph I* (Vienna, 1908), 128 ff.

20 Alec Nove, ed., *The Soviet Seven Year Plan* (London, 1960), 75 ff.; Harry Schwartz, *Russia's Soviet Economy* (2 ed., New York, 1954), 453 ff.; Robson, 384 ff.

21 Arthur H. Cole, "The Tempo of Mercantile Life in Colonial America," *Business History Review,* XXXIII (1959), 277 ff.; *Golden Ages,* 44, 45.

22 On the problem of time, see Pitirim A. Sorokin and Robert K. Merton, "Social Time: A Methodological and Functional Analysis," *American Journal of Sociology,* XLII (1937), 615 ff.

23 Kaufmann, 509 ff.; Rosenau, 121, 133.

24 See, e.g., Catherine E. Reiser, *Pittsburgh's Commercial Development 1800–1850* (Harrisburg, 1951), 28, 191 ff.

25 Louis Wirth, "Urbanism as a Way of Life," *American Journal of Sociology,* XLIV (1938), 20 ff.; Patterson, 222 ff.; Dore, 71 ff.

26 See, in general, Lloyd Rodwin, ed., *The Future Metropolis* (New York, 1961), 23 ff. For specific illustrations see Louis Chevalier, "La Formation de la population parisienne au XIXe Siècle," Institut National d'Etudes Démographiques, *Travaux et Documents,* X (1950); Alphonse Daudet, *Numa Roumestan—Moeurs parisiennes* (Paris, 1881), ch. iii; Dore, 255 f.; Alexander Campbell, *The Heart of Japan* (New York, 1961), 3 ff.; William A. Jenks, *Vienna and the Young Hitler* (New York, 1960), 4.

27 Société Jean Bodin, *Receuils,* VII (1955), 398 ff.; J. B. Sansom, *The Western World and Japan* (New York, 1958), 242; J. D. Chambers, *Nottinghamshire in the Eighteenth Century* (London, 1932), 40 ff.; Besant, *London in the Eighteenth Century,* 475 ff.; George Rudé, *The Crowd in the French Revolution* (Oxford, 1959), 232 ff.

28 Robson, 210 ff.

29 See Petermann, 331 ff.; Jenks, 11; George, 21 ff.; Besant, 140 ff., 263 ff.; Fisher, 18 ff.

30 Georg Simmel, "Die Grosstädte und das Geistesleben," *Jahrbuch der Gehe-Stiftung zu Dresden,* IX (1903), 187 ff.; Kurt H. Wolff, ed., *Georg Simmel, 1858–1918* (Columbus, Ohio, 1959), 100 ff., 221 ff.; Emile Durkheim, *De la Division du travail*

social (5 ed., Paris, 1926), *passim,* but especially the preface to the second edition; Oswald Spengler, *The Decline of the West* (New York, 1950), II, 92 ff.; Mumford, *passim.* See also Wirth, 20 ff.

31 Jean Jacques Rousseau, *Emile ou de l'éducation* (Paris, 1854), Book I, p. 36; Robert A. Kann, *A Study in Austrian Intellectual History* (New York, 1960), 63; see also the point of view implicit in such novels as E. M. Forster, *Howard's End* (London, 1910).

32 Walt Whitman, *Complete Writings* (New York, 1902), I, 196.

33 See also Weber, *Growth of Cities,* 368 ff., 441 ff.

34 See Percy E. Schramm, *Hamburg, Deutschland und die Welt* (Hamburg, 1952), 350 ff.; Mumford, 395 ff.

35 Robson, 30 ff., 60 ff., 75 ff.; Sam B. Warner, *Street Car Suburbs* (Cambridge, 1962); Weber, *Growth of Cities,* 469 ff.; H. J. Dyos, *Victorian Suburbs* (Leicester, 1961).

36 Rosenau, 130 ff.; Robert Owen, *Book of the New Moral World* (London, 1842), II, 16; Ralph Neville, *Garden Cities* (Manchester, 1904); G. Montague Harris, *The Garden City Movement* (London, 1906); Mumford, 514 ff.

37 David H. Pinkney, *Napoleon III and the Rebuilding of Paris* (Princeton, 1958), 25 ff.

38 Robson, 685; Schramm, 187 ff.

39 Oscar Handlin, *John Dewey's Challenge to Education* (New York, 1959), 33 ff.; George D. Painter, *Proust; the Early Years* (Boston, 1959); Robert Musil, *The Man Without Qualities* (London, 1953); Hans Rosenberg, *Bureaucracy, Aristocracy and Autocracy* (Cambridge, 1958), 182 ff.; Hannah Arendt, *The Origins of Totalitarianism* (New York, 1951), 54 ff.; Norman Jacobs, ed., *Culture for the Millions?* (Princeton, 1961), 43 ff.; Kann, 146 ff.

40 Jacobs, 64 ff.

41 Oscar Handlin, *Adventure in Freedom* (New York, 1954), 174 ff.; Kann, 50 ff., 109 ff.

42 Dore, 291 ff.; Arendt, 301 ff.; Jenks, 40 ff., 74 ff., 126 ff.

43 Mumford, 511 ff.; Louis Wirth, *Community Life and Social Policy* (Chicago, 1956), 206 ff.

44 Weber, *The City,* 11 ff.; Wirth, "Urbanism," 8 ff.; Sjoberg, 4 ff., 321 ff.

3

If All the World Were Philadelphia: A Scaffolding for Urban History, 1774–1930

SAM BASS WARNER, JR.

Although Sam Warner's primary purpose in the following essay is to establish a set of variables to be used as a framework for further investigation in urban history, he does provide support for many of Oscar Handlin's generalizations. For example, Warner's data shows a close relationship between changes in the American and Atlantic economy as a whole and in the microcosm of Philadelphia. With the continuing advance in technology and increase in organizational scale, much of Philadelphia's labor force has shifted from direct production activities to white-collar, educational, and governmental work.

The urban economist views the city primarily as a labor market. The urban historian, therefore, can properly ask what kind of labor market the city has been at various periods in its history given the state of the economy of which it is part. Both Handlin and Warner emphasize that the urban historian can use the periodization developed by economic historians in gathering and organizing their own data. In contrast to Sjoberg, Warner pinpoints the size of the work group, rather than the source of power, as the key change in the first stage of the industrial revolution. He notes that industrial entrepreneurs incurred significant costs by bringing people together to labor in groups rather than by putting work out in a domestic system where men, women, and children labored in their own homes or in small shops. Often the use of power-driven machinery, as well as the productivity gains resulting from a division of labor, supplied the impetus for this social organization of work.

Warner's suggestion that historians study the relationship between occupation and residence is a fruitful one. Several scholars have pointed out that occupational and residential stability promote group consciousness, and ties are likely to be much stronger among those who both live and work together.[1] In another essay, Warner has suggested that the textile workers of Philadelphia resisted mechanization longer than those of New England because of the cohesiveness derived from their residential clustering.[2]

■ ■ ■ ■ For Further Reading

Sam B. Warner, Jr., *The Private City: Philadelphia in Three Periods of Its Growth* (Philadelphia: University of Pennsylvania Press, 1968) is a valuable essay on Philadelphia in the years 1774–1775, 1830–1860, and the 1920s. Warner puts heavy emphasis on the concept of privatism to explain the patterns of development and distortion in the city's history. Roy Lubove, *Twentieth-Century Pittsburgh: Government, Business, and Environmental Change* (New York: John Wiley and Sons, 1969) is an analysis of the motivations and limitations of the "Pittsburgh Renaissance" of the post–World War II period. Lubove supports Warner's picture of the forces molding and distorting the twentieth-century city.

■ From the moment American historians began writing self-conscious urban history they assumed the city was a particular kind of place, an environment, or set of environments, that called for special historical investigation. In his pioneering *Rise of the City, 1878–1898* (New York, 1933), Arthur M. Schlesinger, Sr., took the common-sense view that the crowding in slums, the intense social and economic interactions of the downtown, and the diurnal rhythms of the suburbs, all forced men to learn new styles of life if they were to prosper, indeed if they were to survive. Subsequent urban historians, whether their subject was immigrants, industrial cities, or colonial towns, repeatedly asserted that the city, either as a whole or by its parts, bore uniquely upon the lives of the men and women whose stories they told. Thus far, however, historians have failed to study the sources of this uniqueness in any systematic way.

Perhaps because the idea of a city as a special place, or a cluster of special places, seemed such a truism, it appeared not to be worthy of investigation in its own right. Perhaps because the demands for environmental history forced historians to labor so long to master the detail of a locale, few of them would contemplate a comparative study or a survey of a long time period. Or, perhaps the tradition of local history that has long stressed the distinctiveness of each urban portrait has prevented historians from considering the comparative and sequential aspects of urban environments. Whatever the cause of the lack of system, now thirty-five years after Schlesinger began the specialty, urban history still lacks a study of the succession of urban environments for any major city and the custom of research that would allow a reader to compare the history of one city to the history of any other.

This failure to examine the environment of cities in any systematic way has had serious consequences for the specialty. Teachers of urban history courses in American colleges must patch together chronological series out of books that do not treat comparable events, although the entire selection purports to deal with urbanization. A common sequence touching some of the important areas in American urban history might leap, for example, from Carl Bridenbaugh's description of colonial towns, to Oscar Handlin's analysis of Boston from 1830 to 1880, to Jacob Riis' account of New York's Lower East Side, to Lincoln Steffens' survey of municipal corruption, to Gilbert Osofsky's history of Harlem.[3] There is analysis of urban environments in Handlin, Riis, and Osofsky, although the data presented do not allow strict comparison without much outside knowledge. There is no concept of environment in Bridenbaugh and Steffens. The latter's argument rests on an interpretation of the structure of urban industry in the early twentieth century, but none of the other books give information on the earlier or later industrial structure. There are immigrants in Bridenbaugh's towns, but no information on acculturation. Just as frustrating to teacher and student as this lack of consistent information from book to book is the fact that no outline of the process of urbanization can be elicited from a chronological reading of our major urban histories. Except to the most imaginative reader, the usual shelf of urban history books looks like a line of disconnected local histories.

From time to time more systematic methods of viewing change in urban environments have been proposed. Soon after Schlesinger's work appeared, Lewis Mumford wrote his wide-ranging urban history of Europe and America, *The Culture of Cities* (New York, 1938). In it he divided urban history according to technological periods, arguing that urban environments responded to a regular sequence of technological events.[4] Economic historians have also worked with the concept of a process of development, and their periods complement the technological periods that Mumford derived intuitively. The economists have related the size of cities to economic functions and thereby tied urban history directly to the history of industrialization.[5] By extension of their reasoning, it is possible to relate internal environments to general economic change by regarding these environments as products of the developing scale and complexity of local, national, and international markets. Thus, the colonial American town becomes a product of an Atlantic system for the exchange of staples and manufactured goods; the big city to which the immigrants came in the early nineteenth century becomes a product of increased interregional commerce; the modern metropolis becomes a product of highly specialized regional and interregional exchanges in which services of all kinds have grown to supplant in significance older manufacturing and commercial functions. The idea of such urban sequences is as old as the concept of industrialization. What is new is the growing ability of economic historians to specify the relationships that determine urban growth and change.

Today it is possible to arrange the kind of basic facts that urban historians tend to gather in the course of their studies in such a way as to reveal the sequences suggested by Mumford and the economic historians. Such an arrangement gives the writer, and later his readers, a measure by which to judge the typicality of the subject; it also enables the writer and his readers to get some idea of where the particular events under discussion fit within the process of Atlantic urbanization. An orderly presentation of a few facts can, in short, provide a kind of intellectual scaffolding for urban history.

This article will demonstrate a systematic arrangement of a few facts about the population of Philadelphia during the years 1774, 1860, and 1930. It will discuss, in order, the growth of the population, the course of industrialization, the changing locations of workplaces and homes, the shifting intensity of residential clusters, and the group organization of work. Philadelphia has special merit for such a demonstration because it became a big city early in our history and because it industrialized early.

By the best current estimate the population of urban Philadelphia in 1775 (Philadelphia, Northern Liberties, and Southwark) was 24,000.[6] Such a size did not make it the rival of Edinburgh and Dublin, as it has often been described,[7] but rather an ordinary provincial town comparable to many towns throughout Europe and Latin America. Though a new town, its physical, social, and economic environments must have been long familiar to the European world. This very typicality of Philadelphia suggests that comparative studies of contemporary European and Latin American provincial cities would reveal important dimensions of the preindustrial world.

In 1860 the consolidated city of Philadelphia (consolidated in 1854 to include all of Philadelphia County) held a population of 566,000, second only to New York in numbers of inhabitants.[8] So rapid had been its growth that it had become one of the great cities of the world, about the same size as the old cities of Vienna and Moscow or the new city of Liverpool. As in the case of Liverpool, industrialization, immigration, and boomtown conditions were its hallmarks.

In 1930 Philadelphia's population (within the same boundaries as in 1860) had risen to 1,951,000. It was then, as it has remained, one of the nation's "big five," grouped with New York, Chicago, Los Angeles, and Detroit. In comparison to other cities of the world it ranked twelfth, behind Osaka, Paris, Leningrad, and Buenos Aires.[9] In this period the key social issue was the manner in which a city of such unprecedented size structured its masses of people and its heavy volume of economic activities.

It is impossible to classify with precision the occupations of city dwellers over a century and a half of modern history. Crude listings can, nevertheless, give useful perspectives on the nature of urban economic life. The statistics for Philadelphia suggest two quite different perspectives: a view of continuity and a view of change.

In terms of continuity, differences of a few percentage points may be read both to suggest the stability of urban life and to point to fundamental change. Note, for example, in Table I the move in the Manufacturing category from 52.4 per cent to 45.3 per cent, in the professions from 3.1 per cent to 6.3 per cent, or in the building trades from 7.6 per cent to 8.1 per cent. Although the span from 1774 to 1930 is generally treated by historians as a time of major revolutions, over the entire 150 years the city fulfilled a basic set of functions: it provided clothing, food, and housing for its residents, and professional services, markets, and manufactures for its residents and its trading region. From such a placid viewpoint, even a sharp decline, such

Table I. A Comparison of Some Elements of the Work Structure
of Philadelphia, 1774–1930*

	1774	1860	1930
Occupation:			
Laborers, all industrial categories	13.3	8.1	8.7
Clerks of all kinds, office, and sales	0.8	3.4	13.9
All other occupations	85.9	88.5	77.4
	100.0%	100.0%	100.0%
Workers by industrial categories:			
Manufacturing and mechanical industries	52.4	54.9	45.3
Building	7.6	8.3	8.1
Clothing	7.6	11.7	4.5
Bakeries	3.3	0.9	1.2
Iron, steel, and shipbuilding except autos and blast furnaces	6.2	4.5	4.7
Metalworking except iron and steel	2.0	2.4	0.6
Paper and printing	0.8	3.2	2.9
Miscellaneous textiles except wool and knitting	1.8	4.8	3.8
Balance of manufacturing	23.1	19.1	19.5
Nonmanufacturing	47.6	45.1	54.7
Wholesale and retail except autos	21.1	11.2	15.3
Transportation except railroads and transit	12.3	3.6	2.6
Professional and semiprofessional except entertainment	3.1	4.3	6.3
Hotels, laundries, and domestic service except slaves and indentured servants	5.9	21.8	12.8
Other nonmanufacturing industries	5.2	4.2	17.7
	100.0%	100.0%	100.0%
Total Classified	3,654	3,012	864,926

* The classification of the Philadelphia work force of this table is that of the 1930 US Census, *Fifteenth Census, Classified Index of Occupations* (Washington, D.C., 1930), and *Alphabetical Index of Occupations* (Washington, D.C., 1930). One exception only has been made: wooden shipbuilding trades have been placed with the iron, steel, and shipbuilding categories for 1774 and 1860. The categories chosen for this table are those showing some specificity and continuity through all three periods and did not, like banking, contain so many unspecified clerks, or, like cotton mills, contain so many unspecified operatives as to defy 1774 or 1860 restoration. Occupations that could not be distributed by industry, like gentleman, widow, clerk, agent, operative, laborer, foreman, and helper, have been omitted from the industrial categorization of 1774 and 1860 and therefore do not enter into the percentage distributions of those years. These variations in classification between 1774, 1860, and 1930 probably account for small fluctuations in the Index of Dissimilarity of Table III. In a few cases the census names of some industrial categories have been altered for clarity. The census' Other Iron and Steel category appears in the table as Iron, steel, and shipbuilding except autos and blast furnaces; the census' Other Textiles appears as Miscellaneous textiles except wool and knitting; the census' Other Professional appears as Professional and semiprofessional except entertainment. The table's category Hotels, laundries, and domestic service except slaves and indentured servants is a grouping of three census categories: Hotels, Restaurants, and Boarding Houses; Laundries and Cleaning Shops; Other Domestic Services. The 1774 list of occupations was drawn up from a careful comparison of names given on the 1774 Provincial Property Tax List for Philadelphia County with the 1775 Constable's Return for Philadelphia. The tax list is deposited in the Pennsylvania Historical and Museum Commission, Harrisburg; the Constable's Return is in the Archives of the City of Philadelphia, City Hall, Philadelphia. The 1860 material was drawn from a random sample of 3,666 persons taken from the original Eighth Census schedules for Philadelphia County now deposited in the National Archives. The 1930 data were transcribed from unpublished schedules of the Fifteenth Census now in my possession.

as that of the transportworkers, or an equally sharp rise, such as that of the clerks, can be regarded as merely a shift in the nature of the city's commerce, not a departure from its historic functions. This perspective of continuity is especially useful to political history since it helps to explain the enduring power of urban businessmen, the commercialism of urban leadership, and the perseverance of business ideology at all levels of city politics.

The grouping of occupational statistics can also be used to place a city's history in a perspective of change. One can, for instance, interpret the shifts in the percentage of persons engaged in manufacturing and mechanical industries in the three years we are using (1774, 52.4 per cent; 1860, 54.9 per cent; 1930, 45.3 per cent) to suggest a steady decline in the proportions of Philadelphians engaged in manufactures from a peak in 1774. This interpretation seems proper because the 1774 percentage radically understates manufacturing activity. Colonial tax lists did not report the contribution of female domestic labor although such labor constituted an important fraction of the city's output. Indeed, one economic historian has estimated that on the eve of the Revolution four thousand Philadelphia women were spinning and weaving.[10] If this interpretation is correct, then the course of urban industrialization takes on a special character. Not only did successive changes in industrial organization and machine processes free men and women from manufacturing for other occupations, but urban industrialization was a progressive sequence, ever lessening the commitment of the urban work force to manufacturing. Such a long trend differs from our common-sense impression that manufacturing occupied more and more city workers from President Jackson's time to the Hoover era.

More detailed comparisons of occupational and industrial groupings can also be made. Such groupings reflect changes in the structure of Philadelphia's economy that accompanied changes in the city's role in the Atlantic and American economy. During the first wave of industrialization, from 1774 to 1860, the proportions of unskilled laborers fell rapidly while the numbers of office and sales clerks multiplied. General wholesaling and retailing, however, declined with the differentiation of the old importing merchant's and general storekeeper's functions into distinct specialties. The labor force tied to marine transport and drayage declined sharply, while new industries like clothing, paper, and printing and some lines of textiles rose to great importance.

In the second wave of industrialization, during the interval 1860–1930, office and sales clerks again multiplied, but unskilled laborers remained a more or less steady proportion of the working population. Clothing, printing, baking, and textiles declined in relative importance, though they remained heavy users of Philadelphia's labor force. New industries, especially electrical machinery and auto parts, surged into prominence.[11] Such changes in manufacturing went forward within the context of a general decline in the proportion of Philadelphians engaged in manufactures and a strong rise in professions, government, commerce, and some services.

In sum, even such a crude table (Table IV) shows that Philadelphia, despite its unique historical mixture of manufacturing, banking, and transportation, participated in the general trend of American and European industrialization suggested by Colin Clark.[12] Philadelphians' economic effort shifted steadily from an early concentration on manufactures and commerce toward a modern emphasis on services, education, and government.

As in the case of all large American cities, Philadelphia's growth was propelled by heavy in-migrations of rural native and foreign immigrants. The successive waves of foreign migration have been well documented, and now recent internal migrations have been estimated in state-by-state detail.[13] Today's practical concern with the social and political problems of black core cities and white metropolitan rings has obscured some of the history of urban settlement. The modern core of poverty and ring of affluence date from the late nineteenth century and were not characteristic of the first wave of urban growth.[14]

A kind of core and ring distribution of city dwellers manifested itself from the beginning, but it was much weaker and the reverse of the later distribution. In 1774 the poor seemed to have been pushed to the fringes of the city by the high cost of land near the Delaware River wharves. Then, during the early nineteenth century, Philadelphia grew so rapidly, and from such small beginnings, that no large stock of old housing existed to absorb or to ghettoize the waves of poor people flooding into the city.

Like inhabitants of a booming Latin American city today, Philadelphians of all income levels had to locate in new construction. Shanties, shacks, backyard houses, and alley tenements, as well as the monstrous conversions of the early nineteenth century, all so movingly reported by the nation's first sanitary inspectors, testify to the unpleasant clash of low incomes with the costs of new construction.[15] Under these conditions the poor tended to settle in backyards everywhere, in any old, decaying street that was not being seized by business, and especially at the outer edge of the city where land was cheapest, or could be squatted on.

If laborers are taken as proxies for low-income families, then Table II shows the tendency of poverty to concentrate at the ring of the city in 1860, not at the core; clerks concentrated next to the downtown. Such commonplace occupations as carpenters, machinists, shoemakers, and tailors settled in reasonably even proportions in both parts of the city. By 1930 the large stocks of old, cheap housing in the core of the city had completely reversed this pattern; low rents concentrated in the core, homeowners and middle-income rentpayers ($50.00–$99.00) at the ring.

Complementary patterns can be observed in the location of immigrants. In 1860, except for the British who clustered in the ring to be near the city's outer textile mills, immigrants were rather evenly distributed between core and ring. In 1930 the major immigrant groups, the Italians, Poles, and

Table II. *Location of Foreign-Born, Negroes, and Selected Occupations,*
Tenures, and Rents, by Per Cent in Core or Ring,
1860, 1930*

1860

	Negro	For-eign-Born	Britain	Ger-many	Ireland		Total Popu-lation
Ring	34.9	62.1	73.7	60.4	60.8		61.9
Core	65.1	37.9	26.3	39.6	39.2		38.1
Total Number	22,185	168,556	22,398	43,833	94,989		565,529

	Laborer	Clerk	Car-penter	Ma-chinist	Shoe-maker	Tailor	Sample
Ring	75.5	40.6	61.7	69.5	66.9	68.9	58.9
Core	24.5	59.4	38.3	30.5	33.1	31.1	41.1
Number in Sample	442	283	149	82	181	122	4,740

1930

	Negro	Britain	Ger-many	Ireland	Italy	Poland	Russia	Total Popu-lation
Ring	19.7	52.6	43.8	52.0	29.5	27.4	30.0	70.4
Core	80.3	47.4	56.2	48.0	70.5	72.6	70.0	29.6
Total Number	222,504	36,593	38,066	31,359	68,156	30,582	80,959	1,950,961

	Own Their Home	Rent at under $15	Rent $15–$29	Rent $30–$49	Rent $50–$99	Rent $100+		Total Families
Ring	52.4	10.9	16.8	40.3	60.5	44.2		44.2
Core	47.6	89.1	83.2	59.7	29.5	55.8		55.8
Number of Families	232,591	10,142	63,432	96,026	36,427	6,538		448,653

* The core is the original municipality of Philadelphia, 1860, Wards 5–10; the ring is the eighteen outer wards. The location of the Negroes was given in *U.S. Ninth Census: 1870,* I, *Population,* 254; the location of the foreign-born was determined by transcribing the original eighth census schedules at the National Archives. The error in the transcription was less than 1.0 per cent. The location of the occupations was determined from a sample of *McElroy's Street Directory* for 1860. The ring wards are northeast 23, 35, 41; south 48; west 34, 46, 40; northwest 38, 21, 22, 42; the core is the thirty-seven inner wards of the city. All figures calculated from unpublished tract statistics of the fifteenth census, 1930. The owning families plus the renting families do not quite add to 100 per cent because there were 3,497 families who were listed as renting, but did not specify their rental group. (*U.S. Fifteenth Census: 1930, Population, Families,* IV, 1162–63.)

Russians, and the incoming Negroes concentrated in the cheap housing in the core. By the twentieth century, income, ethnic, and racial segregation had become as characteristic of the giant industrial metropolis as jumble and huggermugger had characterized the earlier big city.

As significant to the social geography and social history of the city as the general placement of income, ethnic, and racial groups by core and ring is the question of the intensity of residential clustering. For example, are the shops and houses of the printers so tightly clustered together in one neighborhood that they encourage the establishment of benevolent societies and unions somewhat in the manner of the medieval city with its guilds? Or are the printers' homes so dispersed that only the conditions in the shops themselves contribute to association? Are the immigrants of a given period so tightly clustered that they experience American culture only through the strong filter of an ethnic ghetto? Or are the immigrants mixed in with large proportions of other poor people so that their assimilation is a process of adapting to some more general culture of the American poor? Variations in the intensity of clustering will also affect the historian's evaluation of the functions of political bosses and their ward machines and of the services of city institutions like hospitals, schools, theaters, and saloons. By noting the ward location of the workers classified according to their industrial groups for Table I, and by adding information on the foreign-born and on rents, as it became available, one can compare the intensity of residential clustering in 1774, 1860, and 1930.

In the history of Philadelphia, the general trend in concentrations of settlement was striking. Between 1774 and 1860 necessity and convenience caused the members of some industries to cluster their homes. Then, with the improvement in intracity transportation and the creation of large business organizations, the necessity to hive faded away. As this industrial cause of clustering lapsed, intense segregation based on income, race, foreign birth, and class rose to prominence as the organizing principle of the metropolis. (See Table III.)

A value of twenty-five on the accompanying Index of Dissimilarity (Table III) makes a convenient boundary between strong and weak clustering.[16] Some groupings of industry like the building trades, wholesaling, and retailing never established strong residential clusters. In 1774 the laborers' homes clustered most intensely at the outer fringe of town; the other strong gatherings were the printers; the shipbuilders near the port; blacksmiths, tinsmiths, and coppersmiths (these occupations are included within the US census categories of Table III, namely, Metalworking except iron and steel; Iron, steel, and shipbuilding; Paper and printing).

The big city of 1860 continued some of these tendencies toward industrial concentration: professionals such as lawyers and doctors lived and practiced near the downtown; bakers lived and worked there, too, and also clustered near the city's eleven public markets. The strongest industrial cluster of this era, and remaining so in 1930, was the textileworkers. Another sign of the future, visible from the tabulation for 1860, was the concentration of the hotel, laundry, and domestic workers. In this case their stronghold lay on the south side of the downtown, the site in 1930 of Philadelphia's sin

Table III. *Index of Dissimilarity, Philadelphia, Southwark, and Northern Liberties, 1774; Philadelphia, 1860; 1930**

1774	Index No.	1860	Index No.	1930	Index No.
				Rental under $15 per month	56.0
				Italy, foreign-born	50.7
				Negro, native and foreign	50.7
				Rental $100+	50.2
		Negro, free, native-born	47.3		
				Russia, foreign-born	44.4
				Poland, foreign-born	44.0
				Miscellaneous textiles	42.3
		Miscellaneous textiles	40.3		
Laborers	37.2				
		Germany, foreign-born	34.1	Rental $15–$29	35.3
Metalworking except iron and steel	32.5				
				Germany, foreign-born	32.4
				Rental $50–$99	31.5
				Hotels, laundries, and domestics	30.8
		Bakeries	30.7		
Iron, steel, and shipbuilding	29.4				
Paper and printing	29.4				
		Iron, steel, and shipbuilding	29.0	Clothing	27.7
				Transportation except railroads and transit	27.2

Table III (continued)

1774	Index No.	1860	Index No.	1930	Index No.
				Britain, except Northern Ireland, foreign-born	26.6
		Hotels, laundries, and domestics	25.9		
		Metalworking except iron and steel	25.6		
		Professional except entertainment	25.4		
Transportation except railroads and transit	24.7				
Miscellaneous textiles	24.3				
				Professional except entertainment	23.1
				Owned occupied home	22.6
Clothing	22.3				
		Laborers	21.9		
		Clothing	21.8		
				Ireland, Northern and Southern, foreign-born	21.5
Building trades	21.2				
				Iron, steel, and shipbuilding	20.8
Wholesale and retail	20.5				
		Ireland, Northern and Southern, foreign-born	19.8		
German patronyms	19.7				

1774	Index No.	1860	Index No.	1930	Index No.
Professional except entertainment	19.7				
		Transportation except railroads and transit	19.6		
		Paper and printing	19.0		
				Rental $30–$49 (the median)	17.7
Bakeries	16.7				
		Building trades	16.4	Metalworking except iron and steel	16.4
				Bakeries	15.2
Hotels, laundries, and domestics	15.1				
				Paper and printing	11.4
				Building	10.4
		Pennsylvania, native-born	10.1		
		Wholesale and retail	9.6		
Homeowners	6.1				
				Wholesale and retail	5.3

* This Index of Dissimilarity should give the reader some measure by which he can compare the intensity of residential clustering in Philadelphia in 1774 to clustering in 1860 and clustering in 1930. The index has been frequently used by sociologists to discuss segregation in modern American cities. The values of the index in this table are lower than for modern studies because all the tabulations had to be based upon ward data, the ward being the only subdivision of the city for which material was available in all three periods. To construct the index, proportions of each group (laborers, foreign-born Irish, and so forth) to the total population of each ward were calculated. Next the proportion of the group to the total population of the city was calculated. Then the index was computed. The index measures the degree to which the group in question clustered in some wards in higher proportions than its proportion to the total population of the city. It is a measure of the variation of the ward-by-ward distribution of one group as compared to all others in the city. If the index number were 0, then in each ward of the city the group in question would be distributed in precisely its proportion to the entire city's population. If the index number were 100, the group would be entirely concentrated in its ward, or wards, and present in no others. A full explanation of the index and other methods of measuring clustering appears in Taeuber and Taeuber, *Negroes in Cities,* 203–204, 223–38. The sources for the occupations and origins of this table were the same as those mentioned in the note to Table I. For a more complete description of the archival research behind the data for 1774, see Sam Bass Warner, Jr., *The Private City: Philadelphia in Three Periods of Its Growth* (Philadelphia, 1968), 225–28.

and slum district. The evidence of the free Negroes also tells of the long-standing caste rules against that race. Theirs was the most intense segregation. The foreign-born Germans had created a strong cluster on the north side of town, but the largest immigrant group of all, the Irish, was evenly distributed throughout the city. They lived in basements, alleys, and attics on every block.[17]

In 1930, except for the textile group, well-paid skilled workers were scattered through the city's wards without much regard as to their industries. The new clusters of industry groupings shown in Table III were those who lacked skills and were not well paid: truckers, expressmen, sailors, clothing-workers, and workers in hotels, laundries, and domestic service. These were also the trades of the Negroes and the new immigrants. The index for 1930, then, shows the modern metropolitan pattern: high concentration of low skills and low rents. All the disfavored groups did not live in the same place, to be sure, but these groups divided up what was available wherever cheap old housing prevailed. In Philadelphia in the 1920's these conditions could be found especially in the core and in the old industrial sections of the north side. The rich, of course, huddled together, as segregated in their way as the poorest Negro.

These trends nicely match the general trend in the building of the American metropolis and the aging of its structures. They also reflect the strong early twentieth-century prejudice against foreigners and the intense caste feeling against Negroes. In this sense, the history of Philadelphia seems to conform to the general national history of urban growth, immigration, and industrialization.[18]

Because most of our social historians who are interested in big cities have been concerned with immigrants, and because our labor historians have not been concerned with cities, American history has failed to deal with the interaction between urban environments and the social organization of work. The simplest statistical computation shows that we have ignored a series of events of wide implication and enormous magnitude. The arrangement of most of the economic activities of a city into work groups is as much of a revolution in the environments of cities as the introduction of the automobile or electricity. In this important dimension of social structure, the town of 1774, the big city of 1860, and the industrial metropolis of 1930 all differed markedly from each other.

In eighteenth-century Philadelphia, with but very few exceptions, most people labored alone, with their family, or with a partner or a helper or two.[19] The first wave of industrialization brought a large fraction of the city's manufacturing workers into a group organization of work. (See Table IV.) The technique of rationalizing tasks so that they could be performed by groups of men and women working within one shop, rather than as individuals laboring in a neighborhood of households, was to my mind the

Table IV. *Average Size of Establishments in Major Lines of Manufacture, Philadelphia, 1860, 1930**

Total Persons Employed	1860	Average No. Persons Per Establishment
98,397	All lines of manufacture	15.6
1,255	Locomotives	627.5
4,793	Cotton goods	94.0
1,131	Gas fixtures	75.4
3,258	Cotton and woolen goods	63.9
1,021	Umbrellas and parasols	48.6
3,290	Shirts, collars, etc.	45.7
14,387	Clothing, men's and boys'	40.9
1,219	Silk fringes and trimmings	39.3
1,876	Bricks	38.3
2,285	Hosiery, woolen	32.2
1,613	Machinery, general, of iron	26.4
2,680	Carpets	21.6
1,190	Bookbinders	20.0
1,038	Carriages and coaches	20.0
1,326	Leather	15.8
8,434	Boots and shoes	12.0
1,627	Furniture and cabinetmakers' wares	10.1
1,290	Cigars	5.6
1,138	Millinery, laces, etc.	4.9
54,851		

	1930	
292,616	All lines of manufacture	52.6
1,986	Sugar refining	662.0
3,103	Iron and steel mills	443.3
20,280	Electrical machinery	375.6
1,535	Paper	307.0
5,105	Leather	204.2
8,321	Worsted goods	180.9
8,564	Cigars and cigarettes	161.6
26,693	Knit goods	134.1
1,861	Chemicals	124.1
1,245	Dental goods and equipment	113.2
13,806	Printing and publishing, newspaper and magazine	99.3
3,479	Silk and rayon manufacture	94.0
2,219	Cotton, small wares	92.5
1,829	Druggists' preparations	91.5
5,692	Cotton goods	79.1
3,002	Woolen goods	73.2
3,327	Shirts	72.3
1,840	Meat packing, wholesale	59.4
13,083	Foundry and machine-shop production	59.2
3,227	Boxes, paper	50.4

Table IV (*continued*)

Total Persons Employed	1930	Average No. Persons Per Establishment
4,056	Dyeing and finishing textiles	41.4
4,676	Furniture, including store fixtures	41.0
11,680	Clothing, men's and boys'	39.6
3,884	Confectionery	39.2
2,070	Paints and varnishes	37.6
1,432	Ice cream	36.7
1,114	Structural and ornamental iron	35.9
9,304	Clothing, women's	31.3
1,464	Fancy and miscellaneous articles	30.5
1,463	Planing mill products	28.7
1,513	Nonferrous metals	28.0
1,293	Copper, tin, sheet ironwork	21.9
8,413	Bread and bakery products	16.5
7,319	Printing and publishing, book and job	15.2
189,878		

* A major line of manufacturing is one that employed one thousand or more persons in the city of Philadelphia. Office help is included with the mill hands, supervisors, owners, and employers. Many children are omitted in 1860 in those lines, like cigar making, that were dominated by small shops. (Philadelphia Board of Trade, *Manufactures of Philadelphia* [Philadelphia, 1861], 5–18; *U. S. Fifteenth Census: 1930, Manufactures*, III, 466–67.)

largest component in the first wave of urban industrialization. The early increases in productivity in most lines of urban manufacture came from the work of groups, not from the new machines. The violent strikes and the anti-Catholic and anti-Negro riots of the 1830's and 1840's testify to the painful and revolutionary effect of this social change.[20] By 1930 three-quarters of Philadelphia's work force—in office, factory, store, and government—labored in groups.[21]

In the simplest sense this transformation of the organization of work had the effect of creating a new lattice of loyalties and social relationships in the city. If factoryworkers may be taken as indicative of the behavior of clerical and retail help, then the University of Pennsylvania's Wharton School studies show that most city dwellers in the 1920's settled down to more or less permanent jobs after four or five years of shopping around.[22] It seems fair to reason that in time the men and women of his work group must have become important members of a worker's social life and that the group must have become a source of discipline, loyalty, and culture in its own right. These were some of the positive results of removing a large fraction of the city's work force from entrepreneurial roles.[23]

Research on the historical interactions between the group organization of work and urban residential environments is not yet fairly begun, yet such research seems to hold great promise for extending our comprehension of the processes of urban history. In my own study of Philadelphia I have found that even such simple information as the average size of establishment by industry adds significantly to the understanding of such important events as the rise and decline of unions and strikes, epidemics of street violence, and the development of an isolated mill-town culture in one quarter of Philadelphia as opposed to the suburban-downtown white-collar culture of another quarter.[24]

To sum up, what in the way of intellectual scaffolding for urban history does this survey of Philadelphia offer? It provides a descriptive framework relating changes in scale to changes in structure.

First, at each period of Philadelphia's history (1774, 1860, 1930) the city had grown to a radically different size, from 24,000 to 566,000 to 1,951,000. The proportions of the social elements of the city were thoroughly altered by such shifts, as were all the city's environments. The basic distribution of the city's jobs and houses according to core and ring varied with each period, and the variations depended directly upon rapid urban growth. The implications of such changes in social geography for political institutions, communications within the city, municipal institutions, and informal associations have yet to be explored with any thoroughness. Here is a great opportunity for studies of small areas that would reinterpret the materials of local history.

Second, the occupational history of the city changed according to the sequences suggested by current generalizations of economic history. The very conformity of Philadelphia to these generalizations suggests that the city responded to advances in transportation, business organization, and technology as a member of a large Atlantic economy and society.

Third, the social geography of industrialization appears to have been one of complex changes. The interaction of the events of industrialization with those of rapid growth seems to have shifted residential segregation away from clustering by occupations toward clustering by classes, ethnicity, and race. Studies of these events are just beginning.[25]

Fourth, industrialization populated the city with a new set of social units: work groups. The nature of these groups, their number, and their impact upon other events in the history of large cities changed significantly over time. Again, the subject is unexplored and calls for research that combines local and institutional history.

Altogether the Philadelphia data confirm the utility of Mumford's descriptive sociotechnical categories and the economic historians' developmental sequences as a useful basis for analysis of the history of any large modern city, or for the comparison of different cities. The unities of scale, social structure, economic institutions, and technology at various stages in the modern process of industrialization and urbanization are inescapable.

This article is offered as the first attempt to discover and arrange the data for one large modern city in such a way that historians may find evidence of the processes they have long speculated upon. It is hoped, further, that the data concerning Philadelphia will give urban historians a scaffolding on which to build the studies of small areas that are required for the history of changing urban environments. Since the data are simple, moreover, their systematic arrangement should encourage historians of other cities to make comparisons that will enable us to say if all the world really was Philadelphia.

■ ■ ■ ■ **Notes**

1 Joan W. Scott, "The Glassworkers of Carmaux, 1850–1900," in *Nineteenth-Century Cities: Essays in the New Urban History,* ed. Stephan Thernstrom and Richard Sennett (New Haven: Yale University Press, 1969), 3–48.
2 Sam B. Warner, Jr., "Innovation and the Industrialization of Philadelphia 1800–1850," in *The Historian and the City,* ed. Oscar Handlin and John Burchard (Cambridge: The M.I.T. and Harvard University Presses, 1963), 63–69.
3 Carl Bridenbaugh, *Cities in the Wilderness: The First Century of Urban Life in America, 1625–1742* (New York, 1938), and *Cities in Revolt: Urban Life in America, 1743–1776* (New York, 1955); Oscar Handlin, *Boston's Immigrants: A Study in Acculturation* (Cambridge, Mass., 1941); Jacob Riis, *How the Other Half Lives: Studies among the Tenements of New York* (New York, 1890); Lincoln Steffens, *The Shame of the Cities* (New York, 1904); Gilbert Osofsky, *Harlem: The Making of a Ghetto. Negro New York, 1890–1930* (New York, 1966).
4 In this work and its predecessor, *Technics and Civilization* (New York, 1934), Mumford elaborated a scheme first proposed by the Scottish biologist and city planner, Patrick Geddes, in his *Cities in Evolution* (London, 1915).
5 Eric E. Lampard, "History of Cities in Economically Advanced Areas," *Economic Development and Cultural Change,* III (Jan. 1955), 81–136; Eugene Smolensky and Donald Ratajczak, "The Conception of Cities," *Explorations in Entrepreneurial History,* 2d Ser., II (Winter 1965), 90–131; and a useful survey of various systematic methods of urban study, Philip M. Hauser and Leo F. Schnore, *The Study of Urbanization* (New York, 1965).
6 This figure is calculated from manuscript tax lists and constables' returns. Other colonial statistics in this paper are from 1774. This size of population is of the same magnitude as that used by Everett S. Lee, "Population," in *The Growth of Seaport Cities, 1790–1825,* ed. David T. Gilchrist (Charlottesville, Va., 1967), 28.
7 Bridenbaugh, *Cities in Revolt,* 217.
8 New York's population was 805,651, Brooklyn's 266,661, giving a combined urban population of 1,072,312. (*U. S. Eighth Census: 1860, Population,* I, xxxi–xxxii.) Baltimore was third with 212,418.
9 The 1860 and 1930 world population data are from Vladimir S. Woytinsky and Emma S. Woytinsky, *World Population and Production* (New York, 1953), 120–22. The population of all cities is according to their political boundaries, not their metropolitan regions.
10 Anne Bezanson, *Prices and Inflation during the American Revolution: Pennsylvania, 1770–1790* (Philadelphia, 1951), 129.
11 See Table IV; and Gladys L. Palmer, *Philadelphia Workers in a Changing Economy* (Philadelphia, 1956), 20–52.
12 Colin Clark, *The Conditions of Economic Progress* (2d ed., London, 1951), Chap. ix.
13 Conrad Taeuber and Irene B. Taeuber, *The Changing Population of the United*

States (New York, 1958); Simon Kuznets *et al., Population Redistribution and Economic Growth, United States, 1870–1950* (3 vols., Philadelphia, 1957–64).

14 Sam Bass Warner, Jr., *Streetcar Suburbs: The Process of Growth in Boston, 1870–1900* (Cambridge, Mass., 1962), gives a detailed account of the development of this core and ring pattern in Boston; Leo F. Schnore, *The Urban Scene, Human Ecology and Demography* (New York, 1965), demonstrates three quite different patterns for race, education, and income in large American metropolitan regions, 1950–1960.

15 *Transactions of the American Medical Association,* II (1849); John H. Griscom, *The Sanitary Condition of the Laboring Population of New York* (New York, 1845).

16 Karl E. Taeuber and Alma F. Taeuber, *Negroes in Cities: Residential Segregation and Neighborhood Change* (Chicago, 1965), 43–62.

17 I have compared these Philadelphia Index of Dissimilarity values for foreign-born in 1860 with those of Boston at about the same period. The results are similar: they indicate that the Irish assimilation in Boston also took place in mixed poor neighborhoods of both foreign-born and native poor as well as in heterogeneous wards of all classes and backgrounds. The Index of Dissimilarity values for Boston (twelve wards, 1855) were: foreign-born Irish, 8.0; foreign-born Canadians, 13.9; foreign-born Germans and Dutch, 33.8. (*Census of Massachusetts: 1855* [Boston, 1856], 124–27.)

18 Students in my seminar at Washington University did some computations of the Index of Dissimilarity for 1910 and 1950 and arrived at values consistent with those given here for Philadelphia in 1930 for Baltimore, Boston, Chicago, Cincinnati, Houston, Kansas City, Los Angeles, Louisville, Manhattan and Brooklyn, St. Louis, and San Francisco. Stanley Lieberson did a careful study of ethnic group patterns in Boston, Buffalo, Chicago, Cincinnati, Cleveland, Columbus, Philadelphia, Pittsburgh, St. Louis, and Syracuse, using similar methods. His results also fit with my values for Philadelphia. (Stanley Lieberson, *Ethnic Patterns in American Cities* [New York, 1963], 209–18.)

19 The exceptions were shipyards, ropewalks, and distilleries in the city. In the country the plantation for manufacture or agriculture was the setting for group work. The only other common cases were ships and the army. (Richard B. Morris, *Government and Labor in Early America* [New York, 1946], 38–40; Carl Bridenbaugh, *The Colonial Craftsman* [New York, 1950], 126–29, 136–39, 141–43.)

20 *History of Labour in the United States,* ed. John R. Commons (4 vols., New York, 1918–35), I, 185–230.

21 It seems reasonable to estimate that conditions of work in groups prevailed in all lines of activity where the average size of the establishment was fifteen or more. (William M. Hench, *Trends in the Size of Industrial Companies in Philadelphia for 1915–1930* [Philadelphia, 1948], 7–8, 21–23; *U. S. Fourteenth Census: 1920,* IX, *Manufactures,* 1277; *U. S. Fifteenth Census: 1930, Manufactures,* III, 444, *Wholesale Distribution,* II, 1262–67; Pennsylvania Department of Labor and Industry, "Employment Fluctuations in Pennsylvania 1921–1927," *Special Bulletin 24* [Harrisburg, 1928], 30.)

22 Anne Bezanson *et al., Four Years of Labor Mobility: A Study of Labor Turnover from a Group of Selected Plants in Philadelphia, 1921–1924* (Philadelphia, 1925), 70–96.

23 A good way to get some feeling for the issues of urban work groups would be to look at the data in *The Pittsburgh Survey,* ed. Paul U. Kellogg (6 vols., New York, 1909–14), in the light of the suggestions of Robert Blauner, *Alienation and Freedom: The Factory Worker and His Industry* (Chicago, 1964); and Marc Fried, "The Role of Work in a Mobile Society," *Planning for a Nation of Cities,* ed. Sam Bass Warner, Jr. (Cambridge, Mass., 1966), 81–104.

24 Warner, *The Private City.*

25 There is a suggestive study of Manhattan in 1840 that unfortunately suffers from the incompleteness of street directory data: Allan R. Pred, *Annals of the Association of American Geographers,* LVI (June 1966), 307–38.

4

Economic Development and Social Structure in Colonial Boston

JAMES A. HENRETTA

In the previous essay, Sam Warner urged historians to gather and arrange various kinds of statistical data to help shed light on questions of social structure and social process. The following study by James Henretta of the comparative distribution of wealth in Boston in 1687 and 1771 is an excellent example of the possibilities of this technique. Along with other younger scholars, Henretta has not been satisfied with impressionistic descriptions of social class, and therefore he has examined the prevailing ownership of property in quantitative terms. In his hands phrases like the "better sort," the "middling sort," and the "meaner sort" acquire a useful precision, and he makes us aware that the social structure of Boston in 1771 was not simply an enlarged version of that of 1687. Even before the industrial revolution in America, the forces of modernization outlined by Oscar Handlin had brought about an increase in the number and proportion of the propertyless, and had concentrated more of a greatly increased total wealth among a small group of owners.

Henretta also indicates the close parallel between property ownership and political power. Town-meeting democracy rested upon the premise that a man's social and political position should reflect the size of his property holdings. Not until the 1830s did the close connection between wealth and officeholding begin to ebb in American cities. Then the wealthy found more important and congenial ways to spend their time, and new men advanced from below using politics as a vehicle for upward mobility.

Urban and social historians are turning more and more to sources which will allow them to make statistical and quantitative comparisons and judgments. Unfortunately, the statistical material for early cities is inadequate and not often as reliable as we would like. Moreover, not all the questions to which we need answers can be dealt with quantitatively. Yet, as Henretta's essay shows, with some luck, imagination, and skill with modern computers, a quantitatively sophisticated scholar can broach new questions and force us to reconsider our answers to old ones.

■ ■ ■ ■ For Further Reading

Carl Bridenbaugh, *Cities in the Wilderness: Urban Life in America, 1625–1742* (New York: Capricorn Books, 1964) and Carl Bridenbaugh, *Cities in Revolt: Urban Life in America, 1743–1776* (New York: Capricorn Books, 1964) provide a richly researched and detailed study of the five major colonial seaports, Boston, Newport, New York, Philadelphia, and Charleston, from their foundations until the beginning of the American Revolution.

■ A distinctly urban social structure developed in Boston in the 150 years between the settlement of the town and the American Revolution. The expansion of trade and industry after 1650 unleashed powerful economic forces which first distorted, then destroyed, the social homogeneity and cohesiveness of the early village community. All aspects of town life were affected by Boston's involvement in the dynamic, competitive world of Atlantic commerce. The disruptive pressure of rapid economic growth, sustained for over a century, made the social appearance of the town more diverse, more complex, more modern—increasingly different from that of the rest of New England. The magnitude of the change in Boston's social composition and structure may be deduced from an analysis and comparison of the tax lists for 1687 and 1771. Containing a wealth of information on property ownership in the community, these lists make it possible to block out, in quantitative terms, variations in the size and influence of economic groups and to trace the change in the distribution of the resources of the community among them.[1]

The transformation of Boston from a land-based society to a maritime center was neither sudden nor uniform. In the last decade of the seventeenth century, a large part of the land of its broad peninsula was still cultivated by small farmers. Only a small fraction was laid out in regular streets and even less was densely settled. The north end alone showed considerable change from the middle of the century when almost every house had a large lot and garden. Here, the later-comers—the mariners, craftsmen, and traders who had raised the population to six thousand by 1690—were crowded together along the waterfront.[2] Here, too, in the series of docks and shipyards which jutted out from the shore line, were tangible manifestations of the commercial activity which had made the small town the largest owner of shipping and the principal port of the English colonies. Over 40 per cent of the carrying capacity of all colonial-owned shipping was in Boston hands.[3]

Dependence on mercantile endeavor rather than agricultural enterprise had by 1690 greatly affected the extent of property ownership. Boston no longer had the universal ownership of real estate characteristic of rural Massachusetts to the end of the colonial period. The tax list for 1687 contained the names of 188 polls, 14 per cent of the adult male population, who were neither owners of taxable property of any kind nor "dependents" in a household assessed for the property tax.[4] Holding no real estate, owning no merchandise or investments which would yield an income, these men constituted the "propertyless" segment of the community and were liable only for the head tax which fell equally upon all men above the age of sixteen.[5] Many in this group were young men, laborers and seamen, attracted by the commercial prosperity of the town and hoping to save enough from their wages to buy or rent a shop, to invest in the tools of an artisan, or to find a start in trade. John Erving, a poor Scotch sailor whose grandson in 1771 was one of the richest men in Boston, was only one propertyless man who rose quickly to a position of wealth and influence.[6]

But many of these 188 men did not acquire either taxable property or an established place in the social order of Boston. Only sixty-four, or 35 per cent, were inhabitants of the town eight years later. By way of contrast, 45 per cent of the polls assessed from two to seven pounds on the tax list, 65 per cent of those with property valued from eight to twenty pounds, and 73 per cent of those with estates in excess of twenty pounds were present in 1695. There was a direct relation between permanence of residence and economic condition. Even in an expanding and diversifying economic environment, the best opportunities for advancement rested with those who could draw upon long-standing connections, upon the credit facilities of friends and neighbors, and upon political influence. It was precisely these personal contacts which were denied to the propertyless.[7]

A second, distinct element in the social order consisted of the dependents of property owners. Though propertyless themselves, these dependents— grown sons living at home, apprentices, and indentured servants—were linked more closely to the town as members of a tax-paying household unit than were the 188 "unattached" men without taxable estates. Two hundred and twelve men, nearly one sixth of the adult male population of Boston, were classified as dependents in 1687. The pervasiveness of the dependency relationship attested not only to the cohesiveness of the family unit but also to the continuing vitality of the apprenticeship and indenture system at the close of the seventeenth century.

Yet even the dependency relationship, traditionally an effective means of alleviating unemployment and preventing the appearance of unattached propertyless laborers, was subjected to severe pressure by the expansion of the economy. An urgent demand for labor, itself the cause of short indentures, prompted servants to strike out on their own as soon as possible. They became the laborers or semiskilled craftsmen of the town, while the sons of the family eventually assumed control of their father's business and a share of the economic resources of the community.[8]

The propertied section of the population in 1687 was composed of 1,036 individuals who were taxed on their real estate or their income from trade. The less-skilled craftsmen, 521 men engaged in the rougher trades of a waterfront society, formed the bottom stratum of the taxable population in this pre-industrial age. These carpenters, shipwrights, blacksmiths, shopkeepers owned only 12 per cent of the taxable wealth of the town.[9] Few of these artisans and laborers had investments in shipping or in merchandise. A small store or house, or a small farm in the south end of Boston, accounted for their assessment of two to seven pounds on the tax list. (Table III)

Between these craftsmen and shopkeepers and the traders and merchants who constituted the economic elite of the town was a middle group of 275 property owners with taxable assets valued from eight to twenty pounds. Affluent artisans employing two or three workers, ambitious shop-keepers with investments in commerce, and entrepreneurial-minded sea masters with various maritime interests, bulked large in this center portion of the economic order. Of the 275, 180 owned real estate assessed at seven pounds or less and were boosted into the third quarter of the distribution of wealth by their holdings of merchandise and shares in shipping. (Table III) The remaining ninety-five possessed real estate rated at eight pounds or more and, in addition, held various investments in trade. Making up about 25 per cent of the propertied population, this middle group controlled 22 per cent of the taxable wealth in Boston in 1687. Half as numerous as the lowest group of property owners, these men possessed almost double the amount of taxable assets. (Table I)

Merchants with large investments in English and West Indian trade and individuals engaged in the ancillary industries of shipbuilding and distilling made up the top quarter of the taxable population in 1687. With taxable estates ranging from twenty to 170 pounds, this commercial group controlled 66 per cent of the town's wealth. But economic development had been too rapid, too uneven and incomplete, to allow the emergence of a well-defined merchant class endowed with a common outlook and clearly distinguished from the rest of the society. Only eighty-five of these men, one third of the wealthiest group in the community, owned dwellings valued at as much as twenty pounds. The majority held landed property valued at ten pounds, only a few pounds greater than that of the middle group of property holders.[10] The merchants had not shared equally in the accumulated fund of capital and experience which had accrued after fifty years of maritime activity. Profits had flowed to those whose daring initiative and initial resources had begun the exploitation of the lucrative colonial market. By 1687, the upper 15 per cent of the property owners held 52 per cent of the taxable assets of the town, while the fifty individuals who composed the highest 5 per cent of the taxable population accounted for more than 25 per cent of the wealth. (Table I)

By the end of the seventeenth century widespread involvement in commerce had effected a shift in the locus of social and political respectability in Boston and distinguished it from the surrounding communities. Five of the nine selectmen chosen by the town in 1687 were sea captains.[11] This was more than deference to those accustomed to command. With total estates of £83, £29, £33, £33, and £24, Captains Elisha Hutchinson, John Fairweather, Theophilus Frary, Timothy Prout, and Daniel Turell were among the wealthiest 20 per cent of the population.[12] Still, achievement in trade was not the only index of respectability. Henry Eames, George Cable, Issac Goose, and Elnathan Lyon, the men appointed by the town to inspect the condition of the streets and roads, had the greater part of their wealth, £105 of £130, invested in land and livestock.[13] And the

Table I. *Distribution of Assessed Taxable Wealth in Boston in 1687**

Total Value of Taxable Wealth	Number of Taxpayers in Each Wealth Bracket	Total Wealth in Each Wealth Bracket	Cumulative Total of Wealth	Cumulative Total of Taxpayers	Cumulative Percentage of Taxpayers	Cumulative Percentage of Wealth
£ 1	0	£ 0	£ 0	0	0.0%	0.0%
2	152	304	304	152	14.6	1.8
3	51	153	457	203	19.5	2.7
4	169	676	1,133	372	35.9	6.8
5	33	165	1,298	405	39.0	7.8
6	97	582	1,880	502	48.5	11.3
7	19	133	2,013	521	50.2	12.1
8	43	344	2,357	564	54.4	14.2
9	22	198	2,555	586	56.6	15.4
10	45	450	3,005	631	60.9	18.1
11	17	187	3,192	648	62.5	19.2
12	30	360	3,552	678	65.4	21.4
13	13	169	3,721	691	66.6	22.4
14	12	168	3,889	703	67.9	23.4
15	22	330	4,219	725	69.9	25.4
16	21	336	4,555	746	72.0	27.5
17	1	17	4,572	747	72.0	27.6
18	18	324	4,896	765	73.8	29.5
19	1	19	4,915	766	73.9	29.6
20	30	600	5,515	796	76.8	33.2
21–25	41	972	6,487	837	80.7	39.0
26–30	48	1,367	7,854	885	85.4	47.3
31–35	29	971	8,825	914	88.2	53.1
36–40	21	819	9,644	935	90.2	58.1
41–45	19	828	10,472	954	92.1	63.1
46–50	16	781	11,253	970	93.6	67.8
51–60	16	897	12,150	986	95.1	73.2
61–70	19	1,245	13,395	1,005	97.0	80.7
71–80	7	509	13,904	1,012	97.8	83.8
81–90	3	253	14,157	1,015	97.9	85.3
91–100	7	670	14,827	1,022	98.6	89.3
100–	14	1,764	16,591	1,036	100.0	100.0

* Money values are those of 1687. Many of the assessments fall at regular five pound intervals and must be considered as an estimate of the economic position of the individual. No attempt was made to compensate for systematic overvaluation or undervaluation inasmuch as the analysis measures relative wealth. The utility of a relative presentation of wealth (or income) is that it can be compared to another relative distribution without regard to absolute monetary values. See Mary Jean Bowman, "A Graphical Analysis of Personal Income Distribution in the United States," *American Economic Review*, XXXV (1944–45), 607–628, and Horst Mendershausen, *Changes in Income Distribution during the Great Depression* (New York, 1946).

presence of Deacon Henry Allen among the selectmen provided a tangible indication of the continuing influence of the church.

These legacies of an isolated religious society and a stable agricultural economy disappeared in the wake of the rapid growth which continued unabated until the middle of the eighteenth century. In the fifty years after 1690, the population of the town increased from 6,000 to 16,000. The farms of the south end vanished and the central business district became crowded. In the populous north end, buildings which had once housed seven people suddenly began to hold nine or ten.[14] Accompanying this physical expansion of Boston was a diversification of economic endeavor. By 1742, the town led all the colonial cities in the production of export furniture and shoes, although master craftsmen continued to carry on most industry on a small scale geared to local needs. Prosperity and expansion continued to be rooted, not in the productive capacity or geographic position of the town, but in the ability of the Boston merchants to compete successfully in the highly competitive mercantile world.[15]

After 1750, the economic health of the Massachusetts seaport was jeopardized as New York and Philadelphia merchants, exploiting the rich productive lands at their backs and capitalizing upon their prime geographic position in the West Indian and southern coasting trade, diverted a significant portion of European trade from the New England traders. Without increasing returns from the lucrative "carrying" trade, Boston merchants could no longer subsidize the work of the shopkeepers, craftsmen, and laborers who supplied and maintained the commercial fleet. By 1760, the population of Boston had dropped to 15,000 persons, a level it did not exceed until after the Revolution.[16]

The essential continuity of maritime enterprise in Boston from the late seventeenth to the mid-eighteenth century concealed the emergence of a new type of social system. After a certain point increases in the scale and extent of commercial endeavor produced a new, and more fluid, social order. The development of the economic system subjected the family, the basic social unit, to severe pressures. The fundamental link between one generation and another, the ability of the father to train his offspring for their life's work, was endangered by a process of change which rendered obsolete many of the skills and assumptions of the older, land-oriented generation and opened the prospect of success in new fields and new places. The well-known departure of Benjamin Franklin from his indenture to his brother was but one bright piece in the shifting mosaic of colonial life.

The traditional family unit had lost much of its cohesiveness by the third quarter of the eighteenth century. The Boston tax lists for 1771 indicate that dependents of property owners accounted for only 10 per cent of the adult male population as opposed to 16 per cent eighty-five years earlier. Increasingly children left their homes at an earlier age to seek their own way in the world.

A second factor in the trend away from dependency status was the decline in the availability of indentured servants during the eighteenth century. Fewer than 250 of 2,380 persons entering Boston from 1764 to 1768 were classified as indentured servants.[17] These were scarcely enough to replace those whose indentures expired. More and more, the labor force had to be recruited from the ranks of "unattached" workers who bartered their services for wages in a market economy.[18]

This laboring force consisted of the nondependent, propertyless workers of the community, now twice as numerous relative to the rest of the population as they had been a century before. In 1687, 14 per cent of the total number of adult males were without taxable property; by the eve of the Revolution, the propertyless accounted for 29 per cent. The social consequences of this increase were manifold. For every wage earner who competed in the economy as an autonomous entity at the end of the seventeenth century, there were four in 1771; for every man who slept in the back of a shop, in a tavern, or in a rented room in 1687, there were four in the later period. The population of Boston had doubled, but the number of propertyless men had increased fourfold.

The adult males without property, however, did not form a single unified class, a monolithic body of landless proletarians. Rather, the bottom of society consisted of a congeries of social and occupational groups with a highly transient maritime element at one end of the spectrum and a more stable and respected artisan segment at the other. Although they held no taxable property, hard-working and reputable craftsmen who had established a permanent residence in Boston participated in the town meeting and were elected to unpaid minor offices. In March 1771, for instance, John Dyer was selected by the people of the town as "Fence Viewer" for the following year. Yet according to the tax and valuation lists compiled less than six months later, Dyer was without taxable property.[19] At the same town meeting, four carpenters, Joseph Ballard, Joseph Edmunds, Benjamin Page, and Joseph Butler, none of whom was listed as an owner of taxable property on the valuation lists, were chosen as "Measurers of Boards."[20] That propertyless men should be selected for public office indicates that the concept of a "stake in society," which provided the theoretical underpinning for membership in the community of colonial Boston, was interpreted in the widest possible sense. Yet it was this very conception of the social order which was becoming anachronistic under the pressure of economic development. For how could the growing number of propertyless men be integrated into a social order based in the first instance on the principle that only those having a tangible interest in the town or a definite family link to the society would be truly interested in the welfare of the community?[21]

Changes no less significant had taken place within the ranks of the propertied groups. By the third quarter of the eighteenth century, lines of economic division and marks of social status were crystallizing as Boston approached economic maturity. Present to some degree in all aspects of town life, these distinctions were very apparent in dwelling arrangements.

In 1687, 85 per cent of Boston real estate holdings had been assessed within a narrow range of two to ten pounds; by the seventh decade of the eighteenth century, the same spectrum ran from twelve to two hundred pounds. (Table III) Gradations in housing were finer in 1771 and had social connotations which were hardly conceivable in the more primitive and more egalitarian society of the seventeenth century. This sense of distinctiveness was reinforced by geographic distribution. Affluent members of the community who had not transferred their residence to Roxbury, Cambridge, or Milton built in the spacious environs of the south and west ends. A strict segregation of the social groups was lacking; yet the milieu of the previous century, the interaction of merchant, trader, artisan, and laborer in a waterfront community, had all but disappeared.[22]

The increasing differences between the social and economic groups within the New England seaport stemmed in part from the fact that craftsmen, laborers, and small shopkeepers had failed to maintain their relative position in the economic order. In the eighty-five years from 1687 to 1771, the share of the taxable wealth of the community controlled by the lower half of the propertied population declined from 12 to 10 per cent. (Table II) If these men lived better at the end of the century than at the beginning, it was not because the economic development of Boston had effected a redistribution of wealth in favor of the laboring classes but because the long period of commercial prosperity had raised the purchasing power of every social group.

The decline in the economic distinctiveness of the middle group of property holders, the third quarter of the taxable population in the distribution of wealth, is even more significant. In 1771, these well-to-do artisans, shopkeepers, and traders (rising land values had eliminated the farmers and economic maturity the versatile merchant–sea captain) owned only 12½ per cent of the taxable wealth, a very substantial decrease from the 21 per cent held in 1687. These men lived considerably better than their counterparts in the seventeenth century; many owned homes and possessed furnishings rarely matched by the most elegant dwellings of the earlier period. But in relation to the other parts of the social order, their economic position had deteriorated drastically. This smaller middle group had been assessed for taxable estates twice as large as the bottom 50 per cent in 1687; by 1771 the assets of the two groups were equal.

On the other hand, the wealthiest 25 per cent of the taxable population by 1771 controlled 78 per cent of the assessed wealth of Boston. This represented a gain of 12 per cent from the end of the seventeenth century. An equally important shift had taken place within this elite portion of the population. In 1687, the richest 15 per cent of the taxpayers held 52 per cent of the taxable property, while the top 5 per cent owned 26.8 per cent. Eighty-five years later, the percentages were 65.9 and 44.1. (Tables I and II and Chart A)

Table II. Distribution of Assessed Taxable Wealth in Boston in 1771*

Total Value of Taxable Wealth	Number of Taxpayers in Each Wealth Bracket	Total Wealth in Each Wealth Bracket	Cumulative Total of Wealth	Cumulative Total of Taxpayers	Cumulative Percentage of Taxpayers	Cumulative Percentage of Wealth
£ 3–30	78	£1,562	£1,562	78	5.0%	0.3%
31–40	86	2,996	4,558	164	10.6	0.9
41–50	112	5,378	9,936	276	17.9	2.2
51–60	74	4,398	14,334	350	22.6	3.5
61–70	33	3,122	17,456	383	24.7	3.8
71–80	165	12,864	30,320	548	35.4	6.5
81–90	24	2,048	32,368	572	36.9	7.0
91–100	142	13,684	46,052	714	46.1	10.0
101–110	14	494	46,546	728	47.1	10.1
111–120	149	17,844	64,390	877	56.7	13.9
121–130	20	2,570	66,960	897	58.0	14.5
131–140	26	4,600	71,560	923	59.7	15.5
141–150	20	2,698	74,258	943	60.9	16.1
151–160	88	14,048	88,306	1,031	66.6	19.1
161–170	11	1,846	90,152	1,042	67.4	19.6
171–180	18	3,128	93,280	1,060	68.6	20.3
181–190	10	1,888	95,168	1,070	69.2	20.7
191–200	47	9,368	104,536	1,117	72.2	22.7
201–300	126	31,097	135,633	1,243	80.4	29.4
301–400	60	21,799	157,432	1,303	84.2	34.1
401–500	58	24,947	182,379	1,361	88.0	39.6
501–600	14	7,841	190,220	1,375	88.9	41.3
601–700	24	15,531	205,751	1,399	90.4	44.6
701–800	26	19,518	225,269	1,425	92.2	48.9
801–900	20	17,020	242,289	1,445	93.4	52.6
901–1,000	16	15,328	257,617	1,461	95.4	55.9
1,001–1,500	41	48,364	305,963	1,502	97.1	66.4
1,501–5,000	37	85,326	391,289	1,539	99.5	84.9
5,001–	7	69,204	460,493	1,546	100.0	100.0

* The extant tax list is not complete. In ward 3, there are two pages and 69 polls missing; in ward 7, one page and 24 polls; in ward 12, an unknown number of pages and 225 polls. Only the total number of polls (224) is known for ward 11. The missing entries amount to 558, or 19.3 per cent of the total number of polls on the tax list. Internal evidence (the totals for all wards are known) suggests that the absent material is completely random. Nevertheless, it should be remembered that this table represents an 80 per cent sample.

The value of shipping investments and of "servants for life" was not included in the computation of the table as it was impossible to determine the assessor's valuation. For the law regulating the assessment, see *The Acts and Resolves, Public and Private, of the Province of the Massachusetts Bay . . .*, IV (Boston, 1881), 985–987. Money values are those of 1771.

Certain long-term economic developments accounted for the disappearance of a distinct middle group of property owners and the accumulation of wealth among a limited portion of the population. The scarcity of capital in a relatively underdeveloped economic system, one in which barter

Table III. Real Estate Ownership in Boston in 1687 and 1771*

1687			1771		
Assessed Total Value of Real Estate	Number of Owners	Cumulative Total of Owners	Assessed Annual Worth of Real Estate	Number of Owners	Cumulative Total of Owners
£ 1	0	0	£ 1	0	0
2	168	168	2	1	1
3	75	243	3	9	10
4	203	446	4	49	59
5	85	531	5	22	81
6	167	698	6	79	160
7	3	701	7	0	160
8	54	755	8	115	275
9	2	757	9	3	278
10	107	864	10	91	369
11	0	864	11	4	373
12	24	888	12	43	416
13	0	888	13	163	579
14	3	891	14	10	589
15	25	916	15	3	592
16	8	924	16	148	740
17	0	924	17	6	746
18	7	930	18	7	753
19	1	931	19	5	758
20	46	932	20	236	994
21–30	25	1,003	21–25	41	1,035
31–40	11	1,014	26–30	163	1,198
41–50	2	1,016	31–35	93	1,291
			36–40	92	1,383
			41–45	5	1,388
			46–50	42	1,430
			51–60	32	1,462
			61–70	10	1,472
			71–80	9	1,481
			81–90	3	1,484
			91–100	3	1,487

* The assessed annual worth of real estate in the 1771 valuation must be multiplied by six to give the total property value.

transactions were often necessary because of the lack of currency, required that the savings of all members of the society be tapped in the interest of economic expansion. The prospect of rapid commercial success and the high return on capital invested in mercantile activity attracted the small investor. During the first decade of the eighteenth century, nearly one of every three adult males in Boston was involved directly in trade, owning at least part of a vessel. In 1698 alone, 261 people held shares in a seagoing vessel.[23]

Trade had become "not so much a way of life as a way of making money; not a social condition but an economic activity."[24] This widespread ownership of mercantile wealth resulted in the creation of a distinct economic "middle class" by the last decades of the seventeenth century.

A reflection of a discrete stage of economic growth, the involvement of disparate occupational and social groups in commerce was fleeting and transitory. It lasted only as long as the economy of the New England seaport remained underdeveloped, without large amounts of available capital. The increase in the wealth and resources of the town during the first half of the eighteenth century prompted a growing specialization of economic function; it was no longer necessary to rely on the investments of the less affluent members of the community for an expansion of commerce. This change was slow, almost imperceptible; but by 1771 the result was obvious. In that year, less than 5 per cent of the taxable population of Boston held shares in shipping of ten tons or more, even though the tonnage owned by the town was almost double that of 1698. Few men had investments of less than fifty tons; the average owner held 112 tons. By way of contrast, the average holding at the end of the seventeenth century had been about twenty-five tons.[25] Moreover, on the eve of the Revolution ownership of shipping was concentrated among the wealthiest men of the community. Ninety per cent of the tonnage of Boston in 1771 was in the hands of those whose other assets placed them in the top quarter of the population.[26] With the increase in the wealth of the town had come a great increase in the number of propertyless men and a bifocalization of the property owners into (1) a large amorphous body of shopkeepers, artisans, and laborers with holdings primarily in real estate and (2) a smaller, somewhat more closely defined segment of the population with extensive commercial investments as well as elegant residences and personal possessions.

A similar trend was evident in other phases of town life. In the transitional decades of the late seventeenth and early eighteenth century, the fluidity inherent in the primitive commercial system had produced a certain vagueness in the connotations of social and economic status. Over 10 per cent of the adult males in Boston designated themselves as "merchants" on the shipping registers of the period from 1698 to 1714, indicating not only the decline in the distinctiveness of a title traditionally limited to a carefully defined part of the community but also the feeling that any man could easily ascend the mercantile ladder. Economic opportunity was so evident, so promising, that the social demarcations of the more stable maritime communities of England seemed incongruous.[27] By the sixth decade of the eighteenth century, however, rank and order were supplanting the earlier chaos as successful families tightened their control of trade. The founding in 1763 of a "Merchants Club" with 146 members was a dramatic indication that occupations and titles were regaining some of their traditional distinctiveness and meaning.[28]

An economic profile of the 146 men who composed this self-constituted elite is revealing. Of those whose names appeared on the tax and valuations lists of 1771, only five had estates which placed them in the bottom three quarters of the distribution of wealth. Twenty-one were assessed for taxable property in excess of £1,500 and were thus in the top 1 per cent of the economic scale. The taxable assets of the rest averaged £650, an amount which put them among the wealthiest 15 per cent of the population.

That 146 men, 6½ per cent of the adult male population, were considered eligible for membership in a formal society of merchants indicates, however, that mercantile activity was not dominated by a narrow oligarchy. The range of wealth among the members of the top quarter of the propertied population was so great and the difference of social background so large as to preclude the creation of a monolithic class or guild with shared interests and beliefs.

Yet the influence of this segment of society was pervasive. By the third quarter of the eighteenth century, an integrated economic and political hierarchy based on mercantile wealth had emerged in Boston to replace the lack of social stratification of the early part of the century and the archaic distinctions of power and prestige of the religious community of the seventeenth century. All of the important offices of the town government, those with functions vital to the existence and prosperity of the town, were lodged firmly in the hands of a broad elite, entry into which was conditioned by commercial achievement and family background. The representatives to the General Court and the selectmen were the leaders of the town in economic endeavor as well as in political acumen. John Hancock's taxable wealth totaled £18,000; James Otis was assessed at £2,040, while Colonel Joseph Jackson had property valued at £1,288. Other levels of the administrative system were reserved for those whose business skills or reputation provided the necessary qualifications. Samuel Abbot, John Barrett, Benjamin Dolbeare, John Gore, William Phillips, William White, and William Whitewell, Overseers of the Poor in 1771, had taxable estates of £815, £5,520, £850, £1,747, £5,771, £1,953, and £1,502 respectively. All were among the wealthiest 7 per cent of the property owners; and Barrett and Phillips were two of the most respected merchants of the town. John Scollay, a distiller with an estate of £320, and Captain Benjamin Waldo, a shipmaster assessed at £500, who were among those chosen as "Firewards" in 1771, might in an earlier period have been dominant in town affairs; by the seventh decade of the century, in a mature economic environment, the merchant prince had replaced the man of action at the apex of the social order.

Gradations continued to the bottom of the scale. Different social and occupational levels of the population were tapped as the dignity and responsibility of the position demanded. It was not by accident that the estates of the town assessors, Jonathan Brown, Moses Deshon, and John

Kneeland, were £208, £200, and £342. Or that those of the "Cullers of Staves," Henry Lucas, Thomas Knox, and Caleb Hayden, totaled £120, £144, and £156. The assumption of a graded social, economic, and political scale neatly calibrated so as to indicate the relation of each individual to the whole was the basic principle upon which the functioning of town-meeting "democracy" depended. William Crafts, with a taxable estate of £80, was elected "Fence Viewer." Half this amount qualified William Barrett to be "Measurer of Coal Baskets," while Henry Allen and John Bulfinch, "Measurers of Boards," were assessed at £80 and £48. The design was nearly perfect, the correlation between town office and social and economic position almost exact.[29]

As in 1687, the distribution of political power and influence in Boston conformed to the standards and gradations of a wider, more inclusive hierarchy of status, one which purported to include the entire social order

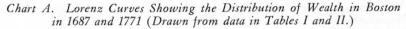

Chart A. Lorenz Curves Showing the Distribution of Wealth in Boston in 1687 and 1771 (Drawn from data in Tables I and II.)

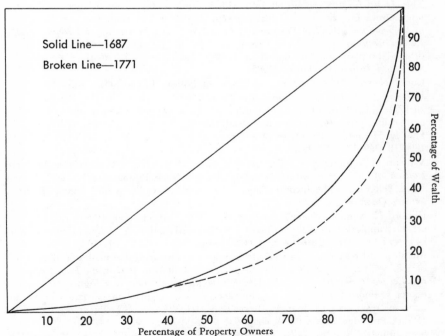

within the bounds of its authority. But the lines of force which had emerged on the eve of the American Revolution radiated from different economic and social groups than those of eighty-five years before, and now failed to encompass a significant portion of the population. The weakening of the "extended" family unit and the appearance of a large body of autonomous wage earners, "proletarians" in condition if not in consciousness, had introduced elements of mobility and diversity into the bottom part of society. Equally significant had been the growing inequality of the distribution of wealth among the propertied segment of the community, notably the greater exclusiveness and predominance of a mercantile "elite." Society had become more stratified and unequal. Influential groups, increasingly different from the small property owners who constituted the center portion of the community, had arisen at either end of the spectrum. Creations of the century-long development of a maritime economy in an urban setting, these "merchant princes" and "proletarians" stood out as the salient characteristics of a new social order.

■ ■ ■ ■ **Notes**

1 "Tax List and Schedules—1687," in *First Report of the Record Commissioners of the City of Boston, 1876* (Boston, 1876), 91–133; "Tax and Valuation Lists—1771," in Massachusetts Archives, CXXXII, 92–147, State House, Boston.

2 The tax list for 1687 shows 80 polls with holdings of five acres or more within the town limits. For the size and location of most Boston real estate holdings from 1630 to 1645 see the "Book of Possessions" (and "Appendix"), *The Second Report of the Record Commissioners of the City of Boston*, 2d ed. (Boston, 1881) and also the detailed property maps compiled by George Lamb, *Series of Plans of Boston . . . 1630–1635–1640–1645* (Boston, 1905).

3 Curtis Nettels, "The Economic Relations of Boston, Philadelphia, and New York, 1680–1715," *Journal of Economic and Business History*, III (1930–31), 185–215.

4 In 1771, in Concord, Middlesex County, only 26 of 396 polls (6.5 per cent) were without taxable property; in Easton, Bristol County, 26 of 261 (10 per cent); and in Hadley, Hampshire County, 8 of 157 polls (5.1 per cent). Mass. Archives, CXXXII, 199–210, 269–274, 251–254.

5 William H. Whitmore, ed., *The Colonial Laws of Massachusetts. Reprinted from the Edition of 1672, with the Supplements through 1686* (Boston, 1887), 22–23. Edwin R. A. Seligman, "The Income Tax in the American Colonies and States," *Political Science Quarterly*, X (1895), 221–247.

6 Clifford K. Shipton, *Sibley's Harvard Graduates*, XII (Boston, 1962), 152–156. For other examples of mercantile success, see Bernard Bailyn, *The New England Merchants in the Seventeenth Century* (Cambridge, Mass., 1955), 192–197.

7 Mobility and residence data were determined by comparing the names on the tax list of 1687 with those of a list of the inhabitants of Boston in 1695 in the *First Report of the Record Commissioners*, 158–170. While the death rate was higher among the poorer sections of the population, this alone does not explain the variation in permanence of residence. See John B. Blake, *Public Health in the Town of Boston, 1630–1822* (Cambridge, Mass., 1959), chap. 6.

8 See Samuel McKee, Jr., *Labor in Colonial New York, 1664–1776* (New York, 1935), chaps. 2, 3; also, Richard B. Morris, *Government and Labor in Early America* (New York, 1946), 147–149.

9 The lower 50 per cent of the property owners is treated as a whole as Tables I and II and Chart A indicate that the proportion of wealth held by this section of the population is approximately the same in 1687 and 1771.

10 See Table III; and Edwin L. Bynner, "Topography and Landmarks of the Provincial

Period," in Justin Winsor, ed., *The Memorial History of Boston . . .* , II (Boston, 1881), chap. 17; Bailyn, chaps. 6, 7; Nettels, 185–200.

11 Robert Francis Seybolt, *The Town Officials of Colonial Boston, 1634–1775* (Cambridge, Mass., 1939), 74.

12 *First Report of the Record Commissioners,* 99, 116, 126, 99, 95; Table I.

13 Seybolt, 74; *First Report of the Record Commissioners,* 98, 109, 127, 109; Bailyn, chaps. 6, 7.

14 Clifford K. Shipton, "Immigration to New England, 1680–1740," *The Journal of Political Economy,* XLIV (1936), 225–238; Boston's population was 9,000 in 1710; 13,000 in 1730; 16,382 in 1742; 15,731 in 1752; and 15,520 in 1771. Lemuel Shattuck, *Report to the Committee of the City Council Appointed to Obtain the Census of Boston for the Year 1845* (Boston, 1846), 3–5. In 1687 there were 850 houses for 6,000 people or 7.05 persons per house. "Tax Lists and Schedules—1687." The average number of persons per house in 1742 was 9.53; in 1771, 8.47. Shattuck, 54.

15 Samuel Eliot Morison, "The Commerce of Boston on the Eve of the Revolution," in American Antiquarian Society, *Proceedings,* New Ser., XXXII (Worcester, 1922), 24–51.

16 See the table of entries and clearances in 1773 for the major colonial ports, American Antiquarian Society, *Proceedings,* 28. By 1760 Philadelphia had 23,750 inhabitants and New York 18,000. Carl Bridenbaugh, *Cities in Revolt, Urban Life in America, 1743–1776* (New York, 1955), 5.

17 Compiled from "Port Arrivals—Immigrants," in Record Commissioners of the City of Boston, *A Volume of Records Relating to the Early History of Boston* (Boston, 1900), 254–312. See, also, Mildred Campbell, "English Emigration on the Eve of the American Revolution," *American Historical Review,* LXI (1955–56), 1–20.

18 For most of the 18th century, Negro slaves compensated for the lack of white servants. From 150 in 1690, the number of Negroes rose to 1,100 in a population of 13,000 in 1730. In that year, they made up 8.4 per cent of the population; in 1742, 8.4 per cent; in 1752, 9.7 per cent; but only 5.5 per cent in 1765. Computed from data in Shattuck, 4–5, 43. The 1771 tax list indicates that only 17 of 318 Negro "servants for life" were held by persons whose property holdings placed them in the lower 50 per cent of the distribution of taxable wealth; 70 by individuals in the third quarter of the economic scale; and 231 or 72.6 per cent by the wealthiest 25 per cent of the population. A somewhat different picture is presented by Robert E. Brown, *Middle-Class Democracy and the Revolution in Massachusetts, 1691–1780* (Ithaca, 1955), 19; and McKee, 171.

19 Seybolt, 341; "Tax and Valuation Lists—1771," ward 1. Dyer apparently paid rent for part of a house assessed at £20.

20 Seybolt, 340–341; "Tax and Valuation Lists—1771," wards 1 and 2.

21 For a different view, see Brown, 28–30, 79–95.

22 Walter Muir Whitehill, *Boston, A Topographical History* (Cambridge, Mass., 1959), chaps. 1–3; Bridenbaugh, 25.

23 Bernard and Lotte Bailyn, *Massachusetts Shipping, 1697–1714, A Statistical Study* (Cambridge, Mass., 1959), 56, 79 (Table II).

24 Bailyn, *New England Merchants,* 194.

25 In 1771, Bostonians owned 10,396 tons of taxable shipping; the town's tonnage was 6,443 in 1698. See Bailyn and Bailyn, *Massachusetts Shipping,* 79 (Table II).

26 Only 2.3 per cent of the 8,898 tons of shipping for which the owners are known was held by individuals in the bottom half of the distribution of wealth (estates of £100 or less in Table II); 5.9 per cent more by those with estates valued from £100 to £200; and an additional 19 per cent by persons with wealth of £200 to £500. 73 per cent of Boston's shipping was held by the wealthiest 12 per cent of the propertied population, those with estates in excess of £500. See Table II.

27 Bailyn and Bailyn, *Massachusetts Shipping,* 57–58.
28 "Society for the Encouraging of Trade and Commerce Within the Province of Massachusetts Bay," Ezekiel Price Papers, Massachusetts Historical Society, Boston. See also, Charles M. Andrews, "The Boston Merchants and the Non-Importation Movement," in Colonial Society of Massachusetts, *Publications,* XIX (Boston, 1918), 159–259.
29 Seybolt, 339–343; "Tax and Valuation Lists—1771."

5

The Working Classes of the Pre-Industrial American City, 1780–1830

DAVID MONTGOMERY

David Montgomery shares James Henretta's belief in the value of quantification, and in the essay below he pays careful attention to the various subgroups within the working classes and the surviving data on wage rates in preindustrial American cities. Montgomery also asks, however, that his fellow scholars consider those questions of belief, attitude, and perception which cannot be measured in statistical or quantitative terms. For instance, how did journeymen, laborers, and seamstresses of the early nineteenth century view their society and their own position within it? From what perspective did they regard the rise of the factory system and the domination of the economy by impersonal market forces? By raising such questions, Montgomery hopes to prompt historians to investigate the meaning of the working people's experience, and thereby enlarge our understanding of the human element in relation to economic change and development. Henretta showed how increasing trade and wealth affected property distribution; following Montgomery's research program, the next step would be to assess the psychological impact of these factors on the various groups affected, especially those on the lower levels of the social scale.

The author's concern with the working classes reflects a growing belief among historians that scholars have concentrated too exclusively upon the literate, the articulate, and the well-to-do, and that it is now time to look at history from the bottom. It is not simply class bias which has accounted for this myopia, although there has been plenty of that. It is much easier to uncover the beliefs of men who put pen to paper easily and frequently, than of those who spent their lives as cartmen and tailors. Although, as Montgomery indicates, material about some groups is relatively abundant, scholars who wish to recapture the experience and the perceptions of workers will often have to exercise ingenuity in searching out sources and imaginative insight when studying them.

■ ■ ■ ■ For Further Reading

Carl Bridenbaugh, *The Colonial Craftsman* (Chicago: Phoenix Books, 1950) is a delightful book which was originally presented as a series of lectures at New York University. Richard Walsh, *Charleston's Sons of Liberty: A Study of the Artisans 1763–1789* (Charleston: University of South Carolina Press, 1959) is a study of the working classes of one city. Raymond Mohl's *Poverty in New York: 1783–1825* (New York: Oxford University Press, 1971) is a major contribution to the subject.

■ In the years since Raymond W. Goldsmith submitted to Congress his statistical findings on the rise of per capita income in the United States many economic historians have come to date the beginnings of sustained industrial growth at some time during the 1830s.[1] This chronology has provided historians of the working class with a significant bench-mark to guide their own research and analysis. Among other things it raises questions concerning the sources, size, and character of the labor supply which was at hand before the acceleration of economic growth and the ideological baggage (attitudes, customs, institutions) which the available workers carried with them when they entered the industrial era. The objective of this article is to suggest some parameters for both sets of questions derived from an examination of the working classes in the young nation's four northern cities: Boston, New York, Philadelphia, and Baltimore.

During the five decades before 1830 these cities were essentially depots for trans-oceanic shipping, and their labor force was largely tied to maritime commerce. Surrounding each of them was "a vast scene of household manufacturing" where, wrote Alexander Hamilton, country folk produced clothing, shoes, and other necessities, "in many instances, to an extent not only sufficient for the supply of the families in which they are made, but for sale, and even, in some cases, for exportation."[2] Such a countryside Albert Gallatin found twenty years later in New Hampshire, where the average farmer's house had at least one spinning wheel, and every second house boasted a loom on which from 100 to 600 yards of saleable cloth were woven annually (at a time when journeymen weavers in their homes averaged only 829 yards per year and factory looms, 1,111 yards).[3] Most manufacturing, in other words, was carried on outside of the major cities. By 1820 some 12 percent of the nation's labor force was engaged in manufacturing and construction, and 28 percent in all non-agricultural occupations, but at that time the residents of these cities and their contiguous suburbs totalled only 356,452, or 3.7 percent of the American people.[4]

The merchant elite of these communities, furthermore, was concerned not so much with hiring labor as with vending the produce of labor, both agricultural and mechanical. Mathew Carey went so far as to accuse the merchants of hostility toward manufacturing interests, of striving "to impress upon the public mind, that the national prosperity depended almost altogether on commerce; that the protection of manufactures by duties on imports was impolitic and unjust."[5] Understandably the broadsides of Carey, Gallatin, Tench Coxe, and other promoters of manufacturing bore the aspect of appeals to the dominant agricultural and commercial interests of the land to pay some heed to the needs of industry and to believe that the growth of domestic manufactures could take place without depriving farmers and merchants of either manpower or customers.

But Carey's conception of the merchant as industry's relentless foe slighted the encouragement offered manufacturing by the commercial city itself.

The concentration of population in seaports required by a growing flow of commerce prevented urban residents from producing their own necessities in the fashion of farm families. It generated a social division of labor within the city itself and hence a need for sedentary artisans. The accumulation of merchant fortunes, furthermore, created a demand for luxury goods and thus for expert craftsmen: for silversmiths, goldbeaters, clockmakers, wig and peruke makers, printers of books and journals, tailors, and cordwainers familiar with European fashions and capable of reproducing them. By the end of the eighteenth century, moreover, seaboard merchants had opened a substantial oceanic trade in shoes, clothing, barrels, and ironwares with the regions of slave plantations. This trade encouraged the development of both the putting-out system and the early efforts toward factory organization of production.

Although most manufacturing was carried on outside the great urban centers, the seaport itself, therefore, generated a demand for labor in production as well as trade. In the eighteenth century most manufacture had been performed in the workshops of mechanics who, with the aid of family, apprentices, and occasional journeymen, made the wares they vended themselves.[6] The printer, for example, was usually a bookseller and a journalist as well, in the manner of Mathew Carey, who in the 1790s composed his own editorials in type and then hawked the paper about Philadelphia. Only after 1810 did urban newspapers gravitate into the hands of publishers who were not printers but, in the language of the journeymen, "speculators on the labor of printers" who installed "hireling editors" to write the columns printers now set in type.[7]

The colonial conception of a journeyman as tomorrow's master mechanic was neither dead nor fully obsolete by 1820, for vertical mobility was still remarkable. Among the early members of the Franklin Typographical Association of New York, a trade society of journeymen founded in 1799, were David Bruce, the future owner of the city's largest printing shop and a pioneer typefounder; Thurlow Weed, a future boss of state politics; Samuel Woodworth, the poet of "Old Oaken Bucket" fame; and Peter Force, America's most eminent historical archivist.[8] Two of the master shoemakers who testified against the cordwainers union in Philadelphia's 1805 conspiracy trial were former journeymen and union members, as were two of the employers at the similar Pittsburgh trial ten years later.[9] But by the first two decades of the nineteenth century the emergence of distinct societies of journeymen and of masters among printers, tailors, shoemakers, carpenters, stone cutters, and other trades in every seaport indicated a new awareness of distinct class interests. The seventeen benevolent societies of Philadelphia carpenters, ship masters, stone cutters, and other trades listed by James Mease in 1811 were clearly organizations of master mechanics. Their initiation fees ranging from $10 up and their annual dues of four or five dollars contrast remarkably with the one dollar initiation and the 25 cents monthly dues (waived after ten years' membership) charged by that city's printers union.[10] Societies of journeymen that sought to combine benevolent functions with the enforcement of union wage scales ultimately found it necessary to either expel members who had risen to the rank of employers, or to succumb to the urgings of "alimoners" in their midst and abandon the effort to regulate trade conditions. Thus the printers' organizations in Philadelphia and Boston during the 1820s converted themselves into friendly societies open to employers and workmen alike, while the New York society, bent on controlling wages and aware that "the interests of the journeymen are separate and in some respects opposite to those of the employers," resolved in 1817 "that when any member of this society shall become an employing printer he shall be considered without the limits of this society."[11]

The myth of harmonious personal relationships among masters, journeymen, and apprentices in a setting of domestic paternalism may be quite anachronistic when applied to post-Revolutionary decades. Ian Quimby's study of apprentice contracts in eighteenth century Philadelphia revealed a persistent erosion of filial duties and loyalties by the emerging ethos of commercialism. The mutual moral obligations of apprentices and masters in such matters as work expected of the boy, and the education and clothing due him were converted over the course of the century into money values and specified in ever-increasing detail in the contracts.[12] The experience of cabinetmakers, furthermore, suggests that journeymen seldom remained long enough with any master to develop a sense of personal attachment. The journeymen of Samuel Ashton's Philadelphia cabinet shop between 1795 and 1803 averaged scarcely six months in his employ. So rapid was the turnover of craftsmen that, though Ashton rarely needed more than five workmen at a time, forty-nine different men worked for him during those eight years.[13] Under such circumstances class antagonisms based on chronic disputes over wages could be quite consistent with a high level of upward social mobility.

By the 1820s, therefore, the urban working classes comprised recognizable and self-conscious elements of urban society. The "classes . . . who are wholly dependent upon wages," wrote Reverend Joseph Tuckerman, "are very numerous" and, he continued:

> would, indeed, be numerous, if we looked for them among only those who have no trade, and who are generally distinguished alone, as labouring men. This large division includes shop, market, and other porters; carmen; those who are employed in lading, and unlading vessels; wood-sawyers; hod carriers; house servants; those employed by mechanics in a single branch of their business; and multitudes, who are men and women of any work, occasionally required in families, as washing, scouring, etc.; or on the wharves, or in the streets of the city. Besides these, the number is great of those, who are journeymen, and many of whom will never be anything but journeymen, in the

various mechanic arts; and considerable numbers are also employed in the different departments of large manufactories, who possess no capital; and who know, and will continue to know, little or nothing in any other department of these establishments, except that in which they are themselves employed. All these, in the strictest sense, and in the common acceptation of the term, are dependent on the wages which they obtain for their services.[14]

Tuckerman's definition of the wage earning classes suggests that journeymen, mechanics, casual laborers, and factory operatives must be analyzed separately. Even though many mechanics would "never be anything but journeymen," they enjoyed the highest incomes and status of any wage earners and were psychologically the most firmly wedded to the social values and practices of the traditional artisan. Apprenticeship was the historic route of access to "the art and mysteries" of any trade, and the journeymen of this period strove to bar any other avenue of entry. The Philadelphia Typographical Society, which sought with occasional success to reserve all printing positions in town for its own members, excluded from membership anyone "who shall not have served an apprenticeship satisfactory to the board of directors" of the union, and subsequently tried to keep from the presses anyone who had "broken into the trade" after he was twenty-one years old.[15] Both the income and the honor associated with the printer's art were thus to be reserved to those who elected to ply it when they first attained the age of productive manhood at fifteen or sixteen years old. Altogether Philadelphia's complete records of apprentices bound between October 1771 and October 1773 revealed 1,075 youths apprenticed to sixty-eight trades (including many girls indentured to learn "housewifery"). Ten percent of them were to learn the cordwainer's art, and the trades of tailor, mariner, carpenter, and cooper followed shoemaking in order of preference.[16]

Sons of mechanics apprenticed to trades were supplemented by those of farmers who, for example, constituted the bulk of Massachusetts' supply of shoemakers,[17] and in Baltimore by young slaves. The emancipation of northern slaves meant the eclipse of Negro apprenticeship in most urban trades elsewhere. Because the training of slave craftsmen had rarely been complete, freed Negro artisans, who faced intense animosity from white craftsmen and had lost the protection of their masters, rarely survived in positions where they could train apprentices of their own race, and even fewer whites would engage black youth for training.[18] The influx of white farm boys to urban trades, on the other hand, was inhibited by that "desire of being an independent proprietor of land" which Alexander Hamilton believed would always keep small the numbers of those "who would be diverted from it towards manufacturers."[19] Youths who did elect urban trades, furthermore, often fled their apprenticeships after only a year or two of service and, to the great distress of established journeymen, easily found employment as half-trained workmen at substandard wages. The supply of labor was thus rapidly increased at the expense of its quality. The founding of mechanics' institutes (vocational schools) in every major northern city in the 1820s bears witness to the breakdown of traditional apprenticeship training.[20]

The fact remains that residents of rural areas in the Northeast were being lured toward the city, just as others were migrating westward, and frequently such migrants had been craftsmen, rather than (or as well as) farmers. In every decade between 1790 and 1840, the population of all four cities under review grew at a rate substantially above the 33 percent to 36 percent growth for the nation as a whole, with two exceptions: both Philadelphia and New York grew at less than the national rate between 1810 and 1820, and Baltimore's increase after 1820 was chronically below the national pace.[21] This urbanization of native Americans was supplemented by the arrival of European immigrants, but the extent of the trans-oceanic contribution to the growth of these seaports is difficult to measure. Although newcomers to America totalled 400,000 between 1790 and 1830, with 1801–1807, 1816 and 1828–1830 being the years of greatest influx, the bulk of them came not to the American seaport but through it.[22] It was the demand for farm laborers in the hinterland which produced, for example, the large scale trafficking in redemptioners Frances Wright witnessed in the Philadelphia of 1818.[23]

Among the immigrants who tarried in the city, however, were many skilled mechanics. British emigrants and British trade union practices (complete to the oaths sworn over union scales and the trappings of secrecy necessitated in the old country by the Combination Acts but retained here as a matter of custom) showed up in every conspiracy trial of union journeymen. When the prosecutor charged Philadelphia cordwainers in 1805 with "crimes" committed by union members a decade earlier, the defense replied with only slight exaggeration that none of the journeymen on trial had been in America when those acts were committed.[24] Stocking weavers in Germantown and Kensington outside of Philadelphia had almost all learned their trade in Leicester or Nottingham or the Rhineland. Linen weavers had poured out of northern Ireland in the 1770s and again at the close of the American Revolution, many of them coming to the new republic. In 1784 alone 11,000 passengers embarked from Dublin, most of them emigrants of this type.[25]

An extreme case of immigrants' providing an industry with its skilled labor was offered by the thousand or so carpet weavers in the country in the early 1830s, at least nine-tenths of whom were Scots, largely from Kilmarnock and Ayr. So well did these mechanics know each other that when sixty-three of them struck the Thompsonville Carpet Manufacturing Company in Connecticut, they quickly assembled, compiled from memory a list of the eleven other principal carpet manufactories in the nation, wrote personal letters to friends in each of them explaining the dispute, notified the Blue Bonnet Tavern in New York City, which served as the country's hiring hall for carpet weavers, to divert men from the struck plant, and dispatched an appeal to the *Old Countryman* in that city to warn off any Scots not reached by the other methods.[26]

Such incidents suggest the hypothesis that America was then a land of opportunity for handicraftsmen whose skills were being undermined by the industrial revolution in England but still in high demand in the more backward American economy. True, the number of handloom weavers and stockingers working in England continued to grow rapidly down to 1820 and perhaps beyond, despite the unmistakable deterioration of income and status in those trades. Many older craftsmen, Arthur Redford found, moved to manufacturing cities in England, there continuing to ply their obsolete trades while depending increasingly on the earnings of their factory-employed children.[27] The Scottish carpet weavers brought to trial in Connecticut for their strike, however, were remarkably young men, twenty-two years of age or less. The presumption is that the craftsman-immigrant tended to be neither the daring innovator nor the veteran artisan who could not quit his obsolescent trade, but the mobile youth who spurned Briton's factory for the possibility of plying the (to him) preferable family trade in a new location.

This hypothesis is consistent with Hamilton's belief that "the disparity" between the "dearness of labor" in America and that in England was "much less in regard to artificers and manufacturers, than in regard to country labourers," a belief recently concurred in by H. J. Habakkuk and Stuart Bruchey.[28] During the first two decades of the nineteenth century skilled tradesmen in England engaged in "honourable work" (a high quality work not yet subjected to a division of labor and deterioration of apprenticeship standards), looked upon 30s. weekly ($7.50) as an expected income, while some earned £3 and over. Such a 30s. standard fell below the $8.25 of an American shoemaker or the $9 a more seasonal carpenter might ordinarily have expected when working at union standards by precisely the differential of 12 percent–20 percent in America's favor which J. Leander Bishop found for glass workers.[29] True, American workmen paid considerably fewer taxes than their English counterparts, and as D. B. Warden observed of Philadelphia, "Smiths, shoemakers, weavers, and tailors have generally one or two acres of land, which afford pasture for a cow, fuel, and esculent plants."[30] But such bucolic benefits were by no means unknown to English weavers, croppers, and shoemakers, most of whom still worked in their cottages in rural villages.

Far more extreme was the contrast between the American municipal or canal laborer's expectation of some $4.50 a week (often paid partly in board) and the earnings of the English casual laborer, which then ranged from perhaps 11s. weekly in cotton factories to 1s. a day for wheelbarrow men in Birmingham. Taking 10s. (i.e., $2.50) as good weekly pay for such laborers in the second decade of the century, the unskilled American enjoyed a premium of 80 percent over his British counterpart.[31] That the wage differential was less rather than greater for the artisan than for casual labor is thus evident even without investigation of the real values of money wages in the two countries. Yet British craftsmen did migrate, spurred by the deteriorating conditions in their trades at home and lured, as one emigrant manual declared, by the openings in American trades left by "the strong emulation of the *cute* native Yankee to elevate himself above the common labour class."[32]

Whether graduates of American or British apprenticeships, urban tradesmen were both geographically mobile enough and sufficiently well informed about the state of the labor market elsewhere to maintain rather uniform wage standards throughout the northeastern cities. When Philadelphia shoemakers demanded a schedule of prices based on $4 a pair for back strap boots in October 1805, they were aware that the New York union had established precisely that scale in March. Similarly, when Pittsburgh shoemakers unionized at the end of that decade, they quickly drove up their prices from 75 cents below the Philadelphia wage to parity with it—but when they sought a scale higher than Philadelphia's, they were roundly defeated by their masters.[33] Both the New York and Washington societies of printers undertook—by correspondence with their counterparts in Philadelphia, Baltimore, Boston, and Albany—to establish uniform scales, and all these societies exchanged "rat lists" with each other, so that typographers who violated union rules and standards could not find refuge in other communities.[34] At times employers cooperated with these efforts of the journeymen, as did master printers in New York in 1815, or, more dramatically, the master weavers of Baltimore, who in 1829 did everything in their power to ostracize a fellow employer for slashing his journeymen's wages below the city norm.[35]

Although the mechanic was ranked by Tuckerman within the wage-earning classes, there is little evidence that prior to the 1830s he either identified himself with "the poor" or felt in any way alienated from the existing social order. Despite the absence from common American parlance of the rigid British distinction between "honourable" and "dishonourable" work, only the scale of the New York shoemakers out of all the union price lists which have been preserved from that period (mainly those of printers, shoemakers, tailors, and weavers) included a specified wage for coarse work, partially completed work, or the work of helpers. While the Pittsburgh shoemakers union did explicitly deem coarse work "out of society" and posed no objections to non-members performing such tasks, there is no such clear evidence from any of the seaport cities. It is remarkable, however, that the prosecutor in the New York shoemakers' trial, while conceding that many journeymen were not members, insisted that "all the best workmen were of the society." Similarly Philadelphia shoemakers considered themselves fully unionized between 1798 and 1804, when their society had 100 to 150 members, while the city directory for 1798 listed 292 shoemakers and cord-wainers.[36] A plausible inference is that cheap shoes for slaves and for auction sale, which did not appear in the union's scale of prices, were deliberately relegated to inferior workmen whom the society made no effort to recruit.

The mechanics proudly preserved an ideological heritage blended of Ben Franklin's maxims and Tom Paine's "rights of man." The best local legal talent defended their societies in the several conspiracy trials to which they were subjected, as witness Philadelphia's shoemakers enlisting Caesar Rodney, whom President Jefferson was soon to appoint Attorney General of the United States. When seventeen years earlier that city's mechanics had paraded with their masters in joyous celebration of the ratification of the federal constitution, they had borne such emblems as "the weavers' flag, a rampant lion in a green field, holding a shuttle in his dexter paw—motto—'*may the government* protect us,'" the boat builders' flag (atop the thirty-three foot schooner *Federal Union* drawn down Market Street for the occasion) bearing "an axe and an adze crossing each other—motto, 'by these we live,'" or the bricklayers' flag, with "the federal city rising out of a forest, workmen building it, and the sun illuminating it," motto, "'*both buildings and rulers are the works of our hands.*'" At the close of the procession, bakers distributed bread to the poor, victuallers slew their "two stately oxen" and gave away the meat, and millers provided the needy with flour.[37] The best the printers could do was to read the destitute a poem, but clearly the citizen craftsmen were dispensers, not recipients, of charity.

Very different was the outlook of the impoverished residents of the Rittenhouse Square vicinity, who petitioned the Philadelphia city council in 1830 to halt the dumping in the square of offal swept from neighboring streets, "which being in heaps, occasions numerous ponds of stagnant and putrescent water in the immediate spots, which in summer send forth pestilential vapours wafted by every breeze to the dwellings of your petitioners, whose only comfort, health, is thus destroyed." These poor argued that "being of the working class, their whole time is indispensably employed in various labour to maintain their families," so that sickness is "a scourge the most severe."[38] Here was a group whose annual incomes ranged far closer to $200 than to $400 or $425 expected by craftsmen, a group who Reverend Tuckerman feared "have lived, and to a great extent are living, as a *caste*—cut off from those in more favoured circumstances; and doomed to find their pleasures, and sympathy in their sufferings, alone among themselves."[39]

The seaport poor were by no means a new phenomenon at the end of the 1820s. James Henretta has clearly traced their emergence in eighteenth-century Boston as a function of the growth of overseas commerce. He discovered from the Boston tax rolls of 1687 that only 14 percent of the adult male population of the city, that is, 188 men, were neither "dependent" nor owners of property. In contrast to them stood the 17 percent of the adult males who as servants, apprentices, or participants in family home enterprise were classified as dependent. The propertied classes numbered 1,036 (69 percent of the adult males) and included 521 poor craftsmen, 275 artisans of the "middling sort" with two or three journeymen apiece, and the wealthier tradesmen, professionals, and merchants. By 1771 only 10 percent of the adult males were dependent in the traditional sense, while 29 percent were neither dependent nor propertied. These were wage earners in the full meaning of the term, and while the city's population had doubled between the two counts, their number had increased fourfold. They ranged in occupation from seamen and longshoremen at one end of the scale to journeymen at the other, but, while the latter ranked close to the small property-holding mechanic, the division of wealth between the upper and lower halves of property owners was far sharper than had been the case in the seventeenth century.[40]

Most day laborers participated directly in transportation and commerce. It was the demand for seamen, longshoremen, carters, and domestic servants which absorbed unskilled wage earners already in the eighteenth century. By the early nineteenth century, construction work, wood cutting, and road building employed many, while thousands of Philadelphia's poor, Mathew Carey found, "travel hundreds of miles in quest of employment on canals at 62½, 75 and 87½ cents per day, paying a dollar and a half or two dollars per week for their board, leaving families behind, depending on them for support."[41] By 1830 Carey estimated "labourers, hodmen, seamstresses, families of workmen on canals and rail-roads" at 40 percent of the working classes and 25 percent of the total population of Philadelphia.[42]

Many laborers reached the city from the farm by way of the sea. The merchant fleet of Massachusetts, wrote Samuel Eliot Morison, "was manned by successive waves of adventure-seeking boys, and officered by such of them as determined to make the sea their calling." The great majority on the crew lists professed "to be native-born Yankees, and probably were."[43] Seamen would register with federal revenue agents after 1796 and receive, for a fee of 25 cents, papers certifying their United States citizenship. Between that year and 1812, 106,757 seamen collected their papers, and of them only 1,530, or 1.4 percent were naturalized citizens. The registrations reported for the years after 1808 were certainly still incomplete, for district revenue collectors were very tardy in submitting their reports to Washington. The fact that registration was heaviest in years such as 1797 and 1805, when the danger of British impressment was most severe, indicates that enrollment was never very thorough.[44] These figures, nevertheless, can suggest the large number of native Americans who took to the sea.

So high were the rates of promotion, death, and desertion that the man who spent more than twelve years before the mast was rare indeed. No other occupation offered an unskilled farmboy so great an opportunity to rise quickly in wealth and standing—or to topple from yardarm into the cold Atlantic. Few seamen dwelt long in any port, but while ashore they augmented the local casual labor supply significantly. Illustrative of their role was young Charles Erskine, whose mother moved to Boston in the early 1820s after his father (a currier) had deserted her. Playing about the docks, Erskine heard the tales of sailors and through them was lured to sea. Between voyages he and his mates earned their keep ashore by whatever employment was available wherever they happened to be. He once helped construct an aqueduct in Washington and at another time worked in a Philadelphia hook and eye factory.[45]

In marked contrast to the artisan's tendency to ply for life the trade he had learned in his adolescence, the laborer was the epitome of versatility. To move from sea to canal digging to hod carrying to factory work was well within the realm of possibility. Many of the half-trained journeymen and "botches" who bedevilled mechanics' efforts to retain high quality and wage standards were of this sort. New England's first factory to use cotton spinning machinery, founded in Beverly, Massachusetts, in 1787, wasted precious quantities of material in training its workmen, then was driven close to ruin when it had to raise wages to prevent its partly-taught employees from deserting to rival firms. Mercifully, perhaps, the factory burned down in 1808.[46] A happier experience with such labor was reported by a cotton mill near Providence, which employed fifty-three workers in the factory and 125 on putting-out by 1810. The owners, reported Albert Gallatin, at first suffered "in being put to much expense by English workmen, who pretended to much more knowledge in the business than they really possessed." But the phony Samuel Slaters were discharged, "and Americans, as apprentices, &c. are getting the art very fast," though the company did not anticipate dividends "for a considerable time."[47]

The fact that machine operatives could be trained made the "factory controversy" of this period focus not on the fate of the workers, as was to be the case in the 1830s and 1840s, but on the potential impact of manufacturing upon the nation's supply of farm labor. Wages of farm hands, Henry Carey reported, were higher in the vicinity of the cities than in more rustic settings.[48] Whether this differential in money wages was a sign of competition from urban employments or simply an indication that the market economy was more mature near the cities (that a smaller portion of the farm laborer's income was paid in kind and more in cash than was the case to the West) is not clear. Whichever it meant, advocates of governmental aid to manufactures from Coxe through Carey felt obliged to echo Hamilton's famous assurance that manufacturing would not attract able-bodied men away from the land, that it would rather "afford occasional and extra employment to industrious individuals and families," through which farmers could profit by the home produce of their wives and daughters, and provide steady employment for "persons who would otherwise be idle, and in many cases a burthen on the community," and render women and children "more useful, and the latter more early useful . . . than they should otherwise be."[49]

At this period, therefore, it was impossible to speak of the factory labor force without directing attention to women, children, and charitable institutions. This was the case long before the mills of Lowell arose. Philadelphia's first large-scale use of spinning jennies was undertaken by the United Company of Philadelphia for Promoting American Manufactures, founded by patriotic subscriptions in 1775. By the late 1780s it employed 400 women, most of them recruited from the city's poor rolls. Despite the pride with which the Society displayed a jenny of eighty spindles in the Federal Procession of 1788, and boasted that the woman operating it was "a native of and instructed in this city," the company's building was destroyed by an arsonist only two years later.[50] Newly-inaugurated President Washington found a similar labor force when he visited a Boston sail duck factory. Here pairs of little girls spun and wove flax from eight in the morning until six at night, but their demeanor favorably impressed the President, who described them as "daughters of decayed families" and "girls of character—none others are admitted."[51]

Two decades later the Secretary of the Treasury reported that eighty-seven cotton mills then in operation or about to commence operations in the United States needed a labor force of about 500 men and 3,500 women and children.[52] Such a work force was for Gallatin proof positive that manufacturing need not lure men from the farm. Tench Coxe agreed:

> Female aid in manufactures, which prevents the diversion of men and boys from agriculture, has greatly increased. Children are employed, as well as the infirm and the crippled. The assylums of the poor and unfortunate, and the penitentiaries of indiscretion and immorality are improved and aided by the employment and profits of manufactures.[53]

The markets of seamstresses were especially crowded with unmarried and widowed women, not to speak of those whose husbands were "travelling"—in the informal divorce procedure of the day. When such women bid on sewing work, they competed with both married women trying to supplement their own families' meager incomes and recipients of work relief. While female operatives in Philadelphia factories earned two or three dollars a week in the 1820s, seamstresses rarely surpassed $1.25, and the city's home relief system helped keep those earnings low. In slack seasons so many women applied to the Provident Society and other charities for work to tide them over that the scale offered by almshouses became, during the 1820s, the standard price offered by private firms. Thus the U. S. War Department offered seamstresses 12½ cents a shirt, the very wage given by the Provident Society. In reply to a plea that such a price reduced the seamstresses "to the degradation of pauperism," the Secretary of War termed the subject "of such delicacy, and so intimately connected with the manufacturing interests, and the general prices of this kind of labour in the city of Philadelphia" that he dared not change his Department's practice.[54]

While the seamstress stood with one foot in the poor house, this was not the case with the weaver, for in the urban areas most cloth was still put out to families with handlooms. The city and county of Philadelphia in 1809 produced 65,326 yards of cloth in its six factories on both hand and power looms, but its home production amounted to 233,232 yards.[55] Furthermore, the spinning mills, while they continued to be staffed primarily by women and children, tended to free themselves by the second decade of the century from dependence on public charities. The reason is that unmarried women, widows, and orphaned families gravitated toward them by free choice.

Especially was this the case in New England, where the textile mill became a means of emancipation for the "maiden aunts" who lived with so many of the region's families. In Massachusetts the 1810 male population under the age of sixteen outnumbered females of the same age in the ratio of 104 to 100. Between the ages of sixteen and forty-five, however, the proportions were reversed. During the marrying season (ages sixteen through twenty-five) there were 103 women for every 100 men, but in the post twenty-six age of the spinster, women outnumbered men by a ratio of 107 to 100. And Massachusetts had 3,335 more women of that age than it had men.[56] Theirs was the choice, at best, of boarding with parents, or a married sister, or entering a mill. Since the loss of males was a result of the westward movement, it would seem that, as far as New England's early textile industry is concerned, the famous "safety-valve" worked in reverse. The migration of men to the West created a surplus of female labor in the East.

Neither New York State nor Pennsylvania exhibited such an imbalance of the sexes, for both were receiving substantial immigration, and considerable westward movement still occurred within their boundaries. But within the cities of New York and Philadelphia free white women between the ages of sixteen and twenty-five sharply outnumbered the men of the same age. The New York ratio in 1820, for example, was 119 women to 100 men in that age bracket, while in Philadelphia women of this marriageable age outnumbered men 122 to 100. Similarly, the Boston ratio was 127 to 100, and that of Baltimore 108 to 100.[57] Although the terrible toll of childbirth, among other hazards, more than corrected the balance of the sexes in all four cities after the age of twenty-six, each of the seaports was naturally provided with a sizeable force of women for whom there was no prospect of marriage and for whom entry into the labor market was a necessity.

Each of these groups of city workers of the pre-industrial epoch (journeymen mechanics, male laborers, and women) merits careful historical study. Little new work has been done in this area since David J. Saposs contributed his chapters to John R. Commons' *History of Labour in the United States* in 1917, and because of this deficiency the labor historian's view of this period has fallen seriously out of phase with that of the economic historian. For example, Saposs' contention that "the wages of the unskilled were going up while those of the skilled were kept down by the merchant-capitalist" in the century's first two decades finds no support in the wage data of this article or in recent economic studies.[58]

The problem assumes considerable significance in the light of George Rogers Taylor's hypothesis that per capita income in America declined rather steadily between 1807 and the early 1830s.[59] The impact of such a trend could logically have been different for mechanics, for factory operatives, for casual laborers, and for women sewing in their rented rooms. Only specific studies of particular groups of workers can yield conclusive data on the standard of living. Jackson Turner Main and James Henretta have shown that enough evidence exists in tax rolls, judicial records, and the press of the eighteenth century to enable the historian to reconstruct patterns of property and income distribution quite clearly.[60] Their work challenges other historians to trace the evolution of these patterns in early nineteenth century city life and to reduce their reliance on impressionistic evidence.

Still greater is the need for research into the cultural and intellectual life of the working classes of this period. We need to know what the urban poor expected of life, how they reacted to the commercial ethos of their cities, and how they conceived their relationship to the governing merchant elites. Were they, as some historians have recently portrayed the poor of Naples or London, simultaneously devoted to the traditional social order, aware of their power as a mob, confident the city would care for them in times of want, and, profoundly hostile toward the emerging impersonal and amoral market economy?[61] Was it such a mentality which made some 200 assembled New York sailors, idled by the embargo, respond obediently when Mayor Marinus Willet commanded them to disperse, with assurances that the embargo was "the *Captain's Orders*," and that the city would "do everything possible for your relief"?[62] Such questions cannot yet be answered because a fixation on the clash of "agrarian" and "industrial" values has distracted us from exploring pre-industrial urban values and customs.

Similarly American historians have yet to probe the culture of the American mechanic as, say, E. P. Thompson did for his British counterpart. Our concern has been either with the journeyman's economic circumstances (where there is still much to be learned) or with whether he voted for Andrew Jackson (and may we be spared that debate for a while). Because the mechanics were frequently organized and far more articulate than the urban poor, research into the mind of the journeyman should prove relatively easy. The ideas suggested in this article need careful testing, to begin with, and beyond them lie several major issues for research. How open was economic mobility for the journeymen, and what changes did the post-

Revolutionary generation experience in this regard? Why did this class provide most of the country's early nineteenth century adherents to deism, and just how widespread and significant was infidelity among them?[63] What new circumstances made craftsmen in every major city between 1827 and 1837 expand the horizons of their concern beyond the limits of their own trades, create city Trades' Unions as new institutions to fuse the efforts of the several crafts, undertake unprecedented united action with the unskilled laborers, giving rise to something worthy of the name labor movement?

These problems suggest that we have rushed ahead to evaluate labor's response to industrialism without first ascertaining labor's pre-industrial behavior and attitudes. In exploring the shock of change after the Civil War our attention has been directed half a century too late, and our concern with the fate of agrarian values has led us to ignore the impact of the spreading factory system on the cultural heritage of urban America's lower orders.

■ ■ ■ ■ **Notes**

1 U.S. Congress, Joint Economic Committee, *Hearings [on] Employment, Growth and Price Levels,* "Part 2—Historical and Comparative Rates of Production, Productivity, and Prices," 86th Cong., 1st Sess., 1959, 230–279; George Rogers Taylor, "The National Economy Before and After the Civil War," in *Economic Change in the Civil War Era,* edited by David T. Gilchrist and W. David Lewis (Greenville, Del., 1965), 1–22; Douglass C. North, *Growth and Welfare in the American Past* (Englewood Cliffs, N.J., 1966), 15–17, 75–89; Robert Gallman, "Commodity Output, 1839–1899," in *Trends in the American Economy in the Nineteenth Century, National Bureau of Economic Research Studies in Income and Wealth, Volume Twenty-Four* (Princeton, N.J., 1960), 13–67. Stuart Bruchey finds indices of significant industrial growth before the 1830s, *The Roots of American Economic Growth, 1607–1861, An Essay in Social Causation* (New York, 1965), 76–91.

2 Alexander Hamilton, "Report on Manufactures," in Hamilton, *Papers on Public Credit, Commerce, and Finance,* edited by Samuel McKee, Jr. (Indianapolis and New York, 1957), 222.

3 Albert Gallatin, "Manufactures," *American State Papers,* Finance, II, 434–435.

4 Figures on distribution of labor force are calculated from U.S. Department of Commerce, Bureau of the Census, *Historical Statistics of the United States, 1789–1945* (Washington, D.C., 1949), 29. Population figures for city and suburban areas are taken from those presented by Professor Everett S. Lee at the 1966 Eleutherian Mills–Hagley Foundation Conference on the Growth of Seaport Cities, 1790–1825.

5 Mathew Carey, *Autobiography* (Research Classics, Number One, Brooklyn, 1942), 95.

6 See Carl Bridenbaugh, *Colonial Craftsman* (New York, 1950); Richard B. Morris, *Government and Labor in Early America* (New York, 1946); Staughton Lynd and Alfred Young, "After Carl Becker: The Mechanics and New York City Politics, 1774–1801," *Labor History,* V (Fall, 1964), 215–224.

7 Carey, 11–25; Ethelbert Stewart, "Documentary History of the Early Organization of Printers," in U.S. Department of Commerce and Labor, *Bulletin of the Bureau of Labor,* No. 61 (Washington, D.C., 1905), 912.

8 George A. Stevens, *New York Typographical Union No. 6* (Albany, 1913), 38, 81–102.

9 *Commonwealth v. Pullis,* in John R. Commons, *et al., Documentary History of American Industrial Society* (10 vols., Cleveland, 1910), III, 59–248; *Commonwealth v. Morrow,* in *History of American Industrial Society,* IV, 15–88.

10 Thomas Wilson, *Picture of Philadelphia, for 1824, Containing the "Picture of Philadelphia, for 1811, by James Mease, M.D." with All Its Improvements since that Period* (Philadelphia, 1823), 267–276; Stewart, 943.

11 Stevens, 76.

12 Ian M.G. Quimby, "Apprenticeship in Colonial Philadelphia" (unpublished Master's Thesis, University of Delware, 1963), 60–63.

13 Morrison H. Hecksher, "The Organization and Practice of Philadelphia Cabinet-making Establishments, 1790–1820" (unpublished Master's Thesis, University of Delaware, 1964), 22–25.

14 Joseph Tuckerman, *An Essay on the Wages Paid to Females for Their Labour . . .* (Philadelphia, 1830), 8.

15 Stewart, 877, 943.

16 Quimby, 30.

17 Blanche Evans Hazard, *Organization of the Boot and Shoe Industry in Massachusetts before 1875* (Cambridge, Mass., 1921), 322–323.

18 Leonard Price Stavisky, "The Negro Artisan in the South Atlantic States, 1800–1860: A Study of Status and Economic Opportunity with Special Reference to Charleston" (unpublished Ph.D. dissertation, Columbia University, 1958), 16–22; Morris, 182–188; Leon Litwack, *North of Slavery. The Negro in the Free States, 1790–1860* (Chicago, 1961), 153–162.

19 Hamilton, 203.

20 See Bruchey, 188–189.

21 Everett S. Lee, Growth of Seaport Cities. See also D.B. Warden, *Statistical, Political, and Historical Account of the United States of North America* (3 vols., Edinburgh, 1819), I, xlii. Between 1775 and 1790 the growth rates of these cities had fallen well behind the national rate. George Rogers Taylor, "American Economic Growth before 1840: An Exploratory Essay," *Journal of Economic History,* XXIV (Dec., 1964), 439.

22 *Historical Statistics of the United States,* 34; Curtis P. Nettels, *Emergence of a National Economy, 1775–1815* (New York, 1962), 133; Marcus Lee Hansen, *Atlantic Migration, 1607–1860* (Harper Torchbook edition, New York, 1961), 84; E.P. Thompson, *Making of the English Working Class* (New York, 1966), 430–432.

23 Frances Wright, *Views of Society and Manners in America,* edited by Paul R. Baker (Cambridge, Mass., 1963), 240–241. Compare the observations of Johann David Schoepf in Baltimore in 1783, *Travels in the Confederation,* translated and edited by Alfred J. Morrison (2 vols., Philadelphia, 1911), I, 339–340.

24 Commons, III, 108.

25 Edwin T. Freedley, *Philadelphia and Its Manufactures* (Philadelphia, 1858), 241–242; Arthur Redford, *Labour Migration in England 1800–1850,* edited and revised by W.H. Chaloner (Manchester, 1964), 166–167.

26 *Thompsonville Carpet Manufacturing Company vs. William Taylor . . .* in Commons, IV—Supplement, 16–125.

27 Thompson, 279–296; Redford, 186.

28 Hamilton, 208; H.J. Habakkuk, *American and British Technology in the Nineteenth Century: The Search for Labour-Saving Inventions* (Cambridge, 1962), 21–43; Bruchey, 162–164.

29 J. Leander Bishop, *History of American Manufactures from 1680–1860* (2 vols.,

Philadelphia, 1864), I, 242. For a description of "honourable work" in England see Thompson, 234–268.

30 Warden, II, 107.

31 For data on wages of unskilled labor see Mathew Carey, *Appeal to the Wealthy of the Land* . . . (Philadelphia, 1833), 17; Warden, II, 85; Christopher Roberts, *The Middlesex Canal* (Cambridge, Mass., 1938), 78–82. For comparable wages in England see Thompson, 310, 313; Redford, 39.

32 Patrick Matthew, *Emigration Fields, North America, The Cape, Australia, and New Zealand* (Edinburgh and London, 1839), 40.

33 Commons, III, 106, 368–369, IV, 34.

34 Stewart, 866, 871–872, 877, 881, 886, 888. Compare the efforts of Philadelphia's union curriers, Leonard Bernstein, "The Working People of Philadelphia from Colonial Times to the General Strike of 1835," *Pennsylvania Magazine of History and Biography*, LXXIV (July, 1950), 325.

35 Stewart, 877; "Report of the Trial of the Journeymen Weavers in Baltimore City Court," in Commons, IV, 269–272.

36 Commons, III, 368–370; Commons, III, 72–81, 84–85; Commons, IV, 28–40; Cornelius Wm. Stafford, *Philadelphia City Directory for 1798*.

37 *American Museum*, IV (July, 1788), 57–78.

38 Samuel Hazard, ed., *Register of Pennsylvania*, V (Feb. 20, 1830), 124. Rittenhouse Square became a wealthy neighborhood only after 1850. See Nathaniel Burt, *The Perennial Philadelphians. The Anatomy of an American Aristocracy* (Boston and Toronto, 1963), 531.

39 Tuckerman, 25.

40 James A. Henretta, "Economic Development and Social Structure in Colonial Boston," *William and Mary Quarterly*, Third Series, XXII (Jan., 1965), 75–92. See also Jackson Turner Main, *Social Structure of Revolutionary America* (Princeton, 1965), 37–40.

41 Carey, *Appeal*, II. On canal laborers see William A. Sullivan, *Industrial Worker in Pennsylvania 1800–1840* (Harrisburg, 1955), 71–73.

42 Carey, *Appeal*, 7.

43 Samuel Eliot Morison, *The Maritime History of Massachusetts 1783–1860* (Sentry Edition, Boston, 1961), 106, 108.

44 *American State Papers*, Commerce & Navigation, I, 955, 968; Act of May 28, 1796, *Public Statutes at Large of the United States of America* (17 vols., Boston, 1850), I, 477.

45 See J. Grey Jewell, *Among Our Sailors* (New York, 1874), 1–50; Charles Erskine, *Twenty Years before the Mast* (Philadelphia, 1896), 2–9, 272.

46 Bishop I, 399–401.

47 Gallatin, 434.

48 Henry C. Carey, *Essay on the Rate of Wages: with an Examination of the Causes of the Differences in the Conditions of the Labouring Population throughout the World* (Philadelphia, 1835), 91.

49 Hamilton, 193.

50 Bishop, I, 384–387; *American Museum*, V (July, 1788), 60.

51 Edward Everett, *Mount Vernon Papers* (New York, 1860), 112.

52 Gallatin, 427.

53 Tench Coxe, *Statement of the Arts and Manufactures of the United States of America, for the Year 1810* . . . (Philadelphia, 1814), xiv.

54 Exchange of correspondence with the Secretary of War, printed in Mathew Carey, *Appeal to Common Sense and Common Justice* (Philadelphia, 1822), xii–xiii. On the role of charities in fixing urban wage levels see Mathew Carey, *Essays on the Public Charities of Philadelphia* . . . (Philadelphia, 1829), 18–19; Benjamin J.

Klebaner, "The Home Relief Controversy in Philadelphia, 1782–1861," *Pennsylvania Magazine of History and Biography*, LXXIVII (Oct., 1954), 420.

55 Coxe, 44.

56 Warden, I, 200.

57 The ratios are calculated from statistics presented by Everett S. Lee, Growth of Seaport Cities.

58 John R. Commons, *et al., History of Labour in the United States* (4 vols., New York, 1918–1935), I, 105. *Cf.,* Sullivan, 31, 72–73.

59 Taylor, "American Economic Growth before 1840," 437.

60 Henretta, 75–92; Main, 37–40.

61 See E.J. Hobsbawm, *Primitive Rebels. Studies in Archaic Forms of Social Movement in the 19th and 20th Centuries* (New York, 1965), 108–125; Thompson, 55–76.

62 George Daitsman, "Labor and the Welfare State in Early New York," *Labor History,* IV (Fall, 1963), 250.

63 See Herbert M. Morais, *Deism in Eighteenth Century America* (New York, 1934); Albert Post, *Popular Freethought in America, 1825–1850* (New York, 1943); Lewis Masquerier, *Sociology: Or, The Reconstruction of Society . . .* (New York, 1877).

6
Urban Life in Western America, 1790–1830

RICHARD C. WADE

The westward movement of the American people has been a consistent and enduring source of fascination. The "western" is a perennial staple of popular fiction, films, and TV series. In 1893 Frederick Jackson Turner read his famous paper on "The Significance of the Frontier in American History" which emphasized the role of the West in molding the American character and in creating a society unique and distinct from that of Europe. Turner invested popular interest in the West with scholarly and intellectual significance, and, following his example, several generations of historians spent their lives supporting or refuting the frontier thesis.

Turner saw the settling of the West as the result of successive waves of migration. "Stand at Cumberland Gap and watch the procession of civilization, marching single file—the buffalo following the trail to the salt springs, the Indian, the fur-trader and hunter, the cattle-raiser, the pioneer farmer —and the frontier has passed by. Stand at South Pass in the Rockies a century later and see the same procession with wider intervals between." This suggests that the West was a rural area and was distinctly western only so long as its people were rural folk.

Yet, as Richard C. Wade points out in the following essay, towns often spearheaded the westward movement. Men went west not only searching for furs and farmland, but also for promising town sites and urban opportunities. The establishment of urban communities for trade and defense often preceded the settlement of surrounding farmlands. In the developing West, he believes, towns provided focal points of trade and cultural activity as well as supplying disproportionate numbers of political leaders.

The themes of economic development, cultural growth, emergence of urban problems and political response to them, and urban rivalry discussed by Wade in this essay are developed at greater length and in more detail in his book, The Urban Frontier: The Rise of Western Cities, 1790–1830.

■ ■ ■ ■ For Further Reading

Richard C. Wade, *The Urban Frontier: Pioneer Life in Early Pittsburgh, Cincinnati, Lexington, Louisville, and St. Louis* (Chicago: Phoenix Books, 1964) and Richard C. Wade, *Slavery in the Cities: The South 1820–1860* (New York: Oxford University Press, 1964) are both excellent studies in comparative urban history. *The Urban Frontier* is a full exposition of the themes of the following article, while *Slavery in the Cities* provides considerable information on southern urbanism generally. Kenneth Wheeler, *To Wear a City's Crown: The Beginnings of Urban Growth in Texas, 1836–1865* (Cambridge, Mass.: Harvard University Press, 1968) compares the early history of four Texas frontier cities, San Antonio, Galveston, Houston, and Austin. Robert R.

Dykstra, *The Cattle Towns* (New York: Atheneum, 1968) is a sophisticated study of five Kansas cattle towns. Dykstra provides important material on rural–urban conflict and on the processes of decision-making and internal conflict within the towns.

■ The towns were the spearheads of the American frontier. Planted as forts or trading posts far in advance of the line of settlement, they held the West for the approaching population. Indeed, in 1763, when the British drew the Proclamation Line across the Appalachians to stop the flow of migrants, a French merchant company prepared to survey the streets of St. Louis, a thousand miles through the wilderness. Whether as part of French and Spanish activity from New Orleans or part of Anglo-American operations from the Atlantic seaboard, the establishment of towns preceded the breaking of soil in the transmontane West.

In 1764, the year of the founding of St. Louis, settlers made the first plat of Pittsburgh. Twelve years later and four hundred miles down the Ohio, Louisville sprang up at the Falls, and the following decade witnessed the beginnings of Cincinnati and Lexington. Before the century closed, Detroit, Buffalo, and Cleveland were laid out on the Great Lakes. In fact, by 1800 the sites of every major metropolis in the old Northwest except Chicago, Milwaukee, and Indianapolis had been cleared and surveyed.

Furthermore, these urban outposts grew rapidly even in their infant decades. By 1815 Pittsburgh, already a thriving industrial center, had 8,000 inhabitants, giving it a slight margin over Lexington. Cincinnati estimated its population at 4,000 at the end of the war with Great Britain, while farther west Louisville and St. Louis neared half that figure.

The speed and extent of this expansion startled contemporaries. Joseph Charless, the editor of the *Missouri Gazette,* who had made a trip through the new country in 1795, remembered the banks of the Ohio as "a dreary wilderness, the haunt of ruthless savages," yet twenty years later he found them "sprinkled with towns" boasting "spinning and weaving establishments, steam mills, manufactures in various metals, leather, wool, cotton and flax," and "seminaries of learning conducted by excellent teachers."[1] The great transformation moved a Cincinnati bard to a somewhat heroic couplet:

> Here where so late the appalling sound
> Of savage yells, the woods resound
> Now smiling Ceres waves her sheaf
> And cities rise in bold relief.[2]

Not all the towns founded in the trans-Allegheny region in this period fared as well, however. Many never developed much beyond a survey and a newspaper advertisement. Others, after promising beginnings, slackened and settled down to slow and unspectacular development. Still others flourished briefly then faded, leaving behind a grim story of deserted mills, broken buildings, and aging people—the West's first harvest of ghost towns. Most of these were mere eddies in the westward flow of urbanism, but at flood tide it was often hard to distinguish the eddies from the main stream. Indeed, at one time Wheeling, Virginia, St. Genevieve, Missouri, New Albany, Indiana, and Zanesville, Ohio, were considered serious challengers to the supremacy of their now more famous neighbors.

Other places, such as Rising Sun, Town of America, or New Athens, were almost wholly speculative ventures. Eastern investors scanned maps looking for likely spots to establish a city, usually at the junction of two rivers, or sometimes at the center of fertile farm districts. They bought up land, laid it out in lots, gave the place a name, and waited for the development of the region to appreciate its value. Looking back over this period one editor called it a "city-making mania," when everyone went about "anticipating flourishing cities in vision, at the mouth of every creek and bayou."[3] This speculation, though extensive, was not always profitable. "Of the vast number of towns which have been founded," James Hall declared, "but a small minority have prospered, nor do we think that, as a general rule, the founders of these have been greatly enriched by their prosperity."[4]

Despite many failures, these abortive attempts to plant towns were significant, for they reveal much about the motives of the people who came West in the early period. Many settlers moved across the mountains in search of promising towns rather than good land, their inducements being urban opportunities rather than fertile soil. Daniel Drake, who was among the earliest urbanites of the frontier, later commented on this process:

It is worthy of remark, that those who made these beginnings of settlement, projected towns, which they anticipated would grow into cities. . . . And we may see in their origins, one of the elements of the prevalent tendency to rear up towns in advance of the country which has ever since characterized Ohio. The followers of the first pioneers, like themselves had a taste for commerce and the mechanic arts which cannot be gratified without the construction of cities.[5]

Proprietors competed for these urban migrants, most of whom came from "those portions of the Union which cherish and build up cities."[6] In fact, the preference of some settlers for towns was so great that in 1787 Lexington petitioned the Virginia legislature for incorporation to be "an inducement to well disposed persons, artizens [*sic*] and mechanics who from motives and convenience do prefer Town life."[7]

The West's young cities owed their initial success to commerce. All sprang from it, and their growth in the early years of the century stemmed from its expansion. Since the Ohio River was the chief artery of trade and travel, the towns along its banks prospered most. Pittsburgh, where the Allegheny meets the Monongahela, commanded the entire valley; Cincinnati served the rich farm lands of Kentucky and Ohio; Louisville fattened on the transshipment of goods around the Falls; and St. Louis, astride the Mississippi, was the focus of far-flung enterprises, some of which reached to the

Pacific Ocean. Even Lexington, landlocked in a country of water highways, grew up as the central mart of Kentucky and Tennessee.

Though these cities were firmly established by the first decade of the century, the coming of the steamboat greatly enhanced their size and influence.[8] By quickening transportation and cutting distances, steam navigation telescoped fifty years' urban development into a single generation. The flow of commerce down river was now supplemented by a northward and eastward movement, giving cities added opportunities for expansion and growth. "The steam engine in five years has enabled us to anticipate a state of things," a Pittsburgher declared enthusiastically, "which in the ordinary course of events, it would have required a century to have produced. The art of printing scarcely surpassed it in beneficial consequences."[9] The "enchanter's wand" not only touched the established towns but created new ones as well. A French observer noted that "in the brief interval of fifteen years, many cities were formed . . . where before there were hardly the dwellings of a small town. . . . A simple mechanical device has made life both possible and comfortable in regions which heretofore have been a wilderness."[10]

As these commercial centers grew, some inhabitants turned to manufacturing. Indeed, this new interest spread so rapidly in Pittsburgh that in 1810 a resident likened the place to "a large workshop," and already travelers complained of the smoke and soot.[11] Between 1803 and 1815 the value of manufactured goods jumped from $350,000 to over $2,600,000, and the city's iron and glass products became known throughout the new country.[12] Watching this remarkable development, the editor of *Niles' Register* exclaimed: "Pittsburgh, sometimes emphatically called the 'Birmingham of America,' will probably become the *greatest manufacturing town in the world."*[13] Lexington also turned increasingly to industry, her ropewalks and textile mills supplying the whole West. Beginnings were more modest in other places, but every city had at least a few ambitious enterprises.

Some of this urban expansion rested on a speculative base, and the depression of 1819 brought a reckoning. Lexington, already suffering from its landlocked position, received fatal wounds, while Pittsburgh, the West's foremost city, was crippled for a decade. Elsewhere, however, the setback proved only momentary and the mid-twenties saw the old pace renewed. Population growth again provides a convenient index of development. Cincinnati quickly overtook its faltering rivals, the number of its residents leaping from 6,000 in 1815 to over 25,000 in 1830. By the latter date the census recorded Pittsburgh's recovery. Though the figure had dropped to 7,000 during the depression, it rose to 13,000 in 1830. Farther west Louisville and St. Louis enjoyed spectacular expansion, the former boasting over 10,000 inhabitants at the end of the period, while the Mississippi entrepôt passed the 6,000 mark. Lexington alone lagged, its population remaining stable for the next two decades.

Even these figures, however, do not convey the real growth. In most places municipal boundaries could no longer contain the new settlers, and many spilled over into the suburbs. For instance, Allegheny, Bayardstown, Birmingham, Lawrenceville, Hayti, and East Liberty added nearly 10,000 to Pittsburgh's population, bringing the total to 22,000.[14] The same was true of Cincinnati where 2,000 people lived in the Eastern and Northern Liberties.[15] In Louisville, Preston's and Campbell's "enlargements" and Shippingport and Portland swelled the city's total to 13,000.[16] Ultimately, the urban centers annexed these surrounding clusters, but in the meantime local authorities grappled with early manifestations of the suburban problem.

As the cities grew they staked out extensive commercial claims over the entire West.[17] Timothy Flint calculated that Cincinnati was the central market for over a million people, while a resident asserted that its trade was "co-extensive with steamboat navigation on the western waters."[18] Louisville's economic penetration was scarcely less impressive. As early as 1821, a local editor declared that "the people of the greater part of Indiana, all Kentucky, and portions of Tennessee, Alabama, Illinois, Missouri, now report to this place for dry goods, groceries, hardware and queensware."[19] St. Louis' empire touched Santa Fe on the south, Canada on the north, and the Pacific on the west. "It is doubtful if history affords the example of another city," wrote Hiram M. Chittenden, "which has been the exclusive mart for so vast an area as that which was tributary to St. Louis."[20]

In carving out these extensive dependencies, the young metropolises overwhelmed their smaller neighbors. The rise of St. Louis destroyed the ambitions of Edwardsville across the Mississippi, which once harbored modest hopes of importance. Pittsburgh's recovery in the late twenties condemned Wheeling and Steubenville to minor roles in the upper Ohio region. And Louisville's development swallowed two Kentucky neighbors while reducing Jeffersonville and New Albany on the Indiana side of the river to mere appendages.

Not satisfied with such considerable conquests, the cities reached out for more. Seeking wider opportunities, they built canals and turnpikes and, even before 1830, planned railroads to strengthen their position. Cincinnati, Pittsburgh, and St. Louis tried to tap the increasing trade on the Great Lakes by water links to the North. Pennsylvania's Iron City also hoped to become a major station on the National Road, and for a decade its Washington representatives lobbied to win that commercial bond with the East. Lexington, suffocating in its inland position, frantically strove for better connections with the Ohio River. A turnpike to Maysville was dashed by Jackson's veto, technical difficulties made a canal to the Kentucky River impractical, but some belated hope rose with the possibility of a railroad to Louisville or Cincinnati.

The intensive search for new advantages brought rivalry and conflict. Though the commerce of the whole West lay untouched before them, the cities quarreled over its division. Thus Louisville and Cincinnati fought over a canal around the Falls of the Ohio. The Kentucky town, feeling that its strength depended upon maintaining the break in transportation, obstructed every attempt to circumvent the rapids. Only when Ohio interests threatened to dig on the Indiana side did Louisville move ahead with its own project. Likewise, harsh words flew between Wheeling and Pittsburgh as they contended for the Ohio River terminus of the National Road. Smaller towns, too, joined the struggle. Cleveland and Sandusky, for instance, clashed over the location of the Ohio Canal, the stake being nothing less than control of the mounting trade between the Valley and the lakes. And their instinct to fight was sound, for the outcome shaped the future of both places.

Urban rivalries were often bitter, and the contestants showed no quarter. In the late twenties when only the success of Transylvania University kept Lexington's economy from complete collapse, Louisville joined the attack which ultimately destroyed the school. In a similar vein Cincinnatians taunted their upriver competitor as it reeled under the impact of the depression of 1819. "Poor Pittsburgh," they exclaimed, "your day is over, the sceptre of influence and wealth is to travel to us; the Cumberland road has done the business."[21] But even the Queen City found her supremacy insecure. "I discovered two ruling passions in Cincinnati," a traveler remarked, "enmity against Pittsburgh, and jealousy of Louisville."[22] This drive for power and primacy, sustained especially by merchants and articulated by editors, was one of the most consistent and striking characteristics of the early history of Western cities.

As they pursued expansive policies, municipalities also ministered to their own growing pains. From the beginning, urban residents had to contend with the problems of living together, and one of their first acts was to petition the territory or state for governing authority to handle them. The legislatures, representing rural interests and generally suspicious of towns, responded with charters bestowing narrow grants of power which barely met current needs and failed to allow for expansion. As localities grew, however, they developed problems which could be met only with wider jurisdiction. Louisville's charter had to be amended twenty-two times before 1815 and Cincinnati's underwent five major changes between 1815 and 1827. Others, though altered less often, were adjusted and remade until finally scrapped for new ones. Reluctantly, and bit by bit, the states turned over to the cities the responsibility of managing their own affairs, though keeping them starved for revenue by strict tax and debt limitations.

Despite inadequate charters and modest incomes, urban governments played a decisive role in the growth of Western cities. Since these were commercial towns, local authorities paid special attention to mercantile requirements. They not only constructed market houses but also extended municipal regulation over a wide variety of trading activity. Ordinances protected the public against adulterated foods, false measurements, and rigged prices. Some municipalities went even farther and assumed responsibility for seeing that "justice is done between buyer and seller."[23] In search of this objective, officials fixed prices on some goods, excluded monopolies from the market, and tried to equalize opportunities for smaller purchasers. To facilitate access to the exchange center, they lavished time and money on the development of wharves and docks and the improvement of streets.

Municipalities also tackled a wide variety of other problems growing out of urban life. Fire protection, at first casually organized, was placed on a more formal basis. Volunteer companies still provided the manpower, but government participation increased markedly. Local councils legislated against many kinds of fire hazards, and public money furnished most of the equipment. Moreover, some places, haunted by the image of Detroit's disaster in 1805, forbade the construction of wooden buildings in the heart of the city, a measure which not only reduced fire risks but also changed the face of downtown areas. The development of adequate police was much slower. By 1830 only Lexington and Louisville had regular patrols, and these were established with the intent more of control of slaves than the general protection of life and property. In other towns law enforcement was lax by day and absent at night, though the introduction of gas lighting in Pittsburgh and Cincinnati in the late twenties made the after-dark hours there less dangerous than before.

Congested living created new health hazards and especially increased the likelihood of epidemics. Every place suffered, but none like Louisville, which earned a grim reputation as the "Graveyard of the West" because of the constant visitations of yellow fever and malaria.[24] Cities took preventive measures, such as draining stagnant ponds and clearing streets and lots, and also appointed boards of health to preside over the problem. Municipal water systems, introduced in Pittsburgh and Cincinnati before 1830, made life healthier and certainly more comfortable, while the discussion of installing underground sewers pointed to still more extensive reform in sanitation.

In meeting urban problems, Western officials drew heavily on Eastern experience. Lacking precedents of their own, and familiar with the techniques of older cities, they frankly patterned their practice on Eastern models. There was little innovation. When confronted by a new question, local authorities responded by adopting tested solutions. This emulation characterized nearly every aspect of development—from the width of streets to housing regulations. No major improvement was launched without a close study of established seaboard practices. St. Louis' council, for example, instructed its water committee to "procure from the cities of Philadelphia and New Orleans such information as can be obtained on the subject of conveying water and the best manner of clearing it."[25] When Cincinnati discussed introducing underground sewers, an official group was designated to "ascertain from the city authorities of New York, Philadelphia, Baltimore and Boston, how far the sinking of common sewers is approved in those cities."[26]

Pittsburgh undertook gas lighting only after exhaustive research and "very full enquiries at New York and Baltimore."[27]

Though the young towns drew upon the experience of all the major Atlantic cities, the special source of municipal wisdom was Philadelphia. Many Western urbanites had lived or visited there; it provided the new country with most of its professional and cultural leadership; it was the model metropolis. "She is the great seat of American affluence, of individual riches, and distinguished philanthropy," a Pittsburgh editorial declared in 1818. "From her . . . we have everything to look for."[28] Newspapers often referred to it as "our mother city."[29]

From street plans to cultural activity, from the shape of market houses to the habits of people, the Philadelphia influence prevailed. Robert Peterson and John Filson, who had a hand in the founding of Louisville, Lexington, and Cincinnati, borrowed the basic grid pattern of the original plats from the Pennsylvania metropolis.[30] Market location and design came from the same source, as did techniques for fire fighting and police protection. Western towns also leaned on Philadelphia's leadership in street lighting, waterworks, and wharving. Even the naming of suburbs—Pittsburgh's Kensington and Cincinnati's Liberties—came from the mother city. The result was a physical likeness which struck many travelers and which Philadelphians themselves recognized. Gideon Burton, for instance, remembered his first impression of Cincinnati in the 1820's: "How beautiful this city is," he remarked, "how much like Philadelphia."[31]

The Quaker City spirit, morever, went beyond streets, buildings, and improvements, reaching into a wide range of human activity. Businessmen, yearly visitors in the East, brought marketing and promotion techniques from there;[32] young labor movements lifted their platforms from trade union programs in the mother city; employment agencies were conducted "principally on the Philadelphia plan."[33] The same metropolis trained most of the physicians of the West and a large share of the teachers and ministers. Caspar Wistar's famed Sunday evening gatherings of the intelligentsia provided the idea for Daniel Drake's select meetings of Cincinnati's social and cultural elite. Moreover, Philadelphia furnished the model of the perfect urbanite, for the highest praise that Western town dwellers could bestow upon a fellow citizen was to refer to him as their own "Benjamin Franklin."[34] In short, Philadelphia represented the highest stage of urban development, and progress was measured against this ideal.

Such borrowing was a conscious policy. In 1825 Mayor William Carr Lane of St. Louis, the most able urban statesman of the period, provided the justification. "Experience is the best guide . . . ," he told his councilmen. "The records of other towns are a source from which we may expect to derive useful hints. . . . It is therefore incumbent upon us to examine carefully what other communities similarly situated have done."[35] The process, however, was selective, not slavish. Investigation usually revealed a wide variety of possibilities, allowing Western cities to choose the most appropriate technique. Nevertheless, young towns preferred to meet their urban problems by adopting the established ways of the East. The challenge of the new country, far from producing a bold and fresh response, led to greater dependence on the older sections of the Union.

As transmontane cities developed they created societies whose ways and habits contrasted sharply with those of the countryside. Not only was their physical environment distinct, but their interests, activities, and pace of life also differed greatly. In 1811 a farmer near Lexington expressed the conflict as contemporaries saw it in a dialogue between "Rusticus" and "Urbanus." The latter referred to the "rude, gross appearance" of his neighbor, adding: "How strong you smell of your ploughed ground and corn fields. How dismal, how gloomy your green woods. What a miserable clash your whistling woodland birds are continually making." "Rusticus" replied with the rural image of the town dweller. "What a fine smooth complexion you have Urbanus: you look like a weed that has grown up in the shade. Can you walk your streets without inhaling the noxious fumes with which your town is pregnant? . . . Can you engage in calm contemplation, when hammers are ringing in every direction—when there is as great a *rattling* as in a storm when the hail descends on our house tops?"[36]

One of the most conspicuous differences was in social structure. The stratification of urban societies was in marked contrast with the boisterous equality of the countryside. Social lines developed very quickly in the city. Though not as tightly drawn as in the East, they represented the meaningful distinctions in Western communities. The groupings were basically economic, though professional people were set apart by their interest and training, and Negroes by their color. No rigid boundaries divided the classes, and movement between them was constant. Yet differences did exist; people felt them and contemporaries thought them significant. It is suggestive in this regard that the first great literary product of the West, *Modern Chivalry,* satirized the notion of equality, and the author, Hugh Henry Brackenridge, was one of Pittsburgh's leading citizens.

These divisions deepened in the postwar years. As the cities grew the sense of neighborliness and intimacy diminished, giving way to the impersonality characteristic of urban living. To old-timers the changing social configuration bred a deep nostalgia and raised the image of happier, simpler days. "We cannot help looking back with sorrowful heart, in that time of unaffected content and gaiety," a Pennsylvanian lamented, "when the unambitious people . . . in the village of 'Fort Pitt' in the yet uncharted town of Pittsburgh, were ignorant and careless of all invidious distinctions, which distract and divide the inhabitants of overgrown cities. Then all was peaceful heartfelt felicity, undisturbed by the rankling thorns of envy; and equality . . . was a tie that united all ranks and conditions in our community."[37] Town life in the West had never been that idyllic, but the distortion of the vision was itself a measure of the rapid change. "We have our castes of society, graduated and divided with as much regard to rank and dignity as the most scrupulous Hindoos maintain in defense of their religious prejudices," the same source admitted in 1826. Moreover, social distances were great. "Between the . . . classes . . . there are lines of demarcation drawn wide, distinct and not to be violated with impunity."[38] Nor was this stratification surprising. Having come from places where differences mattered, early city dwellers tried to re-create them in a new setting. The urge for status was stronger than the appeal of equality, and as the towns expanded cleavages deepened.

Urban ways were further distinguished from rural habits by the collective approach to many problems. City living created issues which could not always be solved by the highly individualistic methods of agrarian society. Local governments assumed an ever wider responsibility for the conduct of community affairs, and voluntary associations handled a large variety of other questions. Merchants formed chambers of commerce to facilitate cooperation on common problems; professional people organized societies to raise the standards of their colleagues and keep out the untrained. Working people, too, banded together in unions, seeking not only greater economic strength but also fraternity and self-improvement. Religious and philanthropic clubs managed most charity and relief work, while immigrants combined to help new arrivals. In addition, other associations grew up to promote literature and music, encourage debating, advocate social innovations, support public causes, and conduct the welter of amusements which larger cities required. Just as conditions in the countryside placed greatest emphasis on individual effort, so the urban situation made cooperative action seem more appropriate.

Rural and metropolitan West were also separated by distinctive social and cultural developments. The towns very quickly produced a surprisingly rich and diversified life, offering opportunities in many fields similar to those of Eastern cities but lacking on the farm or frontier.[39] They enjoyed a virtual monopoly of printing presses, newspapers, bookstores, and circulating libraries. Theaters sprang up to encourage local players and traveling troupes, while in larger places museums brought the curious and the scientific to the townfolks.[40] In addition, every week brought numerous lectures and debates on all kinds of topics, keeping urban residents abreast of the latest discoveries and developments in every field. By 1815 these amenities had already lost their novelty. Indeed, some thought the civilizing process was getting out of hand. "Twenty sermons a week—," a Cincinnatian wearily counted, "Sunday evening Discourses on Theology—Private assemblies—state Cotillion parties —Saturday Night Clubs, and chemical lectures— . . . like the fever and the ague, return every day with distressing regularity."[41]

Of course, the whole transmontane region matured culturally in this period, but the towns played a strategic role. "Cities have arisen in the very wilderness . . . ," a St. Louis editor noticed in 1821, "and form in their respective states the *foci* of art and science, of wealth and information."[42] A Cincinnatian made a similar observation. "This *city,* in its growth and cultural improvements has anticipated the western country in general."[43] The hinterland, already bound to urban communities by trade, readily admitted its dependence. The *Pittsburgh Gazette* merely stated the obvious when it remarked in 1819 that the surrounding region "looks up to Pittsburgh not only as a medium through which to receive the comforts and luxuries of foreign commodities, but also a channel from which it can most naturally expect a supply of intellectual wealth."[44] Thus while the cities' merchants staked out markets in the countryside, their civic leaders spread a cultural influence into the same area.

This leadership extended into almost every field. For example, the educational opportunities of town children greatly exceeded those of their rural neighbors. Every municipality developed a complex of private tuition schools topped by an academy and, in every place except Louisville, a college. Moreover, the cities organized the movement for public schooling. Ohio's experience is illustrative. The movement for state legislation started in Cincinnati, received its major impetus from the local press, and was carried in the Assembly through the efforts of representatives from Hamilton county. It is also significant that the first superintendent of common schools in Ohio was Samuel Lewis of Cincinnati. Nor was this urban leadership surprising. The cities, as the great population centers, felt the educational pressure first and most acutely. In addition, they alone had the wealth needed to launch ambitious projects for large numbers of children. Hence the towns were ready for comprehensive public programs long before the countryside.

The most striking illustration of the cultural supremacy of the cities, however, was Lexington's unique reign as the "Athens of the West."[45] The area's largest town until 1810, it was early celebrated for its polish and sophistication and was generally conceded to be the region's capital of arts and science. But the coming of the steamboat and the depression of 1819 combined to undermine its economic position. To offset this commercial and industrial decline, Lexington's civic leaders inaugurated a policy of vigorous cultural expansion.[46] They built schools, subsidized Transylvania University, and advertised the many opportunities for advancement in learning and letters in the metropolis. Throughout the twenties this campaign was a spectacular success. The town became the resort of the most talented men of the new country. Educators, scientists, painters, lawyers, architects, musicians, and their patrons all flocked there. Transylvania University attained national eminence, attracting most of its faculty from the East and drawing students from better than a dozen states. Like a renaissance city of old Italy, Lexington provided the creative atmosphere for a unique flowering that for a decade astonished travelers and stimulated the best minds of the West.

In its golden age the town boasted the most distinguished collection of intellectuals the new country had ever seen in a single city. The central figure in this awakening was Horace Holley, a Unitarian minister from Boston and the president of Transylvania. Though not an accomplished scholar himself, he recruited a remarkable faculty and raised the institution from a small denominational college to a university of the first rank. The medical department achieved a special distinction. Its dean was Charles Caldwell, one of Benjamin Rush's favorite pupils, who turned down important posts in New York, Philadelphia, and Baltimore to join the Kentucky experiment. Members of the staff included the botanist, Charles Wilkins Short, Daniel Drake, later the author of a pioneering study of diseases in the Mississippi Valley, and the surgeon, Benjamin Winslow Dudley. Among them, too, was the furtive and erratic, yet highly talented, Turkish-born naturalist, Constantine Rafinesque, whose most fruitful years were spent in Lexington.[47]

The graduating class of the medical school in 1826 demonstrated the extent of the university's reputation and influence. With sixty-seven degrees granted in that year, twenty-eight of the recipients came from Kentucky, ten from Tennessee, five each from Virginia, South Carolina, and Alabama, three from Ohio, two each from Mississippi, Illinois, and Louisiana, and one each from North Carolina and Georgia. During the twenties the college trained many of the West's most distinguished people. In politics alone it turned out at least seventeen congressmen, three governors, six United States senators, and the president of the Confederacy. In the same decade the school produced scores of lawyers, clergymen, and physicians, who did much to raise professional standards in the new country. Few universities have left such a clear mark on a generation; in its heyday Transylvania fully deserved its title of the "Harvard of the West."[48]

The college was the center of this wilderness renaissance, but around it moved other figures—artists, architects, musicians, and poets—who gave added luster to the movement. In Matthew Jouett the city had the West's most famous painter. A student of Gilbert Stuart and a portraitist of considerable gifts, he made his studio the exciting headquarters for a group of promising young artists. Gideon Shryock provided Lexington with an architect equal to its enlightenment. After studying with William Strickland in Philadelphia, he brought the Greek revival across the mountains. His work, especially the state capitol at Frankfort and Morrison College at Transylvania, brought him immediate fame and has led a modern critic to assert that he "was almost a decade ahead of his time even when judged by sophisticated eastern standards."[49] Music shared the upsurge, and in 1817 townsfolk heard Anthony Phillip Hennrich conduct the first performance of a Beethoven symphony in the United States.

The glitter of this city drew young people from all over the transmontane region, including many from the countryside. In doing so, it provoked a familiar lament from the rural areas whose children succumbed to the bewitchment of Lexington. "We want our sons to be practical men," wrote a Kentucky farmer, "whose minds will not be filled with those light notions of refinement and taste, which will induce them to believe that they are of a different order of beings, or that will elevate them above their equals."[50] Later, agrarian representatives in the legislature joined the attack on Transylvania by voting to cut off state financial assistance.

No less striking than cultural cleavages were the differences in rural and urban religious development. Progress in the cities was steadier and more substantial—though less spectacular—than in the back country. Traveling ministers might refer to Pittsburgh as "a young hell, a second Sodom,"[51] and Francis Asbury might complain in 1803 that he felt "the power of Satan in those little, wicked western trading towns,"[52] but both churches and membership multiplied rapidly in urban centers. Furthermore, the growth owed nothing to the sporadic revivals which burned across the countryside at the beginning of the century. These movements were essentially rural, having their roots in the isolation of agricultural living and the spiritual starvation of people unattended by regular services. The city situation, with its constant contacts and settled church organizations, involved neither of these elements. Instead, religious societies proliferated, sects took on such additional functions as charity and missionary work, and congregations sent money back East to aid their seminaries. Far from being sinks of corruption, Western cities quickly became religious centers, supplying Bibles to the frontier, assisting foreign missions, and, in the twenties, building theological schools to provide priests and ministers for the whole region.

Political life also reflected the growing rural-urban division. Though the rhetoric of the period often obscured them, differences existed from the very beginning. Suspicion of the towns led states to avoid economic and cultural centers when locating their capitals. Nearly all these cities sought the prize, but none was successful. The *Missouri Gazette* candidly stated the issue in 1820. "It has been said that St. Louis is obnoxious to our Legislature—that its growth and influence . . . are looked on with a jealous eye, and its pretensions . . . ought to be discouraged."[53] The same clash had earlier occurred in Kentucky, where state leaders virtually invented Frankfort to keep the capital away from Louisville or Lexington.

As the region developed, however, the conflict became increasingly apparent, though it was still expressed cautiously. "We must be permitted to say," an editor asserted in 1820, "that in Cincinnati we have separate interests" from the countryside.[54] Likewise, a Pittsburgher prefaced a strong attack on the neighboring areas by declaring that "we think it wrong to stir up a jealousy between city and country."[55] Nevertheless, the split represented one of the fundamental facts of Western politics.

Of course, farm dwellers easily outnumbered urbanites, but the latter wielded disproportionate power. The case of Jefferson and Oldham counties in Kentucky was illustrative. In the mid-twenties the combined vote reached

3,200, Louisville residents casting roughly a quarter of them. Yet the state senator and both representatives came from the city. In 1829 when a third assemblyman was added, the rural interests pleaded with Louisville leaders to name someone from the surrounding area. "It may seem strange," wrote an observer, "that it would be necessary thus to ask for the liberality of 800 voters in favor of 2,400. . . . Nevertheless, the concentrated energies of 800 do entirely outweigh the scattered influence of the 2,400—that all past experience teaches."[56] The situation was the same elsewhere. At one time all of Missouri's representatives in Washington—two senators and one congressman—as well as its governor came from St. Louis.

The cities' political influence rested on their ability to produce leadership. As the economic and intellectual centers of transmontane life they attracted the talented and ambitious in all fields. Politics was no exception. Nearly all the great spokesmen of the West had important urban connections and their activity often reflected the demands of their town constituents. Henry Clay was one of Lexington's most prominent lawyers when he went to the United States Senate in 1806. Thomas Hart Benton held local offices in St. Louis before moving on to the national scene, and William Henry Harrison, though he lived in nearby North Bend, had deep roots in Cincinnati affairs through most of his long public life. Moreover, all were alive to the interests of their city. Benton's successful attack on government factories in the Indian territory culminated a long and intense campaign by St. Louis merchants to break federal trade control on the Missouri. Clay's enthusiasm for an ample tariff on hemp derived at least as much from the pressure of Lexington's manufactures as from that of the growers of the Blue Grass. And Harrison, as state senator, led the campaign for public schools in Ohio largely at the behest of his Cincinnati supporters. These were not isolated cases; an examination of the careers of these men demonstrates the importance of their urban connections.

By 1830, then, the West had produced two types of society—one rural and one urban. Each developed its own institutions, habits, and living patterns. The countryside claimed much the larger population, and often gave to transmontane affairs an agrarian flavor. But broadcloth was catching up with buckskin. The census of 1830 revealed the disproportionate rate of city growth. While the state of Ohio had four times as many inhabitants as it counted in 1810, Cincinnati's increase was twelvefold. The story was the same elsewhere. Louisville's figure showed a growth of 650 per cent compared with Kentucky's 50 per cent, and Pittsburgh tripled in size while Pennsylvania did not quite double its population. By 1830 the rise of these cities had driven a broad wedge of urbanism into Western life.

Though town and country developed along different paths, clashes were still infrequent. The West was large enough to contain both movements comfortably. Indeed, each supported the other. The rural regions supplied the cities with raw materials for their mills and packinghouses and offered an expanding market to their shops and factories. In turn, urban centers served the surrounding areas by providing both the necessities and comforts of life as well as new opportunity for ambitious farm youths. Yet the cities represented the more aggressive and dynamic force. By spreading their economic power over the entire section, by bringing the fruits of civilization across the mountains, and by insinuating their ways into the countryside, they speeded up the transformation of the West from a gloomy wilderness to a richly diversified region. Any historical view which omits this aspect of Western life tells but part of the story.

■ ■ ■ ■ Notes

1 *Missouri Gazette* (St. Louis), July 13, 1816.
2 *Liberty Hall* (Cincinnati), June 11, 1815.
3 *Missouri Republican* (St. Louis), Aug. 29, 1825.
4 James Hall, *The West: Its Commerce and Navigation* (Cincinnati, 1848), p. 227.
5 Daniel Drake, "Dr. Drake's Memoir of the Miami County, 1779–1794," Beverley Bond, Jr., ed., Historical and Philosophical Society of Ohio, *Quarterly Publications,* XVIII (1923), 58.
6 Drake, 58.
7 James R. Robertson, ed., *Petitions of the Early Inhabitants of Kentucky to the General Assembly of Virginia, 1769–1792* (Louisville, Ky., 1914), p. 106.
8 Louis C. Hunter, *Steamboats on the Western Rivers, An Economic and Technological History* (Cambridge, Mass., 1949), pp. 27–32.
9 Morgan Neville, "The Last of the Boatmen," *The Western Souvenir for 1829* (Cincinnati, Ohio, n.d.), p. 108.
10 [Jean Baptiste] Marestier, *Mémoire sur les Bateaux à vapeur des États-Unis d'Amérique* (Paris, 1824), pp. 9–10.
11 Zadock Cramer, *Pittsburgh Almanack for the Year of Our Lord 1810* (Pittsburgh, Pa., 1810), p. 52.
12 Pittsburgh's industrial foundations are discussed in Catherine Elizabeth Reiser, *Pittsburgh's Commercial Development, 1800–1850* (Harrisburg, Pa., 1951), pp. 12–21.
13 *Niles' Register,* May 28, 1814.
14 *Pittsburgh Gazette,* Nov. 16, 1830.
15 *Cincinnati Advertiser,* Aug. 18, 1830.
16 United States *Census,* 1830, pp. 114–15.
17 For an appreciation of the economic importance of the cities in the growth of the West, see Frederick Jackson Turner, *Rise of the New West, 1819–1829* in *The American Nation: A History,* A. B. Hart, ed., XIV (New York, 1906), pp. 96–98.
18 Timothy Flint, "Thoughts Respecting the Establishment of a Porcelain Manufactory at Cincinnati," *Western Monthly Review,* III (1830), 512; Benjamin Drake and Edward W. Mansfield, *Cincinnati in 1826* (Cincinnati, Ohio, 1827), p. 71.
19 *Louisville Public Advertiser,* Oct. 17, 1829.
20 Hiram M. Chittenden, *The American Fur Trade of the Far West* (2 vols., New York, 1902), I, p. 99.
21 *Pittsburgh Gazette,* Dec. 18, 1818.
22 *Pittsburgh Gazette,* Feb. 5, 1819.
23 *Pittsburgh Gazette,* Mar. 9, 1810.
24 Benjamin Casseday, *The History of Louisville from Its Earliest Settlement till the Year 1852* (Louisville, Ky., 1852), p. 49.

25 St. Louis City Council, Minutes, Court House, St. Louis, June 12, 1829.

26 Cincinnati City Council, Minutes, City Hall, Cincinnati, Oct. 6, 1827.

27 Pittsburgh City Council, City Council Papers, City Hall, Pittsburgh, May 10, 1827. The extent of Western urban indebtedness to the East is perhaps best illustrated in the establishment of the high school in Louisville. The building was "mainly after the plan of the High School of New York, united with the Public School Rooms of Philadelphia." Most of the teachers came from the East, while the curriculum and even reading assignments derived from "the High School of New York and some of the Boston establishments." *An Account of the Louisville City School, Together With the Ordinances of the City Council, and the Regulations of the Board of Trustees for the Government of the Institution* (Louisville, Ky., 1830), pp. 5 ff.

28 *Pittsburgh Gazette,* Oct. 27, 1818.

29 For example, see *Pittsburgh Gazette,* June 23, 1818.

30 For example, see Rufus King, *Ohio First Fruits of the Ordinance of 1787* (Boston, 1888), p. 209.

31 Gideon Burton, *Reminiscences of Gideon Burton* (Cincinnati, Ohio, 1895). The strategic location of Western cities in the life of the new country reminded some visitors of the regional supremacy of Philadelphia. Lewis Condict, for example, referred to Lexington as "the Philadelphia of Kentucky." "Journal of a Trip to Kentucky in 1795," *Proceedings of the New Jersey Historical Society,* n.s., IV (1919), 120.

32 *Cincinnati Enquirer,* Apr. 22, 1923.

33 *Pittsburgh Mercury,* Aug. 7, 1827.

34 The phrase was constantly used in characterizing John Bradford of Lexington and Daniel Drake of Cincinnati, but it was applied to others as well.

35 St. Louis City Council, Minutes, Court House, St. Louis, Apr. 25, 1825.

36 *Kentucky Reporter* (Lexington), July 2, 1811.

37 Samuel Jones, *Pittsburgh in 1826* (Pittsburgh, Pa., 1826), p. 43.

38 Jones, p. 43.

39 For a day-to-day account of the cultural offerings of a Western city between 1820 and 1830 see the highly informative but unpublished diary of William Stanley Merrill in the library of the Historical and Philosophical Society of Ohio (Cincinnati).

40 The development of the theater in Western cities is outlined in Ralph Leslie Rush, *The Literature of the Middle Western Frontier* (New York, 1925), I, pp. 352–400. For a detailed study of a single town see William G. B. Carson, *The Theatre on the Frontier, The Early Years of the St. Louis Stage* (Chicago, 1932), pp. 1–134.

41 *Liberty Hall,* Dec. 9, 1816.

42 *Missouri Gazette,* Dec. 20, 1820.

43 *Liberty Hall,* June 29, 1819.

44 *Pittsburgh Gazette,* Apr. 30, 1819.

45 For Lexington's growth and brief supremacy see Bernard Mayo, "Lexington, Frontier Metropolis," in *Historiography and Urbanization,* Eric F. Goldman, ed. (Baltimore, Md., 1941), pp. 21–42.

46 See, for example, *Kentucky Reporter,* Oct. 4, 1820.

47 Transylvania's "golden age" is treated in detail in Walter William Jennings, *Transylvania, Pioneer University of the West* (New York, 1955), pp. 99–124, and Niels Henry Sonne, *Liberal Kentucky, 1780–1828* (New York, 1939), pp. 160–242.

48 The reputation of Lexington in Cincinnati is charmingly portrayed in the letters of young Ohioans attending Transylvania University to their friends back home. See especially the William Lytle Collection in the library of the Historical and Philosophical Society of Ohio (Cincinnati).

49 Talbot Hamlin, *Greek Revival Architecture in America: Being an Account of Important Trends in American Architecture and American Life prior to the War between the States* (New York, 1944), p. 244.
50 *Kentucky Reporter,* Feb. 16, 1824.
51 *Pittsburgh Gazette,* Sept. 23, 1803.
52 Francis Asbury, *Journal of Rev. Francis Asbury, Bishop of Methodist Episcopal Church* (n.p., 1821), III, p. 127.
53 *Missouri Gazette,* Dec. 6, 1820.
54 *Cincinnati Advertiser,* Sept. 16, 1829.
55 *Pittsburgh Statesman,* Aug. 26, 1823.
56 *Louisville Public Advertiser,* July 28, 1824.

7

Patterns of Mid-Nineteenth Century Urbanization in the Middle West

BAYRD STILL

In the preceding article Richard C. Wade surveyed the early years of the Ohio Valley cities, and in the next essay Bayrd Still examines the Great Lakes cities in the middle decades of the nineteenth century. He finds that Buffalo, Cleveland, Detroit, Chicago, and Milwaukee exhibited a remarkable uniformity in economics, social structures, and institutional arrangements. Imitation rather than innovation was the watchword for these villages rapidly becoming cities.

Professors Wade and Still both point up the fact that migration and the establishment of new communities was often a conservative process. Men tried to reproduce the patterns they had known in the past and borrowed heavily from existing communities. Western cities looked to eastern cities and to each other when deciding what obligations the municipality should assume and how best to meet those responsibilities. Rather than increase the scope of public services offered, they repeated the patterns set by older cities at a comparable stage of development. When the Lakes cities did enlarge their public role, they did so in response to their increased size and complexity, not because of a more expansive philosophic conception of the services a city should provide its citizens.

In the middle of the nineteenth century, editors and civic leaders stressed the individual's obligation to promote the growth and prosperity of his city by enlarging its trade and especially its industrial activities. Residents of all these cities wanted their community to become the metropolis of an entire region; they also hoped that flourishing industry would provide a more secure and stable economic base than reliance on a seasonally concentrated trade. Subscription libraries and other fee-supported institutions and services were often promoted because they would make the city more attractive to newcomers and contribute to its growth and prosperity.

■ ■ ■ ■ For Further Reading

Bayrd Still, *Milwaukee: The History of a City* (Madison: State Historical Society of Wisconsin, 1948, rev. ed. 1967) is a thorough and well-documented history of one major Great Lakes city. Bessie L. Pierce, *A History of Chicago,* 3 vols. (New York: Alfred A. Knopf, 1937–1957) is thorough and competent but smothers much of the drama of the city's history. Daniel Boorstin, *The Americans: The National Experience* (New York: Vintage Books, 1967) has fascinating material on urban boosterism and the processes of city building. Harold M. Mayer and Richard C. Wade, *Chicago: Growth of a Metropolis* (Chicago: University of Chicago Press, 1969) is a magnificently illustrated book with a highly readable text.

■ Until recently a persistent preoccupation with the agrarian aspects of the westward march of American settlement has to some extent obscured the fact that the prospect of future towns and cities as well as the promise of broad and fertile acres lured settlers to the "sunset regions." On many a frontier the town builder was as conspicuous as the farmer pioneer; the western city, through the efforts of its founders to extend its economic hinterland, actually facilitated the agrarian development of the West; and the opportunities attending city growth as well as those afforded by cheap farm lands contributed to the dynamic sense of economic abundance felt by Americans of the mid-nineteenth century. As early as 1845 one middle western editor identified this urban growth with the rapid development of the West when he wrote:

> The tide of emigration to the West seems to increase daily. . . . What an enterprising spirit characterizes the American people. . . . This . . . activity and enterprise . . . are the result of free institutions, which give an impetus to the human mind. In no other country have towns and villages sprung up so suddenly as in this. Everything seems to go ahead with railroad velocity. Well might Marryat remark that cities grow up here to more importance in ten years than they do in Europe in a century.[1]

The growth of cities is admittedly a significant aspect of the history of the West. But any precise estimate of the bearing either of urbanization upon the expansion of the American frontier or of the westward movement of population upon city growth in the United States awaits a more adequate exposition of urban development in specific sections of the country than has as yet been set forth.[2]

The migrants who poured into the Mississippi Valley in the middle of the nineteenth century built cities as well as cultivated farms. By the seventies, when the American people were first becoming conscious of the drift of population to the city, the Middle West showed a spectacular urban growth. It could then boast seven cities of more than a hundred thousand people,[3] whereas thirty years before only New Orleans had achieved that size. To be sure, the total population of the ten major mid-western cities in 1870 still fell slightly short of the more than 1,800,000 city dwellers then living in New York, Philadelphia, and Boston; but in the rate of their growth the former were putting to shame the cities of the Atlantic coast. Among these mushroom metropolises of the West, the lake cities—Buffalo, Cleveland, Detroit, Chicago, and Milwaukee—rather than the valley cities— Pittsburgh, Cincinnati, Louisville, Nashville, and St. Louis—showed the greatest proportional increase in numbers.[4] By 1870 the five lake cities had attained a combined population of more than sixteen times their total of 1840, although the population of the states in which they were located had barely tripled.[5]

Because of their rapid and parallel growth, a comparative analysis of these five lake cities provides a useful means of studying the nature of the emerging city in the Middle West. With striking similarity, they all limited themselves to those duties of the urban community which were common to eighteenth century cities. They all responded to the democratic movement by extending popular participation in municipal government and then by broadening the authority of the executive or administrative commission. Not only did they rely upon the individual to provide most of the services which are demanded today of the city itself but they also expected him to promote the city's growth—a promotion which in every case involved substituting the encouragement of manufacturing for an earlier emphasis on trade. And with equal uniformity they imitated the experience of one another in ordering the details of their municipal life. While it is never too wise to try to compress the variety of human behavior into patterns, the common responses of the five cities suggest the conclusion that these at least are qualities which may well be characteristic of mid-nineteenth century urbanization in the upper Middle West.

A comparative study of the charters under which the Great Lake cities were governed between 1830 and 1870 discloses the imitation of form and limitation of function in which the powers of the urban community were at that time conceived. These charters were cut from an almost identical constitutional pattern, laid down in the spirit of eighteenth century America. Admittedly the creature of the legislative will of the state, each city never- theless resorted frequently to the public meeting for the purpose of proposing charter changes and civic improvement.[6] With the advance to city status the meagre functions of the village period—protection against fire, opening and repairing streets, regulating markets, licensing shows, and sinking public wells—were considerably expanded. These functions were enlarged by a uniform extension of regulatory powers, services, and guarantees—additions which were, however, more boldly granted than enforced if one judges from the charges of nonenforcement levied against the city administration by the Milwaukee press.

The first city charters of Buffalo (1832), Cleveland (1836), and Chicago (1837) were strikingly similar in form. The Chicago charter is almost an identical copy of the Buffalo document save for certain local references. In the more than thirty clauses enumerating the powers of the council, the wording of the Chicago charter is different from that of Buffalo in less than half a dozen instances. The Chicago charter added provisions with respect to street lamps and ferries, but lacked the provision for the assize of bread that is found in the Buffalo framework of government. Significantly, the contemporaneous government of Milwaukee, organized at virtually the same time (1836), was still confined to the restricted duties of a village. Ten years later, however, when it emerged as a city, its citizens sought, and the state legislature granted, an expansion of powers quite similar to those of its sister cities of the Great Lakes. The Chicago consolidation act of 1851 found an echo in a like measure for Milwaukee in 1852 and in a revision of Buffalo's charter in 1853. These charters elaborated rather than expanded the powers of the municipality in ways dictated by closer acquaintance with the problems of city government. Again the customary parallelism in form stands out both in the general pattern of the documents and in the many identical clauses, such as those setting up the fire department and compelling the removal of ill-smelling nuisances.[7]

The advance from village to city brought an extension of municipal responsibilities, but only to an extent normally resulting, especially in America, from the crowding of people into small compass. These new powers were limited in general to the protection of life and property, although the results of each extension of authority were recognized as having a bearing on the promotion of trade and hence on the prosperity of the municipality. Concern for securing property against the chronic fire hazard of the western city made possible the enactment of building restrictions and encouraged the organization of fire-fighting facilities. Concern for health prompted the authorities to establish pesthouses, to quarantine immigrants coming through the lake ports, and to abate such nuisances as stagnant pools, foul-smelling substances, and slaughter houses—reforms stimulated not so much by aesthetic considerations as by the prevailing conviction that urban filth and the spread of cholera went hand in hand. While thus exhorting cleanliness, the authorities at the same time, perhaps paradoxically, laid restrictions on wasting water and prohibited bathing in the rivers from which the city water supply was drawn.

In the interests of urban order, the city councils were empowered to provide watchmen and police; to suppress disorderly houses; to impound animals running at large; to prevent immoderate driving, rolling hoops or playing ball in the streets, and the cluttering of sidewalks with snow, dirt, firewood, awnings, or cigar store Indians; to restrain "runners" for boats and stages; and to curtail city noises. Nor were these idle grants of authority. The Cleveland council, as one of its first acts, passed an ordinance on May 9, 1836, which provided that the streets were to be swept semi-monthly on Friday mornings by the owners or occupants of property; that horses should not be fastened so as to obstruct passage in the streets nor be driven on the sidewalks; and that the huge wooden replicas of boots, saddles, and kettles with which merchants advertised their wares were not to project over three feet into the street. In addition to providing for quarantine and hospitalization of the sick poor, the health ordinances of Milwaukee required that physicians report cases of contagious diseases and that records of burials show the cause of death lest criminal or dangerous causes be left unknown; decreed a fine of ten dollars for refusal to be vaccinated on the request of a physician employed by the city council; set up barriers to the immigration of the diseased, going so far as to empower constables to call upon the aid of bystanders in forcibly keeping immigrants from landing; and banned slaughter houses within the city limits. The Buffalo council prohibited interment within certain limits and ordered that graves be not less than five feet deep. Anti-noise ordinances in Buffalo and Milwaukee prevented the playing of musical instruments on docks or wharves on Sunday, and in Milwaukee the ringing of bells or loud outcries at public sales were forbidden.

In providing for markets and the regulation of traffic in necessary commodities, these western cities followed practices by which frontier and colonial communities had attempted to protect an often insufficient food supply, prevent monopolistic practices detrimental to the public health and security, avoid the competition of foreign vendors and hucksters, and at the same time force competition upon the licensed merchants.[8] In 1849 Chicago had three markets for the retailing of perishable foods. Butchers were forced to hold stalls there until an act of 1851 permitted the establishment of meat shops outside the market.[9] City markets and strict market ordinances were justified as a means of supplying large cities with fresh and wholesome provisions, because leniency in this respect, it was felt, might encourage disease. Vendors of fresh meat, poultry, eggs, butter, lard, fruit, and vegetables were forced to sell their goods at the market during the market hours unless licensed to sell at some other place or in some other way. To guarantee the wholesomeness of the products, cleanliness of the stalls, and orderliness of the market, prohibitions were set up against pitching quoits, the presence of dogs, and the use of obscene and profane language in the vicinity of the market place. Purchasing goods at the markets for resale elsewhere or forestalling country producers for the purpose of buying their produce for resale was prohibited.[10]

Similar regulations for supervising weights and measures affected the purchase of boards, brick, coal, firewood, casks, hay, flour, tobacco, potash, and salted provisions such as fish. According to a Cleveland ordinance of May 8, 1939, vendors of hay without a certificate of weight were subject to a fine of twenty-five dollars. In 1859 Milwaukee farmers opposed as an inequitable tax the weighing charge of five cents per load of wood and twenty-five cents per load of hay—a concession sold by the city to the highest bidder.[11] The assize of bread, customary in the colonial city charter and in early charters in the West, was apparently abandoned in Chicago and for a while in Cleveland, though provided for elsewhere.[12] In these young urban communities, commerce in such necessary commodities as food, fodder, and firewood was of sufficient public interest to warrant close regulation. Other pursuits related to the public welfare were also restricted. For instance, ordinances regulating the fees of hackmen and carters were not unusual. Chapter XIII of the Buffalo ordinances of 1855 stipulated that a hackman might be fined for refusing to carry a passenger or for going by other than the shortest route. Interest in attracting immigrants prompted a Milwaukee ordinance of May 3, 1849, which fixed a maximum charge of ten cents per article on the goods of immigrants and other passengers landed on the piers of the city.

These principal activities of the mid-nineteenth century city were laid down at the inception of cityhood and were based upon the regulations commonly existing during the colonial period. Later amendments elaborated these functions of municipal government as specific problems arose, and occasionally a measure was passed which suggested an expanding concept of city government, as in the Chicago provision of 1851 with respect to planting and preserving ornamental trees along the streets and in the public grounds of the city. In general, however, the close of this middle period saw only a limited expansion of urban responsibilities beyond those assumed with the grant of the original charter. Nor did these differ in any marked way from the eighteenth century pattern of powers granted the government of New York City at the close of the colonial period.

However, in defining the political authority underlying municipal management, these cities, developing in the current of nineteenth century democracy, left eighteenth century limitations far behind. Here again is a striking uniformity of behavior in the five lake cities. Each began its career as a city with a property qualification, in addition to a residence requirement of varying length, for at least one class of voters—whites, aliens, or Negroes. Detroit in 1824 required its electors to be freemen who had paid a city tax. Buffalo extended the suffrage to United States citizens but required Negro voters to have a freehold estate of $250 on which taxes had been actually rated and paid. A tax qualification was prerequisite to voting in Cleveland in 1836, and Chicago in 1837 expected its voters to be householders or to have paid a city tax of not less than three dollars within the year. As late as 1846 Milwaukee exacted payment of a property tax or required highway or fire duty of male aliens who had declared their intention of becoming citizens. At the outset of cityhood in Chicago, Detroit, and Buffalo, only those owning a freehold estate were eligible for the major elective posts; Milwaukee, having demanded a similar qualification of her village trustees, abandoned this provision upon becoming a city in 1846.

Chicago took the lead in a democratic movement which brought by the early fifties the abolition of property qualifications for suffrage and office holding. Milwaukeeans called a proposal to restrict the suffrage to United States citizens an "odious and anti-republican" attempt to deprive "one-half of the citizens of Milwaukee, who will be taxed for the support of the city government, of their right to a voice in electing their officers or making their laws."[13] Like the framers of the state constitutions of the middle period, these mid-western city dwellers believed in representative government closely responsive to the popular will. A proposal to allow aldermen to hold their offices for three years was opposed in Milwaukee as "placing them beyond the reach of public opinion for a time almost equal to an age in older communities."[14] Consequently, annually-elected councils were endowed with wide authority and the power of the executive office was greatly curtailed. In Buffalo the mayor was the creature of the council, and in the other cities little more than a figurehead. Chicagoans in 1840 openly resented the fact that their mayor was given a salary and pointed to Detroit and Buffalo where, they said, the mayors "in fact receive nothing."[15] Adherence to the democratic principle of passing jobs around was the practice if not the provision. In Cleveland between 1836 and 1870 only five mayors succeeded themselves in office, and of the twelve available council positions the yearly average of councilmen who were reëlected was two. A study of the situation in Chicago and Milwaukee shows a similar rotation in office. In Detroit it became necessary to force men by threat or danger of fine to serve once they had been elected, although they were specifically exempted from holding the same office two years in succession. The municipal legislators served without salary, but this did not prevent many of them from amassing fortunes, especially when they held the office of street commissioner.[16] To judge from an analysis of the trades and occupations of those who were councilmen in Cleveland and Milwaukee in the first twenty years of their cityhood, commission merchants, grocers, joiners, builders, masons, and attorneys took a predominantly active part in the government of these young western cities.

Charter changes both in the early fifties and after the financial crisis of 1857 brought some decrease in the amateur management of these governments and a consequent strengthening of the executive arm. In 1852 Milwaukee was provided with an appointed comptroller, soon made elective, to manage city finances. In 1858 the state legislature devised a bicameral council for the city in the hope of retarding hasty legislation. The mayor was granted the veto power in Chicago in 1851 and in Milwaukee in 1859, a negative that was strengthened in the latter city in 1861 and in the former in 1872 by requiring two-thirds rather than a majority of the elected councilmen to override it. The major development in all the Great Lakes cities at the close of the period under discussion was in the direction of establishing boards and commissions as a means of divorcing city management from amateur direction and political interference. This trend, realized in the late sixties and early seventies, was motivated, according to the Milwaukee *Sentinel,* by a feeling that it was inefficient and costly to commit the complicated problems of street improvements and urban services to elected councilmen. It would be better, said the editor, to trust the outlay of great sums of the people's money to "three capable, honest, experienced business men . . . with a moderate compensation for their services, than take the chances under the elective principle of having men of doubtful qualities . . . without compensation . . . under the constant imputation of petty frauds and speculations upon the ward funds."[17] Vesting in the mayor the power of appointing the members of these boards and commissions is an index of the increased prestige of the executive and the decreasing influence of the legislative branch of city government at the opening of the seventies. The Great Lakes cities, growing to maturity in the environment of nineteenth century democracy, thus broadened the base of urban politics but narrowed the administration of municipal affairs.

These major cities of the Middle West did not "just grow." The promotional activities of the original speculator-founders were only the beginning of a long-time program in which newspaper editors, merchants, and citizens at large combined their efforts to attract settlers and business to a given city and away from its neighboring rivals.[18] The promoters of the embryo village on the east side of the Milwaukee river expended nearly $100,000 laying out streets and effecting other improvements designed to attract the settler. By the exertion of political influence and the donation of land they secured the county courthouse for their growing community. Across the river, the promoters of the "west side" were spending similar sums upon improvements, filling the columns of the Milwaukee *Advertiser* with glowing reports of their city's promise, and, by employing a river boat to meet the lake steamers that touched Milwaukee harbor, preempting immigrants possibly destined for their rivals' village. Subsequently many a subterfuge was devised by Chicago and Milwaukee in an attempt to discredit the other in the eyes of European immigrants and eastern capitalists. Only the combination of geography and the railroad left Milwaukee a tired but still confident second in the race. "Forcing" immigrants was accomplished through the use of representatives and promotional advertising in eastern cities. For example, propaganda concerning deaths from cholera, or the absence of them, figured prominently in such campaigns.[19]

The promotion of business in these cities followed a common pattern. A predominant concern for trade and commerce gave way in the middle sixties to the encouragement of manufacturing. Economic developments in Milwaukee and Cleveland substantiate this interpretation. The early interest in trade was reflected by the editor of the Milwaukee *Daily Sentinel and Gazette* in 1846: "It is . . . clearly to the interest of our merchants, millers, forwarders, and business men generally to unite upon some plan for extending and improving roads leading to Milwaukee."[20] Even before this, popular contributions had subsidized a bridge that promised to facilitate the trade of neighboring farmers with the village merchants. Plank roads and railroads were heralded as a means of tapping the markets of the hinterland. Connections by rail with the Columbia River, with the Mississippi River (completed by 1857), and with the Minnesota country, and routes eastward by steam ferry across Lake Michigan and by the Detroit and Michigan railroad were only a few of the projects. They were supported by city funds, by loans of city credit, and by popular subscription—contributions often appealed for and given as a matter of civic duty.[21] Clevelanders were equally convinced of the importance of roads and railways for prosperity. The editor of the Cleveland *Daily True Democrat* wrote in 1849: "Let us, like the wise Cincinnati merchants, spend liberally for these [plank] roads and do all to arouse our farmers and everybody to the importance of increasing our facilities for trade and travel and thus make Cleveland the center of a large region."[22] By 1856 it was asserted in the Cleveland *Leader* that railroads were responsible for the city's growth. The establishment of Boards of Trade in Buffalo (1844), Detroit (1847), Cleveland and Chicago (1848), and Milwaukee (1849); the organization and promotional excursions of merchants; the contesting of disputed trade areas through the use of runners and drummers—these activities suggest the early emphasis on trade and commerce as the key to civic prosperity. In 1857, Milwaukee merchants were urged to compete for trade in Iowa and Minnesota where

> already Chicago, St. Louis, Dubuque, Galena, Cincinnati even, have their runners, posters, and advertisements scattered broadcast . . . offering tempting inducements to merchants to come and buy. . . . Now is the time for our merchants, manufacturers, and traders to . . . scatter their cards, handbills, circulars, and advertisements up and down the Mississippi. Let them dispatch some of their shrewdest clerks to La Crosse, Winona, Prescott, Hudson, St. Paul . . . and canvass thoroughly for orders.[23]

By 1855, however, Cleveland editors were sounding a warning note. Business men were blinded, they said, "by the belief that commerce alone" would make the city great. The *Leader* asserted in 1856 that "no thinking man with capital will stop here when we have only commerce to sustain us. A manufacturing town gives a man full scope for his ambitions."[24] That newspaper encouraged popular subscriptions to factory enterprises, urged the reduction of real estate prices as an inducement to capital, and agitated for the protection and consumption of home manufactures.[25] An appeal to civic duty attended this promotion as it had the earlier agitation for railroad connections. By the late sixties when Cleveland had become a manufacturing center, earlier arguments used there were being echoed in Milwaukee. Vigorous newspaper agitation, together with the organization of the Milwaukee Manufacturers Association in January 1863, excited industrial ambitions. "Commerce alone can never give us a permanent prosperity," counselled a Milwaukee editor in 1866.[26] By 1872, as a result, one-third to one-half of the working population of Milwaukee was engaged in manufacturing goods valued at $20,000,000.[27] Stimulated by the economic developments of the Civil War period, pressed by the expansion of population into areas farther west of them, and in a sense taking a cue each from the economic experiences of the other, the lake cities had turned by 1870 from an almost exclusive interest in commerce to endorse sentiments to the effect that "a thousand dollars put into manufacturing does more to gather population than a million dollars put into trade."[28]

A major source of the urban services of these young communities developed from the sense of individual responsibility which prompted thousands of city dwellers to invest their savings in the railroads and factories that were supposed to bring prosperity to the urban center. The mid-nineteenth century saw the Great Lakes cities in what might be called the "subscription period" of their municipal growth. Two to three days' work on the streets, for which money payments could be substituted, was expected of all able-bodied men.[29] Street and sidewalk improvements as well as the eradication of nuisances were to be taken care of individually or charged against the property benefited. For protection against theft and riot Milwaukeeans had to rely upon occasional watchmen, volunteer firemen, and members of free military companies until a night watch and a police force were organized in 1852. As late as 1855 men carried weapons for their own protection, and an ordinance of that year compelled all citizens to aid the police when called upon to do so. In 1837 the Cleveland *Herald and Gazette* referred to the "Mutual Protecting Society," and in 1839 a number of the citizens "with commendable spirit formed themselves into companies for a city watch." In 1859 the merchants of Detroit, where as early as 1825 volunteer watchmen had been mobilized by passing around a subscription paper, subscribed to the support of a patrol for the business district, and the Milwaukee Board of Trade offered a bonus for additional protection in 1860.[30] By the late fifties and early sixties police service was generally provided at city expense, and the management of the police by a commission was agitated or passed in Milwaukee (1864), Detroit (1865), and Cleveland (1866).

Fire protection came also in a major degree from individual contributions of time and money. In the middle thirties Clevelanders were fined when they refused to serve in the bucket line at fires. Local editors appealed to property owners to contribute their share of volunteer firemen and in 1840 congratulated Phoenix Company Number Four for having won the premiums offered annually by the insurance companies to stimulate competitive-minded fire fighters to efficiency and accomplishment. Milwaukeeans from all levels of society were members of the organized volunteer firemen, who met a portion of the costs of their own equipment and whose service exempted them from highway or militia duty. Donations, benefit concerts, and dinners raised $2,500 in 1851 to swell the funds by which the Ocean, Neptune, and Cataract companies of volunteer firemen carried on their work. Despite the pleas of property owners for more efficient service than unpaid volunteers could give, it was not until the appearance of the steam fire engine in the sixties that professional fire fighters were generally maintained from public funds.[31]

Aside from a meagre and inadequate tax to support almshouses and to furnish medical care for the sick poor, urban relief, too, was provided by individual donation. Invariably the cessation of navigation in the winter season brought demands from the unemployed of the city. Out of public meetings came plans for raising money and organizations for dispensing relief. Mayor D. A. J. Upham of Milwaukee expressed a general opinion in 1849 when he held that private enterprise was best equipped to meet the problem. The Cleveland *Daily True Democrat* said the poor could not be taken care of "unless individual activity and associated effort act."[32] Women's organizations, such as the Martha Washington Society of Cleveland and the Ladies Benevolent Society of Milwaukee, were soon supplanted by more systematically managed relief groups, like the Milwaukee Provident Association and the Cleveland Relief Association. The Milwaukee group advertised its cause as a community responsibility, raised over $20,000 in the five years ending in 1867, and distributed fuel and provisions only after careful investigation of the needy. Private contributions were the chief means of support of the Chicago Relief and Aid Society, incorporated in 1857. Soup kitchens were also subsidized by private gifts and meal tickets were sold to those citizens who wished to offer them to the poor. The Milwaukee women who managed these enterprises trusted "to the benevolence of our citizens . . . for the food to be supplied."[33]

To a large extent the cultural services of the city, beyond the provision for public schools, were the result of support by subscription. Forerunners of the public libraries of the seventies were the membership libraries of such organizations as the Young Men's Associations in Chicago and Milwaukee and the Reading Room Association in Cleveland.[34] Imitating Chicago's example, and realizing that the lack of private libraries compelled "voluntary association," several Milwaukeeans organized to promote a library in 1847.[35] In canvassing for funds and members they did not neglect to stress community obligation and the example of other cities. The promotional value of good libraries to the city was "a pretty safe index of the mental advancement . . . of a city." They also emphasized the "gallantry of the Association [which] admits even ladies to a full participation of the advantages of membership, with the exception, we think, of voting."[36] Chartered in 1848, the Cleveland Library Association issued stock certificates and charged yearly dues. Soliciting subscriptions in 1851 for a reading room, the editor of the Cleveland *Daily True Democrat* was convinced that "nothing . . . adds so much to the reputation of a city as a good Reading Room and Library."[37]

Many other cultural activities were fostered by subscription. Local musicians and actors volunteered their services in aid of the fire department, orphan asylum, and other causes. The Milwaukee Musical Society when soliciting members in 1857 advised the public that its monthly dues of forty cents plus a two dollar initiation fee were "but a moderate tax to pay towards the support of an organization which ministers so largely to the enjoyment of our citizens and which reflects such credit upon our city."[38] The founders of academies and colleges in asking for endowments also appealed to civic duty.[39] By 1870 the beginning of public libraries[40] and the agitation for parks—following New York's example with Central Park —were slight but indicative signs of the rôle that the urban government was ultimately to play in providing aesthetic satisfaction and social and cultural benefits to its citizens.[41] A Cleveland editor went so far as to start a crusade in 1870 against city noises—"an evil rapidly becoming unendurable." He wrote: "While suppressing so rigorously all offences to the sight and smell, and punishing in general all disturbances of the peace, it would be only consistent to include in the proscription the still greater plague of noise." Yet he concluded a year later that the cure for city noises still lay in the field of individual responsibility: "We have not yet reached that point where the law will guard the nerves of the aged, the tender, and infirm from unnecessary torture."[42] Such a concept of city function did not square with the "subscription period" of city growth.

These striking parallels in the institutional history of the five major cities of the Great Lakes are to be explained in part by the contemporaneous character of their growth, by the common sources from which their population sprang, and by the similarity of the economic forces influencing their behavior. In all five cities, the foreign born provided about half the population, with natives of Germany, Ireland, and Great Britain distributing themselves in nearly uniform proportions, except in Milwaukee where European immigrants were more predominantly German. In the sectional origins of native Americans these cities were also similar. New York, Massachusetts, and Pennsylvania contributed most abundantly to each of the five cities save Chicago, which drew a large number from neighboring Michigan. The census of 1870 showed as well a remarkable uniformity in the percentages of people engaged in various occupational pursuits. But it was not simply a matter of similar social ingredients, for this municipal development of the Great Lakes area was apparently following a pattern or process not unusual to urban evolution elsewhere. As they grew to comparable size these cities were in many ways merely repeating the experience of the coastal cities half a century earlier. For example, after a generation of city growth the expanded powers of the lake cities in 1870, like those of the seaboard cities in 1800, represented a response more to the problems of size than to any changed philosophy of the functions of urban communities for which a difference in environment or personality might have been responsible. By 1870 each of these lake cities was a more conscious "municipal entity" than in its village period. Commercial regulations for the common good, cooperation through taxes and subscriptions for the promotion and improvement of the city, and the recognition of some of the social responsibilities presented by the interdependence of city life certainly had fostered a group consciousness—a group attitude, however, still very largely articulated by and pivoting around the individual. The "municipal consciousness," twentieth century pattern, was more than a generation in the future. Its full development awaited the flow of population, new economic needs, and changing social philosophy of the late nineteenth and early twentieth centuries.

In these urban centers of the Middle West in the mid-nineteenth century, the houses, to one traveller's surprise, were not "wigwamified," the dress and ornament not "wampumized."[43] As Anthony Trollope said, the "general level of . . . material and intellectual well-being—of beef . . . and book learning" was "no doubt infinitely higher than in a European town."[44] These cities sprang from beginnings closely associated in practice and attitude with the westward expansion of the American people. As they grew, their concern for popular management and their emphasis upon the intrinsic rôle of the individual in the promotion of the physical and cultural growth of the city reveal attitudes often observed by students of the agrarian frontier. At the same time, they showed a willing dependence upon eastern sources in the transmission of culture, a studied imitation of tested forms of municipal practice and urban service, and an expanding assumption of community responsibility. Such influences suggest that in the rise of the large city in the West, as elsewhere, one sees another—perhaps equally important if less explored—side of American social history in the nineteenth century.

■ ■ ■ ■ **Notes**

1 Milwaukee *Daily Sentinel*, May 26, 1845.
2 The following are the most useful titles for making comparative studies of urban development in the Mississippi Valley. Buffalo: Robert W. Bingham, *The Cradle of the Queen City: A History of Buffalo to the Incorporation of the City* (Buffalo, 1931); Henry W. Hill, ed., *Municipality of Buffalo, New York; A History, 1720–1923* (4 vols., New York, 1923); Josephus N. Larned, *A History of Buffalo, Delineating the Evolution of the City* (2 vols., New York, 1911). Cleveland: Elroy M. Avery, *A History of Cleveland and its Environs* (3 vols., Chicago, 1918); William R. Coates, *A History of Cuyahoga County and the City of Cleveland* (3 vols., Chicago, 1924); Samuel P. Orth, *A History of Cleveland, Ohio* (3 vols., Chicago, 1910). Detroit: George B. Catlin, *The Story of Detroit* (Detroit, 1923); Clarence M. Burton, ed., *The City of Detroit, Michigan, 1701–1922* (4 vols., Chicago, 1922); Silas Farmer, *History of Detroit and Michigan* (Detroit, 1884); Arthur Pound, *Detroit, Dynamic City* (New York, 1940); Robert B. Ross and George B. Catlin, *Landmarks of Detroit* (Detroit, 1898). Milwaukee: William G. Bruce, *History of Milwaukee City and County* (3 vols., Milwaukee, 1922); John G. Gregory, *History of Milwaukee, Wisconsin* (4 vols., Chicago, 1931); Bayrd Still, "The Growth of Milwaukee as Recorded by Contemporaries," *Wisconsin Magazine of History* (Madison), XXI, 1938, 262–292, and "Milwaukee, 1870–1900: the Emergence of a Metropolis," *Wisconsin Magazine of History*, XXIII, 1939, 138–162. Chicago: Alfred T. Andreas, *History of Chicago, 1670–1885* (3 vols., Chicago, 1884–1886); J. Seymour Currey, *Chicago: Its History and Its Builders* (3 vols., Chicago, 1912); Bessie L. Pierce, *A History of Chicago* (2 vols., New York, 1937, 1940), and *As Others See Chicago* (Chicago, 1933). Pittsburgh: Leland D. Baldwin, *Pittsburgh, the Story of a City* (Pittsburgh, 1937); George T. Fleming, *History of Pittsburgh and Environs* (5 vols., New York, 1922);

Frank C. Harper, *Pittsburgh of Today, Its Resources and People* (4 vols., New York, 1931); Sarah H. Killikelly, *The History of Pittsburgh, Its Rise and Progress* (Pittsburgh, 1906). Cincinnati: Clara Chambrun, *Cincinnati: Story of the Queen City* (New York, 1939); Henry A. and Kate B. Ford, *History of Cincinnati, Ohio* (Cleveland, 1881); Charles T. Greve, *Centennial History of Cincinnati and Representative Citizens* (2 vols., Chicago, 1904). Louisville: Reuben T. Durrett, *The Centenary of Louisville* (*Filson Club Publications,* no. 8, Louisville, 1893); L. A. Williams and Co., eds., *History of the Ohio Falls Cities and their Counties* (Cleveland, 1882); J. Stoddard Johnston, ed., *Memorial History of Louisville from its first Settlement to the Year 1896* (2 vols., Chicago, n.d.). Minneapolis: Norman S. B. Gras, "The Significance of the Twin Cities for Minnesota History," *Minnesota History* (St. Paul), VII, 1926, 3–17; Mildred L. Hartsough, *The Twin Cities as a Metropolitan Market: a Regional Study of the Economic Development of Minneapolis and St. Paul* (Minneapolis, 1925); Calvin F. Schmid, *Social Saga of Two Cities: An Ecological and Statistical Study of Social Trends in Minneapolis and St. Paul* (Minneapolis, 1937). St. Louis: John T. Scharf, *History of St. Louis City and County, from the Earliest Periods to the Present Day* (2 vols., Philadelphia, 1883); Walter B. Stevens, *St. Louis, the Fourth City, 1764–1911* (2 vols., St. Louis, 1911). Memphis: Gerald M. Capers, Jr., *The Biography of a River Town; Memphis: Its Heroic Age* (Chapel Hill, 1939). New Orleans: Henry Rightor, ed., *Standard History of New Orleans, Louisiana* (Chicago, 1900).

3 St. Louis, 310,864; Chicago, 298,977; Cincinnati, 216,239; New Orleans, 191,418; Pittsburgh, 139,256; Buffalo, 117,714; Louisville, 100,753. *Fifteenth Census of the United States, 1930, Population,* I, 18–19.

4 Between 1860 and 1870 the total population of the lake cities increased over 100 per cent; that of the valley cities, 60 per cent; that of New York, Philadelphia, and Boston, 20 per cent; that of the United States, 22.6 per cent. *Fifteenth Census, Population,* 12 *et passim.*

5 Comparative population of the Great Lakes cities:

	1820	1830	1840	1850	1860	1870
Buffalo	2,095	8,668	18,213	42,261	81,129	117,714
Cleveland	606	1,076	6,071	17,034	43,417	92,829
Detroit	1,422	2,222	9,102	21,019	45,619	79,577
Chicago			4,470	29,963	109,260	298,977
Milwaukee			1,712	20,061	45,246	71,440

Fifteenth Census, Population, 19. The total population of the East North Central States increased during 1840 to 1870 from 2,924,728 to 9,124,517. *Fifteenth Census, Population,* 11.

6 Chicago's first charter was the result of popular agitation. It was submitted to a mass meeting for popular approval, there slightly altered, and sent to the legislature. Edmund J. James calls it a self-proposed charter, "a practical recognition of local self-government on a large scale." Edmund J. James, *The Charters of the City of Chicago* (Chicago, 1898), 23. Such local participation did not prevent imitation in selecting the form of the charter.

7 For an example of identical clauses in these city charters see *Laws of the State of New York, 1853* (Albany, 1853), 461; *Laws of Wisconsin, 1852* (Madison, 1852), 81; and *Statutes of Illinois, Private Laws, 1851* (Springfield, 1851), 143.

8 For colonial legislation on this subject consult Henry W. Farnam, *Chapters in the History of Social Legislation in the United States to 1860* (Washington, 1938), 92–115.

9 Pierce, *Chicago,* II, 461, note.

10 As an example of this type of early municipal regulation see "An Ordinance Relating to the First Ward Market, and to License and regulate Butcher's Stalls, Shops and Stands for the sale of Butcher's Meat, Poultry, Game, and Fresh Fish," in *Charters*

and Ordinances of the City of Milwaukee (Milwaukee, 1857), 464–465. Of similar nature is a Buffalo ordinance of April 23, 1855, and one in Cleveland, June 3, 1851.

11 Milwaukee *Sentinel,* January 4, 1859.

12 An act regulating the "Assize of Bread" seems to have been in force in Detroit as late as 1820. The price of bread was fixed according to a sliding scale based on the price of flour. George N. Fuller, *Economic and Social Beginnings in Michigan, 1805–1837* (Lansing, 1916), 126. A Massachusetts regulation, based on the price of grain plus a reasonable allowance for labor, was abandoned in 1801. Farnam, 110. The Milwaukee ordinance regulating the manufacture and sale of bread (July 13, 1836) required registration of the baker's place of business, the use of wholesome flour, and the marking of loaves with the weight of the loaf and the initials of the baker. This was virtually the same bread legislation as that of New York in 1839 and of Boston as late as 1834. A similar provision is found in Chapter XXXVII of the Cleveland ordinances as codified in 1877.

13 Milwaukee *Courier,* January 27, 1845, quoted in Milwaukee *Evening Wisconsin,* October 15, 1895.

14 *Courier,* quoted in *Evening Wisconsin,* October 15, 1895.

15 Pierce, *Chicago,* I, 328, note.

16 Laurence M. Larson, *A Financial and Administrative History of Milwaukee (Bulletin of the University of Wisconsin,* no. 242, *Economics and Political Science Series,* Vol. IV, no. 2, Madison, 1908), 27–28; Milwaukee *Sentinel,* June 27, 1857.

17 Milwaukee *Sentinel,* April 5, 1869. See also *Sentinel,* March 11, 1852, and March 23, 1864; Gregory, I, 253.

18 The Cincinnati *Gazette,* quoted in the Milwaukee *Sentinel* of June 10, 1859, asserted that a newspaper served the founders of towns by acting as a kind of credential to the reality of the inchoate city, and as a light to direct the pioneer to a new home and to direct business and emigration into new channels.

19 The Boston *Chronotype,* as quoted in the Milwaukee *Daily Sentinel and Gazette,* August 29, 1846, referred to the "forcing process" as circulating "numberless libels in handbills" in the East. Milwaukeeans claimed that Chicago newspapers were libeling their health record, and Cleveland papers labored during the thirties to deny that the village was sickly.

20 Milwaukee *Daily Sentinel and Gazette,* March 11, 1846. In his inaugural address, Mayor D. A. J. Upham averred that "the improvements we most need . . . are the roads and facilities of securing trade from the country." *Sentinel and Gazette,* April 12, 1849.

21 The city of Milwaukee soon substituted the issuance of bonds as loans to railroad companies for the earlier practice of buying railroad stock. Substantial security and a popular vote of authorization were required. This popular support was freely given, and by 1858 the loans to railroad companies totaled $1,614,000, all of which was ultimately repaid except two issues of $100,000 each. Larson, 74–75. By contrast the city of Chicago had made no railroad investments by 1870, and individual Chicagoans had not found it necessary to invest much in enterprises that eastern capitalists were eager to finance. Pierce, *Chicago,* II, 75.

22 Cleveland *Daily True Democrat,* June 1, 1849.

23 Milwaukee *Sentinel,* March 17, 1857.

24 Cleveland *Leader,* October 31, 1855, and March 10, 1856.

25 Cleveland *Leader,* March 30, 1858.

26 Milwaukee *Sentinel,* October 20, 1866. See also *Sentinel,* April 16, 1869, for an assertion by manufacturers that Milwaukeeans were still putting all their eggs in one basket.

27 Frederick Merk, *Economic History of Wisconsin During the Civil War Decade* (Madison, 1916), 127.

28 Cleveland *Leader*, April 10, 1873.

29 Chicago in 1847 required males between the ages of twenty-one and sixty to work on the streets three days each year, with commutation at the rate of fifty cents per day. Milwaukee in 1846 required two days' work with commutation at seventy-five cents per day.

30 Cleveland *Herald and Gazette*, June 28, 1837; Gregory, II, 1123; Milwaukee *Daily Sentinel and Gazette*, April 16, May 20, 1847, and February 6, 1850; Milwaukee *Sentinel*, August 16, 1855, and January 14, 1860; Cleveland *Herald*, November 28, 1839; Burton, I, 406.

31 Cleveland *Herald and Gazette*, December 22, 1837; Cleveland *Herald*, June 24, 1840; Cleveland *Leader*, November 25, 1862, and April 14, 1863; Milwaukee *Sentinel*, January 22, 1852, March 4, 1861, and March 4, 1862; Gregory, II, 795 ff.; Burton, I, 402.

32 Cleveland *Daily True Democrat*, December 20, 1850.

33 Milwaukee *Sentinel*, November 30, 1857. See also *Sentinel*, November 23, 1857, November 12, 1866, and December 20, 1867; Milwaukee *Daily Sentinel and Gazette*, April 12, 1849; Pierce, *Chicago*, II, 445–446.

34 The Young Men's Association organized in Chicago in 1841 was modeled after a similar organization in Albany. Members were asked to donate books to the library and non-members might use the reading room at a charge of fifty cents a month. By 1847 the library had a thousand volumes, plus current newspapers. Pierce, *Chicago*, I, 286–288. The Cleveland Reading Room Association was supported by voluntary subscriptions. Avery, I, 188. Judging from an advertisement in the Cleveland *Herald*, November 30, 1836, dues were five dollars a year.

35 The charge for life members was twenty-five dollars. Regular members paid an entrance fee of two dollars and fifty cents quarterly thereafter. The sum of $1,513 was collected in the first two months. The association had 810 books at the end of the first year. The librarian donated his services, and the library was open two afternoons a week. By 1867 the association had three thousand members and more than ten thousand volumes. Gregory, II, 1077–1078.

36 Milwaukee *Sentinel*, December 2, 1857.

37 Cleveland *Daily True Democrat*, January 29, 1851. "Lucy Ann," having come to Cleveland from the East, wrote to the editor of the Cleveland *Herald*, July 14, 1845, bemoaning the lack of a Young Men's Association or a Reading Room Association. "There are enough young men here to support a . . . library, but . . . they are more fond of riding . . . in buggies, eating ice cream, and smoking cigars . . . than they are of obtaining worth of mind."

38 Milwaukee *Sentinel*, December 7, 1857.

39 Milwaukee *Sentinel*, March 4, 1852, November 26, 1853, and August 3, 1855.

40 The nucleus of Cleveland's public library was a collection of books provided under the school library law of 1853. A free public library was authorized by an act of 1867 and realized in 1869. According to the Cleveland *Leader*, March 16, 1869, "A free library is proof of the enlightened liberality in a community and of the intellectual culture and refinement thereof." Detroit's public library was formally opened in 1865. Burton, I, 838. The library of the Young Men's Association of Milwaukee was transferred to the city of Milwaukee in 1878. Gregory, II, 1078.

41 Public parks, according to the press, would counteract "the downward tendencies of city life" (Milwaukee *Daily Sentinel and Gazette*, April 24, 1845); enhance the value of property (Cleveland *Herald*, December 31, 1840); and offset urban congestion as a consequence of which "few grounds around the city remain occupied" (Milwaukee *Sentinel*, December 18, 1865). Detroit was agitating for an extensive park and Cleveland for three of them in 1865. The park question was discussed in

a desultory way in Chicago during the fifties and sixties, but not until the late sixties was much accomplished. Pierce, *Chicago,* II, 339–341.

42 Cleveland *Leader,* September 3, October 18, 1870, and May 9, 1871. See also May 7, 1869.

43 A narrative of Nathaniel P. Willis of 1860, quoted in Gregory, II, 1320.

44 Anthony Trollope, *North America* (New York, 1862), I, 182.

8

The Beginnings of Mass Transportation in Urban America

GEORGE ROGERS TAYLOR

In recent decades Americans have become increasingly critical about the impact of the automobile upon American cities, especially in encouraging urban sprawl and bringing about the physical separation of social classes. The predominant theme of their argument is that the automobile has caused social fragmentation by promoting a pattern of residential development whereby people having similar incomes live together in areas separate from those of different economic levels.

George Rogers Taylor shows, on the other hand, that the process of residential dispersion began a half century or more before the first automobiles appeared on American streets. In the "walking city" of the 1820s, city dwellers of almost all economic positions had to live close to their work and thus to each other. As population grew and congestion increased, the development of the omnibus, the commuter railroad, the steam ferry, and the horse-drawn streetcar made more land available for settlement and enabled the more fortunate to escape some of the negative aspects of urbanization.

Public, rather than private, transportation permitted this dispersion. In many American cities today, only those who are too young, too old, or too poor to drive use public transportation, and it becomes difficult to imagine the pre–Civil War situation when public transportation was the property of the well-to-do. Only businessmen, professionals, and the most highly paid workers could afford the fares, and in some instances the time, to live several miles from the center of the city. They and their families could enjoy some open space and suburban amenities; the mass of working people had to continue living in physically crowded, noisy, and unhealthy environments. The familiar urban ecological pattern of poor core and affluent ring that we associate with the automobile had its genesis in transportation developments of the pre–Civil War period, although, as Sam Warner indicated in his essay on Philadelphia, the process was by no means complete by 1860.

■ ■ ■ ■ For Further Reading

John W. Reps, *The Making of Urban America: A History of City Planning in the United States* (Princeton: Princeton University Press, 1965) is a richly illustrated history of street layouts in American cities up to the beginning of the twentieth century. Sam B. Warner, Jr., *Streetcar Suburbs: The Process of Growth in Boston, 1870–1900* (New York: Atheneum, 1969) is a very important study of the interaction, at a later period, between transportation developments and patterns of urban and suburban growth.

■ The need to develop means for facilitating the mass movement of people in the largest American cities first became insistent in the late 1820s. Two circumstances helped create pressure for improved urban transportation of persons: First, the closely built-up sections of the most populous cities began to extend beyond an area in which people could conveniently walk to and from work. Second, economic changes began to affect long-established relationships between the places where men worked and where they lived and to encourage the growth of specialized subcenters within the business districts. To provide increased mobility within the central city and its metropolitan area, omnibuses, steam commuter trains, and horse-cars were introduced during the three pre–Civil War decades. Each of these innovations served to encourage urban growth and to further ecological developments, many of which were already under way.

Urban Population Expansion, 1820–1860

Three of the five most populous American cities, New York, Philadelphia, and Boston, have been selected for this study. Both Brooklyn and Baltimore were larger than Boston in 1860. However, Brooklyn is treated as part of New York's suburban area. Boston, while smaller than Baltimore in 1860, grew more rapidly between 1820 and 1860 and earlier provided for mass transportation.

The almost continuously increasing importance of large cities in American history is an old story, but the rate of urban expansion from 1820 to 1860 and especially during the two decades preceding the Civil War merits more attention than it has received. The rate of urban growth (cities of 2,500 or more) remained extraordinarily high from 1820 to 1860 with the increase in the urban population reaching an all-time peak of 92.1 per cent over the decade of the 1840s. The decennial rate of increase in the 1850s exceeded 75 per cent and was close to 63 per cent during both the 1820s and the 1830s. And the larger cities registered the most rapid growth for, while all cities over 2,500 increased in population by nine times between 1820 and 1860, the population of places of over 50,000 in 1820 rose more than twelve times.

Detailed statistics of population growth for the three cities studied appear in Table I.[1] Most striking is the absolute increase in total (central city plus suburbs) population for each metropolis. New York, numbering about 150,000 in 1820, rose by over 1,000,000 between that date and 1860. Philadelphia, with only 138,000 at the earlier date, increased by more than 400,000 during the following forty years. Boston, with a total of 63,000 in 1820, added 225,000 by 1860. The percentage rates of population growth in the four decades preceding the Civil War maintained a remarkably high level, with 1840–1850 registering the highest growth rates for both the central cities and the suburbs in each of the three cities. In that banner decade New York's

Table 1. Population and Decennial Rates of Increase for New York, Boston, and Philadelphia and Their Suburbs, 1810–1860

	Boston			New York			Philadelphia		
	City*	Suburbs**	Total	City***	Suburbs†	Total	City††	Suburbs†††	Total
Population 1810	33,787	15,867	49,654	96,373	23,361	119,734	53,722	58,488	112,210
Population 1820	43,298	19,949	63,247	123,706	28,350	152,056	63,802	73,295	137,097
Percentage increase 1810–1820	28.1	25.7	27.4	28.4	21.4	27.0	18.8	25.3	22.2
Population 1830	61,392	26,962	88,354	202,589	39,689	242,278	80,462	108,335	188,797
Percentage increase 1820–1830	41.8	35.2	39.7	63.8	40.0	59.3	26.1	47.8	37.7
Population 1840	85,000	39,037	124,037	312,710	78,404	391,114	93,665	164,372	258,037
Percentage increase 1830–1840	38.5	44.8	40.4	54.4	97.5	61.4	16.4	51.7	36.7
Population 1850	136,881	72,091	208,972	515,547	180,568	696,115	121,376	287,386	408,762
Percentage increase 1840–1850	61.0	84.7	68.5	64.9	130.3	78.0	29.6	74.8	58.4
Population 1860	177,840	110,895	288,735	813,669	361,110	1,174,779	137,756	427,773	565,529
Percentage increase 1850–1860	29.9	53.8	38.2	57.8	100.0	68.8	11.0	48.8	38.4

* The area of the City of Boston expanded as mud flats and salt marshes were filled in. The population of islands in Boston harbor is included except for Thompson's Island before 1840. No adjustments have been made for small changes in the legal boundaries of the city effected between 1810 and 1860. For details of these changes see George Wingate Chase, *Abstract of the Census of Massachusetts, 1860* (Boston, 1863), 233.

** The suburban population includes that of the contiguous towns with their boundaries as of 1840. The towns are Chelsea, Charlestown, Cambridge, Brighton, Brookline, Roxbury, and Dorchester. See Jesse Chickering, *A Statistical View of the Population of Massachusetts, from 1765 to 1840* (Boston, 1846), 54–55. For 1850 the population of North Chelsea and for 1860 that of North Chelsea and Winthrop are included as both of these towns were part of Chelsea in 1840.

*** Manhattan Island only.

† The suburbs include the four boroughs, Bronx, Brooklyn, Queens, and Richmond, as constituted under the Act of Consolidation in 1898. Newark and Jersey City, New Jersey, were not included because data were lacking for the early decades.

†† Including only the restricted area within the city limits as they existed before 1854.

††† Includes Philadelphia County less the population within the city limits as they existed before 1854.

suburban population increased 130 per cent, Boston's 85 per cent, and Philadelphia's 75 per cent.

Over the time period covered in Table I the respective areas of each central city and its suburbs have been held constant. This permits a meaningful comparison of the decennial growth of population in each central city and its metropolitan area unaffected by changes in the boundary of either.[2] But comparisons *among* the cities must be made with caution not only because of the wide variations in the size and expansion possibilities of the central cities but also because the size of the suburban areas varies significantly from city to city.

As the table indicates, a large part of the constantly growing numbers of urban dwellers crowded into the older sections of the great cities. Even in the America of open spaces and cheap, abundant land where city walls never set limits to expansion, city people lived for the most part huddled close together in row houses and solid blocks as was common in the great cities of Europe. So it was that foreign visitors to New York, Boston, and Philadelphia in the early 19th century took note of the restless energy of the inhabitants and often complained of filthy streets, even less well cared for than those in European centers. But significantly, they seldom commented upon the crowded compactness of American cities, for in this respect cities in the new country closely resembled those in the old. In the years of accelerated population growth following 1830, older portions of American cities often became even more crowded than the congested areas of London and Paris. By 1850 New York had reached in its "fully settled area" a population density of 135.6 persons to the acre; the comparable figure for Boston was 82.7, for Philadelphia 80.0, and for London 116.9.[3] In an age when most residences in American cities were two- or three-story wooden or brick structures, such densities meant that living conditions in the poorer districts became intolerably congested. Of course, had it been possible for the cities to spread out uniformly in all directions, the excessive crowding as well as the onset of the urban transportation crisis might have been at least temporarily postponed. But for each of the cities under consideration, rivers, mud flats, or arms of the sea imposed a constricted pattern of settlement, with the growing edge increasingly distant from the commercial center.

The towns and cities clustered about each of the central cities constituted the suburbs. Most of these, including even settlements as closely adjacent to Philadelphia as the Northern Liberties, had their own economic focus. They did not serve, at least until the 1840s and 1850s, as places of residence for any considerable number of persons employed in the central city. But increasing population pressures developing in the forties made the suburbs more attractive as places in which to live. The unprecedented rate of suburban growth as shown in Table I at least partially reflects this development.

Year after year New York City spread northward on Manhattan Island between its two "rivers." Until about 1820 the built-up area of the city reached to a little below Fourteenth Street on the west side of the island and a good half mile lower on the east side. As a result, no part of the thickly settled area was more than about one and three-quarters miles from the City Hall or Canal Street. Population spread slowly northward in the 1820s and 1830s, actually pushing out less than one-half mile in most neighborhoods. Then in the next two decades the densely settled area expanded rapidly, though unevenly, northward across the width of the island. By 1860 the heavily settled district reached Forty-second Street and passed it in one sector to extend as far north as Fiftieth Street. Distances of three and four miles now lay between City Hall and the heavily populated sections of the city.

As the closely built-up area of New York shifted northward with increasing acceleration during the forties and the fifties, nearby suburban areas accessible by water became attractive as places of residence for those employed in lower Manhattan. Ferry service from Long Island and the New Jersey shore remained too slow and undependable to encourage large numbers to commute to New York City, at least until well into the forties. But this service improved in the late forties, and the number of commuters rose rapidly. The population of suburban New York increased at a rate unexampled at the time. The number of inhabitants in the four boroughs outside Manhattan Island doubled in the fifties, came close to doing so in the thirties, and rose by 130 per cent in the forties. Brooklyn, closest borough to downtown New York and by far the largest of the four, increased in population from a mere 21,000 in 1820 to 279,000 in 1860. With improved ferry service, two nearby New Jersey cities, Newark and Jersey City, became, in fact, a part of suburban New York City. Between 1840 and 1860 the size of the first rose from 17,000 to 72,000 and that of the second from 3,000 to 29,000.

Boston, like New York, was surrounded by water, except for a narrow neck of land connecting with Roxbury. But its area was so limited that as early as 1820, when its population totaled only 43,000, it had already begun to seem crowded. However, by building bridges, filling in mud flats and shallow bays, and by leveling down hills Boston continuously added to its habitable limits. With the opening of a direct bridge to South Boston in 1828 population began flowing into that sparsely settled area bringing its population to 17,000 by 1855. Noodle's Island, East Boston, practically uninhabited in 1831, achieved a population of 16,000 twenty-five years later. Despite some expansion, Boston's area measured only about two square miles by 1840, or less than one-tenth that of Manhattan Island.[4]

As Boston became more crowded, the adjacent and nearby towns provided room for expansion. Of the seven contiguous towns none was more than five miles from the center of Boston, and though routes to some were necessarily roundabout, others were conveniently direct.[5] From Roxbury a direct overland route led to Boston on the neck of the peninsula. Charlestown, only one mile distant, and Cambridge, three miles, were easily reached by bridges and ferries. Each one of the nearby towns had its own local, commercial, or manufacturing focus, but increasingly in the prewar decades each also provided a haven for those who, while working in the city, sought to live in the suburbs.[6]

The area of the city of Philadelphia, until its limits were enlarged in 1854 to correspond with those of the county of the same name, slightly exceeded two square miles, as did that of Boston in 1840. Bounded by Vine Street on the north and Cedar Street (South Street) on the south, it extended for about a mile along the Schuylkill River on the west and the Delaware on the east. The eastern half became solidly built up by 1830, the whole rectangle by 1850. Adjoining areas like the Northern Liberties and Southwark had become densely populated before 1830. In the immediate prewar decades suburbs and satellite cities spread rapidly northward and even westward across the Schuylkill. When in 1854 the boundaries of the city became identical with those of the county the total area rose from about two to one hundred twenty square miles. As a result, except for a small section across the Delaware River at Camden, the city limits then included the whole suburban or commuting area. So, although the Delaware River to the east and mud flats to the south limited growth, wide, thinly settled, adjacent areas to the north and west invited expansion.

Changing Urban Patterns

As late as the 1820s the ecology of the leading American cities still closely resembled that of the pre-industrial cities of western Europe.[7] At the center of the metropolis clustered the churches, the public buildings, and the homes of the most prominent and well-to-do citizens. Nearby lived lesser merchants and leading craftsmen, their residences frequently intermingled with commercial buildings. Often their stores or workshops were on the first floor of their houses, their living quarters on the second. Junior partners, journeymen, or apprentices might "live in" as part of the employer's family. Where a combination of home, shop, and living quarters no longer served, or where a considerable number of employees was required, as in shipyards, ropewalks, distilleries, and sugar refineries, the workers lived close to their employment, necessarily within walking distance. The chief business of the great seaports was commerce; the location of the wharves determined the focus of activity. Warehouses and countinghouses, the establishments of great merchants and the retail outlets of petty tradesmen, the taverns and grogshops all crowded close to the waterfront, and the longshoremen, hustlers, clerks, ship chandlers, sailmakers, and coopers lived nearby.

Revolutionary developments in manufacturing, transportation, and communications during the three pre–Civil War decades, an increasing specialization of economic institutions, and the phenomenal surge in city population already described combined to effect important changes in the pattern of urban living. In each seaport commerce and industry expanded as never before. In the area adjacent to the water front a greatly increased work force lived under intolerably crowded conditions; beyond the densely settled part of the central city and in the suburbs, thanks to new transportation facilities, many merchants, professional men, and members of a growing middle class established their homes.

The tendency, continuing from colonial times, for business activity to focus on or near the water front of the leading seaport cities intensified as foreign trade expanded, exceeding all previous growth records, and the American merchant marine reached its most glorious age. At the same time industries long established in the harbor areas grew prodigiously: not only establishments catering to the merchant marine like shipbuilding and the manufacture of ship's supplies such as sails, rope, and bread, but also plants dependent upon sea-borne raw materials like distilling, sugar refining, and tobacco processing.

As long as the new system of factory production introduced into the United States early in the 19th century required water power to operate heavy machinery, inland cities located on favorable river sites like Lowell and Chicopee became the chief centers of manufacturing development. But the situation changed when, beginning in the 1840s, abundant supplies of cheap coal became available along the Atlantic seaboard. Stimulated by this cheap fuel, improvements in the construction and operation of steam engines, and a growing demand for manufactured products, factory production expanded phenomenally in the chief seaport cities. Clusters of manufacturing plants, especially those devoted to the production of metal products such as castings, machines, engines, and transportation equipment, grew out from older locations or formed new focuses of population growth along the edges of the central city, commonly where railroad lines terminated. Such expansion not infrequently accompanied the boom in shipbuilding already under way along the East River of New York City, the Delaware River at Philadelphia, and in East Boston at the New England port.

The growing volume of business combined with an increasing differentiation of function, as specialists continued to take over the manifold activities of the great merchants of an earlier day, led to the rapid enlargement of the business section in each of the three cities. Banks, countinghouses, markets, exchanges, factories, warehouses, lumber yards, coffee houses, and taverns crowded into the old residential areas near the water front. More workers were needed in the business district, but fewer could make their homes there. As a result, living conditions became ever more congested in adjacent neighborhoods. Thus, the wards bordering on the old harbor area of lower Manhattan actually lost inhabitants. The population of the Second Ward, having crested close to 9,000 in 1825, declined to about 2,500 in 1860. The Third Ward, with nearly 12,000 in 1845, mustered only about 4,000 at the later date.[8] As the population was pushed out of these areas, displaced persons crowded into the nearby neighborhoods to the north contributing to the notorious slum conditions in wards Six, Eleven, and Thirteen, where by 1860 population density reached more than 300 to the acre.[9] Boston's Fourth Ward, the business and financial center of the city, lost more than half its residents between 1850 and 1860. During the same decade the population of the adjoining Seventh Ward to the south tripled as Irish immigrants continued to press into that already congested area.[10] A similar situation arose in Philadelphia where, during the same decade, the central city showed a relatively small population increase. (See Table I.)

The city workers, their numbers growing more rapidly than ever before, partly by natural increase but largely from an unprecedented inflow from the countryside and from foreign countries, pressed into the older residential areas of the central city, turning them into slums notorious even for that day. Whole families often lived packed into single rooms or damp cellars, and social and sanitary conditions became intolerably bad. A study of living conditions in New York City in 1864 found nearly a half million people living in tenement houses and over fifteen thousand living in cellars. In these crowded areas household industry or take-home work commonly played an important role. In the suburbs just north of Philadelphia male weavers worked hand looms under their own roofs. In all three cities seamstresses found employment in these congested areas doing piecework at home. Especially in New York and Boston, slum sections became havens for hordes of recently arrived immigrants. There, unaccustomed to city living and with low wages and irregular employment, they often formed ethnic islands. Sharing their poverty and their squalor with their own countrymen, they remained within walking distance of the water front where the great majority found employment as unskilled laborers. Some of the most impoverished of the recently arrived German and Irish immigrants to New York City lived as squatters in shanties erected on unoccupied rocky or hilly ground within the city or on open land beyond the settled area. They secured a precarious living as ragpickers, cinder gatherers, or day laborers engaged in the building of new streets and sewers.[11]

For the great majority of low-income workers, improved mass transportation failed, as this study will show, to provide an opportunity to escape from the congestion of the central city at least before 1860. Riding to work continued to be prohibitively expensive for most city dwellers. So, as the metropolis grew and its thickly settled area spread out, the distance between the places where men lived and where they found employment lengthened. Most workmen continued, as they had from time immemorial, to walk to work. Some may have gone considerable distances on foot—perhaps as much as three or even four miles night and morning. But this must have been most exceptional. We do know from an official count on September 6, 1851, that 14,310 persons entered Boston on foot.[12] But it seems unlikely that many of these walked farther than about two miles—a distance which would normally require at least thirty minutes. One authority observes that ". . . few workingmen can afford to spend more than half an hour in going to their work. . . ."[13] The case of the employees of a gas company in the Northern Liberties (Philadelphia), as indicated by the payroll for December 3, 1852, may be fairly typical. Of twenty-one workers none lived more than one and two-thirds miles from the gas plant and all but five lived within one mile.[14]

In the years of rapid urban growth following the twenties, the great merchants and professional men (some of whom already had "country" homes) were not alone in fleeing from the noise and confusion of the water front, the dirt, the stench, and the intolerably crowded conditions of the old central city. They were joined by many businessmen of intermediate means, retailers, managers, contractors, speculators, and junior partners. Even some better-paid clerks, accountants, and specially skilled craftsmen fled from the noise and confusion. Thus, in New York City, those financially able to do so moved ever northward on the island as business establishments and slums pressed in behind them.[15] Describing the situation in Manhattan, an editorial in the *American Railroad Journal* stated, "The gradual appropriation of the whole lower part of the Island to places of business, compel the greater part of our business men to reside from two to four miles 'up town'."[16]

As late as the 1840s, some merchants in Boston still had their fine residences on Summer Street, only a few minutes walk from the wharves, but most had already moved on to Beacon Hill or Roxbury and others had homes in nearby suburbs such as Cambridge.[17] Of course, some wealthy individuals and even those in a few exclusive neighborhoods held out against the tide, forcing the city to surge around and beyond them. This was notably true in conservative Philadelphia where until after the Civil War some of the élite clung to the area south of Washington Square along Second, Third, and Fourth Streets, only a short distance from the busy wharves on the Delaware. But most of the rising business and professional men there as elsewhere pushed outward, in this case toward the north in the vicinity of Broad Street, farther northwest to suburban areas, and westward across the Schuylkill River.

The growth in population of the suburban areas resulted only in part, and doubtless in rather small part before the latter 1840s, from an increase in the number of those who worked in the central city but lived in nearby towns. Many of the suburban towns and cities were of about the same age as the central city itself. Like Brooklyn, Cambridge, and Kensington, they originally developed as, and, in fact, continued in some degree to be, relatively autonomous commercial and manufacturing centers. Nevertheless, strong centralizing influences which tended to bind the great city together as one economic unit predominated. One of these was certainly improved urban transportation by which the limits of the walking city were enlarged, chiefly for those of moderately high incomes before the Civil War, and more generally for those with lower incomes thereafter. A Philadelphian wrote with rare insight in 1859, ". . . already the great mass of our population 'lives along the line' of a [horse] railway; and before the next decade shall have far advanced, every rural vicinage within our corporate limits will be 'grappled with hooks of steel' to the steps of the Exchange."[18] Without effective mass transportation it is difficult to see how the great, highly centralized cities of the late 19th century could have emerged.[19] In any case, the growth in the size of the cities and their suburbs and the accompanying differentiation in the economic services performed led to major developments in urban transportation. Or, stating the matter the other way around, improvements in urban transportation made possible the expansion of the great city and increased functional specialization.

The Era of the Omnibus

The omnibus was the earliest important innovation introduced to promote urban mobility. Of French origin, the term "omnibus" came into common American use in the early 1830s.[20] Usually drawn by two horses, the omnibus carried about twelve passengers, operated over a fixed route on city streets, and picked up and dropped passengers at frequent intervals. Fares charged were ordinarily a fixed amount seldom varying with the distance traveled.

Before the introduction of the omnibuses and the transition vehicles immediately preceding them, hacks or hackney coaches, the forerunners of modern taxis, provided rapid transportation within the city. But coach fees were so high that their use was commonly restricted to the very well-to-do. The rate charged in New York City for a single passenger varied from twenty-five cents to thirty-seven and a half cents for any distance not exceeding a mile, for more than one mile and less than two the rate was fifty cents.[21] Of course many of the relatively affluent owned their own carriages,[22] but for the great mass of city dwellers movement within the urban area required walking.

The need for a public system of mass transportation appeared earliest in New York City where, as in Boston and Philadelphia, the true omnibus evolved as a compromise between the long distance stagecoach and the hackney coach. As early as 1811, a few stagecoaches operated on infrequent schedules from lower Manhattan to Greenwich. In 1816 they ran every two hours, charging a fare of one shilling.[23] The service appears to have developed slowly at first, but by the closing years of the 1820s numerous lines had begun operation. Hackney coaches also came into use over regular routes. They began to operate "from a certain place or places to any other certain place or places," stopping to let down or take up passengers on the way.[24] Most important, however, were stagecoaches whose operation to Greenwich and up and down Broadway was already presenting New York's Common Council with problems concerning license fees and regulation.[25]

In Boston the evolution from stagecoach to omnibus came rapidly during the 1820s. The great Back Bay area had not yet been reclaimed, and the small peninsula on which the city stood began to be closely built up. So Roxbury across the neck and the nearby villages connected with Boston by bridges and ferries became increasingly attractive as places of residence. Short stage lines were operating once a day at least as early as 1823 between Boston and such towns as Dedham, Waltham, and Dorchester and twice daily to Cambridge.[26] Though such lines soon spread to other nearby communities, stagecoach service remained infrequent and fares high. In 1825 the rate by stagecoach to such nearby towns as Medford (five miles) and Milton (seven miles) was thirty-seven and a half cents, and to Lexington (ten miles) fifty cents.[27] Then, early in 1826, an hourly stage established within the city itself began operating from Roxbury to Boston with a fare of nine cents.[28] In a single week late in April it was reported that ". . . about eleven hundred passengers passed *to and fro* by this conveyance. . . ."[29] The success of this experiment apparently encouraged the development of other similar short stagecoach or "omnibus" lines. The July 4, 1826, issue of *Badger & Porter's Stage Register* listed not only the service between Roxbury and Boston but also an hourly stage between Charlestown and Boston, and less frequent service on lines from Cambridge to Boston and from Dorchester and South Boston into the city. Moreover, as in New York, the hackney coach was pressed into service as an omnibus. A hack is reported to have operated every other hour between Cambridgeport and Boston as early as 1826, and three years later a similar conveyance ran on a regular schedule between South Boston and Boston.[30]

In Philadelphia the evolutionary process from stagecoach to omnibus came more slowly but developed much as in New York and Boston. Apparently one of the first omnibus-like coaches in Philadelphia began operation in December, 1831. It ran hourly from the Merchants' Coffee House on Second Street to Schuylkill Seventh (now Sixteenth) and Chestnut Streets with fares at ten cents or twelve tickets for one dollar. It soon proved a failure, but two years later two omnibus lines were in regular operation within the city and numerous short stagecoach lines gave service, mostly only twice a day, to such nearby places as Germantown, Frankford, Darby, and Fairmount.[31]

In urban United States history the years from about 1830 to the early 1850s may well be termed the Era of the Omnibus. During this period of unprecedented city growth, the omnibus facilitated and helped to make possible the urban expansion. As early as 1830, "upwards of seventy unwieldly omnibus coaches" were operating in New York City,[32] and William Dunlap recorded in his diary on July 4, 1833, that he waited on Broadway but "after long standing was obliged to walk home, all the stages numerous as they are being throng'd."[33] At about this time the term "omnibus" began to come into common use and the shape and construction of the vehicle became more or less standardized. Somewhat larger than the usual long-distance stagecoach, the omnibus normally seated twelve persons, though more might be crowded in when traffic was heavy. A coachman mounted on an elevated seat at the front of the vehicle, collected the fares, and drove a span of horses. At times these vehicles were larger and more elaborate. At least some omnibuses were luxuriously upholstered, were drawn by four to six horses, and carried a boy attendant to collect the fares.[34] In the winter they provided a smooth and quiet ride on the snow-packed streets when, as was usual at least in New York, runners replaced the wheels.[35]

By 1833 the age of the omnibus had arrived in New York City. In that year eighty of these vehicles, still referred to by some as "city stages," were licensed to operate on the streets. Of these only sixteen went beyond the city proper to Harlem, Manhattanville, and Yorkville. The license fee which had been one dollar per annum became twenty dollars for four-horse and ten dollars for two-horse vehicles in 1834. Yet the number of omnibuses rose to ninety-seven in that year and stood at one hundred eight in 1837.[36] Commenting on the "noise and bustle" contributed by these vehicles, the New York *Gazette and General Advertiser* for August 5, 1834, said New York might well be termed "The City of Omnibuses."[37] In 1839, sixty-seven omnibuses were counted passing a point on Broadway during one-half hour at a "comparatively dull hour in the afternoon."[38]

The number of these vehicles increased at a much more rapid rate than the population of the city. A visitor to New York City in 1846, commenting on the constant increase in the number of omnibuses, reported that 12 of them could be seen at one time.[39] The licenses granted by New York City for omnibuses numbered 260 in 1847, rose to 425 in 1850, and reached a high point, 683, in 1853. A committee of the New York Board of Aldermen reporting in 1850 found the facilities quite inadequate for public needs. "During certain periods of the day and evening," their report stated, "and always during inclement weather, passengers are packed into these vehicles, without regard to comfort or even decency, sometimes, and many are utterly unable to secure seats, even after waiting for hours."[40] A guidebook published in 1853 reported omnibuses were daily averaging 13,420 trips and collecting 120,000 fares from passengers.[41] But the competition of the newly introduced horsecars soon made itself felt. Annual declines in the number of omnibus licenses issued reduced the total by 1858 to the level attained at the beginning of the decade. The number then rose for a few years, but had fallen to 231 by 1865. (See Table II.)

In Boston, too, the number of omnibuses rose rapidly. Greatly increased travel to Roxbury was reported by 1840. In that year *The Boston Almanac* listed eighteen lines, some operating to points within the city, and others to more than a dozen nearby suburban communities.[42] But the traffic within Boston was confined to a very large extent (nearly 50 per cent in 1848) to the Roxbury route and outside the city to Cambridge and Charlestown

Table II. Number of Omnibus Licenses Issued by New York City, 1846–1865

1846	255	*1851*	568	*1856*	588	*1861*	589
1847	260	*1852*	561	*1857*	489	*1862*	574
1848	327	*1853*	683	*1858*	424	*1863*	565
1849	370	*1854*	622	*1859*	439	*1864*	397
1850	425	*1855*	593	*1860*	536	*1865*	231

SOURCE: D. T. Valentine, *Manual of the Corporation of the City of New York*, annual volumes, 1845–46 through 1865. For most years the data are for the year ending February 1.

(close to 40 per cent). The total number of omnibuses and stages operating was reported as two hundred fifty in 1847.[43]

In Philadelphia, as in Boston, the omnibus was well established during the 1830s and became essential to city transportation during the 1840s. Heavy coaches drawn by four horses served suburban areas such as German-town and Chestnut Hill. One company operated eight of these daily between Philadelphia and Chestnut Hill. *Disturnell's Guide* for June, 1847, lists fourteen omnibus routes leaving from the Merchants' Exchange, some of them at five-minute intervals. By the end of 1848, omnibuses numbering one hundred thirty-eight and operated by eighteen different lines departed from the Exchange. The congestion became so great at that place in 1849 that the City Council required some omnibuses to change their starting point.[44] In 1857 when horsecars were being introduced, Philadelphia had three hundred twenty-two omnibuses in operation.[45]

In most other American cities of appreciable size, omnibus lines began regular operation well before 1860. Washington, reported to have had service between Georgetown and the Navy Yard as early as 1830, was by 1850 imposing fines for reckless driving and limiting the occupancy of each vehicle to twelve passengers. In the middle forties omnibuses operated regularly in Baltimore and Pittsburgh, and by the opening of the next decade they provided mass transportation in such rapidly growing centers as Chicago and Toronto.[46]

Within all three cities to which this study is directed the usual omnibus fare during the 1830s was twelve and a half cents, although rates on very short lines were often less. Thus the charge to the South Street ferry in Philadelphia was only five cents in 1838. For those who could afford to buy small blocks of tickets or to purchase season tickets the cost was considerably lower. At least by 1837 a price reduction of one-third was made in New York when six or twelve tickets were purchased, and in Philadelphia an annual subscription permitted persons who used the omnibuses four times a day to reduce the cost to one cent for each ride. By the late forties omnibus fares for single tickets had generally fallen to six and a quarter cents—a reduction roughly equivalent to the decline in the general level of prices. In the early fifties six cents appears to have been the usual fare in New York and six and a quarter cents in Boston. In 1852 severe competition among omnibus lines forced fares in Philadelphia as low as three cents over most routes, and by 1860 fares in New York varied from four to six cents.[47]

Who rode in the omnibuses? A New Yorker reported in 1849 that it depended upon the time of day: "In the early morning . . . the omnibus is chiefly occupied by junior clerks with big iron keys in their hands, or laborers with tin kettles between their feet, on their way to their downtown avocations." Later in the morning come the "sleek and rotund burghers of above Bleecker . . ." And not long after them "Gotham's fair wives and daughters" on their way to shop, to see the dentist, or to visit the milliner or dressmaker. The same author also notes the patronage of omnibuses by young gentlemen on the way to the theater who "thus preserve their patent leather pumps."[48] It seems most unlikely, however, that many ordinary wage earners customarily patronized the omnibuses. In the forties and fifties, when common laborers ordinarily received wages of less than one dollar a day and skilled craftsmen seldom earned more than two, very few could afford to spend twelve or even six cents a day for omnibus fare.[49] Certainly budgets for workers' families printed in the early fifties made no provision for such expenditures.[50] The shocking living conditions associated with overcrowding spread throughout the central portion of all of these cities during the omnibus era and grew worse with the increased flow of immigrants after 1846, and this congestion arose, in no small degree, because most common laborers were forced by brute necessity to live within walking distance of their work.[51]

But for the relatively well-to-do and a growing middle class, the omnibus proved a great convenience. Omnibuses, wrote a New Yorker in 1837 ". . . are particularly convenient for merchants and others doing business in the lower part of the city, and living in the upper part. After staying till three o'clock to settle their money affairs in Wall Street, they would be late to dinner, were they obliged to foot it a mile or two; and most of them would not like to pay from three to four shillings for coach hire."[52] So the overcrowding of downtown areas led many of those who could afford it to move outward from the business districts, and the omnibus made this change of residence feasible for merchants, traders, professional men, and possibly some skilled workers. The situation is well described by Sir Charles Lyell, who, on his visit to New York City in May, 1846, wrote that since he had been in the city five months earlier ". . . whole streets had been built, and several squares finished in the northern or fashionable end of town, to which the merchants are now resorting, leaving the business end, near the Battery, where they formerly lived. Hence there is a constant increase of omnibuses passing through Broadway, and other streets running north and south."[53] And conditions appear to have been similar in Philadelphia where, as in New York, the bulk of the population was compressed in the area between two "rivers." In Boston proper, distances were short and omnibuses proved a convenience for the well-to-do, especially those who lived in the suburbs and entered the city by suburban train, for among the most popular omnibus lines were those running from the railroad stations into the central city. Omnibuses also operated between nearby suburbs and Boston, but the service was too limited and the fares much too high to attract many common laborers.[54]

Several other factors help to explain the heavy patronage of the omnibus lines. Most businessmen still followed the practice of going home for their midday meal and then returning to their offices around three or four in the afternoon. For many this entailed added use of public transportation. Also, the spreading out of the business area and the accompanying differentiation of function necessitated an increased amount of travel within the city. Couriers sent with messages or documents made use of the omnibus lines and merchants and other businessmen, no longer located close to the exchange or the financial district, found the use of the horse-drawn vehicles a great convenience. Finally, when the weather was cold or wet, few who could afford to do so failed to seek the shelter of the omnibuses even though the distance to be traveled might be only a few blocks.

The Commuter Railroads

The first crude railroads reached out from the leading seaport cities during the 1830s, the same decade which saw the rise of the omnibus. Not originally designed to facilitate travel between the suburbs and the central city, the railroads had, by the end of the decade, developed substantial commuter services. In the forties and fifties, commuter trains played a most important role in metropolitan Boston, a less important one in Philadelphia and New York.

By 1838 four railroad lines branched out from Boston: the Boston & Lowell, the Boston & Worcester, the Boston & Providence, and the Eastern. The total was raised to seven by 1845, with the addition of the Fitchburg, the Boston & Maine, and the Old Colony. Except for the Eastern, which used a ferry from East Boston until its railroad bridge was completed in 1854, each one of these railroads entered into the city proper. The railroad stations were so located as to make even the most distant not more than about a half hour's walk from the business district. Omnibuses operating at frequent intervals into the central city from each of the railroad stations served those who did not wish to walk and could afford the six and a fourth cents fare.[55]

Railroad fares from nearby towns into Boston were at first so expensive as to be beyond the reach of workingmen and most middle-class persons. Nor did early attempts to provide a somewhat cheaper service in second-class coaches attract many patrons. Season tickets by the full, half, or quarter year were first offered in 1838 and 1839. Prices of these tickets, though high at first, fell rapidly during the early and middle forties and remained at a uniquely low level later in that decade and during the early fifties. Thus, three-month [season] tickets between Malden and Boston (five miles) on the Boston & Maine cost $10.00 in 1846, fell to $6.87 in 1848, and were priced at $8.25 during the early 1850s. On the Boston & Worcester the three-month ticket from Brighton (five miles) had been $15.00 in 1846 and fell to $10.00 in 1850. The rate to Dedham, almost twice as far (nine and a half miles), held at $12.00 in the early fifties. Charges as low as these compared favorably with the fare charged by omnibuses within the city: six and a fourth cents in the late forties and five cents in the fifties. Commutation tickets at $12.00 a quarter came to a little over eight cents a ride and at $6.87 to less than five cents a ride. If Roxbury commuters purchased season tickets in 1850, they paid only about three and a half cents on the railroad, while each omnibus ride cost six cents.[56]

Low as were these commutation fares, they were beyond the reach of most ordinary workmen. But, for a considerable number of small merchants and tradesmen and perhaps a few skilled mechanics and better-paid clerks, living in the nearby suburbs now became feasible. Contemporary evidence indicates that, at least by the early 1850s, commuter railroad service permitted "by far the larger part of her [Boston's] business men [to] reside out of the city."[57] A writer in *Hunt's Merchants' Magazine* reports, somewhat ambiguously, that old Boston residents, giving way before foreign workers, have moved to the suburbs where, "availing themselves of the frequent omnibuses, or of special trains run almost hourly, and commuting for passage at $20.00 to $40.00 a year; they reach their stores and offices in the morning; and at night sleep with their wives and children in the suburbs."[58]

The number of commuters increased rapidly after the late 1840s. A stockholders' committee of the Boston & Providence Railroad reported that commuters between Boston and Dedham numbered only 320 in 1848–49, but that a great increase had come about by 1854.[59] The average number of passengers entering Boston daily by railroad train apparently increased from about 20 to 50 per cent between 1848 and 1851.[60] By 1850 the passenger trains entering or leaving Boston numbered 240. Almost all of these carried commuters and more than half were strictly commuter trains going no more than fifteen miles from the Boston station.[61] In his book published in 1856, E. B. Grant estimates the number of season tickets sold annually to have been 6500.[62]

Why did railroads prove much less important for commuters in New York and Philadelphia than in the Boston area? Partly because in the extensive, solidly built-up areas of New York and Philadelphia, omnibuses provided convenient service over the short distances involved. The stretches of water surrounding the Boston isthmus and the relatively few bridges necessitated roundabout and expensive omnibus trips from suburban areas into that city. Also, since the steam railroads entering Boston across waterways or tidal flats penetrated only a short distance into the city, they aroused less opposition from those who deplored the operation of locomotives on city streets.[63] But, in New York and Philadelphia, railroads utilized the city streets for considerable distances through the central city. When operated by steam locomotives, they were disliked because of their noise and smoke, and feared because of the danger to persons and property. Consequently, regulations in both cities required passenger coaches to be detached from the locomotive at the entrance to the more thickly settled areas and pulled into the central city by horses or mules.[64] The inconvenience and delay caused by these regulations, as well as the slower time possible under animal power, somewhat reduced the attractiveness of distant suburban living in the vicinity of these two cities.

Two railroads served New York City before 1860: the Hudson River Railroad Company and the New York & Harlem Railroad Company. The former, chartered in 1846, entered the city on the west side along the Hudson River. Steam engines provided power as far as the depot at Tenth Avenue and 31st Street, and horses provided it from there to the terminal in lower New York City at Chambers and Hudson Streets. This railroad provided neither a local nor a commuter service for New Yorkers.[65] The New York & Harlem Railroad, however, played an important role in urban transportation. Chartered by a special act of the state legislature in 1831, it began operations from Pine to 14th Streets late in 1832. The railroad extended its tracks both to the north and south in the next few years so that, by 1839, passenger cars operated between the City Hall and Harlem.[66] The original charter permitted the use of steam locomotives but the company relied chiefly on horses and mules. In 1838 the Harlem Railroad owned four locomotives, forty cars, and one hundred horses.[67] The New York City Council prohibited the use of steam locomotives in 1845 below 32nd Street and in 1856 below 42nd Street. The railroad companies seem to have evaded strict compliance with this regulation. In 1850 the editor of the *American Railroad Journal* noted that the Hudson River Railroad was quietly operating a locomotive which ate its own smoke. He urged that New York City should not, like Boston, restrict the use of steam within the city.[68] Nevertheless, prohibition against steam continued and became effective below 42nd Street at least by the late fifties.[69]

The phrase "ate its own smoke" refers to a Dummy locomotive operated by the Hudson River Railroad in 1850. The entire locomotive was enclosed in a box to disguise the mechanism, and the engine condensed its steam instead of emitting an exhaust. These features were designed to make the machine as silent and inoffensive as possible when it was used within New York's city limits. The Dummy locomotive, devised by Henry Waterman, a mechanic of the railroad, was created to replace the horses formerly used for this service. It was expected to result in a great operating economy, but mechanical deficiencies and public alarm against the use of steam locomotives on city streets temporarily ended the Dummy's operation. Several years later, however, the idea was revived with considerable success.

Traffic on the Harlem Railroad grew rapidly over the years. For the year ending August 1840 the road carried over one million passengers. This total rose to three and a half million by 1859.[70] The Harlem appears to have been unique in that it both carried large numbers of local passengers within the central city and also provided important commutation services to the more remote northern end of the island. Over relatively short distances within the city where horses were used, from the City Hall to 27th Street or 32nd Street, and after 1854 as far as 42nd Street, the Harlem Railroad competed effectively with the omnibuses. Fares (six cents in 1853) were about the same as the omnibus fares, and the service was frequent: about every five or six minutes during the day.[71] At the same time, traffic from the suburban and country areas expanded as business and professional men sought homes away from crowded lower Manhattan. The fare from City Hall beyond 42nd Street to Yorkville (five and a half miles) was usually about twelve cents. To Harlem (eight miles) the charge for single tickets in 1838 was twenty-five cents. The fare remained twelve cents in the late forties and early fifties, and went up to fifteen cents by 1855.[72] Season tickets were also expensive: $25.00 for six months or about twenty-three cents for each round trip. The annual number of commuters as reported early in 1853 was 804, a sum apparently between one-fourth and one-fifth of the total number of commuters in the Boston area.[73] Though few, if any, city workers could afford to expend such sums to go to and from work, they could and did crowd the Harlem cars to get into the country for a Sunday holiday.[74]

Steam ferries operating in the waters about Manhattan also brought an increasing number of commuters into New York City. Fifteen regular ferry lines served New York City from nearby places in 1853, a number which rose to 26 by 1860. In 1853, the popular Fulton Street ferry from Brooklyn left every five minutes during the day, that from Jersey City every ten minutes. The fare on the former was one cent, on the latter three or four cents. Most Brooklyn residences were actually nearer the New York business district than were those in the upper part of New York City. Convenient and cheap transportation, therefore, as well as what the guidebook describes as the "pure air and delightful prospects of Brooklyn," led many who worked in New York to live in that suburb.[75]

A growing number of businessmen lived in more distant areas and depended upon steam trains to bring them into the ferry terminals. Thus, as early as 1849, between eighty and one hundred commuters made the trip to New York by means of the Flushing, North Shore & Central Railroad, and the connecting ferry. As the one-way through fare, including the ferry charge, varied from ten to twenty cents, these commuters clearly had relatively high incomes.[76] The New Jersey Railroad and Transportation Company, reported in the *American Railway Times*[77] to be the first commuter railroad in the United States, ran 58 trains in 1849 and 144 in 1859 between New Brunswick and Jersey City. By the latter date, yearly commutation tickets were priced at $50.00, about sixteen cents a round trip. This must have been one of the busiest commuter lines in the country. It seems likely that many of the commuters continued to ferry across New York harbor to Manhattan, but it is again obvious that they must have been chiefly business-men rather than workmen.

Only one of the railroads diverging from Philadelphia in the pre–Civil War years became an important commuter line, the Philadelphia, German-town & Norristown Railroad Company. Serving a pleasantly rolling residen-tial area northwest of the original city limits, this railroad had two branches. One led seven miles to Germantown, where after the middle fifties it con-nected with the Chestnut Hill Railroad, which continued four miles beyond to Chestnut Hill. The other, more southern branch ran along the Schuylkill River through Manayunk to Norristown. The railroad's passenger station located at Ninth and Green Streets provided a convenient terminal in the congested Spring Garden area. From there to the centrally located Mer-chant's Exchange was about fifteen blocks: a rather long walk, but omni-buses were available for those wishing to ride.

Primarily a passenger railroad, the Philadelphia, Germantown & Norris-town received nearly three-fourths of its revenue (in 1850) from the trans-portation of passengers. Beginning in the late forties, commuter business expanded rapidly, especially on the Germantown branch. The number of trains to and from Germantown, which had varied from three to six in the late forties, rose to 40 by 1859. Between 1850 and 1860, the annual number of passengers on the Germantown branch increased over sevenfold. A con-siderable portion of the increased traffic resulted from the growing number of daily commuters. The directors of the railroad reported in 1859 that more than six hundred yearly tickets were issued to residents of Germantown, ". . . whose business requires their daily attendance in the city [Philadel-phia]."[78] In 1860 they observed that "hundreds have gone from the densely settled portions of the city to those places [Germantown, Roxborough, and Manayunk] with the intention of permanently remaining. . . ."[79]

In Philadelphia, as in Boston and New York, however, commuting by railroad trains (even to nearby suburbs) was limited largely to the relatively affluent. Quarterly commutation tickets from Germantown cost $10.00 and yearly tickets $30.00 during the fifties, and even this price was raised in 1860.[80] Such rates were apparently not too expensive for the Philadelphia businessmen of whom a contemporary wrote, "Many . . . have summer residences in the vicinity of the road, while others permanently reside in the country."[81]

None of the other railroads entering Philadelphia could match the Philadel-phia, Germantown & Norristown in speed and convenience for commuters.

It alone brought its steam trains directly into the densely settled area. Three New Jersey Railroads, the Camden & Amboy, the Camden & Atlantic, and the short West Jersey, terminated at Camden across the Delaware from Philadelphia. The five lines entering Philadelphia from the west across the Schuylkill depended upon horses to bring their coaches into the central city. None of these lines operated suburban trains. Apparently horse-drawn cars were utilized only to a limited extent for local passenger transportation within the city.[82] On two roads which led northward, passengers encountered similar difficulties or delays. The tracks of the Philadelphia and Trenton Railroad terminated at Tacony on the Delaware River, whence passengers were transported seven miles by steamboat to Philadelphia.[83] The North Pennsylvania Railroad, not in full operation until 1855, ran almost directly north from its terminal at Front and Willow Streets only two blocks from the Delaware River. Horses or mules drew the passenger cars one mile northward from this terminal to Master Street where a steam locomotive took over. Neither of these two railroads provided important commuter services before the Civil War.[84]

Beginnings of the Horsecars

The era of the omnibus and the beginnings of the commuter railroads extended into the early 1850s. Their important contribution has often been overlooked because the sensational success of the horse railways revolutionized the urban transportation of persons in the years immediately preceding the Civil War. The moving of railroad cars by means of animal power had been common since the early 1830s. Yet between 1852 and 1860 construction of street railways proceeded so rapidly and their popularity became so great that contemporaries hailed them as the "improvement of the age."[85] Summarizing the extent of this change, a student of urban transportation states:

> In 1840 omnibuses in the Boston area carried about 1,000,000 passengers. In 1857, the Boston and Worcester Railroad carried about 500,000 to the neighboring cities. But in 1860 the Metropolitan Railroad Corporation, the largest horse-drawn railroad in Boston, alone carried 6,410,850, and the various horse railroads in the city carried a total of 13,695,193.[86]

Powered by horses, cables, and finally electric motors, the streetcar dominated urban transport during the latter half of the 19th century. In this study, our attention centers on the horsecar's beginnings in New York, Boston, and Philadelphia, its advantages over established methods of local transportation, and its contribution to early city growth.

The first horsecars were little more than omnibuses operating on rails laid in city streets. The cars in operation during the late 1850s were ordinarily drawn by two horses and easily accommodated about 40 persons. A contemporary reported that "the cars will hold sitting and standing, from 60 to 65 passengers, and will, at a pinch, hold 74."[87] A light, open, one-horse car suitable for warm-weather use carried almost as many passengers. Larger and heavier passenger cars, such as those in common use on steam railroads, required as many as four or six horses to move them through the streets.[88]

A wave of enthusiasm for horse-railway construction struck first in New York City, where a special committee of the Board of Aldermen recommended the chartering of horse-railway companies in 1850.[89] The Common Council granted charters to the Sixth and Eighth Avenue lines in 1852 and to the Second and Third Avenue lines in the following year. Quickly constructed through city streets, these pioneer horse railways enjoyed a tremendous patronage.

The horsecar lines proved profitable investments despite huge bribes to politicians and the purchase of the existing omnibus companies at inflated prices. The Third Avenue line reportedly paid about $400,000 to buy out five omnibus companies.[90] By September 30, 1857, horse railways in New York City including Brooklyn extended for 44 miles, by 1860 for 142 miles. In the earlier year the streetcars of metropolitan New York carried 32,000,000 passengers, and by 1860 the number was close to 45,000,000.[91]

The street-railway building boom in Boston followed that in New York by about two years. The state legislature approved two lines in 1853: the Cambridge Railroad Company, to be built from Cambridge to Boston, and the Metropolitan Railroad Company to connect Boston and Roxbury.[92] By 1856, when these pioneer lines had gone into operation, many similar projects were under way. Fifty-seven miles of horse-railway lines were in operation by November 30, 1860, and 13.7 million passengers had been transported during the year then ending. The passenger total exceeded the number of passengers carried on steam trains in the whole state during the same twelve-month period.[93]

Last of the three cities to accept the street railway, Philadelphia made up for the delay by rushing construction so enthusiastically that a local publication referred to "its epidemic character."[94] Progress had been slow at first. A special committee of the city council reported favorably in 1855; a company was chartered to operate a line on Fifth and Sixth Streets in 1857, and the first cars ran in January 1858. Then, as opposition collapsed, eighteen companies secured charters by the end of 1859. By the close of 1860, eighteen street railways were operating 155 miles of line in Philadelphia, a total slightly greater than that for metropolitan New York and more than twice that for the city of Boston.[95]

As the omnibuses seemed to become indispensable for urban transportation and their numbers increased, they gave rise to increasing complaints. Often dirty, crowded, and ill-ventilated, they surged from side to side of the street, picking up and putting down passengers on signal without plan or system. They cluttered up busy streets, caused traffic jams, invited accidents endangering life and damaging property, and made a terrific din as they clattered over the cobblestones. An editorial writer called the omnibus "a perfect Bedlam on Wheels" and declared that "Modern martyrdom may be succinctly defined as riding in a New York omnibus."[96] Another report stated: ". . . the omnibuses are . . . a constant source of peril to both pedestrians and vehicles, everywhere threatening with opposite and confusing dangers, requiring a constant vigilance to avoid them, and often impossible to be avoided, as is attested by so many serious, and sometimes fatal, accidents."[97]

Although horsecars might also become stuffy, dirty, and overcrowded, they possessed marked advantages over the omnibuses. The rails provided a relatively smooth, quiet, and accident-free ride in cars with a capacity two to four times that of an ordinary omnibus. The average speed of the streetcars, six to eight miles an hour, exceeded that of the omnibuses by about one-third. Pulling wheeled vehicles over smooth rails proved more efficient and cheaper than dragging them over the rutted and uneven cobblestones of the city streets. One horse, pulling over rails, it was held, could do the work of three or four on a common road. Furthermore, as the cars moved down the middle of the street, they caused a minimum of interference with other traffic. Drivers of wagons and carriages often found it advantageous to keep the wheels on one side of their vehicles rolling on a street-car rail. In Philadelphia both wheels could be engaged, for the city required the tracks to be laid with the usual wagon gauge of five feet two and a half inches. These matters were important, since major streets in the central city were becoming seriously choked with traffic by the early fifties.[98]

Why, despite the obvious advantages of the streetcar, was its general adoption postponed until the 1850s? Before the development of the steam railroads and the coming of the omnibus car around 1830, Americans were familiar with the tramway. All of the early American tramways, including the "railroad" operated in 1826 at Quincy, Massachusetts, depended upon horse power. And the use of rails laid through city streets to transport horse-drawn passenger and freight cars was as old as the railroad itself in New York, Philadelphia, and elsewhere.

The delay in the building of street railroads in New York seems especially surprising. At the same time that the Harlem Railroad developed its long-distance and commuter business, its local horse-drawn streetcars had become increasingly important for short distance city transportation. It may well be that the success of the Harlem line helps to account for New York's priority in building horse railroads, but the question remains as to why the building of other horsecar lines did not come about until after the Harlem Railroad had been in operation for nearly twenty years. In Boston, where the steam railways entered the central city, no important experiment with street railways seems to have been made prior to the 1850s. The first genuine horse-railway service in Philadelphia appears to have originated, as in New York, on the lower end of a steam-railroad line. The North Pennsylvania Railroad having extended its tracks from its terminal at the corner of Washington and Cherry Streets about one and a half miles to the corner of Front and Willow Streets, there began on January 3, 1855, the operation of so-called "passenger (Omnibus) cars." This, the Philadelphia *Evening Argus* reported, marked "the commencement of Railroad omnibuses in this city."[99]

On the city portions of the early steam railroads in New York and Philadelphia, horses were engaged in pulling not only the relatively light cars serving local traffic but also the heavier commuter and long-distance passenger coaches, as well as freight cars of every description. Under such circumstances, perhaps it is not surprising that the advantages of specialized, horse-drawn street passenger railways were not more quickly recognized. An anonymous writer said regarding Philadelphia: ". . . burden-cars are drawn by animal power through Market and Broad Streets and the obstruction of these thoroughfares by the continuous transit of coal, lime and freight cars, is a serious detriment to the streets. . . ."[100] Another commentator referred to the delays caused by "long strings of mules, of a dozen each, constantly passing and repassing with a single car."[101] Steam engines were prohibited on the tracks laid through the city streets connecting the Philadelphia railway lines with each other and with the docks along the Delaware River. The use of these railways for local passenger transportation appears to have been limited and sporadic.[102]

Arguments advanced against the construction of street railways lost most of their persuasiveness as experimentation progressed. Owners of retail stores, especially those dependent on the "carriage trade," discovered location on a horsecar line to be a positive advantage. Traffic was clearly expedited instead of being slowed down as some had feared. And the interference of the tracks with other vehicles decreased as builders learned to lay the tracks more nearly flush with the surface of the streets.[103] Nevertheless the rails did make ". . . the streets inconvenient for all other vehicles. . . ."[104]

Such considerations as those noted above, along with a not unusual amount of popular prejudice and inertia, helped to delay the building of street railways. Also, in all three cities, vested interests, especially those of the omnibus companies, and the cupidity of politicians strongly reinforced conservative influences. In New York the Board of Aldermen had, in 1850, accused the omnibus interests of standing in the way of the construction of needed streetcar lines. A year later the Aldermen granted street railway company charters to political favorites who, in buying out the omnibus companies at inflated prices, enriched themselves as owners of the companies purchased. It will be remembered that these were the years when the Tammany Hall boss, Fernando Wood, enlivened New York City politics. The editor of the *American Railway Times,* noting the extremely high cost of building the New York street railways—$213,988 per mile for the Sixth Avenue line as against an average per-mile outlay of $43,000 for all United States steam railroads—commented that the costs of "Common Councils and Aldermen are included in the right of way."[105]

In Boston, where political corruption was only slightly less notorious than in New York, the editor of the *American Railway Times* asserted that the "Metropolitan Company today rules the city with a rod of iron" and said there had been a "dishonest doubling and octupling of the cost by those who are building and control the roads."[106] Conditions in Philadelphia differed from those in the other two cities chiefly in that the political influences appear to have been more effective in delaying approval of charters for street railways. The Pennsylvania legislature finally granted its first street railway franchise in 1857. A rash of special acts granting charters followed in the next two years, accompanied by the usual charges of illegal rewards to members of the legislature and the Common Council.[107]

Other large American cities, including Baltimore, Chicago, Cincinnati, Pittsburgh, and St. Louis, acquired their first horse railways in 1859 or 1860.[108] Horsecars began operating in Paris in 1853, but an experiment in London with horsecar lines (tramways) in 1861–1862 failed dismally. Not until 1870 did they operate successfully on London streets. The original failure in London, surprising in view of the widespread success elsewhere, warrants brief comment. George Francis Train, an American whose exuberance and sensational promotional methods antagonized at least a part of the British public, finally obtained official authority and built three short tramways in London in 1861. Their failure and removal the next year appears to have resulted from their location in fashionable neighborhoods where neither much support nor much patronage could be expected; their rails which, especially when not properly seated, seriously interfered with other traffic; and their misfortune in being overshadowed in public interest by the great railways building boom then attracting the enthusiastic attention of investors in the London area.[109]

Steam trains moved in limited degree on the rails in the three cities under study. But steam power was nowhere regularly used for local, short-distance transportation. In Boston, where railroads penetrated at most only a short distance into the city, the issue did not become important. In New York, and especially in Philadelphia, strong opposition arose to the use of steam engines within the city. This opposition stemmed in part from the supposed danger threatened by the steam engine, not entirely an imaginary one, since two early Harlem engines had blown up within the city limits.[110] Also, at least on the earliest trains, the crude braking system did not permit quick stops. Small efficiency units with the engine located at one end of the car proved unpopular with passengers who feared to ride in them even when the engine was concealed. By 1850 such objections had lost much of their validity, but the prejudice remained. Vested interests in Philadelphia playing on popular fears prevented steam railroads from making connections through the central city until after the Civil War.[111] A handbill circulated by Philadelphia interests, shows a child being run over by a railroad engine and warns mothers of being "hurried home to mourn a Dreadful Casualty!" The real opposition appears to have come from Philadelphia commercial interests which opposed through railroad connections in the city in the belief that their business would suffer and Philadelphia would become, as the handbill claimed, a mere "SUBURB OF NEW YORK!"[112]

Cheaper, more convenient, and faster than the omnibuses, the horsecars proved tremendously popular as soon as they were introduced. Fares within the central city were ordinarily five cents.[113] This was a reduction of only one cent below the usual omnibus charge of six cents, but the streetcar lines were ordinarily considerably longer than omnibus routes, and transfers to other streetcar lines were often available at a small additional charge.[114] So, wherever streetcars operated, they soon took away most of the omnibus trade. But, where the demand was great and horsecars were not permitted, as on Broadway in New York City, the omnibuses continued to do a thriving business.[115]

As pointed out earlier, the railroads entering Boston built up a very substantial commuter business by charging low prices to those who purchased yearly, half-yearly, or quarterly tickets. In the early fifties the railroad managements found that, with growing expenses, the commuter passengers did not cover their added cost at the low season ticket rates. Despite vigorous public protests, the railroad substantially increased commuter fares. When the Fitchburg Railroad raised its charges, angry commuters burned the president in effigy, and traffic fell off as some people returned to patronizing the slower, less convenient omnibuses. The situation was ripe for the introduction of the horsecars. When in 1856 a streetcar line began operating on the Cambridge-Boston route, travel on the main line of the Fitchburg fell off drastically, and the following year the Harvard Branch Railroad, operated between Cambridge and Watertown by the Fitchburg Railroad, suspended operation as a result of horsecar competition.[116]

The commuter trains were faster than the horsecars, and they continued to serve the more distant suburbs, but the streetcars drew a larger and larger share of the total traffic. They offered greater convenience because they ran more often and made more frequent stops.[117] It is true that, in some cases, seasonal commutation fares on the steam roads were as low as and occasionally even lower than single fares on the horsecars. But this was only rarely the case, and prices of single tickets on the railroads were always considerably higher. In fact, the low commuter fares charged by the steam railroads could be maintained only when they led to increased single-fare purchases by commuters' families and others.

At the same time that the relatively cheap single fares of the street railways[118] hurt the suburban railroads, they benefited the professional men and skilled workers who sought to live out of the central city. Many of these people who could manage to pay the necessary single streetcar fares would have found it difficult, even impossible, to advance the considerable sums necessary to invest in season commutation tickets. In Philadelphia the only important commuter railroad, the Philadelphia, Germantown & Norristown Railroad,[119] was forced to reduce its single-ticket fares in 1859 when it had to meet competition from a horse railroad. By 1860 the horse railroads had established their leading position in urban transportation. A contributor to the *American Railway Times* wrote: "They are steadily drawing the settlement of new population to their lines, and a large proportion of the persons who are now going into the country to build homes, prefer the location on the line of the Horse rather than on the Steam Railways; that is, everywhere within eight or ten miles of the cities."[120]

As the area of the city expanded, the inhabitants, whether bent on business or pleasure, felt an increasing need for expeditious transportation. This demand developed more and more from those who sought to move to the outskirts from their residences in the older and increasingly crowded part of the city. In 1850, the year before the first horsecar lines were chartered in New York City, a report to the Aldermen declared that as crowding grew in the central city and high rents were charged for ". . . undesirable, crowded, and unwholesome tenements in the lower part of the city . . . ," all who could sought homes ". . . in the upper portions and suburbs of the city. . . ."[121] The streetcar apparently facilitated this trend. Thus a newspaper comment in 1860 refers to the horse railways as ". . . spreading . . . the laboring population to the suburbs. . . ."[122] A report of 1866 concerning New York stated that, "In the morning, between six and seven, and the same hours at night, the cars are filled with mechanics, labourers, clerks, factory girls, while later in the morning, and the earlier eve, our more wealthy business men favor these roads."[123] Oscar Handlin indicates that the extension of horsecar lines to the nearby Boston suburb of Roxbury before 1860 led a considerable number of immigrant workers to make their homes there.[124]

So the horsecars appear to have made possible some migration from the congested central city, although contemporaries' reports appear to be based as much on expectation as realization. At any rate, so far as can be judged for the years before the Civil War, the chief benefits of the horsecars were less for the unskilled workers than for the middle- and upper-income receivers who had patronized the omnibuses. The speed of the horsecars was too slow (about eight miles an hour) and their fares too high to make them very useful to the great mass of the poorest workers. Men who labored ten hours a day (or even two or three hours longer) could not spend unlimited time going to and from work. And even though the horse railway fare was only five cents each way, the cost came to a considerable sum for men who earned between one and two dollars a day. Under these circumstances, the facilities for rapid transit did not meet the needs of the tenement dwellers in the most crowded districts, and the density of population in the slums of the great cities grew rapidly despite the spread of horse railways. In 1860 more than half of the inhabitants of New York City still lived below 14th Street, an area about one-tenth the size of the whole island, and the crowding was almost as excessive in Boston and Philadelphia.[125]

The development of new methods of urban transportation between 1830 and 1860 thus encouraged a centralized pattern of metropolitan growth which retained the focus of commerce and communications in the business district of the old walking city. This resulted as much from the effectiveness of the innovations in urban transportation as from their defects. The improved means of transportation provided mobility for high- and middle-income groups, thus facilitating the emergence of specialized business and residential districts and promoting the division of the business districts into separate sections for the performance of particular functions. But half or more of the persons inhabiting the great cities lived in the slums of the walking city, typically crowded between the business district on one side and desirable residential suburbs on the other. By facilitating this differentiation, the innovations in urban transportation contributed to the profound social and economic changes of the 19th century and no doubt played a part in making possible the phenomenally high level of per capita economic growth which characterized that epoch. On the other hand, it should not be overlooked that the innovations in urban transportation brought with them concealed costs of considerable significance. Against increases in workers' income must be counted the necessary outlays for transportation.[126] And, offsetting other advantages, including the decreased hours of labor which became substantial only much later, should be placed the time necessarily consumed in going to and from work. It must also be emphasized that the failure to provide really cheap and rapid mass transport condemned hundreds of thousands of the poorer workers to live in the crowded, unsanitary slums of the central city.[127] The beginnings of mass urban transportation in New York, Boston, and Philadelphia brought significant technological progress, as this paper has shown, but increased urban mobility also brought economic and social developments whose impact merits much further study and whose end is not yet.

▪ ▪ ▪ ▪ Notes

1 Data from various decennial United States census reports except for Boston in 1840. See Lemuel Shattuck, *Census of Boston for the year 1845* . . . (Boston, 1846), 7–16. Range of error in the early enumerations probably ran about ±6 per cent. Computations are the author's.

2 Except for a few small variations which could not be avoided. See footnotes to Table

1. The determination of geographical boundaries for central city and suburban areas in each population center was necessarily influenced by the availability of continuous series.

3 J. D. B. DeBow, *Statistical View of the United States* (Washington, 1854), 193; Adna F. Weber, *The Growth of Cities in the Nineteenth Century* (New York, 1899), 463.

4 Jesse Chickering, *A Statistical View of the Population of Massachusetts, from 1765 to 1840* (Boston, 1846), 105.

5 See Table I.

6 Issac Smith Homans, *History of Boston, from 1630 to 1856* (Boston, 1856), 61, 130–136; Sam B. Warner, Jr., *Streetcar Suburbs, The Process of Growth in Boston, 1850–1900* (Cambridge, Massachusetts, 1962), 17–19; Walter Muir Whitehill, *Boston: A Topographical History* (Cambridge, Massachusetts, 1959), 75 ff.; Chickering, *passim*.

7 Gideon Sjoberg, *The Preindustrial City, Past and Present* (Glencoe, Illinois, 1960), 323.

8 Robert Ernst, *Immigrant Life in New York City, 1825–1863* (New York, 1949), 191.

9 Edward Ewing Pratt, *Industrial Causes of Congestion of Population in New York City* (New York, 1911), 35.

10 *The Seventh Census of the United States: 1850* (Washington, D.C., 1853), 52, and *The Eighth Census of the United States: 1860* (Washington, D.C., 1864), 225.

11 Oscar Handlin, *Boston's Immigrants, 1790–1865* (Cambridge, Massachusetts, 1941) *passim;* Ernst, especially chaps. III and IV. For a contemporary account of conditions in the Philadelphia area in the early 1830s see Mathew Carey, *Appeal to the Wealthy of the Land* (Philadelphia, 1833). See also Pratt; Edward Bowmaker, *The Housing of the Working Classes* (London, 1895); Kate K. Liepmann, *The Journey to Work, Its Significance for Industrial and Community Life* (London, 1944); David Ward, "Nineteenth Century Boston: A Study in the Role of Antecedent and Adjacent Conditions in the Spatial Aspects of Urban Growth" (unpublished dissertation, University of Wisconsin, 1963), chap. IV.

12 Damrell Y. Moore and George Coolege, *The Boston Almanac for the Year 1854* (Boston, 1854), 48.

13 Weber, 471.

14 Records of the Northern Liberties Gas Works in the Eleutherian Mills Historical Library, Wilmington, Delaware.

15 Ernst, 19–20; Letter of John J. Davenport on *The . . . Population of the City of New York* (New York, 1884), 9–10 (pamphlet in the Army Medical Library, Washington, D.C.).

16 XXIII (Aug. 3, 1850), 488.

17 "Dr. Chickering's Report," Nov. 7, 1850, in *State Census of Boston,* City Document No. 42 (Boston, 1850), 39–42; Whitehill, 112 ff; Ward, 31–32.

18 *The Stranger's Guide in Philadelphia* (Philadelphia, 1859), 270.

19 For an excellent analysis see Warner.

20 For references on the European origin of the omnibus, see Foster M. Palmer, "The Literature of the Street Railway," *Harvard Library Bulletin,* XII (Winter 1958), 117–118. Successful omnibus operation is said to have begun in Paris in 1819 and in London ten years later. Charles Henry Moore, *Omnibuses and Cabs: Their Origin and History* (London, 1902), 8–12.

21 *The Picture of New York and Stranger's Guide* (New York, 1818—preface dated 1817), 234; *American Railroad Journal, and Advocate of Internal Improvements,* V (Aug. 27, 1836), 543; Charles H. Haswell, *Reminiscences of an Octogenarian of the City of New York (1816–1860)* (New York, 1897), 215; New York (City) Common Council, *Manual of the Corporation of the City of New York for the Years 1841 & 1842,* 45.

22 Sir Charles Lyell reports that in Boston "many of the wealthiest families keep no

carriages. . . ." *A Second Visit to the United States of North America* (New York and London, 1849), I, 125.

23 Elizabeth Bisland, "Old Greenwich," in *Halfmoon Series, Papers on Historic New York*, eds. Maud Wilder Goodwin and others (New York and London, 1897), 292–293; Haswell, 9.

24 *Minutes of the Common Council of the City of New York, 1784–1831* (New York, 1917), XVII, 246.

25 *Minutes of New York*, XVI, 431; XVII, 246; XVII, 64, 107, 665.

26 *The Christian Almanack, 1823* (Boston, 1823), 46.

27 *Badger & Porter's Stage Register, 1825* (Boston, 1825), 7–10.

28 *The City Record and Boston News-Letter*, I (February 25, 1826), 112.

29 *City Record and News-Letter*, I (April 29, 1826), 226.

30 *A Hand-Book for Passengers over the Cambridge Railroad* (Boston, 1859), 6; Thomas C. Simonds, *History of South Boston* (Boston, 1857), 224.

31 Joseph Jackson, *Encyclopedia of Philadelphia* (Harrisburg, Pennsylvania, 1933), IV, 941; *The Stranger's Guide to the City of Philadelphia* (Philadelphia, 1833), 16–21; Frederic William Speirs, *The Street Railway System of Philadelphia, Its History and Present Condition* (Baltimore, 1897), XV, 9–10.

32 John Mason, President, *A Statement of Facts in Relation to the Origin, Progress and Prospects of the New York and Harlem Railroad Company* (New York, 1833), 3.

33 *Diary of William Dunlap*, ed. Dorothy C. Barck, Collections of the New York Historical Society for the Years 1929–1931, LXII–LXIV (New York, 1931), III, 719. Traffic was unusually heavy because of the holiday.

34 Charles R. Barker, "Philadelphia in the Late 'Forties,'" *Philadelphia History*, II (Jan. 1931), 249. But most omnibuses were drawn by two horses.

35 J. S. Buckingham, *America, Historical, Statistic and Descriptive* (New York, 1841), I, 164–165.

36 *New-York as It is In 1833*, ed. Edwin Williams (New York, 1833), 160; *New-York as It is In 1834*, 172; *New-York as It is In 1837*, 208.

37 Cited by I. N. Phelps Stokes, *The Iconography of Manhattan Island* (New York, 1915–1928), III, 611.

38 *Hazard's United States Commercial and Statistical Register*, I (July 31, 1839), 87.

39 Lyell, II, 249.

40 Report of a Special Committee on Railroads, Sept. 7, 1850, New York City Board of Aldermen, Doc. 59, 971.

41 *Francis's New Guide to the Cities of New-York and Brooklyn, and the Vicinity* (New York, 1853), 97–98.

42 S. N. Dickinson, *The Boston Almanac, for the Year 1840*, 83–84; *Report of the Committee of Investigation of the Western Railroad, March 12, 1840*, "'D' Fare on Rail-Roads. No. 1," 44.

43 Nathaniel Dearborn, *Boston Notions* (Boston, 1848), 221.

44 Barker, 250; *Disturnell's Guide through the Middle Northern and Eastern States*, June, 1847, 23; Edward W. Hocker, *Germantown 1683–1933* (Germantown, Pennsylvania, 1933), 216.

45 Speirs, 10.

46 William Tindall, "Beginnings of Street Railways in the National Capital," *Columbia Historical Society Records*, XXI (1918), 25; J. Thomas Scharf, *The Chronicles of Baltimore* (Baltimore, 1874), 512; Leland D. Baldwin, *Pittsburgh, The Story of a City* (Pittsburgh, 1937), 240; Bessie Louise Pierce, *A History of Chicago* (New York, 1937–1940), II, 323–324; Louis H. Pursley, "Street Railways of Toronto 1861–1921," *Interurbans*, XVI (June 1958), 5.

47 Information on rates of fare is widely scattered. Among the more useful sources of

information are Charles R. Barker, "Philadelphia, 1836–1839, Transportation and Development" in *Philadelphia History* (Philadelphia, 1933), II, 346–348; Jackson, IV, 942; W. Williams, *A Hand-Book for the Stranger in Philadelphia* (Philadelphia, 1849), 98; Nathaniel S. Dearborn, *Historical and Geographical Remarks for Map of Boston and Vicinity, 1841* (Boston, 1840), 17; *Pathfinder Railway Guide for the New England States,* Sept. & Dec., 1849 (Boston, 1849); *New-York As It is: In 1833, . . . 1834, . . . 1835; A Glance at New York* (New York, 1837); O. L. Holley, *A Description of the City of New York* (New York, 1847); *Phelps' New York City Guide* (New York, 1852), 58; J. H. French, *Historical and Statistical Gazetteer of New York State,* 8th ed. (Syracuse, 1860), 429.

48 [George G. Foster], *New York in Slices* (New York, 1849), 64–66.

49 Stanley Lebergott, *Manpower in Economic Growth: The American Record since 1800* (New York, 1964), chap. VII, 541–547; Jackson, IV, 940–942.

50 New York *Daily Tribune,* May 27, 1851, 7; New York *Times,* Nov. 8, 1853, 4.

51 For an early example of crowded conditions in New York City see the New York *Observer,* Nov. 30, 1833, 191. See also Handlin, chap. IV, and Ernst, chaps. IV and V.

52 *A Glance at New York,* 261.

53 Lyell, II, 249.

54 In December, 1849, the fare one way between Boston and Cambridge or Roxbury was ten cents, that to Brighton twenty-five cents. In some cases small reductions resulted from the purchase of ten tickets. See *Pathfinder Railway Guide,* Dec. 1849.

55 *Pathfinder Railway Guide,* Dec. 1849 (Boston, 1849), 81.

56 Issac Smith Homans, *Sketches of Boston Past and Present* (Boston, 1851), 14; *Pathfinder Railway Guide,* July 1850, 18.

57 Editorial, *American Railroad Journal,* XXIII (Nov. 30, 1850), 758.

58 E. H. D[erby], "City of Boston," *Hunt's Merchants' Magazine and Commercial Review,* XXIII (Nov. 1850), 485.

59 *Report of the Committee for Investigating the Affairs of the Boston and Providence Railroad Corporation Appointed by the Stockholders,* Jan. 9, 1856 (Boston, 1856).

60 *Report of the Committee . . . of the Boston and Providence Railroad;* Dearborn, *Boston Notions,* 221; *Hunt's* XXV (Nov. 1851), 639–640.

61 D[erby], 485; *Pathfinder Railway Guide,* 1850.

62 *Boston Railways: Their Condition and Prospects* (Boston, 1856), 98. The *American Railroad Journal,* XXVI (Feb. 26, 1853), 131–133, indicates the total for the year previous as 3661. The article also refers to 4560 commuters who transact business in Boston. A valuable recent study is Charles J. Kennedy, "Commuter Services in the Boston Area, 1835–1860," *Business History Review,* XXXVI (Summer 1962), 153–170.

63 A city ordinance forbidding locomotives to cross Causeway Street induced the Boston and Maine Railroad, at least for a time, to bring its coaches into the Haymarket Square Station by means of oxen. Efforts to prevent the use of steam locomotives by railroads entering from the west and south were unsuccessful. Alvin F. Harlow, *Steelways of New England* (New York, 1946), 147; Boston Records, XXXII (March 20, 1854), 157–163 and (May 10, 1854), 335; XXVI (Dec. 22, 1858), 706.

64 Dionysius Lardner, *Railway Economy* (New York, 1850), 338.

65 Harry J. Carman, *The Street Surface Railway Franchise of New York City,* Studies in History, Economics, and Public Law, LXXXVIII (New York, 1919), 17–28; J. H. French, 428; *Stranger's Handbook for the City of New-York* (New York, 1853), 96; Erastus Cornelius Benedict, *New York and City Travel, Omnibus and Railroad* (New York, [ca. 1851]), 8.

66 Carman, 17–30; Joseph Warren Greene, Jr., "New York City's First Railroad, The New York and Harlem, 1832 to 1867," *New-York Historical Society Quarterly Bulletin,* IX (Jan. 1926), 107–123.

67 *Hazard's Register,* I (Sept. 4, 1839), 166.
68 *American Railroad Journal,* XXIII (Aug. 3, 1850), 488; Greene, 108–112; Carman, 25–27; French, 429.
69 French, 429, n. 1.
70 *Report of the Committee Appointed at a Meeting of the Stockholders of the New York and Harlem Railroad Co.,* Aug. 30, 1841, 10; John W. Barber, *Historical Collections of the State of New York* (New York, 1851), 208; *Hunt's,* XLIII (Sept. 1860), 373.
71 *Francis's Guide,* 97; *Daggett's United States Railroad and Ocean Steam Navigation Guide for 1847,* 62; *American Railroad Journal,* XXVI (May 7, 1853), 296–297; *Report of the Committee . . . of the New York and Harlem Railroad,* 38; see also Greene, 107–123.
72 *Report of the Committee . . . of the New York and Harlem Railroad; Daggett's Guide,* Oct. 1847; and other contemporary railway guides.
73 *American Railroad Journal,* XXVI (Feb. 26, 1853), 131–132.
74 Foster, 87; *Francis's Guide,* 97.
75 *Francis's Guide,* 26, 94–96, 137; J. Judd, "A Tale of Two Cities: Brooklyn and New York, 1834–1855," *Journal of Long Island History,* III (Spring 1963), 19–33; French, 427–429.
76 Vincent F. Seyfreid, *The Long Island Railroad, A Comprehensive History* (Garden City, New York, 1963), 2, 14–18.
77 XII (Sept. 1, 1860), 341.
78 Report of the President and Managers of the Philadelphia, Germantown & Norristown Railroad Company, Sept. 30, 1859, 5. The annual reports of the Philadelphia, Germantown & Norristown Railroad, 1850 through 1860, are available at the Historical Society of Pennsylvania in Philadelphia.
79 Report of . . . the Philadelphia, Germantown & Norristown Railroad Company, Sept. 30, 1860, 5.
80 See pertinent issues of the *American Railway Guide* and the report of the Philadelphia, Germantown & Norristown Railroad for 1860. On the basis of a six-day week, $10.00 a quarter is about six cents a ride.
81 William Bromwell, *Off-Hand Sketches. A Companion for the Tourist and Traveller over the Philadelphia, Pottsville, and Reading Railroad* (Philadelphia, 1854), 38.
82 Barker, 247–248, and "Philadelphia, 1836–39, Transportation and Development," *Philadelphia History,* II (Dec. 1932), 340–344; *American Railroad Journal,* XXXII (Sept. 3, 1859), 567; Joseph Jackson, *Market Street Philadelphia* (Philadelphia, 1918), 45–46.
83 *Disturnell's Railway, Steamship, and Telegraph Book* (New York, July 1852), 30.
84 Jay V. Hare, *History of the North Pennsylvania Railroad* (Philadelphia, 1944), 4–7, 11.
85 Alexander Easton, *Practical Treatise on Street or Horse-Power Railways* (Philadelphia, 1859), 4.
86 Yasuo Sakakibara, "The Influence of the Introduction of Street Railways upon Urban and Industrial Growth in Eastern Massachusetts, 1855–1875" (unpublished Master's thesis, Amherst College, 1956), 2.
87 *American Railroad Journal,* XXXII (Jan. 8, 1859), 20; see also *Argument of Amos B. Merrill, for . . . the Citizens' Horse Railroad Co.,* Mar. 4, 1863 (Boston, 1863), 15.
88 *American Railroad Journal,* XXXV (July 12, 1862), 537.
89 Report of a Committee on Railroads, September 7, 1850, New York City, Board of Aldermen, Doc. 59, *passim.*
90 Easton, 25.
91 *American Railroad Journal,* XXXII (April 23, 1859), 265, and XXXII (Oct. 8, 1859), 649; J. L. Ringwalt, *Development of Transportation Systems in the United*

States (Philadelphia, 1888), 167; *Hunt's*, XLV (Sept. 1861), 295. Carman, 145, reports passenger traffic annually, 1853–1875. His figures show an increase from 6,800,000 in 1853 to 36,500,000 in 1860.

92 Edward S. Mason states that an unincorporated street railway operated by the owner served in Cambridge in 1852: *The Street Railway in Massachusetts* (Cambridge, Mass., 1932), 3, n. 1.

93 *Returns of the Railroad Corporations in Massachusetts, 1860* (Boston, 1861), Public Doc. No. 46, unnumbered summary page. *United States Census of 1860; Mortality and Miscellaneous Statistics*, 332, gives 67.39 as the Boston mileage; see also *Hunt's*, XLV (Aug. 1861), 117.

94 *The Strangers Guide in Philadelphia* (Philadelphia, 1859), 270. See also "The Diary of Sidney George Fisher 1859–1860," *Pennsylvania Magazine of History and Biography*, LXXXVII (April 1963), 191–192, 207.

95 Frederick William Speirs, XV, 11, 17–18; *American Railroad Journal*, XXXIII (Nov. 10, 1860), 994. Ringwalt, 167, gives the total Philadelphia mileage as 148, as does also *United States Census of 1860, Mortality and Miscellaneous Statistics*, 332.

96 New York *Herald*, Oct. 8, 1864, quoted by Carman, 29, n. 1. See also Easton; New York City, Board of Aldermen, Doc. 59, Sept. 7, 1850, 967–968.

97 Report of the Special Committee Relative to Constructing a Railroad in Broadway, Nov. 15, 1852, New York City, Board of Aldermen, Doc. 57, 1420.

98 New York City, Board of Aldermen, Doc. 59 (Sept. 7, 1850), 971–972, and Doc. 57 (Nov. 15, 1852), 1413; Boston, "Report of a Committee on the Meeting of Horse Railroads at a Central Point . . .", Doc. 58 (Oct. 10, 1859), 6; Walter Spooner Allen, *Street Railways* (New Bedford[?], Massachusetts, 1889), 4; Easton, *passim;* George Francis Train, *Observations on Horse Railways* (London, 1860), 46–47; Charles MacKay, *Street Tramways for London* (London, 1868), 8–9; *American Railroad Journal*, XXIV (May 7, 1853), 296; and *Hunt's*, XLIV (May 1861), 672.

99 Hare, 7; *Philadelphia: A Guide to the Nation's Birthplace* (Harrisburg, Pennsylvania, 1937), 142–143.

100 *Improved Railway Connections in Philadelphia* (Philadelphia, 1863), 12.

101 *The Railroad Record* (Cincinnati), X (July 17, 1862), 253. See also Barker, "Philadelphia in the Late 'Forties,' " 245–250, and "Philadelphia, 1836–39," 342–347; *American Railroad Journal*, XXXII (Sept. 3, 1859), 567.

102 *American Railroad Journal*, XXXII (Sept. 3, 1859), 567; Barker, "Philadelphia in the Late 'Forties,' " 245–249, and "Philadelphia, 1836–39," 340; Jackson, *Market Street*, 45–46.

103 New York City, Board of Aldermen, Doc. No. 57 (Nov. 15, 1852) 1413–1429; Train, 46–47; Mackay, 4–10.

104 "Diary of Sidney George Fisher," 207, also 192.

105 XXII (June 30, 1860), 259. See also Carman, 11–107; New York City, Board of Aldermen, Doc. 59 (Sept. 7, 1850), 961 ff. A writer in *Hunt's* declared that horse railways of good quality could be constructed at a cost of "$10,000 to $15,000 per mile in cities, exclusive of the equipage, stables, and change of grade," XLV (Aug. 1861), 117.

106 *American Railway Times*, XXII (March 24, 1860), 118 and (Jan. 7, 1860), 8.

107 Speirs, 13–17, 93.

108 *United States Census of 1860, Mortality and Miscellaneous Statistics*, 332, gives the length of track in St. Louis as 26.30 and that in Cincinnati as 17.38 miles.

109 T. C. Barker and Michael Robbins, *A History of London Transport*, Vol. I. *The Nineteenth Century* (London, 1963), 178–188; see also Train, *passim*.

110 Greene, 115, 118.

111 *American Railroad Journal*, XXXV (July 12, 1862), 537; *American Railway Times*,

XVI (May 21, 1864), 166; Easton, 54–60; Q. A. Gillmore, *A Practical Treatise on Roads, Streets, and Pavements,* 5th ed. (New York, 1876), 240–244.

112 Even the direct movement of passenger cars from one Philadelphia terminal to another was prevented by "carriage and bus" interests: G. W. Baker, *A Review of the Relative Commercial Progress of the Cities of New York and Philadelphia* (Philadelphia, 1859), 6–7; New York *Times,* Jan. 21, 1863, 4.

113 Fares to points very far into Boston's suburbs were substantially higher; Easton, 98.

114 The Metropolitan Railroad of Boston was required in 1860 to offer 28 tickets for one dollar; Boston Records, XXXVII (April 23, 1860), 253–254, 361–366. In Philadelphia, tickets permitting transfers to another line sold for seven cents: Speirs, 49; J. Thomas Scharf and Thompson Westcott, *History of Philadelphia. 1609–1884* (Philadelphia, 1884), 2201; *The Stranger's Guide in Philadelphia* (1859), 272; *American Railroad Journal,* XXXII (Jan. 8, 1859), 20; Easton, 22–24.

115 *American Railroad Journal,* XXXIII (Jan. 28, 1860), 65.

116 Kennedy, 163–167.

117 E. B. Grant wrote: ". . . nothing contributes as much to increase the . . . travel on a railroad as the frequency of the trains." *Boston Railways; Their Condition and Prospects* (Boston, 1856), 97.

118 Reductions were often made when customers bought a dollar's worth of tickets.

119 Hocker, 224–226.

120 *American Railway Times,* XII (April 28, 1860), 168.

121 New York City, Board of Aldermen, Doc. 59 (Sept. 7, 1850), 972.

122 *American Railroad Journal,* XXXIII (Nov. 10, 1860), 994; see also XXIX (Sept. 27, 1856), 619: *Facts Respecting Street Railways* (London, 1866), 26; Handlin, 95–105.

123 *Facts Respecting Street Railways,* 619.

124 Handlin, 99–105. Many immigrants, however, must have found unskilled employment in construction and in suburban factories; see Ward, 64–65.

125 Letter of Davenport.

126 In Belgium and England, provision for special low-fare commuter trains for workmen was made as early as 1861: Liepmann, 29–31.

127 Letter of Davenport, *passim.* Although the letter was written for the special purpose of promoting the building of a subway in New York, the writer's conclusions appear justified. See also Richard L. Meier, *Science and Economic Development* (Cambridge, Massachusetts, 1956), 125–129.

9

Italians in Urban America: A Study in Ethnic Adjustment

HUMBERT S. NELLI

Many of the men, women, and children who crowded into the less desirable sections of America's cities came from Europe. The foreign-born, their children, and their grandchildren still make up a considerable portion of the urban population forty years after the United States legislated an end to virtually unrestricted immigration. Before the Civil War most immigrants to American cities came from Ireland and Germany; by the 1890s the major sources of immigration were from southern and eastern Europe—countries such as Italy, Russia, and Austria-Hungary.

In the following essay, Humbert Nelli provides an overview of the Italian experience in urban America. He notes the similarity between the situation of the Italians and that of other nationalities from southern and eastern Europe who came to the United States to take advantage of urban rather than rural economic opportunities. All these groups produced the institutions of the "colonial" press, the immigrant banker, the benefit society, and the padrone, *or labor contractor.*

The padrone was most common in the early stages of a group's migration, when there were few established members who could aid later arrivals in finding work and a place to live. The padrone acted as the intermediary between employers seeking laborers and his fellow-countrymen seeking work. In addition to finding jobs, he often boarded the men, and exchanged their American money for Italian money to remit to the old country. For these services he frequently took a sizable percentage of the men's earnings, often so much that publicists frequently described the padrone as little better than a racketeer. Nelli, however, argues that the padrone served a useful though temporary function in the first years of migration, and that the relationship between padrone and worker was not always exploitative.

As Nelli observes, the migration from southern Italy to New York and Chicago involved a dual adjustment, from a rural or village society to a complex urban culture, as well as from Europe to America. Consequently, the cultural patterns of the ethnic group resulted from interaction between the European village background and the American urban environment. We badly need some comparative studies of how the same group fared in different cities. For example, what was the "critical mass"? How large did a group have to be to create viable institutions? Were the rates of social mobility different in eastern and midwestern cities? How did the Italian experience in Kansas City, where there were few other immigrants, compare to New York, where minorities were in the majority? Nelli's essay on Chicago is a useful starting point for such a comparative study, as well as being a valuable contribution in its own right.

■ ■ ■ ■ **For Further Reading**

Humbert S. Nelli, *The Italians in Chicago: 1880–1930* (New York: Oxford University Press, 1970) is a full history of the Italians in Chicago. M. A. Jones, *American Immigration* (Chicago: University of Chicago Press, 1960) is a valuable survey by a British scholar of the entire spectrum of immigration to the United States. William Whyte, *Street Corner Society* (Chicago: University of Chicago Press, 1955) is a classic participant–observer study of Italian-Americans in Boston's North End in the 1930s.

I

■ Nearly four million Italians entered the United States between 1890 and 1921, when restrictive legislation enacted by the federal government ended the period of free and large-scale immigration to this country. Contemporaries expressed deep concern about the influx of this alien horde, composed, many claimed, of criminals, paupers, ignorant peasants, and illegal contract laborers, all congregated in closely-packed colonies where they infected American life by perpetuating old-world traits and compounding city problems. Few discerned that settlement in America's urban environment profoundly affected not only the receiving society, but newcomers as well.[1]

Life centered around the family in southern Italy and Sicily (and eastern Europe), where needs and problems were handled from the standpoint of the family group or its individual members. Political scientist Edward C. Banfield, in a recent study widely accepted by immigration scholars and students of Italian history, described a Sicilian–southern Italian society dominated by amoral familism. Banfield found peasants and gentry alike unwilling to act "for any end transcending the immediate, material interest of the nuclear family." If this study is accurate, one can reasonably conclude that community and ethnic consciousness found among Italians and Sicilians in the United States was not an old-world transplant, but a development of the new world.[2]

In the United States, one leader of a Sicilian–southern Italian community described his neighborhood in Chicago as possessing "unusual unity and strength." He believed that his colony had "to a very great extent the same kind of warmth, friendliness and intimacy in our community life that was to be found in the small towns of Sicily from whence our parents came." It is ironic that this community feeling, which developed in response to the American environment, was assumed to be a carry-over of old world habits.[3]

Because it served as a staging area where new arrivals remained until they absorbed new ideas and habits which made possible their adjustment to the alien environment, the community of the immigrant generation fulfilled a vitally important function both to its inhabitants and the receiving society. It bridged the gap between rural (old-world) traditions and the new urban world; it acquainted a succession of immigrant groups with American ideas and values, although obviously not all members of any group reacted in the same way to the colony, its available institutions, or its urban surroundings.

II

The pattern of Italian settlement in cities east of the Mississippi and north of the Ohio began with the founding of the immigrant community by northern Italians, who tended to predominate until the 1880s; after that time, southerners and Sicilians formed the bulk of the new arrivals. The original enclave started in or near the city's central portion—that is, the business area—and was characterized by the movement of economically successful newcomers out of the settlement and into the American community. New arrivals from overseas swarmed into the colony, filling vacancies and creating or aggravating overcrowded, rapidly deteriorating neighborhoods.

In general, settlement in Chicago typified the Italian experience in urban America.[4] Northern Italians, most of them from Genoa and Tuscany, formed the early colony in the years after 1850. Whether from the north, in the first three decades of immigration, or from the south and Sicily after the 1880s, newcomers tended at first to settle along the same streets and in the same tenements. They lodged according to town or province of origin, doubtless seeking familiar faces, names, and dialects. They lived together and—if possible—worked together.[5] This early concentration broke down as immigrants met and mingled with newcomers from other towns and provinces in the homeland and with non-Italians who lived and worked in close proximity. In the process, they began for the first time to think of themselves as Italians rather than as members of a particular family or emigrants from a particular locality. This new concept comprised a considerable expansion of provincial horizons, and was one of the first results of Chicago's impact upon them.

Not only did they live and work with Italians from throughout the Kingdom as well as with Irishmen, Poles, Germans, Scandinavians, and others; many went to church with these "foreigners" and their children attended the same schools. In contrast to the homeland tradition of seeking a spouse from the same place of birth, they began to intermarry with "outsiders" from elsewhere in Italy. Despite strong northern prejudices, by 1900 marriages had begun to take place between Tuscans (and other northerners) and Sicilians (and other southerners). On occasion newcomers even married non-Italians. Both choices represented a shifting away from old-world attitudes, although of individually varying significance.[6]

Continuing the pattern set by their predecessors, southern Italians and Sicilians who obtained the financial means moved away from the colony. If migration from the ethnic settlement—a sign of economic mobility and an indication of desires for better housing and living conditions—did not take place in the first generation, it generally occurred in the second or third.[7] Nevertheless, the continued presence of numbers of Italians in neighborhoods led contemporaries to the erroneous conclusion that Italians, their children, and their grandchildren after them, remained on the same streets and in the same tenements from the time they arrived in the city until they died. Americans also assumed that compact, unchanging settlements grouped according to place of immigrant origin. While this description fitted the initial phase of settlement, new relationships quickly formed, both with other Italians and with members of different nationality groups. A major cause of this constant regrouping and expanding of relationships was the fact that the composition of Italian colonies (like that of other ethnic groups) remained in constant flux, with at least half the community residents changing their place of dwelling each year.[8]

Contrary to popular belief, Chicago, like other urban areas, contained few blocks inhabited exclusively by Italians, and even fewer solidly Italian neighborhoods.[9] Between 1890 and 1920, only limited sections of certain Chicago streets held a 50 percent or higher concentration of Italian immigrants and their children. The population density of Italians in the city's various Italian districts fell considerably below 50 percent.

Throughout the four decades following 1880, the Near West Side community in the vicinity of Hull House made up the largest and most heavily concentrated Italian group in the city. According to the City Homes Association *Report* of 1901, this "Italian district" extended from Polk to Twelfth Streets and Halsted to Canal. Here, while first and second generation Italians constituted 50 to 70 percent of the population in portions the size of blocks or slightly more, they formed only one-third of the area's total population. This mixture of nationalities, of course, brought about innumerable contacts among members of different nationality groups. By 1920 the major Italian community had shifted to the west of Halsted, where similarly scattered concentrations could be found.[10]

Observers of immigrant life in Chicago and other cities ignored or did not recognize the gradual shift in location of Italian districts. Thus the area discussed in one study often differed from that in another, even though the colony in both instances might be labelled "The West Side" or "The North Side" community. In addition, the composition of Italian communities underwent rapid and continual change. Hence the miserable, poorly fed, and ragged residents described in one survey probably were not the same individuals examined in subsequent studies of the same area.

III

Americans concerned over slums and the effects which incoming European peasants might have in perpetuating miserable conditions and multiplying city problems sincerely believed that urban difficulties could be alleviated or even solved by encouraging immigrants to move into rural surroundings. Shifting Italians into agriculture appeared to be "the natural solution of the problem of Italian concentration in the slums," wrote I. W. Howerth in 1894. "Henceforth the tendency of Italians to congregate in large cities will decrease." In order to bring about this desired event, the Italian and American governments, individual states, and private agencies (such as local Italian-American chambers of commerce) supported the establishment of agricultural colonies for Italian immigrants throughout the United States and especially in Texas, Arkansas, Mississippi, Louisiana, and Alabama.[11]

Despite auspicious beginnings and official support, most rural ventures came to nothing. For example, Alessandro Mastro-Valerio (later editor of *La Tribuna Italiana Transatlantica* of Chicago, and head of the Italian Chamber of Commerce's Agricultural Section) founded an Italian agricultural colony at Daphne, Alabama in 1892. This enterprise received counsel and financial aid from Jane Addams and the residents of Hull House. Italian inhabitants of Chicago, however, gave it little support and soon it failed. Truck gardens in the vicinity of large urban centers of the East and Midwest, and in California, achieved a greater measure of success than did efforts to attract immigrants to rural colonies.[12]

Contemporaries wondered why more Italians did not move to farms. Some maintained that "new" immigrants, trapped in cities, lacked the strength, ability, and knowledge required to take advantage of the marvelous agricultural opportunities offered in the United States. According to this thesis, "old" immigrant groups had seized these opportunities and thus had proven themselves to be superior to "new" arrivals. In this vein, labor economist and historian John R. Commons observed that "in the immigrant stage they [Italians] are helpless." In contrast, "immigrants from Northwestern Europe, the Germans and Scandinavians," had been from the start "the model farmers of America" because of their "thrift, self-reliance, and intensive farming." He added, "The least self-reliant or forehanded, like the . . . Italians, seek the cities in greater proportions than those sturdy races like the Scandinavians, English, Scotch and Germans."[13]

Commons believed that serious consequences would follow the massing of recent immigrants in American cities because cities did not create the spirit of independence and initiative achieved by farm workers. He distrusted new immigrant groups and feared the phenomenal growth of urban areas and the changes being wrought there by technology and increasing populations. "The dangerous effects of city life on immigrants and the children of immigrants cannot be too strongly emphasized," he wrote. Foreigners in urban centers "are themselves dragged down by the parasitic and dependent conditions which they [cities] fostered among the immigrant element."[14]

Others held similar views and expressed them in magazines, books, and reports. "The illiterate races, such as the Hungarians, Galicians, and Italians, remain in the cities to lower the standards of the already crowded Atlantic territory," declared one. Said another, "The illiterate immigrants congregate chiefly in the slums of our great cities."[15]

Alessandro Mastro-Valerio reported to the United States Industrial Commission in 1901 that Italian immigrants wanted desperately to farm but did not know "how to get the land and the means to work it until it produces." Consequently, he said, they remained caged in cities. Because most of the immigrants had engaged in farm labor in Italy, it seemed logical that they should hope to settle on the land in America. As country people, "they should have been established in the country." Americans, he said, had a responsibility for moving immigrants out of urban areas and into agriculture.[16]

An Italian visitor to an early farming settlement in the American South indicated some reasons for the immigrant preference for crowded cities rather than rural "opportunities":

> The colony lives in poorly constructed houses, made of wood, without the most elementary precautions against the weather; frequently . . . the dwellings are really tents, where members of the colony sleep together without distinction as to age and sex . . . . Hygiene is unknown . . . . Our people are eternally deeply in debt . . . and the current agricultural contracts, for sharecropping or renting, are not to the advantage of the Italians.[17]

Overwhelming as these disadvantages appear, Robert Foerster has shown that factors such as ignorance of opportunity, unfamiliar climate, squalid living conditions, and cost of land did not form the primary deterrents to successful farming colonies. In Argentina, for example, Italians overcame similar obstacles and farmed to great advantage, adapting without difficulty to new-world crops, soils, markets, and rural living conditions. Another and more important factor contributed to immigrant distaste for settlement in the country: most Italians simply did not emigrate to North America with hopes or intentions of farming.[18]

Like the majority of immigrants, "old" as well as "new," Italians arrived seeking economic opportunities. In the last decades of the nineteenth century and the early ones of the twentieth, prospects of financial gain existed in commercial and industrial centers of the North and East and not in agriculture. This fact resulted in the failures of agricultural colonies, such as the one at New Palermo, Alabama, as reported in *L'Italia* of Chicago on May 21, 1904. The immigrants, reported the paper, who "went with the delusion of finding riches," instead "found nothing but misery." The United States Industrial Commission recognized the desire for economic betterment in its summary volume, published in 1902, where it examined the factors responsible for immigrant concentration in cities. The Commission noted first "the general movement of all modern industrial peoples toward urban life—a movement quite characteristic of the American people themselves."

For the foreign-born, additional factors reinforced this trend: (1) the isolation of farm life in the United States, in contrast with more crowded conditions in rural areas of Europe; (2) immigrant memories of "hardship and oppressions of rural life from which they are struggling to escape"; (3) ready employment in cities directly upon arrival and for higher wages than those paid farm laborers.[19]

In the period after 1890, as English historian Frank Thistlethwaite has pointed out, the great migrations proceeded "from farm to factory, from village to city, whether this meant from Iowa to Chicago, Silesia to Pittsburgh or Piedmont to Buenos Aires." Writing in 1906, demographer Walter F. Willcox found no evidence that "immigrants tend disproportionately toward cities." He claimed that recent immigrants showed no stronger tendencies to crowd into cities than had earlier groups. Nevertheless, during the years between 1890 and 1905, writers and speakers repeated the idea that immigrants—especially illiterate ones—clung to the slums of large cities. The American public in general accepted this view.[20]

The cultural problem of adjusting to new living patterns, the result of moving to an urban environment, constituted a key factor responsible for immigrant difficulties in urban America. Contemporaries failed to recognize that adjustment would have been necessary had the villagers migrated to a city in Italy or to some other European city rather than across the Atlantic. Americans of rural background who moved to urban areas faced many of the same problems encountered by Sicilians who journeyed to the new world, to Milan, or to other cities in the Italian peninsula and Europe.[21]

Significantly, Americans and Italians who encouraged agricultural colonies did so at least in part because of the conviction that foreigners would become Americanized more rapidly and completely in a rural setting than they could in a city. Commissioner General of Immigration Frank Sargent maintained that "if, instead of crowding into our large cities," immigrants would go to rural areas, "there would be no need to fear for the future."[22] Probably the opposite was true. As the experience of German agricultural colonies in Pennsylvania and the Midwest made clear, assimilation slowed or halted in rural environments where there existed only limited contacts with outside agencies and individuals. In sparsely populated areas, an ethnic community is forced in upon itself, or can maintain a desired isolation. In cities, on the other hand, contacts of one type or another are (and were) virtually impossible to prevent.

University of Chicago sociologist Robert E. Park noted in 1921 that the rural experience "is naturally in the opposite direction" of the urban. Country life "emphasizes local differences, preserves the memories of the immigrants, and fosters a sentimental interest in the local home community." An expert on foreign-language newspapers, Park cited the example of the "German provincial press, which is printed in a dialect no longer recognizable by the European press, and which idealized German provincial life as it existed fifty years ago and still lives in the memories of the editors and readers of these papers." This comment paralleled an observation made several years previously by John Foster Carr, who noted that by 1906 "only two poor fragments remain of the numerous important German and Irish colonies" that had flourished in New York City in the 1870s and 1880s. In contrast, "the ancient settled Pennsylvania Dutch, thanks to their isolation, are not yet fully merged in the great citizen body."[23]

Clearly, new arrivals to the United States faced the basic problem not of escaping from a mythical urban "trap" or of finding agricultural jobs, but rather of settling into a new way of life, that of the city community.

IV

Italians who, in the Kingdom, never considered the possibility of cooperation or even of contact with co-nationals from other towns and provinces, found themselves forced to deal with urban difficulties in the United States as members of groups. In the process, newcomers modified familiar institutions (like the Church), organized some which had scarcely touched their lives in Italy (such as the press and mutual benefit societies), and established agencies which did not exist in the home country (notably the immigrant bank). Thus while some immigrant institutions had counterparts in the old world, southern Italians and Sicilians either came in contact with them for the first time in America or cast them in new molds.

Many Americans assumed that ethnic communities and their institutions reproduced homeland surroundings and encouraged "isolated group life"; hence through "churches and schools, and in social, fraternal, and national organizations," immigrants could maintain "the speech, the ideals, and to some extent the manner of life of the mother country." In reality, of course, the colony represented an important step away from old-world patterns. Because the city prevented isolation, neither the community nor its institutions were fully Italian in character; nor were they American. They served an interim group, the immigrant generation with its old-world traditions and new-world surroundings.[24]

Community institutions of all new immigrant groups in the United States resembled each other and native American counterparts more closely than they did any homeland organizations. Mutual benefit and fraternal societies, for example, existed among Poles, Ukrainians, Lithuanians, Jews, and others. Italian publishers used similar techniques and faced the same problems as those of other foreign-language press groups. Non-Italians also depended upon services provided by immigrant bankers and padroni. "In America," sociologist Robert E. Park noted, "the peasant discards his [old-world] habits and acquires 'ideas.' In America, above all, the immigrant organizes. These organizations are the embodiment of his needs and his new ideas."[25]

Many newcomers sought to solve life's complexities by joining benefit groups. These were not "transplanted" institutions carried by southerners to the United States.[26] In southern Italy and Sicily, where strong family ties ensured aid in times of need, group life featured recreational activities in a few social clubs (*circolo sociale*), most of which had small memberships and limited community importance.[27]

The mutual aid society (*società di mutuo soccorso*), although known in Italy, existed almost exclusively among middle classes, and especially among artisans, in urbanized areas of the northern and central parts of the Kingdom. By the 1890s, mutual aid groups had begun to appear in the Italian south and Sicily, as J. S. McDonald has pointed out, but not in those portions of the south from which emigration flowed. The development of mutual aid societies among Italians in the United States contrasted with that in the homeland, where benefit groups closely intertwined with the growth of labor unions; societies were, in the words of historian Daniel L. Horowitz, "the linear predecessors of the trade unions in Italy." Societies in the United States, on the other hand, concentrated on insurance and social functions, aiding newly arrived immigrants to deal with sickness, loneliness, and death rather than labor organization.[28]

Benefit societies in the United States antedated the period of large-scale immigration from southern and eastern Europe. Assessment mutual aid methods found popularity with working-class Americans, native as well as foreign-born, by the middle of the nineteenth century. Groups like the Mechanics Mutual Aid Society, founded in 1846, provided strong competition for regular life insurance companies. Benefit societies in America apparently grew out of English friendly societies, which provided working-class points of view plus sickness, old age, and funeral benefits along with features from secret societies, ideas about organization and self-government, and an interest in social activities, ritual, and symbolism. "The prototype societies," according to insurance historian J. Owen Stalson, "were active in England while we were still colonies." American groups, however, developed a stronger social and fraternal character than English friendly societies. In a highly mobile country like the United States, vast numbers of the native-born as well as immigrants from Europe found themselves uprooted from familiar surroundings, people, and life patterns. For them the lodge filled a great social and psychological void. Furthermore, the practice of "passing the hat" for unfortunate group members guaranteed aid in the event of need at minimum expense for all concerned, at least during the early years of the society when members were young and vigorous, and death or illness appeared to be problems of the distant future.[29]

Immigrants (and native Americans) who joined mutual benefit organizations contributed small monthly sums, usually between 25 cents and 60 cents, to guarantee that the group would look after them when they were sick and provide a decent burial when they died. In addition, societies required all members to attend funeral services or pay a fine as penalty for non-attendance. In this way the organization assured each member of a proper burial and a well-attended service, with the result that funerals tended to become social events. Over the years the burial service grew into an opportunity for old acquaintances to gather at irregular intervals and to reminisce about old days. Since young and vigorous members predominated at first, most deaths resulted from accidents or disease growing out of employment conditions. Societies also generally handled other related activities, particularly the payment of sickness and accident expenses.[30]

In early years of settlement, societies formed typically on the basis of place of origin, either town or province of birth. This development in itself indicated a significant movement away from old-world distrust of anyone outside the family circle. In the new urban environment, and in the absence of sufficient family members to provide the resources necessary to meet all emergencies, immigrants found it necessary to cooperate with "outsiders." Consequently natives of a particular town or province—men who would have regarded each other as strangers in Italy—found that in the United States they possessed in common enough traditions to warrant banding together.

It is difficult to determine both membership figures and the number of societies in existence,[31] because of the basis of group organization—in many cases, not merely town or province of birth, but neighborhood and even street or building of residence—and the fact that some societies formed with goals other than mutual aid or recreation. Some existed to satisfy political, religious, or military functions. Through necessity, small units which had organized on a town or provincial basis consolidated into, or were absorbed by, larger organizations encompassing all Italians regardless of place of birth or residence. In all these respects the Italian experience with societies paralleled that of other nationalities. Thus the merging of small groups into the Sons of Italy had its counterpart in the establishment, for example, of the Polish National Alliance.

The function and value of the "colonial" press (as those in Italy and many in the immigrant community referred to Italian-language newspapers in the United States) were temporary, specialized in nature, and vital only so long as a sufficiently large group needed its services. The press saw itself in a nobler role. According to Italian-American journalist Luigi Carnovale, the best and truest friend available to the immigrant was his Italian-language journal. "In the colonial press, in short, the Italian immigrants have always found all that is indispensable—wise advice, moral and material assistance, true and ardent fraternal love—for their success and triumph in . . . America."[32] The major significance of colonial tabloids lay on a less grand, but undeniably important level, that of easing the first critical years of immigrant adjustment to America. Articles about events in Italy and in towns and provinces of origin, news of other immigrant communities, reports of societies and listings of collections for needy newcomers, all helped Italian-Americans to develop and nurture a sense of belonging within their new surroundings. Information about local and national American events, emphasis on the values of education and participation in politics, and advice regarding behavior and modes of expression acceptable to Americans were editorial attempts to lessen adjustment problems for readers. The press served as a crutch for immigrants having difficulties in adapting to their new surroundings, or those unable to break away from homeland traditions. To many of the second generation and a number of self-reliant newcomers, colonial journals offered little of interest or value; hence readership reached its height during the first two decades of the twentieth century, the time of arrival of great masses of immigrants desperately in need of services which foreign-language newspapers could provide.[33]

During this period also, Italian-language tabloids employed technological advances pioneered by American papers in order to attract attention and hold readers. Immigrant periodicals in the United States bore a stronger resemblance to the popular American press than to homeland journals, and featured headlines, brief articles, special columns, simple language, and profuse illustrations. Because of inadequate staffs, they also contained typographical errors, slang, plagiarisms, and unverified news items. Editors who valued literary excellence over sensational news, pictures, and frequent protestations of loyalty to Italy generally lasted but a short time.[34]

Unlike the other institutions, the Church existed for newcomers before they left Europe, and formed an integral part of their lives. Yet it had undergone changes in the new world. Italians found the Church in America to be a cold and puritanical institution, controlled and often operated, even in Italian neighborhoods, by the hated Irish. Devout Catholics and critics of religion alike resented Irish domination of the Church, demanded Italian priests and sought to control churches in their communities. Liberals and nationalists decried the Roman Church's opposition to Italian unification and its continued refusal to recognize the Kingdom.[35]

By 1900, Italians appeared to be so dissatisfied that many Catholics believed the situation posed a serious threat to the Church's future in the United States. Laurence Franklin wrote an article for *Catholic World,* appearing in April, 1900, which showed how Italian disillusionment developed. The study contrasted the religious turmoil among immigrants in the United States with conditions in Italy. "At home a chapel or church stood at their very door," Franklin pointed out. "Their parish priest was their personal friend, who had baptized them at their birth, taught them their catechism, and watched over them like a father or elder brother." In an American city, on the other hand, "they are suddenly thrown back upon themselves, without either tradition or public opinion to foster their sense of moral and social responsibility . . . . No church is to be found in the long row of tenements which form their horizon line, and the priests whom they meet speak another tongue." As a result of these factors, "like sheep without a shepherd, they too often go astray, wandering into some other fold, through interest or ignorance."[36]

In following years the Italian immigrant "Problem" remained a source of deep concern within the Church. By early 1914 the *Catholic Citizen* of Milwaukee concluded that the religious condition of Italian immigrants and their children in the United States was "our biggest Catholic question," a view widely held among American Catholics. Between the beginning of the century and 1921, various aspects of the "Italian Problem" received frequent examination in the Catholic press, including discussion of religion in the homeland, parochial education in America, the need for Italian-speaking priests, and analyses of proposed solutions to the "Problem."[37]

Protestants saw in Catholicism's difficulties an ideal foundation for proselytizing. They lost no opportunity to proclaim Protestant recognition and support of the Italian Kingdom, in contrast to the attitude of the Church. Protestant clergy condemned the papacy as a reactionary institution—"it could not be the papacy and be anything else"—and branded Catholicism as a "papal cult," a "fetish materialism," "image worship and spiritualism," entirely opposed to the simple truths of the Protestant interpretation of the gospels.[38]

Some Protestant sects, especially Methodists, Baptists, and Presbyterians, worked actively among Italian immigrants in urban America, supporting a total of 326 churches and missions with more than two hundred pastors, printing several Italian-language newspapers and publishing a steady stream of books, articles, pamphlets, and leaflets in English and Italian.[39]

Contacts with Protestant settlements, social workers, public school teachers, ministers, and missions profoundly influenced some Italians, who turned to Protestantism because it seemed to be one road to Americanization. Protestants believed that conversion formed an integral and essential element of immigrant adjustment; as one minister proclaimed in 1906, "If the immigrant is evangelized, assimilation is easy and sure." Nevertheless, despite costly and prodigious efforts by non-Catholic churches and settlements, relatively few Italians converted; those who did quickly transferred to American congregations.[40]

The tendency of many newcomers simply to turn away from all religious activities created a greater menace to the Church than did Protestantism. Undoubtedly what Father Joseph Schuyler calls "the stress of disorganization," the impact of migration and the influence of the American environment, distracted many immigrants from traditional organizations like the Church.[41]

Appearances to the contrary, the bulk of the Italian immigrants remained nominally or actually loyal Catholics, but in a way differing from other Catholic groups (like Irish- or Polish-Americans). National consciousness, which developed among all three groups in the United States, strongly influenced ethnic attitudes toward religion. While for Irish and Polish Catholics religion made up a central part of national loyalty, for Italians Catholicism and nationalism exerted opposing forces.[42]

At the same time that they attacked abuses of the Church in both Italy and the United States, Italian-Americans rallied to support the "Italian Church" against Irish "usurpers" and Protestants. One Protestant clergyman who worked zealously to convert Italians complained that some who talked and acted like "rationalists, atheists, free-thinkers and the like," called themselves Catholics, strongly opposed Protestantism, and urged other Italians to "stand fast to the traditions of their fathers' religion."[43]

Critics who "saw" an irreligious attitude in immigrant superstition and idolatry[44] ignored the fact that image-worship, especially of the Virgin, and anthropomorphic views of nature and religion made Catholicism comprehensible to the unlettered mind. In the same way, critics considered Italians' addiction to festivals, processions, and feasts as a perversion of religion, although to participants they formed an integral part of worship. Immigrants who celebrated these functions in America did so not only in an effort to reestablish those elements of religion which had strongly appealed to them in Italy, but also to counteract Irish influences in their new churches.[45] Thus what seemed to Americans to be a falling away from religion was at least in part an adaptation of old habits to new conditions. Prior to 1921, however, the Catholic Church did not occupy the position of prestige among Italian-Americans that it later assumed, particularly after 1945.[46]

In order to gain and hold the support of immigrants and their children, the Church in the United States found it necessary to offer a variety of services which were partly or entirely non-theological in nature and which were unnecessary in the static, unchanging homeland village. Among these new facilities were missions, hospitals, lay societies and organizations, and Sunday Schools. These expanded functions formed part of a general movement in the American Catholic Church during the period between 1890 and World War I toward providing social services in order to meet the needs of Slavic as well as Italian immigrants.[47]

V

Identification with the colony, and use of its facilities and institutions, signified not only a growth away from homeland outlooks but also, for many newcomers, a vital step in assimilation. It is important to note, however, that Italians exhibited a variety of responses to urban America. Some ignored all community institutions and never expanded their loyalties or interests from the district of origin; even the Italian Kingdom lay outside their comprehension.[48] Others made full use of some or all existing community institutions and enlarged their personal horizons to include Italy, a concept which did not exist for them before their emigration from it.[49]

A third group preferred to make limited use of press, societies, and churches as intermediaries through which to learn American customs and ideas. Often these first generation arrivals came as young adults or children and absorbed or consciously adopted American habits and speech in the outside community, from politics as well as schools, settlement houses, and streets.[50]

From politics Italians gained patronage jobs and neighborhood conveniences like bathhouses as well as a voice in city government. In the early years of settlement, this influence extended only to occasional machine support for Italian candidates for precinct or ward positions, in exchange for delivering the vote for Irish politicians (who generally controlled Italian and other "new" immigrant wards).[51] Over the passage of time Italians won control of Italian wards; victories in city-wide elections occasionally occurred, but not with any regularity until the 1930s and 1940s.[52]

Social workers reached and influenced many through classes in English, courses in sewing, handicrafts, and other activities for women, the support of Italian theatre groups, summer camps for children, and the sponsoring of political and social clubs for men. Along with public schools, social workers and settlement houses offered alternate channels of contact with the American community to those provided by American political bosses, Italian *prominenti,* bankers, and padroni. Some reformers sought to establish and support free employment agencies for immigrants and to destroy the padrone labor system, while others worked to procure the passage of child labor laws and strict observance of compulsory education legislation.[53]

Italian immigrants won notoriety (and the wrath of social workers) because they seldom permitted their children to obtain adequate schooling. While complaining that their own lack of education kept them from getting better jobs, parents sent their offspring out to work in order to supplement family incomes. Although in time most Italians complied with minimum requirements of compulsory education laws, they secured jobs for their children after school hours. When Italian children reached the legal withdrawal age of fourteen, they were "to an alarmingly high degree" withdrawn from school and put to work.[54]

Despite dire predictions that Italians, caught in a "cycle of poverty," would remain destitute and a burden to society, by 1900 they had begun progressing from unskilled labor into commercial, trade and professional classes, including printing, bricklaying, carpentering, import and export, banking, law, and medicine.[55] Notwithstanding complaints of reformers and laments of immigrant workers about education, financial success at this time did not depend entirely on schooling; ambition, hard work, and cunning could, and did, overcome illiteracy.[56] Crime, one means of economic advancement independent of education, social background, and political connections, provided for all classes of Italians opportunities for quick and substantial monetary gain and sometimes for social and political gains as well. Within the colony bankers and padrone labor agents, blackhanders and other lawbreakers all realized small but important profits by swindling or terrorizing compatriots. The "syndicate," business operations reaping vast profits from the American community, offered almost limitless opportunities within the hierarchy. Thus, for some, crime offered means of advancement inside the ethnic community and for others, opportunities outside it.[57]

By the same process that many Americans believed Italians to be naturally criminal, contemporaries assumed that certain nationalities were predisposed to a particular occupation because of inborn traits or old-world influences. The Irish, for example, were "natural politicians," although comparison with Irish experiences in other parts of the world would have challenged this belief. Irish immigrants and their children did not achieve political successes in London, Liverpool, or other urban centers in England and Scotland (to which Irish immigration was "more numerous though less celebrated" than to American cities) comparable to their achievements in New York, Chicago, and other cities in the United States.[58] Opportunities for political success were simply not present for Irish immigrants in England and Scotland, and Irish preeminence in American political life, like the later prominence of Italians in crime and Jews in the clothing industry, was due primarily to availability of opportunity rather than to inborn characteristics or old-world habits.[59]

VI

Willingly or unwillingly, immigrants began the process of assimilation as soon as they arrived in the urban environment. The community and its institutions fulfilled the function not of prolonging old-world traits and patterns, but of providing important first steps in introducing newcomers to American life, and they did so most effectively. Schools and settlement houses introduced many directly to middle-class ideas and living patterns and thus served as an outside force influencing the second generation and some of the more independent newcomers. Economic achievement played a vital role in furthering adjustment as well as in spurring movement out of early ethnic districts. Over the passage of years newcomers and their children moved up the economic ladder, progressing from unskilled labor into commercial, trade, and professional lines. Channels of progress also appeared within organized labor and politics, while criminal activities provided a lucrative means of financial advancement, both within the Italian colony and in the larger urban environment. Critics complained of the slow upward progress of the immigrants, and compared Italians (and other "new" groups) with their predecessors, ignoring the fact that the "old" elements arrived in Chicago and other northern cities considerably earlier than did the bulk of Italians, Russian Jews, Poles, Lithuanians, and Greeks. They thus had the opportunity, as sociologist Richard Ford has pointed out, of profiting economically and socially in cities that had not developed rigid political or financial patterns. "The process of acculturation," notes Ford, "has been going on considerably longer for the Swedish, German and Irish immigrants than for the Italians and Russians."[60]

Like most recent immigrants, Italians appeared to move outward from the urban core more slowly and reluctantly than had Irish, Germans, and other older groups. Contemporaries did not see the extensive amount of residential mobility among Italians and other late arrivals. From the early years of residence, movement took place not only inside colonies and from one community to another, but also from the early, centrally located districts toward outlying areas of the city and even into suburbs. By the 1920s the suburban trend was noticeable and significant. World War I and the immigration laws of 1921 and 1924 closed new sources of immigration, and Italian districts began perceptibly to decline. The cumulative effect, noted by sociologist Harvey W. Zorbaugh in the late 1920s, was that "few Italians are coming to America . . . . The community without any influx from the old country is fast becoming Americanized." Depression in the 1930s and housing shortages in the 1940s slowed the pace of this dispersion from the ethnic colony, but it has again accelerated since 1950.[61]

■ ■ ■ ■ **Notes**

1 A sampling of available literature includes: Frank Julian Warne, *The Immigrant Invasion* (New York, 1913); M. Victor Safford, *Immigration* (Boston, 1912); Jacob A. Riis, *How the Other Half Lives* (New York, 1890); Samuel P. Orth, *Our Foreigners* (New Haven, Conn., 1920); Henry Cabot Lodge, "Efforts to Restrict Undesirable Immigration," *Century Magazine*, LXVII (January, 1904), 466–469; Frank E. Sargent, "The Need of Closer Inspection and Greater Restriction of Immigration," *Century Magazine*, LXVII (January, 1904), 470–473.

2 William I. Thomas and Florian Znaniecki, *The Polish Peasant in Europe and America*, I (Chicago, 1918), pp. 87–89; Edward C. Banfield, *The Moral Basis of a Backward Society* (Glencoe, Ill., 1958), p. 10. Among others who accept the Banfield position are Herbert J. Gans, *The Urban Villagers: Group and Class in the Life of Italian-Americans* (New York, 1962), p. 203 and Norman Kogan, *The Politics of Italian Foreign Policy* (New York, 1963), pp. 4–5.

3 Statement by Dr. A. J. Lendino, quoted in William Foote White, "Social Organization in the Slums," *American Sociological Review*, VIII (February, 1943), 36.

4 U. S. Senate, *Reports of the Immigration Commission*, XXVI (1911); George La Piana, *The Italians in Milwaukee, Wisconsin* (Milwaukee, 1915); Frederick A. Bushee, "Italian Immigrants in Boston," *Arena*, XVII (April, 1897), 722–734; Walter I. Firey, *Land Use in Central Boston* (Cambridge, Mass., 1947), chap. v; Charles Loring Brace, *The Dangerous Classes of New York* (New York, 1872), chap. xvii; Charlotte Adams, "Italian Life in New York," *Harper's Magazine*, LXII (April, 1881), 676–684; Charles W. Coulter, *The Italians of Cleveland* (Cleveland, 1919).

5 U. S. Commissioner of Labor, *Ninth Special Report. The Italians in Chicago, A Social and Economic Study* (1897); Frank O. Beck, "The Italian in Chicago," *Bulletin of the Department of Public Welfare of Chicago*, II, No. 3 (February, 1919), 2–12; Alessandro Mastro-Valerio (at times Mastrovalerio, Mastro Valerio, and Valerio), "Remarks upon the Italian Colony in Chicago," *Hull House Maps and Papers* (New York, 1895), pp. 131–139; Edith Abbott and Sophonisba P. Breckinridge,

"Chicago Housing Conditions, IV, The West Side Revisited," *American Journal of Sociology,* XVII (July, 1911), 1–34; Grace Norton, "Chicago Housing Conditions, VII. Two Italian Districts," *American Journal of Sociology,* XVIII (January, 1913), 509–542; Natalie Walker, "Chicago Housing Conditions, X. Greeks and Italians in the Neighborhood of Hull House," *American Journal of Sociology,* XXI (November, 1915), 285–316; Esther Quaintance, "Rents and Housing Conditions in the Italian District of the Lower North Side of Chicago," unpublished Master's thesis, University of Chicago, 1925.

6 Observations based on examination of marriage records of parishes in Italian communities.

7 Edith Abbott, *The Tenements of Chicago, 1908–1935* (Chicago, 1936), p. 97, maintained that while the second generation was moving from immigrant colonies to communities such as Columbus Park and Oak Park, many members of immigrant generations refused to move away from "the Italian church and their circle of old village cronies."

8 Jane Addams, *Newer Ideals of Peace* (New York, 1907), p. 67; Chicago Department of Public Welfare, *First Semi-Annual Report to the Mayor and Aldermen of the City of Chicago* (Chicago, 1915), p. 89. Residential mobility patterns are examined in a forthcoming book.

9 New York City was a possible exception, but there is every reason to believe that the remarks that follow in the text apply to that city as well. See, for example, Leo Grebler, *Housing Market Behavior in a Declining Area* (New York, 1952), pp. 135–137, 245–246, on Manhattan's lower east side Italian community during the period from 1910 to 1930.

10 Robert Hunter, *Tenement Conditions in Chicago. Report of the City Homes Association* (Chicago, 1901), pp. 56, 188, 195–196; Ernest W. Burgess and Charles Newcomb (eds.), *Census Data of the City of Chicago, 1920* (Chicago, 1931).

11 I. W. Howerth, "Are the Italians a Dangerous Class?" *Charities Review,* IV (November, 1894), 40. The U. S. Bureau of Immigration published *Agricultural Opportunities. Information Concerning Resources, Products and Physical Characteristics* [of various states] (Washington, 1912–1920). Under the direction of Alessandro Mastro-Valerio, the Agricultural Section of the Italian Chamber of Commerce of Chicago was very active in its efforts to settle Italians in rural colonies located in the southern states. See also A. H. Stone, "Italian Cottongrowers in Arkansas," *American Monthly Review of Reviews,* No. 35 (February, 1907), 209–213; L. Mathews, "Tontitown," *Everybody's Magazine,* No. 20 (January, 1909), 3–13; G. Rossati, "La colonizzazione negli stati di Mississippi, Louisiana ed Alabama," *Bollettino dell'Emigrazione* (Hereafter *Boll. Emig.*), No. 14 (1904), 3–30; G. Moroni, "Gli italiani in Tangipahoa," *Boll. Emig.,* No. 7 (1910), 3–6; Luigi Villari, "Gli italiani nel distretto consolare di New Orleans," *Boll. Emig.,* No. 20 (1907), 3–46; U. S. Congress, *Industrial Commission,* XV (1901), 405–507; U. S. Senate, *Immigration Commission,* XXI.

12 Adolfo Rossi, "Per la tutela degli italiani negli Stati Uniti," *Boll. Emig.,* No. 16 (1904), 74–80; *Hull House: A Social Settlement, An Outline Sketch* (pamphlet dated February 1, 1894), p. 21; Florence Kelley, "The Settlements: Their Lost Opportunity," *Charities and the Commons,* XVI, No. 1 (April 7, 1906), 80; Alberto Pecorini, "The Italian as an Agricultural Laborer," *Annals of the American Academy of Political and Social Science,* XXXIII (March, 1909), 383–384.

13 John R. Commons, *Races and Immigrants in America* (New York, 1907), pp. 133, 166.

14 Commons, pp. 167–168.

15 U. S. Congress, Senate, *Report from the Committee on Immigration,* 54th Congress, 1st Session, 1896, Rept. 290, p. 9; Lodge, 468. See also Jeremiah W. Jenks and W. Jett Lauck, *The Immigration Problem* (New York, 1912). The authors argued

on the basis of the findings of the U. S. Immigration Commission, of which both were members, that the "old" immigration naturally went into agriculture while the "new" immigrants remained in the cities (p. 26).

16 U. S. Congress, *Industrial Commission*, XV, 497. Mastro-Valerio's argument was open to question, as he himself ought to have recognized, since both colonies that he founded in Alabama failed. For a view similar to Mastro-Valerio's see G. E. Di Palma Castiglione, "Italian Immigration into the United States, 1901–4," *American Journal of Sociology*, XI (September, 1905), 183–206.

17 Giovanni Preziosi, *Gl'italiani negli Stati Uniti del Nord* (Milan, 1909), p. 81.

18 Robert F. Foerster, *The Italian Emigration of Our Times* (Cambridge, Mass., 1919), pp. 370–371.

19 U. S. Congress, *Industrial Commission*, XIX (1902), 969–971.

20 Frank Thistlethwaite, "Migration from Europe Overseas in the Nineteenth and Twentieth Centuries," *Population Movements in Modern European History* (ed. Herbert Moller; New York, 1954), reprinted from *XIe Congrès International des Sciences Historiques, Stockholm, 1960, Rapports V: Histoire Contemporaire*, p. 91; Walter F. Willcox, *Studies in American Demography* (Ithaca, 1940), pp. 159, 169, 174. This is from chap. x, "The Foreign-Born," which is largely a reprint of an earlier article by Willcox, "The Distribution of Immigration in the United States," *Quarterly Journal of Economics*, XX (August, 1906), 523–546.

21 Pauline Young, "Social Problems in the Education of the Immigrant Child," *American Sociological Review*, I, No. 3 (June, 1936), 419–429. P. 420 discusses urban adjustment problems of rural Americans.

22 Sargent, 470.

23 Robert E. Park, "Cultural Aspects of Immigration. Immigrant Heritages," *Proceedings of the National Conference of Social Work*, XLVIII (1921), 494; John Foster Carr, "The Coming of the Italian," *Outlook*, LXXXII (February 24, 1906), 429.

24 Edith Abbott and Sophonisba P. Breckinridge, *The Delinquent Child and the Home* (New York, 1912), p. 55. Constantine M. Panunzio, himself an immigrant, wrote of an Italian colony in which he had resided in Boston: "This was in no way a typical American community, neither did it resemble Italy." *The Soul of an Immigrant* (New York, 1922), p. 231.

25 Grace Abbott, *The Problem of Immigration in Massachusetts. Report of the Commission on Immigration* (Boston, 1914), pp. 202–207, presented an examination of the various institutions mentioned here among Greeks, Italians, Jews, Lithuanians, Poles, and Syrians in Massachusetts. Robert E. Park, "Foreign Language Press and Social Progress," *Proceedings of the National Conference of Social Work*, XLVII (1920), 494. On the foreign-language press among other immigrant groups see Thomas Capek, *The Czechs in America* (Boston, 1920), pp. 172–173 and Edmund G. Olszyk, *The Polish Press in America* (Milwaukee, 1940).
The padrone and the immigrant banker are examined in detail elsewhere and will not be discussed here. For an analysis of the activities and role in the community of the former see Humbert S. Nelli, "The Italian Padrone System in the United States," *Labor History*, V, No. 2 (Spring, 1964), 153–167, and of the latter, Nelli, "Italians and Crime in Chicago: The Formative Years, 1890–1921," *American Journal of Sociology*, LXXIV, No. 3 (January, 1969), 380–382.

26 Rudolph J. Vecoli, "*Contadini* in Chicago: A Critique of *The Uprooted*," *Journal of American History*, LI, No. 3 (December, 1964), 412, cites as proof an article which appeared in one of Chicago's Italian-language newspapers, *L'Unione Italiana*, on March 18, 1868. This date was at least ten years before southern Italians became an important element in Chicago and other urban centers.

27 William E. Davenport, "The Exodus of a Latin People," *Charities*, XII, No. 18 (May 7, 1904), 466, and Banfield, pp. 16–17.

28 J. S. McDonald, "Italy's Rural Social Structure and Emigration," *Occidente*, XII

(September–October, 1956), 443–446; Daniel L. Horowitz, *The Italian Labor Movement* (Cambridge, Mass., 1963), p. 12. The Italian background of the mutual benefit society is discussed in Edwin Fenton's excellent "Immigrants and Unions, A Case Study: Italians and American Labor, 1870–1920," unpublished Ph.D. dissertation, Harvard University, 1957. See also two sources on which Fenton relied heavily: Renaldo Rigola, *Storia del Movimento Operaio Italiano* (Milan, 1946), pp. 9–22, and Humbert L. Gualtieri, *The Labor Movement in Italy* (New York, 1946), p. 137.

29 J. Owen Stalson, *Marketing Life Insurance: Its History in America* (Cambridge, Mass., 1942), pp. 446–449; Josef M. Baernreither, *English Associations of Working Men* (London, 1889), chap. i, "Origins and General Character of Friendly Societies."

30 Antonio Mangano, "The Associated Life of the Italians in New York City," Charities, XII, No. 18 (May 7, 1904), 479–480; G. Abbott, pp. 202–206; Giovanni E. Schiavo, *The Italians in Chicago: A Study in Americanization* (Chicago, 1928), p. 59. On the vital importance of death benefits to immigrants, see Robert E. Park and Herbert A. Miller, *Old World Traits Transplanted* (New York, 1921), pp. 124–128.

31 "Le Società italiane all'estero," *Bollettino de Ministero degli Affari Esteri* (April, 1898), 7; "Le Societa italiane all'estero nel 1908," *Boll. Emig.*, No. 24 (1908), viii; "Le Societa italiane negli Stati Uniti del'America del Nord nel 1910," *Boll. Emig.*, No. 4 (1912), 20.

32 Luigi Carnovale, *Il Giornalismo degli emigrati italiani nel Nord America* (Chicago, 1909), p. 34; also pp. 33, 74, 77. Carnovale worked for *La Tribuna Italiana Transatlantica* in Chicago, *Il Pensiere* and *La Gazzetta Illustrata* (a magazine) in St. Louis.

33 *The Bulletin* (later changed to *The Interpreter*), I, No. 9 (December, 1922), 10, noted that not only did American-born children of immigrants prefer to read American papers, but also that "the foreign-born . . . as soon as they have acquired sufficient English, turn to the American papers for American and general news, depending on the press of their language for little more than news of the home country."

34 Carnovale, *Il Giornalismo*, pp. 33–34, 74, 77; Giuseppe Prezzolini, *I trapiantati* (Milan, 1963), pp. 62–63. These remarks refer specifically, of course, to the bourgeois press. Anarchist, religious, and socialist papers reached a very small and specialized audience.

35 *La Tribuna Italiana Transatlantica*, Jan. 14, 1905; June 4 and 18, July 2, Aug. 13 and 20, 1904; Apr. 22, 1905; Oct. 27, 1906; Aug. 24, Nov. 9, 1907; Feb. 29, 1908; *L'Italia* (Chicago), Nov. 1, 1890. Italian resentment over Irish control of the Church in the United States was shared by other Catholic groups as well. On the "Americanist controversy" see Thomas T. McAvoy, C.S.C., *The Great Crisis in American Catholic History, 1895–1900* (Chicago, 1957); Robert D. Cross, *The Emergence of Liberal Catholicism in America* (Cambridge, Mass., 1958); Colman J. Barry, O.S.B., *The Catholic Church and German Americans* (Milwaukee, 1953).

36 Laurence Franklin, "The Italian in America: What he Has Been, What he Shall Be," *Catholic World*, LXXI (April, 1900), 72–73.

37 D. Lynch, "The Religious Condition of Italians in New York," *America*, X, No. 24 (March 21, 1914), 558. At least 25 articles appeared in *America*, *American Ecclesiastical Review*, and *Catholic World*, the leading Catholic scholarly reviews, during the years between 1900 and 1921.

38 *La Fiaccola* (New York), Sept. 10, 1914; Sept. 19, 1912. See "Vatican Notes," a regular weekly feature of the journal. "The Vatican and Italy," Oct. 3, 1912, described the struggle between the Italian state and the Church. "Italian Evangelical Chronicle" was a regular feature devoted to Protestant activities among Italian

immigrants in various cities of the U.S. On the growth of Protestantism among Italians see "The Secret of Our Success," Oct. 31, 1912, and "The Italian Mission," Oct. 24, 1912.

39 Aurelio Palmieri, "Italian Protestantism in the United States," *Catholic World,* CVII (May, 1918), 177–189; Antonio Mangano, *Sons of Italy: A Social and Religious Study of the Italians in America* (New York, 1917); Enrico C. Sartorio, *Social and Religious Life of Italians in America* (Boston, 1918); William P. Shriver, *Immigrant Forces: Factors in the New Democracy* (New York, 1913); Mary Clark Barnes and Lemuel Call Barnes, *The New America: A Study in Immigration* (New York, 1913).

40 Local Community Research Committee, *Chicago Communities,* III, "The Lower North Side," Document 27; Howard B. Grose, *Aliens or Americans?* (New York, 1906), p. 256; *Literary Digest,* No. 47 (October 11, 1913), 636.

41 *La Fiaccola,* Aug. 26, 1920; Joseph Schuyler, S. J., *Northern Parish: A Sociological and Pastoral Study* (Chicago, 1960), p. 228.

42 Thus bourgeois and proletarian papers alike condemned the pope's temporal claims in Italy, the former primarily out of loyalty to the Kingdom. Protestant as well as leftwing journals fully upheld the Kingdom, in part to embarrass the Church and in part to further their own particular objectives. *L'Italia,* Sept. 15, 1888; Oct. 20, Nov. 5, 1890; *Il Progresso Italo-Americano* (New York), Nov. 3, 1890; Apr. 30, 1895; *La Tribuna Italiana Transatlantica,* Oct. 27, 1906; *La Fiaccola,* Jan. 30, Feb. 13 and 27, 1913; *Il Proletario* (Philadelphia), Sept. 15, 1911; *La Parola dei Socialisti* (Chicago), Sept. 27, 1913.

43 A. Di Domenica, "The Sons of Italy in America," *Missionary Review of the World,* XLI (March, 1918), 193.

44 Vecoli, 415. On the situation in Italy see Joseph M. Sorrentino, S. J., "Religious Conditions in Italy," *America,* XII, No. 1 (October 17, 1914), 6–7.

45 Robert A. Woods (ed.), *Americans in Process* (Boston, 1902), pp. 228–229. Such celebrations met strong opposition from liberals and socialists within the Italian community. *La Tribuna Italiana Transatlantica,* Aug. 5 and 12, 1905; *Il Proletario* (Philadelphia), Aug. 11, 1909; *La Parola dei Socialisti* (Chicago), Nov. 8, 1913.

46 François Houtart, *Aspects Sociologiques du catholicisme américain* (Paris, 1957), pp. 204–206.

47 Andrew Shipman, "Immigration," *Official Report of the Second American Catholic Missionary Congress, 1913* (Chicago, 1914), pp. 154–171; Aaron I. Abell, *American Catholicism and Social Action: A Search for Social Justice* (New York, 1960), especially chap. v.

48 Park, 495; Park and Miller, pp. 147–151. This last is a discussion of a colony of Sicilians living much as they did in their home village of Cinisi, a situation of note in the United States because of its uniqueness.

49 C. A. Price, "Immigration and Group Settlement," *The Cultural Integration of Immigrants* (ed. W. D. Borrie; Paris, 1959), pp. 267–268; Prezzolini, p. 63; Caroline F. Ware, "Cultural Groups in the United States," *The Cultural Approach to History* (ed. C. F. Ware; New York, 1940), pp. 62–65.

50 Foerster, p. 395. This third group of immigrants, comprised of those who adjusted quietly and with a minimum of difficulty, did not attract the attention of Americans.

51 John Palmer Gavit, *Americans by Choice* (New York, 1922), p. 372: J. T. Salter, *Boss Rule* (New York, 1935), pp. 75–86; Humbert S. Nelli, "John Powers and the Italians: Politics in a Chicago Ward, 1896–1921," *Journal of American History,* LVII (June, 1970), 67–84.

52 See Arthur Mann, *La Guardia: A Fighter Against His Times: 1882–1933* (Philadelphia, 1959), pp. 109–116; Samuel Lubell, *The Future of American Politics* (3rd ed., rev.; New York, 1965), pp. 77–83.

53 Federal Writers' Project, Works Progress Administration, *The Italians of New York* (New York, 1938), pp. 105–107; Coulter, pp. 32–34; Edward Corsi, *In the Shadow of Liberty* (New York, 1935), pp. 25–28; Jane Addams, *Twenty Years at Hull House* (New York, 1910), chaps. x and xiii.

54 Alberto Pecorini, *Cli Americani nella vita moderna osservati da un italiano* (Milan, 1909), pp. 397–398; Sophia Moses Robison, *Can Delinquency be Measured* (New York, 1936), pp. 143–144; Beck, 9. On attitudes toward education in southern Italy see Leonard Covello, "The Social Background of the Italo-American School Child, A Study of the Southern Italian Family Mores and their Effect on the School Situation in America," unpublished Ph.D. dissertation, New York University, 1944, p. 399.

55 Carr, 429; Alberto Pecorini, "The Italians in the United States," *The Forum,* XLV (January, 1911), 21–24; U.S. Congress, *Industrial Commission,* XV, 435–436; U.S. Senate, *Immigration Commission,* XXVIII, 169–176; Edwin Fenton, "Italians in the Labor Movement," *Pennsylvania History,* XXVI, No. 2 (April, 1959), 113–148 and "Italian Workers in the Stoneworkers Union," *Labor History,* III, No. 2 (Spring, 1962), 188–207.

56 Filippo Lussana, *Lettere di illetterati* (Bologna, 1913); Letter from Grace Abbott to Julia Lathrop, January 14, 1913, located in The Papers of Edith and Grace Abbott, University of Chicago, Box 57, Folder 7.

57 Nelli, "Italians and Crime in Chicago: The Formative Years, 1890–1920," 373–391.

58 Cecil Woodham Smith, *The Great Hunger* (New York, 1962), p. 266. For the presentation of a widely held (although exaggerated) view that the Irish dominated American urban politics, see John Paul Bocock, "The Irish Conquest of Our Cities," *Forum,* XVII (April, 1894), 186–195.

59 On the role of the American environment in Italian criminal activity see William S. Bennet, "Immigrants and Crime," *Annals of the American Academy of Political and Social Science,* XXXIV, No. 1 (July, 1909), 120–121, and Nelli, "Italians and Crime in Chicago: The Formative Years, 1890–1920," 386–391.

60 Richard C. Ford, "Population Succession in Chicago," *American Journal of Sociology,* LVI (September, 1950), 160. It is tempting to compare the Italian experience with that of the American Negro. For Italians, as well as for other European immigrant groups, settlement in core area ethnic colonies formed the vital first step in the assimilation process. The core community has also functioned effectively for Negroes from the American rural South, but the process has typically ended at that point. The basic reason for this difference between the immigrant and the Negro urban experience was described in 1931 by a federal committee investigation of Negro housing conditions. In the case of the immigrant who had learned American speech and habits within the core community, movement "to more desirable sections of the city" was possible. "In the case of Negroes, who remain a distinguishable group, the factor of race and certain definite racial attitudes favorable to segregation, interpose difficulties to . . . breaking physical restrictions in residence areas." The President's Conference on Home Building and Home Ownership, *Report of the Committee on Negro Housing* (1931), p. 5. As historian Gilbert Osofsky observed in his recent study, *Harlem: The Making of a Ghetto. Negro New York, 1890–1930* (New York, 1966), p. 131, this situation has continued to exist.

61 Local Community Research Committee, *Chicago Communities,* III, "The Lower North Side," Document 30 (excerpts from the notes of Harvey W. Zorbaugh). A similar situation existed elsewhere in urban America. See Caroline F. Ware, *Greenwich Village, 1920–1930. A Comment on American Civilization in the Post-War Years* (Boston, 1935), pp. 156–157.

10
The Study of Corruption

ERIC L. MC KITRICK

Eric McKitrick's following essay is an excellent example of fruitful use by an historian of concepts developed in another discipline, in this case political sociology. McKitrick employs Robert Merton's model of the structure and functions of the political machine to raise questions about and to order the data for twentieth-century urban political history. In so doing, he throws considerable light on American political culture, on the relations between government and legitimate and illegitimate business, on social welfare, and on the complex interlocking of crime, corruption, and social mobility.

The tone and content of the essay reflect the time of its writing, the 1950s—those years of the Eisenhower administration when the "bland were leading the bland." Like the American people generally, historians and other scholars emphasized the successes of American society more than its failures. They assumed the nation's problems were not very great to begin with and, in any case, were in the process of improvement if not solution. Note McKitrick's discussion of the welfare problem: scientific welfare had replaced the indiscriminate charity of the political bosses. Scarcely anyone today would view our welfare system in such a positive light. The 1954 school desegregation decision led men of good will to believe that our racial problems would soon disappear, and that Negroes and Puerto Ricans would follow the patterns of other immigrant groups in upward social mobility.

The reader might compare this essay to Nathan Glazer and Daniel Moynihan's article on New York written at the end of the 1960s after so many assumptions of the 1950s had proved false. But McKitrick is worth reading for reasons other than simply understanding the mood of the 1950s. He effectively demonstrates the historian's role in studying change over time, and shows how, in order to accomplish this function best, the historian can, and indeed must, borrow relevant concepts from the social sciences.

■ ■ ■ ■ For Further Reading

Lincoln Steffens, *The Shame of the Cities* (New York: Hill and Wang, 1957) is the classic muckraking study of municipal government at the turn of the century. Moisei Ostrogorski, *Democracy and the Organization of Political Parties,* vol. II, *The United States,* edited and abridged by Seymour Martin Lipset (New York: Doubleday Anchor Books, 1964) presents the penetrating observations of a European scholar on the heyday of municipal bossism. Walton Bean, *Boss Ruef's San Francisco* (Berkeley and Los Angeles: University of California Press, 1952) is a study of one of the most famous municipal graft prosecutions in American history. Robert K. Merton, *Social Theory and Social Structure* (New York: The Free Press, 1957) contains his essay on the

"Latent Functions of the Machine." Merton used Steffens and others to construct his model. James F. Richardson, *The New York Police: Colonial Times to 1901* (New York: Oxford University Press, 1970) has considerable material on the continuing relations between illegitimate enterprise, the political structure, and the police. Edward N. Costikyan, *Behind Closed Doors: Politics in the Public Interest* (New York: Harvest Books, 1966) is a perceptive reform Democratic leader's personal view of the current state of municipal government, including corruption.

■ The investigation of corruption (in the analytical sense) does not seem to present a subject of very intense interest to social scientists these days. Past research in this area has for the most part taken its stimulus from a basic commitment to *reform,* rather than from the intrinsic charm of the subject, and most of it has tended to be done during times when a general concern with reform was fairly high. We are not living in such a period today. Actually such periods have been very productive, yielding rich materials in the form of journalism, histories, memoirs of reformers, and treatises on "good government" which, in their very devotion to the overthrow of the "machine" system, could hardly help producing, in the course of things, a number of insights into the nature of that system. Such bursts of energy have, in their turn, even begotten certain idiosyncratic by-products, such as an occasional "apology" for the system, or occasional sympathetic sketches of the more legendary "bosses," showing the genial side of their activities—all of which has not only multiplied the raw data, but has also given them depth.[1]

It may be regrettable—in the interest of sustained energy—that the moral tensions which formerly served to foster such investigation are at present so noticeably relaxed. But, on the other hand, there may also be reason to think that this very relaxed emotional climate itself offers a peculiarly promising setting in which future work might take a new and fruitful turn. In this setting, we are now able to recognize that further "reform" activity, for its own sake, will probably yield us very little that we do not already have in the way of insights; it is difficult, for instance, to mistake the indiscriminate Kefauver diggings for much that resembles "knowledge." Moreover, in this setting, we have perceived that, amid the conflicting claims of a disorderly democratic political society, the corrupt machine system has historically performed certain stabilizing functions: it was David Riesman who referred to the local politician as "soaked in gravy which we can well afford." And finally, it is in this same setting of detachment that we are free to appreciate the attributes of that remarkable technician—and gentleman—DeSapio of Tammany Hall. These, at any rate, are a few of the straws in the wind.[2]

What we ought to see in the future—assuming a picking-up of interest —will be various studies in which political machines and their auxiliary activities are examined in a structural and functional way: that is, in terms of such questions as, what have they done for society—how do they work

—what gaps have they filled in our political life—what has been needed to maintain them—what are the limits within which they have had to operate —what sort of future may be expected for them?

The closest approach to a theoretical model for dealing with such questions has been that offered by Robert K. Merton in his *Social Theory and Social Structure*,[3] and no new investigation could very well afford not to take this model as its starting point. So far as I know, very little, if anything, has been done with it. I am not even sure that it has been subjected to critical examination.

An important thing to note with regard to the Merton scheme is that it seems to have been postulated for what might be called a "classical" period in the history of American machine politics. The most perceptive field work ever done in this area is still probably that of Lincoln Steffens—and since it is from Steffens that Mr. Merton has taken his major cues, it is inevitable that the balance and arrangement of his categories should be most appropriate to a state of things which existed about fifty years ago: a period roughly centering on the year 1905.

This is not meant to intimate that the model does not apply today. It is valid and accurate in all its major details. It is so set up that any alterations in it would have to be more in the nature of refinements than of basic changes. But the subject matter itself has changed in a great many ways since Steffens' time, and I emphasize this in order to make my key point. In the absence of outside stimuli—such as a general public interest in "reform" (or, for that matter, a primary *need* for reform)—pressure for new work and new insights will have to come from somewhere within the social sciences, and, specifically, I would say that it will have to come from the field of American history. Its raw data will be found in the form of substantial materials which must now be called "historical": material covering the period in which our cities underwent their most phenomenal phases of growth—material which dates back at least to the end of the Civil War. Any theoretical model for the explanation of social phenomena has a tendency, in spite of all precautions, to be static. But if there is anything about our social scene that is insistently dynamic, it is the tempo of our political life—and to get the sense of dynamism in political structures (that is, *change,* and the things that produce it), one needs the sense of time. We know a great deal about the functions of such structures at given points in time. But of equal, if not greater, importance to political sociology today is the course of transformation which these structures—these "machines"—have undergone over the past two generations. This is now what makes "history" such a vital dimension. An understanding of such change, and of the reasons for it, is bound to "feed back" into one's understanding and judgment of the very functions themselves.

What are—or have been—these "functions"? To repeat, they have been no better itemized than by Mr. Merton, and probably the best way to set up points of reference for the present discussion would be to recapitulate very briefly the principal elements of his model.

A "structural context" is first established: a general setting or environment in which, for one reason or another, the "need" for such an establishment as the political machine has arisen. The principal element in this environment is the diffusion and fragmentation of power—and therefore of responsibility—which tends to be inherent in a transitory, non-authoritarian, elected, democratic officialdom. It is easy to see how this could emerge as a critical limitation in the mushrooming cities of the United States during the seventies, eighties, and nineties, amid an urban life proliferating in complexity and tangled with a bewildering maze of conflicting needs and claims. Here an alternative, informal focus of responsibility was located in the "boss," a leader of unofficial executive status who had a freedom and flexibility made possible by his ability to work, as it were, in the back room. Another element in this context—if I myself may add one—would be the fact that any organization of a political nature which did have the power and numbers to furnish these needs and umpire these claims was bound to have no more than a semiprofessional status. Such an organization, constantly requiring money to keep itself going, would have to derive a certain amount of it from sources no more than quasi-official in nature. All this would follow in the absence of centralized, professionalized, bureaucratic traditions of administration.[4]

In this setting, Mr. Merton enumerates four of the major "latent functions" which have been performed by the machine system, in relation to the various subgroups making up its constituency. The first of these functions involves various kinds of welfare services for the poor and powerless; such services would include the widest range of things—food, jobs, intercession with the law in times of difficulty, and so forth. Their price, quite logically, would be votes. Another set of functions appears in response to some of the manifold and perennial problems of business men—such problems as the need of smaller business men for protection against each other, the occasional need of larger business men to have cumbersome and expensive projects expedited, and the constant need of all classes of business men for unofficial protection against a snarl of contradictory and overlapping laws, codes and regulations. The prices here, graded as they would be according to the services, add up to "routine graft"—the "oil" that keeps the machine in running order. A third type of function is one which requires a certain conceptual subtlety to recognize. For certain critical ethnic groups, and for groups situated in lower social brackets generally, the large urban political machine has traditionally afforded very important channels of social mobility—avenues to personal advancement—which would doubtless otherwise be closed.[5] For example, the availability of careers in politics served as a significant safety valve for the surplus social energies of the New York Irish from the 1870s on. The price which these groups were asked to pay was, from their viewpoint, hardly excessive: unstinting party loyalty—unquestioning devotion to the organization. A final category of functions is one in which services analogous to those performed for "legitimate" business were also made available to the underworld—to "illegitimate" business. Here the machine could actually operate as a kind of stabilizing mechanism: by maintaining communication—and actual connections—with the underworld, it could act as an umpire for activities carried on outside the law; it maintained, in effect, a measure of control; it could set standards and define limits. The price, of course, was the familiar "protection money"—the kickback.

Such, then, is the pattern. To what extent does it hold today? It is a pattern whose formal outlines are still in some way to be recognized in all our major cities. However, the specific activities and operations represented by these formal categories have been so immeasurably altered and transformed as to change the very *symmetry* of the pattern, and to raise certain very crucial questions. Has the old system for practical purposes (as some writers have begun to assert) really "broken down"? Or does it continue to operate within a more limited area? What has been the effect of the reform tradition? Has the boss "gone straight"? What kinds of loyalties can the machine command today? What kinds of things can it still do—and are there things that it can no longer do?

Certain kinds of historical problems immediately suggest themselves—problems having to do with the *persistence* of the "corrupt machine." For instance: under what conditions has it been possible for a reform movement to be successful? We find that it has never quite been a matter of civic affairs reaching a given point of "rottenness," with the honest citizens at that point making common cause to strike down the machine. What seems to have been required, as a matter of historical experience, is the combining of other factors, fairly complex and not always easy to identify. Such factors include points at which the machine has ceased to serve its clients responsibly—points at which services could no longer be considered worth the prices asked. The arrival of hard times could quickly precipitate such a situation. An even more sensitive point could be the one at which (for whatever reason) the machine's internal solidarity had become weakened—because of power struggles, some temporary loss of internal responsibility, perhaps a weakening of loyalties resulting from inequitable distribution of spoils. Variations on these themes will be found, if one is looking for them, recurring again and again in the literature. They are admirably spelled out in the downfall of the Tweed machine. Here we see the Boss having lost all bearings, all sense of proportion, launching a series of insane depredations, and alienating his followers by refusing to distribute the loot honorably. The Ring had become virtually a *personal* operation, with Tweed's raids upon the city treasury far exceeding what could reasonably be afforded. Here, moreover, we see the critical increment of reform energy coming from *within:* Samuel Tilden's success was in large measure due to strategic assistance from the Tammany organization, and to the invaluable inside knowledge which was the product of having himself worked, for years, with Tammany Hall.

A situation of this sort may undoubtedly be matched by numerous others —and, in fact, by still others turned, as it were, inside out. For, conversely, it may be assumed that a reform government which offers nothing as a substitute for the functions performed by the machine will find itself very shortly in a state of paralysis. The mayoralty of Seth Low in New York in the early 1900s furnishes such a case; another is found in the efforts of Joseph Folk to "reform" St. Louis in 1902; and numerous others may be located all through the reform annals of the Progressive Era.

Such might be called the "functional" approach on the simplest and most straightforward plane. But it leads into parallel problems of even greater interest and greater subtlety. Take this question: what is the function of the reform movement—not for destroying the machine but for reinvigorating it, for renewing its vitality, for *helping* it to persist? At this point the "machine" metaphor itself becomes misleading. It has in no case, apparently, been a thing that could be smashed in the way that an engine can be rendered useless by the destruction of a few key parts. Rather, its very complexity, the very functional autonomy of so many of its parts, makes it more like an *organism.* For instance, solidarity at the ward level seems to persist almost by habit: Plunkitt of Tammany Hall—then a ward leader—survived the destruction of Tweed and flourished, and his experience must have been reenacted by many another in comparable circumstances. How might this be explained?

Taking this situation as the focal point for a whole range of problems, one might attempt to picture the scene at local headquarters the day after an election in which smashing victories had been won by the reform ticket. One may picture the post-mortem (a proceeding built into American politics): it would most surely include a highly critical reappraisal of the power situation in the ward—and those present would be the first to understand why the organization had lost. A further result would compare very closely with Durkheim's analysis of what happens at funerals: a ritual reaffirmation of group solidarity. Still another consequence would be that the demands normally made on the machine would (in view of lean times to come) tend to drop off. Therefore—assuming that the lean period did not last too long—it might be predicted that the aftermath of defeat would coincide with precisely that phase of the machine's greatest moral solidarity.[6] Some highly interesting conclusions might be expected to flow from this. Granting any other functions remaining for the machine to perform—and by definition they always exist—might not these be precisely the conditions in which they would be discovered? A crude example is afforded by the breakup of the Whisky Ring in Grant's time; the "army of termites" (as

Matthew Josephson put it) promptly marched into the Post Office Department. Or, let the setting be a little less extreme and more refined: such conditions as those just described might simply serve as a test for activities whose *style* must be altered from time to time in order to remain acceptable. Boss Kelly of Chicago, according to legend, was always pleased to have Paul Douglas somewhere on the scene; his use of Douglas was as a standing threat to "any of the boys who got too hungry." A final point to be made along these lines is that the very informal nature of the machine will set limits at *any* time upon its stability—which would mean that its internal leadership must remain aggressive and dynamic to keep from being unhorsed by disaffected henchmen. The most natural alliance that an insurgent group could reach for would be an alliance with reformers. Other factions standing by could then, like Lord Stanley on Bosworth field, take their choice. The machine, in other words, has been anything but a torpid institution: a perennial state of internal "yeastiness" has made it a dynamic one.

Another set of problems, in which historical analysis and the use of historical materials are indispensable, would have to do with *long-term* changes in the entire system of machine rule. Here the reform tradition must be given its due in another way, for the very process of evolution in civic politics has been accompanied by reform groups taking up the slack and calling the turn as change occurs. The city manager and city commission plans never quite produced—in themselves—the effects hoped for by their early exponents, but they may still be considered as symptoms of a long-term process whose tendency has been toward ever-continued extension, rationalization, and stabilization of official administrative agencies. Probably the most specific and most important single expression of this has been the extension of civil service into municipal government. Today, for example, a considerable sector of Tammany's former patronage preserves in New York City is blanketed by a very efficient system of civil service.

The notion of evolutionary change could be carried directly into the specific functions enumerated in Mr. Merton's conceptual scheme. Upon the welfare functions, for instance, time has unquestionably left its mark. Here, a considerable number of the services once performed for unassimilated immigrant groups and for the economically underprivileged are today no longer needed. The need has been eroded away by the assimilation process itself, by the development of scientific welfare on municipal and state-federal levels, and, most especially, by a relatively long period of full-employment capitalism. The result has been mobility, a constant turnover of population in urban areas—all of which has been deeply subversive of neighborhood solidarity.[7] Or, take those functions performed for legitimate business. If it is kept in mind that the protection, the controls, and the umpiring have been "*un*official," as opposed to "official," there can be little doubt as to which direction the curve has gone over time, since one of the most dramatic features of our political history since 1933 has been the extension of official public controls into every aspect of business and over all kinds of businesses. Such change is, of course, anything but absolute; the old pattern, in some form, is still there. I am only indicating what the time dimension has been doing to it.

The most fascinating changes of all, and by far the most complex and difficult to trace down, are those connected with Mr. Merton's other two functions—the functions involving social mobility and relationships with the underworld. One of the most remarkable of recent discoveries in the social sciences has been the manner in which these two areas are related—the manner in which (whether the political machine is directly involved or not) they grade into one another. Somewhere along the way a conceptual block has been removed, and we are now able to see that not only do the values of mobility, status, and respectability operate in the underworld in a way precisely analogous to their workings in the "upperworld," but also, that the extent to which the two worlds *overlap* in shared values is considerable. All of this furnishes us a final set of problems directly related to those already touched upon.

In drawing a pattern of corruption (loosely used here as a generic term for covering a wide variety of things) might it not be possible to trace not only the obvious shifts and transformations but also a pattern of *energy*? What happens when obstacles are placed in a particular area of corruption? Is the result an alternative pattern? Perhaps—but what about the stabilization of *existing* patterns? The same question could be put in another way —in terms of the social-mobility function (either in politics or the underworld) for socially deprived ethnic groups. Is there a possible correlation between the rise to social acceptability and the stabilization of particular forms of corruption in which members of these groups have specialized? Might not the very high value which American society at large sets upon mobility serve over time as a built-in check—as a stimulus for (say) "cleaning up" the rackets?[8] This surely goes back at least to the days of Plunkitt —he was the man who made the virtuous distinction between "honest" and "dishonest" graft.[9]

The Italian community of a generation ago may provide the clue to the way the mechanism works. Assume at the outset a series of status gradations all the way up through narcotics, prostitution, and ultimately gambling—and in which the gamblers would be, as it were, the "gentlemen." Costello would handle the gambling, Luciano the girls and dope. Now what has, in fact, happened between then and today? As the entire Italian community has moved up, the higher-status brackets of the underworld have apparently come under tremendous crowding and pressure (gambling at large having become almost respectable), whereas the lower grades have been vacated to unorganized riffraff. No one of comparable prestige has arisen to fill the shoes of Lucky Luciano, and probably no one will. Moving up, then, into politics, we see the New York civic scene today liberally dotted with substantial citizens of Italian origin.[10] Indeed, it appears that the same mechanism just described (simple mobility—with or without an "ethnic" dimension) has been at work within Tammany Hall itself. One of Mr. DeSapio's current problems seems to be the presence of significant numbers of liberal, civic-conscious young people working in the local clubs simply for the fun of it. The "Boss" is not finding it easy to give away what patronage he has, since the very people to be rewarded are turning out to be better placed elsewhere, in business and in the professions.[11]

Let me now return to my original point. I would like to repeat my belief that those studies which can most appropriately embrace the kinds of questions I have raised will come more and more to have a historical framework. An excellent type of investigation, simple in format but with the flexibility needed for moving into any number of related areas, would be the life-study of a machine. Here, with the historical dimension, one could get the very crucial sense of a *cycle*. For cycles are long, and they embrace much change. One might further predict that the historian to whom this kind of project will be of interest will tend more and more to come into it equipped with analytical tools which he has appropriated from elsewhere but domesticated for his own special requirements. They may not ease his task, but they will make him sensitive to a whole range of vital connections which, admittedly, past historical studies (and many "scientific" ones as well) have left untouched.[12]

I cannot resist a final question. Is the machine headed for extinction? Is it getting "cleaner and cleaner"? Conceivably not—not necessarily. New predictions could very well center on a new mobility-cycle for ethnic groups still not yet "arrived"; and this might involve a period of renewed machine activity in which the tone of politics could once more drop quite noticeably. For instance, what might happen when municipal patronage and civil service jobs are no longer attractive to (say) bright young Jewish and Italian lawyers—no longer within their dignity? One clear sign of rising mobility among Negro and Puerto Rican groups would be the appearance of substantial numbers of them in minor political leadership rôles. Along with it would come, of course, a great deal of tension as such groups increased in power and numbers, and the first phase would probably not be attractive in its quality and style. We might expect, moreover, that the very same liberal, socially conscious groups now urging a "fair shake" for our minorities may themselves soon be embarking on new reform crusades without quite realizing what was happening. It has all happened in the past.

But what *would* be happening? It would be the same process of assimilation and socialization, the same "mobility-cycle" (though they did not call it that) which was undergone by the Irish after the Civil War, and after them the Jews and Italians. It is a process full of corruption and full of vitality. What we know about *those* groups may well give us the clues we need for plotting what is still to come.

■ ■ ■ ■ **Notes**

1 The work which combines all the best in the tradition is, of course, that of Lincoln Steffens: *The Shame of the Cities* (New York, 1904), and especially the *Autobiography* (New York, 1931). Early inquiries (more or less theoretical) from a reform viewpoint are Robert C. Brooks, *Corruption in American Politics and Life* (New York, 1910); John J. Hamilton, *Government by Commission: The Dethronement of the City Boss* (New York and London, 1911); Frank J. Goodnow, *City Government in the United States* (New York, 1904); and Frederic C. Howe, *The City: The Hope of Democracy* (New York, 1906). A more recent summation of early reform efforts is Clifford W. Patton, *The Battle for Municipal Reform* (Washington, 1940). That "muckraking" itself is not quite dead, even today, is evident in Estes Kefauver's *Crime in America* (Garden City, 1951). The machine, on the other hand, had its literary apologists as early as the 1890s: Daniel Greenleaf Thompson, *Politics in a Democracy* (New York, 1893); Alfred Henry Lewis, *Richard Croker* (New York, 1901); and *The Boss* (New York, 1903). Material on Tammany Hall is very rich. It includes Denis Tilden Lynch, *"Boss" Tweed* (New York and London, 1927) and *The Wild Seventies* (New York and London, 1941); M. R. Werner, *Tammany Hall* (New York, 1928); Roy V. Peel, *The Political Clubs of New York City* (New York and London, 1935); William L. Riordon, *Plunkitt of Tammany Hall* (New York, 1948); and especially Lothrop Stoddard's fascinating *Master of Manhattan: The Life of Richard Croker* (New York and Toronto, 1931). A number of active reformers have left us their memoirs. Outstanding among them are Brand Whitlock, *Forty Years of It* (New York, 1914); Fremont Older, *My Own Story* (San Francisco, 1919); Tom L. Johnson, *My Story* (New York, 1911); and Carter Harrison, *Stormy Years* (Indianapolis and New York, 1935). An attempt to deal "scientifically" with city politics is Harold F. Gosnell, *Machine Politics: Chicago Model* (Chicago, 1937); also in this vein is Sonya Forthal, *Cogwheels of Democracy: A Study of the Precinct Captain* (New York, 1946). More humane, and consequently more illuminating, is John T. Salter, *Boss Rule: Portraits in City Politics* (New York and London, 1935).
2 Another such "straw," surely, is the immense popularity of Edwin O'Connor's novel, *The Last Hurrah* (Boston, 1956).
3 Glencoe, Ill., 1949. See pp. 71–81.
4 Max Weber, acutely sensitized to bureaucracy and its implications, was very impressed by the responsibility of the American "boss," recognizing that in him and in his organization lay the natural functional substitute for bureaucracy in a growing democratic political culture. See "Politics as a Vocation," in *From Max Weber: Essays in Sociology,* translated and edited by H. H. Gerth and C. Wright Mills (New York, 1946), pp. 108–111.
5 The significance of this function may be confused unless an important analytical distinction is made. It should be thought of in terms, not of the "number" of careers it provides for these groups at large, but rather of a critical ratio of outlets for the potential *leadership* among such groups.
6 I have been told that some of the Wallace groups reached the high point of their solidarity about a month *after* the 1948 election. After this high point—with nothing to look forward to—the groups tended to disintegrate.
7 Some present-day consequences of this mobility are discussed in G. Edward Janosik, "Suburban Balance of Power," *American Quarterly,* VII, 123–141 (Summer 1955);

and Harvey Wheeler, "Yesterday's Robin Hood," *American Quarterly,* VII, 332–344 (Winter 1955).

8 A real landmark of analysis in this area, one whose importance cannot be too much emphasized, is Daniel Bell's brilliant essay, "Crime as an American Way of Life," *Antioch Review,* XIII, 131–154 (Summer 1953).

9 There have, of course, been exceptions, but it appears that city bosses (who have by definition "risen to the top") have in general tended to be men who were fairly honest personally, and who remained aloof from police corruption (the "shaking down" of disorderly houses and other illegal enterprises), even while tolerating it among their vassals. Such activity was considered dirty and disreputable, and beneath their personal dignity. "Honest graft," on the other hand (business dealings to which the city was a party, and in which the politician, as business man, had advantages of prior knowledge), was on a considerably higher moral plane. See Riordon, pp. 3–8. For a comparative survey in standards of honesty—standards surprisingly high—see Harold Zink, *City Bosses in the United States* (Durham, 1930).

10 Throughout William Foote Whyte's *Street Corner Society* (enlarged ed., Chicago, 1955) are examples of how the universally coercive values of respectability and the drive for status and success operated among the Italian community both in the rackets and in politics, as well as elsewhere. Especially illuminating is Mr. Whyte's story of how a leading racketeer of "Cornerville" forbade his son to play with the riffraff of the neighborhood, and how gratified he himself was to associate with a Harvard professor—until he discovered the "professor" hanging out with the street-corner and poolroom crowd. Very perceptive observations on the social, political and geographical mobility of the Italian community are also to be found in chapter 4 ("The Frontier Reappears") of Samuel Lubell's *The Future of American Politics* (New York, 1952), pp. 62–80.

11 See Robert L. Heilbroner, "Carmine G. DeSapio: The Smile on the Face of the Tiger," *Harper's Magazine* (July 1954), 23–33.

12 Since the above was written, an excellent and illuminating monograph, conceived along these very lines, has come to my attention. It is A. Theodore Brown's "The Politics of Reform: Kansas City's Municipal Government 1925–1950" (Ph.D. Thesis, University of Chicago, 1956).

11
Boss Tweed's Public Welfare Program

JOHN W. PRATT

As Eric McKitrick noted in the previous essay, the political boss developed in a fragmented, diffused governmental system having no tradition of civil service nor continuity of officeholding. In a system devised by men primarily motivated by fear of unified political power, somebody had to pull the disparate strings of government together so it could operate. The boss played this role.

The boss and the machine also provided rudimentary social services at a time when even the dubious benefits of our current system of public welfare were lacking. Bosses like Tim Sullivan of New York's Bowery, and Johnny Powers of Chicago became famous for their charity and their ability to provide jobs for their chronically underemployed constituents. As John Pratt indicates in the following article, the most famous boss of all—William Marcy Tweed—found ways of using the public purse to finance his own charitable activities.

Tweed went to the state legislature with the intention not only of funneling state money into Catholic schools and orphanages, but also of influencing appointment of the state officials who controlled much of the city administration. Beginning in 1857, the legislature created a series of boards to administer various facets of New York City's government. The police, fire, and health departments, and the excise and liquor regulation of the city, came under the control of commissioners appointed either by the governor or by the legislature. Republicans dominated the state government until Tweed succeeded in getting John Hoffman, former mayor of New York City, elected governor, and in securing a Democratic majority in the legislature. In 1870 Tweed drafted a new charter for New York City transferring control of city government back to municipal officials, and with the help of $600,000 distributed in the right places, pushed it through the legislature. The following year the Tweed Ring came to grief after the New York Times *exposed mammoth frauds, and politicians like Samuel Jones Tilden joined the opposition and forced Tweed out.*

Two useful recent studies of Tweed are Alexander B. Callow, Jr., The Tweed Ring *(New York, 1966) and Seymour Mandelbaum,* Boss Tweed's New York *(New York, 1965). Callow's book is lively and well-written political history, while Mandelbaum makes imaginative use of social science concepts, especially communication theories, in assessing Tweed. He views the machine and the big payoff as attempts to govern a city which had outgrown its communication network and which lacked any other mechanism for arriving at decisions except the marketplace, with its basic questions—what do you want, how much are you willing to pay? Through a system*

*of payoffs—of something for everyone—Tweed managed to hold the frag-
mented city together until many citizens decided that the cost-graft was
higher than his services were worth.*

▪ ▪ ▪ ▪ For Further Reading

John W. Pratt, *Religion, Politics and Diversity: The Church State Theme in New
York History* (Ithaca, N.Y.: Cornell University Press, 1967) is a full-scale examination
of church-state problems. Jerome Mushkat, *Tammany: The Evolution of a Political
Machine, 1789–1865* (Syracuse, N.Y.: Syracuse University Press, 1971) is a detailed
history of Tammany Hall and its political role from its formation to the end of the
Civil War.

▪ William Marcy Tweed, Grand Sachem of Tammany Hall and
the political boss of New York City in the 1860s, has long personified
the corruption of America's cities in the decades following the Civil War.
Over the years historians have turned to the accounts of the Tweed Ring
for their stock illustrations of municipal corruption in the later 19th century,
and they continue to do so. "The career of Boss William M. Tweed of
New York city," in the words of one survey of the period, "is the classic
example of municipal fraud."[1] The authors of another recent American
history text conclude: "The most infamous of all the corrupt city governments of the era was the Tweed Ring in New York."[2] Such judgments are
a common reaction to the standard accounts of the Ring's gargantuan frauds
and peculations in an age when many of our cities were being looted by
cynical and greedy politicians who were not known for their restraint.
Because the Tweed Ring stole more than the others, and in a more brazen
fashion, we are told, it "has remained through the years the synonym of
civic corruption."[3]

But despite the prodigious scale of Boss Tweed's thefts, a reading of the
monographic literature on the Tweed Ring suggests another reason why it
is that historians of the period have turned to the events of Tweed's rise
and fall for their examples. In the argot of the newspaper trade, the Tweed
story has continued to be good copy. The accounts of his life offer an
unmatched succession of sordid and lurid details that is prime material for
popular consumption. Among the references most frequently cited in the
standardized textbook treatments of the Tweed Ring are the familiar works
by Gustavus Myers, M. R. Werner, and Denis T. Lynch.[4] These old stand-
bys, together with the biting cartoons of Thomas Nast, are the sources for
most of the well-known, even stereotyped, details of Boss Tweed's dramatic
career which have enlivened the pages of countless history books.[5]

Unfortunately, these colorful accounts are not always as dependable as
they might be. Judged by almost any current standard of historical scholarship, they are often uncritical and overly dependent on sources fanatically
hostile to Tweed. Time and again Myers, Werner, and Lynch are guilty of

selecting the sensational or entertaining anecdote, though it may not reflect the whole truth, while bypassing the more prosaic facts indispensable to any serious understanding of the Tweed years. Therefore, the heavy reliance of later writers on these and other conventional accounts has too often resulted in the overlooking of pertinent details. One particularly significant omission deals with the means by which the Ring assiduously courted the political favor of New York City's poorer classes.

That a great part of the city's poor, many of them recent immigrants, gave their unquestioning allegiance to the Tweed machine has long been known and commented upon. The bloc-voting of New York City's working class districts for Tweed candidates is widely recognized to have been one of the Ring's major sources of strength.[6] Generally this electoral support has been attributed to the self-interested concern shown by Tweed and his henchmen for the welfare of their poorer constituents. The Tweed Ring practiced what one writer has termed a "kind of unofficial social insurance."[7] Tweed and other district leaders assisted the needy with gifts of food and fuel. They found jobs on the city payroll for the unemployed, helped immigrants to become naturalized, and protected these people when they ran afoul of the law. In return for this assistance, the Ring expected and received the votes of the poor at the polls.[8]

It has never been pointed out, however, that the Tweed Ring did not rely exclusively upon the private charities of its ward leaders to build up its mass electoral following. Boss Tweed also superintended an extensive program of public aid to private institutions with which large numbers of the city poor came in direct contact at some time in their lives. In contrast to the random gifts of groceries and coal to deserving constituents by the district leaders, Tweed's public aid was systematic and sustained throughout the years of the Ring's greatest power. Through his access to the City treasury and to the resources of the State government, Boss Tweed managed to subsidize parochial schools in New York City and to dispense regular monetary grants to private charitable institutions in the metropolis. The schools educated many of the children of Tweed's constituents, while the private charities cared for the numerous orphaned and diseased victims of urban poverty. Tweed's program of official social insurance came at a time when rapid urban growth was placing ever greater demands upon these private institutions, and it was accepted with gratitude. The funds so liberally dispensed by the Ring from the public coffers were an important complement to the "unofficial social insurance" to which students of the Tweed machine have given so much attention. Public aid became quite as important as private charity in the calculations of the Boss and his fellow plunderers. Together, they were meant to inspire that blind loyalty and gratitude among the poor which made them impervious to the accusations of Tweed's enemies until the very end.

The Tweed Ring's philanthropies, as well as its other designs upon public funds, hinged on Tweed's election to the New York State Senate in 1868. Boss Tweed's foray into State government, as the leader of New York City's delegation in the legislature, usually is interpreted as a maneuver to advance his schemes for plundering the city. The State legislature held the ultimate power of the purse over the great metropolis. Its approval was required for the proposed annual tax rates and expenditures of both the City and County of New York. If the Tweed Ring was to carry out its grandiose plans for enriching its members, it had to secure control over the yearly financial deliberations at Albany.[9]

What historians have never pointed out is that Boss Tweed's position of power at the State Capitol also made possible the Ring's expanded welfare program. Because it would involve public expenditure by the City, Tweed had to have legislative approval before he could hope to support parochial schools or to divert State tax moneys to charitable institutions in the city. It is significant of Tweed's intentions that the two committees of the State Senate upon which he secured places were the Committee on Municipal Affairs and the Committee on Charitable and Religious Societies.[10] In the former he was able to promote his plans for raiding the City treasury, while in the latter committee he pursued his philanthropic interests.

Tweed's school-subsidy arrangement was an ill-concealed appeal to the Irish and Germans of New York City, most of them Roman Catholics, who made up a large part of the Ring's electoral strength.[11] For years, Catholics in the city had been claiming that their church schools should be permitted to share in the division of public school funds. Periodically they protested against the city's public schools on the grounds that they were either too Protestant or else too godless. Good Catholics, it was asserted, could not in conscience send their children to such institutions. Beginning in the early 1840s under Bishop Hughes, when eight parochial schools were teaching about 5,000 New York City pupils, New York Catholics had been making a determined effort to build up their own church schools in order to compensate for the alleged defects of the public schools. The poverty of much of the Catholic population in the city, however, plus the denial to Catholic schools of their rightful share (as Catholics viewed it) in public funds for education, prevented anything like an adequate system. Thus formal requests for regularized support of parochial schools, directed sometimes to the City and sometimes to the State, were based on claims of right as well as need. But these appeals had always been turned down on the State level (where, however, occasional appropriations for specified church schools were sometimes included in the general charity bills) through the combined opposition of militantly anti-Catholic Protestants and of believers in a strictly nonsectarian public education. Despite these rebuffs, Catholics retained their conviction that parochial schools were entitled to a fair return from their school-tax payments.[12]

Tweed, as a good politician, could not have been unaware of this conviction.

In March 1869, he introduced a bill in the legislature which would have permitted the City and County of New York to pay a portion of the annual expenses of parochial schools within their jurisdiction.[13] Because of the history of opposition to such proposals, the bill was carefully phrased to omit any specific mention of Roman Catholic schools. Yet the purpose was fairly obvious. The aid which Tweed recommended was to be confined to free schools where "not less than two hundred children have been or are taught and educated gratuitously. . . ."[14] The terms implicitly excluded the existing public schools, already financed under present laws, as well as private tuition schools. Neither were there many, if any, Protestant or Hebrew church schools in heavily Catholic New York City that could meet the bill's enrollment requirement. By process of elimination, this left only the overcrowded and poorly equipped Catholic parish schools to benefit from the projected aids.

The bill was quickly reported out of Tweed's own Committee on Charitable and Religious Societies, where he had been careful to have it sent for initial perusal. It was accompanied back to the floor by a strong recommendation from the Tweed committee for its immediate passage. In order to lend an appearance of bipartisanship, the favorable committee report was presented jointly by Tweed, a Democrat and Episcopalian, and a Senator Crowley, a Republican and a Catholic. But despite its carefully worded terms and the display of unity from the committee, the bill's true intent did not escape the notice of the Republican majority. The Albany *Argus* reported that the Senate Republicans "smelt a savor of Popery in the provisions, and called a caucus and agreed to kill it."[15]

Repulsed but not defeated, Tweed adopted another expedient to achieve the same end. He had the school proposal inserted in the annual tax-levy bill providing for the government of New York City in the coming fiscal year. Embedded in this lengthy and complex budget statement, prepared by Tweed's Committee on Municipal Affairs, was a section empowering the City authorities to set aside a yearly sum equal to twenty percent of the City's income from excises in 1868—this money then to be disbursed by a Tweed-controlled official for the support of free schools other than public or charity schools. As part of the larger Tweed money-grab bill, the school provision passed the legislature with very little dissent and became law. The editorial organ of the State Republican Party, the Albany *Evening Journal,* confirmed a widespread suspicion that the smooth passage of the tax-levy bill was made possible by Tweed's "fixing" of several Republican legislators. That the potentially explosive section relating to schools provoked no serious opposition suggests that it, too, was part of the "fix."[16]

A public storm over the school question could not be avoided so easily outside the legislative halls. Tweed's school measure presented a ready-made issue to his opponents. Shortly after its passage, the New York *Times* launched an attack upon the law, terming it a serious threat to the public school system. The cry was taken up by a leading Methodist organ in New York City. Its editors attributed the school measure to a corrupt desire on the part of the "Irish Democratic party" for votes, and solemnly warned that it gave evidence of a general "Papal conspiracy" against American institutions. In September, New York Republicans, meeting in State convention at Syracuse, inserted a rousing plank in the party platform denouncing the appropriation of public money to sectarian schools. The New York City wing of the Republican Party, marshaled by the Union League Club, began an intensive statewide campaign for the repeal of Tweed's school arrangement in the next session of the legislature. In sweeping terms, the anti-Tweed forces described the school law as part of a Catholic-Democrat plot to overthrow the religious freedom of non-Catholic Americans, and to subvert the hallowed principle of Church-State separation. With a tough re-election fight drawing near for Tweed's hand-picked occupant of the governor's chair, John T. Hoffman, the New York Democracy was being indicted all over the State as the "State Church" party—even as a pliant tool of the Catholic hierarchy, but without any concrete evidence of the New York clergy's having instigated the school-aid bill or any other Tweed measure for support of Catholic institutions. When the legislature reconvened in early 1870, it was deluged by petitions from all sides demanding in outraged and often inflammatory terms the immediate repeal of Tweed's school "steal."[17]

Threatened with the loss of votes upstate and the possible defeat of Governor Hoffman in the fall if the religious issue were allowed to occupy the campaign, Tweed appears to have decided upon a strategic retreat. While the Boss remained in the background, prudently disassociating himself from the move which might prove damaging to his standing with his city following, his legislative supporters made the necessary arrangements. With a great display of reluctance, they accepted an amendment to the current New York City tax-levy bill for 1870 repealing the previous year's provision for parochial schools. As a parting shot, however, the repealer was amended by the Tweed forces to postpone its effective date until the schools which had received aid for the 1869–70 school year should obtain their subsidy for the coming academic year. Tweed may have been forced to give way, but not before he had secured public funds for the religious schools of his Catholic supporters over a period of two years. Moreover, he had thrown the onus for killing the program upon the Republican Party. This was the only time in New York's history that Catholic parochial schools received regular public grants avowedly intended for general instructional purposes. The following year (1871) the legislature made sure that it would not happen again by forbidding the City to raise by taxation or borrowing, or to appropriate or apply, money for support of "any institution or enterprise that is under the control of a religious denomination."[18]

Boss Tweed's presence in the State legislature was beneficial not only to

Catholic schools but also to private charitable institutions in New York City. For several years, the State of New York had been granting funds to private orphanages, hospitals, dispensaries, and charity schools. Successive legislatures appropriated money to these private, and usually sectarian-operated, charities in order to relieve the State of caring directly for certain classes of unfortunates. This practice soon became institutionalized in the form of an annual charity bill. Most New Yorkers seem to have preferred to support existing private facilities rather than pay for the construction and operation of a network of costly public-welfare institutions.[19]

The annual charity bill was subjected to increasing abuse in the 1860s. Even before Tweed arrived in Albany it had become a logrolling instrument to accommodate the political needs of individual legislators. Hatched in committee and generously amended on the floor of each house, the charity bills had been mounting in cost each year.[20] Such an arrangement was admirably suited to Boss Tweed's purposes. Skillfully employing his disciplined following in the legislature, Tweed was able to add significantly to the number of institutions receiving public largess while also increasing the total sums to be expended.[21] This new zeal for ever-larger charity appropriations indicates the importance attached to them by the Tweed forces. The funds were quite obviously intended to promote good will for the Ring among its impoverished constituents in the metropolis.

That Tweed went to Albany in part, at least, to have a hand in shaping the State charitable program is evident from his appointment to the Senate Committee on Charitable and Religious Societies. It was this committee that entertained requests for funds, and drew up the annual charity appropriation bills. During Tweed's ascendancy at Albany, both the sums voted and the number of participating institutions increased steadily. Over the seventeen years immediately preceding the advent of Senator Tweed, in 1869, the State had spent a total of $2,199,000 on private charities. During the three years in which Tweed superintended the passage of the charity bills, $2,225,000 was appropriated. Private orphanages and homes for the friendless—the largest category of State-aid recipients—numbered a pre-Tweed high of sixty-eight in the 1868 bill. By 1871, the number of these recipient institutions had grown to one hundred and six. This program of expanded State subsidies, initiated and carried out under the leadership of Boss Tweed, was aptly described by a friendly observer as "the open door policy in State Aid. . . ."[22]

The moneys voted by the legislature for charity were distributed to participating institutions through the agencies of local government. Some idea of New York City's share is conveyed by a contemporary estimate of the sums channeled through the City authorities. From 1869 to 1871, the years of Tweed's greatest power in city and State, the City of New York distributed approximately $1,893,000 to private institutions. Of this total, $1,396,000 went to Catholic-operated charities and schools. About $500,000 represented the subsidies to parochial schools obtained through Tweed's efforts in 1869 and 1870. The balance, $896,000, was paid over to Catholic orphanages, charity schools, hospitals, and dispensaries. While political expediency as well as considerations of relative need required that institutions sponsored by the city's Catholic majority receive the lion's share of the funds, Tweed did not overlook the opportunity to spread cheer among non-Catholic institutions. Over the same span, Protestant organizations received $83,000, Hebrew charities were paid $26,000, and the unaffiliated institutions obtained $194,000 of State money.[23] During floor debate on the 1871 charity bill, Tweed recited his philanthropic creed for the benefit of the Republican contingent in the State Senate: "I believe in supporting all deserving charities, without asking what denomination control [*sic*] them. . . . We, on this side, are in favor of aiding all the charities. So now, gentlemen on the other side, offer your amendments, inserting deserving charities, and we will accept them."[24] Few Republican legislators could resist such an offer.

It was only after the Tweed Ring's downfall in late 1871 that an end was brought to Tweed's "open door" policy of State aid. In response to the general public revulsion against all that Tweed stood for, following his exposures in the New York *Times* and by the Committee of Seventy in New York City, the legislators sanctimoniously refused to pass any charity appropriations for the next three years. When this proved to be a costly economy, the State once more began to make grants, but with great caution and never again with the complete abandon of the Tweed years.[25]

To summarize: from 1869 to 1871, when the Tweed Ring was. riding high, Boss Tweed did not forget his constituents in the slums who had helped put him into power. While Ring members continued their private benefactions to the poor, Tweed was engaged in the more important work of assisting Catholic school children and the underprivileged of New York City with public money. One of the main purposes behind Tweed's election to the State legislature in 1868 was to secure the necessary State authorization and financial resources for his policy. In these acts of public assistance, as distinct from the personal favors and gifts of the Tweed leaders which students of the era have emphasized, the Ring appears to have seen a major means for tightening its hold over the allegiance of the city's poor. Tweed's public-welfare program was considered by contemporaries to be another and very important reason for the Tweed Ring's continued support among the working classes of the city. While more prosperous citizens howled for economy, only the Tweed organization seemed to care for the needs of the underprivileged. It is a phase of the Tweed story that has never been revealed by the host of Tweed's critics.[26] Ironically, this welfare program, while cynically conceived to promote the selfish interests of the Tweed Ring, served a beneficial and much-needed end. It helped to soften some of the rigors of urban life years before the majority of Americans were persuaded that the public had a continuing responsibility for the welfare of society's unfortunates.

■ ■ ■ ■ Notes

1 Richard Hofstadter, William Miller, Daniel Aaron, *The American Republic* (2 vols.; Englewood, N.J.: 1959), II, 265.
2 Dumas Malone and Basil Rauch, *Empire for Liberty: The Genesis and Growth of the United States of America* (2 vols.; New York: 1960), II, 64.
3 Malone and Rauch, 65.
4 Myers, *History of Tammany Hall* (New York: 1901); Werner, *Tammany Hall* (New York: 1928); Lynch, *"Boss" Tweed: The Story of a Grim Generation* (New York: 1927).
5 See, for example, Charles A. and Mary R. Beard, *The Rise of American Civilization* (2 vols. in one; New York: 1933), II, 309–11, 862; Samuel E. Morison and Henry Steele Commager, *The Growth of the American Republic* (4th ed., 2 vols.; New York: 1950), II, 836; Harry J. Carman, Harold C. Syrett, Bernard W. Wishy, *A History of the American People* (2d ed., 2 vols.; New York: 1960–61), I, 707–9; John D. Hicks, *The American Nation: A History of the United States from 1865 to the Present* (3d ed., Cambridge, Mass.: 1955), 84–85, 103.
6 Myers, 217, 230; Lynch, 329.
7 Hicks, 84.
8 Myers, 214; Lynch, 169, 349–50; a recent account is in Hofstadter et al., II, 265.
9 Myers, 220–21; Lynch, 283.
10 New York (State) Senate, *Journal, 1869,* 277; New York *Times,* March 25, 1869, March 15, 1871.
11 Lynch, 329, 374.
12 John W. Pratt, "The Politics of Tolerance: A History of Church-State Relations in New York, 1624–1900," doctoral dissertation, Harvard University, 1959, 278–81, 284–304, 310–13.

The first Catholic church school in New York (St. Peter's Free School, established in 1800) received in 1806 a State grant ($1,565.78) proportional to the amounts distributed in 1801 among ten Protestant schools from the remainder of a five-year appropriation by the 1795 "Act for Encouragement of Schools." No further public money, however, was granted to it or to any other denominational schools in the city until 1813. The legislature then made a fund available for annual distribution (to be prorated among the beneficiary institutions according to the total number of pupils taught gratuitously in the schools each operated, but to be used exclusively for teachers' salaries) to "the Free School Society in New York City, . . . the Orphan Asylum Society, the Society of the Economical School, the African Free School, and to such incorporated religious societies as now support or hereafter shall establish charity schools within the city. . . ."—New York (State), *Laws, 1795,* Chap. 75; *1801,* Chap. 189; *1806,* Chap. 63; *1813,* Chap. 52.

The purpose of this act, like the act of 1795 but unlike the general school law of 1812 which applied only upstate, was to save on public costs of education by making use of private schools already in being rather than to establish a new system of common schools. Under the terms of the 1813 law, the Free School of St. Peter's Roman Catholic Church, along with a number of Protestant charity schools and the secular schools under the privately run Public School Society, appears to have received public moneys yearly up to 1825. In the latter year, under a statutory authorization of 1824 and in response to pressure from the Public School Society, the Common Council enacted an ordinance depriving all religious schools then and thereafter of any share in the school fund.—New York (State), *Laws, 1812,* Chap. 242; *1813,*

Chap. 52; *1824,* Chap. 226; *Minutes of the Common Council of the City of New York 1784–1831* (New York: 1917), XIV, 498–99 (April 25, 1825).

When present and future financial support from public revenues was prohibited to all religious schools in 1825, there were but two Catholic parochial schools in the city. By 1840, despite their deprivation of public funds, six more had been established. The eight Roman Catholic church schools in the city when Bishop Hughes assumed their leadership were: St. Peter's, St. Patrick's, Transfiguration's, St. James', St. Nicholas', St. Paul's, St. Joseph's, and St. John's, with a claimed enrollment—all told—of some 5,000 pupils.—*The Metropolitan Catholic Almanac and Laymen's Directory, 1841* (Baltimore: Fielding Lucas, 1842), 191.

Although these schools and those to come never enjoyed regularized support from City or State as part of the educational system, except through Tweed's short-lived annual tax-levy bill of 1869, a few of them had been named along with a growing number of charitable institutions upstate and down in the annual charity bills of the mid-1860s: in 1865, "For Saint Mary's Church in the city of New York, to aid in the maintenance of schools under its charge, one thousand dollars"; in 1866, for St. Mary's, St. Bridget's, and the Church of the Immaculate Conception, $1,000 each; and in 1867, for the Church of Transfiguration, St. Mary's, St. Bridget's, and Church of the Immaculate Conception, $1,000 each. New York City parochial schools were dropped from the 1868 and all subsequent charity bills although, after Tweed's tax-levy provision for the city's Catholic schools had been repealed, the 1871 charity bill granted aid to certain parochial schools outside New York City.—New York (State), *Laws, 1865,* Chap. 641, sec. 2; *1866,* Chap. 774, sec. 2; *1867,* Chap. 751, sec. 2; *1871,* Chap. 869, sec. 2.

13 Senate, *Journal, 1869,* 277.

14 Quoted in New York *Times,* March 26, 1869.

15 Albany *Argus,* March 27, 1869. See also Senate, *Journal, 1869,* 355, and the comments of the Presbyterian New York *Observer,* April 1, 1869, in an editorial titled "An Abominable Bill."

16 New York (State), *Laws, 1869,* Chap. 876, sec. 10; Senate, *Journal, 1869,* 626, 701–4, 1126–37, 1176–80; Assembly, *Journal, 1869,* 2053–64, 2165; New York *Times,* May 10, 11, 13, 1869.

In the wording of the act, the "annual amount" provided was "to be distributed under the direction of an officer to be appointed . . . by the board of education . . . for the support of schools, educating children gratuitously in said city who are not provided for in the common schools thereof, excepting therefrom schools receiving contributions for their support from the city treasury [i.e., the charity schools]." Catholic parochial schools in New York City were no longer designated "charity schools," as they had been in the 1813 school act and, by implication, in the charity bills of 1865–1867 (see note 12). Indeed, the 1871 tax-levy bill for the City specifically excludes denominational schools from the category of charitable institutions. Tweed's motive for distinguishing parochial from charity schools in the 1869 tax-levy act was to make possible regularized aid for New York City parochial schools as educational institutions, whereas the motive in 1871 was, by emphasizing their denominational character, to prohibit any kind of public support for them.—New York (State), *Laws, 1871,* Chap. 582.

17 [New York] *Christian Advocate,* June 3, Oct. 14, 1869; New York *Times,* May 12, September 30, 1869, February 16, March 31, 1870; New York (State) Assembly, *Documents, 1870,* Doc. 169; Albany *Evening Journal,* March 31, April 1, 1870; Senate, *Journal, 1870,* 128ff.; Assembly, *Journal, 1870,* 273ff.

18 New York *Times,* April 23, 26, 1870; Albany *Argus,* April 26, 1870; Albany *Evening Journal,* April 26, 1870; New York (State), *Laws, 1870,* Chap. 383, sec. 50; *1871,* Chap. 582, sec. 6.

Section 50 of this 1870 bill, before its amendment, would have made the repeal of the 1869 provision for parochial schools effective immediately upon passage (actually April 26th)—well before distribution time for the next school-year subsidy. But the amendment postponed the effective date to "the thirtieth day of September next," thereby extending the 1869 provision until after the 1870–1871 school-year fund had been legally distributed among the city's parochial schools in accordance with its still unrepealed terms.

The specific wording of the prohibition against church-school aid, passed April 19, 1871, reads: "It shall not be lawful for the mayor, aldermen, and commonalty of the city of New York, or the board of supervisors of the county of New York, or the board of apportionment herein created, to appropriate or apply any portion of the tax herein authorized to be raised in aid of any private or sectarian school, or to any institution or enterprise that is under the control of any religious denomination, or to borrow any money on the faith or credit of the city to be applied to any such purpose. . . ."

19 Pratt, 325–34.

20 Constitutional Commission of the State of New York, 1872–73, *Journal* (Albany: 1873), 313; Citizens Association of New York, *The Constitutional Convention: Alterations in the Fundamental Law of the State* (New York: 1867), 17; Edward M. Connors, *Church-State Relationships in Education in the State of New York* (Washington, D.C.: 1951), 93.

21 Frederick J. Zwierlein, *The Life and Letters of Bishop McQuaid* (3 vols.; Rochester, N.Y.: 1925–27), III, 313–14; David M. Schneider and Albert Deutsch, *The History of Public Welfare in New York State* (2 vols.; Chicago: 1938–41), II, 20; Constitutional Commission, 1872–73, *Journal,* 313.

22 Zwierlein, III, 314 (quoting Bishop McQuaid); Senate, *Journal, 1869,* 277; New York *Times,* March 25, 1869; Constitutional Commission, 1872–73, *Journal,* 313; Schneider and Deutsch, II, 20.

23 These figures were compiled by a leading opponent of State aid to sectarian charities in the 1860s and '70s, Dexter Hawkins of New York City, and are cited in Werner, 194. Werner is in error when he attributes these grants to New York City rather than to their correct source: the State. The sum of $500,000 for parochial schools is based on estimates appearing in the New York *Times,* May 12, 1869, and in the *Christian Advocate,* May 27, 1869.

24 New York *Times,* April 7, 1871.

25 New York City Council of Political Reform, *Proposed Amendments of the Constitution of the State of New York* (New York: 1874), 22; Zwierlein, III, 314; Albany *Evening Journal* and Albany *Argus,* May 15, 1872; Pratt, 344–50.

26 Tweed's public-welfare program seems to have been dismissed by historians on the basis of a statement first appearing in Myers, 229, that the institutions receiving public aid were often fictitious, serving as fronts behind which the Tweed Ring was stealing from the public in yet another way. This charge, for which Myers offers no evidence and which I have been unable to substantiate, has nevertheless been repeated in several later works. See, for example, DeAlva S. Alexander, *A Political History of the State of New York* (4 vols.; New York: 1906–23), III, 224.

12

Boss Cox's Cincinnati: A Study in Urbanization and Politics, 1880–1914

ZANE L. MILLER

Bosses existed outside of New York, and Tammany was not the only urban machine. In this selection Zane Miller examines the reasons for, and the workings of, a spectacular boss in Cincinnati. Miller provides a case study based on an idea proposed by his mentor, Richard Wade. According to Wade's hypothesis, political conflicts within cities and metropolitan areas are more significant historically than any division between rural and urban areas. Secondly, he believes these intra-city conflicts often pit the periphery of the city against the core.

By the 1880s and 1890s Cincinnati had developed an ecological form consisting of three separate districts, which Miller calls the Circle, the Zone, and the Hilltops. The coming of electrification to the street railways in the 1890s increased the area open to settlement and completed the process—noted by George Rogers Taylor and Sam Warner—of physically separating the social classes. The Circle, Miller's term for the residential belt surrounding the Central Business District, was inhabited by the most recent arrivals, and the poorest and most demoralized of Cincinnati's citizens. The Zone of Emergence housed those people who had made some economic progress. Miller borrowed the term and the concept from Boston social workers of pre–World War I days who used it to describe areas inhabited by the American-born children of the foreign-born—the second generation. James T. Farrell's Studs Lonigan is a brilliant fictional depiction of life in a similar area of Chicago. Finally, on the Hilltops resided the most well-to-do, those who had really arrived. (Like the military, the most prosperous urbanites have always sought the high ground.)

Each of these areas developed its own political style based on the needs and perceptions of its citizens. It was the genius of Boss Cox and his machine to provide some links between these areas at a time when the city seemed threatened with disintegration. The machine did supply order and positive government to a city badly in need of them, but eventually it proved impossible to satisfy the Circle without alienating the Hilltops, and the Cox machine was overthrown.

In a later essay in this book, Herbert Gans argues against an ecological explanation of urban differences, emphasizing instead the concepts of social class and the stage-of-life cycle in accounting for variations in social characteristics and life style. In other words, he suggests that residence is not an independent variable, but rather relates to income, marital status, number

201

and ages of children, and value systems—whether the desire is to be where "*the action is*," *or to seek open space and quiet neighbors.*

Keeping these factors in mind, Miller's formulation becomes even more useful. People of similar income and background did tend to cluster in his threefold pattern, and there were recognizable political differences between the Circle, the Zone, and the Hilltops.

■ ■ ■ ■ **For Further Reading**

Zane L. Miller, *Boss Cox's Cincinnati: Urban Politics in the Progressive Era* (New York: Oxford University Press, 1968) and Sam B. Warner, Jr., *Streetcar Suburbs: The Process of Growth in Boston* (New York: Atheneum, 1969) both assess the impact of the expanded area open to urban settlement by the development of the streetcar system in the late nineteenth century. Miller also has a good deal to say about the strengths and weaknesses of the municipal, political, and governmental system.

■ Many observers of the turn-of-the-century urban scene have depicted bossism as one of the great unmitigated evils of the American city, as a tyrannical, authoritarian, relentlessly efficient, and virtually invulnerable political system. Between 1904 and 1912, for example, George B. Cox was castigated by writers in four national magazines. Gustav Karger called him the "Proprietor of Cincinnati." Lincoln Steffens declared that "Cox's System" was "one great graft," "the most perfect thing of the kind in this country." Frank Parker Stockbridge claimed that "The Biggest Boss of Them All" had an organization "more compact and closely knit than any of the political machines which have dominated New York, Philadelphia, Chicago, St. Louis or San Francisco." And George Kibbe Turner concluded that in the 1890s "the man from Dead Man's Corner . . . seated himself over the city of Cincinnati. For twenty years he remained there—a figure like no other in the United States, or in the world."[1] Yet these knowledgeable and sensitive journalists obscured as much as they revealed about the nature of Queen City politics in the Progressive era. A new kind of city had developed, and "the boss" comprised only a fraction of its novel political system.

Paradoxically, Cox and his machine[2] were produced by, fed on, and ultimately helped dispel the spectacular disorder which engulfed Cincinnati in the late-nineteenth century and threatened the very survival of the democratic political process. In these years, increasing industrialization, technological innovations in communication and transportation—especially the coming of rapid transit—and continued foreign and domestic migration had reversed the physical pattern of the mid-century walking city and transformed Cincinnati into a physically enlarged, divided, and potentially explosive metropolis.[3]

Old citizens were shocked as familiar landmarks and neighborhoods vanished. By 1900, railroads and warehouses had monopolized the Ohio River bottoms. The financial and retail districts had moved up into the Basin around Fountain Square, the focus of the street railway system; new club, theater, and tenderloin districts had developed; and industries had plunged up Mill Creek Valley, converting Mohawk-Brighton into "the undisputed industrial bee-hive of the Great Queen City of the West," surrounding once fashionable Dayton Street, creating a new community called Ivorydale, and reaching out to the villages of Norwood and Oakley in search of cheap land, ready access to railroads, and less congested and more cheerful surroundings.[4]

The Over-the-Rhine entertainment section along Vine Street became tawdry with commercialism. It now had, complained one habitué, "all the tarnished tinsel of a Bohemianism with the trimmings of a gutter and the morals of a sewer"—a repulsive contrast, he felt, to "the old-time concert and music halls . . . where one could take wife, sister, or sweetheart and feel secure . . . that not one obnoxious word would profane their ears."[5]

The fashionable residential districts which had flanked the center of the walking city began to disintegrate. One family after another fled the East End for the hills around the Basin, leaving only a small coterie led by the Charles P. Tafts to stave off the advance of factories and slums.[6] The elite West End seemed to disappear overnight. It "did not go down imperceptibly," recalled one old resident. "It went to ruin almost as if a bombshell sent it to destruction."[7]

The Hilltops, at mid-century the private preserve of cemeteries, colleges, and a handful of wealthy families,[8] became the prime residential district in the new city. The crush to get in generated new tensions. In 1899 one observer acidly remarked: "when rapid transit came the Hebrews . . . flocked to" Walnut Hills

> until it was known by the name of New Jerusalem. Avondale was then heralded as the suburb of deliverance, but again rapid transit brought the wealthy Hebrews . . . in numbers greater than the flock of crows that every morning and evening darkens her skies, until now it has been facetiously said that the congregation has assembled in force and . . . when Avondale is roofed over the synagogue will be complete.[9]

The diffusion of wealthy families, the reduction in casual social and business contacts, and the construction of new communities made ardent joiners of the Hilltops elite. Each neighborhood had an improvement association, and between 1880 and 1905 five new businessmen's organizations devoted to boosting the city's lethargic economy had appeared. In the same period six social clubs opened downtown facilities, and three country clubs were started. By 1913, moreover, there were twenty-two exclusive clubs and patriotic societies and innumerable women's groups.[10] These developments helped counteract the disruptive effects of the "country movement," as one visitor labeled it, which was "so general that church-going became an affair of some difficulty" and "society itself . . . more or less disintegrated."[11]

But not all those moving out were affluent. Liberated by rapid transit, skilled and semiskilled workers and moderately prosperous professional and white-collar men with life savings, the courage to take out a mortgage, an equity in a building and loan association, or a willingness to rent a flat in a double or triple decker, also fled the Basin.[12] They took refuge in a no-man's-land between the center of the city and the Hilltops frontier which was similar to an area dubbed the Zone of Emergence by Boston social workers.[13]

Zone residents formed what the Cincinnati *Post* referred to as "the so-called middle class . . . , the class that makes any city . . . what it is . . . [,] the class that takes in the great body of people between wealth and poverty" and builds up "many organizations, societies, associations, fraternities and clubs that bring together people who are striving upward, trying to uplift themselves, and hence human society."[14]

> When I lived down on Richmond in a little house we cooked the corn beef and cabbage in the house and ate in there, and when we wanted to go to the toilet we went out into the yard, now I live in a fine house, I am made to eat . . . out in the yard, and when I want to go to the toilet I have to go into the house.[15]

Graham R. Taylor had noted that since most Zone residents commuted they suffered a severe "dislocation of the normal routine of factory and home": they had to adjust to "the need for travel and its curtailment of leisure and income . . . ," to eating lunches away from home, to doing without "customary city facilities," and to knowing the feeling of "isolation from their fellows."[16] Price Hill—like the rest of the Zone a heavily Catholic area—felt itself conspicuously cut off. In the 1890s the editor of the *Catholic-Telegraph*, denouncing the traction company as the "octopus," joined the Price Hill Improvement Association in begging both city and traction company officials to bring the area "within range of the civilized world" and suggested secession as a means of dramatizing to the "people east of Millcreek" that a new public school, "granted by the unbounded munificence of the City of Cincinnati," did not amount to a redemption of the city's annexation pledges.[17]

The exodus, however, did not depopulate the Basin. Instead, a great residential Circle formed around the central business district. It filled with newcomers and those who lacked the means to get out—rural whites and Negroes from the South, Germans, Irish, Greeks, Italians, and Jews from eastern Europe. Working at the poorest paying jobs available, they were jammed into the most congested quarters. The Circle led all other areas of the city in arrests, mortality, and disease.[18]

Although the pressure to escape was enormous, the barriers were formidable. Ignorant of the ways of the city, as an Associated Charities report put it, Circle dwellers had to be "shown how to buy, how to cook, how to make the home attractive, how to find employment." Many, "utterly friendless and discouraged," succumbed to "the damnable absence of want or desire" and grew "indifferent . . . to their own elevation."[19] Plagued by "physical bankruptcy,"[20] they found it difficult to find and hold jobs, let alone form and maintain the kind of organizations which enabled Zone residents to shield themselves from economic disaster, legal pitfalls, social isolation, and apathy.[21]

The immediate impact of the emergence of the new city pushed Cincinnati to the brink of anarchy. In March 1884, the *Enquirer* complained that the police had failed to choke off a crime wave although, in the last year alone, there had been twelve arrests for malicious shooting, twenty-nine for malicious cutting, forty-seven for cutting with intent to wound, 284 for shooting with intent to kill, ninety-two for murder and manslaughter, and 948 for carrying a concealed weapon. The total number of arrests came to 56,784. The city's population was 250,000.[22] Later that same month, a lynch mob descended on the county jail. While police and militia fought off the mob, gangs looted stores and shops on the fringe of the downtown district. In three days of riot the courthouse was burned to the ground, fifty-four people were killed, and an estimated 200 people wounded.[23]

During the fall elections, violence erupted in the lower wards; two policemen and one Negro were killed. Congressman Benjamin Butterworth remarked that he had "never witnessed anywhere such coarse brutality and such riotous demonstrations. . . ." Cincinnati, he concluded, "seems . . . doomed to perdition."[24]

Less than two years later the city faced another major crisis. On May 1, 1886, Cincinnati workers joined in nationwide demonstrations for the eight-hour day. These were followed by a series of strikes. The militia was called out, and for two weeks the city resembled an armed camp. Only the show of force and, perhaps, the memory of the courthouse catastrophe prevented another riot.[25]

Yet labor remained restive, and a rash of strikes followed. By 1892, the paternalistic system which had dominated the breweries was smashed.[26] And in 1894, Judge William Howard Taft spent the hot days of June and July "trying to say nothing to reporters" and "issuing injunctions" in an effort to control and prevent the railroad strike from leading to mass violence.[27]

The Sunday-closing question was another explosive issue. The *Post*, the *Catholic-Telegraph*, a Committee of Five Hundred, and many Protestant clergymen all leveled scathing attacks on the continental Sabbath. "Sunday in Cincinnati," asserted one Methodist minister, "is a high carnival of drunkenness, base sensuality, reeking debauchery and bloody, often fatal crime." Other spokesmen tied the open Sunday to anarchism, atheism, corrupt politicians, a decadent daily press, indifferent public officials, and the ruthless exploitation of labor.[28] "The modern Puritan," insisted Charles P. Taft, "intends to rise up and oppose to the uttermost this kind of Sunday."[29]

When, in 1889, the mayor announced his intention to enforce the Sunday-closing law for saloons, the city almost faced another riot. Some 1,000 saloonkeepers vowed to ignore the new policy. When a cadre of police and firemen marched over the Rhine to close Kissell's saloon, an unruly crowd gathered, epithets were hurled, but no violence occurred. Kissell's was closed; the "era of the back door," with "front doors locked and curtains up, but back doors widened," had opened.[30]

These spectacular outbreaks plus other pressures overwhelmed city hall. Indeed, scarcely a residential area, economic interest, or social or occupational group was left unscathed by the multidimensional disorder. As the physical area of the city expanded, officials were besieged by demands for the extension, improvement, and inauguration of public services of all kinds and for lower taxes. Simultaneously, the relative decline of the city heightened the urgency of the agitation. Municipal institutions and agencies, established to meet the needs of the walking city, became overburdened, outmoded, and dilapidated.[31]

The new city, with old ways shattered, provided a fertile breeding ground for turmoil and discontent and, as it turned out, for innovation and creative reconstruction. Initially, however, this unprecedented change accompanied by unprecedented demands for government action produced only the hope of reform. In 1885, on the eve of the repudiation of a Democratic administration, William Howard Taft predicted that "the clouds are beginning to break over this Sodom of ours and the sun of decency is beginning to dispel the moral miasma that has rested on us now for so many years. It's the beginning of an era of reform."[32]

Yet for almost a decade no party could put together a decisive ruling majority.[33] The city's political processes seemed frozen by a paralyzing factionalism. The division of the city into residential districts which roughly coincided with socio-economic lines made it difficult for the wealthy and well-educated[34] to keep in contact with and control ward politics. As a result, extreme factionalism developed which could, apparently, be surmounted only by appealing to a host of neighborhood leaders and by constructing alliances which crossed party lines.

According to close observers, the chief products of this system were the use of money in city conventions and the rise of what Charles P. Taft called the "bummer," a "queer creature" who "evolves somehow from the slums. . . ." In youth "a bootblack, a newsboy or a general loafer," he matured into "an Arab" who needed only "a good standing with a saloon that has a fine layout during the day." A "hustler at the polls and conventions," the bummer was in such demand that he could accept money from competing candidates, thus lengthening the convention and contributing to interfactional dealing. After studying the influence of the "bummer," Taft gloomily concluded that the "day of pure politics can never be . . . until a riot, a plague or flood kills off all the ward bummers."[35]

By 1897, however, and without divine intervention, all this had changed. In January of that year, three months before the city election, the *Post* gravely announced its intention to describe "impassionately and without bias the means employed" in Cincinnati's "superior and unrecorded government." It was controlled by "the boss, whose power is absolute"—George B. Cox.[36]

The *Post*'s analysis closely paralleled those made after the turn of the century. It dissected the patronage system, outlined the sources of financial support, and noted the attempted appeasement of the city's various special groups—the soldiers, the Germans, the Republican clubs, the Reform Jews, the legal and medical professions, the socially prominent Hilltops businessmen, and certain cooperative Democrats. It excitedly reported the effectiveness of the organization's intelligence system, the way the "plugger" and the "knocker" wore "beaten paths to the office of the boss to urge the appointment of this man, the discharge of that [,] or to report some feature of misconduct or expression. . . ." The paper noted that Cox was always available for consultation with any citizen regardless of station or status and that he had been little more than one of several important factional leaders until, in 1886, Governor Joseph B. Foraker selected him to serve as chief adviser on patronage and political affairs in Hamilton County.[37]

Foraker made a shrewd choice; Cox had grown up with the new city and received a liberal education in its ways. The son of British immigrants, he was born in 1853 and reared in the Eighteenth Ward, a district which by the 1880s contained fashionable as well as slum housing, factories, and its share of saloons and brothels. His father died when Cox was eight. Successively, Cox worked as a bootblack, newsboy, lookout for a gambling joint, grocery deliveryman, bartender, and tobacco salesman. His school principal, who later became superintendent of schools, claimed that Cox was frequently in boyish trouble in classes, exhibited an "undisguised love for his mother," and "never lied . . . bore malice, sulked, whined or moped." Cox had also been exposed to religion. Although not a churchgoer, as an adult he had, according to one journalist, "dormant powerful sentiments, which rest on foundations of the firmest faith."[38]

In the mid-1870s Cox acquired a saloon in his home neighborhood. He entered politics and served on the city council from 1878 until 1885 when, after joining forces with the Republican reform mayoralty candidate, he ran unsuccessfully for county clerk. He tried for the same post in 1888, failed, and never again stood for public office.[39]

At that time, moving away politically from the Circle, Cox worked with George Moerlein, perhaps the strongest of the GOP professionals in the Zone. In 1890, he and Moerlein quarreled over patronage; and in the city convention of 1891, Cox was able, with the support of the Blaine Club, a kind of political settlement house that he had helped to establish, to defeat Moerlein's candidate for police judge and nominate his own man.[40] Moerlein men now became Cox men. So, too, did Charles P. Taft and the *Times-Star,* which had been one of the last, the most influential, and the most outspoken of Cox's critics in the Hilltops Republican ranks. It accepted Cox, the paper announced, to secure a "New Order" for Cincinnati.[41] And the president of the gas company, sensing the political drift, confided to his diary that he had "concluded [an] arrangement with Geo. B. Cox for services at $3500 per year quarterly to last for three years."[42] In the spring election of 1894 the Republicans carried the city with a plurality of over 6,500 votes, the first decisive municipal election in a decade.[43] In 1897, Cox was the honest broker in a coalition composed of Circle and Zone Negroes, Zone politicians, the gas and traction companies, and Hilltops Republican reformers.[44]

Election returns after 1885 disclose a clear pattern. The GOP won five successive contests by uniting powerful Hilltops support with enough strength in the Zone to overcome the Democratic grip on the Circle.[45] Until 1894 the margins of victory were perilously thin. The substantial triumph of that year merely marked the completion of the alliance which pitted a united periphery against the center of the city.

The heart of the Republican "New Order" coalition, and the critical factor in the election of 1894, was its appeal to voters in the Hilltops fringe who demanded order and reform. To satisfy the Hilltops, Cox and his associates eliminated the bummer, provided brief and decorous conventions, enfranchised Negroes by suppressing violence at the polls, reduced the rapid turnover in office, and cut down the incidence of petty graft and corporation raiding.

Moreover, the "machine" heeded the advice of its reform allies from the Hilltops. Cox accepted the secret ballot, voter registration, and a series of state laws which, though retaining the mayor-council form of government with ward representation, were designed to give the city a stable and more centralized government. The administrations which he indorsed started to build a professional police force, expanded and reequipped the fire department, pushed through a $6,000,000 water-works program, renovated municipal institutions, supported the growth of the University of Cincinnati, launched extensive street-paving and sewer-constructing projects, and tried to reduce the smoke problem and expand the city's park acreage. They also opened the door to housing regulation, suppressed the Sunday saloon, flagrant public gambling, and disorderly brothels (the city was never really closed), began to bring order into the chaotic public-utilities field by favoring privately owned, publicly regulated monopolies under progressive management, and succeeded in keeping the tax rate low. The Republican regime, in short, brought positive government to Cincinnati.[46]

While this program also won votes in the Zone, it was not the sole basis for the party's popularity there. Many of the lieutenants and captains closest to Cox were Zone residents. They composed a colorful group known variously as "the gang," "the sports," or the "bonifaces"—a clique which met nightly Over-the-Rhine either at Schubert and Pels, where each had a special beer mug with his name gilded on it, or at the round table in Wielert's beer garden. Three of them owned or operated combination saloons, gambling joints, and dance halls; one was prominent in German charitable associations and the author of several textbooks used in the elementary schools; another served twenty consecutive terms as president of the Hamilton County League of Building Associations; and one was a former catcher for the Cincinnati Redlegs.[47]

Their tastes, behavior, and attitudes were conveniently summarized in the biographical sketches of ward leaders and city officials in the 1901 *Police and Municipal Guide*. All were characterized as friendly, well-known, "All Around Good-Fellows" who liked a story, belonged to several social and fraternal groups, gave generously to charity, and treated the poor and sick with special kindness. They were all among the most ardent supporters of any project to boost the city.

Cox is pictured in the *Guide* as an adherent to the code of the Zone who had risen to the top. He was a *bon vivant* who enjoyed good cigars and good jokes, a man of wealth whose recently completed Clifton mansion was luxuriously decorated and adorned with expensive works of art, a man of impressive but quiet and private charity. Above all, he was true to his word, loyal to his friends, yet quick to reprimand and replace those who betrayed his trust by misusing public office.[48]

Cox and his top civil servants—surrounded by a motley crowd of newspaper reporters, former boxers and ball players, vaudeville and burlesque performers, and other Vine Street characters—provided an attractive model for men awed by the glamor, wealth, and power which was so visible yet so elusive in the new city. Cox's opponents in the Zone seldom attacked him or this inside group directly. Even in the heat of the 1897 campaign, the *Volksfreund,* the German Catholic Democratic daily, carefully described Cox as an "amiable man" who had to be "admired" for his "success" and, either ignoring or unaware of the process of negotiation and mediation by which he ruled, criticized him only for his illiberality in imposing "dictatorial methods" on the GOP.[49] Indeed, most Zone residents, like those of the Hilltops, found it difficult to object to a government which seemed humane, efficient, and progressive.

Yet it would be a mistake to overestimate the strength of the "New Order" Republican coalition. Its victories from 1885 to 1894 were won by perilously close pluralities. The organization, moreover, failed to carry a referendum for the sale of the city-owned Southern Railroad in 1896 and lost the municipal contest in 1897 to a reform fusion ticket, and the fall elections of 1897, 1898, and 1899 to the Democrats.[50] In all these reversals, crucial defections occurred in both the Hilltops and the Zone. Skittish voters grew indignant over alleged corruption, outraged by inaction on the traction and gas questions, piqued by the rising cost of new city projects, annoyed by the slow expansion of the educational program, or uneasy over the partial sacrifice of democracy to efficiency within the Republican organization.[51]

Thereafter, however, the Republicans rallied and won three of the next four city elections by unprecedented margins. The strategy and tactics remained essentially the same. Although not wholly averse to raising national issues, Cox's group gave local affairs the most emphasis.[52] The organization was occasionally purged of its less savory elements. Cox and his Zone advisors continued to consult with their Hilltops allies on nominations. The party promised and, in fact, tried to deliver order and reform. Without abolishing ward representation in the city council, it strengthened the mayor and streamlined the administration. The party also broadened and deepened its program as civic associations, women's clubs, social workers, social gospellers, and spokesmen for the new unionism—all novel forces in urban politics—expanded and elaborated their demands.[53]

But voting patterns underwent a fundamental and, for the GOP, an ultimately disastrous change. By 1903 the Republicans dominated the entire city, carrying not only the Zone and Hilltops but also the center. The Circle was now the invincible bulwark of Cox's power.[54]

There were several factors involved in the conversion of Circle Democrats to Republicanism. First, Cox had extensive personal contacts with them which dated back to his unsuccessful races for county clerk in the 1880s. Second, the Democrats had been unable to put down factionalism. By the late 1890s there were two reform elements in the party, both of which belabored the regulars from the center of the city as tainted with corruption, too cozy with Cox, and perhaps worst of all, as a discredit and burden to the party because they wore the charred shirt of the courthouse riot.[55]

In the wake of the fusionist victory of 1897, Mike Mullen, the leader of a riverfront Democratic ward, explained why he would henceforth work with the Republican party.

> I have worked hard [for the Democratic party] have suffered much and have won for it many victories. Yet all the while there was a certain element . . . that looked on me with distrust. . . . [L]eaders of the Fusionist Party did not think enough of me to let me look after the voting in my own ward, but sent down a lot of people to watch the count. That decided me.[56]

He was later joined by Colonel Bob O'Brien who, like Mullen, specialized in Christmas turkey, soupline, and family-service politics.[57] These Democrats led their constituents into the Republican fold.

It was this alliance with the Circle which ultimately destroyed Cox. Antimachine spokesmen were convinced that they had to educate the city before they could redeem it. They felt, too, that politics was a potent educational tool. But campaigns had to be spectacular in order to engage the voters' attention and participation. As A. Julius Freiberg notes, the "psychology" of the electorate was such that years of "speaking, writing, explaining, even begging and imploring" had been "to no purpose." The "reformer and his fellow students may sit about the table and evolve high principles for action, but the people . . . will not be fed by those principles unless there is a dramatic setting, and the favorite dramatic setting is the killing of a dragon." And all the people "love the dramatic; not merely the poor, but the rich, and the middle class as well." All that was needed was a situation that would enable the right man to "bring to book the boss himself."[58]

Reformers hammered relentlessly at the theme that Cox was not a good boss; he was the head of a "syndicate" which included the worst products of slum life.[59] In "that part of the city where vice and infamy hold high revel," went one version of the charge, "the boss-made ticket finds its most numerous supporters. Every dive keeper, every creature who fattens upon the wages of sin . . . , all the elements at war with society have enlisted." Men "who claim to be respectable," the chief "beneficiaries of this unholy alliance . . . , go down into the gutter and accept office from hands that are reeking with the filth of the slums." Worse still, this "alliance of the hosts of iniquity with the greed of special privilege and ambition for power and place" plays so successfully "upon the prejudices and . . . superstition of the many that wrong is often espoused by those who in the end are the victims of the wrong."[60]

The reformers also impugned Cox's personal integrity. Democratic County Prosecutor Henry T. Hunt secured evidence that Cox had perjured himself in 1906 when he said he had not received a cent of some $250,000 of interest on public funds which Republican county treasurers had been paid by bankers. In the spring of 1911, Hunt and the grand jury indicted Cox and 123 others during a broad investigation of politics, corruption, and vice.[61]

Finally, Hunt, stressing the issue of moral indignation, ran for mayor in the fall of 1911 on a Democratic reform ticket. Using the moral rhetoric of the muckraker, Hunt and his associates tied bossism, the chaos, poverty, and vice of the slums, and the malefactors of great wealth together and pictured them as a threat to the welfare of the whole city. Once again the Hilltops and Zone voted for order and reform. Hunt's progressive coalition swept the periphery, lost only in the Circle wards, and won the election.[62]

By that time, however, Cox was no longer boss. President Taft and Charles P. Taft had wanted Cox to step aside as early as 1905, but they found him indispensable. After the grand jury revelations, however, they were able to convince the "bonifaces" that Cox was a liability. With the organization against him, Cox retired. For a time, he insisted that his two chief assistants, August Herrmann and Rudolph Hynicka, should also quit, apparently convinced that they, like himself, could no longer command the confidence of the periphery. Charles P. Taft's *Times-Star* agreed. The two men, backed by the Blaine Club, merely resigned their official party positions, but refused to get out of politics entirely.[63]

What, then, was Cox's role in politics and government in the new city? He helped create and manage a voluntary political-action organization which bridged the racial and cultural chasms between the Circle, Zone, and Hilltops. He and his allies were able to bring positive and moderate reform government to Cincinnati and to mitigate the conflict and disorder which accompanied the emergence of the new city. With the crisis atmosphere muted, ardent reformers could develop more sophisticated programs and agitate, educate, and organize without arousing the kind of divisive, emotional, and hysterical response which had immobilized municipal statesmen in the 1880s. In the process, while battering at the boss, the slums, and the special-privilege syndicate, they shattered the bonds of confidence which linked the Zone "bonifaces" and the moderate reformers of the Hilltops to Cox's organization. Cox, it seems, said more than he realized when, in 1892, he remarked that a boss was "not necessarily a public enemy."[64]

■ ■ ■ ■ Notes

1 Gustav J. Karger, "George Barnesdale Cox: Proprietor of Cincinnati," *Frank Leslie's Popular Monthly,* LVII (Jan. 1904), 273; Lincoln Steffens, "Ohio: A Tale of Two Cities," *McClure's Magazine,* XXV (June 1905), 309; Frank Parker Stockbridge, "The Biggest Boss of Them All," *Hampton's Magazine,* XXVI (Jan.–June 1911), 616; George Kibbe Turner, "The Thing Above the Law: The Rise and Rule of George B. Cox, and His Overthrow by Young Hunt and the Fighting Idealists of Cincinnati," *McClure's Magazine,* XXXVIII (March 1912), 580. See also Wallace S. Sayre and Nelson W. Polsby, "American Political Science and the Study of Urbanization," Philip M. Hauser and Leo F. Schnore, eds., *The Study of Urbanization* (New York, 1965), 115–23.

2 It operated, according to William Howard Taft, "as smoothly . . . as a nicely adjusted Corliss engine. . . ." Cincinnati *Enquirer,* Oct. 22, 1905.

3 Zane L. Miller, "Boss Cox and the Municipal Reformers: Cincinnati Progressivism, 1880–1914" (doctoral dissertation, University of Chicago, 1966), Part I, Introduction, 2–5.

4 For the quotation see Max Mosler, Jacob Hoffman, and James D. Smith, *Historic Brighton: Its Origin, Growth and Development* (Cincinnati, 1902), 91. See also James A. Green to Joseph C. Green, March 28, 1913, James A. Green Papers (Cincinnati Historical Society); Andrew Hickenlooper, "Reminiscences," 524, Andrew Hickenlooper Papers (Cincinnati Historical Society); Graham Romeyn Taylor, *Satellite Cities: A Study of Industrial Suburbs* (New York, 1915), 91–93; Willard Glazier, *Peculiarities of American Cities* (Philadelphia, 1886), 135.

5 Frank Y. Grayson, *Pioneers of Night Life on Vine Street* (Cincinnati, Aug. 1924), 63–65, 123–25. Interviews: William C. Smith, Dec. 19, 1962; Alfred Segal, Nov. 2, 1962; Robert Heuck, Nov. 27, 1962; and Edward F. Alexander, Nov. 13, 1962.

6 Cincinnati *Post,* June 20, 1912; Ruth M. Heistand, "A Social History of Cincinnati's Eastern Basin Area: An Inquiry into the Character, Interests, Attitudes, and Social Services of this Primary Neighborhood" (master's thesis, University of Cincinnati, 1936), 55, 72–75.

7 James Albert Green, *History of the Associated Charities of Cincinnati, 1879–1937: A Record of Service* (Cincinnati, n.d.), 18–19.
8 Sidney D. Maxwell, *The Suburbs of Cincinnati: Sketches Historical and Descriptive* (Cincinnati, 1870), 2, 96–97, 99–100, 118–28, 148, 177–85.
9 Cincinnati *American Israelite*, Oct. 26, 1899.
10 Cincinnati *Civic News*, I (Oct. 1911), 3; Frank F. Dinsmore, Chas. W. Dupuis, Martin H. Fischer, and Walter A. Draper, *History of the Queen City Optimists Club* (Cincinnati, Jan. 1955), 1–2; *Mrs. Devereux's Blue Book of Cincinnati Society for the Year 1912–1913* (Cincinnati [1912?]), 183–241.
11 Charles Dudley Warner, "Studies of the Great West, Cincinnati and Louisville," *Harper's New Monthly Magazine*, LXXVII (Aug. 1888), 430.
12 For a full analysis of this region see Miller, Part I, 58–124.
13 Robert A. Woods and Albert J. Kennedy, *The Zone of Emergence* (Cambridge, 1962), 31–183.
14 Cincinnati *Post*, June 11, 1913.
15 Quoted in Joseph Stacy Hill, "Further Chats With My Descendants," Typescript ca. 1933, p. 42 (Cincinnati Historical Society).
16 Taylor, 95–96.
17 Cincinnati *Catholic-Telegraph*, March 20, 1890, Nov. 2, 16, 1893.
18 For a detailed analysis see Miller, Part I, 15–57.
19 Cincinnati *Charities Review*, I (April 1908), 8; United Jewish Charities, *Fourteenth Annual Report, 1910* (Cincinnati, n.d.), 59.
20 One social worker speculated that the Circle dwellers' "lack of energy and initiative" was due "to physical bankruptcy . . . which, although largely imaginative, is the result of [a] neurotic and temperamental condition . . . and incapacitates . . . as effectively as real physical disability." See United Jewish Charities, *Eighteenth Annual Report, 1914* (Cincinnati, n.d.), 7–8.
21 Boris D. Bogen, "Politics in Jewish Settlements," *Jewish Charities*, II (Sept. 1911), 10–11.
22 Cincinnati *Enquirer*, March 9, 1884. See also Joseph D. Emery, *Thirty-Five Years Among the Poor and Public Institutions of Cincinnati* (Cincinnati, 1877), 16.
23 Perhaps the best among the many contemporary accounts of the riot is J. S. Tunison, *The Cincinnati Riot: Its Causes and Results* (Cincinnati, 1886). The casualty totals are from "Annual Report of the Department of Police," *Annual Reports of the City Departments of the City of Cincinnati for the Fiscal Year Ending December 31, 1884* (Cincinnati, 1885), 311.
24 Benjamin Butterworth to Alphonso Taft, June 5, 1885, Taft Papers, Family Correspondence, Box 25 (Manuscript Division, Library of Congress). For other accounts of the election disorders in the fall of 1884 see Cincinnati *Catholic-Telegraph*, Oct. 16, 1884; Butterworth to Joseph B. Foraker, Jan. 5, 9, 1885, Joseph B. Foraker Papers, Box 31 (Cincinnati Historical Society).
25 Oscar Ameringer, *If You Don't Weaken: The Autobiography of Oscar Ameringer* (New York, 1940), 44–47; Sidney D. Maxwell to Mrs. Emma Maxwell, May 5, 6, 11, 12, 1886, Sidney D. Maxwell Papers (Cincinnati Historical Society); Cincinnati *Times-Star*, May 3, 13, 1886.
26 Cincinnati *Freie Presse*, Jan. 23, 1921. For the strikes see Cincinnati *Times-Star*, Feb. 3, Oct. 6, 1892; Cincinnati Central Labor Council *Chronicle*, June 5, 1886, Sept. 29, 1901.
27 Henry F. Pringle, *The Life and Times of William Howard Taft: A Biography* (2 vols., New York, 1939), I, 134–36.
28 Rev. T. H. Pearne, *What Shall Be Done with the Cincinnati Sunday Saloon? An Address Before the Cincinnati Methodist Preachers' Meeting, May 13th and May 19th, 1887* (Cincinnati, 1887), 7. See also Cincinnati *Times-Star*, March 29, 1889; Cincinnati

Post, March 29, 1889; Cincinnati *Catholic-Telegraph,* June 5, 1884; *Address of the Bund für Freiheit und Recht* (Cincinnati, May 1886), 4, 5, 6–7.

29 Cincinnati *Times-Star,* Dec. 2, 1889.

30 Jno. Pearson to Foraker, July 26, 1889; Foraker to John B. Mosby, July 26, 1889, Foraker Papers, Boxes 38, 29; "Report of the Non-Partisan Board of Police Commissioners," *Annual Reports of the City Departments of the City of Cincinnati for the Fiscal Year Ending December 31, 1889* (Cincinnati, 1889), 199–200; Joseph Benson Foraker, *Notes of a Busy Life* (2 vols., Cincinnati, 1916), I, 411–16. For the "era of the back door" see Grayson, *Pioneers of Night Life,* 18.

31 See the reports of the city boards, departments, and agencies, and the mayor's annual messages in the *Annual Reports* of the city, 1884–1891. See also Cincinnati Commercial Club, *Report of [the] Special Committee to [the] Commercial Club . . . on Deficient Water Supply to the City, Aug. 25, 1890* (Cincinnati, n.d.); Cincinnati Chamber of Commerce, *A Canal Town in a Railroad Era* (Cincinnati, Feb. 1887); Charles B. Wilby, "What is the Matter with Cincinnati?" *Extracts of a Paper Read before the Young Business Men's Club, Nov. 30, 1886* (Cincinnati, n.d.).

32 William Howard Taft to Mother [Louisa Taft], March 27, 1885, Taft Papers, Family Correspondence, Box 25.

33 In 1885 the Republican reform mayoralty candidate won by 4,000 votes out of a total of nearly 53,000. See Cincinnati *Times-Star,* April 6, 1885. But the elections of 1887 and 1889 were three-cornered affairs resulting in a total Republican plurality of 1,153. In 1891, with only two strong tickets in the field, the Republican mayoralty nominee won by a margin of 138 votes over his Democratic opponent. Cincinnati *Times-Star,* April 5, 1887; Hamilton County Board of Elections, "Record of City Elections, Commencing in 1888" (Offices of the Hamilton County Board of Elections, Cincinnati).

34 Richard C. Wade, *The Urban Frontier: The Rise of Western Cities, 1790–1830* (Cambridge, 1959), 112–17, 204–06.

35 Cincinnati *Times-Star,* Sept. 27, 29, 1890.

36 Cincinnati *Post,* Jan. 2, 1897.

37 Cincinnati *Post,* Jan. 2, 8, 15, 20, 26, 30, Feb. 1, 1897.

38 Karger, 274.

39 See notes 1 and 37.

40 George B. Cox to Foraker, Dec. 24, 1888; Foraker to T. W. Graydon, March 16, 1889; Foraker to Murat Halstead, March 18, 1889, Foraker Papers, Boxes 32, 29; Diaries, Feb. 2, 16, March 23, 25, 1891, Hickenlooper Papers; Cincinnati *Post,* Feb. 3, March 4, 9, 1891; Hickenlooper to Milton A. McRae, March 26, 1891, Hickenlooper Papers.

41 Cincinnati *Times-Star,* April 4, 1891.

42 Diaries, May 8, 1891, Hickenlooper Papers.

43 Hamilton County Board of Elections, "Record of City Elections."

44 Although Cox avoided publicity, his few public statements succinctly summarize his technique. Bossism, he believed, evolved with the modern city. He never consciously aspired to leadership but acquired it naturally—or had it thrust upon him. A good and successful boss, he felt, claimed and held power by adhering to a few principles. He kept graft at a minimum, kept his word, and demanded that those responsible for securing nominations and winning elections receive consideration when favors were passed out. See Cincinnati *Commercial-Gazette,* Jan. 29, 1892; Cincinnati *Post,* Feb. 22, 1911, May 20, 1916.

45 Election returns from Cincinnati *Times-Star,* April 6, 1885, April 5, 1887; Hamilton County Board of Elections, "Record of City Elections."

46 See *Annual Reports of the City Departments of the City of Cincinnati . . . , 1885–*

1897; Cincinnati Municipal Reference Bureau, *The March of City Government, City of Cincinnati (1802–1936)* (Cincinnati, 1937), 15–16.

47 The Cincinnati *Times-Star,* March 27, 30, 1891, lists all the Republican councilmen, gives their occupations, and comments on their backgrounds. See also Cincinnati *Citizens' Bulletin,* Aug. 29, 1903.

48 Cincinnati Police Department, *Police and Municipal Guide, 1901* (Cincinnati, n.d.). Perhaps the best description of the "bonifaces" and the Vine Street characters is in Grayson, 63–65. Grayson was a reporter for the Cincinnati *Times-Star* and a member of the coterie.

49 Cincinnati *Volksfreund,* March 8, 1897. The Cincinnati *Catholic-Telegraph* and the *Chronicle,* the Cincinnati Central Labor Council organ, both spoke essentially to a Zone constituency. Even when in a reform mood they did not attack the "bonifaces" personally in these years.

50 In the 1899 gubernatorial election the Zone, apparently attracted by the Democratic reform platform, went Democratic along with the Circle. The Hilltops, however, voted Republican. See Hamilton County Board of Elections, "Abstract of Votes Cast from 1896–1899, Incl., . . . 1899" (Offices of Hamilton County Board of Elections, n.d.). In 1897 both the Zone and the Hilltops went for the fusion reformers against the GOP. See Hamilton County Board of Elections, "Record of City Elections."

51 The accumulation of Zone grievances is quite clearly seen in the 1897 election which the fusionists won by 7,400 votes out of a total of 64,000. For the campaign and post-election analyses see Miller, 818–81. Nonetheless, it was the massive defection of the heretofore solidly Republican Hilltops which put the fusionists on top in 1897.

52 Although national issues were irrelevant, the general pattern of politics in Cincinnati was similar to national developments. Carl N. Degler has suggested that the Republican party attained national dominance after 1884 in part because it was identified by urban voters as the party of positive action. See Carl N. Degler, "American Political Parties and the Rise of the City: An Interpretation," *Journal of American History,* LI (June 1964), 41–50.

53 For the new forces in politics see Miller, 305–37. The Cincinnati *Citizens' Bulletin,* Aug. 15, 29, 1908, Oct. 23, 1909, Sept. 30, 1911, among other contemporary sources, recorded Republican strategy. For the policy of the Republican administrations see the *Annual Reports of the City Departments of the City of Cincinnati . . .* for the years 1900–1905 and 1907–1911.

54 Before this time, only two Circle wards had been reliably Republican. One, the Eighteenth, was Cox's former district; and the other, the old Ninth, was entrusted to Rudolph K. Hynicka who, with August Herrmann, served as Cox's closest associates. See also Hamilton County Board of Elections, "Record of City Elections."

55 Cincinnati *Times-Star,* Nov. 7, 1888. For the Democratic factions see *Times-Star,* March 25, 1885; C. W. Woolley to John Sherman, April 7, 1885, John Sherman Papers (Manuscript Division, Library of Congress); Cincinnati *Volksfreund,* April 8, 1887; Cincinnati *Times-Star,* April 2, 1889; Cincinnati *Post,* April 2, 1889, Feb. 26, 1894; and especially R. B. Bowler to Charles T. Greve, Sept. 13, 19, 20, Oct. 8, 29, Dec. 19, 26, 1893, Jan. 6, 12, March 23, 1894, Charles T. Greve Papers (Cincinnati Historical Society).

56 Cincinnati *Post,* April 12, 1897.

57 Cincinnati *Citizens' Bulletin,* April 11, May 9, Aug. 29, 1903; Cincinnati *Volksblatt,* April 7, 1903; Henry C. Wright, *Bossism in Cincinnati* (Cincinnati, 1905), 48–49.

58 A. Julius Freiberg, "Mayor Hunt's Administration in Cincinnati," *National Municipal Review,* III (July 1914), 518.

59 See, for example, Cincinnati *Post,* Oct. 5, 11, 13, 1905; Cincinnati *Enquirer,* Nov. 1, 17, 1905; Cincinnati *Citizens' Bulletin,* May 6, July 8, Sept. 30, 1905, April 27, 1907.

60 Cincinnati *Citizens' Bulletin,* Oct. 19, 1907.

61 Ohio General Assembly, Joint Committee on the Investigation of Cincinnati and Hamilton County, *Who got the quarter million graft and who paid it back?* . . . *History and Work of the Special Committee Created Under and by Virtue of Senate Joint Resolution No. 54 and House Bill No. 1287* (Columbus, n.d.), 6–11; Cincinnati *Citizens' Bulletin*, Feb. 22, 1908, April 8, 1911; Charles P. Taft to William Howard Taft, Feb. 28, 1911, Taft Papers, Presidential Series, No. 3, Box 523.

62 Henry T. Hunt, *An Account of My Stewardship of the Office of Prosecuting Attorney* (Cincinnati, n.d.), 1–11; Cincinnati *Citizens' Bulletin*, Sept. 30, 1911; Cincinnati *Post*, Oct. 25, 1911; Hamilton County Board of Elections, "Abstract of Votes . . . 1908–1911" (Offices of the Hamilton County Board of Elections). The language of the Cincinnati reformers regarding democracy, morality, and politics was very much like that of the Muckrakers as described in Stanley K. Schultz, "The Morality of Politics: The Muckrakers' Vision of Democracy," *Journal of American History*, LII (Dec. 1965), 527–47. Yet they were primarily interested in devising institutions, including a positive government, which would mold moral citizens and make politics democratic. Their goal was not destructive, nor their rhetoric ceremonial.

63 Cincinnati *Times-Star*, Nov. 8, 1905; William Howard Taft to Rudolph K. Hynicka, July 15, 1910, Taft Papers, Presidential Series 8, Letterbooks; William Howard Taft to Horace D. Taft, Nov. [?], 1911, Taft Papers, Presidential Series 8, Letterbook; Cincinnati *Post*, May 22, 1911; Cincinnati *Commercial-Tribune*, Nov. 5, 1911.

64 Cincinnati *Commercial-Gazette*, Jan. 29, 1892; Cincinnati *Post*, Feb. 22, 1911.

13

The Small Businessman as Big Businessman: The City Commissioner and Management Movements

JAMES WEINSTEIN

In recent years, a number of scholars, most notably Samuel P. Hays and James Weinstein, have drastically revised the prevailing conception of municipal reform in the early twentieth century—the period historians have called the progressive era. Textbooks and general histories presented the process of urban political reform as an uprising of the people against an unholy alliance of bosses, the underworld, and crooked businessmen; more simply, good men banding together to throw the rascals out. Lincoln Steffens recognized that the boss and his machine filled some real needs, and that the reform process was more complicated than just getting rid of evil politicians. Hays contends, however, that Steffens and the later writers who took their cues from him badly misread both the character of opposition to the machine and the forces leading to the transformation of municipal government.[1]

With the increased scale and the more highly developed organization of American society in the late nineteenth century, new groups arose including men who conducted business on a metropolitan or nationwide scale, and professionals who acquired and used highly specialized knowledge in their practices. Such men and women objected to inefficient government that catered to the values and parochialisms of lower-class groups. Immigrants and workers generally took interest in their own particular neighborhoods and wards, and lacked much concern for the city as a whole. Their values centered around home, family, church, and saloon; honest, efficient, business-like government might even be injurious to them. Efficiency might mean cutting the public payroll; impartial law enforcement might close their saloons and give them no place to turn when a son ran afoul of the police; and civil service procedures might reduce access to needed jobs.

On the other hand, forward-looking businessmen and professionals wanted a government that would provide maximum services for minimum taxes and would be oriented toward city-wide rather than local interests. To accomplish these goals, they wished to see members of the upper and upper-middle classes take over in the political sphere as they had already done in the economic and social spheres. In a number of cities "reform" groups, heavily weighted toward the upper end of the social scale, acted to put an end to the traditional decentralized and lower-class dominated political system. One method they employed was changing the form of representation from a fairly large council elected on a ward basis to a small

217

council elected at large. The purpose and the result was to eliminate blue-collar workers and small businessmen as representatives on the councils. Securing election in an at-large system usually required access to the newspapers, substantial campaign funds, and a reputation as one of the city's leading citizens. Prominent business or professional men could easily meet these requirements, while workers and small shopkeepers could not.

As James Weinstein points out in the article below, the commission and the city-manager forms of government achieved most directly the goals of rational, efficient, and businesslike government. Adoption of the corporation structure in business enterprise promoted rationality and efficiency in the American economy; what better model could be chosen by those who wished the same values to prevail in urban government? Whether rationality or efficiency, conceived in business or engineering terms, could solve the problems of cities is another question.

■ ■ ■ ■ **For Further Reading**

Samuel P. Hays, "The Politics of Municipal Reform in the Progressive Era," *Pacific Northwest Quarterly*, 55 (October 1964): 157–169 is an important article that shows the elitist nature of many urban reform movements. Allen Davis, *Spearheads for Reform: The Social Settlements and the Progressive Movement 1890–1914* (New York: Oxford University Press, 1967) illustrates another facet of urban "reform," that of dedicated women and men who tried to make life more livable for the immigrant poor of the great metropolitan centers.

■ On a national scale big businessmen tended to be the leaders for reform and regulation, while the smaller manufacturers and commercial men often took a narrower, or more immediately interest-conscious, view. In the movement for an interstate trade commission, later embodied in the Federal Trade Commission, and in the agitation for workmen's compensation, the executives of leading financial institutions and of large corporations (especially those associated with the National Civic Federation), assumed the initiative. The National Association of Manufacturers, which represented small manufacturers and was suspicious of financiers, dragged its feet until its membership was gradually converted to support for, or acquiescence in, the new reforms. But on a municipal level the small businessman sometimes displayed a broader vision. He was in his own domain and tended, on this scale, to assume attitudes of social responsibility. As participants in local chambers of commerce and boards of trade, local businessmen could identify the future of their cities with that of their own business interests. To rationalize and make more attractive a particular city meant more business for its local entrepreneurs. The centralization of power, or the removal of decision making from "politics," favored businessmen over workingmen or white collar employees. In no area of political or social reform did small businessmen more clearly demonstrate the force of this logic than in the movements for city commission and manager governments.

The idea later embodied in commission and council manager government was enunciated as early as 1896 by Dayton, Ohio, industrial pioneer, John H. Patterson. In a speech at the Dayton centennial, the founder and president of the National Cash Register Company argued that "a city is a great business enterprise whose stockholders are the people." If Patterson had his way, "municipal affairs would be placed on a strict business basis" and directed "not by partisans, either Republican or Democratic, but by men who are skilled in business management and social science."[2] It was not until five years after Patterson spoke that the first commission government came into being, and it was a dozen years before the movement took root and began rapidly to spread. At first, the commission idea was only one plan in what a leading civic reformer described in 1903 as a "hopeless diversity" of remedies for the inefficiency and poor service of American city governments.[3] Yet so well did this "most far reaching progressive proposal for institutional change"[4] fulfill the requirements of business that it was quickly adopted by hundreds of boards of trade and chambers of commerce. Today commission and council manager governments are the prevailing forms of municipal organization, in use in almost half of all American cities.

Of course, the drive for municipal reform at the turn of the century did not come from businessmen alone. Graft, corruption, and the misery of slum life had been given wide publicity by reformers and journalists, and by single taxers and socialists. Muckrakers Jacob Riis, Lincoln Steffens, B. O. Flower, and others had exposed the "Shame of the Cities"; successful reform movements had been led by mayors Tom Johnson of Cleveland and Samuel (Golden Rule) Jones of Toledo, and by many other men less well known. The business community did not support this variety of reform, tinged as it was with radical social theories. Indeed, many early reformers concluded that business interests strongly supported the old system of corruption. In 1906 the Cleveland reformer, Frederick C. Howe, wrote that it was "privilege of an industrial rather than a personal sort that has given birth to the boss." Howe had entered political life "with the conviction that our evils were traceable to personal causes"—to the "foreign voter" and to the indifference of the "best" citizens. But experience forced him to a new belief: democracy had failed "by virtue of the privileged interests which have taken possession of our institutions for their own enrichment." From a belief in a "businessman's government" he, like Lincoln Steffens and journalist-reformer Brand Whitlock, had come to believe in a "people's government."[5] Even so conservative a man as William J. Gaynor, mayor of New York City, commented in 1910 that the true corrupters were the "so-called 'leading' citizens" who "get a million dollars out of the city dishonestly while the 'boss' gets a thousand."[6]

As Howe understood, businessmen opposed social reformers such as Jones and Johnson because their administrations disrupted the working relationships between business and the local political machine without providing a suitable and dependable alternative—and also because Jones and Johnson increased the political power of labor and radicals.[7] Aversion to graft, alone, was not enough to move businessmen to sponsor reform. Though costly, business had accepted and lived with graft for many years. What converted these men into civic reformers was the increased importance of the public functions of the twentieth-century city. Streets had to be paved for newly developed motor vehicles; harbors had to be deepened and wharves improved for big, new freighters. In addition, electric lighting systems, street railways, sewage disposal plants, water supplies, and fire departments had to be installed or drastically improved to meet the needs of inhabitants, human and commercial, of hundreds of rapidly growing industrial centers.

Municipal services had always been expensive, but as they increased in magnitude and number, costs tended to grow more and more burdensome. In city after city, business circles came to realize that something had to be done. Boston in 1909 was described as "another city whose businessmen have awakened to a new sense of their civic responsibilities" because "the debt of the city was increasing by leaps and bounds, apparently out of all proportion to the improvements for which it was incurred." At the same time the "extraordinary expenses" of municipal services in Chicago moved the Commercial Club of that city to work out a "general scheme of public improvements," known as the "Plan of Chicago."[8] In the search for alternatives, the commission and manager plans emerged as most promising. They offered stability; they were less expensive; they were devoid of commitment to radical social theories; and they assured businessmen of a more direct and central role in municipal affairs.

The first commission government emerged from the backwash of the great tidal wave that virtually destroyed Galveston, Texas, in 1900. Left in ruins, with a government unable to cope with the situation, the city was on the edge of bankruptcy. In the emergency, the old, corrupt aldermanic system was abandoned and an organization of local businessmen, the Deepwater Committee, took control. This group, which had been formed earlier to promote harbor improvements, looked on Galveston "not as a city, but [as] a great ruined business." Setting out to establish a new government capable of quick, efficient action in rebuilding a modern city and port, these businessmen evolved a plan for government that closely followed the most efficient form of organization known to them: the business corporation.[9] The theory of the commission plan echoed John H. Patterson's view. It was that "a municipality is largely a business corporation," and, as such, that it should seek "to apply business methods to public service." The voters were seen as stockholders, and the commissioners as corresponding to the board of directors of "an ordinary business corporation."[10]

As adopted, the Galveston plan provided for a five man commission vested with the combined powers of mayor and board of aldermen. Each commissioner headed a city department and functioned as legislator and administrator. The Commission, because it handled all city business, could act promptly and efficiently, and the relative prominence and broad powers given each commissioner "assured" the attraction of "good" men to office. In short, it was a plan to make government more businesslike and to attract businessmen to government.

Commission government spread rapidly through Texas: first to Houston in 1903, then by 1907 to Dallas, Dennison, Fort Worth, El Paso, Greenville, and Sherman. In 1907 Des Moines, Iowa, enacted a commission charter, and to the accompaniment of nationwide publicity the "Texas Idea" was renamed for its Northern imitator. By 1913 over 300 cities from coast to coast had adopted the "Des Moines Plan."

Yet even while commission government was winning quick and widespread acceptance, serious structural weaknesses appeared. The election of popular but incompetent administrators, men who played politics better than they ran city departments, revealed the disadvantages of combining executive and legislative functions in the commissioners. Individual commissioners often attempted to consolidate their positions by securing excessive appropriations in order either to strengthen their own departments or simply to reward their supporters with city jobs. Since the commissions as a whole fixed both appropriations and policy, the consent of the other commissioners was necessary, and a system of favor-trading often developed in the commissions, side by side with interdepartmental rivalries. In many cases "five separate governments" tended to develop around the five commissioners.[11]

To overcome these weaknesses, municipal reform leader H. S. Gilbertson drew up a "commission-manager" plan in 1910, and the board of trade of Lockport, New York, sponsored it as its proposed new city charter.[12] The Lockport proposal, as Gilbertson's plan was called, separated the legislative and executive functions by retaining an elected commission to legislate for the city, while providing for an appointed manager to assume all executive functions. Under this plan executive ability was no longer a prerequisite for successful commissioners. At the same time the day-to-day management of city affairs was removed from more direct political pressures by the creation of an independent office for the manager, who was hired on a contractual basis to carry out the policies set by the commission.

Under the Lockport proposal departmental appointments, as well as the expenditure of city funds, were, for the most part, placed in the manager's hands. Despite the efforts of the Lockport board of trade, the manager charter was defeated in the New York legislature in 1911, and once again the South took the lead when Sumter, South Carolina, secured a "commission-manager" charter the same year. But, as with the original commission plan, the manager movement received national impetus only after a Northern city, Dayton, Ohio, adopted the plan in 1913. Thereafter, the "Dayton Plan" spread rapidly, and in six years more than 130 cities had put through manager charters.[13]

The initiative for commission and manager government came consistently from chambers of commerce and other organized business groups; they were the decisive element, in coalition with civic reformers, which made the movement a sweeping success. We have seen that the businessmen's Deepwater Committee originated the commission plan in Galveston, and that the Board of Trade sponsored the manager plan in Lockport. Similarly, in Des Moines, the Commercial Club led the commission movement after a local lawyer, James G. Berryhill, had discovered "a city government approaching the ideal" on a business trip to Galveston in 1905. Berryhill, exulting over the idea that the commission managed Galveston "as a board of directors manages a bank," returned home a champion of the new reform.

After securing its adoption in Des Moines he turned his attention to Pennsylvania, where the plan won approval of the Pittsburgh chamber of commerce in 1909. In turn, the Pittsburgh businessmen organized a convention of representatives of commercial bodies of all the second- and third-class cities of Pennsylvania, which met at Williamsport in 1910. After hearing Berryhill describe the advantages of commission government, the delegates—bankers, merchants, and manufacturers who stood in the first rank of Pennsylvania businessmen—voted unanimously to support legislation to permit the adoption of commission charters. They also pledged to press a campaign of education for the new form of civic government and went home to do battle with their local political machines. In June 1913, their efforts bore fruit when an act passed the Pennsylvania legislature *requiring* all cities of the third class to adopt commission charters.[14]

In individual cities, too, business leaders pushed through commission charters. In Dallas, Texas, a "prominent banker" headed a "citizen's committee" that drafted a charter enacted by the state legislature in 1907. In Columbia, South Carolina, the local chamber of commerce recommended a commission charter in 1912. And in Charlotte, North Carolina, the chamber of commerce led the movement for commission government in 1917.[15]

The manager movement, like the commission, also was led by chambers of commerce and boards of trade. The first manager charter in Sumter, South Carolina, for example, was promoted by the local chamber. Dayton was a model of business sponsorship. There the chamber of commerce set up a committee of five members, headed by John H. Patterson. He set up a Bureau of Municipal Research, which, in turn, "plunged into an aggressive campaign of public education."

Meanwhile, the chamber "began to suspect that its open sponsorship of a new charter might seem an evil omen to many of the ordinary working-class voters." Accordingly, it ceased its official participation, and the original committee was increased, first to fifteen, and finally to one hundred. The new citizens' committee then hired the former secretary of the Detroit Board of Commerce, who built a broad coalition in support of the reform. Despite these efforts the opposition to the new charter on the part of the Democratic and Socialist parties appeared to doom the manager plan in Dayton, until, as in Galveston, an act of God intervened in behalf of the businessmen. A short time before the charter election, Dayton suffered a devastating flood; when the mayor proved unable to cope with the problems it created, John H. Patterson took charge of the city. Patterson used his factory, fortunately located on high ground, as a rescue headquarters; quickly manufactured many makeshift boats; housed and fed flood victims; and as the waters receded stood out as hero and leader.[16] In the election, the manager charter carried easily.

After Dayton installed its new manager, chambers of commerce rapidly extended their activity in behalf of the plan. In Glen Falls, New York, the local chamber conducted a canvass for a manager charter. In Jackson, Michigan, the chamber proposed a "commission-manager system," which carried despite opposition from working class wards. In Kalamazoo, the newly organized chamber of commerce listed manager government as the second point on its program. In Defiance, Ohio, the chamber sponsored a high school oratorical contest on city government: the winner spoke on "One Man Management of Cities." In St. Augustine, Florida, the chamber prepared a manager charter and secured its adoption. In Benton Harbor, Michigan, the manager charter was twice rejected at the polls; undaunted, the local chamber of commerce pressed again for its acceptance.

Commission and manager government had become the favorite of local business—because the new municipal governments met their most obvious needs.[17] From the beginning the new form of government permitted substantial increases in the services provided by the city, at little or no extra cost, and often at considerable savings. In Galveston, for example, the commission found the city bankrupt in 1901. By 1906 it had brought the value of the city's paper to above par. In these years the entire city had been rebuilt, a giant seawall erected, the grade of most of the city raised, and the harbor improved by the addition of many new deepwater wharves: all at an annual saving of $220,000, one third of the old budget. In Houston, too, after five years of commission government, the tax rate had been reduced 30¢ per $100, while the cost of city water had been reduced from 50¢ to 15¢ per 1,000 gallons. During this period the commission expended $1,865,757 for improvements, all out of current revenue. In Des Moines, after one year the commission showed a saving of $184,000 over the old system of "graft and extravagance." During this year new public buildings were built, the civic center was landscaped, and the river banks were walled. Similarly, in Leavenworth, Kansas, a saving of $26,000 was anticipated in the first year of the commission, despite the expense of better services.[18]

Manager cities followed the same pattern. In the three years from 1908 to 1911, Staunton, Virginia, was "lifted from mud to asphalt" and placed on a sound financial basis, with no increase in expenditures. The new manager paved streets at ten times the former pace, improved the water system, and installed modern lighting; in the process he increased the value of the city's paper by almost one hundred percent. In Austin, Texas, similar improvements were made. In Dayton, under the manager, the tax rate was increased slightly, but improvements were achieved in all areas of municipal activity.[19]

In addition to the money saved and the indirect benefits to business in the form of improved facilities and services, some commission and manager governments directly subsidized their local entrepreneurs. When, for example, the Oakland, California, commission floated a bond issue of $2,500,000 for harbor improvements it also imposed a tax of $2\frac{1}{2}$¢ per $1,000 for municipal advertising and the entertainment of visitors. And in Amarillo, Texas, the commission-manager government imposed a direct tax of two mills to maintain the local chamber of commerce.[20]

The argument that commission and manager charters would assure the election of "good" (i.e., business) men to office usually proved valid. The first commission in Galveston comprised five businessmen—"a veteran wholesale merchant," a "promising young . . . banker," "an active partner in a prosperous wholesale house," "a successful real estate dealer," and the secretary-treasurer of a livestock concern—all "good, clean, representative men." In Austin, Mayor A. P. Wooldrige, himself a prominent banker, headed a "businessman's government" that stayed in office for ten years. In Janesville, businessmen were in the leadership under both the commission and manager charters. In Dayton, John H. Patterson and the chamber of commerce put up a hand-picked slate that won easily. In Springfield, Ohio, five experienced businessmen made up the commission, while in Jackson, Michigan, most of the councilmen from 1914 to 1919 were business executives, bankers, or merchants, and the mayor during these years was also president of the chamber of commerce. In Illinois, too, the new commissions generally included several active businessmen, some of whom had not previously been active in politics.[21]

Even in cities where businessmen did not constitute a majority of its members, the commission remained strongly under their influence. In Des Moines, for example, the city council frequently met with the advisory board of the Commercial Club to consult on matters of public importance. In Omaha, the Commercial Club organized an advisory committee with the intention of meeting regularly with the seven-man commission, so that the commissioners might "profit by the advice of men who know." The logical culmination of this development occurred in Beaufort, South Carolina, where the offices of city manager and secretary of the board of trade were combined, with the city government and the local businessmen each paying one half the manager's salary. Commission and manager governments did, indeed, encourage businessmen to play a more direct role in municipal affairs.[22]

This being so, most businessmen were well satisfied with the operation of the new form of municipal government. In 1915, in an effort to decide whether or not to sponsor a commission-manager charter in its city, the chamber of commerce of Fulton, New York, sent a confidential inquiry to bankers and other leading businessmen in cities that had adopted the manager plan. Replies were received from thirty-two cities. In twenty-eight, business leaders found the manager system highly satisfactory; in three they were disappointed; in one city they were divided.

Many reported substantial savings in the operation of their city government, while almost all boasted of increased services with no extra cost. Bank presidents and cashiers were almost unanimous in their praise of manager government. The assistant cashier of the River National Bank in Springfield, Ohio, wrote that "the business class of our citizens are very well satisfied." A bank president from Sherman, Texas, reported that "those who pay taxes are generally satisfied with the new system." The cashier of the Union Bank in Jackson, Michigan, wrote, "Its effect on business is favorable." From Montrose, Colorado, Charles A. Black replied, "I am one of the largest property owners and taxpayers here. . . . I find that our present city manager government is far superior and more satisfactory all around." Finally, the city manager of Manistee, Michigan, advised: "You cannot make any mistake in adopting this business form of government."[23]

Reformers in organizations of the genteel, such as the National Municipal League, often praised commission and manager government in traditional terms—for its simplicity, its concentration of responsibility, its intelligibility to the average voter.[24] But the main burden of defense of the new reform fell on business organizations, and they carried on the debate in business parlance. At the various conventions of state leagues of municipalities and at meetings of commercial bodies both critics and champions addressed themselves to the merits (or demerits) of businesslike government. At the 1910 convention of the League of Cities of the Third Class of Pennsylvania, for example, the delegates were told that "the controlling idea" of commission government was the creation of a governing body which would conform as nearly as possible "to the organization of a great business corporation"; conventions of the League of Virginia Municipalities in 1909 and 1911 heard similar arguments. At the later meeting, E. A. Sherman, who described himself as "a practical businessman . . . and nothing else," told the delegates they should adopt the commission in order to attract new business concerns to their Southern cities—thus placing himself squarely in the mainstream of the concern of the new Southern progressives.[25]

The evolution of the commission into the council-manager plan only refined the argument. Defenders of the modification explained that it simply brought municipal government more closely into correspondence with corporate organization. The first manager charter, adopted in Sumter, South Carolina, was described as the "concentration of the administrative organization under the control of a single appointive manager in exactly the same way as a private business corporation." Similarly, in Dayton, the procedure of looking for a manager followed "precisely that of a large corporation looking for an executive head." In Cleveland a local newspaper urged that city "to adopt the modern method of managing a city like a stock company."[26]

The opponents of the new plans attacked the concept of the city-as-business. At the 1913 meeting of the League of Kansas Municipalities, the visiting secretary of the Iowa League argued that "a city is more than a business corporation," and that, while business principles should control financial actions, this was not the primary function of municipal government. "Good health," he concluded, "is more important than a low tax rate."[27] The same year the Washington League of Municipalities convention heard Spokane's commissioner of public safety complain of the tendency to run municipal government from a "cold-blooded business standpoint." Municipal government, the commissioner observed, "is more than a mere organization for business."[28]

Other opponents, particularly political machines in Northern cities, Socialists, and trade unionists, had more specific grievances. Their fears and opposition came from a belief that the commission and manager charters would, by design or not, eliminate workers or their representatives from active participation in the process of government.

The Socialist Party, which between 1910 and 1919 elected various municipal officers in over 300 cities, led in opposing many features of commission and manager plans. Three major features of the plans bore the brunt of Socialist criticism: the elimination of ward representation, which meant the end of minority representation; the extreme concentration of power in the hands of the commission, which meant quick decisions and little time to mobilize opposition; and the "fallacy" of the nonpartisan ballot, which meant the elimination of three-way contests for office and an emphasis on personality, rather than party.

One report of a Connecticut Socialist found that commission government was the product of the " 'merchant and capitalist class,' " and that commission-governed cities afforded a fine medium for " 'capitalists to advertise their business.' " In Pocatello, Idaho, the Socialist party took the lead in defeating a commission government charter, arguing that it was an " 'autocratic and exclusive form of city government.' " In Manitowoc, Wisconsin, where a Socialist was mayor, the party opposed a proposal for commission government and defeated the new charter by a vote of 298 to 1,049. In Hamilton, Ohio, a few days after the United States entered the First World War, the Socialists defeated an attempt to form a manager government. In Dayton, the Socialists became the main source of opposition to the manager charter, although the United Trades and Labor Council also opposed the new reform. There, the Socialists, Democrats, and Prohibitionists issued a pamphlet entitled *Dayton's Commission Manager Plan: Why Big Manufacturers, Bond Holders, and Public Franchise Grabbers Favor It, and Workingmen and Common People Oppose.*[29]

The elimination of patronage undoubtedly moved political machines in many cities to oppose commission government, but the opposition of the Socialists and labor, neither of which had much patronage to lose, cannot be so easily dismissed. Several features of the electoral process in commission and manager cities did favor business groups against labor and its political allies. The first of these was simple limitation of the right to vote. In Galveston, the original plan provided for the appointment of all five commissioners. The state legislature modified this to provide for the election of two of the five, but it took a court decision decreeing appointive government unconstitutional to make the Galveston commission fully elective. In Houston, the second commission city, a poll tax of $2.50 limited democracy by eliminating 7,500 "irresponsible" voters in a potential electorate of 12,000. And in Newport, Rhode Island, there was a similar restriction of the right to vote.[30] Overt limitation of suffrage, however, was out of keeping with the prevailing spirit of these years. Thus, when James G. Berryhill— himself a Progressive—introduced the plan in Des Moines, he added the initiative, the referendum, and the recall, as well as the nonpartisan ballot. These features became characteristic of commission and manager charters.[31]

Nevertheless, the heart of the plan, that of electing only a few men on a citywide vote, made election of minority or labor candidates more difficult and less likely. Before the widespread adoption of commission and manager government it was common for workingmen to enter politics and serve as aldermen, or even mayor. Socialists elected teamsters, machinists, cigar makers, railroad conductors and trainmen, tinners, carpenters, miners, and other workers to the mayoralty of dozens of cities and towns in these years.[32] But once the commission plan was in effect this became rare. Workingclass aldermen were hard hit because the resources needed to conduct a citywide campaign were much greater than those needed for ward election, and because minorities—political, racial, or national—were usually concentrated in specific wards. In Dayton, for example, the Socialists received twenty-five percent of the vote in the election immediately preceding the adoption of the manager reform, electing two ward councilmen and three assessors. In 1913, after the manager charter was adopted, they received thirty-five percent of the vote and elected no one to the commission. In 1917 the party again increased its vote, this time to forty-four percent; again they elected no candidate.[33]

The nonpartisan ballot, a feature of most commission-manager plans and widely heralded as a great advance in democracy, also tended to operate against minority groups. Socialists claimed that the nonpartisan ballot gave great advantage to men of wealth and prominence, and that it gave a "terrific advantage" to the commercial press—although in fact, the Socialist Party often maintained its strength better in nonpartisan elections than did the major parties which depended heavily on patronage to hold together their organizations. To some degree, however, the nonpartisan ballot did handicap the workingclass candidates—most of whom were known only in their own neighborhoods and were without access to the press or adequate campaign funds. Theirs was a double task: to present themselves and their principles to the public. The nonpartisan ballot was a boon to the well-known man, and the well-known man, more often than not, was a leading merchant, manufacturer, or the lawyer of one or the other.[34] In addition, the combination of administrative and executive functions in the commission plan meant that the city could function smoothly only when experienced business executives were chosen to run it. The people of Wichita, Kansas, learned this when a former street laborer was elected to the commission. Being a street laborer, wrote reformer H. S. Gilbertson, was "an honest calling," and workers did have a right to representation. But, he asked, does this give "a man quite the preparation for managing one of the departments of a city?"[35]

Although the manager plan eliminated the problem of electing incompetent administrators, it strengthened the already strong tendency to regard the city as a "stock company." The method of electing the commission or council remained the same, and the manager, chosen by the commission or council, proved most often to be a man of limited social outlook, one who tended to think purely in business or, more narrowly, engineering terms. The reduction of expenditures made by the manager, while of great benefit to the taxpaying citizens, was often made at labor's expense. In Staunton, Virginia, for example, the new manager saved money by paying formerly full-time city employees only for those hours actually worked.[36]

The managers were usually proficient at increasing the efficiency of a fire department or reducing the cost of street paving, but social and political problems were often outside their range of interest. In 1918 Richard S. Childs (under whose direction H. S. Gilbertson had drawn up the Lockport Manager charter) suggested to the City Managers' Association, "Some day we shall have managers here who have achieved national reputation, not by . . . running their cities for a freakishly low expense per capita, but managers who have successfully led their commissions into great new enterprises of service." The advice was met with hostility. The managers, Leonard D. White notes, told Childs "directly that theorists were not welcome at the meetings of the Association."[37] Civil engineering, not social engineering, interested the manager; economy, not service, was his basic principle.

Because of his training, the manager tended to share the corporate concept of the city: All elements of the community must be harmonized, but in the interest of the major stockholders. He identified with the growing tendency among Progressives to remove as many areas of social and economic decision making as possible from the realm of politics. An extreme statement of this view appeared in the magazine *Engineering and Contracting:* ". . . our entire system of 'representative government,' in which representation comes solely through elections, is an uneconomic system, and is destined shortly to be changed."[38]

There were many, besides the Socialists, who thought commission government had already changed the system of representation and had guaranteed business rule. Most of these men did not oppose the new plans *in toto,* but only wished to assure that the commissions reflect the makeup of the entire community. To this end, they proposed proportional representation in the elections to the commission, and revived the Proportional Representation League to lead the fight.

The League, which had been in existence since the early 1890's, had lain dormant for many years. In 1914, a year after Dayton installed its first city manager, the *Proportional Representation Review* renewed publication, and that year and the next many new members joined the League's council. Active in the rejuvenated League were Progressives like John R. Commons, William S. U'Ren, Charles A. Beard, and Ben B. Lindsey. The genteel reformers were represented by Charles W. Eliot, Albert Shaw, Charles Francis Adams, and DeLancy Verplanck, and the Socialists by Carl D. Thompson and Charles P. Steinmetz. Despite the activity of the League, however, proportional representation made little headway. In the eight years from 1914 to 1922 only five cities adopted this reform.[39]

In Dayton, where opposition to the unrepresentative council developed rapidly after the adoption of the manager charter, proportional representation failed because business groups opposed a reform which they believed could benefit only Socialists and Negroes.[40]

Nor was the fear of the Dayton businessmen without basis. In Kalamazoo, in the first proportional representation election in 1918, Truxton Talbot, a "radical Socialist," was elected to the commission. Thereafter, the inclination of Kalamazoo's "really representative" commission to do something "more directly of benefit to the people than cleaning the streets and lighting them" disturbed the business interests of the city, or so the manager claimed.[41] What happened in Kalamazoo must have confirmed the fears of many chambers of commerce and thereby strengthened their opposition to modifications of commission or manager charters. At any rate, the proportional representation movement had no more success than did Socialist and trade union attacks on the commission plans.

Business leaders did not intend to share with other classes in their cities any more than was necessary. They were willing to make concessions on program, however, particularly since many of the programs supported or demanded by reformers and workingmen made for greater efficiency and lessened class antagonisms. This led them, perhaps unknowingly in some instances, in the direction of municipal ownership, of increased planning, and, especially where the competition from radicals was keen, even toward social reform. In Dayton, for example, after five years of manager government, municipal garbage collection had been instituted, a municipal asphalt plant built, new sewers (based on the projected needs of 1950) constructed, parks improved, new bridges erected, and a Department of Public Welfare established. The Welfare Department instituted milk inspection, free legal aid, a municipal employment agency, a municipal lodging house, medical examinations for school children, free vaccination, playgrounds, play festivals, and other social services, all on the theory that "happy workers are more efficient."[42]

The achievements in Dayton followed closely the ideology of John H. Patterson, a pioneer in the field of enlightened paternalism, as well as Dayton's leading citizen. Patterson, in consultation with the National Civic Federation, established a welfare organization of the National Cash Register Company to further the health and education of his employees, and to improve their working conditions. In addition, he built a schoolhouse on the factory grounds, which were landscaped as an "industrial garden." His motives as much "materialistic" as "humanitarian," Patterson boasted that he made the improvement because "it pays." Often a ruthless employer, he demanded and received maximum efficiency from his workers. His paternalism applied also to Dayton. For example, he created a vast park of several hundred acres and made it "as public as if it belonged to the city," but he retained the title to it.[43]

Dayton's attitude toward the functions of city government had much in common with other commission and manager cities. In Houston, for instance, there were no outstanding personalities like Patterson, no radical opposition, and the poll tax restricted the electorate to a minority of the adult males. Yet the commission took over operation of the water works (and saved the city $400 per month), and at the same time the Health commissioner set up a city pharmacy and surgical room for the city poor in which he saved $100 to $150 per month by filling prescriptions and treating patients in the municipally owned clinic.[44]

All commissions aimed to reduce costs and increase services, and, since these were their first principles, most followed a policy of municipal planning and municipal ownership of some, if not all, utilities. To a large degree, therefore, the programs of the various business groups which led the commission and manager movements had points in common with those of many social reformers, and even with those of the Socialists.[45]

Fundamental differences between business groups and the genteel reformers, on the one hand, and Socialists, labor, and some of the more radical social reformers, on the other, did exist both in regard to what class should administer these programs and what the ultimate purpose of the programs should be. But the similarity of many immediate goals often debilitated the political opposition and helped assure the adoption of the commission and manager charters. Developed and led by business groups, the movement fulfilled the requirements of progressivism by rationalizing city government and institutionalizing the methods and values of the corporations that had come to dominate American economic life. The end result of the movements was to place city government firmly in the hands of the business class. And, interestingly, at what is normally considered the end of the Progressive Era, 1917, the manager movement spurted ahead at its highest rate of growth. This occurred in the five years from 1918 to 1923, when 153 cities adopted manager charters, as compared to 87 in the five years before 1918, and 84 in the five years after 1923.[46]

During the First World War, chambers of commerce and boards of trade greatly intensified their antiradical and antilabor activities, and in hundreds of small cities and towns Socialist locals were destroyed by the superpatriotic business groups. Just as the war would serve to institutionalize corporation-controlled regulatory agencies on a national level so on a local level the business organizations were able rapidly to press forward their political domination of American municipalities.

■ ■ ■ ■ **Notes**

1 Samuel P. Hays, "The Politics of Reform in Municipal Government in the Progressive Era," *Pacific Northwest Quarterly*, LV (October 1964), pp. 157–169.

2 Quoted in Landrum C. Bolling, "Dayton, Ohio," in Frederick C. Mosher, *et al., City Manager Government in Seven Cities* (Chicago, Public Administration Service, 1940), p. 266.

3 Clinton R. Woodruff, "An American Municipal Program," *Political Science Quarterly*, XVIII (March 1903), p. 48.

4 Arthur S. Link, *American Epoch: The History of the United States since the 1890's* (New York, Alfred A. Knopf, 1958), p. 85.

5 Frederick C. Howe, *The City, The Hope of Democracy* (New York, Charles Scribner's Sons, 1906), quoted in *Arena*, XXV (May 1906), pp. 512–513; see also Lincoln Steffens, *Autobiography* (New York, Harcourt Brace, 1931), pp. 430–435, 572–574.

6 William J. Gaynor, "The Problem of Efficient City Government," *Century*, LXXX (September 1910), p. 666.

7 Frederick C. Howe, *Confessions of a Reformer* (New York, Charles Scribner's Sons, 1925), pp. 98 ff. Neither Jones nor Johnson, both of whom were single taxers, succeeded in building a permanent political base. This instability was typical of reform administrations in those years; it was rare that one lasted two terms or more. See, for example, Bird S. Coler, "Mistakes of Professional Reformers," *Independent*, LIII (June 20, 1901), pp. 1405–1407; Joseph D. Miller, "The Futilities of Reformers," *Arena*, XXVI (November 1901), pp. 481–489; E. R. L. Gould, "Civic Reform and Social Progress," *International Monthly*, III (March 1901), pp. 344–358.

8 Arthur H. Grant, "The Conning Tower," *American City* (October 1909), p. 68; Walter B. Snow, "The Cost of Inefficiency in Municipal Work," *American City*, pp. 77–82; Charles H. Wacker, "The Plan of Chicago," *American City*, p. 50.

9 George K. Turner, "Galveston: A Business Corporation," *McClure's*, XXVII (October 1906), p. 612.

10 Carl Doheney, "Commission Government and Democracy," *American City,* II (February 1910), p. 77.

11 H. S. Gilbertson, "Some Serious Weaknesses of the Commission Plan," *American City,* IX (September 1913), pp. 236–237; Charles M. Fasset, "The Weakness of Commission Government," *National Municipal Review,* IX (October 1920), pp. 642–647.

12 Staunton, Virginia, had appointed a manager in 1908, but because of charter limitations the Staunton experiment did not include commission government and was not conceived as a refinement of that plan. See Henry Oyen, "A City with a General Manager," *World's Work,* XXIII (December 1911), p. 223.

13 Richard S. Childs, "The Lockport Proposal," *American City,* IV (June 1911), pp. 285–287; F. D. Silvernail, "The Lockport Proposal," *Annals of the American Academy of Political and Social Science,* XXXVIII (November 1911), pp. 884–887; City Managers' Association, *Fifth Yearbook* (New York, 1919), p. 161; Harold A. Stone, Don K. Price, and Katherine H. Stone, *City Manager Government in the United States* (Chicago, Public Administration Service, 1940), pp. 10–11; Don K. Price, "The Promotion of the City Manager Plan," *Public Opinion Quarterly,* V (Winter 1941), pp. 563–578.

14 "The Originator of the Des Moines Plan," *Hampton's Magazine* (February 1911), pp. 248–249; Benjamin F. Shambaugh, "Commission Government in Iowa: The Des Moines Plan," *Annals,* XXXVIII (November 1911), pp. 698–718; A. M. Fuller, "Commission Government of all Third-Class Cities of Pennsylvania," *American City,* IX (August 1913), pp. 123–124; "League of Cities of Third Class of Pennsylvania," *Proceedings of the Annual Convention* (1910), p. 126; *Board of Trade and Engineering Journal* (Scranton, Pennsylvania), VI (November 1910), pp. 7–8.

15 Stone, Price, and Stone, *City Manager Government in Dallas* (Chicago, Public Administration Service, 1939), p. 9; Stone, *et al., City Manager Government in Janesville (Wisconsin)* (Chicago, P.A.S., 1939), p. 6; Christie Benet, "A Campaign for a Commission Form of Government," *American City,* III (December 1910), pp. 276–278; Stone, *et al., City Manager Government in Charlotte* (Chicago, P.A.S., 1939), p. 4.

16 "The City Manager Adopted by Sumter, South Carolina," *American City,* VII (July 1912), p. 38; Fred W. Francher, "Two Epoch-Making Campaigns in Dayton, Ohio," *American City,* IX (July 1913), pp. 47–49; Isaac F. Marcosson, "Business Managing a City," *Collier's,* January 3, 1914, pp. 5–6; Bolling, pp. 268 ff.

17 *American City,* XII (May, June 1915), pp. 416, 515; XIII (July, August, November 1914), pp. 44, 136–137, 421; Stone, *et al., City Manager Government in Jackson (Michigan)* (Chicago, P.A.S., 1939), p. 8.

18 Turner, pp. 610–620; William O. Scroggs, "Commission Government in the South," AAP&SS *Annals,* XXXVIII (November 1911), pp. 682–687; H. J. Haskell, "The Texas Idea: 'City Government by a Board of Directors,'" *The Outlook,* LXXXV (April 3, 1907), pp. 839–843; *American City,* II (April 1910), p. 190; "The Des Moines Plan of City Government," *World's Work,* XVIII (May 1909), p. 11533.

19 Oyen, pp. 221, 228; Burton J. Hendrick, "Taking the American City out of Politics," *Harper's,* CXXXVII (June 1918), pp. 106–113; Bolling, pp. 276–277; Stone, *et al., City Manager Government in Austin* (Chicago, P.A.S., 1939), pp. 5 ff.

20 *American City,* V (October 1911), p. 225; Fulton, New York, Chamber of Commerce, Commission Manager Form of Government, August 19, 1915 (New York, New York Public Library), p. 1.

21 Turner, p. 613; Stone, *et al., City Manager Government in Austin,* p. 5, *City Manager Government in Janesville,* pp. 4–6; Francher, pp. 47–49; Fulton Chamber of Commerce, Commission Manager Form of Government, p. 15; Stone, *et al., City*

Manager Government in Jackson, p. 15; John A. Fairlie, "Commission Government in Illinois Cities," AAP&SS *Annals,* XXXVIII (November 1911), p. 755.

22 Ray F. Wierick, "The Development of Des Moines," *American City,* IV (May 1911), p. 203; VII (November 1912), pp. 567–568; X (April 1914), p. 381.

23 Fulton Chamber of Commerce, Commission Manager Form of Government, pp. 1–16.

24 See, for example, William B. Munro, "Ten Years of Commission Government," *National Municipal Review,* I (October 1912), pp. 567–568; also Childs, pp. 285–287.

25 Joshua C. Taylor, "Causes and Effect of Commission Government," League of Cities of the Third Class of Pennsylvania, *Proceedings of the Annual Convention, 1910,* p. 117; League of Virginia Municipalities, *Sixth Annual Convention Report,* pp. 77–89. See, also, *Fourth Annual Convention Report.*

26 "The City Manager Plan Adopted by Sumter, S.C.," p. 38; Hendrick, p. 110; *Literary Digest,* LIV (February 17, 1917), p. 99.

27 League of Kansas Municipalities, *Proceedings, 1913,* p. 25.

28 Washington League of Municipalities, *Proceedings, 1913,* p. 176.

29 William C. Seyler, "The Rise and Decline of the Socialist Party in the United States" (unpublished Ph.D. thesis, Duke University, 1952), pp. 237–238; *American City,* XII (June 1915), pp. 509–510; *Wisconsin Comrade,* I (June 1914), p. 1; Howard White, "Hamilton, Ohio," in Mosher, *et al.,* p. 183; Bolling, p. 269.

30 Childs, p. 285; Haskell, p. 842; "Three Great Experiments," *Independent,* LXIV (June 18, 1908), pp. 1409–1410. Newport imposed a $134 property restriction on the right to vote.

31 "The Originator of the Des Moines Plan," pp. 248–250. Berryhill had agitated for state regulation of railroads, when he was a state legislator in the late 1880's.

32 See James Weinstein, *The Decline of Socialism in America, 1912–1925* (New York, Monthly Review Press, 1967), pp. 42–44.

33 Seyler, p. 237; *Dayton News,* November 7, 1917.

34 Seyler, p. 239. Socialists did not always oppose commission government. Home rule was the decisive test for them. In North Dakota, where a system of preferential voting was in effect, the Socialists were quite pleased with the commission plan. See William E. Walling (ed.), *Socialism of Today* (New York, Henry Holt, 1916), pp. 549 ff. In Birmingham, Alabama, Arlie Barber, a Socialist who campaigned as a party member, was elected to the commission on a nonpartisan ballot in 1915 but was defeated for re-election in 1917 after he had opposed the United States intervention in the war, and conscription. *Cleveland Citizen,* December 4, 1915; *Birmingham Age-Herald,* April 10, October 5, 9, 1917.

35 Gilbertson, p. 237.

36 Oyen, p. 220.

37 Leonard D. White, *The City Manager* (Chicago, 1927), p. 149.

38 Quoted in *Literary Digest,* LIV (February 17, 1917), p. 399.

39 *Proportional Representation Review,* s.3 (October 1914–January 1922). The cities were Ashtabula, Ohio, 1915; Kalamazoo, Michigan, 1918; Sacramento, California, 1921; West Hartford, Connecticut, 1921; and Cleveland, Ohio, 1921.

40 White, pp. 77–78.

41 *Proportional Representation Review,* s.3 (January 1920), p. 9.

42 Hendrick, pp. 111–113; the quotation is from Marcosson, p. 24.

43 Harry A. Toulmin, Jr., "John Henry Patterson," *Dictionary of American Biography,* XIV, pp. 304–305; Fred C. Kelly, "Dayton's Uncle Bountiful," *Collier's* (August 1, 1914), p. 8; *Encyclopedia of American Biography,* XXVII, p. 18.

44 Haskell, pp. 840–841.
45 See, for example, Raymond Moley, "Representation in Dayton and Ashtabula," *National Municipal Review,* VI (January 1918), pp. 28–29.
46 Stone, *et al., City Manager Government in the United States* (Chicago, Public Administration Service, 1940), p. 30.

14
The Church and the City, 1865–1910

ROBERT D. CROSS

Robert Cross wrote the following essay as the introduction to a very useful source collection, The Church and the City, 1865–1910. *In his introduction, Cross brilliantly delineates the variety and the complexity of the churches' responses to urbanization, while in the documents he provides first-hand testimony of the many mansions of American religion.*

It seems safe to say that religious and church history (the two are not necessarily synonymous) have been neglected in the United States. Those historians who are not church members often are not particularly interested in the area, while those who are usually do not wish to be typed as denominational scholars. Yet, as Cross observes, the churches have long been key social institutions providing many urbanites some element of stability and meaning in their lives.

We cannot recapture the social experience of previous generations of city dwellers without asking what they expected of their churches, and how well these institutions responded to the challenges posed by urban growth. It is not enough to read the denominational press and the books written by the more articulate churchmen who taught in seminaries and universities. These men tended to be more liberal and innovative than the average clergyman faced with a conservative vestry, board, or congregation. Historians, being bookish fellows and sharing the values of the liberals, have found reading the social gospelers a congenial task; congenial, but also misleading, unless supplemented by other sources. Cross's great contribution has been to survey and conceptualize the entire range of religious response to the emergence of the large, heterogeneous city. His analysis combines understanding and sympathy.

■ ■ ■ ■ **For Further Reading**

Robert D. Cross, *The Emergence of Liberal Catholicism in America* (Cambridge, Mass.: Harvard University Press, 1958) surveys the conflicts during the latter part of the nineteenth century between the immigrant and European-oriented Catholics and those who wished to embrace, selectively, American culture. Henry F. May, *Protestant Churches and Industrial America* (New York: Harper & Row Torchbooks, 1949) studies the evolution of the social gospel in American Protestantism. Moses Rischin, *The Promised City: New York's Jews, 1870–1914* (New York: Harper & Row Torchbooks, 1962) is a sympathetic and informed study of the interaction between the city and the east European Jewish religious and cultural community.

I

■ In the fifty years between the close of the Civil War and the onset of World War I, American cities grew rapidly. Although early in the nineteenth century religious spokesmen like Lyman Beecher had been aware of the need to "evangelize" the growing city populations, most had been preoccupied with the challenges and opportunities presented by the "frontier." The emphasis shifted after the Civil War. A flood of books with titles like *The Challenge of the City, The Redemption of the City, If Christ Came to Chicago,* and *Christianity's Storm Centre: A Study of the Modern City* demonstrated how acute the problem had come to seem.[1] It was not, of course, in the bookstore that religion's response was most authoritatively rendered, but in the behavior of the churches—not only the churches which found the community in which they were established swelling into a metropolis, but also the new churches of one kind or another appearing in the cities. No more in this era than in any other in American history was all religious life lived within the churches; then as always there were sturdy individualists to whom religion was gravely important but to whom church membership seemed an irrelevance if not a spiritual handicap. But for the vast majority of religiously concerned Americans, the churches were the normal vehicle of religious life, making the conduct and welfare of these churches the best barometer of American religion's response to the city.

It was clear from the start that the response would be remarkably multiform. There were already in the 1840's many mansions in American religion; each variant form reflected a unique set of notions not only about church membership and organization and worship, but also about the church's proper role in "the world."[2] Furthermore, in practice if not always in ecclesiastical theory, initiative in responding to new situations rested mostly in the hands of the local church. When such a varied and decentralized institution was confronted with the fact of city growth, dynamic both in its pace and in its apparent unpredictability, it is hardly surprising that church life in the cities was soon almost incredibly diverse in character. (So diverse, in fact, that for many years it was regarded as simple chaos, a judgment of God upon American religiosity.) About the turn of the century, churchmen like H. Paul Douglass began to survey the urban scene more matter-of-factly, and to discern patterns in the kind of religious responses they found.[3] In recent years, such churchmen have been joined by professional sociologists, and together they have evolved quite sophisticated typologies—never in the belief, however, that any typology could do full justice either to the whole range of response or to the uniqueness of the individual churches.[4] Still, these efforts at classification make it possible now to distinguish four general modes of churchly response.

Transformations include the changes that took place in long-established churches when the towns in which they stood rapidly expanded into cities.

Suddenly they found themselves "downtown" churches with a conspicuous location, an equally conspicuous loss of neighborhood membership, and consequently a pressing need to redefine their mode of preaching to the community.

Transplantations characterize the attempts—always unsuccessful in the long run—to create, in the midst of a city, churches identical to warmly remembered ones in town or country. Immigrant groups usually created "ethnic churches," and migrants from the American countryside often founded "village churches" in a fond attempt to create at least one bulwark against urban demoralization.

Adaptations, by far the largest category of urban churches, resulted from single-minded attempts to cope with some specific challenge of the city. Viewed from the perspective of the traditional church in America or Europe, these adaptations seemed heretical for their emphasis or overemphasis on some belief or practice. (1) Neighborhood churches, on the way to becoming the "suburban church" of the mid-twentieth century, defined their ambit in terms of a neighborhood that was not the whole of a community, nor even a cross section of it, but a highly stratified segment. (2) Some churches came to specialize as centers of revivalist exhortation. (3) Adventism, always stimulated by untoward developments in the surrounding culture, was given renewed expression by Charles Taze Russell and the group that came to be known as Jehovah's Witnesses. (4) A congeries of short-lived but intense Pentecostal churches matched the Witnesses' hostility to the culture in which they found themselves, but drew upon the opportunities the city offered for an autonomous religious life. (5) Christian Science exemplified the special anxiety of city-dwellers about health and well-being, and their receptivity to "new thought" which offered a gnostic solution to uncertainties about both this world and the next.

Reintegrations were typified by the "institutional church," which self-consciously sought to restore the old identification of the church with the whole community. Since the population of most cities was far too large for a single congregation to encompass, the institutional church resolved at least to draw its membership from a real cross section of the city, not simply some congenial social class or ethnic group. "Transplanted" or "adapted" churches might in time follow the path of "reintegration"; in the late nineteenth and early twentieth centuries, however, it was the churches "transformed" by urbanization into downtown churches which were most likely to make this transition. But there was nothing inevitable about it, even for the "transformed."

II

The churches located near the center of a growing city faced a difficult choice. Almost inevitably, the bulk of the congregation of "Old First

Church"—of "Center Church"—of "Trinity Church"—moved to less crowded, more fashionable neighborhoods; their former homes were made over into places of business, or were subdivided into boarding houses, or were replaced by barracks and tenements to accommodate a flood of new inhabitants. Many of the newcomers were immigrants from Europe, deterred by language and faith from joining the old church on the green. Others, fresh from the American countryside, were nearly as uprooted psychologically, and at least as unlikely to find the old church a purveyor of the kind of religious life they had been accustomed to. Some were the "derelicts" that find shelter in the heart of large cities. In the middle of the nineteenth century, the old churches in the southern reaches of Manhattan found themselves surrounded by Irish and German Catholics, by people from the provinces, by a large fraction of the Negro population, and by the city's professional criminals. In the area known as the Five Points, all of these lived in close proximity, physically near the old churches, but in spirit hopelessly remote.[5] Some of the congregations, in despair, sold their buildings to commercial enterprises (or, occasionally, to immigrant religious groups) and built new churches "uptown" or in the suburbs. Those that resolved to stay where they had always been encountered the vicissitudes of the "downtown" church.

There were, of course, a few compensations. Trinity Church in New York, for example, benefited from the steady increase in the value of its extensive property holdings. But for the bulk of the people in the neighborhood the church as landlord did not arouse the same affection as had the church as house of worship. By the turn of the twentieth century, in fact, Trinity had become a byword for its profit-minded operation of some of the worst tenement-houses in the city. Trinity's role changed in other ways as well. Increasingly, it became a kind of cathedral, in effect if not in ecclesiastical law. Testifying by its presence to the existence in city culture of religion as an institution, it ceased being the meetinghouse around which the life of the city, or even a fair cross section of the city, revolved.

In most "downtown" churches the number of religious services declined; even so, attendance became increasingly sparse. By the end of the century, it had become conventional for city newspapers to note the meager congregations at Sunday morning services in the famous old churches. Budgets were met by income from property, from pew rents, and from the large donations of the few wealthy families that maintained a traditional loyalty; some contributions also came from parvenus seeking the prestige which conspicuous support of the older churches—Trinity, Brick Presbyterian, Temple Emanu-El—still brought. Great emphasis was placed on church architecture, on carefully elaborated ritual and liturgy; organized religion would thus demand respect from the passer-by, even if it did not bring in flocks of members. It became increasingly important to have a minister of high social standing; Episcopalians, Reformed Jews, and others frequently imported them from Europe. Dignity, social grace, learning, and eloquence were required of him. It would be an especial accolade for the church if ceremony and sermon were so distinguished that prominent visitors to the city regarded a visit to the church as one of "the things to be done." Such visitors fit easily into Sunday congregations made up not of the families of the neighborhood but of a handful of individuals from various parts of the city.

Under such circumstances, it would have been miraculous if the minister proved a pastor to his neighborhood. Phillips Brooks, of Trinity Church, Boston, was admirably suited by the remarkable sweetness of his character to be such a pastor. But his influence extended little beyond the narrow circle of his upper-class Episcopalian congregation. Much the same might be said about Morgan Dix of Trinity Church, New York, and about Gustav Gottheil of Emanu-El. Priests to their "own" people, they felt little incentive to explore the way religion affected, or failed to affect, the rest of the city.

Though the downtown church of the late nineteenth century touched the lives of a far smaller percentage of the population than had its ancestor on the village green, it preserved, simply by staying in the center of the city, a potential for future importance which the churches which moved uptown or to the suburbs decisively abdicated. Its location gave it the moral right, and its financial resources gave it the means, to experiment with new techniques of "churching" the urban population. An easy but in the long run unsuccessful mode was to support a flock of mission churches or chapels. Premised, tacitly, on the belief that different social classes "do not like to worship together," such colonialist enterprises sometimes developed into viable churches—especially if they were planted in the midst of a population group so bound together by a common foreign language, national consciousness, or color as to be able to resist the disintegrating forces in urban life. More often, the life of a mission church was short, and marred by feelings of dependence and hostility. Charles Stelzle remembered about his youth in lower New York City that "none of the chapel people were ever invited to a business meeting of the home church, even though legally they were members of the church. They had nothing whatever to say, not even with reference to the chapel which they attended and helped support. . . . No wonder it was hard to get workingmen to take an interest in that kind of enterprise."[6] The decision of Trinity Church in 1908 to close St. John's Chapel in the belief that the money could be expended better elsewhere led the conservative Episcopal newspaper *The Churchman* to complain that "no account was taken of the people in St. John's parish, of their rights, of their hopes or of their souls."[7]

The major alternative to creating separate chapels was to make unusual efforts to attract to the downtown churches themselves the large unchurched population. As early as 1856, the New York Sunday School Union had tried to allocate to each downtown church responsibility for a certain territory of the city; members of that church were to visit each person in the area at least weekly in order to bring him into active church life. Essentially similar plans were experimented with in other cities before the Civil War; and the Home Evangelization program, the Evangelical Alliance, and the Federation of Churches and Christian Workers in New York made brave efforts in the late nineteenth century. On the whole, they were no more successful than had been the chapels and mission churches.[8] Only very slowly some of the downtown churches came to realize that the transformation worked on society by the city was so intense that the character of the church had to be transformed if a genuine reintegration of church and culture was to be accomplished. The institutional church, about which more will be said later, emerged between 1890 and 1910 as the most ambitious attempt at this larger task.

III

Just as some of the older residents tried to preserve what they remembered as the major characteristics of their churches, so many of the newcomers tried to transplant the rural or small-town church into their new environment. Especially in the first years of industrial cities like Holyoke, Massachusetts, in the mid-nineteenth century, or Gastonia, North Carolina, in the 1920's, a high percentage of the Protestant population was right off the farm, and right out of the rural churches.[9] For them, the old-time religion was the strongest surrogate of the continuity they wished to preserve with their former lives. In the churches they built and supported, they tried to keep much the same patterns of service. They wanted no doctrinal or theological concessions to the spirit of the times, or the ethos of city culture; "you have to carry a bucket of blood into the pulpit to satisfy these people," a Gastonia minister remarked.[10]

Baptists and Methodists predominated in the countryside, and so it was natural that the bulk of the transplanted churches were of these denominations. But a sizable number of the emigrants to the cities brought with them such a compelling concern for "perfection" that many "holiness" churches were also founded. The origins of such churches lay in the revivalism of the early and middle nineteenth century. As Timothy Smith has shown, the ardent search for God's grace not only led many leaders of the old Calvinist faiths—like Charles G. Finney—to stress the possibility of perfectionism; it also gave renewed intensity to Methodist belief in sanctification through the benefits of the "second blessing."[11] The National Holiness Association represented a massive attempt to foster personal holiness. Most of its leaders were Methodists, and most hoped to intensify religious life within Methodist churches, rather than to create a new denomination. But like earlier awakening or reform movements in American Protestantism, the holiness group encountered opposition within the settled churches. Not all bishops, conferences, or ministers could approve of the emotionalism the holiness meetings engendered and found praiseworthy. Churches, whether in the country or the city, sometimes boggled at the willingness of the holiness advocates to experiment with new measures of preaching revival, of seeking out converts, and of caring for the needy. As a result, the late nineteenth century saw the gradual, often reluctant, coalescence of new denominations, such as the Church of the Nazarene and the Church of God.[12] Some migrants to the city had made the transition before leaving the country; for them, membership in a holiness congregation was completely natural, an act that reaffirmed a previous commitment. Others left the countryside before breaking with an older denomination, but, faced in the city with the need to affiliate with a different congregation in any event, chose a holiness group as best fulfilling long-cherished preferences. For both, the holiness congregation was a kind of transplantation—a re-creation of the rural past.

A similar spirit characterized the attempts of immigrant groups to preserve unmodified in American cities the religious life they had known in European villages. Such people were doubly alienated from the "downtown" churches they encountered. So, within a few months of the arrival of the first sizable numbers of Jews from Eastern Europe, New York was dotted with synagogues, each seeking to re-create the special religious life of a *shtetl,* or small village. Those Lutherans from Germany or Scandinavia who settled in the cities tried to find, in churches effectively limited to members speaking the mother tongue, something of the church life they remembered. Catholic immigrants, belonging to a Church which in theory organized local churches by territorial rather than ethnic boundaries, were not always so successful in finding churches limited to their own "kind."[13] But by the end of the nineteenth century, many American dioceses had provided "national" parishes which encompassed all those speaking a similar foreign language. In those national parishes where the Church could also provide a priest of the same nationality, parishioners were able to enjoy the round of services and festivals cherished in the old country.

Such churches were inevitably transient. Sometimes, a peculiarly rigid social-economic structure such as prevailed in a small Southern industrial city would keep a group together for a generation or more; sometimes the centripetal forces of a foreign-language ethnic group enabled its members for a period of time not only to renounce the opportunity to scatter through the whole city but also to resist temptations to adapt their "country" church to city life. (Of course, the country churches willy-nilly made some adaptations immediately; the very determination to transplant and maintain an institution exotic to the city created a beleaguered spirit which they had not previously had.) But usually within a decade or so, the transplanted churches from the country, like those older churches which had experienced the transformation of their community into a city, were forced to make much more radical adaptations. Though at any given moment a considerable proportion of a city's churches might be striving to remain country churches, a growing number had adapted in dramatic fashion.

IV

The much more complex, heterogeneous life of the cities produces institutions that are far more specialized than those which flourish in rural culture. Furthermore, just as city-dwellers expect of such institutions rather precise intellectual and moral services, so the leaders of such institutions come to approximate functionaries with highly specialized skills. So it was with most of the churches which adapted to the ways of city life in late nineteenth-century America. Compared with the traditional churches, many of these adaptations—even some of those the age most admired—seem almost grotesque, heretically preoccupied with responding to some limited aspect of urban life, and stressing some limited theme in the churches' armory of beliefs and modes of worship.

The "neighborhood" church neatly illustrates both the plausibility and the peril of adaptation. As Springfield, Massachusetts, grew from a frontier town to a considerable city and its population spread out away from the original cluster on the Connecticut River, those who thought of themselves as Congregationalists but did not wish to journey into the center of town to "Old First Church" founded successively a North and a South Congregational Church, a Faith Church, a Hope Church, until more than a dozen neighborhood churches had been created. Such cellular division was sometimes justified as creating new, reasonably sized and reasonably located churches, each as concerned as the original church with the total gospel of the Church to the World. But Springfield was not, any more than were other cities, a cluster of generally similar neighborhoods, but an area that was highly stratified according to income, class, and ethnic group. As a result, each new congregation tended to be markedly segregated, and thereby highly susceptible to a very specialized notion of the nature of the Church and of its proper relations with the World. An extreme but illuminating example of the neighborhood church was Plymouth Congregational, founded in the 1840's in the City of Brooklyn, for many decades a suburb for up-and-coming New Yorkers. For forty years its minister and central figure was Henry Ward Beecher.

Perhaps because of his expansive, ebullient personality, perhaps because he was the son of Lyman Beecher, one of the great churchmen of the prewar years, but mostly because of the demands of his congregation, Beecher enjoyed a singularly close relationship with his flock. Instead of speaking from a pulpit far back from or high above the congregation, Beecher had one constructed as much in the center of the church as possible. His sermons frequently elicited emotional outbursts. At the weekly prayer meeting, he delighted to emphasize his communion with his people by sitting on a chair where he could share rather than direct the flow of testimony. Everything about his role militated against prophetic preaching against the sins of his people. It was not that Beecher felt inhibitions about the subjects to which the minister ought to address himself. Shrugging off the tradition that enjoined the minister to concentrate on simple evangelical truths, Beecher claimed the right and duty to speak on politics, economic life, the most recent innovations in the world of culture—all the themes of interest to his congregation. But the evils which excited his alarm were those that came from without the circle of his congregation's lives, and threatened their social and psychological well-being. The old doctrines of hell and eternal damnation, for example, seemed increasingly incongruous to both Beecher and his thriving, prospering people, and Beecher soon avowed that the God they all worshiped was a God of love, who would not conceivably deal harshly with creatures made in His own image. "You are Gods," he once told his congregation; "you are crystalline, your faces are radiant."[14] Aware that the newly bruited doctrines of Darwinism threw into doubt the power of God as well as His amiability, Beecher was not long in assuring his people that evolution, rightly construed, implied only that God chose to create by retail, rather than wholesale. (The metaphor, no less than the sentiment, was harmonious to the sensibilities of his bourgeois audience.) Equally important, he vindicated the righteousness of middle-class economic behavior against the polite innuendoes of the wealthy, and the protests and occasionally obstreperous revolts of the poor. Justifying the *douceurs* of prosperity, he slashed at the immoralities that luxury induced in the wealthy; preaching a Protestant ethic of hard work, he denounced working-class demands for better wages and living conditions, as evidence of unfitness to life. If few neighborhood or suburban churches were so imaginatively and fulsomely served as was Plymouth Congregational, most of them encountered a version of the Gospel so edited and distorted as to be almost a parody. Many developments in American culture helped promote this kind of Christianity, but it could hardly have been sustained in the churches if the sociology of metropolitan life had not produced parishes so stratified and so unrepresentative of the full spectrum of potential churchgoers.

No doubt the social homogeneity of the suburban or neighborhood church sometimes allowed a congregation to transcend other kinds of stratification. In a new area, representatives of different denominations often found it possible to unite in a community church which ignored theological or liturgical distinctions which had long lost their meaning. A similar development was possible for the children and grandchildren of European immigrants who wished to belong to a church which preserved the central faiths of their fathers without the admixtures of language and custom which now seemed alien and un-American. The unification movements among the bewildering variety of Scandinavian Lutheran churches were markedly aided by the proliferation of community churches. Some of the ethnic tensions in American Catholicism were allayed by the same development. Probably the most dramatic example was the emergence in suburban areas of Conservative Judaism which proffered a more plausible, more American version of Judaism than the Orthodoxy that had been transplanted from *shtetl* to urban ghetto; Conservatism also provided a viable common ground for Jews of "German" and of "Eastern European" origin.[15]

For former country folk deprived of a genuinely country church and not yet settled into a neighborhood church, revivalism often afforded a consoling sense of continuity. (It had been one of the strong appeals of the transplanted holiness churches, but it also proved powerful even when sharply separated from regular congregational life.) To church leaders it seemed wholly natural that revivals, which had played a crucial part in bringing religion to the unchurched West, should be used to Christianize the "city wilderness." As early as 1857, the Baptist minister Henry Clay Fish had exclaimed, "What can save our large cities, but a powerful revival of religion?"[16] Superficially, at least, the city seemed an even easier place to conduct a revival than the open country, where the people had to be collected, housed, and supervised, or the small town, where the numbers available were strictly limited. But early nineteenth-century revivalists had noticed that their success was greater in small towns than in cities. To Finney, city people were too engrossed in worldly ambitions; "see how crazy these are who are scrambling to get up . . . ," he said, "enlarging their houses, changing their styles of living. . . . It is like climbing up [the] masthead to be thrown off into the ocean. To enjoy God you must come down, not go up there," as the city continually tempted.[17] By the 1840's, however, it appeared that the right kind of revival could "succeed" in the great city. Emphasis upon the theological niceties of a single denomination was inappropriate for a heterogeneous city audience; furthermore, the newspapers and other impersonal modes of communication on which a city revival depended for its notoriety were not inclined to herald purely sectarian efforts. As a consequence, revivalism developed in considerable autonomy from the congregations existent in the city. Churches developed, like Tremont Temple in Boston, which offered a steady fare of revival services. Inevitably they came to place emphasis not on the continuing religious life of their audiences, but on the success of the revivals in producing numerous convictions of sin.

The dramatic but curiously limited effect of urban revivalism was perfectly illustrated by the career of its greatest exponent, Dwight L. Moody. After a pious upbringing in East Northfield, Massachusetts, he sought a business career in Boston. When converted, he felt that the cities in England and America were his destined field; "if we can stir them, we shall stir the whole nation," he said.[18] Never ordained as a minister, he felt no obligation to any denomination, and preferred to conduct his revivals in a special tabernacle rather than a church. He recognized that careful planning was necessary to provide the advance publicity; to secure the necessary funds; to coordinate the ushers, choirs, and auxiliary ministers; to keep the meeting to a brisk schedule of sermon, gospel hymn, and exhortation; to obviate—and if necessary to suppress—hysterical outbreaks. He would no doubt have been gratified by the contemporary's observation that Moody made the business of revivals businesslike.[19] His goal was so simple that it was easy to pursue it matter-of-factly. He once defined his duty as to ask at least one stranger a day, "Are you a Christian?" By the end of his life, he had asked several million, with an energy and persuasiveness unsurpassed in his era. Speaking as he felt he was to people no more than a generation away from active church life, he did not imagine that complicated arguments were necessary; the main task would be to confront as many hearers as possible with the challenge: were they for or against Christ?

Concentrating on this one task, he made no effort to respond to the peculiar difficulties of urban culture. "The old-time religion" was "good enough" for him; knowing the Bible, he saw no need to read or consider Darwin. A natural kindliness made him worry about difficulties of the poor in keeping warm in the winter, but he refused to be distracted from his revivalist efforts into any prolonged consideration of the social-economic order. Critics of a later era could without much difficulty construct from Moody's occasional remarks a ready acquiescence in *laissez faire,* but his attitude was less affirmation than simple indifference. No doubt his aloofness to worldly concerns was strengthened in Moody by a belief in an imminent Second Coming. (But even those revivalists without millennial expectations showed far more interest in the moment of grace than in the subsequent life of the faithful in the world.)

This same set of priorities conditioned Moody's attitude toward the urban churches. Though he supported their work, it did not seem to worry him greatly that revivalists like himself were not notably successful in persuading non-church members who "decided" for Christ to join a congregation. Sometimes he seemed to be reconciled to the prospect that his converts would maintain a vicarious relationship to the churches; once, seeking money for a Sunday School, he sold "stock certificates" which would entitle investors to *watch* Sunday School members studying. Earlier, in the smaller cities and towns, "seasons of revival" had meant revival for the congregations as well as for the individuals. But big-city revivalism in Moody's day developed into a functional substitute for church life. Like the "adaptations" of the neighborhood church, revivalism forfeited much that it purportedly sought to preserve.

Like the neighborhood church, too, revivalism appealed only to special segments of the city population. Moody believed that the poorer classes were those most cut off from religion; he made them the target of his revivals, and when he founded the Moody Bible Institute in 1886 he charged its students to devote their lives to evangelizing the poor. Yet, like most other urban revivalists, he drew most of his audiences from the middle and lower-middle classes, especially those who in their own lives or family traditions had had some contact with organized Protestantism. When he tried to conduct a revival on Fourteenth Street and Second Avenue in New York, the attendance was so sparse that he sent out men to try to round up listeners from the nearby cafés." 'Don't you want to come up to the church . . . and hear Dwight L. Moody preach?' the chairman said to four men who sat at a cardtable near the door. 'Who the hell is Moody?' one of them replied. And that was all there was to it."[20] Moody's complete defeat on the Lower East Side neatly symbolized the limits of revivalism's ability even to begin the process of reestablishing the old church order among the city's poorer people.

The striking growth of what came to be known as Jehovah's Witnesses demonstrated that many of those whom revivalism could not reach sought a more radical rejection of contemporary culture than men like Moody demanded. In the 1840's pre-millennialism had attracted a large following; when William Miller's predictions of a day of judgment had not been fulfilled, some had been disillusioned, but a variety of adventist churches remained in existence. Then in 1872, Charles Taze Russell, dissatisfied not only with his early Congregationalism but also with the "infidelity" to which "science" and "modern thought" had led him, found in the eschatological promises of the Bible a guarantee that Christ would soon return to rule on earth. In that overwhelming perspective, the creeds and practices of the churches seemed worse than temporizing; not preaching the truth, they were necessarily diabolic agencies. Zion's Watch Tower Society, which Russell organized in 1884, tolerated no compromise with the world, no participation in rituals or worship which tried to sanctify modes of accommodation. Society members were to devote all their efforts to "witnessing" and "publishing" Christ's imminent coming. Free of the need to follow conventional modes of action, Russell was able to develop modes of "evangelism" peculiarly suited to the masses of unchurched city dwellers. He developed an illustrated lecture, or sermon, "The Photo Drama of Creation," and transcribed his words on to phonograph records that could be played to many more people than Moody could ever have reached, and in situations and places where neither Moody nor any other regular revivalist would ever have been accepted.[21] Unencumbered by a theological tradition (Russellites declared for example that the Trinity was a vulgar error), he could depict "the divine plan of the ages" with the clarity of an architectural drawing; even the barely literate could see in the chart which prefaced most collections of Russell's writings the point in history where mankind stood. Though the movement avoided stipulating an exact day in which Christ would sit in judgment, 1914 was generally thought to mark the beginning of Christ's reconquest of the world. As important as the danger was the promise, epitomized in the slogan made popular by the Witnesses in the twentieth century, that "millions now living will never die." Simple in the demands they made upon the believer, unqualified in the denunciations they uttered against the government, the other churches, indeed modern culture generally, Jehovah's Witnesses exerted a growing appeal to the lower social and economic classes in American cities. By the twentieth century, observers recognized that the Witnesses were proselyting successfully among the habitués of city missions, which apparently could reach down-and-outers, but could not mold them into any kind of church.[22] Symbolically, when Jehovah's Witnesses established themselves in Brooklyn, they turned a former mission of Plymouth Church into their headquarters. Though they did not themselves develop congregational life of the once familiar type, they made out of one strain of traditional religion an adaptation to felt needs that was more viable than either the mission ventures of transformed churches or the adaptations of revivalism.

The Witnesses were held to their single religious purpose first by the charismatic leadership of Russell and later by a highly centralized organization dominated by "Judge" Rutherford. In marked contrast were the flock of largely autonomous local groups which began to appear, as it seemed, spontaneously in many of the large cities about the turn of the century. Sharing with the Holiness churches an almost unlimited trust in the leadings of religious emotion, and with the Witnesses a strong conviction of a not too distant Second Coming, these churches were often lumped with Holiness groups and the Witnesses as manifestations of Pentecostalism. But while all did indeed believe that the special gifts of the Pentecost would be bestowed on men again, both Witnesses and Holiness groups remained extremely wary toward contemporaries claiming the gift of "tongues" and of healing.

The gift of tongues, or *glossolalia,* was not only an easy development of the hyper-excitement of the protracted religious meetings these groups treasured; it met the needs of simple, untutored people anxious to take a leading part in meetings.[23] Honorific distinctions in favor of a professional minister disappeared; formal training, logic, even Biblical scholarship lost most importance. Above all, command of the language, which more than anything else inhibited European immigrants and slow-speaking country folk from masterful participation in urban culture, now was irrelevant, for might not God choose to speak through His people in any language, any accent?

The gift of tongues first came to public attention in 1905 in Los Angeles, but it is likely that there had been manifestations earlier.[24] From the first, Pentecostalists were an affront to most other churches. H. Paul Douglass, one of the most devoted workers for the Christianization of the city in the twentieth century, declared after a survey of St. Louis in the early 1920's: "It is a challenging and indeed shocking discovery that there are so many examples of these wild religious tendencies in St. Louis, and that so many of the humbler and newer people of the city are actually receiving from them a poor and unnourishing imitation of the Bread of Life." It appalled Douglass to realize that this "spiritual underworld" serving so crudely "that seething, unregulated and untamed stream of emotional religion" should provide so many "humble believers" the "only congenial religious home in St. Louis." Moreover, these sects were often impossibly "dogmatic, perhaps conceited, critical, and impatient with others."[25] But if the Pentecostals sneered at the churches of the "world," they did not discriminate among social classes and ethnic groups; nothing better illustrated their sectarian preoccupation with the leadings of the Holy Spirit than their obliviousness to the "color line" which cut across almost every aspect of American life. Shortlived, tumultuous, and strife-torn as some of these Pentecostal churches were, they brought congregations of striking catholicity together in worship services that were uniquely absorbing.

One of the prized Pentecostal gifts was that of healing. Like the gift of tongues, it proved to have extraordinary appeal to the lower-class folk who flocked into "storefront" churches. But the conviction that organized religion should assume responsibility for bodily ailments was not confined to any one sect or any one social class. In the Episcopal Church, a group of ministers led by Drs. Elwood Worcester and Samuel McComb of Emmanuel Church, Boston, began to treat parishioners suffering from "functional nervous disorders." But the shining example of the attempt of religion to guide the faithful to victory over illness was Christian Science. It was the achievement of Mary Baker Eddy that the Church of Christ (Scientist) which she founded in 1879 was premised on the guidance given by the Scriptures to "Science and Health."

The central strategy of Christian Science was a denial of the reality of matter; for this there were abundant precedents in American transcendentalism, and Mrs. Eddy not surprisingly always had to cope with numerous competing brands of gnosticism. But Mrs. Eddy had unusual powers both of inspiration and organization. Students spoke "of a certain spiritual and emotional exaltation which she was able to impart . . . , a feeling so strong that it was like the birth of a new understanding and seemed to open to them a new heaven and a new earth." Those who "were imaginative and emotional, and especially those who had something of the mystic in their nature, came out . . . to find that for them the world had changed. They lived by a new set of values; the color seemed to fade out of the physical world about them; men and women became shadow-like. . . . The reality of pain and pleasure, sin and grief, love and death, once denied, the only positive thing in their lives was their belief. . . ."[26] Once Mrs. Eddy became convinced that the only way to preserve the purity of this gospel against the distortions of her "enemies" (whom she believed informed with "malicious animal magnetism") was to establish a church, she created an institution which placed all power in her hands, and which made the study of her words the primary religious duty. She built and ruled so well that at her death in 1910 her church was able to survive her.

It was, however, a church with a very special appeal as well as a very special doctrine and government. Most of the members had not long before been members of the older Protestant churches; most were middle or upper-middle class; almost all were living in cities; the preponderance of woman members was exceptional, even for the American churches.[27] All of this seemed reasonable and natural to Mrs. Eddy. Though she would have denied that Christian Science was simply an adaptation of Protestantism, she always believed that a sound Protestant background was virtually a prerequisite for seeing the light. Christian Science, like Beecher's Plymouth Church, purveyed a singularly straitened version of Christianity to a peculiarly middle-class segment of the urban population.

V

By the last decades of the nineteenth century there was an enormous variety of urban churches—downtown, country, immigrant, neighborhood, revivalist, Witnesses, Pentecostal, Christian Science; but those which were churches were not urban in anything but location, and those which were urban were not churches, at least in the traditional sense of being the religious expression of the community. Many prominent churchmen made no secret of their sense that the many expedients did not constitute a triumph of religion in its new tasks.

Among Catholic leaders, much of the discontent focused on the difficulties posed for the Church by the ethnic heterogeneity of the city. Once these were overcome it was plausible to imagine that urban Catholic churches would suffer none of the distortions obvious in Protestant adaptions. Parish boundaries seldom coincided with lines dividing social classes, so that most parishes would come closer to approximating "the whole Church in microcosm" than the average Protestant downtown or neighborhood church. The Church's hierarchical structure seemed also to guarantee that no parish, whatever its social composition, would become too parochial in outlook. Furthermore, by the late nineteenth century, urban Catholic parishes had begun to develop that bewildering array of parochial schools, sodalities, confraternities, and societies—something for every condition of man—for which the modern American Catholic parish is famous. Yet, as a few of the more "Americanist" clergy recognized, the typical urban parishes fell short in two ways of being the authentic voice of their communities—as by ancient rural custom, and theological claim, they ought to be. Recoiling from the city because it was not the country, and because it seemed, to a Catholic population still of immigrant stock, formidably "American," they tended to remain aloof from attempts to civilize the city. Also, obsessed by the dangers to the faith engendered in a religious heterogeneous city, most

Catholics contented themselves with resisting error; they were almost sect-like in their disposition to preserve Catholicism from contact with the non-Catholic world.[28] Though Protestants regularly hailed the success of Catholics in transcending the social divisions rending urban Protestantism, the more perceptive Catholics were anything but satisfied with the Church's response to the city.[29]

A growing number of Protestant leaders concluded that churches could not simply react to urban life; if they hoped to re-establish the harmonious relationship between religion and culture, they would have to take an active responsibility for reshaping that culture, even if that required marked departures from the usual modes of church action. In reaching this perception, churchmen were aided not only by their recognition of the partial failures of the city churches, but also by the partial successes of such enterprises as the YMCA and the Salvation Army. Though making no claims to being churches, such responses to what Aaron Abell has felicitously called "the urban impact" demonstrated that religion could be presented to some elements in the city, only if the men of God would seek to meet certain creaturely needs.[30] Equally influential was the gradual formulation of a "social gospel"—what Henry May and Charles Hopkins have ably discussed in terms of the Protestant churches, but which had parallels in Catholicism and Judaism as well.[31] Finding its great appeal among those least trammeled with congregational responsibilities—among seminary teachers, bishops, and denominational officials—the social gospel gave sanction to those ministers and laymen anxious to redefine the gospel to meet specifically urban needs.

This attitude was especially attractive to Episcopalians, who maintained a disproportionate number of "downtown" churches; who had, as a church, never acquiesced completely in the "denominational" assumption that the responsibility for the welfare of society could be shared with other religious organizations; and whose parishes frequently included enough of the city's wealthiest citizens to permit very costly innovations in the ministry to the city. St. George's, for example, on the East Side of New York, had been surrounded by new immigrants, few of them Episcopalian. The handful of wealthy members, including J. P. Morgan, invited to the pulpit the Reverend William S. Rainsford, an English cleric of considerable experience with the problems of London and Toronto as well as New York. Determined to preside over a community church, even if that required using much of the church's resources to create the community, Rainsford soon had developed a parish program to meet the social and economic needs of every sort and condition of urban man. He attained notoriety by his proposal to establish, as an alternative to the saloon, a church club where the workingman could enjoy his glass in edifying circumstances; more important were his programs of industrial education. That such enterprises were not simply alternatives to church life—like the earlier ventures of city missions, or the Salvation

Army and YMCA—seemed demonstrated when the membership of St. George's grew from 200 to 4,000, with much of the increase coming from people of humble circumstances, both foreign-born and American. This mode of reintegrating church and community became celebrated as the institutional church.

Although the majority of institutional churches grew out of "downtown" Episcopal and Congregational churches of high social standing and low membership, Grace Church in Philadelphia illustrated that a city Baptist church might also become "institutional." In 1882, Russell Conwell brought to the pastorate of Grace no majestic ecclesiastical tradition, but the conviction that churches to succeed must prove more relevant to social problems than they had been to him as a country boy seeking his fortune in the city.[32] As an adjunct to Grace Church, he built Samaritan Hospital, and also Baptist Temple, eventually the center for Temple College and for a whole complex of recreational and social clubs. Grace Church soon claimed to have the largest congregation in the United States.

The conspicuous success of congregations like St. George's and Grace made it plausible for the Open and Institutional Church League, founded in 1894, to boast that "the burning question, 'how to reach the masses,' is practically solved,"[33] for the institutional church seemed to possess the "comprehensiveness" essential to a true congregation. But the League failed to recognize just how precarious was the life of most institutional churches. Both St. George's and Grace at the end of the century depended too much on charismatic ministerial leadership to prove that many churches could reach, let alone hold, the "masses." Rainsford had to struggle continuously to preserve the peaceful coexistence of rich and poor in one church. J. P. Morgan found it almost intolerable to imagine that the vestry, whom he was accustomed to entertain at his home, should contain men he did not "know socially"; and Alfred Mahan quit St. George's in revulsion against Rainsford's democratizing policies. Conwell, spared such problems by the relative absence of wealthy men in his congregation, was continually obliged to seek outside funds to continue his institutional church. Whether he secured money from friendly businessmen like the Wanamakers, or raised it by touring the country delivering his paean to self-help, entitled "Acres of Diamonds," he symbolized the adventitious existence of his church—a missionary venture if not in its character at least in its dependence upon other churches and churchmen. Even the League, acknowledging that more cooperation between denominations would be necessary to sustain institutional churches in some parts of some cities, implicitly retreated from the old faith in the autonomous congregation.

Furthermore, commitment to the social gospel involved the institutional churches in some of the ambiguities of that movement. Faith that a program of action satisfactory to all social classes could be agreed on was soon shaken by the intransigence of the congregations. Early in the twentieth century,

Charles Stelzle became convinced that the institutional church would never even consider the socialistic ideas which, he thought, were talismanic to many city workers; his own inability to get support from the Presbyterian Church for radical congregational experiments was paralleled in subsequent decades by the rebuffs many social gospelers received from their denominations.[34] Most congregations would endorse the social gospel only if it did not involve pronounced departures from middle-class values.

Conversely, to the extent that institutional churches committed themselves to programs of more or less radical social action, they did so on the assumption—explicit in Rainsford's case—that either a healthy community would be swiftly restored, or that the state would see its duty and relieve the churches of their social responsibilities. Either eventuality was conducive of disillusion. As the municipalities, or private agencies like the settlement houses, increased the range of community service, the institutional churches lost much of their sense of mission. Perhaps more ominous was the discovery that social amelioration did not by itself automatically produce a population naturally inclined toward congregational life. The dawning realization that alienation from the churches was not simply a by-product of problems of society was central to the neo-orthodox revolt of the 1930's from the social gospel on which the institutional churches were premised.

VI

For all its limitations, the institutional church constituted the most coherent effort to re-establish the congregation as the normal vehicle of religious life in the city. Its obvious successes encouraged churches threatened by a changing city environment not to desert to the suburbs. Its very willingness to experiment with new modes of evangelism made it an important precedent for contemporary enterprises like the East Harlem Protestant Parish, with its determination to construct a congregational life in a demoralized neighborhood.[35] On the other hand, the institutional church has never been so generally accepted as to preclude the continued existence— and in some cases the steady growth—of more specialized adaptations to the urban scene.

The number of neighborhood churches has increased during the twentieth century. As suburbia has grown more rapidly than center-city, new congregations have been established at an astonishing rate, each usually drawing on a highly stratified segment of the population. The consequence has been much like that exhibited in Beecher's Plymouth Church; within the last decade some Protestant, Catholic, and Jewish spokesmen have gloried in the obvious vitality of these churches, while others have deplored the "suburban captivity."[36]

The relatively steady abandonment in many suburban churches of traditional theology in favor of a gospel of social adjustment and mental health has further narrowed the gap separating them from the gnostic cults once represented almost exclusively by Christian Science, but now including New Thought, Unity, Psychiana, and I Am. Of these, only Christian Science maintains any semblance of congregational life, but the strong group identification of their members renders these cults almost as close to the old church order as many of the suburban churches.

The rural churches established in the cities in the late nineteenth century have been markedly affected by urban life. The Church of God (Anderson, Indiana), for example, one of the larger holiness bodies, has steadily accommodated to the religious diversity of the city by shedding its hostility to other denominations. As members slowly abandon their peculiarities of dress and expression, the church concentrates on maintaining the allegiance of the younger generation; it

> relaxes its program of grab-him-by-the-lapel evangelism, puts robes on the choir and candles on the altar, divides the chancel, replaces folding chairs with oaken pews, and calls a college-trained minister. . . . It moves out of its plain rectangular white frame building into a stone gothic or redwood contemporary structure. It is now respectable.[37]

Such transformed churches, of course, do not appeal so strongly any more to the migrants from the countryside. But with the restriction in the 1920's of immigration from abroad, and with the reduction of the American rural population, the number of country folk in the city has decreased; the likelihood has therefore decreased of creating a church which continues the special version of religious life cherished in one's own country or region. However, the ability of revivalists like Billy Graham to mount revival crusades demonstrates that there are still many people in the cities who are not completely satisfied with the ethos of the city churches.

Meanwhile, the probability has steadily grown that newcomers will be attracted to one of the cultic or Pentecostal groups authentic to the cities. Some of these groups owe their existence to a charismatic leader like Daddy Grace or Father Divine; others are sustained by a special myth like that which connects the "Black Jews" with the Lost Tribes; still others have stressed a single doctrine like the rapidly growing Jehovah's Witnesses, or a single gift, like some of the healing cults.[38] In 1958, Henry Van Dusen, President of Union Theological Seminary, estimated that a third of all believers now adhere to radical sects or cults, and that, taken together, they comprise the most rapidly growing component of American religion.[39] About the same time, two sociologists noted how Puerto Rican migrants to New York, not strongly drawn to the Roman Catholic parishes, have flocked into Pentecostal churches. Not only do these churches offer a stringent moral code in reassuring contrast to the apparent normlessness of the city; they also provide frequent meetings, in which newcomers are welcomed, in which the modes of worship are simple, and in which participation in songs and "tongues" is warmly cherished. "The first time I went there, I was impressed by the way everyone shook hands with me," reported one member. Another said that "I was sick, they came to my home to say a prayer for me." "I used to go to the Catholic Church," a third explained; "there nobody knew me. . . . Now in my church they call me sister."[40] Such testimonies reaffirm that a need for congregational communion continues to be a strong theme in American religious life. Under the social confusions, the economic difficulties, and the psychological tensions engendered by urban life, congregationalism has developed in ways often unfamiliar and almost always profoundly unsatisfactory to leaders whose ideal has remained the village church on the green.

■ ■ ■ ■ Notes

1 Josiah Strong, *The Challenge of the City* (New York: Missionary Education Movement, 1907); Charles H. Sears, *The Redemption of the City* (Philadelphia: Griffith and Rowland Press, 1911); William T. Stead, *If Christ Came to Chicago* (Chicago: Laird and Lee, 1894); Charles Stelzle, *Christianity's Storm Centre: A Study of the Modern City* (New York: Fleming Revell, 1907).

2 Two useful nineteenth-century surveys of the range of religious organization are Robert Baird, *Religion in the U. S. of A.* (Glasgow: Blackie, 1844) and Daniel Dorchester, *Christianity in the United States* (New York: Hunt and Eaton, 1888). The classic analysis of the correlation in America between sectarian difference and social attitude is H. Richard Niebuhr, *The Social Sources of Denominationalism* (Hamden, Conn.: Shoe String Press, 1954).

3 Typical of Douglass' many works on urban religion is his *One Thousand City Churches* (New York: George H. Doran, 1926).

4 A good summary and critique of seven of the most widely accepted typologies is Frederick A. Shippey, "The Variety of City Churches," *Review of Religious Research,* II (Summer, 1960), 8–19.

5 The situation did not become any simpler later in the century; a clergyman in a downtown New York church in the 1890's declared that "on one side of me is a block in which, the police say, thirty-nine languages and dialects are spoken. Within four blocks is a city more foreign than any city in Europe this side of Constantinople." Quoted in Amory H. Bradford (ed.), *Christ and the Church* (New York: Fleming Revell, 1895), pp. 196–197.

6 Charles Stelzle, *A Son of the Bowery* (New York: George H. Doran, 1926), p. 63.

7 Quoted in Ray Stannard Baker, *The Spiritual Unrest* (New York: Frederick Stokes, 1910), p. 42.

8 The failure of most earlier efforts is discussed in Walter Laidlaw, "A Cooperative Church Parish System," *American Journal of Sociology,* III (May, 1898), 795–808.

9 The situation in Holyoke is referred to briefly in Constance M. Green, *Holyoke* (New Haven: Yale University Press, 1939). For Gastonia, see Liston Pope's excellent study, *Millhands and Preachers* (New Haven: Yale University Press, 1942).

10 Pope, p. 88.

11 Timothy Smith, *Revivalism and Social Reform* (New York: Abingdon Press, 1957).

12 Timothy Smith, *Called Unto Holiness. The Story of the Nazarenes: The Formative Years* (Kansas City: Nazarene Publishing House, 1962) is the best study of a holiness group's development. Professor Smith regards the Nazarenes as more of

a creative adaptation to city needs, and less of a transplantation from the country-side, than I.

13 The much controverted "Cahenslyite" episode in American Catholic history turned around the reluctance, or the inability, of Irish-American bishops to provide immigrant Catholics with parishes and priests of their own nationality. See Colman J. Barry, *The Catholic Church and German Americans* (Washington: Catholic University Press, 1953).

14 Constance Rourke, *Trumpets of Jubilee* (New York: Harcourt Brace, Harbinger edition, 1963), p. 129.

15 Marshall Sklare, *Conservative Judaism* (Glencoe, Illinois: Free Press, 1955).

16 Smith, *Revivalism and Social Reform,* p. 49.

17 William G. McLaughlin, *Modern Revivalism: Charles Grandison Finney to Billy Graham* (New York: Ronald Press, 1955), p. 119.

18 McLaughlin, p. 166.

19 Gamaliel Bradford, *Dwight L. Moody, A Worker in Souls* (New York: George H. Doran, 1927), pp. 227–263.

20 The incident is recounted in Stelzle, *A Son of the Bowery,* p. 119.

21 Charles S. Braden, *These Also Believe. A Study of Modern American Cults and Minority Religious Movements* (New York: Macmillan, 1949), p. 361.

22 Theodore Abel, *Protestant Missions to Catholic Immigrants* (New York: Institute of Social and Religious Research, 1933), pp. 54–55.

23 See F. G. Henke, "The Gift of Tongues and Related Phenomena at the Present Day," *American Journal of Theology,* XIII (1909), 196–201.

24 Nils Bloch-Hoell, *The Pentecostal Movement* (Oslo: Universitetsforlaget, 1964), especially pp. 45–51.

25 *The St. Louis Church Survey* (New York: George H. Doran, 1924), pp. 119–120.

26 Quoted in Georgine Milmine, "Mary Baker Eddy," *McClure's Magazine,* XXIX (July, 1907), 108–109.

27 See David O. Moberg, *The Church as a Social Institution* (Englewood Cliffs, N.J.: Prentice-Hall, 1962), p. 396; see also the perceptive English study, Bryan R. Wilson, *Sects and Society. A Sociological Study of the Elim Tabernacle, Christian Science, and Christadelphians* (Berkeley: University of California Press, 1961), p. 350.

28 Robert D. Cross, *The Emergence of Liberal Catholicism in America* (Cambridge, Mass.: Harvard University Press, 1958), especially chapter 2.

29 Robert D. Cross, "The Changing Image of the City among American Catholics," *Catholic Historical Review,* XLVIII (April, 1962), 33–52.

30 Aaron I. Abell, *The Urban Impact on American Protestantism* (Cambridge, Mass.: Harvard University Press, 1943).

31 Charles H. Hopkins, *The Rise of the Social Gospel in American Protestantism* (New Haven: Yale University Press, 1940); Henry F. May, *Protestant Churches and Industrial America* (New York: Octagon Books, 1963). For some reverberations in the Catholic Church, see Abell, *American Catholicism and Social Action* (Garden City, N.Y.: Doubleday, 1960).

32 Agnes R. Burr, *Russell H. Conwell and His Work* (Philadelphia: John Winston, 1917).

33 Quoted in Abell, *The Urban Impact on American Protestantism,* p. 161.

34 For the history of the later years of the Social Gospel, see Paul A. Carter, *The Decline and Revival of the Social Gospel* (Ithaca, N.Y.: Cornell University Press, 1956) and Donald Meyer, *The Protestant Search for Political Realism* (Berkeley: University of California Press, 1960).

35 For the implications of the experience in this parish, as seen by one of its leaders, see George R. Webber, *The Congregation in Mission* (New York: Abingdon Press, 1964). For contemporary Catholic concern about the urban parish, see Dennis Clark,

Cities in Crisis (New York: Sheed and Ward, 1960), and the references in Cross, "The Changing Image."

36 Representative views are those of Andrew Greeley, *The Church and the Suburbs* (New York: Sheed and Ward, 1959); Albert J. Gordon, *Jews in Suburbia* (Boston: Beacon Press, 1959); and Gibson Winter, *The Suburban Captivity of the Churches* (Garden City, N.Y.: Doubleday, 1961).

37 Val B. Clear, "The Urbanization of a Holiness Body," *The City Church*, IX (July–August, 1958), 2–3, 7–11.

38 See G. Norman Eddy, "Store-Front Religion," in Robert Lee (ed.), *Cities and Churches. Readings on the Urban Church* (Philadelphia: Westminster Press, 1962). See also Elmer T. Clark, *The Small Sects in America* (Nashville: Cokesbury Press, 1937).

39 "The Third Force in Christendom," *Life*, XLIV (June 9, 1958), 23.

40 Renato Poblete and Thomas F. O'Dea, "Anomie and the 'Quest for Community': The Formation of Sects among the Puerto Ricans of New York," *American Catholic Sociological Review*, XXI (Spring, 1960), 18–36.

15
The Quest for Community

ROBERT M. FOGELSON

Migration and mobility are key themes in American social history. The United States, said the historian Richard Hofstadter, was born on a farm and moved to the city; and for the last century and a half people have moved from rural to urban communities in search of economic opportunity and social gratification. Movement also takes place from one city to another, a phenomenon which has increasingly become the most important form of internal migration. Even in the early nineteenth century, many residents of pioneer western cities came from Philadelphia and other established cities. After 1880, thousands of men and women from the rural and urban Midwest and Southwest made their way to Southern California, particularly Los Angeles, which has since grown at a phenomenal rate.

Many of the pre–World War I migrants to Los Angeles were attracted by the climate and other amenities, not by superior economic opportunities. As Robert Fogelson indicates in the book from which the following essay is taken, Los Angeles developed its industrial base after it had a substantial population; industry came to tap an already existing market consisting primarily of white, middle-class men and women from the Midwest. These people, like many other Americans, wanted their city to grow but at the same time to retain the values of rural and small town America—values they expressed in patterns of settlement and behavior. They could achieve their goals more readily in Los Angeles than in any other large American city. Even before the automobile, the availability of space and electric traction facilitated the dispersed pattern of settlement and land use for which the city is famous. In effect, Los Angeles was a group of suburbs in search of a city, long before freeways dominated the landscape. It was also no accident that Los Angeles was the only large city to vote for prohibition; in contrast to other metropolises, there were not enough immigrants and other lower-class users of alcohol to prevent its adoption.

Still, Los Angeles's newcomers found they could not create in a metropolitan setting the perhaps mythical neighborliness and sense of community of the small town. The original settlers of the 1870s and 1880s relied on voluntary associations to provide social support. (There seems to be a close relationship between the mobility of Americans and our being a "nation of joiners.") For the later arrivals, voluntary associations, whether churches or state societies, could not fulfill their needs. Nathaniel West's The Day of the Locust *is a chilling fictional portrayal of the resulting rootlessness and isolation of Angelenos. If community was impossible for the native middle-class whites, what of the excluded groups—the Mexicans, the Orientals, and the blacks—who were pressured to adopt the values of the middle-class majority without being allowed to share in its life or to reap its rewards? Fogelson's perceptive account of Los Angeles's social fragmentation goes beyond just that city, which is often taken as the model for future urban America.*

■ ■ ■ ■ **For Further Reading**

E. Digby Baltzell, ed., *The Search for Community in Modern America* (New York: Harper & Row, 1967) is an interesting collection of essays on the general problem of community, or lack of it, in contemporary America. Useful studies of the idea of community are Sebastian de Grazia, *The Political Community* (Chicago: University of Chicago Press, 1958) and Scott Greer and David W. Minar, eds., *The Concept of Community* (Chicago: Aldine, 1969). Mason Drukman, *Community and Purpose in America: An Analysis of American Political Theory* (New York: McGraw-Hill, 1971), argues persuasively that Americans have committed themselves excessively to economic individualism and have therefore not been able to develop a sense of community, either conceptually or in practice.

■ The evolution of a fragmented community accompanied the growth of Los Angeles. Up to 1885, Jackson A. Graves, an early settler and prominent banker, recalled, strong friendship and shared experiences tied the townspeople together. "Somehow or other, we lived nearer each other [in 1875] than we do today," he wrote in 1930. "We were more intimate, more sympathetic, there were fewer of us, and we knew each other better than we know those surrounding us at this time. It also seems that we had more leisure on our hands, time to rejoice with the fortunate, to mourn with those in affliction, to sympathize with those in distress."[1] Although Graves, a conservative appalled by the complexity of modern America, was nostalgic for the simplicity of the nineteenth century, his reminiscences accurately described the attachments of his early life and the integration of his adopted settlement. They revealed that thousands of immigrants of diverse origins, occupations, and positions were successfully assimilated into Los Angeles between 1850 and 1885.

Their assimilation was facilitated by the size, location, composition, and character of the population. After all, Los Angeles had no more than 20,000 people before the boom of the late 1880s, few of whom resided more than one mile from the town's center. Most of them—natives of the New England, Middle Atlantic, and eastern Great Lakes states and immigrants from England, Ireland, and Germany—fully adopted American aspirations and attitudes before coming to Los Angeles. Once there they engaged in commerce, crafts, industry, and the professions and attained satisfactory livelihoods. After a while they settled in desirable residential neighborhoods and adhered to prevailing mores. They were also united, as a European traveler observed in the 1870s, by "a mutual interest in the city's advancement,"[2] for they knew that their personal success depended ultimately on the town's progress. All in all, a midwestern visitor concluded in the 1870s, "The white people here are much like they are in any new and thriving town or city at the east."[3]

But this uniformity was not immediately apparent. From the perspective of the immigrant, everything and everyone seemed different; the town was strange, and the townspeople were strangers. The problems of adjustment appeared formidable. Knowing few, if any, of Los Angeles' inhabitants, how could he meet members of the community? Feeling little or no attachment to the region, how could he gain a position of respect in the town? Subjecting his fortune to precarious urban enterprises, how would he secure protection against the fluctuations of the market? And powerless among so many individuals and interests, how could he impress his designs on the fabric of life in Los Angeles?[4] Notwithstanding the newcomer's best intentions, direct entrance into the community was difficult. Fortunately, the small, compact, homogeneous, and like-minded populace facilitated the formation of voluntary associations that tied him to his fellow citizens and helped him cope with his problems.

The town's groups were legion. They included Masonic and Odd Fellow lodges, French and Italian societies, Baptist and Methodist congregations, drama and literary clubs, fire companies and military brigades, Democratic and Republican parties, Boards of Trade and Chambers of Commerce.[5] Exclusive without being invidious, they served as guideposts for the bewildered immigrant. They identified other residents with like traits and similar interests and encouraged contact on shared grounds and participation in common activities. Membership in these organizations defined the newcomer's place in Los Angeles. Furthermore, fraternal and benevolent societies alleviated his insecurity by providing funds, assistance, and insurance in case of depression, illness, and death. Political and commercial bodies promoted his aspirations in matters involving municipal authorities, transcontinental railroads, and even the federal government. Hence in Los Angeles, as elsewhere in the nation, the voluntary associations first introduced the immigrant to the community and afterwards linked him with it.

Not everyone shared in the town's community life, however. Maladjusted Mexicans, uprooted Chinese, and transient Americans all remained separate from the larger society. Few in number, these people were conspicuous by their differences. They lacked entrepreneurial and professional skills, placed a low priority on material achievement, and held modest expectations of future accomplishments. Considering Los Angeles an ancestral pueblo or a temporary settlement and not their chosen and permanent home, they felt little inclination to improve the town economically or socially. No less important, they were deemed undesirable by the Americans. To one intolerant but not untypical midwesterner, these people made up "a dirty, vile, degraded, unredeemable humanity that sits idly in the shade and suffers the rich gifts of climate and soil to go to waste unused and not even appreciated."[6] From such persons, they could expect little indeed.

Hence they earned poor livings. Most worked as laborers and domestics, some managed as gamblers and thieves, and others survived with no visible means of support whatever. They also lived in dreadful accommodations. They had no money to erect houses in fashionable neighborhoods, and in any case would not have been welcome there. They congregated in the vicinity of the old business district, where they rented crowded quarters in dilapidated dwellings. They took little interest in politics, regarding authority as a threat and avoiding it as a precaution, and politicians showed little concern for them. They did not join fraternal societies or worship in Protestant churches; nor did they cooperate with civic committees or contribute to commercial organizations.[7] Instead, the Mexicans retained and the Chinese created their own institutions, though the transient Americans relied on less formal arrangements and in particular on their wits. Unassimilated, unwelcome, and unprotected, these people were so thoroughly isolated that the American majority was able to maintain its untainted vision of an integrated community.[8]

After 1885 the growth of Los Angeles overwhelmed the original townspeople and their descendants. Not only did the population multiply more than fifty times, and the territory expand more than a hundredfold, in the next forty-five years, but, in addition, the newcomers were far less homogeneous, and their aspirations much less unanimous, than the pioneers. The early settlers now found themselves very few among very many and watched their neighborhoods disrupted by changes in land-use. They were dismayed by the diversity of the recent immigrants and confused by the complexity of public issues. Their response to these changes was ambivalent. They admired the vast metropolis, but defended the "vanished village." "While Los Angeles was small and relatively poor in 1875," a resident wrote a half century later, "do not imagine that we did not enjoy life and have good times."[9] They approved of its material advances, but wondered, as a woman put it in 1931, "how soon the wheels of progress are going to stop rattling long enough for us to hear ourselves think, catch our breath and develop some sort of cohesive social organism."[10]

Incapable of imposing the town's coherence on the metropolis, the older residents tried instead to distinguish themselves from the newcomers. They organized pioneer and historical societies that excluded all but the earliest settlers and their families. They also resided in fashionable neighborhoods that restricted all but the acceptable and the wealthy. Yet these measures failed to set them apart and thereby tie them together. The genealogical gatherings were incidental to their members' lives, and the local subdividers were unmindful of the differences between those truly select and those merely rich. In a related attempt to perpetuate their pre-eminence by honoring the past, these people also simplified the metropolis' problems and celebrated the region's traditions.[11] But though the natives impressed their rhetoric and festivals on the newcomers, they did not control the administration of Los Angeles or the conduct of its residents.

The problems of the pioneers reflected the predominance of the newcomers. They were—admitting their numbers but excepting the Mexicans, Japanese, and Negroes—a remarkably homogeneous group. This is not to deny that they included persons as varied as prosperous farmers and hopeful actors from regions as distinct as New England and the Southwest who left for reasons as diverse as retirement and opportunity in periods as far apart as the mid-1880s and the late 1920s. It is rather to argue that most fit well within the broad range of the middle class, had rural midwestern, or at least native American backgrounds, sought a less arduous and more rewarding life, and migrated between the booms of 1904–1906 and 1920–1925. These similarities deeply impressed visitors to Los Angeles: "There is no other place in America," one wrote in 1927, "where the social stratification is so little marked, where all classes do so nearly the same thing at the same time."[12] Furthermore, these newcomers derived from their past experiences two critical, albeit contradictory, commitments which shaped their aspirations for their community.

First, having repudiated certain traditional values in choosing southern California, they felt a compulsion to justify their decision that could be relieved only by steadfast dedication to Los Angeles. They became unparalleled boosters. "Never anywhere have I seen such continual, consistent and enthusiastic 'boosting,'" an admiring Montana realtor remarked.[13] "You stop a policeman to ask a question and he answers you and then tells you what a wonderful city Los Angeles is," a Utah visitor commented in 1914. "You wait for your change in a store and the salesgirl tells you Los Angeles is a marvelous city. You get your shoes shined and the boy will state that Los Angeles' climate cannot be beaten." After that, he added, "The business man will tell you that all Los Angeles has done isn't a circumstance to what will be done."[14] Far from denying these descriptions, the promoters exulted in them. "If you do not 'come through' and tell us what a beautiful city we have, what a fine country and charming climate," the Los Angeles *Times* advised tourists in 1909, "we shall set you down as lacking in taste, intelligence and eloquence. We shall proceed to tell you, and that will be the worse for you."[15]

Boosterism inhibited dissent in Los Angeles. "There is no room for knockers here," a promoter exclaimed in 1908. "We are too busy going ahead to listen to the man with a tale of woe. The fault-finders are not going to help matters by telling us things are going from bad to worse."[16] Ironically, boosterism reflected the insecurity of the residents. Arthur Letts, a Canadian immigrant who founded the Broadway Department Store, dramatically, though unwittingly, revealed this anxiety in a sign that hung on his downtown building. "DON'T WORRY. WATCH US GROW," it read.[17] The people of Los Angeles did worry, concerned, as they were, not only about the future growth of the metropolis, but also about the inescapable evidence of modernity there. For, though as boosters they endorsed progress, as Americans they feared its consequences. They perceived in urbanization a direct conflict with their second commitment, a devotion, engendered in the country, confirmed in the city, and buttressed by tradition, to a bygone rural community.

Perhaps nothing better illustrated this attitude than their replies to an article, "Los Angeles—The Chemically Pure," published in a sophisticated eastern magazine in 1913. Its author, Willard Huntington Wright, described Los Angeles as a puritanical and ill-governed city destitute of the delights of urbanity. "The spirit of genuine gaiety is lacking," he wrote. "Enjoyment is considered the first step to perdition. Noise is the rumbling of the gates of hell. Music is a sign of immorality, and dancing is indecent." For this attitude he blamed the militant moralists from the Midwest. "These good people brought with them a complete stock of rural beliefs, pieties, superstitions and habits," he explained. "Having, by virtue of numbers, a large voice in municipal affairs, they govern Los Angeles as they would a village." Applying Sunday school precepts to their political decisions, they have transformed a once fascinating and sensible place into a "city of little sociability or hospitality, a city devoid of lenience and cosmopolitanism."[18]

The article outraged the residents of Los Angeles, but, far from denying the author's allegations, they defended the community as he described it. "Los Angeles believes in the home," a southern California spokesman answered. "She believes in the moralities; she believes in the decencies of life; she believes that children born within its precincts should be, as far as possible, freed from that familiarity with vice that renders it difficult properly to bring up children in some American cities . . . She deliberately chooses to be dubbed 'Puritan,' 'Middle-West Farmer,' 'Provincial,' etc., and glories in the fact that she has been able to sweep away many flaunting indecencies that still disgrace older and more vice-complacent communities."[19] "If anything," another Los Angeles citizen wrote, catching the quintessence of this morality, "it is our departure from these 'village ideals,' the simple, comely life of our fathers, that has nurtured the blight of demoralizing metropolitanism, a curse alike to old and young and that embodies in its spirit all those indulgences and immoralities which Mr. Wright seems to think constitute a higher phase of existence than any possible extract of a village."[20]

Thus the people of Los Angeles desired the size but not the character of a modern metropolis. They feared that as the price of progress their adopted community would lose its sense of fellow feeling and lower its standards of personal morality. As the region's population and heterogeneity increased and as its territory and industry expanded—as, in sum, Los Angeles emerged as one of the largest agglomerations in the United States—they therefore strove to recreate the cohesive communal life of their former farms and towns. They longed to perpetuate familiar rural relationships within a strange urban society, to reconcile their material ambitions with their psychic imperatives, to combine the spirit of the good community with the substance of the great metropolis.

This aspiration was faithfully reflected in the thought of the Reverend Dana W. Bartlett. Bartlett, a minister born in Maine, reared in Iowa, and then serving as clergyman, author, and social worker in Los Angeles,[21] had the utmost confidence in his adopted community. A committed environmentalist, he attributed communal deterioration elsewhere to ethnic ghettos and physical congestion; an avowed optimist, he considered Los Angeles capable of avoiding these objectionable excrescences. He appealed to his fellow citizens to design their future accordingly. Let us assimilate the immigrants, he proposed; Americanize the Europeans, and unite the populace. "Let us have a city without tenements, a city without slums," he urged. "Ruralize the city; urbanize the country."[22] The native white majority shared Bartlett's commitments to homogeneity and rusticity. They agreed that the harmony of society depended on the uniformity of its members, and that the integrity of the community required the dispersal of its people. They believed that like-minded persons, joined in voluntary associations and settled in residential suburbs, could prevent "the blight of demoralizing metropolitanism" from spreading over Los Angeles.

From the perspective of the native white Americans, this aspiration seemed eminently practicable. After all, they came from about the same rural, middle-class, native-American backgrounds as their predecessors. They felt no less keen on joining the community and even more committed to their adopted settlement. Moreover, Los Angeles' voluntary associations actively sought their membership. Fraternal orders invited them as brothers; religious congregations welcomed them as worshippers; political clubs appealed to them as voters; commercial organizations solicited their support as businessmen; and civic groups called for their cooperation as citizens.[23] Clearly, no institutional barriers prevented the newcomers from assimilating into the communal life of Los Angeles.

Nor did any insuperable barriers prevent them from settling in the residential suburbs of the metropolis. With few exceptions, they had the necessary wherewithal. Some had enough in savings to live comfortably without working, while others had the skills, capital, and education to gain well-paying jobs, engage in business, serve in professions, and otherwise exploit the opportunities available in an expanding economy.[24] They also allocated a large share of their income to housing. Not only did a suburban home epitomize their vision of the good community, but, in choosing from the many subdivisions in Los Angeles, they encountered no obstacles other than financial in reaching a decision.[25] Sought by subdividers and welcomed by neighbors, the newcomers bought lots and built homes on suburban tracts everywhere in greater Los Angeles. Despite the homogeneity of their voluntary associations, and the rusticity of their residential retreats, however, they failed to recreate the cohesive community so crucial to their personal aspirations.

Voluntary associations integrated the community less effectively in 1930 than in 1885 because they were less relevant to the newcomers. Italian, French, and other ethnic organizations became extraneous as the United States rather than western Europe generated the vast numbers of immigrants. Benevolent societies became superfluous as economic progress, welfare legislation, and insurance companies protected residents against unemployment, accident, and death. Music, literary, and drama clubs became moribund when faced with the relentless competition of the radio, popular magazines, and movies. Commercial associations became specialized and impersonal, as they shifted their attention to the region's industrialization. And civic groups became professional and parochial when they confronted complicated policy questions and profound social conflicts.[26] Homogeneity under modern conditions was thus incompatible with traditional institutions.

The churches too fared poorly. Although most newcomers considered religion beneficial, only one in five was affiliated with a congregation in 1927.[27] "I don't know why, but I have no desire to go to church here in the city," a Protestant woman admitted. "Perhaps it is because it is so hard to get acquainted. Then, too, I thought that all people in church were friendly," she added, "but I found that they do not even bother to say 'Good Morning' to a stranger. That was a shock to me and I just didn't want to go back any more."[28] "When I first came to Los Angeles, I was delighted at the number of new members I was receiving into the church," a Protestant minister acknowledged. "I thought the church was growing very rapidly under my leadership. But when I began to check up, I discovered that the church was constantly losing so many members, that I was doing well if I kept the membership stationary."[29] To overcome the sense of anonymity and the secularization of leisure, most churches stressed social at the expense of spiritual affairs; but, except for a few revivalist cults, the congregations were incapable of binding their communicants.

Residential suburbs did not integrate the metropolis either because they discouraged contact among people. Subdivisions provided little or no acreage for common facilities such as parks and plazas. Deed restrictions prohibited the establishment of nearby commercial enterprises that served as centers of social intercourse in other American cities. Even the layouts separated inhabitants from one another, adults from churches and children from schools. Moreover, the interminable lines of streets and the monotonous rows of houses blurred boundaries between sections of the region, and the widespread use of private automobiles inhibited casual contacts that formerly stimulated personal relationships in Los Angeles. The rustic environment so conducive to community life in the tiny, compact, and well-defined town inhibited social interaction in the immense, dispersed, and sprawling metropolis.

Los Angeles' newcomers did join together on a neighborhood basis. As a means of enhancing the value of their real estate, property holders organized to demand railway connections and street improvements.[30] But these business ties rarely led to social relationships. Also, as a means of maintaining the character and structure of their blocks in the face of an alleged "invasion" of Negroes or Orientals or a projected change in the prevailing land-use, home-owners banded together to enforce deed restrictions, pressure municipal legis-lators, and harass prospective buyers, sellers, and builders.[31] But these outfits mobilized only in response to an immediate challenge. All in all, these asso-ciations were so motivated by a sense of exclusivity and limited to a few parts of the metropolis that they provided a poor foundation for more com-mendable and broader community involvement.

Residential mobility further disrupted voluntary associations and neighbor-hood ties in Los Angeles. As older houses deteriorated, commercial facilities expanded, and ethnic ghettos spread, homeowners in the central district, who gained from rising property values and felt little attachment to any particular tract, moved—often more than once—to outlying subdivisions. There they erected newer and more comfortable homes. For most persons in Los Angeles, the permanent thus became the utopian. Neighbors scattered all over the city, a woman lamented, and newcomers arrived only to leave, joined groups only to quit, and made friends only to part.[32] Neither extreme residential mobility, ineffective voluntary organizations, nor outlying residential subdivisions was unique to Los Angeles. But nowhere else in the United States did people change address so frequently, associations face só perplexing a task, and suburbs so completely dominate a region.

For these reasons most residents felt extremely isolated after 1900. "Why, I don't even know the name of my next door neighbor," one woman admitted. "I hear the water running in their bath tub as well as or better than I hear it in my own tub. I know what they say and can tell what they are doing, but I don't know what their name is and I have never cared to find out."[33] As a result, loneliness became endemic to Los Angeles. "It is strange not to have any home faces round," a young bride confided in her diary. "I felt so odd among so many and so many miles between me and my home folks."[34] "None of the people round here call on each other and not a single neighbor has invited us in," a middle-aged woman remarked not long after. "We don't know anybody and we don't see much sign of neighboring." Isolation and loneliness also engendered suspicion. "I don't know whether I would like to know my neighbors here," the same woman confessed. "I don't like the way some of them act." "Sometimes I think it's an advantage not to know them too well," her daughter interjected. "But we'd like to know a few real well," her mother replied. "It's lonesome when you don't."[35]

To overcome isolation and relieve loneliness, the people of Los Angeles formed other groups. Here they followed the practices of the European im-migrants; but, as they were largely native Americans, membership was based on the state and not the country of birth, and as they sought companionship rather than protection, social intercourse was stressed instead of economic assistance. Pennsylvanians founded the first state society in the 1880s, Iowans organized the largest one in the early 1900s, and nearly all the native Americans established their own by the 1920s. Charles H. Parsons, who federated the state societies of Los Angeles described their appeal as follows: "There are many who come here alone, they have no relatives, possibly no immediate friends; homesickness and lonesomeness naturally follow; possibly one may be almost ready to return to the old home and former friends. Then the opportunity comes to attend one of the famous state picnics or evening social reunions."[36] For the newcomer, Parsons noted, this is the turning point.

"Often one will meet those he knew in the long ago," he explained. "He may only meet those who knew his family and friends, but it is some one from home. Immediately all the outlook changes; homesickness is forgotten, lonesomeness thrown aside. He finds he is not alone out here after all. He went to school with Billy Jones back in Warren county, Ohio. Bill is here. The world grows bright at once. Sure, he will like California and instead of buying a return ticket he buys a home, settles down and becomes a booster for Sunny Southern California."[37] Parsons' enthusiasm aside, the state societies formed only tenuous bonds. Large annual picnics in the city's parks and small monthly meetings in the downtown cafeterias did not compensate for the absence of more frequent contact and more meaningful relationships. Also, the newcomers' children, who knew no state other than California and no life other than the present, found the societies' loyalties incomprehensible and its rustic gatherings dull. In time, therefore, the state societies lost their vigor and deteriorated into sanctuaries for a few elderly and uprooted persons.[38]

Hence many newcomers felt frustrated in Los Angeles. "All their lives," novelist Nathaniel West wrote (with some exaggeration), "they had slaved at some kind of labor, behind desks and counters, in the fields and at tedious machines of all sorts, saving their pennies and dreaming of the leisure that would be theirs when they had enough. Finally that day came." They left for southern California, "the land of sunshine and oranges. Once there, they discover that sunshine isn't enough, however. They get tired of oranges, even of avocado pears and passion fruit. Nothing happens. They don't know what to do with their time. They haven't the mental equipment for leisure, the money nor the physical equipment for pleasure." They become painfully disenchanted with Los Angeles. "Did they slave so long just to go to an occasional Iowa picnic? What else is there? They watch the waves come in at Venice. There wasn't an ocean where most of them came from, but after you've seen one wave, you've seen them all. The same is true of airplanes at Glendale." If only a plane would crash once in a while, West suggested, perhaps their boredom would be relieved. "But the planes never crash."[39]

West expected ennui to incite riot and violence in Los Angeles, but here he misinterpreted the character of its population. It is true that these conditions encouraged eccentric thought and erratic action, an inclination to tinker with ideas and to tamper with institutions, among those native Americans who, as one political leader observed, were "peculiarly susceptible to sentimental appeal . . . goodly people ready to accept any guaranteed panacea for peace on earth and good will to men; rather a shallow thinking lot who take their politics, as they do their religion, largely on faith."[40] These persons— among whom, some were attached to "mind cure" (or "New Thought") before coming to Los Angeles, and others were part of the metropolis' unduly large female, elderly, and otherwise uprooted populace—were particularly responsive to a host of individual cranks and organized cults. They made up the vast audiences that listened to Aimee Semple McPherson, the small congregations that chanted along with revivalist preachers, and the lonely supporters of the "Mankind United," "Mighty I Am," and other mystical movements that flourished more in Los Angeles than any other metropolis.[41]

But it is also true that these people were the exceptions. The others who failed to establish meaningful relationships through voluntary groups and suburban neighborhoods—who, as a British couple observed, "seemed to be almost as destitute of permanent friends as they were of personal furniture" —attempted to resolve the disparities between their expectations and experiences in a less aggressive fashion. They sought companionship in their immediate families and divorced their economic and civic interests from their social lives. They also derived their identities less from organizational affiliations than from material acquisitions; "the wireless, the car, the daily newspaper, or the *Saturday Evening Post,* work, cooking, 'studying how to keep thin,'" the British visitors noted, "seemed to fill their lives to the full."[42] Finally, these people intensified, rather than renounced, their commitment to homogeneity and rusticity; and instead of turning toward an activism that encouraged radical alternatives, they drifted toward a personalism that discouraged involvement per se.

The commitment of the native white majority to homogeneity undermined the position of the foreign and colored minorities in Los Angeles between 1885 and 1930. Southeastern Europeans, Mexicans, Japanese, and Negroes, not, as before, northwestern Europeans and Chinese, they numbered around 200,000 or 15 per cent of the city's population in 1930.[43] Attracted by southern California's extravagant publicity, they came not only from abroad but also from the California and Texas countrysides and from southern farms and northern ghettos. Unlike the midwesterners, they moved for traditional economic (and less political) reasons, for opportunity and a decent job rather than for comfort and a well-rounded life. Nonetheless, except for those Mexicans who intended to return home once they accumulated enough money, these people hoped to find a meaningful place in the Los Angeles community. Unfortunately, the white majority so subordinated and segregated the colored minorities—though, admittedly, not each group in the same way or to the same degree—that they were completely frustrated in this modest aspiration.

Their frustration followed in part from economic subordination. These immigrants were not the least capable of their countrymen. Among them were many Mexican mestizos from active towns, semi-skilled Russian Jews and northern Italians, ambitious American Negroes from northern metropolises, and young Japanese educated in their island's modern cities. But even they suffered severe handicaps in Los Angeles. Whatever their nationality or race, most had been common laborers or agricultural workers in their native lands; many arrived in the United States with less than forty dollars, and few came to southern California with appreciably more. Hence they lacked the skills and capital requisite for advancement in an urban economy. "When one is blind in the house of a money-changer," one Mexican asked, commenting on his dependency, "who does the counting?" "Aie!" his friend replied, "this is like being in the house of the soapmaker. He who does not fall, slips."[44]

A few overcame these disadvantages by grasping the opportunities generated by their own groups or, exploiting their differences, by opening ethnic restaurants and curio shops. But most had no alternative other than to compete in a labor market where, as Table I reveals, they qualified for only the least responsible and rewarding positions. They laid tracks, repaired pavements, slaughtered animals, hauled lumber, labored in factories, fisheries, and canneries, and served as domestics, waiters, janitors, and elevator operators.[45] Those who in time acquired the necessary skills encountered the racial prejudice of employers who claimed that white personnel would not work along-

Table I. Nonwhite Males as a Percentage of the Male Working Force in Selected Occupational Divisions and Occupations, Los Angeles, 1930

Occupations	Negro		Other*	
All occupations	3.1%		9.5%	
Manufacturing and mechanical industries:	2.1		10.7	
Laborers and helpers in construction		8.2		38.0
Managers and officials		0.1		0.6
Transportation and communication:	5.6		13.0	
Chauffeurs and drivers		8.3		6.8
Owners and managers		4.3		2.5
Trade:	1.0		5.5	
Laborers, porters, and helpers in stores		18.3		25.2
Real estate agents and officials		0.8		0.7
Public service:	5.5		2.5	
Laborers		27.1		10.1
Firemen		2.0		0.6
Professional service:	1.6		2.9	
Lawyers, judges, and justices		0.5		0.8
Physicians and surgeons		1.7		2.1
Domestic and personal service:	13.8		19.1	
Janitors and sextons		31.1		14.6
Porters (not in stores)		72.7		10.3
Servants		8.0		32.0

Source: U.S. Bureau of the Census, *Fifteenth Census of the United States: 1930. Population. Volume IV* (Washington, 1933), pp. 199–202.
* Principally Mexicans and Japanese.

side colored persons. Thus the most capable of these immigrants entered private business when they accumulated a little capital or government service where official policy precluded blatant discrimination. Still, so long as they were restricted, as one Oriental complained, to those jobs unwanted by the Americans, they had to accept less challenging and remunerative employment than their abilities warranted.[46]

Their frustration resulted in part from residential segregation too. Many single men who planned to save their earnings and then return home were not inclined to spend much money on housing. Many families that did intend to settle in Los Angeles lacked the confidence to move away from their group and the wherewithal to purchase a house. Hence the Mexicans, American Negroes, Japanese, and, less so, the southeastern Europeans rented quarters in the deteriorating downtown district and outlying industrial sections. There, like immigrants in other American cities, they congregated in ethnic ghettos.[47] "When I first came here," a young Japanese woman remarked about the small fishing colony off the Bay of San Pedro in which she lived, "I never thought that I was in America. Everything was the same as in my small home in Japan. All our neighbors were Japanese. We [all] knew each other."[48]

A few secure and successful Mexicans, Negroes, and Japanese, who shared with the native Americans the rustic ideal, attempted to acquire private homes in residential suburbs after the First World War. But, as the prevailing concept of the good community excluded races other than white and classes other than middle, they found themselves barred from subdivisions in greater Los Angeles by restrictive covenants. "I realize now," one Oriental lamented after a fruitless hunt for a single-family house, "that the Americans do not want to live close to us even though they want us to become Americans."[49] Even where racial covenants had never been imposed or had already expired, nonwhites often encountered the resistance of nearby property holders. "Negroes," a Santa Monica newspaper informed of a proposed development for colored people warned, "We don't want you here; now and forever, this is to be a white man's town."[50] The ethnic minorities were thus confined to undesirable districts, such as Watts, subdivided exclusively for them and to deteriorating neighborhoods, such as West Adams, where the white majority was unwilling to remain. There they formed the colored ghettos of suburban Los Angeles.[51]

The minorities also shared little in the community life of Los Angeles. This is not to deny that public discrimination decreased between 1885 and 1930. The Board of Education ceased separating schoolchildren by race; the Civil Service Commission discontinued drawing lists for nonwhites; and the Playground Board stopped closing its facilities to Negroes. But it is to say that assorted and more subtle kinds of prejudice persisted. *De facto* if not *de jure* segregation pervaded the school system; white persons secured the top positions in the local government; and a court order was required to compel the Playground Commissioners to integrate their swimming pools.[52] Even more upsetting to the Mexicans, Negroes, and Japanese, they were often refused food in restaurants, rooms in hotels, tickets at theaters, rides in jitneys, and other services in public accommodations. They were also denied communion by religious congregations, brotherhood by fraternal orders, affiliations by commercial organizations, and membership in the metropolis' other voluntary associations.[53]

The ethnic groups participated little in politics too. Transient, uninterested, and ill-informed, the Mexicans felt more concern about government in Mexico City than in Los Angeles. They do not vote or otherwise participate in politics, a prominent progressive noted; "the politicians do not base their strength upon them."[54] Deprived by Congress of the privileges of American citizenship, the Japanese refused to accept the corresponding responsibilities. As alien nationals, they sought redress for grievances through the Japanese consulate rather than the municipal legislature. Only the Negroes, who had no other outlet and no other recourse, paid much attention to public affairs in the metropolis.[55] But they had little influence in a city where the electorate was overwhelmingly white and the government was not organized by wards. The weakness of the minorities perpetuated their subordination; and from the viewpoint of the white majority, their inadequacies justified their segregation. Exploited economically, separated residentially, isolated socially, and ignored politically, these people remained entirely outside the Los Angeles community between 1885 and 1930.

Each ethnic group reacted to the situation in its own way. The southeastern Europeans, who diverged least from the native Americans, slowly but steadily assimilated into the majority. The Mexicans, who held the deepest hope and best chance to return home, retained a strong sense of nationality; so long as they could cross and recross the border, they did not feel obliged to recreate Mexico in Los Angeles. The Japanese, to the contrary, fully appreciated the distance to Japan and the irreversibility of their migration; while adhering to the materialistic ethos of their adopted nation, they tried to preserve the traditional rituals of the Orient. And the Negroes, who had no nation other than America, appealed to the native whites to acknowledge and implement their democratic heritage in Los Angeles.[56] Notwithstanding these differences, however, the minorities were all forced to mobilize their own resources and form their own communities.

Like the native Americans, the colored people sought companionship, security, protection, and unity in voluntary associations. The Mexicans established benevolent societies and attended Catholic churches; the Japanese founded nationality groups and built Buddhist shrines; and the Negroes organized state societies and formed colored congregations. These minorities also sponsored commercial organizations and supported ethnic newspapers which, in addition to binding their members socially, served as intermediaries between them and the white community. Created in response to tangible and pressing personal problems, these voluntary associations often showed exceptional vigor. Asked why the Japanese organizations were so strong, one of their leaders replied in terms almost, but not quite, as appropriate for the Mexicans and the Negroes: "If such disadvantages for them did not occur because of the fact that they are Japanese, perhaps the Japanese association would not have so firm a hold."[57]

Conditions in the metropolis were not conducive to the stability of these organizations, however. Many Mexicans left Los Angeles for their homeland, some Japanese quit their jobs to become truck farmers, and a few Negroes sought more promising opportunities in the countryside. Among those who stayed in the metropolis, the more successful moved from crowded commercial sections to outlying suburban ghettos, depriving the voluntary groups of their leaders. Even if the membership and the leadership had remained constant, moreover, these organizations would still have lacked the economic and political resources to realize their aspirations.[58] While these associations fared better than their white counterparts, then, they did not fully compensate the Mexicans, Japanese, or Negroes for the disabilities they labored under in Los Angeles.

To compound these difficulties, the voluntary associations, like the state societies, had little appeal for the second generation. Educated in the public schools and exhilarated by American freedom, the youngsters felt encumbered by the affiliations of their ancestors. The parents, as aware of the frustrations of American life as the children were of its promises, warned against this powerful attraction. But they paid them no heed. "They saw so many changes that they didn't know where to stop," one troubled woman remarked. "They didn't interfere with our plans then as they do now; they didn't talk back to us; they were obedient, but they seemed so excited. They learned English rapidly. Of course, we were glad of it, but we were also sorry. That made them too smart. But we couldn't get along without the language. Besides when they learned English they started to talk English among themselves, and we were at once divided: the 'old Russians' and the 'young Americans.' Oh they were faithful and devoted to us, but we just seemed to lose them right along. And the longer we stay here, the greater the difference between the old and young."[59]

Without the active participation of the second generation, the benevolent societies, religious congregations, and even commercial associations were less able to assimilate the newcomers, tie them together, protect their interests, and promote their goals. Without the firm support of the community organizations, the cohesive southeastern European, Mexican, Japanese (and the less stable Negro) families were gradually fragmented; their traditions were disrupted, their values undermined, and their cultures weakened.[60] In time, moreover, the children discovered that the old could not be thoroughly discarded nor the new entirely assimilated, and that they belonged to the minority they denied even more than to the majority they emulated. "Daily new philosophies are poured into my ear, and new ideas collect around me," a young woman of a separatist Russian sect remarked, "But the voices of those ancient monks rise up within me [and] compel me to admit . . . that I am a random dissatisfied soul."[61]

In response to the disintegration of their communities and cultures, the ethnic minorities also adopted the racism, nativism, and conservatism of the white majority that so effectively excluded them. The Mexicans attempted to dissociate themselves from *los tintos;* the Negroes insisted that the Japanese be treated as foreigners; and the Japanese contrasted their enterprise with the Mexicans' backwardness.[62] They exploited these ideologies as a means of elevating themselves at the expense of others, a practice that was outrageous on the part of the white Americans and pathetic on the part of their colored countrymen. Like the majority, the minorities also attempted to secure personal satisfaction by limiting their horizons to the individual and the family, the job and the home. But they were discriminated against as individuals, frustrated as spouses and parents, offered only the most menial employment, and confined to the least desirable neighborhoods. In a metropolis that promised a fuller life and opportunity to all, their subordination and segregation was particularly appalling.

Throughout these years, as an eminent sociologist wrote, Los Angeles' minority groups existed "in intimate economic dependence, but in more or less complete cultural independence of the world about them."[63] This situation was not, of course, unique here; indeed, nowhere in the United States did minorities enjoy complete equality and integration. But in Los Angeles, where they were distinguished by race rather than nationality, the majority subjugated and excluded them even more rigorously. Their plight reflected the anxieties of the native whites, and yet even they failed to recreate a coherent community. The interpersonal and institutional life of Los Angeles in the early 1930s was thus summarized, according to one scholar, in one word: disintegration.[64] Hence the fragmented society of the white majority complemented the isolated communities of the ethnic minorities and, along with the dispersal and decentralization of the metropolis, emerged as integral features of twentieth-century Los Angeles.[65]

■ ■ ■ ■ **Notes**

1 Jackson A. Graves, *California Memories, 1857–1927,* 2nd ed. (Los Angeles, 1930), p. 100; see also, Marshall Stimson, "Memorandum to Harvard College," Marshall Stimson Papers, Henry E. Huntington Library, San Marino, Calif.
2 Ludwig Louis Salvator, *Los Angeles in the Sunny Seventies: A Flower from the Golden Land,* trans. Marguerite Eyer Wilbur (Los Angeles, 1929), pp. 129–130; Ben C. Truman, *Semi-Tropical California* (San Francisco, 1874), p. 21.
3 Isaac W. Lord to [?], March 24, 1876, Lord Letterbook, p. 142, Lord Papers, UCLA.
4 On nineteenth-century American urban communities in general, see Oscar Handlin, "The Social System," *Daedelus* (Winter 1961), pp. 11–30.

5 See Thompson and West, *History of Los Angeles County California,* 1880 (Reprint Berkeley, 1959), pp. 121–125.

6 Isaac W. Lord Letterbook, p. 50, Lord Papers; see also, Los Angeles *Evening Express,* February 16, 1886.

7 Los Angeles *Evening Express,* July 7, 1876, March 4, 1880, February 2, 1886; Los Angeles *Herald,* April 9, 1882; Charles Loring Brace, *The New West: or California in 1867–1868* (New York, 1869), pp. 277–280.

8 See, for example, T. S. Kenderdine, *A California Tramp . . . Life on the Plains and in the Golden State Thirty Years Ago* (Newton, Pa., 1888), pp. 197–198; T. S. Kenderdine, *California Revisited, 1857–1897* (Newtown, Pa., 1898), p. 161.

9 Graves, *My Seventy Years in California 1857–1927* (Los Angeles, 1927), pp. 437–438; Graves, *California Memories,* pp. 5, 6, 100.

10 Sarah Bixby Smith, *Adobe Days: A Book of California Memories* (Los Angeles, 1931), p. 107; see also, L. J. Rose, Jr., *L. J. Rose of Sunny Slope 1827–1889. California Pioneer, Fruit Grower, Wine Maker, Horse Breeder* (San Marino, Calif., 1959), foreword.

11 "President More's Address," *Historical Society of Southern California, Los Angeles, 1887* (San Francisco, 1888), pp. 11–13; *Annual Report of the Los Angeles County Pioneers of Southern California for the Year 1909–1910,* p. 6.

12 Bruce Bliven, "Los Angeles: The City That Is Bacchanalian—In a Nice Way," *The New Republic,* 51: 198 (July 13, 1927).

13 Los Angeles *Examiner,* March 3, 1912; see also, Mark Lee Luther, *The Boosters* (Indianapolis, 1923), pp. 9–10, 34–35.

14 Los Angeles *Examiner,* March 23, 1914.

15 Los Angeles *Times,* July 11, 1909. See also, *Pacific Municipalities,* 27: 417–418 (August 1913).

16 Los Angeles *Examiner,* May 29, 1913, December 13, 1908; Los Angeles Suburban Homes Company Minutes, May 12, 1910, Whitley Papers; Leo B. Lesperance to Wendell M. Bishop, December 20, 1924, Leo B. Lesperance Papers, Special Collections Division, University of California Library, Los Angeles.

17 William H. B. Kilner, *Arthur Letts 1862–1923* (Los Angeles, 1927), p. 100, illustration facing p. 107. Abbot Kinney, the developer of Venice, Calif., made an even more memorable remark when he said that "In this country . . . the people can have what they talk." Los Angeles *Examiner,* May 30, 1913.

18 Willard Huntington Wright, "Los Angeles—The Chemically Pure," Burton Rascoe and Graff Conklin, eds., *The Smart Set Anthology* (New York, 1934), pp. 90–102.

19 *Out West,* 5: 208–209 (March 4, 1913); see also, Erik Linklater, *Juan in America* (New York, 1931), p. 392.

20 Los Angeles *Examiner,* February 28, 1913; see also, Los Angeles City, *Ordinances Scrapbook,* no. 9610, vol. 15, p. 104, no. 65355, vol. 79, p. 93, no. 19000, vol. 25, p. 97, no. 38456, vol. 46, pp. 128–129, no. 38070, vol. 46, p. 16, no. 36674, vol. 44, p. 121, no. 20640, vol. 27, pp. 17–18, and no. 37699, vol. 45, pp. 114–115, City Hall, Los Angeles; Los Angeles Board of Playground and Recreation Commissioners Minutes, December 1, 1917, October 7, 1920; Gilman M. Ostrander, *The Prohibition Movement in California, 1848–1933* (Berkeley and Los Angeles, 1957), pp. 131–132, 139–140.

21 Dana W. Bartlett, *The Better City: A Sociological Study of a Modern American City* (Los Angeles, 1907), chaps. i–vi, ix–xii.

22 *Report of the Housing Commission of the City of Los Angeles [1909–1910],* p. 26; Los Angeles *Examiner,* June 5, 1909.

23 See, for example, Charles D. Willard, *History of the Los Angeles Chamber of Commerce* (Los Angeles, 1899), pp. 10–11.

24 *Fifteenth Census: 1930. Population, IV,* pp. 199–202.

25 Los Angeles Chamber of Commerce, *Small Farm Home; Cahuenga Suburban,* April 1895; Los Angeles *Examiner,* July 10, 1910; *Pacific Outlook,* 9: 5 (July 16, 1910).
26 See, for example, Willard, *Los Angeles Chamber of Commerce,* pp. 102–104.
27 George Burlingame, "How Religious is the City of Los Angeles?" Los Angeles *Times,* August 28, 1927, quoted in Carl Douglas Wells, "A Changing Social Institution in an Urban Environment: A Study of the Changing Behavior Patterns of the Disciples of Christ in Los Angeles" (University of Southern California Doctoral Dissertation, 1931), p. 5. See also, Jan and Cora Gordon, *Star-Dust in Hollywood* (London, 1931), p. 36.
28 Wells, p. 145; see also, Wells, chaps. ii, iii, iv.
29 Wells, pp. 25–26; see also, H. Paul Douglas, *The Church in the Changing City* (New York, 1927), pp. 373ff.
30 J. F. Sartori to Edward A. Dickson, undated, Edward A. Dickson Papers, Special Collections Division, University of California Library, Los Angeles; the correspondence of the Hill Street Association and Robert C. Gillis; Los Angeles *Ledger* (published by the Greater Pico Street Association), Gillis Papers.
31 *Articles of Incorporation and By-Laws of the Huntington Palisades Property Owners Corporation Ltd.,* Gillis Papers; *Articles of Incorporation and By-Laws of Palos Verdes Homes Association,* Palos Verdes Homes Association Files; see also, Bessie A. McClenahan, *The Changing Urban Neighborhood: From Neighbor to Night-Dweller* (Los Angeles, 1929), pp. 216–218.
32 McClenahan, p. 57; McClenahan, pp. 35, 47, 84; Hollywood *Citizen,* December 29, 1916; J. R. Douglas, "Report on Conditions Affecting the Real Estate Business in Los Angeles," 1923, Security—First National Bank Research Department, Los Angeles.
33 McClenahan, p. 57; McClenahan, pp. 64–65, 68–69.
34 October 22, 1905, September 24, 1906, Mrs. Ernest T. Emery's Diary.
35 McClenahan, pp. 24, 61, 71, 78.
36 C. H. Parsons, quoted in *The Golden West: A Magazine of Progress,* 1: 7 (September 1, 1919); see also, Los Angeles *Times,* February 23, 1909; Los Angeles *Examiner,* December 26, 1909, March 18, 1911; Buford E. Pierce, *Illustrated Annual: Federation of State Societies of Southern California 1914* (Los Angeles, 1914), passim; Carey McWilliams, *Southern California Country: An Island on the Land* (New York, 1946), pp. 165–171.
37 Parsons, quoted in *The Golden West;* see also, Florence C. Parsons, "Story of the Federation of State Societies," *The Golden West,* 1: 7 (May 15, 1919). The magazine later became the "Official Organ of the Federation of State Societies," The purposes of the state societies were described in the Michigan group's constitution as follows: "To promote interest in the mother State, to aid in extending acquaintances among her people whether residents here or merely visitors in this place; to broaden each other's knowledge and information about local conditions whereby all may be benefited; and to arouse and strengthen the interest of visitors and intending settlers in all that pertains to the growth of the community and generally to promote the social welfare and common good of its members." Los Angeles *Examiner,* December 26, 1909.
38 McWilliams, pp. 165–171.
39 Nathaniel West, *The Day of the Locust* (New York, 1939), pp. 224–225.
40 Meyer Lissner to Mark Sullivan, January 8, 1920, Lissner Papers, Stanford University; see also, Los Angeles *Examiner,* August 28, 1905.
41 Nancy Mavitz, *Sister Aimee* (Garden City, N.Y., 1931); H. T. Dohrman, *California Cult: The Story of "Mankind United"* (Boston, 1958); McWilliams, chaps. xiii–xiv;

Charles S. Braden, *Spirits in Rebellion: The Rise and Development of New Thought* (Dallas, 1963), passim.

42 Jan and Cora Gordon, p. 36. "In a land of optimism," they also wrote, "you cannot associate with people who break your heart; in a land where all social positions are fluid one must be prepared to reject those who fall behind in the money race, and to accept rejections philosophically from those who leave us behind . . . therefore a certain cold-bloodedness in acquaintanceship must be cultivated almost in self-defense." Jan and Cora Gordon, p. 24.

43 *Fifteenth Census: 1930. Population, III, Part 1*, pp. 266–267; *Eleventh Census: 1890. Population, I*, p. 451; see also, Charlotta A. Bass, *Forty Years: Memoirs from the Pages of a Newspaper* (Los Angeles, 1960), p. 21; Pauline V. Young, *The Pilgrims of Russian-Town* (Chicago, 1934), chap. i.

44 Ruth D. Tuck, *Not with the Fist: Mexican-Americans in a Southwest City* (New York: 1946), p. 88; see also, Tuck, 65–67; "Reports of the Immigration Commission," vol. 25, pt. III, pp. 125–163, 357–358, 470–471; *Annual Reports of the Commissioner General of Immigration to the Secretary of Labor [1911]*, pp. 38–43, *[1912]*, pp. 92–96, *[1913]*, pp. 64–70, *[1914]*, pp. 62–67, *[1915]*, pp. 82–87; Young, chap. i; Manuel Gamio, comp., *The Mexican Immigrant, His Life Story. Autobiographical Documents* (Chicago, 1921), passim; Eugene S. Richards, "The Effects of the Negro's Migration to Southern California upon His Socio-Cultural Patterns," (University of Southern California Doctoral Dissertation, 1941), pp. 42–49.

45 "Reports of the Immigration Commission," vol. 25, pt. I, pp. 223–248, pt. III, pp. 454–460; *Fifteenth Census: 1930. Population, IV*, pp. 199–202; John R. Haynes to Roy L. Garis, August 29, 1929, Haynes Papers, UCLA: Yamato Ichihashi, *Japanese in the United States* (Stanford, 1932), chaps. vii–xi; J. Max Bond, "The Negro in Los Angeles," (University of Southern California Doctoral Dissertation, 1936), pp. 150–151; Young, chap. ii.

46 Kit King Louis, "A Study of American-Born and American-Reared Chinese in Los Angeles" (University of Southern California Masters Thesis, 1931), p. 80; J. McFarline Ervin, "The Participation of the Negro in the Community Life of Los Angeles" (University of Southern California Masters Thesis, 1927), pp. 45–72; Barton S. Scruggs, *A Man in Our Community: The Biography of L. G. Robinson of Los Angeles* (Gardena, Calif., 1937), passim.

47 Commission of Immigration and Housing of California, *A Survey Made in Los Angeles City* (San Francisco, ca. 1910), p. 23; "Report of the Immigration Commission," vol. 25, pt. I, pp. 223–248,. 361–362.

48 Kanichi Kawasaki, "The Japanese Community of East San Pedro, Terminal Island, California" (University of Southern California Masters Thesis, 1931), p. 50 (combined from her remarks); see also, Young, chap. ii; Richards, pp. 35–37, 47, 218.

49 Louis, p. 114; Bond, pp. 76–77; Emory F. Bogardus, *The Mexicans in the United States* (Los Angeles, 1934), p. 79; Bass, pp. 95–113.

50 Santa Monica *Weekly Interpreter*, April 26, 1922, Robert C. Gillis Papers, Mr. Arthur L. Loomis, Pacific Palisades, California.

51 Clara G. Smith, "The Development of the Mexican People in the Community of Watts" (University of Southern California Masters Thesis, 1933), passim; also Kiyoshi Uono, "The Factors Affecting the Geographical Aggregation and Dispersion of the Japanese Residences in the City of Los Angeles" (University of Southern California Masters Thesis, 1927), pp. 124ff; Bond, pp. 68ff; *Fifteenth Census: 1930. Population, VI*, pp. 156–160, 181–189.

52 *California Eagle*, September 18, 1915, December 8, 1917; Bass, pp. 21, 50–52; Los Angeles Board of Playground and Recreation Commissioners Minutes, September

10, 1925, Department of Parks and Playgrounds, City Hall, Los Angeles; Los Angeles City, *Petitions* (1931), No. 1636.

53 Louis, p. 103; *California Eagle,* September 24, 1914, September 13, 1919, April 29, 1922; Lawrence B. De Graaf, "Negro Migration to Los Angeles, 1930–1950" (UCLA Doctoral Dissertation, 1962), chap. ii; Bass, pp. 13–14, 39–40; Tuck, pp. 197–207.

54 John R. Haynes to Roy L. Garis, August 29, 1929, Haynes Papers; *El Heraldo de Mexico,* January 7, 1920; *La Opinion,* April 2, 1927; Bogardus, pp. 76–77.

55 *California Eagle,* April 24, May 1, August 22, 1914, September 9, 1916, April 28, 1917, April 21, May 12, 1923; Bass, passim; Committee on Immigration and Naturalization, House of Representatives, *Hearings. Japanese Immigration* (Washington, 1921), Part 3, pp. 924, 927; Carey McWilliams, *Prejudice. Japanese Americans: Symbol of Racial Intolerance* (Boston, 1944), pp. 92–96.

56 Bogardus, pp. 76–78; Committee on Immigration and Naturalization, *Japanese Immigration,* p. 934; Bass, pp. 39–42; Young, chap. ii.

57 Committee on Immigration and Naturalization, *Japanese Immigration,* p. 924; Tuck, pp. 152–164; McWilliams, *Prejudice,* pp. 77–78; Fumiko Fukuoha, "Mutual Life and Aid Among the Japanese in Southern California with Special Reference to Los Angeles" (University of Southern California Masters Thesis, 1937), p. 87; *California Eagle,* April 5, 1914; Bass, pp. 16–26.

58 Gamio, p. 27; Bogardus, pp. 37–40; McWilliams, *Prejudice,* pp. 83–92; Louis, pp. 81, 89; *California Eagle,* April 13, 1928; Graaf, chap. ii.

59 Young, pp. 124–125; see also, Smith, p. 59; Louis, pp. 30, 43; Richards, "Negro's Migration to Southern California," p. 136.

60 Some of the observations made then have a chilling immediacy now. "They feel that they are Negroes and that as Negroes they will never get anywhere," remarked one white man. "They face an insecure and hopeless future. They don't have any social mooring. They are cut off from all the things that control people. No jobs to live up to, no home to aspire to and protect, no social agencies to guide them." "The Negro church in Los Angeles has certainly followed its original purpose," a Negro man noted. "The mission of the church is soul saving. Well, they do their work too well; they are so busy saving souls for Christ that the community around them is going to the devil." Bond, pp. 150–151, 214.

61 Young, p. 227; see also, Bogardus, pp. 24–32; Tuck, pp. 106–121; Committee on Naturalization and Immigration, *Japanese Immigration,* pp. 965–996; McWilliams, *Prejudice,* pp. 96–105; Richards, "Negro's Migration to Southern California," p. 128; Bond, p. 214.

62 Bogardus, pp. 85, 97; Tuck, pp. 204–205; *California Eagle,* May 1, 1914, January 23, 1915, April 28, 1917; see also, Gamio, p. 154; Bond, pp. 150–151.

63 Robert Ezra Park, "Education and the Cultural Crisis," *American Journal of Sociology,* 48 (May 1943), reprinted in Robert Ezra Park, *Race and Culture* (Glencoe, Ill., 1950), p. 323.

64 George M. Day, "Races and Cultural Oases," *Sociology and Social Research,* 18: 328, 335–339 (March–April 1934).

65 The reader may well wonder why nothing has been said about education in Los Angeles here. The only answer is that the public schools received remarkably little attention before 1930. Certainly there were no crises comparable to the recent offensive of the radical right. The available materials (including the Board of Education Minutes) yield no simple explanation, and the entire subject probably requires separate study. It might begin with P. W. Search, Superintendent of Schools, *Los Angeles City Schools Report of Conditions with Recommendations* (Los Angeles, 1895) and Walter A. Jessup and Albert Shiels, *Report of the Advisory Committee to the Board of Education of the City of Los Angeles . . .* (Los Angeles, 1916).

16
The Urban Klansman

KENNETH T. JACKSON

In his book The Ku Klux Klan in the City, *from which the following essay is taken, Kenneth Jackson further illustrates Richard Wade's contention that conflict within the city is more significant than conflict between rural and urban areas. In assessing the Klan as a whole, Jackson may have overestimated the urban component and unduly slighted the rural and small-town elements of this "invisible empire"; however, he has raised a very salient point in describing the city arm of the Klan as constituting a reaction to specifically urban tensions. The changes of the 1920s, when so many innovations of modern American culture became more widely disseminated, threatened many urbanites who lacked the money, the flexibility, and the education to benefit from the new age. Most threatening of all was the "invasion" (the military terminology was not accidental) of residential areas by unwanted people—the new immigrants and the blacks—who were thrusting out from the old core of the cities into transitional areas, the "zones of emergence."*

The lower-middle class aspired to respectability and security with limited resources; its vulnerability made it listen to Klan organizers in the 1920s and George Wallace in the 1960s. Jackson has sought to understand, not simply to condemn, the movement and its motivations; for this we owe him much.

Jackson sees the Klan primarily as an attempt to prevent unwanted social change by political means. In addition, the organization supplied meaning and purpose for men psychologically at sea in a world they didn't create and didn't understand. If, as Fogelson contends, the modern metropolis could not arouse a sense of belonging and community among its fragmented residents, societies like the Klan could fill the gap: it had a purpose; it had defined and easily identifiable enemies; it satisfied the need for mystery and ceremony with its robes, hoods, and rituals; and it provided a haven for the frustrated and the alienated. Unfortunately, it attempted to achieve its goals by emphasizing the divisions among people rather than their common needs and interests.

■ ■ ■ ■ For Further Reading

David M. Chalmers, *Hooded Americanism: The History of the Ku Klux Klan* (Chicago: Quadrangle Books, 1965) is a survey of the entire history of the Klan. Charles Alexander, *The Ku Klux Klan in the Southwest* (Lexington: University Press of Kentucky, 1965) is an excellent regional study. Irving Bernstein, *The Lean Years: A History of the American Worker, 1920–1933* (Baltimore: Pelican-Penguin Books,

1960) offers considerable insight into the economic and social problems confronting men who were attracted to the Klan.

> *We invested $21,000 in this place and we're not going to be chased out. We had to move out before, from the southeast side, when all those Negroes moved in and we practically gave that house away. We're not running again.*

> TOM STRAMIK
Chicago, 1966

■ The Bureau of the Census revealed in 1920 that the United States had made the long-awaited transition from a rural to an urban nation. In 1910, 54.2 per cent of its people lived on farms or in crossroads villages of fewer than 2,500 inhabitants; by 1920, only 48.6 per cent could be so classified. For the first time in American history less than half the population conformed to the Jeffersonian ideal.

Recognizing 1920 as a watershed in our national development, historians have tended to interpret the ensuing decade as an era of conflict between two well-defined groups in American life, the one rural, white, dry, Anglo-Saxon, and Protestant, and the other urban, wet, recent immigrant, and Catholic.[1] A contest between conservative and liberal, and past and future, it featured many of the great luminaries of the period: William Jennings Bryan, Clarence Darrow, Billy Sunday, H. L. Mencken, and Al Smith. Viewed in this perspective, Prohibition, Sacco-Vanzetti, the 1924 Democratic Convention, the Scopes Trial, immigration restriction, and the presidential campaign of Governor Smith were but skirmishes in a conflict of vastly greater import.

This neat rural-urban dichotomy tends to veil rather than illuminate the truth when applied to the Ku Klux Klan, however. Considering the city as a single entity obscures the fact that speakeasy and farmhouse were hardly more diverse than elements within the city itself. The urban migration of rural, old-stock Americans is a phenomenon almost as old as the nation itself and ranks in significance with the more celebrated and recent movement of immigrants and Negroes to the city. Thus every metropolis contained a myriad of racial, ethnic, and religious cultures, not all of them congenial. Moreover, the prevailing notion that tolerance and acceptance are more easily spawned in the heterogeneous environment of a large city than in a smaller community is at best too simple, and perhaps mistaken.

An important by-product of the urban confrontation of cultures was the success of the Ku Klux Klan in metropolitan areas. Certainly the Invisible Empire did not have great appeal in every city, but neither did it attract widespread support among the farmers and townspeople of many states.

Generally, whenever the secret order was strong on a statewide basis, it was more attractive to white Protestants in populous communities than in Robert Lynd's Middletown or along Sinclair Lewis's Main Street.

Because the official records have never been found and in all probability no longer exist, the precise size and distribution of membership of the Invisible Empire cannot be determined.[2] But any comparison of rural, small-town, and urban Klan strength must necessarily begin with an evaluation of total membership, which has been variously estimated at between one and nine million.[3] The commonly accepted figure of about four million was first suggested in 1924 by Stanley Frost, author of several articles and a book on the secret order and a reported friend of *Fiery Cross* editor Milton Elrod. Frost was exceedingly vague, however, and greatly over-estimated the size of such realms as Maryland, Oregon, Texas, California, Mississippi, and Tennessee. His evaluation was readily accepted because both the Klan and the anti-Klan camps stood to gain by exaggerating the size of the threat.[4] A more realistic examination would reveal that in actuality the Invisible Empire enrolled approximately 2,030,000 persons between 1915 and 1944, and never at any time numbered as many as 1,500,000 active members (see Table I). Of the two million total, at least one million, or 50 per cent, resided in metropolitan areas of more than 50,000 persons. No fewer than 650,000, or 32 per cent, resided in metropolitan areas which in 1920 contained more than 100,000 persons (see Table II). The traditional ascription of Klan strength to residents in small towns clearly ignores a most important facet of Klan support. On a percentage basis, Indianapolis, Dayton, Portland, Youngstown, Denver, and Dallas were the hooded capitals of the nation, but Chicago's twenty klaverns and 50,000 Knights accounted for the largest single total.

Almost as important as mere numerical representation was the disproportionate influence which urban klaverns exercised within both state and national organizations. Seattle Klan No. 4, Little Rock Klan No. 1, Marion County (Indianapolis) Klan No. 3, or Robert E. Lee (Birmingham) Klan No. 1 never enrolled over one-third of the Klan's statewide total membership, but each was clearly dominant within its realm. Similar, if not greater, supremacy was enjoyed by Denver, Portland, Los Angeles, Chicago, Detroit, Philadelphia, Pittsburgh, and Dallas Klansmen. Ohio had no dominant chapter; those of Akron, Dayton, Columbus, Youngstown, and Cincinnati were all immense.

An important factor in this heavy urban influence was the source of Klan leadership. Most officials at the Imperial Palace had lived their productive lives in a large city, and townspeople or farmers did not win prominence in most state organizations. That Illinois Grand Dragon Charles Palmer hailed from Chicago was typical rather than exceptional. Texas's H. C. McCall, Brown Harwood, Zeke Marvin, and Marvin Childers came from Houston, Fort Worth, Dallas, and San Antonio. Oklahoma's N. Clay Jewett

Table I. *Distribution of Klan Membership by States**

Realm	Total	Realm	Total
Indiana	240,000	Washington	25,000
Ohio	195,000	Virginia	20,000
Texas	190,000	Connecticut	20,000
Pennsylvania	150,000	West Virginia	18,000
Illinois	95,000	Mississippi	15,000
Oklahoma	95,000	Wisconsin	15,000
New York	80,000	Maine	15,000
Michigan	70,000	Massachusetts	12,000
Georgia	65,000	Dist. Columbia	7,000
Florida	60,000	South Carolina	5,000
New Jersey	60,000	Minnesota	5,000
Alabama	55,000	Delaware	5,000
Oregon	50,000	Utah	5,000
California	50,000	Rhode Island	5,000
Louisiana	50,000	Idaho	5,000
Missouri	45,000	South Dakota	5,000
Colorado	45,000	Arizona	4,000
Kansas	40,000	North Dakota	3,000
Tennessee	35,000	Montana	3,000
Kentucky	30,000	New Hampshire	2,000
Iowa	28,000	Vermont	2,000
Nebraska	25,000	Nevada	2,000
Maryland	25,000	Wyoming	1,000
Arkansas	25,000	New Mexico	1,000
North Carolina	25,000		
		Total	2,028,000

* The above totals include all male and female persons initiated into the Klan between 1915 and 1944. The figures are personal estimates, which are based to some degree on the claims of William Joseph Simmons, Edward Young Clarke, Hiram Wesley Evans, and Robert L. Duffus, the estimates of the New York *World*, *Washington Post*, *The New York Times*, and *The Imperial Night-Hawk*, the evaluations of Charles Alexander, Emerson Loucks, and David Chalmers, and the report of the imperial kligrapp at the 1924 Klonvocation.

was from Oklahoma City; Maryland's Frank Beall from Baltimore; Alabama's James Esdale from Birmingham; Wisconsin's William Wieseman from Milwaukee; Oregon's Fred Gifford from Portland; Ohio's Charles Harrod and Clyde Osborne were from Columbus and Youngstown; Colorado's John Galen Locke was from Denver; Indiana's David Stephenson and Walter Bossert were from Evansville and Indianapolis; Connecticut's Harry Lutterman and New Jersey's Arthur Bell from suburban New York City; Tennessee's J. R. Ozier and M. S. Ross from Nashville; and Georgia's Nathan Bedford Forrest was from Atlanta. These grand dragons may have occasionally denounced the iniquities of urban politics or offered lip service to the virtues of farm and country, but they chose the city for themselves and thereby set the pattern for the Invisible Empire.

Predictably, the source and character of the Klan press was also urban. With the exception of such short-lived and insignificant periodicals as the

Tyler (Texas) *American* and the Tullahoma, Tennessee, *Klan Krusader,* almost every Klan-supported newspaper or magazine, including such major journals as *The Fiery Cross, The Kourier, Dawn, Searchlight, The Watcher on the Tower, The Western American, The Kluxer, The Pitchfork, The American Standard,* and Col. *Mayfield's Weekly,* was headquartered and published in a large city and received the bulk of its advertising revenue from urban businessmen.

Among the questions hardest to answer about the urban Klan are those which concern the character of its membership and the nature of its appeal. Who was the urban Klansman? Why did he turn to the Invisible Empire? The questions defy simply answers but must be analyzed if the movement is to be understood. It will not suffice to call Klan members cowards and scoundrels or to dismiss the secret order as a simple manifestation of ignorance and bigotry. Most members were not innately depraved or anxious to subvert American institutions. Rather they regarded their initiation as a patriotic gesture and believed the tenets of "one hundred per cent Americanism" to be both moral and Christian. As sociologist Frank Tannenbaum has observed: "Sincerity is a common virtue, and must not be denied in an analysis of group behavior."

There is general agreement among students of the Invisible Empire that the typical Klansman was decent, hard-working, and patriotic, if narrow-minded. But very little specific research has been done on the socio-economic status of the average member. Most observers have placed the responsibility for nativist resurgence on the "common man" rather than upon either social extreme. Former Kleagle Edgar Fry described his associates as "successful business and professional men, nearly all of them devout church members, married men with families, and just the sort of men to make up a prosperous community." His sentiments were echoed by seventy-three Pennsylvania exalted cyclops, who declared upon oath in 1927 that the Klan membership of their state was "gleaned from the average walk of life and such as composes our Protestant churches, our lodges, commercial clubs, and other civic organizations." John Moffatt Mecklin, surely the most quoted of all authorities, regarded "the good solid middle class, the backbone of the nation" as providing the bulk of the membership; sociologist Guy B. Johnson theorized in 1922 that "prosperous business and professional men" were dominant; and in 1924, Arthur Corning White interpreted the movement as the "middle class, caught between capital and labor."[5] More recently, Irving Leibowitz of Indianapolis described the Invisible Empire as "made up largely of people of substantial and decent standing," and Professor Charles Alexander found the secret order to be "remarkably cross-sectional" in the Southwest, including "a good portion of the substantial people." Less flattering portraits have meanwhile been drawn by Frederick Lewis Allen and Richard Hofstadter. Allen viewed the secret order as

Table II. *Total Size of Klan Membership in Large American Cities, 1915–1944**

City	Total	City	Total
Akron	18,000	Minneapolis-St. Paul	2,500
Albany-Schenectady-Troy	11,000	Mobile	3,000
Allentown-Bethlehem	2,000	Nashville	3,500
Atlanta	20,000	New Bedford	—
Baltimore	5,000	New Haven	2,000
Birmingham	14,000	New Orleans	3,000
Boston-Somerville-Cambridge	3,500	New York-Yonkers-New Rochelle	16,000
Bridgeport	1,500	Newark-Elizabeth, N.J.	5,000
Buffalo	7,000	Norfolk-Portsmouth, Va.	4,000
Charleston, W. Va.	2,000	Oklahoma City	5,000
Chattanooga	2,500	Omaha-Council Bluffs	3,500
Chicago	50,000	Patterson-Clifton, N.J.	4,500
Cincinnati-Covington	15,500	Philadelphia-Camden	35,000
Cleveland	2,500	Pittsburgh-Carnegie	17,000
Columbus	16,000	Portland	22,000
Dallas	16,000	Providence, R.I.-Mass.	3,000
Davenport-Rock Island-Moline	4,000	Reading, Penn.	1,500
Dayton	15,000	Richmond	2,500
Denver	23,000	Rochester	1,500
Des Moines	3,000	St. Joseph	2,500
Detroit	35,000	St. Louis-E. St. Louis	5,000
Erie	3,000	Salt Lake City	1,000
Fall River	—	San Antonio	6,000
Flint	2,000	San Diego	2,000
Fort Wayne	3,000	San Francisco-Oakland	3,500
Forth Worth	6,500	Scranton	2,500
Gary-Hammond	10,000	Seattle	8,000
Grand Rapids	2,000	Spokane	2,500
Hartford	2,000	Springfield, Ill.	2,500
Houston	8,000	Springfield-Holyoke, Mass.	2,000
Indianapolis	38,000	Springfield, Ohio	3,000
Jacksonville	3,500	Syracuse	1,500
Jersey City-Bayonne	4,000	Tacoma	2,000
Kansas City, Mo.-Kan.	5,000	Tampa-St. Petersburg	2,500
Knoxville	3,000	Toledo	1,500
Little Rock-N. Little Rock	7,500	Trenton	2,000
Los Angeles-Long Beach	18,000	Tulsa	6,000
Louisville	3,000	Utica-Rome, N.Y.	1,500
Lowell	—	Washington	7,000
Memphis	10,000	Wichita	6,000
Miami	4,000	Wilmington, Del.-N.J.	3,500
Milwaukee	6,000	Worcester	2,500
		Youngstown-Warren	17,000
		Total	653,000

* All members, male and female, who resided in the standard metropolitan area, are included. The figures are personal estimates.

drawing mostly upon the "less educated and less disciplined elements of the Protestant community," while Hofstadter labeled the average Knight "relatively unprosperous and uncultivated."[6]

This study has sought to re-open the inquiry into the socio-economic character of the Ku Klux Klan. The evidence indicates that in the city the secret order was a lower-middle-class movement.[7] Few men of wealth, education, or professional position affiliated with the Invisible Empire; the exceptions, such as Dr. John Galen Locke in Denver and Vice President Edwin Debarr of the University of Oklahoma, usually served in high Klan office. White-collar workers in general provided a substantial minority of Klan membership and included primarily struggling independent business-men, advertising dentists, lawyers, and chiropractors, ambitious and unprin-cipled politicians and salesmen, and poorly paid clerks. The greatest source of Klan support came from rank and file non-union, blue-collar employees of large businesses and factories. Miserably paid, they rarely boasted of as much as a high school education and more commonly possessed only a grammar or "free school" background. Their religious loyalty was to con-servative, non-ritualistic Protestant denominations such as the Baptist, Methodist, or Christian churches.

Although evidence regarding the geographical background of the mem-bership is meager, there was a statistically significant correlation between Klan success and population growth.[8] For example, the secret order was active and strong in such cities as Detroit, Memphis, Dayton, Youngstown, Dallas, and Houston, all of which claimed high growth rates between 1910 and 1930. Conversely, it was weak in comparatively stable Boston, St. Louis, New Orleans, Providence, and Louisville. But Klansmen were not necessarily urban newcomers. On the contrary, in the only city for which statistics are available (Knoxville), one-third of the members were lifelong residents and the remainder had lived in the community for an average of more than nine years. These figures suggest that urban newcomers were the cause rather than the source of Klan strength.

The appeal of "one hundred per cent Americanism" to urban, lower-middle-class Fundamentalists was undoubtedly complex. It was not, however, related to a suppressed penchant for violence. The notion must be dispelled that Klansmen were essentially sadists reveling in murder and torture. Scores of floggings, tar and featherings, and other forms of physical abuse were reported in the South between 1920 and 1925, and no fewer than six murders were directly attributable to the secret order. But lawlessness had a long tradition in the region, and not all violations of justice could be charged to the Klan account. This basic fact was recognized by both the American Civil Liberties Union and *The New Republic,* which declared in 1927: "Some hoodlums signed up in order to participate in night-riding, but it is safe to say that 90 per cent of the total membership never indulged in such practices." Outside the South only a very small number of members

Table III. Comparative Klan Occupational Chart*

Community	Total Membership	Blue-Collar		White-Collar	
		Number of Persons	Percentage of Membership	Number of Persons	Percentage of Membership
Knoxville	399	283	70.9	116	29.1
Chicago	110	43	39.1	67	60.9
Aurora	73	26	35.6	47	64.4
Winchester	180	134	74.4	46	25.6

* The above percentages include only those members about whom precise occupational information is available. In Chicago and Aurora the information is biased in favor of white-collar workers because anti-Klan elements were quick to identify the names of independent businessmen on the Klan lists. The occupational distribution of Klansmen in other cities could not be determined.

participated in any form of violence. In fact, in many parts of the country (such as Perth Amboy, New Jersey; Niles, Ohio; and Carnegie, Pennsylvania), Klansmen were more often the victims than the instigators of foul play.[9]

Fear of change, not vindictiveness or cruelty, was the basic motivation of the urban Klansman. He was disillusioned by the Great War and its aftermath, by the Senate rejection of the League of Nations, and by the economic recession which came in the summer and fall of 1920. He was aware of the Red Scare and of reports of "petting parties," "wild dancing," and other indications of a revolution in morals. Sensing that the traditional values, religion, and way of life of an older America were in danger, he donated ten dollars to a hypocritical secret society in a vague attempt to halt the forces of time. Ordinarily, the decade of the twenties is thought of as an era of "normalcy." Actually, it was a period of rapid, almost bewildering, change; the Model T, the telephone, the radio, the airplane, and the motion picture were transforming American life. But the changes of greatest concern to the urban Knight were ethnic and racial, not technological.

Two far-reaching, distinct migration patterns provided the basis for the phenomenal career of the Ku Klux Klan. The first was a shift in the sources of European immigration, particularly noticeable after 1890, from the English, Irish, Scandinavians, and Germans of earlier years to the peasantry of southern and eastern Europe—Hungarians, Italians, Slovaks, Czechs, and Poles. The predominantly Catholic and Jewish newcomers frightened nativists by clinging tenaciously to Old World customs and celebrations, by establishing hundreds of foreign-language newspapers, and by voting for the supposedly corrupt and inefficient urban political machines. Spurred by Lothrop Stoddard's *The Rising Tide of Color* and Madison Grant's *Passing of the Great Race,* older Americans made excited appeals for immigration restriction. Their basic fear was that if the immigration flow were not shut off or drastically reduced, then white, Anglo-Saxon Protestants would become a minority in the land of their fathers, and the nation would be ethnically transformed.

The second major migration pattern of concern was that of American Negroes from farm to city and from South to North. First noticeable about 1910, the trend was accelerated by World War I, which restricted the supply of foreign labor, increased the demands of industry, and encouraged many industries to experiment with Negro labor. An additional factor was the boll weevil, which ravaged hundreds of thousands of acres of fertile cotton fields and forced white farmers temporarily to abandon their custom of advancing money to field hands. The traditional Negro dependence upon southern agriculture was weakened; between 1910 and 1920 the Negro rural population fell by 239,000 while the urban total increased by 874,000. Almost four hundred thousand Negroes moved to southern cities in the decade, and an even larger number trekked to the urban North. During the twenties the black stream became a flood and an additional six hundred thousand Negroes crossed the Mason-Dixon line.[10] The impact was startling, particularly in the Midwest. In the twenty years between 1910 and 1930 the non-white population of Chicago increased from 44,000 to 160,000, that of Detroit from 6,000 to 125,000, and that of Indianapolis from 22,000 to 44,000.

Ultimately, both migration patterns posed a threat to white Protestants throughout the United States, but the immediate impact was primarily upon urban residential stability. By both choice and necessity the immigrants and Negroes crowded into ghettos, often located near the center of the city. White Protestants, on the other hand, were more likely to reside nearer the edge of a community. Thus divided geographically as well as religiously, socially, economically, and politically, the inner core and the residential fringe were consistent opponents and created an intra-urban environment favorable for the growth of the Ku Klux Klan.

Neighborhood transition has been a neglected but omnipresent dimension of American urban history for at least the last one hundred years, but its rapidity and extent increased markedly in the first quarter of the twentieth century as immigrants and Negroes crowded into burgeoning cities.[11] Some physical expansion of the bulging racial and ethnic ghettos was inevitable; but equally threatening to the tranquillity of the older (i.e. white Protestant) residents was the desire of ambitious second-generation immigrants and successful Negroes to escape completely from the old neighborhoods and to buy or rent in the "zone of emergence,"[12] the broad belt separating the core of the city from its outer residential fringe. The "zone of emergence" was usually made up of working-class neighborhoods of modest homes and apartments, and it was here, among white laborers, that the Invisible Empire thrived. Unable to afford a fine home far removed from minority problems, the potential Klansman could not live along Chicago's Lake

Shore Drive or Indianapolis's Fall Creek Parkway, or in Memphis's Hein Park or Atlanta's Druid Hills. Rather, he was forced by economic necessity to live in older transitional areas close to his place of employment. He was bewildered by the rapid pace of life and frustrated by his inability to slow the changes which seemed so constant and so oppressive. He perhaps remembered an earlier neighborhood transition and was frightened at the prospect of a Negro or a Pole coming into his block and causing him to sell his house at a low price. Unable to escape and hesitant to act alone, the threatened citizen welcomed the security and respectability of a large group. Seeking to stabilize his world and maintain a neighborhood status quo, he turned to the promise of the Klan. Not a reaction against the rise of the city to dominance in American life, the Invisible Empire was rather a reaction against the aspirations of certain elements within the city.

The problems of the potential Klansman were complicated by his economic condition. Whether a struggling café proprietor in Indianapolis, a lumber mill worker in Knoxville, a milkman in Chicago, or a cotton oil company employee in Memphis, he had obviously been left at the post in an economic race he perhaps only inadequately understood. His wages were below average, his tasks often menial, his responsibilities slight, and his opportunity for advancement remote. Yet this was an age heavily influenced by the Horatio Alger notion that hard work would be rewarded and that all Americans had ample opportunity in the competition for prestige and economic advantage. Having fought his way above the lowest rungs of the financial ladder, the potential Klansman remained something less than a success. Life seemed to offer him little dignity or personal significance. Moreover, he was faced with increasing competition from Catholics and from a new kind of Negro, who seemed anxious to take his job and live in his neighborhood. What was he to do?[13]

Then a kleagle arrived in the city. Capitalizing on the psychological principle that the easiest idea to sell someone is that he is better than someone else, he told his eager listeners that the country belongs to the sons of the men who built it. Catholics, Jews, Negroes, and foreigners could only undermine the national heritage. The recruiter offered enough mystery to be attractive, enough crusading spirit to be appealing, and enough idealism to be impressive. Pointing to the KKK as the greatest Protestant organization on earth, the kleagle tendered the urban worker the opportunity to become a Knight of the Invisible Empire for only ten dollars. Here indeed was new hope. As a member of a vast and secret body of "one hundred per cent Americans," the initiate was able to derive a modicum of self-esteem from comparing himself with members of unfavored groups. As Professor Gordon Allport has observed, snobbery is a way of clutching at one's own social and economic status and is particularly common among those who have little of either. Moreover, the Klansman found solace in the belief that his participation and his patriotism were essential to the continued survival of constitutional freedoms. His kleetokens, "naturalization," and white robes served as a salve for his wounded pride and enabled him to fight rather than face the future.

Every metropolitan chapter of the Invisible Empire was in some respects unique. The environment of heavily Catholic Detroit differed markedly from the atmosphere of smaller Denver, which was more homogeneous racially and ethnically; the situation in Atlanta was unlike that in Portland. Even within the same city conditions were never the same; Chicago's Austin Klan No. 6 was not faced with the same problems as Englewood Klan No. 2 or Logan Square Klan No. 9. The zeal and ability of recruiters, the degree of major newspaper opposition, the year of peak strength, and the quality of local leadership were important variables. Certainly the political situation differed greatly from city to city. Indianapolis, Chicago, Detroit, and Memphis Knights were forced to contend with unfriendly municipal administrations, whereas a neutral chief executive presided in Knoxville, and pro-Klan politicians occupied the mayoral posts in Denver, Portland, Atlanta, and later, Indianapolis.

But whatever the local situation, urban klaverns faced peculiar problems which served to differentiate them from their small-town or rural counterparts. Survival required a significant adjustment in methods and manner from more traditional methods of Klanishness. Urban Knights could rarely defy city police and parade unmolested through busy downtown streets, nor could they drag moral transgressors from their homes or drive errant Negroes from the community. Burning crosses were utilized somewhat more frequently and with greater effect in the small towns. But because urban Klansmen were less ostentatious and spectacular than their rural counterparts is no indication that they were less active or powerful.

"Harvest Jubilee and Rube parties," river excursions, "Kolossal Klan Karnivals," barbecues, picnics, and weekly meetings in rented fraternal halls were among the myriad activities of the Klansmen in the cities. Particularly exciting were the large outdoor initiations which normally required a short drive to nearby "naturalization grounds." While urban Klansmen never participated in organized community drives and rarely conducted large-scale charity campaigns of their own, they did lend much assistance to the individually needy. Most of the giving was spontaneous and haphazard and usually included the distribution of food and gifts at Christmas and financial support for impoverished widows. Particularly ambitious in this regard was Dallas Klan No. 66, which established and operated for several years a seventy-five-thousand-dollar institution for homeless children.

Church visitations were an important part of the urban Klan routine, and many Klansmen long remembered the silent reaction of a startled congregation as robed Knights appeared unexpectedly during their services. The alliance with Protestantism was partly the result of conviction and partly the result of clerical assistance. Caleb Ridley in Atlanta, James R. Johnson in Portland, Oscar Haywood in New York City, A. C. Parker in Dallas, and William Oeschger in Denver were among scores of clergymen who served in high Klan positions. But such men were not typical of their co-religionists, and were frequently, like Ridley, drummed out of their own churches. In 1923 Rabbi Samuel Mayerberg warned in Chicago: "Protestantism is on trial. Protestantism must destroy Ku Kluxism or Ku Kluxism will destroy Protestantism." The church survived the crisis capably; virtually every denomination publicly and officially denounced the Klan, and, with the exception of Chicago, opposition to the Invisible Empire was almost everywhere spearheaded by Protestants.

The most distinguishing characteristic of urban Klansmen was a preoccupation with politics. Usually unable to demonstrate publicly or to achieve their goals through intimidation, they turned early to the ballot box as the best method of preserving "one hundred per cent Americanism" in the cities. State-wide contests sometimes gained prominence, as in the campaign of Walter Pierce and compulsory public education in Oregon, Clarence J. Morley and Rice W. Means in Colorado, Earle B. Mayfield in Texas, Ralph Owen Brewster in Maine, and Ed Jackson in Indiana. But primary emphasis was usually placed upon local elections. Strategy varied from city to city with success coming most often when the secret order functioned as a balance of power within the two-party system rather than as an independent political force. Thus did Klan support elect Republican Mayor John Duvall in Indianapolis and Democratic Mayors Benjamin Stapleton and Walter Sims in Denver and Atlanta. Seeking success outside the two major parties, Klan candidates W. Joe Wood in Memphis and Charles Bowles in Detroit met defeat. Similarly, the Invisible Empire's choices for lesser political offices were unsuccessful when they failed to ally with other independent political pressure groups. Regardless of methods, however, the secret order never earned anything more than short-term political success and was usually forced from power as soon as anti-Klan elements awakened the community to the menace and united behind a single candidate. It is significant and indicative of the fact that the Klan was not a movement of economic protest that its political endorsements were made primarily on the basis of race, religion, and attitude toward the KKK rather than upon economic philosophy.[14]

Although the Invisible Empire had only a minor impact upon presidential politics, its national influence was well demonstrated at the 1924 Democratic Convention. In broiling heat, the delegates at Madison Square Garden split almost evenly on a vote to denounce the Ku Klux Klan by name. The motion failed by one vote. The bitterness engendered carried over into the selection of a presidential nominee and smashed the uneasy coalition between the two great wings of the party. Only after 103 ballots, the longest deadlock in convention history, was John W. Davis of West Virginia nominated for President. By that time the Democratic party was so badly divided that only a major depression and the Roosevelt coalition would restore it to health.

The contending forces in American life that tore apart the 1924 Democratic National Convention were also at work in the nation's cities. Roman Catholic and Fundamentalist, Gentile and Jew, Prohibitionist and wet, Negro and white, old immigrant and new came together in urban America as nowhere else and faced each other in direct political, economic, and social competition. The result was not always harmony, understanding, and tolerance. The Ku Klux Klan provided a focus for the fears of alienated native Americans whose world was being disrupted. In the city the Invisible Empire found its greatest challenge, and in the city it met its ultimate defeat.

■ ■ ■ ■ **Notes**

1 For example, see John Higham, *Strangers in the Land: Patterns of American Nativism, 1860–1925* (New Brunswick, N.J., 1955), pp. 264–99; John M. Blum, *et al., The National Experience: A History of the United States* (New York, 1963), pp. 610–15; Andrew Sinclair, *Prohibition, the Era of Excess* (Boston, 1962), *passim;* Richard Hofstadter, *The Age of Reform* (New York, 1955), pp. 289–99; and William E. Leuchtenberg, *Perils of Prosperity, 1914–1932* (Chicago, 1958), pp. 204–40.
2 Complete records may never have existed because Imperial Wizard Simmons testified in 1921 that the Klan did not maintain a printed roster of the membership. On the local level, the National Council of Grand Dragons and Titans decided at Buckeye Lake, Ohio, in 1925 to continue to conceal membership records. Testimony of William J. Simmons, U.S. Congress, House Committee on Rules, Hearings on the Ku Klux Klan, 67th Cong., 1st Sess., 1921, p. 182; and *The New York Times,* August 28, 1925.
3 The lower estimate is that of Noel P. Gist, "Secret Societies: A Cultural Study of Fraternalism in the United States," *University of Missouri Studies,* XV (October 1940), 36. The figure of 9 million, which includes such oddities as an estimate of 890,000 for Michigan, was offered by the *Washington Post,* November 2, 1930.
4 It is interesting to note that the Klan itself rarely boasted of more than 2 million members. See *The Kourier,* January 1925, p. 10; *Dawn,* September 1, 1923; *Searchlight,* February 24, 1923; *Tolerance,* February 4, 1923; Robert L. Duffus, "The Ku Klux Klan in the Middle West," *The World's Work,* XLVI (August 1923), 363; New York *World,* January 3, 1923; *The New York Times,* February 21, 1926; and *Detroit News,* September 17, 1937.
5 Henry P. Fry, *The Modern Ku Klux Klan* (Boston, 1922), p. 60; Guy B. Johnson, "The New Ku Klux Klan Movement," (unpub. Master's thesis, University of Chicago, 1922), pp. 36–7; and Arthur Corning White, "An American Fascismo," *The Forum,* LXXII (November 1924), 636–42.
6 Irving Leibowitz, *My Indiana* (Englewood Cliffs, N.J., 1964), p. 211; Charles C. Alexander, *The Ku Klux Klan in the Southwest* (Lexington, Ky., 1965), p. 18; Hofstadter, pp. 292–3; and Frederick Lewis Allen, *Only Yesterday* (New York, 1931), p. 47.
7 This conclusion is based primarily upon: (1) the official chapter records of Knox County Klan No. 14 in Tennessee and Winchester Klan No. 72 in Illinois; (2) membership lists of the klaverns of Denver, Indianapolis, Chicago, and Anaheim, California; and (3) precinct returns, particularly of local elections in Atlanta, Denver,

Detroit, Memphis, Chicago, Dallas, Portland, and Indianapolis. Voting results are only semi-reliable, however, because the secret order often received support from upper-middle-class elements that were not sufficiently threatened by minority groups to take an extreme position and actually join the Klan.

8 The author used the Spearman rank correlation coefficient to measure the association between the percentage growth of a city between 1910 and 1930, and the percentage of white natives who joined the Klan. Eighteen cities were ranked according to the two criteria, and the resulting correlation between city growth and Klan size was .627. This correlation is significant at the .01 confidence levels.

9 Perhaps the best sources of information relative to Klan violence are the weekly bulletins and annual reports of the American Civil Liberties Union. In 1922, the ACLU reported that most Klan victims were white. The New York *World* maintained that the secret order was morally responsible for crimes committed by white-sheeted men even if technically innocent. *ACLU 1924 Annual Report*, pp. 5–7; "The Rise and Fall of the K.K.K.," *The New Republic*, LIII (November 30, 1927), 33; "The Klan as a Victim of Mob Violence," *The Literary Digest*, LXXVIII (September 18, 1923), 12–13; New York *World*, September 20, 1921; and *Chicago Tribune*, March 24, 1922. Significant also is the fact that relatively few reports of Klan-related violence between 1915 and 1944 are contained in the files of the United States Department of Justice.

10 For example, in 1920 approximately 74 per cent of all Negroes and 84 per cent of all Negro heads of households who were then living in Chicago were born in the southern and southwestern states, predominantly in rural areas of Tennessee, Alabama, Georgia, and Kentucky. Irene Graham, "Negroes in Chicago, 1920: An Analysis of United States Census Data" (unpub. Master's thesis, University of Chicago, 1929), p. 13.

11 The tendency of the Negro community to segregate within itself on the basis of occupations, intelligence, and ambition has long been recognized. For instance, in Chicago in the 1920's, Negro physicians, lawyers, and musicians sought to escape the deluge of poor and disorganized colored families by moving into the select Woodlawn community west of Cottage Grove Avenue. But these families were soon overwhelmed by the same poor people from whom they had escaped, with the unhappy result that resistance to the movement of the Negro increased solely because of his color. E. Franklin Frazier, *The Negro Family in Chicago* (Chicago, 1932), pp. 97–110.

12 The term and the concept are borrowed from Robert A. Woods and Albert J. Kennedy, *The Zone of Emergence*, Sam B. Warner, ed. (Cambridge, 1962).

13 It is interesting to note that "the only significant association between socio-economic status and level of support for Barry Goldwater in 1964 that appeared to be independent of region was a slight bulge at the lower-middle income level." Irving Crespi, "The Structural Basis for Right-wing Conservatism: The Goldwater Case," *Public Opinion Quarterly*, XXIX (Winter 1966), 537–9.

14 For instance, the Klan supported the Sterling-Towner Federal Aid to Education Bill largely in the hope that it would aid public schools and weaken parochial education. Even the Klan's campaign against the Communists and union organizers in the 1930's could not be considered to be based primarily upon economic self-interest.

17
Harlem Tragedy: An Emerging Slum

GILBERT OSOFSKY

Richard Hofstadter's observation about the importance of rural to urban movement is even truer for the nation's black population than for the American people as a whole. For blacks the migration cityward has been primarily a twentieth-century phenomenon. Although blacks did start moving out of the rural South in the Civil War decade of the 1860s, as late as 1900 almost nine out of every ten Negroes still lived in the South, most of them in rural areas. Poverty, the prevalence of lynching, and the ravages of cotton fields by the boll weevil helped push blacks out of the rural South, while the possibilities of freedom and economic opportunity drew them to northern cities. World War I, with its demands for labor and its curtailment of European immigration, speeded the process considerably. The movement to cities, North, South, and West, continued in the 1920s, slowed considerably in the Depression decade of the 1930s, and reached its greatest intensity in the years since 1940. The black population is now more heavily urbanized than the white, and only about half of the nation's Negroes live in the South.

The migration has spread in three broad streams: from the South Atlantic states to Washington, Baltimore, Philadelphia, New York, and Boston; from the Mississippi Valley and the Gulf coast to Cleveland, Chicago, and Detroit; and from Texas to Los Angeles and San Francisco. Today, there is also considerable movement from one metropolitan area to another. In the last twenty years the population distribution of the United States shows more and more blacks concentrated in central cities, while whites have moved—or fled, if one prefers—to the suburbs. The preliminary figures from the 1970 census indicate the white outflow has intensified since 1966. (For an analysis of the events and values behind this movement see Joseph Boskin's article in this book.)

In the book from which this selection is taken, Gilbert Osofsky shows that New York had never been a "promised land" for blacks. Prejudice, poverty, and police brutality had long been their lot in Gotham; and if anything the "great migration" of 1910 to 1930 intensified the prejudices and the problems. Emancipated and bohemian white contemporaries found the Harlem of the Cotton Club and the Negro literary renaissance fascinating. But the realities of poverty, rent gouging, and high disease rates, although overlooked by many, were only too evident to social workers and a few interested others. The Depression opened more eyes to the pathology of Harlem as whites began to experience what blacks had been living with for a long time. One can hardly say that in this case knowledge led to action.

■ ■ ■ ■ For Further Reading

The bibliography on blacks in cities is large and growing rapidly. Among the more important historical studies are Gilbert Osofsky, *Harlem: The Making of a Ghetto* (New York: Harper & Row, 1966); Seth Scheiner, *Negro Mecca: A History of the Negro in New York City, 1865–1920* (New York: New York University Press, 1965); Allen Spear, *Black Chicago: The Making of a Negro Ghetto, 1890–1920* (Chicago: University of Chicago Press, 1967); and Constance Green, *The Secret City: A History of Race Relations in the Nation's Capital* (Princeton: Princeton University Press, 1967). Horace Cayton and St. Clair Drake, *Black Metropolis*, 2 vols. (New York: Harper & Row, 1962) is a sensitive picture of Chicago's South Side ghetto in the 1930s and early 1940s. William M. Tuttle, Jr., *Race Riot: Chicago in the Red Summer of 1919* (New York: Atheneum, 1970) is a superb study of the background and progress of a riot which took thirty-eight lives and left hundreds homeless.

> *"I sit on my stoop on Seventh Avenue and gaze at the sunkissed folks strolling up and down and think that surely Mississippi is here in New York, in Harlem, yes, right on Seventh Avenue."*
>
> —*The Messenger*, 1923

> *"I have been in places where cattle and dogs sleep with masters, but never before have I been in such a filthy house."*
>
> —Judge William Blau's description of a Harlem tenement, 1922

I

■ The creation of a Negro community within one large and solid geographic area was unique in city history. New York had never been what realtors call an "open city"—a city in which Negroes lived wherever they chose—but the former Negro sections were traditionally only a few blocks in length, often spread across the island and generally interspersed with residences of white working-class families. Harlem, however, was a Negro world unto itself. A scattered handful of "marooned white families . . . stubbornly remained" in the Negro section, a United States census-taker recorded, but the mid-belly of Harlem was predominantly Negro by 1920.[1]

And the ghetto rapidly expanded. Between the First World War and the Great Depression, Harlem underwent radical changes. When the twenties came to an end Negroes lived as far south as One Hundred and Tenth Street—the northern boundary of Central Park; practically all the older white residents had moved away; the Russian-Jewish and Italian sections of Harlem, founded a short generation earlier, were rapidly being depopulated; and Negro Harlem, within the space of ten years, became the most "incredible slum" in the entire city. In 1920 James Weldon Johnson was able to predict a glowing future for this Negro community: "Have you ever stopped to think what the future Harlem will be?" he wrote. "It will be the greatest Negro city in the world. . . . And what a fine part of New York City [the Negro] has come into possession of!"[2] By the late 1920's and early 1930's, however, Harlem's former "high-class" homes offered, in the words of a housing expert, "the best laboratory for slum clearance . . . in the entire city." "Harlem conditions," a *New York Times* reporter concluded, are "simply deplorable."[3]

II

The Harlem slum of the twenties was the product of a few major urban developments. One of the most important was the deluge of Negro migration to New York City then. The Negro press, now largely dependent on the migrant community for support, changed its former critical attitude of migration to one openly advocating urban settlement. (The exodus was so large, a Negro minister preached, that it must have been "inspired by Almighty God.")[4] If one is looking for a dramatic turning point in the history of the urbanization of the Negro—"a race changing from farm life to city life"—it was certainly the decade of the twenties. Between 1910 and 1920 the Negro population of the city increased 66 per cent (91,709 to 152,467); from 1920 to 1930, it expanded 115 per cent (152,467 to 327,706). In the latter year less than 25 per cent of New York City's Negro population (79,264) was born in New York State. There were more Negroes in the city in 1930 than the combined Negro populations of Birmingham, Memphis and St. Louis. Similar population increases occurred in urban areas throughout the country.[5]

Negro migration in the twenties drew on areas of the South that had previously sent few people to New York City. The seaboard states of the Upper South—especially Virginia and the Carolinas—continued to be the main sources of New York's migrant Negro population, but people from Georgia and Florida and other Deep South states formerly under-represented also came in greater numbers: "Harlem became the symbol of liberty and the Promised Land to Negroes everywhere," the Reverend Dr. Powell wrote. "There was hardly a member of Abyssinian Church who could not count on one or more relatives among the new arrivals."[6] In 1930, some 55,000 foreign-born Negroes added to the growing diversity of the city's Negro population.

The following chart presents an exact description of the geographical origins of Negro migrants to New York City in 1930. I have selected states with 900 or more residents in the city.

The rapid settlement of a heterogeneous Negro population coincided with another important population change—the migration of whites from all sections of Manhattan to other boroughs. For the first time since Dutch settlement Manhattan's population *declined* in the 1920's as first- and

Negro In-Migration, New York City, 1930[7]

Born in:

Virginia	44,471
South Carolina	33,765
North Carolina	26,120
Georgia	19,546
Florida	8,249
Maryland	6,656
Pennsylvania	6,226
New Jersey	5,275
District of Columbia	3,358
Alabama	3,205
Massachusetts	2,329
Louisiana	2,182
Ohio	1,721
Tennessee	1,651
Texas	1,592
Kentucky	1,216
Mississippi	969
Foreign-born	54,754

second-generation immigrants moved to nicer residential areas in the Bronx, Brooklyn and Queens. Many of the homes they left behind had deteriorated significantly. By 1930 a majority of New York City's foreign-born and second-generation residents lived outside Manhattan.[8] As whites moved out of Manhattan, Negroes moved in. The population of that borough declined 18 per cent in the 1920's as its Negro population increased 106 per cent. By 1930 Negroes represented 12 per cent of Manhattan's population —although they composed only 4.7 per cent of the population of the entire city.[9]

Harlem was the New York neighborhood most radically revamped by the population movements of the 1920's, although the Lower East Side also changed rapidly. Harlem underwent a revolution—what one contemporary accurately called a "stupendous upheaval." Between 1920 and 1930, 118,792 white people left the neighborhood and 87,417 Negroes arrived.[10] Second-generation Italians and Jews were responding to the same conditions of prosperity that promoted mobility in all the immigrant neighborhoods of Manhattan—they were not *only* moving away because Negroes settled near them. Conditions of life which satisfied immigrant parents were often unacceptable to children: "The tenements which housed their parents," immigration expert Edward Corsi wrote in 1930, "are being left behind by the children. . . ." "East Harlem used to have a great deal larger population," a survey of the Mayor's Committee on City Planning during the Great Depression concluded. "Like others of the older residential districts, it has suffered by the exodus of families to newer surroundings. . . ."[11]

The city's newest migrants moved into the Harlem flats vacated by Italians and Jews. Puerto Ricans came to live in East Harlem, created community organizations, and laid the foundations for "El Barrio" of today. By 1930 some 45,000 Puerto Ricans resided in New York City and most were heavily concentrated in East Harlem.[12] Negroes moved north along St. Nicholas Avenue—"On the Heights," they called it—and south into the heart of "Little Russia," the former Jewish section. "Just Opened for Colored" signs were common in the neighborhood. Mount Olivet Baptist Church occupied, and still occupies, the once exclusive Temple Israel of Harlem. Prince Hall Masons bought a building that "was formerly a home for aged Jews." Graham Court, a magnificent block-length apartment house on One Hundred and Sixteenth Street, with eight separate elevators and apartments of seven to ten rooms, was opened to Negroes in 1928.[13] By 1930, 164,566 Negroes, about 72 per cent of Manhattan's Negro population, lived in Harlem.[14] The Negro ghetto remained and expanded as the other ethnic ghettos disintegrated. The economic and residential mobility permitted white people in the city was, and would continue to be, largely denied Negroes. Most Negroes were "jammed together" in Harlem—even those who could afford to live elsewhere—with little possibility of escape.[15] "One notable difference appears between the immigrant and Negro populations," an important federal study of Negro housing concluded. "In the case of the former, there is the possibility of escape, with improvement in economic status, in the second generation, to more desirable sections of the city. In the case of Negroes, who remain a distinguishable group, the factor of race and certain definite racial attitudes favorable to segregation, interpose difficulties to . . . breaking physical restrictions in residence areas."[16] A rather ponderous paragraph, but a significant truth.

III

The settlement of West Indian Negroes in Harlem in the 1920's added another complicating dimension to the racial problems of this community —one that fostered discord rather than harmony among the city's Negroes. There were ten times as many foreign-born Negroes in New York City as in any other American urban area. In 1930, 54,754 foreign Negroes lived in the city—39,833 of whom resided in Manhattan. Miami, the next largest American city in terms of immigrant Negroes, was settled by only 5,512 people; Boston ranked third with 3,287 West Indians. About 25 per cent of Harlem's population in the twenties was foreign-born. Harlem was America's largest Negro melting pot.[17]

In the era of immigration restriction, West Indian Negroes came to America through what a contemporary called the "side door." The immigration laws of the 1920's seriously restricted the migration of Europeans and totally excluded Orientals but had little effect on peoples of the Caribbean. At first there were no restrictions on West Indian Negroes. After 1924, they could enter the country under quotas set aside for their mother countries. Since these quotas were never filled there was, in reality, a free flow of people from the islands to the United States in the 1920's.[18]

Although American Negroes tended to lump all the migrants together in a uniform image—"There is a general assumption," one migrant wrote, "that there is everything in common among West Indians"—it is important to recognize that Harlem's Negro immigrants represented a diverse group of peoples from dozens of different islands in the Caribbean.[19] Most Negro immigrants felt a strong attachment to their homeland. They demonstrated an "exaggerated" nationalism in America—a buffer against the strangeness of the new culture and the hostility they experienced—which was typical of white immigrant groups. It was common, for example, to find former British subjects at the office of the British consul protesting some difficulty they experienced in America.[20] Nationalistic organizations kept close check on American foreign policy in the Caribbean and often gave banquets for and listened to addresses by West Indian dignitaries. West Indian Negroes from all countries had the lowest rate of naturalization of all immigrant groups. The people white Americans and American Negroes called "West Indians" were really individuals from Jamaica, Trinidad, Barbados, Martinique, St. Vincent, St. Lucia, Dominica, British Guiana, St. Kitts, Nevis, Montserrat, Antigua, Virgin Islands, Bermuda, the Bahamas, and so on. Although the majority spoke English, some considered French their first tongue; others Spanish; a few Dutch. The fraternal and benevolent associations they founded were not inclusive organizations for all Negro immigrants, but exclusive ones—*landsmannschaften*—for people from specific islands. Danish settlers kept pictures of the King of Denmark in their homes; former British subjects held coronation pageants and balls ("Boxes, 12s. 6d.—Loges, 8s. 4d.") and flew the Union Jack in Harlem; Frenchmen had annual Bastille Day dances.[21]

Negro immigrants differed from each other in origin, yet in a broader sense they shared general experiences, desires and mores which set them apart *as a group* from their American brethren. Most came from societies in which class distinctions played a more important role in one's life than the color line—although the latter was certainly significant. Unaccustomed to common American racial slurs, they often refused to accept them without protest. The Pullman Company, for example, hesitated to employ West Indian Negroes, it was said, "because of their refusal to accept insults from passengers quietly."[22] Out of this heightened class consciousness came a small group of political and economic radicals in Harlem—"foreign-born agitators," local Negroes called them.[23] Many of Harlem's street-corner orators in the 1920's, though not all, were West Indian migrants. Hubert H. Harrison, a Virgin Islander, was among the most prominent. Harrison was a socialist, an expert in African history, a militant critic of American society and a proud defender of the "Negro's racial heritage." He conducted formal lectures in what he called the "Harlem School of Social Science," and others from street corners—his "outdoor university." A Harlem church, the Hubert H. Harrison Memorial Church, honors his memory. Others presented talks on "Socialism vs. Capitalism," organized tenants' leagues, published Marxist journals and tried to make Harlemites labor-conscious. Richard B. Moore, Frank R. Crosswaith and the Reverend Ethelred Brown—all Negro immigrants—were prominent local candidates for Board of Aldermen, Assembly and Congress on Socialist and Communist tickets— they usually polled an exceedingly small vote. Some organized rent strikes, "rent parades," lobbied for social legislation at City Hall and Albany and distributed radical literature in Harlem. "There is no West Indian slave, no American slave," the short-lived radical magazine *Challenge* commented. "You are all slaves, base, ignoble slaves."[24]

This concern with "class" led to the emergence of a broader tradition in America. What is striking about the Negro immigrant is the way his response to American conditions, such as his exaggerated sense of nationalism, was similar to the typical reactions of most European immigrants. The Negro immigrant "did not suffer from the local anesthesia of custom"[25] and he tried to create a meaningful economic position for himself within American society. Menial labor was, among most first-generation Negro immigrants, considered a sign of social degradation and looked upon with "disgust." Most were forced to accept such jobs initially, but were strongly motivated by their traditions to improve themselves. As a group, West Indians became noted for their ambition, thrift and business acumen. They were called "pushy," "the Jews of the race," "crafty," "clannish."[26] Negro journalist George S. Schuyler "admired their enterprise in business, their pushfulness."[27] "The West Indians [are] legendary in Harlem for their frugalness and thrift," one student noted. When a West Indian "got ten cents above a beggar," a common local saying ran, "he opened a business." Contemporary surveys of Negro business in Harlem and Columbus Hill demonstrate that a disproportionate number of small stores—the traditional "Race Enterprise"—were owned by Negro immigrants. Dr. P. M. H. Savory, one of the leading spokesmen of New York's foreign-born Negro community from the 1920's to his death in June 1965, owned and published the *Amsterdam News*. Many others achieved economic success within the racial barrier.[28]

Another significant distinction between the foreign-born Negro and the American was their attitude toward family life. Slavery initially destroyed the entire concept of family for American Negroes and the slave heritage, bulwarked by economic conditions, continued into the twentieth century to make family instability a common factor in Negro life. This had not been true for most West Indians, and they arrived in America with the orthodox respect for family ties that was traditional of rural people. The West Indian family was patriarchal in structure—contrasted with the typically matriarchal American Negro home. The father, as key worker and wage earner in the islands, ruled the household with a solid hand. It was beneath his dignity to help with domestic chores. (This led American Negroes to brand West Indian men "cruel.")[29] Children were supposed to obey their parents rigidly—American Negroes considered them strait-laced; have long and formal courtships; and receive parental approval before marriage. Illicit sexual relations were considered the worst form of moral evil.[30] These traditions began to change in the second generation, but throughout the 1920's family solidarity was a pervasive force among New York's Negro immigrants.[31]

These differences in style of life were also evident in another important institution—the church. The majority of Harlemites were Baptists and Methodists; the immigrants were predominantly Episcopalian and Catholic.[32] The beautiful St. Martin's Episcopal Church was founded in Harlem in 1928 to minister to the needs of West Indian migrants. Services in immigrant churches were generally staid and quiet; Sunday a day of prayer, rest and visiting—as it had been on the islands. Observers were impressed with the differences between the emotionalism of a typical Harlem religious service and the moderation and restraint shown in churches of the foreign-born. Negro immigrants also objected to the general frivolity and "fast ways" that were part of a typical Sunday in Harlem.[33]

All these factors combined to make Harlem in the 1920's a battleground of intraracial antagonism. American Negro nativism spilled over to taint Harlemites' reactions to the West Indian. The Negro immigrant was ridiculed; his tropical clothing was mocked; children tossed stones at the people who looked so different; foreigners were taunted with such epithets as "monkey-chaser," "ringtale," "king Mon," "cockney." "When a monkey-chaser dies/Don't need no undertaker/Just throw him in de Harlem River/He'll float back to Jamaica," was a verse from a Harlem ditty of the twenties. West Indians came to Harlem, ran another common saying, "to teach, open a church, or start trouble." "Bitter resentment grew on both sides." Each group called the other "aggressive." "We have . . . in Harlem," NAACP director Walter White wrote, "this strange mixture of reactions not only to prejudice from without but to equally potent prejudices from within." "If you West Indians don't like how we do things in this country," an American Negro said tersely, "you should go back where you came from. . . ."[34]

The obvious hostility of American Negroes forced Negro immigrants to unite in defense organizations larger than their individual national groups. The West Indian Committee on America, the Foreign-Born Citizens' Alliance and the West Indian Reform Association were founded in the twenties to soften these intraracial tensions and promote "cordial relations between West Indians and colored Americans." Radio programs were devoted to discussions of "Intra-Race Relations in Harlem," and immigrants were urged to become naturalized citizens. American Negroes, in turn, were asked to tone down their "considerable prejudice against West Indians." A semblance of co-operation was achieved as mass meetings were held in Harlem churches. The hatreds of the 1920's did not die, however, until West Indian Negroes stopped migrating to New York. During the Depression more immigrants left New York than entered and intraracial tensions slowly eased. Young Harlemites today, even third-generation descendants of Negro immigrants, are often unaware of these old divisions. The unique type of intraracial hostility so prominent in the twenties has never reappeared. While it lasted, however, it served to weaken a Negro community in great need of unity. A divided Harlem confronted major social problems that desperately called for the co-operation of all.[35]

IV

The most profound change that Harlem experienced in the 1920's was its emergence as a slum. Largely within the space of a single decade Harlem was transformed from a potentially ideal community to a neighborhood with manifold social and economic problems called "deplorable," "unspeakable," "incredible." "The State would not allow cows to live in some of these apartments used by colored people . . . in Harlem," the chairman of a city housing reform committee said in 1927. The Harlem slum of today was created in the 1920's.[36]

The most important factor which led to the rapid deterioration of Harlem housing was the high cost of living in the community. Rents, traditionally high in Harlem, reached astounding proportions in the 1920's—they skyrocketed in response to the unprecedented demand created by heavy Negro migration and settlement within a restricted geographical area. "Crowded in a black ghetto," a sociologist wrote, "the Negro tenant is forced to pay exorbitant rentals because he cannot escape." In 1919 the average Harlemite paid somewhat above $21 or $22 a month for rent; by 1927 rentals had *doubled* and the "mean average market rent for Negro tenants in a typical block" was $41.77. In 1927 Harlem Negroes paid $8 more than the typical New Yorker for three-room apartments; $10 more for four rooms; and $7 more for five rooms, an Urban League survey noted.[37] Another report concluded that the typical white working-class family in New York City in the late twenties paid $6.67 per room, per month, while Harlem Negroes were charged $9.50.[38]

Realty values which had declined significantly prior to World War I *appreciated* in Harlem in the twenties.[39] Harlem experienced a slum boom. "The volume of business done in the section . . . during the last year is . . . unprecedented," *Harlem Magazine* announced in 1920. "Renting conditions have been very satisfactory to the owners and the demand for space . . . is getting keener every year [due] to the steady increase in the negro population," a *New York Times* reporter wrote in 1923. There was, in the language of a Harlem businessman, an "unprecedented demand for Harlem real estate."[40] For landlords—Negro and white (Negro tenants continually complained that Negro landlords fleeced them with equal facility as whites)—Harlem became a profitable slum.[41]

High rents and poor salaries necessarily led to congested and unsanitary conditions. The average Negro Harlemite in the 1920's, as in the 1890's, held some menial or unskilled position which paid low wages—work which was customarily "regarded as Negro jobs." There were generally two types of businesses in New York in terms of Negro hiring policy, E. Franklin Frazier wrote: "Those that employ Negroes in menial positions and those that employ no Negroes at all." Macy's, for example, hired Negroes as elevator operators, escalator attendants and cafeteria workers; Gimbel's used none. "We have felt it inadvisable to [hire] colored people," a Metropolitan Life Insurance Company executive explained in 1930, "not because of any prejudice on the part of the company, but because . . . there would be very serious objection on the part of our white employees. . . ."[42] Throughout the city the vast majority of Negro men worked as longshoremen, elevator operators, porters, janitors, teamsters, chauffeurs, waiters and general laborers of all kinds. Negro women continued to work as domestics ("scrub women"), although in the 1920's an increasing number were employed as factory operatives in the garment industry and in laundries. Less than 20 per cent of Harlem's businesses were owned by Negroes.[43] The average Harlem family, according to President Hoover's Conference on Home Building and Home Ownership, earned $1,300 a year in the twenties; the typical white family in the city, $1,570. A variety of social investigations noted that working-class whites expended approximately 20 per cent of their income for rent, considered the proper amount by economists; Harlemites, 33 per cent and more.[44] An Urban League study of 2,160 Harlem families demonstrated that almost half (48 per cent) spent 40 or more per cent of their earnings on rent. A 1928 sample of tenement families found that Harlemites paid 45 per cent of their wages for housing. Similar conclusions were reached in a variety of local community studies.[45] Whatever the exact figure, few Negroes looked to the first of the month with expectancy.

Added to the combination of "high rents and low wages"[46] was the fact that Harlem's apartment houses and brownstones were originally built for people with a radically different family structure from that of the new residents. Seventy-five per cent of Harlem's tenements had been constructed before 1900.[47] The Negro community of the twenties, like all working-class peoples in times of great migration, continued to be most heavily populated by young adults—men and women between the ages of 15 and 44. Family life had not yet begun for many Negro Harlemites—as it had for older Americans and earlier immigrants who lived in the community previously.

In 1930, 66.5 per cent of Harlem Negroes were between the ages of 15 and 44, contrasted with 56.5 per cent for the general population of Manhattan and 54.4 per cent for New York City at large. Harlemites who were married had few children. In 1930, 17.5 per cent of Harlem's population was under 14; the corresponding figure for New York City was 24.5 per cent. The number of Harlemites under the age of 15 declined 14 per cent between 1920 and 1930, as whites left the neighborhood. There was a corresponding decrease of 19 per cent for those over 45 years of age.[48]

What all these statistics mean is simply that apartments of five, six, and seven rooms were suitable for older white residents with larger families and larger incomes—they obviously did not meet the needs of the Negro community in the 1920's. "The houses in the section of Harlem inhabited by the Negro were not only built for another race," E. Franklin Frazier noted, "but what is more important, for a group of different economic level, and consisting of families and households of an entirely different composition from those which now occupy these dwellings." "Unfortunately," Eugene Kinckle Jones of the Urban League stated, "the houses built before [the Negroes'] arrival were not designed to meet the needs . . . of Negroes." "The class of houses we are occupying today are not suited to our economic needs," John E. Nail said in 1921. Negro Harlemites desperately needed small apartments at low rentals: "One of the community's greatest needs [is] small apartments for small families with a reasonable rent limit. . . ."[49] Few realtors were philanthropic enough to invest their capital in new construction; older homes, properly subdivided, produced sufficient income. Only a handful of new houses were built in Harlem in the 1920's.[50]

A variety of makeshift solutions were found to make ends meet: "What you gonna do when the rent comes 'round," had been an old Negro song. The most common solution was to rent an apartment larger than one's needs and means and make up the difference by renting rooms to lodgers—"commercializing" one's home. In the twenties, approximately one white Manhattan family in nine (11.2 per cent) took in roomers, contrasted with one in four (26 per cent) for Negroes. Most lodgers were strangers people let into their homes because of economic necessity. It was difficult to separate "the respectable" from "the fast." "The most depraved Negroes lived side by side with those who were striving to live respectable lives," a contemporary complained. Urban reformers blamed many of Harlem's social problems on this "lodger evil."[51]

Every conceivable space within a home was utilized to maximum efficiency: "Sometimes even the bathtub is used to sleep on, two individuals taking turns!" Negro educator Roscoe Conkling Bruce wrote. Boarding-houses were established which rented beds by the week, day, night or hour. A large number of brownstones were converted to rooming houses: "Private residences at one time characteristic of this part of the city have been converted into tenements. . . ." One landlord transformed apartments in nine houses into one-room flats, a state commission investigating New York housing reported. Space which formerly grossed $40 a month now brought in $100 to $125. People were said to be living in "coal bins and cellars." In an extreme case, one social investigator discovered seven children sleeping on pallets on the floor of a two-room apartment. More common was the "Repeating" or "Hot Bed System"—as soon as one person awoke and left, his bed was taken over by another.[52]

An additional Harlem method devised to meet the housing crisis of the twenties was the "Rent Party." Tickets of admission were usually printed and sold for a modest price (25¢). All who wanted to come were invited to a party. Here is an example:[53]

> If you're looking for a good time,
>   don't look no more,
> Just ring my bell and I'll answer
>   the door.
> Southern Barbecue
> Given by Charley Johnson and Joe
> Hotboy, and How hot!

Chitterlings, pigs' feet, coleslaw and potato salad were sold. Money was raised in this way to pay the rent: "The rent party," *The New York Age* editorialized in 1926, "has become a recognized means of meeting the demands of extortionate landlords. . . ." The white world saw rent parties as picturesque affairs—in reality they were a product of economic exploitation and they often degenerated into rowdy, bawdy and violent evenings.[54]

A significant part of the deterioration of the neighborhood was caused by the migrants themselves. Some needed rudimentary training in the simplest processes of good health and sanitation (Booker T. Washington, it will be remembered, preached the "gospel of the toothbrush").[55] E. Franklin Frazier called many Negro Harlemites "ignorant and unsophisticated peasant people without experience [in] urban living. . . ." They often permitted homes and buildings to remain in a state of uncleanliness and disrepair. Landlords complained that apartments were looted and fixtures stolen, that courtyards and hallways were found laden with refuse. Clothes and bedding were hung out of windows; trash sometimes thrown down air shafts; dogs walked on rooftops; profanities shouted across streets; "ragtime" played throughout the night. "Ragtime is a sufficient infliction of itself," one wag complained, "but when it keeps up all night, it becomes unbearable." "Since the so-called 'Negro invasion,'" a colored woman noted, "the streets, the property and the character of everything have undergone a change, and if you are honest, you will frankly acknowledge it has not been for the . . . improvement of the locality. . . . Are we responsible for at least some of the race prejudice which has developed since the entry of Negroes in Harlem?" Negro journals criticized "boisterous" men who laughed "hysterically" and hung around street corners, and those who used "foul language on the streets." An editorial in the *Age,* one of many, attacked "Careless Harlem Tenants": "A great deal might be said about the necessity for training some of the tenants in the matter of common decency," it suggested. The absence of a sense of social and community responsibility, characteristic of urban life, obviously affected Negro Harlemites.[56]

All these factors combined to lead to the rapid decline of Harlem. The higher the rents, sociologists said, the greater the congestion: "Crowding is more prevalent in high-rent cities than in cities in which rent per room is more reasonable." In 1925, Manhattan's population density was 223 people per acre—in the Negro districts it was 336. Philadelphia, the second most congested Negro city in the country, had 111 Negroes to an acre of land; Chicago ranked third with 67. There were two streets in Harlem that were perhaps the most congested blocks in the entire world.[57]

People were packed together to the point of "indecency."[58] Some landlords, after opening houses to Negro tenants, lost interest in caring for their property and permitted it to run down—halls were left dark and dirty, broken pipes were permitted to rot, steam heat was cut off as heating apparatus wore out, dumb-waiters broke down and were boarded up, homes became vermin-infested. Tenants in one rat-infested building started what they called "a crusade against rats." They argued that the rats in their house were "better fed" and "better housed" than the people. Some common tenant complaints in the 1920's read: "No improvement in ten years"; "Rats, rat holes, and roaches"; "Very very cold"; "Not fit to live in"; "Air shaft smells"; "Ceilings in two rooms have fallen"; "My apartment is overrun with rats"; and so on.[59] There were more disputes between tenants and landlords in Harlem's local district court—the Seventh District Court—than in any municipal court in the five boroughs. Traditionally, municipal courts were known as "poor-men's courts"; Harlemites called the Seventh District Court the "rent court." Occasionally, socially conscious judges of this court made personal inspections of local tenements that were subjects of litigation. Without exception what they saw horrified them: "Conditions in negro tenements in Harlem are deplorable"; "Found few fit for human habitation"; "Negro tenants are being grossly imposed upon by their landlords"; "On the whole I found a need for great reformation"; were some of their comments. One municipal official accurately called the majority of Harlem's houses "diseased properties."[60]

V

And the disease did not confine itself to houses. To touch most areas of Harlem life in the 1920's is to touch tragedy. This was especially true of the health of the community. Theoretically, a section of the city inhabited by relatively young people should have ranked below the general population in mortality and sickness rates. Just the reverse was true. Undertaking was a most profitable Harlem business.[61]

From 1923 to 1927 an Atlanta University professor made an intensive study of Harlem health. His findings were shocking. During these years Harlem's death rate, for all causes, was 42 per cent in excess of that of the entire city. Twice as many Harlem mothers died in childbirth as did mothers in other districts, and almost twice as many Harlem children "passed" as did infants in the rest of New York. Infant mortality in Harlem, 1923–1927, was 111 per thousand live births; for the city, 64.5. Families wept at the processions of "so many little white caskets." Similar statistics are recorded for deaths from tuberculosis (two and a half to three times the city rate), pneumonia, heart disease, cancer and stillbirths.[62] An astounding number of Harlemites had venereal diseases. Negro children commonly suffered from rickets—a disease of malnutrition. More women than ever reported themselves "widows" to census-takers. Negro deaths by violence increased 60 per cent between 1900 and 1925.[63] With the single exception of the Lower West Side Health District, which included the old San Juan Hill neighborhood, Harlem was the most disease-ridden community in Manhattan.[64]

Whatever the causes of Harlem's health problems—and medical investigators continue to search for all the answers—a good deal can be laid at the door of slum environment. Urban reformers consistently showed a high correlation between poverty and congestion on the one hand and disease and death on the other. Mortality rates for infants whose mothers worked away from home, for example—and twice as many Negro women as white women in the city did—was higher than for children whose mothers remained at home; working-class families in old-law tenements (pre-1901) died at a higher rate than those in newer houses; poverty led to the consumption of the cheapest foods, and this in turn fostered diseases of poor diet; working mothers died more readily in childbirth than unemployed women; and so on.[65] Added to all these considerations, however, was a deep strain of peasant ignorance and superstition embedded in the minds of thousands of migrants—foreign-born as well as native—who settled in Harlem. Quackery abounded in the community in the 1920's.[66]

Harlem had the reputation of a "wide-open city." Whatever you wanted, and in whatever quantity, so the impression went, could be bought there. This was certainly true for the variety of "spiritualists," "herb doctors," "African medicine men," "Indian doctors," "dispensers of snake oils," "layers-on-of-hands," "faith healers," "palmists," and phrenologists who performed a twentieth-century brand of necromancy there: "Harlem sick people are flocking to all sorts of Quacksters," an *Age* reporter noted. One man, "Professor Ajapa," sold an "herb juice" guaranteed "to cure consumption, rheumatism, and other troubles that several doctors have failed in."

Health center districts, 1930	Infant mortality per 1,000 live births	TB mortality per 100,000 population	Pulmonary TB new case rate per 100,000 population	Other infectious diseases, rate per 100,000 population	Venereal disease new case rate per 100,000 population	General mortality rate per 1,000 population
Manhattan						
Central Harlem	98	251	487	987	2,826	15.3
Lower East Side	62	116	302	1,160	892	14.0
Kips Bay–Lenox Hill	73	75	184	937	629	12.7
East Harlem	75	137	311	1,326	913	12.0
Lower West Side	83	156	391	1,201	1,318	16.7
Riverside	64	75	196	827	778	12.3
Washington Heights	52	72	203	937	668	10.5
Total	73	122	294	1,049	1,455	13.3

Powders could be purchased to keep one's wife home at night, make women fertile and men sexually appealing. "Black Herman the Magician" and "Sister P. Harreld" held séances and sold "blessed handkerchiefs," "potent powders," love charms, lodestones, amulets and "piles of roots." "Ignorance, cherished superstitions and false knowledge often govern Negroes in illness and hamper recoveries," a colored physician with the Board of Health wrote in 1926. Nine wood lice gathered in a little bag and tied around a baby's neck, some believed, would end teething. An egg fried brown on both sides and placed on a woman's abdomen would hasten labor. If a mother in the course of childbirth kicked a Bible from her bed to the floor, either she or her child would die. People had faith in the medicinal qualities of dried cobwebs, rabbit brains, "dirt-dauber tea," and something called "cockroach rum." In spite of efforts of physicians, health agencies and the Negro press to bring modern-day medical information to the community, quackery "continued to thrive with impunity in Harlem." It aggravated an already tragic situation.[67]

Accompanying the proliferation of healers, and rooted in the same rural consciousness which made quackery possible,[68] was the host of storefront churches founded in Harlem in the twenties. These were places that healed one's soul: "Jesus is the Doctor, Services on Sunday," read a sign which hung over one door. An investigator found 140 Negro churches in a 150-block area of Harlem in 1926. "Harlem is perhaps overchurched," W. E. B. DuBois said modestly. Only about a third—fifty-four—of Harlem's churches were housed in regular church buildings—and these included some of the most magnificent and costly church edifices in New York City. The rest held services in stores and homes and appealed to Harlem's least educated people. "Jack-leg preachers," "cotton-field preachers," as their critics called them, hung out their poorly printed signboards and "preached Jesus" to all who wanted to listen. One self-appointed pastor held meetings in the front room of his home and rented chairs from the local undertaker to seat his small congregation. In Harlem in the twenties one could receive the word of the Lord through such nondenominational sects as: "The Metaphysical Church of the Divine Investigation," "The Temple of the Gospel of the Kingdom," "The Church of the Temple of Love," "Holy Church of the Living God," "Temple of Luxor," "Holy Tabernacle of God," "Royal Fraternity Association," "Knights of the Rose and Cross," "Sons of God," "Sons of Christ," "Sons of Jehovah," "Sanctified Sons of the Holy Ghost," and the "Live-Ever-Die-Never" church. People not only had their worries removed in these places, a Negro clergyman wrote, but "their meager worldly goods as well."[69]

The ministers of these churches preached a fundamentalism which centered around the scheming ways of Satan, who was everywhere, and the terror and joy of divine retribution, with an emphasis on terror. One congregation expelled members who attended the theater or movies. "The devil runs every theatre," its pastor said. "He collects a tax on the souls of men and robs them of their seat in heaven." Services were fervent, loud and boisterous as members felt the spirit of the Lord and shouted and begged for His forgiveness. Tambourines sometimes kept up a rhythmic beat in the background and heightened the emotionalism to a state of frenzy. Neighbors of one storefront church sued the congregation for "conducting a public nuisance." The "weird sounds" which emanated from the building, they complained, seemed like a "jazz orchestra."[70]

> Are you ready-ee? Hah!
> For that great day, hah!
> When the moon shall drape her face in mourning, hah!
> And the sun drip down in blood, hah!
> When the stars, hah!
> Shall burst forth from their diamond sockets, hah!
> And the mountains shall skip like lambs, hah!
> Havoc will be there, my friends, hah!
> With her jaws wide open, hah!
> And the sinner-man, hah!
> And cry, Oh rocks! Hah!
> Hide me! Hah!
> Hide me from the face of an angry God, hah!
> Hide me, Ohhhhhh! . . .
> Can't hide, sinner, you can't hide.[71]

Contemporaries were uniformly critical of these evangelists—there were many Harlem "Prophets"—and most of these preachers were probably charlatans in some form. There was at least one exception, however. A new denomination, the Church of Christ, Apostolic Faith, was founded on the streets of Harlem by the Reverend Mr. R. C. Lawson in 1919. The Reverend Mr. Lawson, of New Iberia, Louisiana, "the only real Apostolic–Holy Ghost–Bible Preacher," presented what he called the "Full Gospel" on street corners of Harlem's worst blocks. He decried the lack of emotionalism in the more established urban churches—copying "the white man's style," he said—and offered recent migrants a touch of fire and brimstone and personal Christianity characteristic of religion in the rural South:

> I have found it, I have found it,
> the meaning of life, life in God,
> life flowing through me by the
> Holy Spirit, life abundant, peace,
> joy, life in its fullness.

Lawson started preaching on One Hundred and Thirty-third Street, east of Lenox Avenue. This area "was to Harlem what the Bowery is to the lower East Side," a Negro journalist recorded. From the streets, the Reverend Mr. Lawson moved into a small building and held services for those "fast drifting to a life of eternal darkness" every day and every night of the week. His Refuge Church of Christ became the founding church of the new denomination, and the Reverend Mr. Lawson its first bishop. By 1930 the Apostolic Church had some forty branches throughout the country and ran an orphanage, elementary school and "Bible Supply House"; it continues to prosper today. Annual conventions met in Refuge Church, "the most honored in the sisterhood of the Apostolic Church," and local leaders praised and publicized its good works for Harlem Negroes: "This church has had one of the most remarkable growths of any religious organizations in the country."[72]

Harlem was also a "wide-open city" in terms of vice and gambling.[73] The annual reports of the anti-vice Committee of Fourteen, founded in 1905, showed Harlem as the leading or near-leading prostitution center of Manhattan throughout the twenties. The Committee hired a Negro doctor, Ernest R. Alexander, to do a secret study of Harlem vice in 1928. His report emphasized the "openness of vice conditions in this district." Dr. Alexander personally found sixty-one houses of prostitution in the neighborhood—more than the combined totals of four other investigators hired at the same time to survey other districts. "There is a larger amount and more open immorality in Harlem than this community has known in years," Negro alderman George W. Harris noted in 1922. "It is a house of assignation . . . this black city," Eric D. Walrond wrote bitterly in the Negro journal *The Messenger*.[74]

> Her dark brown face
> Is like a withered flower
> On a broken stem.
> Those kind come cheap in Harlem,
> So they say.[75]

The Committee of Fourteen also disclosed that more than 90 per cent of these "daughters of joy" institutions were owned and managed by whites. Other evidence verifies this.[76]

Gambling also prevailed in the neighborhood: "Bootleggers, gamblers, and other panderers to vice have found it profitable to ply their vicious trades in this section." The poorest of the poor sought instant riches through the numbers racket. No sum was too small to bet—starting with pennies. "One can bet with plenty of takers on anything from a horse race to a mule race," the *Age* editorialized. Many Harlemites "would rather gamble than eat," it concluded. People selected numbers to coincide with birthdays, dreams, hymns or chapters and verses of Scripture in expectation that they would coincide with the clearing-house figures of the day. The odds were thousands to one against success, yet the smallest hope for a richer life was better than none and Negroes continued to play "policy" avidly. "The chief pastime of Harlem seems to be playing the numbers," George S. Schuyler wrote in 1925.[77]

"Buffet flats," "hooch joints," "barrel houses," and cabarets supplied Harlemites with illegal liquor, and occasionally other things, in the Prohibition era. Drugstores, cigar stores, sweetshops and delicatessens were used as "fronts" for speakeasies. "Harlem can boast of more drugstores than any similar area in the world," one Negro commented. "A plethora of delicatessen stores may be found in the Negro sections of New York, most of which are simply disguised bootlegging stores," a Harlemite concluded in 1924. "And so many confectioners! One never dreamed the Negroes were so much in need of sugar." "Speakeasies downtown are usually carefully camouflaged," a *New York Tribune* reporter noted: "In Harlem they can be spotted a hundred yards off."[78]

Poverty and family instability also led to a high incidence of juvenile delinquency. A community with fewer young teenagers should have shown a proportionally lower juvenile crime rate; as with Negro health, just the reverse was true. "The records of the Children's Court of New York for every year from 1914 to 1927 show a steady increase in the percentage of all crimes committed by Negro boys and girls," Owen R. Lovejoy of the Children's Aid Society reported. In 1914 Negro children represented 2.8 per cent of all cases before the juvenile court of New York City; in 1930 this figure rose to 11.7 per cent.[79]

Working mothers had little time to care for their children. Youngsters "with keys tied around their necks on a ribbon" wandered around the streets until families came home at night. A substantial portion were products of broken homes—families without a male head. One Harlem school principal testified that 699 of his 1,600 pupils came from families whose fathers were not living at home. Nor did the majority of Harlem schoolchildren ever have time to accustom themselves to the regularity of school life; many families were rootless. Three-fourths of all the Negro pupils registered in one Harlem school, for example, transferred to some other before the end of one school year; some schools actually experienced a 100 per cent turnover. Pupils from the South were seriously deficient in educational training: "They are at times 14 to 15 years of age and have not the schooling of boys of eight," a Harlem principal wrote. "We cannot give a boy back seven years of wasted life. . . ." The typical Harlem school of the twenties had double and sometimes triple sessions. The "usual class size" was forty to fifty and conditions were generally "immensely overcrowded": "The school plant as a whole is old, shabby, and far from modern." In some schools 25 per cent and more of the children were overage or considered retarded.

Negro children in Harlem often led disrupted and harsh lives from the earliest years of their existence: "Testimony has been given before us as to the moral conditions among children, even of tender age," a municipal agency investigating Harlem schools recorded, "which is not to be adequately described by the word 'horrifying.'" These conditions were obviously reflected in high rates of juvenile crime but more subtly, and worst of all, in a loss of respect for oneself and for life in general. Harlem youngsters developed "a sense of subordination of insecurity, of lack of self-confidence and self-respect, the inability . . . to stand on their own feet and face the world with open eyes and feel that [they have] as good a right as anyone else."[80]

This then was the horror of slum life—the Harlem tragedy of the 1920's. "Court and police precinct records show," a municipal agency maintained, "that in arrests, convictions, misdemeanants, felons, female police problems and juvenile delinquencies, these areas are in the lead. . . ." It was no wonder that narcotics addiction became a serious problem then and that Harlem became "the center of the retail dope traffic of New York"; nor that local violence and hatred for the police were continually reported in the press.[81] The majority of Harlemites even during normal times lived "close to the subsistence level." Many were "under care" of charitable agencies in the period of relatively full employment. Those who needed money quickly and had no other recourse were forced to turn to loan sharks, Negro and white, who charged 30 to 40 per cent interest: Harlem "has been infested by a lot of loan sharks," a municipal magistrate who dealt with such cases stated. In one form or another the sorrow and economic deprivation of the Depression had come to Harlem in the twenties: "The reason why the Depression didn't have the impact on the Negroes that it had on the whites," George S. Schuyler said, "was that the Negroes had been in the Depression all the time."[82]

■ ■ ■ ■ **Notes**

1 The Mayor's Commission on Conditions in Harlem, "The Negro in Harlem: A Report on Social and Economic Conditions Responsible for the Outbreak of March 19, 1935" (unpublished manuscript in La Guardia Papers, Municipal Archives), p. 53. This important study, prepared under the direction of E. Franklin Frazier, will hereafter be cited as "The Negro in Harlem."
2 "The Future Harlem," *The New York Age,* January 10, 1920.
3 John E. Nail to James Weldon Johnson, March 12, 1934, Johnson Collection, Yale University; "Harlem Conditions Called Deplorable," *The New York Times,* September 6, 1927.
4 "Let Them Come," "The New Exodus," *The New York Age,* March 3, 1923, October 16, 1920, September 14, 1929.
5 Bureau of the Census, *Fifteenth Census, 1930: Population* (Washington, D.C., 1933), II, 216–218; Walter Laidlaw, *Population of the City of New York, 1890–1930* (New York, 1932), p. 51.
6 Reverend Dr. Adam Clayton Powell, Sr., *Against the Tide: An Autobiography* (New York, 1938), pp. 70–71.
7 Bureau of the Census, *Fifteenth Census, 1930: Population* (Washington, D.C., 1933), II, 216–218. Note the difference in Chicago's migrant population. In order of greatest numbers Chicago Negroes came from Mississippi, Tennessee, Georgia, Alabama and Louisiana.

8 James Ford, *et al., Slums and Housing: With Special Reference to New York City* (Cambridge, Mass., 1936), II, 311–315.

9 Ford, *et al.,* p. 317; Bureau of the Census, *Negroes in the United States, 1920–1932* (Washington, D.C., 1935), p. 55.

10 Winfred B. Nathan, *Health Conditions in North Harlem, 1923–1927* (New York, 1932), pp. 13–14.

11 *Harlem Magazine,* XIX (June 1930), 8; Mayor's Commission on City Planning, *East Harlem Community Study* (typescript in New York Public Library, 1937), p. 16.

12 Ford, *et al.,* p. 370; Antonio T. Rivera to La Guardia, June 24, 1935, La Guardia Papers; "Harlem Puerto Ricans Unite to Prove Faith," *The New York Times,* July 2, August 9, 16, 1926; *Opportunity,* IV (October 1926), 330.

13 *The New York Age,* August 27, 1927, March 31, 1928, January 11, 1930; *The New York Times,* October 19, 1924.

14 Ford, *et al.,* p. 314.

15 The attempt of Negroes to move into Washington Heights, Yonkers and West-chester was opposed in these sections as it had been in Harlem earlier. The Neighborhood Protective Association of Washington Heights urged landlords to sign racially restrictive covenants. Mortgage pressures from financial institutions closed down a Negro housing development in Yonkers. As a result of population pressure, however, another large ghetto was created in the Bedford-Stuyvesant section of Brooklyn in the 1920's. Of the 68,921 Negroes in Brooklyn in 1930, 47,616 lived in what is now called Bedford-Stuyvesant. "Negro Community Near Yonkers Abandoned," *The New York Age,* July 3, 1926, March 24, August 4, 1928, April 19, 26, 1930; Ford, *et al.,* p. 314. For a sketch of Brooklyn's Negro community see Ralph Foster Weld, *Brooklyn Is America* (New York, 1950), pp. 153–173.

16 The President's Conference on Home Building and Home Ownership, *Report of the Committee on Negro Housing* (Washington, D.C., 1931), p. 5.

17 Bureau of the Census, *Fifteenth Census, 1930: Population* (Washington, D.C., 1933), II, 70; Ira De Augustine Reid, *The Negro Immigrant* (New York, 1938), pp. 248–249; Barrington Dunbar, "Factors in the Cultural Background of the American Southern Negro and the British West Indian Negro that Condition their Adjustment in Harlem" (M.A. thesis, Columbia University, 1935), *foreword,* p. 4.

18 Reid, pp. 31–35; Reid, "Negro Immigration to the United States," *Social Forces,* XVI (March 1938), 411–417; W. A. Domingo, "Restricted West Indian Immigration and the American Negro," *Opportunity,* II (October 1924), 298–299.

19 W. A. Domingo, "Gift of the Black Tropics," in Alain Locke, ed., *The New Negro: An Interpretation* (New York, 1925), p. 343.

20 *The New York Age,* July 9, 1924, February 4, 1928; Harry Robinson, "The Negro Immigrant in New York" (WPA research paper, Schomburg Collection), p. 9.

21 Garrie Ward Moore, "A Study of a Group of West Indian Negroes in New York City" (M.A. thesis, Columbia University, 1923), pp. 19–20; Reid, *The Negro Immigrant,* pp. 126–128; *The New York Age,* February 28, 1931, July 29, 1933.

22 "The Negro in New York" (unpublished WPA manuscript, Schomburg Collection), pp. 25–27; Gardner N. Jones, "The Pilgrimage to Freedom" (WPA research paper, Schomburg Collection), p. 25.

23 Reid, *The Negro Immigrant,* p. 159.

24 Reid, *The Negro Immigrant,* p. 123; "Communists in Harlem," *The New York Age,* September 21, 1929, October 2, 9, 1926, December 24, 1927, January 21, May 12, December 8, 1928, September 21, 1929.

25 Domingo, "Gift of the Black Tropics," p. 347.

26 Robinson, pp. 21–22; Moore, p. 26.

27 "The Reminiscences of George S. Schuyler" (Oral History Research Office, Columbia University, 1960), p. 73.

28 Robinson, p. 9; "The Negro in New York," p. 25; Moore, p. 25; Reid, *The Negro Immigrant*, p. 133; *The Messenger*, VII (September 1925), 326, 337–338; *The New York Age*, February 22, 1930; Baltimore *Afro-American*, January 9, 1932.

29 Moore, p. 5.

30 Dunbar, pp. 14–25.

31 Reid, *The Negro Immigrant, passim*.

32 Reid, *The Negro Immigrant*, p. 125; Greater New York Federation of Churches, *Negro Churches in Manhattan* (New York, 1930).

33 Reid, *The Negro Immigrant*, p. 174; Moore, pp. 20–25; Dunbar, chap. IV, pp. 22–23.

34 Roi Ottley, *'New World A-Coming': Inside Black America* (New York, 1943), pp. 47–48; Jones, p. 25; Beverly Smith, "Harlem—Negro City," *New York Herald Tribune*, February 14, 1930; Reid, *The Negro Immigrant*, p. 115; *The New York Age*, July 19, 1924, March 17, 1934; Dunbar, chap. III, p. 4; Walter White, "The Paradox of Color," in Alain Locke, ed., *The New Negro: An Interpretation* (New York, 1925), p. 367.

35 *The New York Age*, March 3, 24, April 21, 1928; Domingo, "The Gift of the Black Tropics," p. 344–345; Reid, *The Negro Immigrant*, p. 235.

36 "Harlem Slums," *The Crisis*, XLVIII (December 1941), 378–381; *The New York Age*, January 22, 1927.

37 New York Urban League, "Twenty-four Hundred Negro Families in Harlem: An Interpretation of the Living Conditions of Small Wage Earners" (typescript, Schomburg Collection, 1927), pp. 16–18.

38 *Report of the Committee on Negro Housing*, p. 64.

39 "Appreciation" of prices "came [when owners] remained calm. . . ." T. J. Woofter, *et al., Negro Problems in Cities* (New York, 1928), p. 75. *The New York Times* printed dozens of articles on Harlem's new business prosperity.

40 "Harlem Real Estate Increasing in Value," *Harlem Magazine*, VIII (February 1920), 18b; "Unprecedented Demand for Harlem Real Estate," *Harlem Magazine*, X (November 1920), 6; "Revival of Speculative Activity on Harlem's Main Thoroughfare," *The New York Times*, January 18, 1920, July 24, 1921, June 10, 1923, February 13, 1927.

41 "Of all the gouging landlords in Harlem, the colored landlords and agents are the worst, according to the records of the Seventh District Municipal Court." "Race Landlord is Hardest on His Tenants," *The New York Age*, November 20, 1920, June 16, September 22, 1923, May 29, 1926.

42 "The Negro in Harlem," pp. 27–32; *The New York Age*, April 26, 1930.

43 Bureau of the Census, *Fourteenth Census, 1920: Population* (Washington, D.C., 1923), IV, 366–367, 1157–1179; *Fifteenth Census, 1930: Occupations* (Washington, D.C., 1933), 1130–1134; Helen B. Sayre, "Negro Women in Industry," *Opportunity*, II (August 1924), 242–244.

44 *Report of the Committee on Negro Housing*, p. 64; Woofter, *et al.*, p. 122.

45 "Twenty-four Hundred Negro Families in Harlem," p. 19; Sidney Axelrad, *Tenements and Tenants: A Study of 1104 Tenement Families* (New York, 1932), p. 15; New York Building and Land Utilization Committee, *Harlem Family Income Survey* (New York, 1935), p. 3; James H. Hubert, "Harlem—Its Social Problems," *Hospital Social Service*, XXI (January 1930), 44.

46 *Report of the Committee on Negro Housing*, p. vii.

47 William Wilson to La Guardia, October 6, 1944, La Guardia Papers.

48 *Health Conditions in North Harlem*, pp. 16–17; *Fifteenth Census, 1930: Population* (Washington, D.C., 1933), II, 733–734; "The Negro in Harlem," p. 20.

49 ". . . The greatest need is the construction of model tenements. These should consist of one, two, three and four room apartments." "Modern Housing Needs," *The New York Age,* February 12, 1921, January 20, 1923, January 26, 1926, January 29, 1927; "The Negro in Harlem," p. 53; Eugene Kinckle Jones, "Negro Migration in New York State," *Opportunity,* IV (January 1926), 9.

50 Victor R. Daly, "The Housing Crisis in New York City," *The Crisis,* XXXI (December 1920), 61–62.

51 National Urban League, *Housing Conditions Among Negroes, New York City* (New York, 1915), *passim;* Ford, *et al.,* p. 338.

52 "Very often it is found that there are two shifts." William Wilson to La Guardia, October 6, 1944, La Guardia Papers; *The New York Age,* March 12, 1921, February 26, 1927; "Along Rainbow Row," *The New York Times,* August 15, 1921, January 27, 1922; "Twenty-four Hundred Negro Families in Harlem," *passim;* Roscoe Conkling Bruce, "The Dunbar Apartment House: An Adventure in Community Building," *The Southern Workman,* LX (October 1931), 418.

53 *New York Herald Tribune,* February 12, 13, 1930.

54 "I promoted a weekly party, to get money to pay rent." "Boisterous rent parties, flooded with moonshine, are a quick and sure resource." "The Reminiscences of Benjamin McLaurin" (Oral History Research Office, Columbia University, 1960), p. 155; *The New York Age,* August 11, 1923, June 21, December 11, 1926; Clyde Vernon Kiser, *Sea Island to City* (New York, 1932), pp. 44–45.

55 Booker T. Washington, *Up from Slavery: An Autobiography* (New York, 1959), pp. 122–123. Note the following statement of a recent study: "There are many cases in which migratory workers do not understand or properly use ordinary living facilities, such as toilets, showers, bedding, kitchen appliances, and garbage cans. The result has been unnecessary damage to property and needless expense for repairs." 87th Cong., 1st Sess., *Senate Report 1098* (1961), p. 8.

56 *The New York Age,* August 1, 1912, June 5, 1920, September 16, 1922, July 14, 1928; National Urban League, *Housing Conditions Among Negroes,* pp. 9–10; "The Negro in Harlem," p. 113; Eslanda Goode Robeson, *Paul Robeson: Negro* (London, 1930), p. 46.

57 Woofter, *et al.,* pp. 79, 84; "The Negro in Harlem," p. 53; Ernest W. Burgess, "Residential Segregation in American Cities," *The Annals,* CXL (November 1928), 105–115; Ford, *et al.,* p. 749.

58 Owen R. Lovejoy, *The Negro Children of New York* (New York, 1932), p. 15.

59 *The New York Age,* October 28, 1922, January 17, 1925; *Housing Conditions Among Negroes, passim;* "Twenty-four Hundred Negro Families in Harlem," *passim.*

60 "I do not think I need to say that our problem of Harlem is one of the most serious we have to face." Langdon W. Post (Chairman of New York City Housing Authority) to La Guardia, April 30, 1936, La Guardia Papers. "The Negro families of the West Harlem section have undoubtedly the most serious housing problem in the City." Ford, *et al.,* p. 326. *The New York Times,* September 16, 1920, October 17, 23, 1921, April 22, 1922, January 17, June 13, 1925; *The New York Age,* February 28, August 8, 1925, January 9, 1926; "Preliminary Report on the Subject of Housing (1935)," La Guardia Papers.

61 "High Cost of Dying," *The New York Age,* February 25, 1928.

62 *Health Conditions in North Harlem, passim;* Lovejoy, p. 22; "Fighting the Ravages of the White Plague Among New York's Negro Population," *Opportunity,* I (January 1923), 23–24; Dr. Louis R. Wright, "Cancer as It Affects Negroes," *Opportunity,* VI (June 1928), 169–170, 187; Louis I. Dublin, "The Effect of Health Education on Negro Mortality," *Proceedings of the National Conference on Social Work, 1924* (Chicago, 1924), 274–279. Hereafter cited as *PNCSW.*

314 | Harlem Tragedy: An Emerging Slum

63 ". . . Syphilitic infection is one of the most fruitful causes of stillbirths, miscarriages, and early death of infants." New York Association for Improving the Condition of the Poor, *Health Work for Mothers and Children in a Colored Community* (New York, 1924), p. 3; "The Negro's Health Progress During the Last Twenty-five Years," *Weekly Bulletin of the Department of Health*, XV (June 12, 1926), 93–96; *Fifteenth Census, 1930: Population* (Washington, D.C., 1933), II, 959; E. K. Jones, "The Negro's Struggle for Health," *PNCSW, 1923* (Chicago, 1923), 68–72.

64 Adapted from Godea J. Drolet and Louis Werner, "Vital Statistics in the Development of Neighborhood Health Centers in New York City," *Journal of Preventive Medicine*, VI (January 1932), 69.

65 In 1920, 30.3 per cent of white women in the city worked, and 57.9 per cent of colored women were employed. *Fourteenth Census, 1920: Population* (Washington, D.C., 1923), IV, 367. Robert Morse Woodbury, *Causal Factors in Infant Mortality* (Washington, D.C., 1925); L. T. Wright, "Factors Controlling Negro Health," *The Crisis*, XLII (September 1935), 264–265, 280, 284; Mildred Jane Watson, "Infant Mortality in New York City, White and Colored, 1929–1936" (M.A. thesis, Columbia University, 1938); Charles Herbert Garvin, "White Plague and Black Folk," *Opportunity*, VIII (August 1930), 232–235.

66 For "voodoo" and "devil worship" among West Indians see Reid, *The Negro Immigrant*, pp. 48–49, 136–138.

67 ". . . Many [are] bringing with them their simple faith in roots, herbs, home remedies, [and are] imposed upon by unscrupulous venders of worthless . . . remedies." Dr. Peter Marshall Murray, "Harlem's Health," *Hospital Social Service*, XXII (October 1930), 309–313; C. V. Roman, "The Negro's Psychology and His Health," *PNCSW, 1924* (Chicago, 1924), 270–274; *Opportunity*, IV (July 1926), 206–207; *The Crisis*, XLII (August 1935), 243; *The New York Age*, September 23, 1922, February 17, July 21, August 11, 25, 1923, January 6, April 5, 1924, February 21, March 14, 1925, January 18, July 23, 1927.

68 Note the striking similarities between the medical and healing superstitions of urban Negroes in the twentieth century and those of slaves in the early nineteenth century. The following is a description of slave superstition by an ex-slave: "There is much superstition among the slaves. Many of them believe in what they call 'conjuration,' tricking, and witchcraft; and some of them pretend to understand the art, and say that by it they can prevent their masters from exercising their will over their slaves. Such are often applied to by others, to give them power to prevent their masters from flogging them. The remedy is most generally some kind of bitter root; they are directed to chew it and spit toward their masters. . . . At other times they prepare certain kinds of powders, to sprinkle their masters' dwellings." *Narrative of the Life and Adventures of Henry Bibb, An American Slave, Written by Himself* (New York, 1849), pp. 25–31.

69 Smith, *New York Herald Tribune*, February 11, 1930; Ira De Augustine Reid, "Let Us Prey!" *Opportunity*, IV (September 1926), 274–278; Reverend James H. Robinson, *Road Without Turning: An Autobiography* (New York, 1950), 231.

70 *The New York Age*, February 19, 1927; *The New York Times*, September 24, 1919.

71 Zora Neale Hurston, *Dust Tracks on a Road* (Philadelphia, 1942), pp. 279–280.

72 *The New York Age*, January 15, 1927, February 9, 1929, August 23, 1930, August 8, September 19, 1931, July 23, 1932, August 26, 1933, September 1, 1934.

73 "A Wide Open Harlem," *The New York Age*, September 2, 1922.

74 Committee of Fourteen, *Annual Reports*, 1914–1930; *The Crisis*, XXXVI (November 1929), 417–418; *The Messenger*, VI (January 1924), 14.

75 Langston Hughes, "Young Prostitute," *The Crisis*, XXVI (August 1923), 162.

76 "Gambling is popular in Harlem, but the big shots of the racket are white." Fiorello La Guardia, "Harlem: Homelike and Hopeful" (unpublished manuscript,

La Guardia Papers), p. 9; "A Summary of Vice Conditions in Harlem," Committee of Fourteen, *Annual Report for 1928* (New York, 1929), 31–34; *The New York Times,* February 13, 1922; *The New York Age,* February 28, 1925, May 18, 1929. Although whites seemed to control most of Harlem vice, Virgin Islander Casper Holstein—well-known as a philanthropist and café owner—was reputed to be a head of the numbers racket.

77 "Harlem—The Bettor," *The New York Age,* March 7, 1925, November 6, 20, 1926, June 4, 1927, June 23, 1928; *The New York Times,* June 12, 1922, March 11, 1927; "New York: Utopia Deferred," *The Messenger,* VII (October, November 1925), 344–349, 370.

78 *The New York Age,* September 16, 1922, April 21, 1923; *New York Herald Tribune,* February 13, 1930; *The Messenger,* VI (August 1924) 247, 262.

79 Lovejoy, p. 37; *New York Herald Tribune,* February 12, 1930; Joint Committee on Negro Child Study in New York City, *A Study of Delinquent and Neglected Negro Children Before the New York City Children's Court* (New York, 1927).

80 Jacob Theobald, "Some Facts About P.S. 89, Manhattan," *The New York Age,* January 17, 1920; "Report of Subcommittee on Education," La Guardia Papers; "The Problem of Education and Recreation," La Guardia Papers; "The Negro in Harlem," p. 73; Lovejoy, p. 22; *The New York Age,* March 12, 1921.

81 "Results of the Crime and Delinquency Study," La Guardia Papers; *The New York Age,* January 6, February 17, June 23, 1923, June 12, 1926, December 3, 1927, July 28, 1928, January 4, 1930. A white Harlem policeman, at a later date, wrote the following: "Every one of [us] is made to feel like a soldier in an army of occupation. He is engulfed by an atmosphere of antagonism." *The Crisis,* LII (January 1945), 16–17.

82 Lovejoy, p. 15; "The Negro in Harlem," p. 110; *The New York Age,* February 9, 1929; "The Reminiscences of George S. Schuyler" (Oral History Research Office, Columbia University, 1960), p. 232.

18

Politics and Relief in Minneapolis During the 1930s

RAYMOND L. KOCH

During the 1920s, manners and morals attracted more public attention than economics. Although millions of Americans shared only fitfully or not at all in the vaunted prosperity of the decade, issues like Prohibition and crime, the Klan, the sexual revolution, and immigration restriction based on the inferiority of non-Nordic (northern European) groups took precedence in the public eye over low wages, long hours, periodic joblessness, and the threat of technological unemployment. The sickening decline in economic activity after the crash of 1929, and especially the persistence of the Great Depression until the advent of World War II, overturned this order of priorities. Poverty and relief now assumed paramount importance as production dropped and bread lines lengthened.

In the essay below, Raymond Koch surveys the relief situation in Minneapolis in the 1930s, concentrating on the political squabbles surrounding the scope and administration of the city's welfare program at a time of massive joblessness. Minneapolis was not Harlem. The metropolis of the northern Great Plains area, it had a predominantly Nordic population which, according to the racial theories common among many Americans in the 1920s, should have assured its prosperity. But the Depression ignored the speculations of racial theorists and raised the specter of unemployment and possible starvation among people previously unaffected by economic insecurity.

Minneapolis, like other American cities, found that the extent of the Depression soon exhausted private and voluntary charity and that only government could mount the resources to provide even minimal relief. Also, like other cities, Minneapolis soon found its own funds drying up as the relief rolls swelled and tax collections lagged in the face of the continuing economic downturn. President Hoover adamantly opposed direct financing of relief by the national government; he saw the federal role only as the coordination of voluntary and local efforts. Anything else would ultimately sap the moral fiber of the American people and profoundly compromise American principles. Franklin Roosevelt's New Deal did involve the federal government in direct aid to the jobless and the needy, but the New Deal relief programs were no panacea, as harassed local officials soon learned. By the summer of 1935, the New Deal had created its basic welfare program in the Social Security Act and the Works Progress Administration. This legislation left the support of the most needy people, the indigent aged and the unemployable, to the state and local governments. Furthermore, as Koch indicates, relief posed complex administrative and political problems in the interaction of federal, state, and local agencies, and especially in local deter-

mination of the scope and control of the program. The traditional American belief that the poor were responsible for their own problems did not disappear, even when it was clear that massive joblessness ignored class and ethnic lines. Nor could those with income divest themselves of the notion that the welfare rolls were filled with chiselers.

Ideological and political groups struggled to further their own views of a proper relief program, and to have men and women of like mind and political affiliation administer it. A variety of local bodies exercised some control over the program, which meant a considerable amount of political and bureaucratic infighting in determining the thrust and administration of relief in Minneapolis. Similar studies would no doubt have shown comparable results in other cities.

Relief recipients and case workers were not passive observers of the political struggle; they organized and agitated just as did taxpayers and conservatives generally. The result was not unlike the current cleavage between welfare rights organizations and Reagan-like budget cutters.

In addition to giving us an interesting case study of one city's response to the relief crisis of the Depression, Koch supplies a useful insight into the application of federal programs on the local level. Scholars of the New Deal are increasingly turning to state and local studies to determine the impact of New Deal programs upon particular communities. Only in this way can we learn what happened on the operative level, the level where people live, in contrast to the sometimes rarified atmosphere of the White House, the committee rooms and floor of Congress, and the offices of federal agencies. Urban history can play a very useful role in this reevaluation by providing background and context for the study of the effects of national policy on the local level. National history that neglects local components is sure to be one-sided and incomplete, just as local history that is anything more than antiquarian cannot neglect the impact of national decisions upon local events.

■ ■ ■ ■ For Further Reading

Two major works on the New Deal are William Leuchtenburg, *Franklin D. Roosevelt and the New Deal, 1932–1940* (New York: Harper & Row Torchbooks, 1963), a thorough and highly competent survey, and the brilliant interpretive essay by Paul Conkin, *The New Deal* (New York: Thomas Crowell, 1967). James T. Patterson, *The New Deal and the States* (Princeton: Princeton University Press, 1969) opens up the subject of relations between the New Deal and the states. Two valuable books on the impact of New Deal policies on local politics are Lyle Dorsett's study of Kansas City, *The Pendergast Machine* (New York: Oxford University Press, 1968) and Bruce M. Stave, *The New Deal and the Last Hurrah* (Pittsburgh: University of Pittsburgh Press, 1970) on Pittsburgh politics. Both studies show that the New Deal did not kill the political machines but rather supplied valuable patronage and funds to keep them in operation. Bernard Sternsher has edited a valuable collection of essays with an excellent introduction—*Hitting Home: The Great Depression in Town and Country* (Chicago: Quadrangle Books, 1970).

■The Great Depression that overshadowed the 1930s brought New Deal reforms which in turn had widespread impact on local government. In particular there was a rapid expansion of public relief departments, with attendant unrest, in larger cities. A study of the turbulent situation in Minneapolis offers insight into the serious difficulties encountered in the almost overnight development of public welfare services. The one overriding factor behind the troubles was the intense pressure for immediate action due to the severity of the economic collapse and the ensuing unemployment. The fact that people had to be kept from starving influenced many of the actions of various organizations and individuals, especially politicians and social workers, throughout a harrowing decade.

At the outset of the 1929 crash, Minneapolis did not experience the immediate rise in unemployment that the Eastern cities did and consequently weathered the winter of 1929–30 remarkably well. The traditional philosophy of relief-giving—that private charitable agencies should care for the temporarily unemployed—prevailed then in Minneapolis as elsewhere.

By the fall of 1930, however, the number of unemployed requesting aid from the Family Welfare Association, the largest cash assistance private agency in Minneapolis, rose at an alarming pace. The Union City Mission, after the onset of an early October cold wave, bedded more than a thousand homeless and jobless men nightly. A similar development occurred at the Salvation Army's Industrial Home where scores of men were forced to sleep under newspapers because of a scarcity of blankets. As a result, by the end of 1930 private agencies were swamped with the first victims of the depression despite the fact that such agencies had long borne only a small proportion of the total cost for cash assistance. The public relief department still shouldered the greatest cost for needy cases, including resident unemployed and aid to dependent children (or mothers' allowances as the program was then called). Estimates of the total number of unemployed in Minneapolis ran as high as 35,000 in January, 1931.[1]

After the fall elections of 1930, which saw the Farmer-Labor party gain prominence at the state level of politics with the election of Floyd B. Olson as governor, pressure for action on relief needs rapidly increased from organizations of unemployed persons which had sprouted immediately after the great crash.[2] The day after Olson's first inaugural speech, a group of Twin Cities Communists arranged a march to the Capitol and staged a demonstration for unemployment relief. They were led by Karl Reeve, district organizer of the Communist party in Minneapolis and leader of a local chapter of the Trade Union Unity League, a Communist-front organization. The group distributed a circular that blasted the American Federation of Labor and the Farmer-Labor party and even accused Olson himself of being a "henchman of the Steel Trust." Several weeks later the Trade Union Unity League scheduled William Z. Foster, a leading national Communist figure, to speak on March 2, 1931, in the Minneapolis Gateway district, a haven for transients and local homeless and jobless individuals. Mayor William F. Kunze banned the speech, but the league tried to hold a meeting anyway. The result was the "Gateway riot," as it was called the next day after police broke up the assembled group.[3]

As the depression intensified with every passing week during its second year, private agency social workers and administrators realized they could no longer assume responsibility for cases ignored by the public relief department. The government—the common social instrument of all the people—was the only effective means of alleviating the situation. So, as pressure mounted on local politicians, tension developed in Minneapolis between the city council, the board of public welfare, and the division of public relief. Although the relief division dated back to the 1890s, the welfare board dictated city relief policies. The board included the mayor, three councilmen, and three lay members. The mayor appointed the latter six for four-year overlapping terms, subject to city council approval. While the board was the official policy-maker, the council voted the relief appropriations to be distributed by the board, a function that in many instances proved to be an effective control device.[4]

Mounting demands for relief gave Farmer-Labor candidates their best issue in the 1931 city elections. Farmer-Labor endorsed William A. Anderson, replaced conservative William F. Kunze as mayor, and the party's representation increased on the Minneapolis city council. Following the Farmer-Labor victories, the welfare board was deluged with complaints about lengthening relief lines, delays in processing applications, and inadequate food orders. Richard S. Tattersfield, long-time superintendent of the division of public relief, came under heavy attack for showing more interest in conserving public funds than in supplying the needy. He resigned effective September 15, 1931, and was succeeded by his chief critic, Alderman Melchior U. S. Kjorlaug, who, unlike Tattersfield, was trained in social work.[5]

The shift of superintendents marked the beginning of a decade-long effort to achieve greater efficiency and effectiveness in processing relief applications. Kjorlaug undertook department reorganization and promoted the adoption of professional casework techniques. Several trained social workers were added to the staff. Also, the intake department took steps to insure at least a measure of privacy during its interviews.[6]

The combined efforts of public and private welfare agencies helped Minneapolis to emerge from the winter of 1931–32 in better condition than many other cities. However, local resources were nearing depletion. Social workers warned that larger expenditures would be needed for the coming year. The arrival of spring failed to decrease unemployment. Families who had already skimped along at a minimum level of subsistence were, in increasing numbers, forced to make their first application for relief. While most private relief-giving agencies had nearly doubled their budgets over the previous year, they could not begin to keep up with demands. In the face of mounting tax delinquencies and persistent agitation by taxpayers' associations for reduced government spending, municipalities had to spend more and more for relief. In 1932 Minneapolis issued over two million dollars in bonds for direct relief alone. The year 1932 also proved to be the last in which private agencies shared any important part of the cost of unemployment relief. The Family Welfare Association of Minneapolis in that year was allocated over $600,000 from the Community Chest, most of which went to aiding jobless families. In 1933 this sum dropped below $500,000 and kept on dropping thereafter to a low of $200,000 in 1938.[7]

Left-wing dissidents intensified their activities in 1932, further compounding the tense relief situation. By summer large numbers of the unemployed were appearing at City Hall, invading council meetings and heckling aldermen whose proposals dissatisfied them, particularly those who suggested a work relief program. Objecting vigorously to any work arrangement, they favored direct relief only, and that preferably in cash. Late in June, when the relief division was faced with an imminent shutdown owing to the inability of the board of estimate and taxation to sell relief bonds at less than the prevailing interest rate, the *Minneapolis Journal* ran an editorial condemning relief division policies which, it said, had led to its current plight. "Beneficiaries now boo and jeer backers of the groceries-for-work system because they were encouraged for many months to believe that the groceries were rightly theirs without any adequate return in labor." Inevitably, the editorial went on to cite instances of "sponging" in which several heads of families were found to have some means of support other than direct relief. The *Journal* misplaced the blame, however, since the relief policies were established by the board of public welfare, not the division of relief. Ultimately, the policies of the board were controlled by the city council, which determined the amount of money to be spent and in what manner it should be granted.[8]

The summer relief crisis reached a peak on July 8, 1932, when approximately seven hundred "hunger marchers" demonstrated again in front of City Hall. They demanded a five-million-dollar appropriation for city relief, an eight-dollar-a-week grant to unemployed workers, and a slum clearance program. Invading the city council chambers, the demonstrators listened to two Farmer-Labor aldermen protest Mayor Anderson's reappointment of one of the conservative members of the board of public welfare—Mrs. H. S. Godfrey—to another four-year term. One of the aldermen, Albert G. Bastis, was a vitriolic politician who contributed considerably to the relief turmoil for the next few years. Bastis declared that the mayor's appointee did not understand the relief problem and that the welfare board was obsolete. He also accused private agencies of making money on the transients, since these agencies charged the city for the price of meals given to homeless men seeking aid. Bastis created a sensational disturbance several weeks later at another council meeting when he brought in a sack of stale bread and other food in various stages of decomposition, saying it had been given to a woman by the relief department. When Alderman Frank H. Brown ventured to challenge Bastis, his remarks were "met by catcalls and imprecations from the rear of the room . . . . 'That is exactly what we get,' 'eat it yourself and see,' and other such cries were heard above the din." Such skirmishes turned out to be the preliminary events of a battle that would continue for a number of years as the Farmer-Labor party increased its membership, both on the council and on the board of public welfare.[9]

In retrospect, 1932 was no doubt the year of discontent. The state and national governments had refused to act. Left-wing agitators were active everywhere. Social workers had long since abandoned the belief that local relief agencies could handle the crisis. Consequently, relief operations in Minneapolis throughout the winter of 1932–33 continued on the precarious pay-as-you-go system. When the situation grew drastic, the relief department threatened to close down, forcing the city council to issue bonds to provide relief for one more month. Relief rolls increased sharply in November with the arrival of bitterly cold weather. Union City Mission reported that it was serving 1,800 homeless men daily. The Community Fund drive fell short of its goal, and a resoliciting campaign had to be initiated to meet its budget. Meanwhile, several studies of city relief operations were being conducted. One report presented to the council recommended the division of the city into four relief districts and a complete reorganization of the relief department. Another study prepared by a committee which included University of Minnesota sociologist F. Stuart Chapin indicated that the relief department was inadequately staffed and placed the blame on the lack of leadership exerted by the board of public welfare. This report pointed out that in September the fifteen investigators each averaged 311 visits, and then they reached only 4,662 cases out of a total of 8,611 families on the relief roll. Professional social workers insisted that 150 visits per month should be the maximum for adequate service. While this recommendation was heeded and the staff increased, the proportionate rise in family cases (to over 13,000 by March, 1933) cancelled out any decrease in the number of visits assigned to each investigator.[10]

The Minneapolis mayoralty campaign in May, 1933, centered almost entirely on the relief issue. Incumbent Mayor Anderson lost the support of his own local Farmer-Labor Association, which contended that he had failed to improve relief standards. The Farmer-Laborites backed Thomas E. Latimer, who had served as an attorney for one of the local organizations of unemployed. Conservatives backed Alexander G. ("Buzz") Bainbridge, a local theater manager and director of a stock company known as the Bainbridge Players. Anderson and Bainbridge survived the primary, while the Communist candidate, Morris ("Red") Karson, for all his popularity among the unemployed groups, polled only 978 votes. Following the primaries, Bainbridge stridently attacked the failure of the board of public welfare to carry out a large work relief program. He advocated a compulsory work program and a complete reorganization of the relief department. Anderson, who tried to steer a middle course between Bainbridge's position and the radical demands of the Farmer-Laborites, was defeated easily by 10,000 votes in June. Thus, while the remainder of the country had swung to the political left in the 1932 elections, seven months later Minneapolis elected a conservative mayor.[11]

Bainbridge erased all doubts about his intentions when, a month after his election, he presented his reorganization plan. Under the guise of economy, he proposed that the relief department's entire investigative staff of fifty-seven social workers be abolished. Bainbridge argued that the police department could better handle investigations. Trained social workers, he declared, were not required in public welfare administration. Bainbridge also contended that Minneapolis had become a haven for "floaters from all over the country" and that the relief department's paternalistic policies toward unemployed transients cost the city an unwarranted thirty cents a day for each case. The new mayor proposed that all aid to nonresident transients be stopped by October 1. A majority of both the board of public welfare and the relief department resolutely objected to Bainbridge's scheme, and the investigative procedure remained intact. The squabble, however, opened up a split between Superintendent Kjorlaug and the mayor, who presided over the board. The feud flared publicly in September when Kjorlaug charged that the relief department had become a "political football" because of Bainbridge's irresponsible charges. Kjorlaug called for a public investigation of his department to clear its name. The mayor responded by demanding Kjorlaug's resignation on the grounds that the superintendent was "temperamentally unfitted for the position."[12]

The dispute was augmented when several workers in the department informed the mayor of procedures they considered unsatisfactory. One social worker, Mrs. Blanche B. van Poll, even congratulated Bainbridge on his election victory. This proved too much for Kjorlaug, who suspended her for ninety days. Throughout the controversy, Kjorlaug could count on support from a large majority of his staff, the board of public welfare, and several prominent civic organizations and church leaders. Eventually Bainbridge retreated from his adamant demands. By winter, 1933, the development of the National Recovery Administration and the creation of the Civil Works Administration had diverted newspaper headlines away from the mayor's scrimmage with the relief department.[13]

The burst of publicity over the relief situation (it made front-page news throughout most of July, August, and September) had both good and bad effects. On the positive side it made many private citizens and most public officials aware of the difficult problems faced by the relief department. For all of Bainbridge's fulminations against relief policies, his battle with Kjorlaug served to educate the mayor on matters he knew little about. By 1934 the fuss simmered down, and Bainbridge took a more moderate position on relief policy. The dispute also produced careful and more reliable checks on outside income of clients, a classification of transients, and an improved rent policy.

The rent issue provided one of the major causes of the periodic "invasions" of the relief offices by client organizations which protested the eviction notices renters all too often received.[14] With the advent of the federal relief programs (Minneapolis received its first shipment of surplus commodities in October, 1933), unemployment demonstrations decreased. Left-wing agitators could not stir up as much sympathy for their marches when stomachs were filled. In addition, a number of civic associations and religious groups became more interested in relief conditions. Such "awareness" served to form at least a measure of public support for the relief department.

The unfortunate aspect of the debate was the continued exploitation of the relief question by city politicians—both liberal and conservative. Ultimately, it was the relief client who suffered. There was little doubt even in the most "liberal" of minds that a small percentage of the clients constituted a "professional relief class" that schemed and contrived to get a living out of relief without any effort to seek work. These usually formed the nucleus of groups which demonstrated at City Hall, where left-wing agitators could count on them for support. By far the largest number of cases, however, were heads of families who would have preferred work could they have found it and who applied for relief only as a last resort against starvation. This group seldom made newspaper headlines.

The rapid expansion of the relief load from 1931 to 1935 was reflected in the size of the department itself. Its 1930 staff of seven had grown to more than 350 by the close of 1935. The average monthly case load was around two thousand during the winter of 1930–31; by December, 1934, it was over 21,000. In the meantime a detailed system of investigative procedures and a comprehensive set of written personnel qualifications had been established. This process of reorganization was accomplished by Kjorlaug, who labored long and hard to bring order and efficiency into his administration.[15]

The year 1935 saw the program involved in another political crisis. Certain politicians—especially those with a large number of needy constituents—had long exerted pressure on relief officials to place their "boys" on the relief rolls. This pressure increased in 1934 after the outbreak of the sensational and violent truck strike, with many of the pickets demanding and getting public relief.[16]

The mayoralty campaign in the spring of 1935, like the one in 1933, was fought primarily on the relief issue. Farmer-Laborites again backed Thomas E. Latimer. While calling for substantial increases in relief allowances, they also demanded the dismissal of Kjorlaug. Incumbent Mayor Bainbridge campaigned mainly for economy—an unpopular issue—and he was ousted in the primary. Enough relief clients and jobless voters turned out at the polls early in June to elect Latimer over Charles F. Keyes. The election also gave liberals and Farmer-Laborites a majority on the city council, leading to a change in the composition of the board of public welfare. Two Farmer-Labor councilmen,

Edwin I. Hudson and I. G. Scott, replaced board members who had lost their council seats. The third councilman on the board was its vice-chairman, William J. McGaughren, chairman of the Hennepin County Farmer-Labor Association, who, paradoxically, was considered a conservative in matters of relief. The lay members included local businessman I. S. Joseph, the only other conservative on the board, and two labor-backed members, Dr. Albert G. Herbolsheimer and Selma Seestrom, a member of the executive board of the Hennepin County Farmer-Labor Women's Federation. Mrs. Seestrom replaced Mrs. H. S. Godfrey, a long-time board member who resigned in August because (so she said) she was threatened with violence by relief clients for her opposition to increases in allowances.[17]

After the election the organizations of unemployed redoubled their efforts to insure that Farmer-Labor campaign promises would be carried out. One factor that undoubtedly contributed to the increased agitation for more relief was the sharp cutbacks in funds made by the Federal Emergency Relief Administration (FERA) during the spring and summer of 1935. Often clients eligible for work relief experienced a considerable delay in receiving assistance. They were not always put on direct relief immediately, and the Works Progress Administration (WPA) did not get under way as quickly as anticipated. The liquidation of the FERA took place by successive steps from month to month. The largest cut in the work program came in August. Many former work relief clients were thrust on the direct relief rolls, placing an unexpected burden on the city.

The Farmer-Labor controlled board of public welfare assumed power on July 1, 1935. Two weeks later it publicized its program, calling for an increase of up to 130 per cent in family relief grants and a doubling of annual relief expenditures by the city council. Board member Joseph predicted that the plan would bankrupt the city in four months.[18] Early in August, however, the majority voted for increases in relief allowances averaging approximately 35 per cent.

Meanwhile, Mayor Latimer frantically held meetings with state relief officials. Along with representatives from St. Paul and Duluth, he asked the state executive council for more funds. The request was denied. Then Latimer asked the State Emergency Relief Administration (SERA) to allocate more money to Minneapolis. Again, help was denied. Moreover, federal and state relief officials threatened immediate withdrawal of financial support unless the board of public welfare rescinded its increased relief schedule. During this time city relief officials saw their funds rapidly dwindling away. The situation finally reached a crisis late in August when the city comptroller stopped honoring all relief orders because the allocated funds were gone. This placed Farmer-Labor officials in an exceedingly awkward position. They had, at the insistence of their constituents, increased relief allowances; yet because of that very policy their followers faced the possibility of receiving nothing. The board had no choice, so it rescinded the higher allowances on August 28. By this time several new WPA projects had taken some of the clients off the direct relief rolls.[19]

The August events were only preliminary skirmishes for the major battle yet to come. For some time city officials had been criticizing the SERA policy of allocating proportionately more funds to the rural counties than to the urban areas. During the summer of 1935 the SERA made a vigorous attempt to force the rural counties to furnish more money—an effort that resulted in the withdrawal of eighteen southern counties from the SERA. With funds from the FERA rapidly decreasing, the SERA found it more and more difficult to keep pace with the increasing demands from city relief officials for assistance.

The majority on the board of public welfare, spurred by Hudson and Scott, now tried a new tactic. In a concerted effort to gain control over the distribution of all relief funds, including state and federal, the board in October denied desk space in the central relief office to SERA's official representative, Edna Dumaresq. Miss Dumaresq's responsibility was to see that city officials did not misappropriate federal and state funds. Hudson and Scott charged that the SERA social service director, Benjamin E. Youngdahl, was trying to run the board. Youngdahl responded by intimating that the SERA would hold up its monthly allocation to Minneapolis if Miss Dumaresq were not immediately reinstated. The dispute brought out into the open the long-simmering conflict between the right and left wings of the Farmer-Labor party. Latimer publicly favored Youngdahl's position—as did the two conservatives on the board, McGaughren and Joseph. Paradoxically, Youngdahl believed in strong central control—the very thing that the conservatives had always objected to in federal programs. To the conservatives, however, the greater evil at the moment was the blatant attempt of local politicians to gain control of city relief funds.[20]

This direct confrontation of federal versus local authority was further complicated by an announcement from Washington that all federal relief aid to the states would cease on November 15. Since the WPA could not employ all of those eligible for work relief, the city council now had to appropriate even larger sums for direct relief. While the welfare board stumped hard for the sale of additional relief bonds, the city council remained obstinate. Council conservatives, weary of the antics of the board and of Hudson and Scott in particular, now saw their chance for revenge. During the 1930s the city council numbered twenty-six aldermen, two from each ward. Only eleven were conservative in 1935, but they could block a bond issue as it required eighteen votes to pass. Consequently, the conservatives declared they would not vote for the sale of any more relief bonds until the council majority (a coalition of Farmer-Laborites and liberals) removed Hudson and Scott from the board

326 | *Politics and Relief in Minneapolis During the 1930s*

of public welfare. There the matter stood—deadlocked—with the conservatives holding the trump card, since relief bonds would have to be issued eventually.[21]

Meanwhile, Youngdahl engaged in a power play of his own. In the spring of 1935 the SERA, following federal instructions to get more local financial participation, had made an agreement with the welfare board. The substance of it was that the state agency would pay direct relief costs for 1935 above the sum of $1,719,000, which the city board agreed to appropriate. When the dispute erupted in October, Youngdahl, after a preliminary investigation, decided that Minneapolis had not lived up to its contract. When the board increased its individual relief grants in August, it spent more than the original agreement had called for. Beyond that, the board had spent over $75,000 for items the SERA did not consider direct relief, such as mothers' pensions, burials, and housing for homeless men. Youngdahl thus refused to release any more funds to the welfare board. This prompted Hudson to retort: "If Youngdahl is running this board and the relief department, we ought to know it right now." On Monday morning, November 18, the Minneapolis relief department did not open its doors. Hudson and Scott were now trapped; their ward constituents could receive no relief funds. After a hasty conference between the antagonists, the board agreed to reinstate Miss Dumaresq, after which the SERA released $250,000 to the board.[22]

City funds, however, were still being held up by the council conservatives. On November 20 the majority liberal bloc attempted to transfer appropriations from the council's permanent revolving fund to the relief department, but City Attorney Richard S. Wiggin (a Farmer-Laborite) overruled this action. He said it was contrary to the city charter. The next day Kjorlaug cut direct relief to food and fuel items only, giving nothing for rent, clothes, or electricity. The board was now confronted with the effects of its own folly. While claiming to represent the interests of relief clients, Hudson and Scott had succeeded in reducing the already inadequate grants to the barest minimum, leading to even more suffering for the recipients. The financial crisis eased somewhat when state Attorney General Harry H. Peterson (Farmer-Laborite) overruled Wiggin and allowed the council to "borrow" money from its revolving fund. This action automatically released additional SERA funds which were still being withheld pending the issuance of relief bonds by the city council. Although Peterson admitted his ruling was contrary to the city charter, he said that provision for the poor was paramount and overrode all other legal considerations. In December the bond question finally was resolved when five liberal aldermen joined the conservatives and ousted Scott and Hudson from the welfare board. The conservatives then quickly voted the necessary relief funds.[23]

The turmoil, however, did not cease. One of the Farmer-Labor campaign slogans during the 1935 mayoralty race had been, "Kjorlaug must go." The basic reason for this demand lay beneath the surface of customary political oratory; it struck at the very nature of social work itself. Although a competent and not unsympathetic administrator, Kjorlaug was a dedicated practitioner of the case-work method developed by Mary E. Richmond, whose emphasis on "adjusting the individual to his environment" had prevailed in social work during the 1920s.[24] After 1929 it became ludicrous to ask a relief client to adjust to an environment that had collapsed about him. Clients objected to the case-work approach. They wanted neither to be "adjusted" nor to be psychoanalyzed; all they wanted was their relief order. They got support from relief investigators, also called "visitors," who by 1935 numbered over a hundred. Most of them belonged to the Minneapolis Social Workers' Council, local branch of the national rank-and-file movement and essentially a trade union for bettering the lot of relief workers who labored long hours with large case loads for low salaries.[25]

Many Minneapolis rank-and-file visitors publicly opposed Kjorlaug's case-work policies. In response to their objections, the welfare board in August, 1935, appointed five special investigators (themselves members of the staff) to examine relief department activities. Apparently the Social Workers' Council was experiencing its own internal power struggle as left-wing relief visitors tried to gain control of the leadership. According to one report, when the "complaint committee" initiated its investigations, "panic and fear began creeping among the staff. In investigating the investigators it was meeting in semi-secret sessions with a few of the least responsible members of the S.W.C. Rumors, veiled threats, promises of better jobs, spying, intimidation served to disrupt morale." The complaint committee made its first report to the welfare board on November 16 at the height of the SERA controversy. Most of the 1,500 client complaints studied, the committee said, were caused by lack of prompt service, but many clients took strong exception to the case-work method of investigation. This report was one reason why the welfare board suspended Kjorlaug on December 4 for ninety days to "discipline" him for policies it said were creating turmoil within the relief staff. The board also recommended immediate reorganization of the relief department. Board conservatives Joseph and McGaughren opposed the suspension, as did practically all of the city's private social agencies. Kjorlaug himself refused to resign. At first the board tried unsuccessfully to return Richard Tattersfield to his old post and then appointed Norma Fodness, a former president of the Social Workers' Council, as acting relief superintendent. She, however, was not acceptable to the council.[26]

Beset by pressure from all sides, Mayor Latimer organized a citizens' committee of fifty prominent civic and labor leaders to investigate all city relief operations. Labor representatives soon split off to form their own investigating committee in conjunction with organizations of unemployed. Among other things, the labor committee recommended the "new system," recently installed by the welfare board in the north and northeast districts, which operated on the premise that granting of relief was primarily a financial transaction. It did not humiliate the client by prying into his personal life.[27]

Meanwhile, increasingly irritated over the state of affairs, SERA Administrator L. P. Zimmerman issued an ultimatum that Minneapolis would receive no additional funds unless all personnel changes in the relief department were submitted to the SERA for approval. Zimmerman also insisted that relief costs be reduced and that the administration of relief be purged of politics. But Mrs. Fodness, unmoved by SERA threats, said she would continue to make personnel changes. She proposed elimination of fifty-five investigators and twenty-one clerks and recommended salary increases of $70 a month for some of the remaining workers. This ignited a violent demonstration by rank-and-file workers whose spokesman declared that the situation had become intolerable with such "snooping and sniping all the time." The board responded by halting staff reductions, removing Mrs. Fodness, and appointing a moderate Farmer-Laborite, Alderman Ole A. Pearson, relief superintendent. Although Joseph held out for Kjorlaug's reinstatement, most of the board felt the internal conflict within the relief department had become so vicious that he must leave. Kjorlaug finally gave up his battle and resigned late in February, 1936.[28]

After Pearson's appointment the staff hoped for a breathing spell in the ferment over relief that had been making headlines since the summer before. But in April, 1936, the administration of relief again appeared in news stories that revealed what many citizens had long suspected.

Throughout the battle between relief workers, politicians, and the welfare board, the city attorney's office had been conducting its own investigation into relief operations. By April, Joseph A. Hadley, assistant city attorney, had uncovered enough evidence to bring charges against several relief department employees and clients for defrauding the city. Five investigators had posed as "clients," filling out orders to themselves and presenting the orders to merchants. Some transient clients were found to have sold books of meal tickets (given to them by the relief department) for "dehorn" liquor. In addition, nearly two dozen cases of irregularities were uncovered among merchants who handled relief orders.[29]

Pearson, determined that all cases of fraud be disclosed, backed the investigations. He himself ordered the relief department onto a five-day week after it became apparent that some clients who had obtained work still remained on the rolls and were coming to the department on Saturday to obtain relief orders. Pearson subsequently reorganized the payroll investigation division in order to examine as many city payrolls as possible to ferret out those relief clients who had acquired jobs. The investigations resulted in the sentencing of two clients, two merchants, and one relief employee to a year in the workhouse. Furthermore, a number of merchants had their licenses revoked, and several investigators resigned. The episode served to increase public criticism of the entire relief program.[30]

Pearson intensified his drive for administrative efficiency throughout the summer of 1936. In July the welfare board ordered a reregistration of all clients on the rolls. This became necessary for two reasons: it was found that clients on WPA jobs had represented themselves as "artisans" (thus making them eligible for higher wages) when they were actually unskilled workers; and the old age assistance program (OAA) recently had been launched, providing help to many former direct relief clients. The procedure for reregistration, which applied a strict means test to close relatives, also required that the applicant take an oath and sign an affidavit that his resources, if any, were correctly represented. This precipitated a great outcry from clients—so much so that Attorney General Harry H. Peterson intervened to rule that the oath was not a part of the relief law and could not be enforced legally. During 1936 the Workers Alliance had emerged as the major organization representing the unemployed. Its leaders appeared at meeting after meeting of the welfare board during the fall of that year to insist upon a higher food allowance to counter fluctuations in food prices. Their persistence eventually brought a small victory; in December the board voted a 10 per cent increase in the amount allotted for groceries.[31]

By 1937 internal relief department conflicts ebbed as Pearson worked hard to bring order and stability to his administration. Outside forces, however, were again at work. Communist control over the left-wing elements in the Hennepin County Farmer-Labor Association was evidenced when Mayor Latimer failed to gain his party's endorsement for the 1937 election. The previous year Latimer had charged publicly that Communists were infiltrating Farmer-Labor ranks, particularly in Hennepin County. Left-wingers responded to Latimer's charge with the demand that he be "thrown out of the Farmer-Labor party." The quarrel intensified during the summer of 1936 when the mayor tried unsuccessfully to remove Selma Seestrom, a left-wing favorite, from the board of public welfare. He thus identified himself with the right-wing Farmer-Laborites and in doing so lost considerable support from the unemployed groups. As a result of this turmoil the Farmer-Laborites gave their endorsement to Kenneth C. Haycraft, state director of old age assistance. Conservatives supported George E. Leach, who had been mayor of Minneapolis four times during the 1920s. The squabbling within the ranks of labor and the Farmer-Labor party took its toll on election day; Haycraft was soundly beaten by Leach. Farmer-Laborites did gain some satisfaction from the aldermanic races; the progressive bloc managed to retain control of the city council.[32]

By the spring of 1937 the national economy had shown enough improvement so that President Franklin D. Roosevelt ordered a sharp cut in WPA rolls. The slash had hardly been made when an acute recession sent the economy downward during the late summer and fall. The recession, coupled with the WPA cuts, thrust a host of families and individuals back onto the direct relief rolls. These events coincided with the return of Leach to the mayor's office. City officials, civic groups, and even moderate Farmer-Laborites such as McGaughren of the welfare board voiced fears about the eventual effects of the high cost of relief. Since Minnesota's recent laws covering old age assistance and aid to dependent children required considerable financial participation from local political units, city relief costs were rising to new heights in 1937.[33]

Efforts were made to lower the city's direct relief load, which continued to average between 12,000 and 15,000 monthly throughout 1937 despite the advent of the old age assistance program. Mayor Leach, pressured by civic groups that had supported him during the election, decided to inaugurate his own drive to reduce the relief rolls. He was supported by McGaughren, who suggested that clients should not own automobiles, telephones, and other such luxuries. Area farmers complained bitterly that the WPA had drastically reduced the available number of harvest workers, and McGaughren felt that all able-bodied single men on relief in Minneapolis should be forced to take jobs in harvest fields or be automatically cut off the direct relief rolls. Leach opened his drive by urging all civic organizations to find jobs for employable relief clients. He requested that at least one be hired in each of the thousand or more manufacturing establishments in Minneapolis. While it was a commendable idea and highly praised by the Civic and Commerce Association, only a handful of businesses hired relief clients. Leach also requested all the case records so that he could go through them and personally investigate any doubtful ones. As far as economy-minded citizens were concerned, this was another praiseworthy idea. The mayor learned, however, that case records were confidential; even he did not have access to them.[34]

The welfare board itself initiated economy steps. Since November, 1936, the board had allowed a monthly supplement of nine dollars to WPA workers. Originally, this supplement covered only fuel, but it was continued through the summer of 1937 as a food supplement, since WPA employees received equal pay (within each of its classifications) regardless of the number of dependents in each family. Early in August, however, the welfare board discontinued giving supplementary assistance to WPA workers. This action brought immediate protests from the Workers Alliance and the Federal Workers Section of General Drivers Union 544, which threatened to lead a general march of WPA workers off their projects and onto the direct relief rolls unless the supplement was restored. The board not only stood firm on its decision but went even further. In September I. S. Joseph, board finance chairman, warned that relief spending must be cut immediately or Minneapolis would suffer a possible taxpayers' strike and almost certain financial ruin. Joseph's report prompted the board to enact a series of policy changes, the most stringent being the removal of all healthy single men under forty-five and all healthy single women under thirty-five from the relief rolls until December when they would then have to reapply for aid. Other new regulations included: the adoption of a clothing-according-to-need policy, replacing the old set clothing budget allowance; insistence on contributions from all employed unmarried children in relief households; removal of automobile owners from the rolls except in emergency cases; and refusal of relief to any client who was able to obtain credit.[35]

These policy changes were brought about by a number of factors. The turmoil within the relief department itself, the lenient attitude toward clients by many relief investigators, the complex of programs which led to considerable case duplication, client reluctance to take jobs (often in fear that wages would be garnished to pay debts)—all these produced a ground swell of public resentment against certain aspects of the mass relief programs. Many still harbored traditional beliefs about relief, feeling that it should be made as difficult as possible to get and that any allowance should cover only the barest of need. Hard-pressed taxpayers resented the use of relief funds to support such "luxuries" as radios, automobiles, telephones, or even a good suit of clothes. In addition, the influence of left-wingers among the organizations of unemployed (which exacted as much as twenty-five cents per month from relief client members) became increasingly distasteful to even those who were moderately liberal. McGaughren charged that "direct relief in Minneapolis has become a racket," that the leaders of relief organizations were attempting to build direct relief into a permanent activity, and that these groups actually tried to prevent clients from performing any work. No doubt most of the criticisms against relief clients were justified to some degree, but they applied only to a small percentage of the total case load. There were still thousands of individuals and families suffering great deprivation not of their own choosing. The simple fact remained that those desperately in need of economic assistance could not get jobs of any kind.[36]

The new regulations served only to increase agitation by organizations of unemployed. Five days after the restrictions became effective, representatives of the Workers Alliance and the Federal Workers Section of Local 544 held a stormy session with the welfare board in which they vigorously protested the new policies. The meeting ended with a promise by Leach that no needy person would be denied relief. Leach also agreed to ask state WPA Director Victor A. Christgau to increase WPA employment, although he knew very well that Christgau could do nothing because all state monthly quotas were determined solely in Washington. Relief Administrator Zimmerman, however, partially sided with the relief clients and threatened to withhold state funds unless the board of public welfare dropped its harsh policy against single men and women.[37]

In the face of the deepening recession and the WPA's refusal to increase its monthly quotas, organizations of unemployed increased their agitation. They were backed by the tacit approval of Governor Elmer A. Benson and his aides. In October, 1937, WPA workers on Minneapolis projects threatened to strike unless the welfare board revoked its new regulations. Late in October the board did rescind the order barring single men under forty-five and single women under thirty-five from direct relief and the order prohibiting clients from owning automobiles. The problem of supplementary aid to WPA workers with large families still remained, however. WPA employees continued to protest by threatening strikes and insisting upon additional support. In December the welfare board voted to supplement WPA wages for needy families up to 25 per cent if necessary. Thus, if a WPA worker with a large number of dependents received a "security wage" of $55 (the maximum wage for an unskilled worker at the time), he could receive an additional sum of nearly $14 from the city relief department.[38]

Through the winter of 1937–38 the recession continued, causing the highest direct relief load in Minneapolis history. There was a peak of 17,654 relief cases in March. By this time President Roosevelt had requested and received increased appropriations for the WPA. Throughout 1938, as WPA quotas for each state rose, the direct relief load declined. How to finance direct relief remained a vexing problem. Aid from the state relief administration was limited to the appropriations passed by the 1937 legislature. The president of the Minneapolis board of estimate and taxation proposed that the Minnesota income tax be increased so that the state could allocate additional sums to the urban areas. The Hennepin County grand jury, conducting its own study of relief costs, suggested a halt to the issuing of bonds and proposed that relief be financed instead by a city sales tax, thus backing Leach's demand. Farmer-Laborite Alderman Harold Kauth proposed that relief funds be raised by a public lottery. This brought an avalanche of criticism from churches, civic leaders, and conservative politicians. In the end, the city council reverted to form. It continued selling relief bonds.[39]

Under the leadership of Pearson, who remained superintendent throughout the 1940s, the relief department gradually worked its way toward a stabilized and effective administration. It was aided immeasurably by the development of a permanent federal program. Also of assistance was a department survey requested early in 1938 by the welfare board and conducted by the American Public Welfare Association (APWA). Among other things, the APWA study concluded that the relief granted was adequate but that the staff lacked knowledge of modern case-work techniques. "Many cases showed an inability to evaluate the situation from any viewpoint other than relief eligibility," the report said. It contended that visitors ought to aid clients in "problem-solving." The study also criticized a lack of co-operation with other agencies as well as the excessive paper work necessitated by the setup of four district intake offices. The welfare board welcomed most of the association's suggestions and gave Pearson authority to pursue reorganization as he deemed necessary. One result was a trend toward employing professional social workers and developing higher minimum qualifications for visitors.[40]

The history of the Minneapolis relief department through the 1930s reveals the consequences of political intrigue in the development of a public relief program. The constant turmoil over the giving of assistance was enhanced by several factors present in the city's relief environment. Obviously, one factor was the general economic condition. Another was the influence of the Farmer-Labor Party on the board of public welfare and in the city council. Organizations comprised of discontented relief clients and led by left-wing agitators exerted considerable pressure on the local Farmer-Labor party, and extreme left-wing members of the Hennepin County Farmer-Labor Women's Federation also became active in relief politics. A third factor contributing to the turmoil in relief administration was the "pay-as-you-go" system of financing. Relief bonds were issued irregularly by the city council on the basis of how much was needed for the next few months. Other unsettling ingredients were the uncertainty about the extent and duration of federal relief programs and the continual debate within the relief division between rank-and-file workers on one side and the more conservative supervisors on the other.

No one could have divined beforehand the extensive changes that developed during the 1930s. Most significant was the federal government's acceptance of responsibility for meeting the economic needs of distressed Americans. One historian has correctly noted that "the New Deal solved a few problems, ameliorated a few more, obscured many, and created new ones. This is about all our political system can generate, even in crisis."[41] Despite this pessimistic observation, relief programs did bring a measure of sustenance and order into the lives of thousands of Minneapolis residents. By keeping people alive, the New Deal and the Minneapolis relief department unquestionably achieved their most important and immediate goal.

■ ■ ■ ■ Notes

1 *Minneapolis Journal,* October 19, sec. 2, p. 2, 15, October 20, p. 15, 1930; Alvin H. Hansen, Nelle M. Petrowski, and Richard A. Graves, *An Analysis of Three Unemployment Surveys in Minneapolis, St. Paul, and Duluth,* 5–7 (University of Minnesota, Employment Stabilization Research Institute, *Bulletins,* vol. 1, No. 6—August, 1932).

2 Several such groups were active in Minneapolis. The major ones were the United Relief Workers Association, the Unemployed Council, the Workers Alliance (which subsequently absorbed the first two), and the Federal Workers Section of Minneapolis Teamsters Local 574 (in the later 1930s, 544), which after 1935 expanded to include not only the unemployed but also direct relief clients and WPA workers. An excellent brief statement on organizations of unemployed in general is Helen Seymour, *When Clients Organize* (American Public Welfare Association, Chicago, 1937).

3 A copy of the circular is in the unemployment file, Olson Papers, 1931, Governors' Archives, in the Minnesota State Archives. For a description of the Trade Union Unity League, see Irving Howe and Lewis Coser, *The American Communist Party: A Critical History,* 255 (New York, 1962). For background on the Minnesota political scene during the 1930s, see Arthur Naftalin, "A History of the Farmer-Labor Party in Minnesota," unpublished doctoral dissertation, University of Minnesota,

1948 (copy in the Minnesota Historical Society), and George H. Mayer, *The Political Career of Floyd B. Olson* (Minneapolis, 1951). *Minneapolis Journal,* March 3, 1931, p. 1 describes the Gateway riot. Unless otherwise noted, all newspaper citations in this article occur on front pages.

4 For information about the administrative structure of the relief department, see Florence W. Hutsinpillar and Clara Paul Paige, *Report of the Division of Relief of the Department of Public Welfare, Minneapolis,* June, 1931, issued in mimeographed form by the United States Department of Labor, Children's Bureau; and Division of Public Relief, *Historical Review: Four Years of Depression 1931–1934,* a mimeographed report prepared for the Minneapolis board of public welfare.

5 *Minneapolis Journal,* July 23, p. 17, September 4, 1931.

6 Under Tattersfield, applications for assistance were taken over the counter in full view and hearing of others in the cramped quarters. Tattersfield would scribble "Same old bum," "Chronic indigents," and other comments on case records. See Hutsinpillar and Paige, 56.

7 Division of Public Relief, *Historical Review,* 7; Family Welfare Association, *Agency Report,* vol. 18 of *Community Survey of Social and Health Work in Minneapolis,* appendix 1, table 1 (Minneapolis Council of Social Agencies, 1938).

8 *Minneapolis Journal,* June 27, 1932, p. 18. By 1932 many professional social workers, public and private, favored some type of work relief program.

9 *Minneapolis Journal,* July 8, p. 1, 8, July 22 (quotations), 1932.

10 *Minneapolis Journal,* November 25, December 7, p. 1, 26, 1932; Division of Public Relief, *Historical Review,* 6.

11 *Minneapolis Journal,* May 9, June 13, June 14, p. 1, 6, 1933. Another factor in Bainbridge's election was that he was a "wet," while Anderson had earlier vetoed a beer ordinance for Minneapolis.

12 *Minneapolis Journal,* July 18, September 9, 1933.

13 *Minneapolis Journal,* September 12, 1933. For background on the NRA and the CWA, see William E. Leuchtenburg, *Franklin D. Roosevelt and the New Deal, 1932–1940,* 64–66, 121 (New York, 1963).

14 Division of Public Relief, *Historical Review,* 22–25.

15 Harry Fiterman, "Relief Shown City's Greatest Problem," in *Minneapolis Journal,* April 20, 1936; Division of Public Relief, *Historical Review,* 6.

16 The strike is dealt with at length in Charles R. Walker, *An American City: A Rank-and-File History* (New York, 1937).

17 *Minneapolis Journal,* June 11, August 7, 1935.

18 *Minneapolis Journal,* July 16, 1935.

19 *Minneapolis Journal,* August 13, 16, p. 1, 28, August 28, 1935. The state executive council was composed of the governor, attorney general, auditor, treasurer, and secretary of state.

20 *Minneapolis Journal,* October 23, 1935, p. 16.

21 *Minneapolis Journal,* November 1, 8, p. 1, 28, 1935.

22 *Minneapolis Journal,* November 14, 17, p. 1, 2 (quotation), November 18, 1935.

23 *Minneapolis Journal,* November 20, 21, 25, December 20, 1935.

24 See Clarke A. Chambers, *Seedtime of Reform: American Social Service and Social Action, 1918–1933,* 97–99 (Minneapolis, 1963).

25 For general interpretations, see Jacob Fisher, *The Rank and File Movement in Social Work, 1931–1936* (New York School of Social Work, New York, 1936).

26 The quotation is from "Shake-up in Minneapolis," in *Social Work Today,* 3:19 (March, 1936). The editors of this decidedly left-wing national organ of the rank-and-file movement attributed the article to "a committee for four members of the Social Workers Council." *Minneapolis Journal,* November 16, December 4, 7, 1935.

27 *Minneapolis Journal,* December 19, 1935; January 7, p. 1, 6, 1936.

28 *Minneapolis Journal,* December 19, 1935; January 14, p. 1, 2 (quotation), February 13, p. 15, February 25, March 10, 13, p. 21, 1936. The welfare board obligingly gave Kjorlaug a clean bill of health on his administration record and praised him for his honesty. For a brief resumé of the battle leading to Kjorlaug's departure, see "Storm Over Minneapolis," in *Survey,* 72:44 (February, 1936). This was reprinted, with a few changes, in *Minneapolis Journal,* February 14, p. 6, 1936.

29 For major accounts, see *Minneapolis Journal,* April 2, 3, 4, 5, 6, 7, 10, 11, 14, 15, 1936. About four hundred merchants were licensed to do business with relief clients on the basis that they give only those articles that were specified in the order. Some were found to have given items other than those specified.

30 *Minneapolis Journal,* May 5, 1936.

31 *Minneapolis Journal,* July 28, September 14, December 1, p. 1, 6, 1936.

32 *Minneapolis Journal,* March 9, p. 6 (quotation), 13, June 28, July 31, p. 15, 1936; June 15, 1937.

33 Leuchtenburg, *Franklin D. Roosevelt,* 243; Minneapolis Council of Social Agencies, *Community Survey of Social and Health Work in Minneapolis,* vol. 1, sec. 5, p. 3 (Summary Report, 1938).

34 *Minneapolis Journal,* July 21, 28, 29, 1937. Leach also advocated a city sales tax to finance relief costs. See *Minneapolis Journal,* August 6, 1937.

35 *Minneapolis Journal,* August 6, p. 9, August 16, September 2, p. 1, 21, September 3, 1937.

36 *Minneapolis Star,* October 5, 1937.

37 *Minneapolis Journal,* September 8, 14, 1937.

38 *Minneapolis Journal,* October 28, p. 1, 28, December 7, 1937. The December meeting, attended by representatives of WPA workers, labor unions, and unemployed groups, was so stormy that a dozen policemen were called into the room to keep order.

39 *Minneapolis Journal,* April 7, p. 1, 23, June 29, 1938.

40 American Public Welfare Association, *Public Welfare Survey of Minneapolis, Minnesota* (June, 1938), a mimeographed report on the Minneapolis division of public relief. The quotation is on p. 23.

41 Paul Conkin, *The New Deal,* 106 (New York, 1967).

19
The Revolt of the Urban Ghettos, 1964–1967

JOSEPH BOSKIN

In the following essay, Joseph Boskin attempts to analyze the ghetto riots of 1964–1967 by referring to the attitudes of white Americans toward their cities. Boskin follows scholars like Anselm Strauss and Morton and Lucia White in their assessment of how Americans view their cities. Strauss noted the pervasive attachment to rural memories and values among city dwellers; Americans managed to become urban without becoming urbane. Morton and Lucia White, in their book The Intellectual Versus the City, *examined the views of a selected number of writers and thinkers from Thomas Jefferson to Frank Lloyd Wright and concluded that American intellectuals, for a variety of reasons, have rejected the city as an inhumane and unlivable environment. Strauss and the Whites have opened a major topic, but they have far from exhausted it. Historians still have much work in tracing past attitudes and in studying groups like urban boosters and businessmen, the reaction of individuals to changes in the size and in the ethnic and racial composition of their communities, and the role of the political system and the communications media in forming beliefs about cities.*

Ideas and beliefs have an intrinsic interest as well as being guides to action. The form and characteristics of cities result in part from what Americans have thought about them. The record indicates that many Americans have viewed their cities primarily as places of individual economic opportunity rather than ideal places to live. They have not defended them with sufficient zeal against destructive forces of physical change. All too often they have allowed bulldozers and house wreckers to destroy gracious old structures and whole neighborhoods to make room for antiseptic new office buildings or superhighways. In the case of demographic or ethnic change, the response of most older urban groups has been ambivalent and, thus, has had ambivalent consequences. On the one hand, they wished their urban neighborhoods to be congenial places to live and they sought to exclude groups considered alien—especially blacks from the South. But their commitment to urbanism was not very strong and, eventually, with the growing affluence of the post–World War II period, whole sections of cities were emptied of whites, to be replaced by poor blacks.

This movement opened more of the central city to Negroes, and undoubtedly expanded the range and quality of housing available to them and other minorities. But it has also created immense social problems: the newcomers are poor, ignorant, and often sick; they need jobs, training, adequate education, and good health services. The problems of providing these ser-

vices has become exceedingly difficult, because the exodus of the white middle class has meant the departure of the city's taxpayers and many of the city's employers.

The deterioration of social services is only one source of urban black discontent. The recent black experience in the cities also includes racial bigotry, restricted opportunity, political powerlessness, economic exploitation, and physical ugliness—not a pleasant list by any standards. Beginning in 1964 these conditions led to a series of upheavals that rocked the nation. In the selection below Joseph Boskin examines the roots and patterns of the 1960s ghetto riots. He also notes that white Americans were able to ignore most of the turbulence and evade efforts to solve the problems producing it, because they were safely ensconced in all-white suburbs. From these insulated vantage points they could look on indifferently and dismiss what they saw as just another manifestation of the urban pathology they had successfully escaped.

Meanwhile the white suburbs remain adamantly opposed to significant black outmigration from the cities, and as states reapportion in line with the 1970 census, most large cities will lose representation in their state legislatures. The suburbs will gain representation, and it remains to be seen whether suburbanites will be sensitive to the fiscal and social plight of the central cities.

■ ■ ■ ■ **For Further Reading**

Important government-sponsored publications are the Kerner Commission, *Report of the National Advisory Commission on Civil Disorders* (New York: Bantam Books, 1968) and Hugh Davis Graham and Ted Robert Gurr, *Violence in America: Historical and Comparative Perspectives: A Report Submitted to the National Commission on the Causes and Prevention of Violence* (New York: Bantam Books, 1969). Paul Jacobs, *Prelude to Riot: A View of Urban America From the Bottom* (New York: Vintage Books, 1968) examines the pre-riot conditions in Watts and the response of government agencies. The Chicago Commission on Race Relations, *The Negro in Chicago* (Chicago: University of Chicago Press, 1922) is an examination of the causes and events of the Chicago riot of 1919. All too much of it reads exactly like the Kerner Commission Report of 1968. William Tuttle's *Race Riot,* previously noted, provides important insight into the role of labor conflict in precipitating that upheaval. Nathan S. Caplan and Jeffery M. Paige, "A Study of Ghetto Rioters," *Scientific American* (August 1968): 15–21 is an important article which dispels many myths. Edward Banfield, *The Unheavenly City: The Nature and Future of Our Urban Crisis* (Boston: Little, Brown and Co., 1970) presents the views of a neo–Social Darwinist who has apparently had great influence upon the policy makers of the Nixon administration. His chapter title, "Rioting Mainly for Fun and Profit," sums up his interpretation of the upheavals. On Americans' attitudes toward their cities, see Morton and Lucia White, *The Intellectual Versus the City* (New York: Mentor Books, 1964) and Anselm Strauss, *Images of the American City* (New York: The Free Press, 1961).

■ Alternating extremes of elation and despair have characterized black protest in the 1960's. Vacillating between the studied nonviolent and the spontaneous violent approaches to the entrapments of ghetto life, Negro behavior has mirrored the dilemma of the exploited, dark-skinned person: whether to withstand the rejection of the majority in the hope that ameliorative actions would bring rewards within the system or to lash out and destroy the hated environment, thus bringing abrupt awareness to the majority and release for oneself. Over one hundred major revolts in as many cities in the incredibly short space of three years have demonstrated that for those blacks outside of the civil rights and other allied protest movements of the mid-1950's and early 1960's, the course of protest was to be disruptive and violent. Clearly, the behavior of blacks in the large and small ghettos connoted a consensus of attitude toward their own communities, one another, and the larger society. Their actions signified the most important underclass revolt[1] in recent American history.

The Continuing Conflict of Race

The urban protest riots proved to be the pivotal black response. The riots affected the course of the civil rights movement; they coalesced the young, lower- and middle-class Negroes in the cities; they marked the growing conflict between the generations and the classes in Negro communities throughout the nation. Further, they symbolized the inability of American democracy to cope effectively with the historical-psychological problem of racism. The riots, in fact, split the nation in the 1960's and prompted the period of polarization. The clashes of the summer of 1967, however, marked an end to the spontaneous outbursts of the previous period of urban violence. A new stance was effected, as militant groups fashioned a framework of sociopolitical objectives essentially absent in the earlier period of protest.

As the incidence of riots marked the departure from the civil rights period, this new expression of protest in the 1960's can be differentiated from the more characteristic form of urban racial violence which prevailed in the past. With the exception of the Harlem riots of 1935 and 1943, which seemed more clearly to be the consequence of economic and wartime conditions, the riots of the past two centuries were initiated by Caucasians and were motivated by racist attitudes.

In these racial episodes, Negroes suffered the bulk of personal and property damage, with little restitution offered from civil authorities. Between 1900 and 1949, there were thirty-three major interracial clashes. Of these, eighteen occurred during the period of World War I and its aftermath, whereas five occurred during World War II. Obviously, the majority of these occurrences reflected situations of a critical nature.

From the end of World War II until 1964, there were several large-scale urban disturbances which reflected the underlying potential for social violence. None of these conflicts expanded into major urban conflagrations.

Rather, most of the clashes were manifestations of what Allen Grimshaw has called "assaults upon the accommodative structure," that is, Negro challenges to the socioeconomic structure of a community. The most intense violence occurred when minority groups attempted to change residential patterns or when a number of Caucasians defined the situation as one in which such an attempt was being made.

The volatility of these situations was constantly reflected in the years following the termination of the war. Resentment against Negroes who moved into all-white neighborhoods resulted in more than a hundred incidents: the Airport Homes violence in Chicago in November 1945; the Fernwood Project violence, also in Chicago, August 1947; the Georgia house-bombings in May 1947; and the highly publicized violence of 1951 in Cicero, Illinois. Some of the weapons employed by white assaulters—bricks, guns, sniping, Molotov cocktails—were those which were utilized by blacks in the 1960's. Racial violence also occurred when Negroes attempted to use public recreational facilities traditionally reserved for Caucasians in northern and midwestern cities. In sum, the race riots which raged in American society from the turn of the century until the mid-1960's reflected extensions of white racism. The rebellions which began in 1964 represented a major response to that racism.

The explosion of the blacks in the urban ghettos from 1964 to 1967 was presaged three decades ago in the lines of poet Langston Hughes:

> Negroes,
> Sweet and docile,
> Meek, humble, and kind:
> Beware the day
> They change their minds![2]

As late as the year of the first riots came the powerful words of Kenneth Clark, the eminent psychologist, in his work *Dark Ghetto:*

> The poor are always alienated from normal society, and when the poor are Negro, as they increasingly are in the American cities, a double trauma exists—rejection on the basis of class and race is a danger to the stability of the society as a whole.[3]

And, in 1965, a shocked but largely lethargic suburban society was admonished by Mayor Robert Wagner of New York:

> There are lions in the streets, angry lions, aggrieved lions, lions who have been caged until the cages crumbled. We had better do something about those lions, and when I speak of lions I do not mean individuals. I mean the spirit of the people. Those who have been neglected and oppressed and discriminated against and misunderstood and forgotten.[4]

Yet, despite a year of violent urban disruptions and countless admonitions from leaders in the Caucasian and black communities, the disturbances were ascribed to a minority of disgruntled blacks. Few were prepared—even after studies had demonstrated that a sizable proportion of Negroes were actively involved in the rebellions—to accept the fact that Negroes were indeed alienated from American society and angry enough to destroy the environments immediately surrounding them which represented the outside repressive world.

That blacks vented their antagonism on the buildings, streets, and businesses within their immediate reach and avoided these same places in exclusively white areas is crucial to an understanding of their motivations. Central to the development of the *zeitgeist* of the revolts were the attitudes of the Caucasian not only regarding the Negro—which, to understate the situation, is well understood as being antagonistic—but regarding the Negro's environment, that is, the city itself. The experience of the blacks in their mass migration into the core cities was inextricably related to the attitudes of whites toward the cities. For it is not merely the fact of high-density populations living in slum conditions which brought blacks to convulsive actions but, more importantly, the approach which predominates in relation to those enclaves which we call the city. The riot was a response to the interaction of both majority and minority in their respective attitudes toward the ghetto and the city. An essential component of its origin was the majority's rejection of the city as a viable and creative environment within which to live. Thus, an ecological malaise was one of the primary causes of the violent protest.

The City: Never the Promised Land

One of the most poignant and enduring conflicts in our national life, frequently subtle, yet constantly gnawing, has been the antagonism between rural and urban America. This has been far more than a conflict between the political and power interests of divergent human locales; it has been a conflict in the American consciousness, and is implicit in the American value system. Since the early nineteenth century, millions of Americans have yielded to a seemingly fatal attraction to make the great migration from farm and village to the city. Whatever may have been the harsh imperatives which guided them, there was a persistent tendency to look back, with a degree of nostalgia and with a sense of irreparable loss, to an idyllic rural setting. In a nation in which the forces of urbanization were unrelenting, where urban living was clearly the shape of the future, there was a deep conviction, as Walter Lippmann wrote, that the city should not be acknowledged as the American ideal. This mood was not limited merely to those who had strayed from the intended ways, but was shared by those who were born in the city environs. The city has never been conceived as being the preferred place to inhabit permanently, nor has it been romanticized in the arts and mass media. It has rarely been regarded as a focus for creative living.

The burgeoning of industry, and the expansion of the middle class, with its increased financial and physical mobility, enabled the nostalgic rural life to be transplanted into suburbia and exurbia. Thus, for this group of urban dwellers, alternatives of living were possible. The actuality of choice, however, gave rise to an ambivalence in which the best and worst of feelings conjoined: the desire for the idealized rural life-style and a strong desire to partake in the activities of the city.

The movement into the cities in the past two centuries, then, was not accomplished without the creation of a basic paradox. The economic means to achieve a fuller life, though associated with the city, was not fulfilled within the city. The compromise of the suburban community seemed to provide a solution to the uncomfortable dilemma of rural versus urban life. Seemingly, one could have the best of both styles. Several difficulties, however, prevented the suburb from becoming the American middle-class nirvana. The magnitude of the march to the suburbs necessitated mass transportation to and from the central cities. The city administrators' choice, the freeway, soon became a strangulated contact with the city, bringing it not close enough, yet too far away. Yet, many who lived in suburbia were economically dependent upon the city, so that contact with the core city was never physically far removed. Ironically, too, transportation arteries made possible the invisibility of the ghettos.

The development of a sophisticated mass communications system, in the form of television, in the early 1950's reinforced the ambivalent antagonisms towards the city. Throughout the 1950's and 1960's, television portrayed the city as a violent, unhealthy, dirty, corrupt, lonely, unseemly place for people to live, develop, and grow. Survival appeared to be the main component dramatized in series after series. With the exceptions of such productions as were borrowed from earlier successful radio shows, the bulk of television performances were antiurban in substance. In such medical series as "Ben Casey," "The Young Interns," and "The Nurses," psychological maladies or life and death were constant themes. The decade of the 1920's, depicted in such series as "The Roaring Twenties" and "The Untouchables," consistently associated the city with gang violence. In such outstanding series as "Naked City," which dealt with some realistic problems of life in New York, and "East Side, West Side," a series based on the experiences of a social worker, the promise and potential of the city were lacking. Television largely reinforced the image of the city earlier perpetuated by literature and the movies. As Herbert Kosower has correctly noted: "Almost all of Hollywood's films deal with contemporary urban life on a superficial fantasy plane."[5] Even *Street Scene, On the Waterfront, The Naked City, The Pawnbroker,* and *A Thousand Clowns* tended to reflect the harsh aspects of urban life.

Resistance to city living grew from several sources. The organization of the city was felt to be antagonistic to basic American values. It bred impersonality, detachment, and unhealthy conditions. Criticism stemmed from the conception of the city as being anti-individualistic. Groups of people were herded together in living and working conditions which placed a premium on co-operative and collectivistic solutions to social problems.

The city was further indicted for altering the landscape of America, for denying its past and playing havoc with its future. As Anselm Strauss has accurately written, the United States managed to develop an industrial economy without developing a thoroughly urbanized citizenry. Americans, he noted, entered upon the great urbanization of the nineteenth century "protestingly, metaphorically walking backward."[6]

The image of the city was capped in the catch phrase originally ascribed to New York City: "It's a nice place to visit but I wouldn't want to live there." Living was to be done in the suburbs, away from the source of corruptions. The "Promised Land," then, was to be sought outside the city.

Aided by affluence, millions fled from the city into the landscaped suburbs —leaving the core cities to the newer migrant and immigrant groups. Negro-, Puerto Rican–, Mexican-, and Japanese-Americans, and other smaller American minority groups with dark or nonwhite skins, filled the central cities. By the 1960's, all major and most smaller cities had sizable numbers of various ethnic groups in the downtown areas, living in slum ghettos, breathing the increasingly foul urban air, and becoming increasingly alienated. They gradually developed an urban consciousness—a consciousness of the entrapped underclass.

The sense of entrapment stemmed from the inability of the ethnic groups to break out of the urban ghetto and become part of the burgeoning middle classes. Alienation grew out of the anger of betrayal, a betrayal that began when the inner-city dwellers were made the inheritors of decaying cities. That they were being deserted, that the promised land in the North and West was drying up, as Langston Hughes caustically expressed it, "like a raisin in the sun," became increasingly clear in the decades of the 1950's and 1960's. Claude Brown, in his *Manchild in the Promised Land,* an affectionate portrayal of Harlem, began his sketch with this denial of the promise:

> I want to talk about the first Northern urban generation of Negroes. I want to talk about the experiences of a misplaced generation, of a misplaced people in an extremely complex, confused society. This is a story of their searching, their dreams, their sorrows, their small and futile rebellions, and their endless battle to establish their own place in America's greatest metropolis—and in America itself.
>
> The characters are sons and daughters of former Southern sharecroppers. These were the poorest people of the South, who poured into New York City during the decade following the Great Depression. These migrants were told that unlimited opportunities for prosperity existed in New York and that there was no "color problem" there. They were told that Negroes lived in houses with bathrooms, electricity, running water, and indoor toilets. To them, this was the "promised land" that Mammy had been singing about in the cotton fields for many years. . . . It seems that Cousin Willie, in his lying

haste, had neglected to tell the folks down home about one of the most important aspects of the promised land: it was a slum ghetto. There was a tremendous difference in the way life was lived up North. There were too many people full of hate and bitterness crowded into a dirty, stinky, uncared-for closet-size section of a great city.

Before the soreness of the cotton fields had left Mama's back, her knees were getting sore from scrubbing "Goldberg's" floor. Nevertheless, she was better off; she had gone from the fire into the frying pan.

The children of these disillusioned colored pioneers inherited the total lot of their parents—the disappointments, the anger. To add to their misery, they had little hope of deliverance. For where does one run to when he's already in the promised land?[7]

One runs to one's soul brother.

The significant consequences of the great migration along the hallelujah trail was the development of an urban consciousness in the ghettos of the industrial cities. Alain Locke, in his important book in the 1920's, *The New Negro,* took cognizance of the ecological forces at work in Harlem. Proscription and prejudice, he noted, had thrown dissimilar black elements into a common area of contact and interaction. Prior to the movement into Harlem, the Negro was "a race more in name than in fact, or to be exact, more in sentiment than in experience." The central experience between these groups, he continued, was that of "a common condition rather than a life in common. In Harlem, Negro life is seizing upon its first chances for group expression and self-determination."[8] The fusing of sentiment and experience in Harlem was repeated over and again in ghettos across the country. Indeed, ghetto experience became a common denominator, its life-style and language and conditions a similarity of experiences.

Had the ghetto become a viable environment within a dynamic city existence, the level of grievance-consciousness shared by Negroes would have been muted. But the opposite occurred. Instead, the ghetto became a dead-end to those who lived in it. It became an object of loathing, a mirror of a squalid existence. Feelings of hopelessness and isolation were recurrent themes in the testimony of the slum residents, wrote the United States Commission on Civil Rights in 1967. When asked what she would do if she had sufficient income, one resident declared, "The first thing I would do myself is move out of the neighborhood. I feel the entire neighborhood is more or less a trap."[9]

Compounding these antagonisms were, of course, the intensifying anti-urban attitudes of whites. "The people in Harlem," wrote James Baldwin in *Nobody Knows My Name,* two years before the first protest riot, "know they are living there because white people do not think they are good enough to live elsewhere. No amount of 'improvement' can sweeten this fact. . . . A ghetto can be improved in one way only: out of existence."[10] These resentments were further exacerbated by the obvious disparity between the

Caucasian and black neighborhoods. Said a young man to Budd Schulberg in the Watts Happening Coffee House immediately after the riots:

> The contrast: the spectacular growth of central and west L.A. vs. the stagnation of Watts. . . . You've conquered it, baby. You've got it made. Some nights on the roof of our rotten falling down buildings we can actually see your lights shining in the distance. So near and yet so far. We want to reach out and grab it and punch it on the nose.[11]

The mythical urban melting pot began to simmer and finally boiled over.

The protest riots which occurred in massive profusion were thus the consequence of a myriad of historical and ecological factors which fused in the 1960's. Their outstanding feature was a collective mode of attitude, behavior, and sense of power.

The Cry: Burn, Baby, Burn

The sudden burst of rage which rent Harlem in July 1964 was the third mass outburst in that community in the twentieth century. On two previous occasions, the first time during the Great Depression and the second during World War II, blacks in one of the most highly concentrated, racially, ethnic ghettos in the nation signified their protest in spontaneous rioting. Unlike the earlier uprisings which were confined to Harlem, however, the actions in 1964 proved to be the beginning of an urban black protest throughout the country. In city after city, summer after summer, blacks took vengeance by wrecking the hated symbols within their own ghetto areas.

The violent protest in Harlem was rapidly repeated in seven other urban Negro ghettos in the next two months: Bedford-Stuyvesant (Brooklyn), Rochester, Paterson, Jersey City, Elizabeth, Philadelphia, and Dixmoor (Chicago). In 1965, eruptions occurred in five cities, the major conflagrations taking place in Chicago and especially in Los Angeles. Large-scale rioting increased in intensity in the following year, when blacks took to the streets in twenty cities, including Cleveland, Chicago, Omaha, East Oakland, and San Francisco. The year 1967 began on a volatile note as disturbances occurred in the spring in the Southern cities of Nashville, Jackson, and Houston. As the heat of the summer increased, so did the temper for violence. There were mass assaults in Roxbury (Boston), Tampa, Dayton, Atlanta, Buffalo, and Cincinnati in the month of June. Within the next two months, Negroes swarmed through the ghettos of twenty-two cities in the North, Midwest, and South, with the largest riots taking place in Toledo, Grand Rapids, Plainfield (New Jersey), Milwaukee, and especially in Newark and Detroit. By 1968 the rioting had subsided, suggesting that the anger had been channeled into aggressive community programs.

The toll of the rioting over the four-year period was devastating. Between 1964 and 1967, approximately 130 civilians, mainly Negroes, and 12 civil personnel, mainly Caucasian, were killed. Approximately 4,700 Negroes and civil personnel were injured. Over 20,000 persons were arrested during the melees; property damages mounted into the hundreds of millions of dollars; many cities resembled the hollowed remnants of war-torn cities.[12]

Despite the disparity of distance, there was a consensus of attitudes and a similarity of actions among those urban blacks who revolted and those who supported the violent protest.[13] Significantly, the riots were largely unplanned, unorganized, and unscheduled. Ray Lewis, a Cleveland youth worker, explained the origins of the outbreak in that city:

> It wasn't that people planned our riot so consciously. But take a Negro ghetto where men sit around for years saying, "we gonna get whitey," and you build up a group knowledge of what to do.[14]

Taken together, the riots were the actions of a people, poor and dispossessed and crushed in huge numbers into large slum ghettos, who rose up in wrath against a society committed to democratic ideals. Their outburst was an expression of class antagonism, resentment against racial prejudice, anger at the unreachable affluence around them, and frustration at their sociopolitical powerlessness. "What are these people riotin' about in other cities?" exclaimed Efelka Brown, of the "Sons of Watts," an organization set up to train young males in trade skills. "They want *recognition* and the only way they goin' get it is to riot. We don't want to overthrow the country—we just want what we ain't got."[15]

The sense of betrayal of expectations brought about a focus on the grievances of the past and present. The visibility of an affluent, comfortable, middle-class life, made possible by a powerful mass communications system, was in itself enough to induce dual feelings of resentment and emulation. Pronouncements by the political establishment, however, served only to increase these emotions. Thus, enticed by advertising of the leisure life, excited by legislative programs such as the Civil Rights Acts and the War on Poverty, lured by television programs depicting middle-class life, and hopeful of change in their environment, the poor anticipated an imminent improvement in their socioeconomic position. The failure of society effectively to raise the status of those trapped in the cities contributed immensely to the smoldering resentments.

The urge to retaliate, to return the hurts and the injustices, played an integral part of the protest. By itself, the riot was not "a major thing," stated James Richards to the United States Commission on Civil Rights after the Hunter's Point riot in San Francisco in 1966:

> It was just an idea to strike out at something and someone. Even if you don't do anything but break a window or a chair or something like this, you feel that you are hurting a white man or something like this because the white man is the one that is doing everything to you that causes you to have all these problems on you now.[16]

Similar expressions of deep-welled anger were heard from Puerto Ricans in Spanish Harlem. Piri Thomas, author of *Down These Mean Streets,* in testimony before the National Advisory Commission on Civil Disorders, described the origins of the explosion in that area:

> Did you ever stand on street corners and look the other way, at the world of muchos ricos and think, I ain't got a damn? Did you ever count the garbage that flowed down dirty streets, or dig in the back yards who in their glory were a garbage dumps dream? Did you ever stand on rooftops and watch night time cover the bad below? Did you ever put your hand around your throat and feel your pulse beat say, "I do belong and there's not gonna be nobody can tell me, I'm wrong?"[17]

Intense grievances vis-à-vis their inability to achieve even the basic promises of American life of work, status, and housing combined with other minor factors to make the cities highly combustible. The National Advisory Commission found in almost all the cities surveyed "the same major grievance topic among Negro communities."[18] The Commission ranked three levels of grievances among Negroes:

First Level of Intensity:

1. Police practices
2. Unemployment and underemployment
3. Inadequate housing

Second Level of Intensity:

1. Inadequate education
2. Poor recreational facilities and programs
3. Ineffectiveness of the political structure and grievance mechanisms

Third Level of Intensity:

1. Disrespectful white attitudes
2. Discriminatory administration of justice
3. Inadequacy of federal programs
4. Inadequacy of municipal services
5. Discriminatory consumer and credit practices
6. Inadequate welfare programs[19]

To strike out against the visible symbols of white society became a sign of brotherhood. In more than one instance, rock-throwing blacks placed missiles into the hands of residents of the community, saying, "You're either with us or against us, man." In the Watts riot, Mervin Dymally, a Negro assemblyman, was asked by one of the rioters to prove his loyalty by heaving an object at a police car. Dymally refused, saying, "No, man, I'm for peace." The boy quickly replied, "No, you're with the man."[20] Many residents of ghetto areas who did not participate in the actions shouted their approval to those on the streets.

That a general approval, a collective behavior, pervaded the ghettos can be borne out by analysis of the actions of blacks. The two groups singled out for attack were the police and Caucasian-owned businesses. Relations between the police and the minorities, particularly members of the dark-skinned ethnic groups, have always been volatile. As an institution, the police have reflected the attitudes of the majority. To have expected the police to act as a social agency oriented towards reform or conflict-ameliora-tion is to misconstrue their primary function as they view it: namely, the maintenance of law and order. Thus, the police have practiced physical attacks and verbal harassment on minority-group members without inter-ference. Though the public was generally unaware of the treatment accorded minority-ethnic-group members, a prejudicial attitude on its part sanctioned police actions. The language of the police vis-à-vis Negroes—"nigger," "monkey," "them," "boy"—were terms in general usage in American culture. For many years, blacks have attempted to bring to light the ample evidence of discriminatory beatings and humiliations. One such attempt in 1965, by furious blacks in the South-Central area of Los Angeles, compiled a listing of the discriminatory remarks of the then Los Angeles Chief of Police William H. Parker—which resulted in a fifteen-page report entitled "Police Chief William H. Parker Speaks"—and distributed it in the community.[21]

Yet, the police became a main focal point for attack not only because of their attitude toward and behavior with minority groups, but primarily because they came to symbolize the despised invisible white power structure. Of the institutional contacts with which ghetto-dwellers have intimate contact—schools, social welfare and employment agencies, medical facilities, business owners—the police embody the most crushing authority. For many blacks, the police had come to represent more than enforcement of law; they were viewed as members of an occupying army and as an oppressive force acting on behalf of those who rule their environment but who fled it for the greener pastures. "A policeman is an object of contempt," Ernie W. Chambers of Omaha bitterly stated in testimony given before the National Advisory Committee on Civil Disorders.[22] The system represented by the police has been oppressive, the method of rule has been heavy with force, and the phrase "maintain law and order" has been directed basically towards the control of Negroes. "Like why, man, should I get home?" angrily inquired a young black during the Watts riot. "These cops have been pushin' me 'round all my life. Kickin' my —— and things like that. Whitey ain't no damn good, he talks 'bout law and order, it's his law and order, it ain't mine [word deleted by the Commission]."[23]

That a collective wrath directed against the police goaded ghetto residents is evident from an analysis of the early stages of the riots. It is significant that most revolts began as a consequence of an incident in which the police were, in some manner, involved. In several instances, the initiating episode was in the line of routine activity. In the Watts situation, for instance, police stopped two men who were driving in an intoxicated condition. Nevertheless, the significance of the specific event bore no relation to the more serious undercurrent of animosity which had been previously created. In other cases, verbal and physical actions by the police were instrumental in increasing a tense situation by inflaming the ghetto people, as happened in the Newark riot of 1967, which really began when the police charged out of the station house towards a large group of demonstrating and jeering Negroes.

Equally instructive is the fact that snipers, despite their numbers, hit extremely few policemen and firemen during the three years of rioting. The low number of deaths of law officials could hardly be ascribed to poor marksmanship. By 1967, especially in Detroit, the incidence of sniper fire had increased considerably; yet, only four law officers were killed, as compared to thirty-nine civilians. Indeed, of the eighty-three persons who died in seventy-five disorders analyzed by the Permanent Sub-committee on Investigations of the Senate Committee on Government Operations in 1967, approximately ten persons were public officials, primarily law officers and firemen, whereas the remainder were civilians, primarily Negroes.[24]

White businessmen were the second most exposed group singled out for attack. Resentment against the practices of exploitation, in the form of hidden and higher interest rates, shoddy goods and lower quality, higher prices and questionable service, had likewise been building for many years. The communications system in the community had long isolated such business establishments. Consequently, the majority of stores damaged and looted were those against which ill-feelings had developed. Negro stores frequently were protected by identifying signs: "Blood Brother," "Soul Brother," "Negro-owned." Not only were black businesses generally left untouched, but so, too, were libraries, schools, hospitals, clinics, and, surprisingly, governmental agencies. There were instances of bricks and sniper fire hitting these various buildings; however, no concerted attack was conducted. Many places burned down because of the refusal of the rioters to permit fire engines into the area.

Nevertheless, retail businesses suffered a much greater proportion of the damage during the violence than public institutions, industrial properties, or private residences. In Newark in 1967, 1,029 establishments listed damage to buildings or loss of inventory or both.[25] Those businesses which were hardest hit by rioters were those which were felt to be the most exploitative in their business practices: liquor, clothing, food, and furniture stores. Indeed, in at least nine of the riots studied by the President's National Advisory Commission on Civil Disorders, the damage was, in part, the result of "deliberate attacks on white-owned businesses characterized in the Negro community as unfair or disrespectful toward Negroes."[26]

The riot brought a sense of exultation in the community. It served as a release of frustration, anger, and helplessness. Even those participants who afterwards regretted their actions admitted to the joy that they had personally experienced. In testimony before the McCone Commission, conducted after the riot in central Los Angeles, Winston Slaughter, age twenty, a junior college student, responded to the question: "Do you think the riot helped or hurt the Negro cause?"

> Well, you can say regret and then you can say there are some who are glad it happened. Now, me personally, I feel that I regret it, yes. But, deep down inside I know I was feeling some joy while it was going on, simply because I am a Negro.[27]

Others felt no regret, but a sense of pride. As the riots spread to other ghetto areas, those communities which experienced no turmoil felt the need to emulate their brothers. An exchange between three young blacks after the Detroit riot indicated the fulfilling exuberance of the historical moment:

> "Those buildings goin' up was a pretty sight," a long-legged kid said. "I sat right here and watched them go. And there wasn't nothin' them honkies could do but sweat and strain to put it out."

> "Yeah, man," a pal chimed in, "it's about time those honkies started earnin' their money in this neighborhood."

> "You know," said Long Legs, "we made big news. They called this the country's worst race riot in history."

> "Yeah," said another gangly kid, straddling the railing. "My kids goin' to study about that in school, and they'll know their old man was part of it."

> "We got the record man," exulted another youth. . . . "They can forget all about Watts and Newark and Harlem. This is where the riot to end all riots was held."[28]

Further, the protest riot assumed certain features of conventional warfare. The weapons and tactics employed were those standardized in the past thirty years: Molotov cocktails, selected targets, visible enemies, harassing tactics, sniping, mobility, and a capitulation to a more powerful military force in the form of national guardsmen or federal troops. Parallels between war as a means of confronting an enemy and the protest riot could also be observed in the attitudes of ghetto residents. Although the term "riot" was used by blacks, it became clear that they meant to describe their actions in a larger sense. "We in a war," a black youth told a reporter. "Or hasn't anybody told you that?"[29]

The attitude of immediacy was heard from many persons. "Many Negroes would rather die than live under conditions as they are now," exclaimed a male at a youth symposium. "For these people, riots present the only chance of ever achieving equality."[30] An absence of fear was notable among those who actively participated in the streets. "The cops think we are scared of them because they got guns," stated a male in testimony before the McCone Commission, "but you can only die once: if I get a few of them I don't mind dying."[31] Thus, the riots were emotionally liberating. The joy in retaliating and the fun in looting reinforced the feelings of communal action. The individual acts fused with the collective act. The term "we" was used with frequency among the protesting rioters: "We put ourselves on the map." "We were whole again." During the civil violences, there was a partial suspension of conscience. "This liberation from conscience and from con-scientiousness made possible for the rioters an involvement and an extreme commitment usually denied them."[32] Moreover, the pride in action played an integral role in the historical consciousness of the community. Two years after the Watts riot, black and brown high school students, selected to participate in an upward-bound educational project, were asked to complete a form which contained the question: "What kinds of civil rights activities have you participated in?" One student answered: "Watts Riot." Such statements and actions indicate a high degree of participation in the protest disturbances.

Several significant studies have pointedly noted a high degree of com-munity participation in the violence of the small and large riots in the 1960's. The Los Angeles Riot Study (LARS), initiated immediately after the 1965 riot, collated the interviews of 2,070 persons living within the curfew area.[33] The group of Negroes interviewed was a random sample, stratified by age, sex, and income. Interviews were approximately two hours in length; the interview covered questions of attitude toward the riot, activity in the riot, general social and political attitudes, and background information. The LARS survey noted that the majority of Negroes had spent their childhood in the South but that over 60 per cent of the sample had matured in urban areas. Significantly, about the same percentage had lived in Los Angeles ten years or longer at the time of the riot. Contrary to reports about the low educational level of the rioters, the study indicated that over half of the sample had completed high school. Contrary to popular assumptions as well, the study indicated that 72 per cent of the males and 35 per cent of the females were employed in August 1965.

With regard to participation in the riot, the LARS survey demonstrated that up to 15 per cent of the Negro adult population, or about 22,000 per-sons, were active at some point during the rioting; that an additional 35 or 40 per cent, or 51,000 persons, were active spectators. Support for the violence was greater among the younger persons, was greater among men than women, and was as great among relatively longtime residents of South-Central Los Angeles as it was among the more recent migrants from the South. The latter point is of particular importance, inasmuch as it under-cut the notion that the riot was largely the work of the unacculturated and of the recent influx of migrants from the South.

A high percentage of the community supported the violence, in attitude if not in action. Approximately 34 per cent of the sample were favorably disposed toward the actions, and 38 per cent of the population in the curfew area felt that the revolt would help in their quest to improve their positions. Only 20 per cent indicated that the riot hurt the community. In sum, a high proportion of persons in the riot area participated in, or gave support to, the action of fellow residents.

Studies undertaken after the LARS report substantially corroborated its conclusions. The National Advisory Commission on Civil Disorders conducted 1,200 interviews in approximately twenty cities, studied arrest records in twenty-two cities, and elicited additional reports from participants. According to the Report of the Commission, the typical rioter was an unmarried male, between the ages of fifteen and twenty-four, born in the state, and a lifelong resident of the city in which the riot occurred. His education was substantially good, having attended high school, and, economically, his position was approximately the same as his counterpart who did not actively participate in the riot. Nonetheless, he was more likely to be working in a menial or low-status job as an unskilled laborer. In special surveys taken after the Newark and Detroit revolts, interviewers noted strong feelings of racial pride, "if not racial superiority."[34] The riot experience was a definite factor in increased self- and communal pride:

INTERVIEWER: You said you were feeling good when you followed the crowd?

RESPONDENT: I was feeling proud, man, at the fact that I was a Negro. I felt like I was a first-class citizen. I didn't feel ashamed of my race because of what they did [Detroit, 1967].[35]

The nature of the rioting which marked the mid-1960's appeared to undergo serious change by the end of the decade. Two indications of this change were, firstly, the Detroit riot of 1967 in which a sizable proportion of Caucasians joined with the Negroes in burning and looting, thus indicating a meshing of an economic underclass; and, secondly, the development and intensity of the Black Power movement. The activists have been concerned with developing cultural, economic, and political programs within the community. These activist organizations have, on more than one occasion, prevented violent outbreaks by ghetto residents who were angered by representatives of the power structure, particularly the police. Within the broad Black Power movement, moreover, militant groups have counseled for the termination of nonviolence as a technique of bringing about necessary change. "We know that we cannot change violent people by nonviolence," read a mimeographed sheet handed out by the Black Student Union at the University of California, San Diego, immediately after the assassination of Dr. Martin Luther King in April 1968. "We must build mass armed self-defense groups. We must unite to get rid of the government and people that oppress and murder Black People." Thus, by the end of the decade, the energies of the younger blacks were oriented towards more specific, militant goals.

In sum, the revolts in the mid-1960's—more than the nonviolent movement of Dr. Martin Luther King and the extraordinarily powerful civil rights movement of the early 1960's—directed attention to the anguished plights of millions of Negroes, Puerto Ricans, and Mexican-Americans living in the urban centers of the country. The spontaneous outbursts, the collective actions, and the consensual attitudes of blacks and browns highlighted the failure of American society to recognize the problems of the racial minority groups in the cities. The events stemmed not only from the tradition of racist mentality but also from the ambiguous attitudes towards the city itself. The enormity of the failure led to one of the most intense social crises in American society in the twentieth century.

▪ ▪ ▪ ▪ Notes

1 The terms "riot" and "revolt" are used interchangably in this study. They describe acts of assault on the status quo and its tangible legitimate authorities, in this instance, the police and business establishments.

2 Langston Hughes, "Roland Hayes Beaten," *One-Way Ticket* (New York: Alfred A. Knopf, 1949), p. 86.

3 Kenneth Clark, *Dark Ghetto* (New York: Harper and Row, 1964), p. 21.

4 Quoted in Gurston D. Goldin, "Violence: The Integration of Psychiatric and Sociological Concepts," *Notre Dame Lawyer,* Vol. XL, No. 5 (1965), p. 513.

5 Herbert Kosower, King Vidor, and Joseph Boshur, "The Arts," *Psychology Today,* Vol. II, No. 3 (August 1968), p. 16.

6 Anselm Strauss, *Images of the American City* (New York: Free Press, 1961), p. 123.

7 Claude Brown, *Manchild in the Promised Land* (New York: New American Library, 1965), pp. vii–viii.

8 Alain Locke, *The New Negro* (New York: Albert and Charles Boni, 1925), pp. 6–7.

9 U.S. Commission on Civil Rights, *A Time to Listen . . . A Time to Act* (Washington, D.C.: U.S. Government Printing Office, 1967), p. 6.

10 James Baldwin, *Nobody Knows My Name* (New York: Delta Books, 1962), p. 65.

11 "Watts—End or Beginning," *Los Angeles Times,* Calendar, May 15, 1966, p. 3, col. 2.

12 The rioting which occurred following the assassination of Dr. Martin Luther King in April 1968 is not covered in this paper. These actions were not specifically related to the origins and spread of the urban revolt.

13 For a further analysis of the "consensus of attitudes and behavior," see Joseph Boskin, "Violence in the Ghettos: A Consensus of Attitudes," in *Violence in Contemporary Society,* ed. Joseph Frank, *New Mexico Quarterly,* Vol. XXXVII, No. 4 (Winter 1968), pp. 317–334.

14 John Allan Long, "After the Midwest Riots," *Christian Science Monitor,* November 10, 1966, p. 11.

15 "The Hard-Core Ghetto Mood," *Newsweek,* Vol. LXX, No. 8 (August 21, 1967), p. 21.

16 *A Time to Listen . . . A Time to Act,* p. 5.

17 Piri Thomas, in testimony before the National Advisory Commission on Civil Disorders, September 21, 1967.

18 U.S. Riot Commission, *Report of the National Advisory Commission on Civil Disorders* (New York: Bantam Books, 1968), p. 143.
19 U.S. Riot Commission, pp. 143–144.
20 *Report of the Governor's Commission on the Los Angeles Riot,* Vol. II (Sacramento, 1966), pp. 88–89.
21 William H. Parker, "Police Chief William H. Parker Speaks" (Los Angeles: Community Relations Conference of Southern California, 1965).
22 Ernie W. Chambers, in testimony before the National Advisory Commission on Civil Disorders, September 23, 1967. The Commission described Chambers as a "grass-roots leader."
23 *Report of Governor's Commission on the Los Angeles Riot,* Vol. I (Sacramento, 1966), p. 43.
24 *Report of the Commission on Civil Disorders,* pp. 115–116.
25 *Report of the Commission on Civil Disorders.*
26 *Report of the Commission on Civil Disorders.*
27 *Report of Governor's Commission on the Los Angeles Riot,* Vol. XIII (Sacramento, 1966), pp. 28–29.
28 "The Hard-Core Ghetto Mood," p. 20.
29 "The Hard-Core Ghetto Mood," p. 20.
30 California, Alameda County, Human Relations Commission, "Youth Discuss Racial Problems," *Human Relations News,* Vol. I, No. 2 (September 1967), p. 1.
31 *Report of Governor's Commission on the Los Angeles Riot,* Vol. I, p. 16.
32 Frederick J. Hacker and Aljean Harmetz, "What the McCone Commission Didn't See," *Frontier,* Vol. XVII, No. 5 (March 1966), p. 13.
33 Institute of Government and Public Affairs, University of California, Los Angeles, 1967.
34 *Report of the Commission on Civil Disorders,* p. 133.
35 *Report of the Commission on Civil Disorders.*

20

How the Catholics Lost Out to the Jews in New York Politics

NATHAN GLAZER AND DANIEL P. MOYNIHAN

Blacks are not the only city dwellers who feel oppressed in these troubled times. Blue-collar and lower-middle-class whites suffer from inflation; agonize over the "deterioration" of their neighborhoods; believe that blacks are "getting something for nothing"; and listen and watch enraged as radical, upper-middle-class youth attacks their most cherished values of commitment to family and flag. In a number of major American cities there is a close association between social class, religion, and ethnic affiliation. In New York most working- and lower-middle-class whites are Catholic; most upper-middle- and upper-class whites are either Jews or Protestants.

In the following essay, Nathan Glazer and Daniel P. Moynihan analyze the ethnic and class basis of recent political changes in New York. Essentially, they argue, upper-status Jews and Protestants have joined with blacks to oust middle- and working-class Catholics, and also lower-middle-class members of their own groups, from positions of political power and influence. To accomplish this, they have charged that the Catholics are bigots, lacking sympathy for the problems of the most recent arrivals—the blacks and the Latin Americans. These accusations constitute a form of bigotry in themselves, and the threatened working- and lower-middle classes (Jewish school teachers for example), suspect that black advances will come at their expense. The affluent, in effect, propose to "do something" for the blacks at the cost of the most marginal and precariously positioned whites.

More and more scholars and public officials are becoming aware of the necessity for taking into account the needs and frustrations of white ethnic America in devising programs and policies to meet the urban crises of poverty and group conflict. How successful the 1970s will be in reversing the unhappy trends of the 1960s may rest on the intelligence, sympathy, and skill exercised in creating a feeling of common interest between blacks and white ethnics.

Glazer and Moynihan's comments about the Puerto Ricans indicate the importance of individual or group perception of one's place in society. Although Puerto Ricans still fall below Negroes in statistical measurements of status, there is still more hope than despair among them. In contrast to the blacks, whose more militant spokesmen use terms like "oppression" and "colonization" to describe the present and talk of the possibility of "genocide" for the future, the Puerto Ricans consider themselves traditional immigrants who have to start at the bottom but can move up the ladder. The decade of the seventies may show which group has the most realistic conception.

■ ■ ■ ■ **For Further Reading**

Glazer and Moynihan, *Beyond the Melting Pot* (Cambridge, Mass.: M. I. T. Press, 1963) has recently appeared in a second edition, the present selection being a portion of the revised introduction. This material appeared as an article in *New York* 3 (August 10, 1970): 39–49, and is reprinted as it appeared there with the exception of illustrations, captions, and editorial insertions. Also useful is Oscar Handlin, *The Newcomers: Negroes and Puerto Ricans in a Changing Metropolis* (New York: Doubleday Anchor Books, 1959).

■ An important contribution to the malaise of the white working and lower middle classes in the city has been the startling decline in the power of the Irish and Italian groups, and, by the same token, of Catholics, for in New York, to name an occupational group or a class is very much the same thing as naming an ethnic group, and to name an ethnic group is very much the same thing as naming a religious group.

Among the most notable events in New York City during the 1960s was the decline, almost the collapse, of Catholic power. This is not a misnomer. "New York," we wrote in 1963 in our book, *Beyond the Melting Pot,* "used to be an Irish city." That meant a Catholic city as well: one in which the Church had temporal as well as spiritual power. This culminated, even as it declined, in the long reign of Francis Cardinal Spellman as Archbishop of New York, ruling from his episcopal throne in St. Patrick's Cathedral until he died in 1967. Spellman was feared, disliked, and heeded. It went on too long by half. His successor, Terence Cardinal Cooke, whom he had chosen (having first, some said, laid it down to Rome that either he would be permitted personally to pick the next man or he would refuse to die), seemed almost to sense this and promptly assumed a posture much more in keeping with reality. New York's Catholics might still be, probably were, a majority of the population, but in all other senses—of political power, of wealth, of intellect, of energy—they were a minority and had best get used to behaving as such.

A series of events brought all this about. As with all ethnic history in New York, the most important event was the arrival of new groups. The era of Catholic ascendancy in New York came to an end in the aftermath of the arrival, for the first time in large numbers, of the Jews and then the Negroes. The process was slow at first but then accelerated and became almost vengeful. By the end of the sixties, in the entire hierarchy of government officials elected in statewide or citywide elections, there was but one lonely Catholic, Malcolm Wilson, the lieutenant governor. In New York City, following the 1969 election, the powerful Board of Estimate, consisting of the mayor, the controller, the president of the City Council, and the five borough presidents, consisted of five Jews, one white Protestant, one black Protestant, and, again, one lonely Catholic, Robert T. Connor. (Significantly, both he and the lieutenant governor were Republicans. Catholic Democrats had disappeared altogether.) In the weighted voting of the Board of Estimate, Jews had fourteen votes, Protestants six, Catholics two. When *Beyond the Melting Pot* was first published, the Catholic representation was quite the reverse. The Board of Estimate had five Catholics, two Jews, and one black Protestant. The voting strength was Catholics fourteen, Jews six, and Protestants two.

This process had been predictable enough with respect to the decline of Irish power, and we had so predicted. But the decline of Catholic power was not, at least by us, foreseen. Nor, in retrospect, is it easily explained.

One element not to be overlooked is the almost mechanical process whereby a dominant group fractionates and creates the conditions for its own decline. Once securely in power, Catholics began to fall out with one another, in the seemingly fixed pattern of these things. (Al Smith remarked that the only time the Irish stood together was for the Last Gospel at Sunday Mass.) Interestingly, it is the Jews, who have replaced the Irish in power and influence, who are now the most politically divided group in the city. But this is not the whole of the story. The Jews did not merely fill a vacuum; their success involved something more than "just being around," the phrase with which Smith was wont to describe the source of his rise in the scheme of things. The Jews also *ousted* the Catholics. They did this in direct toe-to-toe encounter in a hundred areas of the city's life, and, also, they carried out a brilliant outflanking maneuver involving the black masses of the city, which combined in inextricable detail elements of pure charity, enlightened self-interest, and plain ethnic combativeness.

A full analysis of this complex process has to consider some matter-of-fact political realities. Before the fifties, Jews in New York City were divided among the Democratic party, Republican party, Fusion, and left and liberal third parties—Socialists, American Labor, Liberals. In the fifties and sixties, they increasingly concentrated in the Democratic party. Meanwhile, Catholics, concentrated in the Democratic party in earlier decades, divided by moving into the Republican and new Conservative parties. But simultaneously Jews maintained their attachment to liberals of any party and religion. The result was to eclipse Catholic power within the Democratic party, and limit any rise outside it. But this is only one element in the Catholic decline.

At the beginning of the century, the Catholic population had its share, at the very least, of the most vibrant people of the city in politics, in business, and in the arts; they were quite dominant in areas of immigrant achievement such as sports (where, indeed, they had created a pattern of upward mobility via the prize rings, and the like, that others were to follow precisely). A third of a century later, this was no longer so clearly the case. The Jews were beginning to make their impact. They dominated radical politics, were well established in business, and already intellectually ascendant (withal the nation did not yet realize it). The La Guardia administration for the first time brought Jews in large numbers into positions of political influence.

In the middle third of the century that followed, the Jewish position was expanded and consolidated. This process was hastened, and even in ways made possible, by the rise of Hitler in the 1930s and the extraordinary economic expansion in the United States that commenced in the 1940s. The first led to an intense sense of group identity and group interests among New York Jews—a tradition common enough with them in any event —and also added to their numbers through immigration, a small but amazingly gifted group, the German and Central European refugees. The founding of Israel further intensified this development. Economic expansion brought wealth to the businessmen, influence to the professionals, and something very like power to the Jewish scientists and intellectuals. It may be that the cold war should be listed here as well. Jews were a substantial part of the American Communist party during the thirties and forties. But they were also the dominant group among the Socialist groups, of the left and right, that opposed the Communists, and dominant in the increasingly important intellectual opposition to the Communists that grew in this country in the thirties and the forties. When the cold war broke out, they inevitably supplied a good number of the experts—who else had spent their college (and even high school) years fighting the Stalinists? And, in addition, Jews had entered the new social sciences in enormous numbers: sociology, economics, political science. Thus, Jews were prominent among the intellectuals who developed the military and diplomatic strategies of the 1940s and 1950s—and also among those who opposed them.

In the new scientific elite, which also played its role in the developing cold war, Jews were again everywhere and often on both sides of each issue. Robert Oppenheimer confronted Edward Teller, and A.E.C. Chairman Lewis Strauss turned the issue into one of the great dramas of postwar American history.

The point is that the Jews were everywhere, doing everything. In New York, with the largest Jewish population in the world, they simply outclassed their competition, which was Protestant in business, professional, and intellectual circles, and Catholic in the political ones.

Of all the triumphs of the Jewish style in America of the 1950s, none, surely, was as bizarre or unlikely as the radicalizing of the elite youth of the Eastern seaboard patriciate. By the end of the 1960s, the best preparatory schools of the area were torn with doctrinal disputes between leftist factions anathematizing one another over alleged deviations from doctrines setting forth the true role of the working class in a prerevolutionary phase. Pure C.C.N.Y., circa 1937. And if the prep school boys did not do it especially well, it must surely be marveled, as Dr. Johnson said of the lady preacher, that they did it at all.

All this happened to Jews at a time when rather the opposite was happening to Catholics. Intellectual and cultural sterility gave way before the combined influence of Pope John and the *embourgeoisement* of large sectors of the Catholic population, and was followed by a period of considerable vitality, in comparison at least with the past, but also considerable fractioning.[1] The embattled solidarity of the anti-Communist period also broke up as that issue gradually became, or seemed to become, less central to the nation's life. Catholics started popping up on every side of the political and moral issues of the day. Thus, in 1969, Bishop Fulton Sheen declared himself in favor of the United States' getting out of Vietnam, and doing so quickly. The nation, he declared, was suffering a nervous breakdown over the whole affair. Doubtless, good sense. But, also, in a curious way, a confession of failure. All those speeches to the Friendly Sons of St. Patrick had been pretty poor stuff, had they not? Poor *intellectually*. The New York Catholics had been so very right about a limited number of things—Josef Stalin was *not* a nice man—only in the end to be judged to have been wrong about most. Their cultural history, like the history of their politicians, would be written by their enemies or their betters. After 50 years and more of maintaining the loyalty of the American working class to democratic institutions, they would be judged to have done little more than to have contributed the term "McCarthyism" to the language. And now, they couldn't even get elected to the Board of Estimate.

In largest measure, the passing of the Catholic ascendancy, as a normal, predictable, understood fact about the city, arose from a failure of intellect. There just weren't enough smart Catholics around: smart as district leaders, as playwrights, as professors of molecular biology. A century and a half of unprecedented support of a private educational system had come to little, certainly nothing distinctive. But there was a further factor involved. The 1960s brought the issue of race to the city as it had not existed before. In New York, as elsewhere in the North, this created a range of conflict situations in which Negroes confronted *Catholics*. Not just Irish and Italian Catholics, but also a great range of middle Europeans with very little political or public presence (so little that they could all be lumped under the common term "Ethnics") but with a sizable interest in the maintenance of patterns of residency, employment, and education that Negroes now threatened by the simple fact of their presence and consequent need for a place to live, a job to provide income, a school to provide education. There followed a classic encounter between working-class and middle-class styles in politics, which, in New York, had come to be Catholic and Jewish styles, respectively. A clue can be found in labor historian Selig Perlman's analysis of trade unionism, which arose, he concluded, from a pervasive sense among workers of the scarcity of economic opportunity. (Middle-class intellectuals typically get this wrong, ascribing all manner of universalist and egalitarian intention to what is in fact an effort to keep other people from invading what is seen as a limited and threatened means of making a living.) The newcomers inevitably aroused anxieties. Theirs was a very real threat, and it soon acquired substance as black neighborhoods grew, job markets were transformed, schools changed, and so on through the various forms by which a new group makes its presence felt.

In New York a game followed in which there were in essence the five player groups: Negroes, Puerto Ricans, Jews, Italians and Irish, and, in addition, an elite Protestant group. The play went something as follows. The Protestants and better-off Jews determined that the Negroes and Puerto Ricans were deserving and in need and, on those grounds, further determined that these needs would be met by concessions of various kinds from the Italians and the Irish (or, generally speaking, from the Catholic players) and the worse-off Jews. The Catholics resisted, and were promptly further judged to be opposed to helping the deserving and needy. On these grounds their traditional rights to govern in New York City *because they were so representative of just such groups* were taken from them and conferred on the two other players, who had in the course of the game demonstrated that those at the top of the social hierarchy are better able to empathize with those at the bottom. Whereupon ended a century of experiment with governance by men of the people. Liberalism triumphed and the *haute bourgeoisie* was back in power.

The ethnic politics of New York in the 1960s can be understood only if this not especially pleasant process is seen for what it is. Or was. The Catholic ascendancy in New York had been based first on numbers, but second on a reasonably well-grounded assumption that they normally, as Democrats, would best look after the interests of ordinary people, and would be especially concerned for the least well off, being themselves only recently emerged from that condition. The Protestant elite of the city had always challenged that assumption, asserting instead that the Tammany bosses were boodlers, pure and simple, or in a slightly different formulation, such as that of Lincoln Steffens, were merely paid lackeys of the really big boodlers. Either way the charge was that they did not truly represent the people as they claimed to do. In three elections out of four, the masses would choose to believe the old Tammany boss Charlie Murphy's version rather than that of the *New York Times*. But the effort persisted and in the 1950s acquired a new and devastating tactic. The educated middle class, mostly in the form of young Jewish liberals, began competing for control of the Democratic party machinery itself. In the 1960s they succeeded in breaking Carmine De Sapio, who will probably be regarded as the last of the powerful Democratic party chieftains. (They could destroy De Sapio, but they could not replace him. In the process, they had destroyed a style of politics.) And almost at that moment, the central issue of politics in the city turned from "Bossism" to "Racism," and here the Catholics were wholly outclassed. And also, in a way, outmaneuvered. For when the city turned to the issue of race in the mid-1960s, it did not thereby turn away from the issue of who would control the political system. To the contrary, the struggle over racial issues became in many ways a surrogate struggle for control of the city government and the Democratic party. In the end, the Catholics, who had dominated both, lost out.

Many things happened, of which the most important is that from the outset, Jews, in a great variety of roles, defined the new problem. And the first thing they did was to define the difficulties facing the Negroes as being in most respects identical to those earlier faced by Jews. In essence, this was the situation of the approach of a highly competitive group so threatening to the established position of others that artificial barriers are raised to restrict and limit the success experienced by the new group (for example, quotas in medical schools).

Reality was almost completely the opposite. The black immigrants in New York City in the 1950s and 1960s were a displaced peasantry, not at all unlike their Irish and Italian predecessors; most, in truth, like the Irish, who arrived with all the stigmata acquired from living under rulers of a different race. (The gulf between ruler and ruled in, say, eighteenth-century Ireland was just as great as that between black and white in the American South.) The Negroes were not highly competitive; they were undercompetitive. They had been raised that way in the South, and were not instantly transformed by Bedford-Stuyvesant, which became not a ghetto but a slum. Taking all references to racial or ethnic identity out of university admission applications, and forbidding photographs, would not automatically double or triple the proportion of Negroes admitted to the Columbia Medical School. It might have quite the opposite effect. But, nonetheless, in one form or another, the situation of the black masses was likened to that of an earlier group that had been artificially and systematically denied successes that would otherwise have accrued to them but for discrimination. The response of society would have to be to forbid such discrimination and to punish the discriminators by opening up their restricted preserves to equal opportunity.

Stated in these terms, which are simplified but not exaggerated, it will be seen that this interpretation of the situation of the blacks served a very considerable agenda. It was, first of all, responsive to the genuine concern of New York Jews for the desperate conditions in which so many blacks lived in New York, and the hideous past from which they had escaped. (How could they fail to interpret such things in light of their own experience?) It was responsive to the enlightened self-interest of the Jews, and any other group in the city, to see the black newcomers grow prosperous and successful, as had their predecessors in one degree or another. *But it also served to ascribe, or impute, a good deal of wrongdoing to working-class Catholics who weren't especially conscious of wrongdoing at all.* Moreover, it set up situations of conflict between black and white working-class interests which, no matter who won the battle, ended with the white workers losing the war. No matter what happened, *they* ended up as "racists" and "bigots." And at no cost to upper-middle-class players. It was demanded that trade unions be opened up to the newcomers, with all the primitive fears that would arouse. But it was rarely argued that blacks must be admitted to brokerage firms or law offices. (More to the point, when it was so argued, concessions were easy to make. The upper-middle-class persons involved were not gripped by concern over the scarcity of opportunity. They were more likely to be concerned by the scarcity of Harvard Law School graduates to help with the burgeoning practice. Significantly, when the generalized threat of black competition made its way into the school system, where lower-middle-class Jewish teachers—persons not unlike building trade unionists, trained to one job, and not likely to get another one as good—were exposed, New York experienced the most dangerous racial crisis in its history.) In any event, as this process continued, the fitness of the Catholic majority of the city to govern was increasingly and effectively challenged. On the day after Mayor Lindsay, in 1969, was defeated by an Italian Catholic for re-nomination by his own party, be ascribed his defeat to "bigots." And although he was later thought to be paying not a little attention to the bigot vote, the fact is that, on this issue, he won re-election against quite extraordinary odds. It was in this election that the Catholic ascendancy in New York City finally dissolved. Without doubt, there will be periods of Catholic rule in the future. But the era is over.

One aspect of the decline of Catholic power has been the failure of the Italians to make a larger impact on the city scene. Everything we have said of the Catholics generally holds even more strongly for the Italians in particular. The working-class style as against the middle-class style marks them, even as they move in larger and larger numbers into the middle class. Their ability to take over leadership, in the mass media, in education, in the newer sectors of economic development, in politics, even in the Church, has been limited. Some of the aspects of the Italian-American cultural and social style that seem to have contributed to these limitations—the ties of family, neighborhoods, friends, the choice of these as against the claims of higher education and lonely ambition—have produced many of the most attractive families, neighborhoods, and friendships in New York. (Italians have a genius for making cities livable.) But somehow the ethos has not gone beyond that to create a presumption of leadership in city affairs.

The reasons are complex. But high among them would have to be listed the curse of the Mafia. In the 1960s the curse compounded. Not only did the Italian population continue to suffer from the exactions of its criminal element—a basic ecological rule being that criminals prey first of all on those nearest them—but also the charge, or fear, or presumption, of "Mafia connections" affected nearly the entire Italian community. Injustice leading to yet more injustice: that is about what happened. During the 1960s the mass media, *and the non-Italian politicians,* combined to make the Mafia a household symbol of evil and wrongdoing. Television ran endless crime series, such as *The Untouchables,* in which the criminals were, for all purposes, exclusively Italian. Attorneys General, of whom Robert Kennedy was the archetype, made the "war against organized crime" a staple of national politics. As Attorney General, Kennedy produced Joseph Valachi, who informed the nation that the correct designation of the syndicate was not Mafia but "Cosa Nostra"—"Our Thing." True or not, the designation was solemnly accepted by the media, with an air almost of gratitude for the significance of the information thus divulged. On the occasions that a reputed "family head" would pass away (often as not peaceably, amidst modest comfort, in Nassau County), the *New York Times* would discourse learnedly on what the probable succession would be.

This is rather an incredible set of facts. Ethnic sensitivities in New York, in the nation, have never been higher than during the 1960s. To accuse a major portion of the population of persistent criminality would seem a certain course of political or commercial disaster. But it was not. The contrast with the general "elite" response to Negro crime is instructive. Typically, the latter was blamed on white society. Black problems were muted, while Italian problems were emphasized, even exaggerated. Why?

We do not know. There may have been some displacement of anti-black feeling to Italians, possibly as a consequence of the association of the Mafia with the drug traffic, and the latter's association with high rates of black crime. It may be that society needs an unpopular group around, and the Italians were for many reasons available. Democratic reformers, in largest number Jews but also including among them political figures who had come from the Irish Catholic and white Protestant groups, were able to use the Italian association with crime to topple any number of Italian political leaders and, perhaps more important, to prevent others from acquiring any ascendancy.[2] Many political figures thus gained advantage, but the weakness of the group itself was decisive.

This might be symbolized by the near-to-total failure of the Italian-American "Anti-Defamation League" established during the 1960s to combat anti-Italian prejudice. It was not only modeled on, it was apparently named after, the Anti-Defamation League of B'nai B'rith, but the results were in no way similar. The ADL has access to an extraordinary range of Jewish intellectuals, writers, professors, publishers, publicists, moving picture and, more recently, television executives, who happen to be Jewish. These in turn connect with almost the entire network of public-opinion-making in America. In New York this is known as "clout." It is something which in this field Italians simply do not have. Whether they ever shall, as a group, remains to be seen. There are uncertain signs. Mario Puzo's *The Godfather*, a benign, even romanticized, account of the long life and happy death of a particularly repelling brute of a Mafia chieftain, was 40 weeks on the *Times* Best Seller list for 1969, equaling *Portnoy's Complaint*. This is the mark of an emergent self-consciousness, but not necessarily of emerging competence in the encounters that count. It is likely that Portnoy will continue to be "Assistant Commissioner for the City of New York Commission on Human Opportunity" under the Lindsay Administration and its successors (there is money to be made in poverty), while the sons and daughters of Puzo's saga will continue to find themselves exploiting themselves and exploited by others. For the rest of the city it has at least been an example of reasonably good grace under pressure.

Of the Catholic groups of the city, none ended the 1960s in less promising circumstances than did the Puerto Ricans. Our expectation that they would leapfrog their black neighbors does not seem to have occurred. To the contrary, Puerto Ricans emerged from the decade as the group with the highest incidence of poverty and the lowest number of men of public position who bargain and broker the arrangements of the city. They had no elected officials, no prominent religious leaders, no writers, no powerful organizations. In the 1969 municipal elections, all five of the Puerto Rican candidates (among 246 running for office) lost. Their relations with blacks were not good, especially as the latter took advantage of the opportunities for middle-class persons created by the antipoverty programs. But neither could they make much common cause with the coreligionists who had preceded them to the city. In a way, this left the Catholic Church with one of the most serious problems it had yet faced. The religious observance of Puerto Ricans was mixed, but so was that of Italians when they first arrived. Prosperity makes persons more, not less, concerned with such matters. But Puerto Ricans also showed great interest in Pentecostal Protestantism. (An interesting continuity. The first Irish and then Italians to rise to prominence in public affairs in the city were Protestant. So with the first Puerto Rican, Herman Badillo.) If the Puerto Rican mass should abandon Catholicism, or split on the issue, Catholics would shortly become a numerical as well as a political and cultural minority in the city.

And yet, even though Puerto Ricans have done badly economically and politically, the seventies may be the decade in which they emerge. It may still be argued that their poverty and powerlessness is accompanied by little despair and a good deal of hope. Certainly, even though the Negroes are (statistically) better off economically and have much larger representation politically, they show much more despair and much less hope. The explanation for this paradox, we suggest, is that Puerto Ricans still see themselves in the immigrant-ethnic model; that is, they see their poor economic and political position as reflecting recency of arrival and evil circumstances that can still be overcome. Thus, they have an explanation for their poor circumstances that does not demand revolutionary change. This immigrant-ethnic model is strengthened by the fact that so many new Spanish-speaking immigrants to the city during the 1960s are refugee Cubans and voluntary migrants from various Central and South American countries, who, even more than the Puerto Ricans, see themselves as classic immigrants, fleeing political persecution and economic deprivation to find opportunity in a new country. These non–Puerto Rican Spanish-speaking migrants are, willy-nilly, identified by the rest of the city as "Puerto Rican." Perhaps a new ethnic group, the "Spanish-speaking," is emerging to replace the Puerto Rican.

Certainly, the term is coming into widespread use in the city. The Puerto Ricans have to struggle between a conception of themselves as "colonized" and, therefore, "exploited," and a conception of themselves as "immigrants." The first leads to bitterness, the second to hope. The other Spanish-speaking migrants have much less occasion to think of themselves as colonized (though there is an ideology to justify that, too!).

Not that the "colonized" pattern does not have attractions for Puerto Rican youth and intellectuals. There are some stirrings of alliance with blacks who think in this way. A stronger drive in Puerto Rico for independence will affect Puerto Ricans on the mainland. The radical white college youth, who are now so influential in the mass media, will try to convince them they are "colonized." And yet, one detects a strong resistance to this interpretation of the Puerto Rican position's becoming popular.

What are the signs that the Puerto Ricans might be following the ethnic immigrant pattern rather than the colonial pattern? Some are the moderate tone of their politics; their resistance to full identification with militant blacks; the emphasis of their social institutions, few as they are, on personal mobility; their continued emphasis on business, and creating new business, with little outside support (the colonized pattern would be to call for "expropriation"). The 1960s may go down as the worst decade for the Puerto Ricans in New York. Or we may be wrong, and the long-range economic and political changes in city and country may record the continued agony of the Puerto Ricans in the city.

At the close of the 1960s, the Democrats were more completely out of power in New York state and city government than at almost any time in their history. The oldest organized political party in the world was reduced by way of officeholders to the controller in Albany, Arthur Levitt, who had long since become a politically neutral figure, and the controller in New York City, Abraham Beame, whose career would seem to have passed its apogee.

The decline of the Democrats accompanied, and to some degree merely reflected, the collapse of Catholic power. On the other hand, it is not likely to be a permanent or even a prolonged condition. In party politics prolonged failure typically creates the conditions of eventual success. Thus, by 1970, as Governor Rockefeller completed his third term in office, Republicans had controlled the state government for all but four of the preceding 28 years. By definition, Democratic chances became better. Similarly, the prospect of Mayor Lindsay's succeeding to a third term, or of his being followed by another Republican, would not, on form, be good. The Democrats will rise again.

They will not, however, ever be the same. The process of disestablishing the party machinery has continued almost to the point where there is no machinery. In any number of Eastern cities the decline or destruction of the

Democratic working-class parties was followed by the rise of organized crime as the single most effective system for organizing power and influence. (It was, and remains, the theme of many middle-class commentators that organized crime was somehow brought into existence by the "corrupt" party machines. This would seem not at all the case. The relationship was more often that of competing power systems, with an Irish-Italian overlay.) When the Democratic party declined in New York, a quite different group took over, one which had helped engineer that decline, and which benefited from it. It is a group impossible to locate and difficult to describe save perhaps to say that its nucleus, or one of its nuclei, could be said to be those persons who, at a succession of breakfast meetings in Manhattan in 1968–69, raised fortunes for the campaigns of first Eugene McCarthy, then Hubert Humphrey, then John Lindsay, and then began gathering to consider whom they would raise money for in the coming gubernatorial and senatorial campaigns. Although of distinctly liberal cast of mind, the general sociological point could be made that, in terms of occupation and income and social background, the group was not greatly to be distinguished from the patriciate-plutocracy that in most American cities does try to have a say in things, and usually manages to do so.

To identify this group as "limousine liberals," as Mario Procaccino did in the 1969 mayoralty campaign, or to refer it to as "the Manhattan arrangement," is not far from the facts. It is also a fact that this group beat Procaccino. And herein lies the problem that will continue to plague the Democrats and the city for years to come, whatever the ups and downs of party politics. The Democratic coalition in New York City was shattered in the 1960s. It will never be put back together as a normal condition of politics. In rough terms, this was a coalition of Irish, Italians, Jews, and blacks against the field. They added up to a majority, and they usually won, but never again.

There are a number of reasons for Irish- and Italian-Catholic distaste for and fear of the commercial success and high culture of the Jews (a success increasingly taking the form of familiar WASP power). A word may be in order about reciprocal distaste and not so much fear as disdain by the ascendant group.

In an important article that appeared last year in *The American Scholar,* Michael Lerner laid out the essentials of this relationship.

> When white . . . students denounce the racist university or racist American society, one has little doubt about what they refer to. One also has little doubt about the political leanings of the speaker. He is a good left-liberal or radical, upper-class or schooled in the assumptions of upper-class liberalism.
>
> Liberal-to-radical students use these phrases and feel purged of the bigotry and racism of people such as Chicago's Mayor Daley. No one could be further from bigotry, they seem to believe, than they.
>
> But it isn't so. An extraordinary amount of bigotry on the part of elite

liberal students goes unexamined. . . . Directed at the lower middle class, it feeds on the unexamined biases of class perspective, the personality predilections of elite radicals, and academic disciplines that support their views.

There are certainly exceptions in the liberal-radical university society— people intellectually or actively aware of and opposed to the unexamined prejudice. But their anomalousness and lack of success in making an ostensibly introspective community face its own disease is striking.

In general, the bigotry of a lower-middle-class policeman toward a ghetto black or of a lower-middle-class mayor toward a rioter is not viewed in the same perspective as the bigotry of an upper-middle-class peace matron toward a lower-middle-class mayor; or of an upper-class university student toward an Italian, a Pole or a National Guardsman from Cicero, Illinois—that is, if the latter two cases are called bigotry at all. The violence of the ghetto is patronized as it is 'understood' and forgiven; the violence of a Cicero racist, convinced that Martin Luther King threatens his lawn and house and powerboat, is detested without being understood. Yet the two bigotries are very similar. For one thing, each is directed toward the class directly below the resident bigot, the class that reflects the dark side of the bigot's life. Just as the upper class recognizes in lower-class lace-curtain morality the veiled uptightness of upper-middle-class life, so the lower-middle-class bigot sees reflected in the lower class the violence, sexuality and poverty that threaten him. The radical may object that he dislikes the lower middle class purely because of its racism and its politics. But that is not sufficient explanation: Polish jokes are devoid of political content.

Significantly, by way of illustration, Lerner cited a world-famous Yale professor of government who, at dinner, "on the day an Italian-American announced his candidacy for mayor of New York," remarked that "If Italians aren't actually an inferior race, they do the best imitation of one I've seen." (It was later also said of Mario Procaccino that he was so sure of being elected that he had ordered new linoleum for Gracie Mansion. No one said much of anything about John Marchi, the Republican and Conservative candidate, whose Tuscan aristocratic style was surely the equal of Lindsay's WASP patrician manner, and who conducted perhaps the most thoughtful campaign of the three.) Procaccino was made out a clod, and was beaten.

These are not unfamiliar sentiments in the world. But they do destroy coalitions, and that has happened in New York. Moreover, in New York City, ethnic tensions were greatly exacerbated by the rise during the 1960s of a peculiarly virulent form of black anti-white rhetoric that the white elites tolerated and even in ways encouraged because it was, in effect, directed to the same lower-middle-class and working-class groups which they themselves held in such disdain. Lerner noted an essential fact concerning the Yale professor's comment about Procaccino. "He could not have said that about black people if the subject had been Rap Brown."

Even more essential is the reverse fact that Rap Brown was, at this time, in a metaphoric sense, pretty much free to say anything he wished about the professor, or rather, about "whitey." Indeed, the more provocative the remark, the more likely it was to be taken seriously. This constituted a grievous departure from the rules of ethnic coalition and clearly made an enormous impact on the Democratic party.

In the course of the 1960s, the etiquette of race relations changed. It became possible—even, from the point of view of the attackers, desirable—for blacks to attack and vilify whites in a manner no ethnic group had ever really done since the period of anti-Irish feeling of the 1840s and 1850s. This was yet another feature of the Southern pattern of race relations, as against the Northern pattern of ethnic group relations, making its impress on the life of the city. There was, of course, an inversion. The "nigger" speech of the Georgia legislature became the "honky" speech of the Harlem street corner, or the national television studio, complete with threats of violence. In this case, it was the whites who were required to remain silent and impotent in the face of the attack. But the pattern was identical.

The calamity of this development will be obvious. The whites in the North responded much as did the blacks in the South. In New York City it was especially difficult for the white working class to understand. What had *they* done? What were the blacks complaining about? The point here is that the white worker in New York in the 1960s readily enough came to see that a *portion* of the black population of the city had achieved what was, in effect, a privileged status. Thus, Whitney Young, Jr., in a public address, could dismiss whites as "affluent peasants," in the certainty that such abrasiveness would in no way jeopardize his well-paid job as director of the National Urban League, his office as president of the National Association of Social Workers, and so on through the very considerable perquisites of a race man in New York in the 1960s. Young would reply, and with justice, that such rhetoric was necessary to maintain his "credibility" with black militants. (He was speaking to the separatist, or separated, Association of Black Social Workers, whose numbers in New York came to 3,000.) But this hardly improved his credibility with white workers, who almost certainly at this time could sense that social workers are not an especially exploited people.

Doors were opened to blacks everywhere in the city, doors which would never have been opened to a Pole or a Slovak with similar credentials. And the blacks took it as their due. Which, in any large perspective of American history, it most certainly was, but this was not necessarily self-evident to white workers two or three generations away from the life of peasants on the feudal estates of Europe. Their reaction to the black rhetoric, increasingly accompanied by threats of violence (again the Southern model), was predictable, and it was not always attractive. The anguish of the black slums was something they knew too little (or too much) of to keep steadily in mind. The aggression of the black leaders against whites in general was, in any event, too threatening, too disorienting, to maintain a focus on these other matters. On every hand, persons in positions of ostensible authority seemed to be denying reality. (In his address, Young, a fair man, had noted that "being black can be an asset" to a fortunate minority of the black population. This became a self-evident fact in New York in the 1960s. But all the white elite leaders talked about was discrimination. A similar phenomenon arose as the white elites persistently denied the growing problem of crime, imputing racist motives to anyone who made an issue of it, when for the great mass of the city population it had become a very real issue indeed.) The result was a further delegitimization of authority, a general rise in fear of aggression from other groups (many Negroes at this time became obsessed with the prospect of genocide), and a spreading conviction that the city was "sick" and "ungovernable."

In New York, the 1960s ended much worse than they began. It will now be much more difficult to bring about the gradual incorporation of blacks into the ethnic pattern of the city. If it should turn out to be impossible, the 1960s will be the period in which the direction of things turned.

■ ■ ■ ■ Notes

1 The 1960s were not at all a barren period for Catholic scholarship. To the contrary, in a period when Jewish and Protestant radical intellectuals became political actors of some consequence, with an accompanying decline in the quality of their work, theologians at institutions such as Fordham began to do quite serious work. It was just that—serious work—and had no popular impact save indirectly through the peace movement, but the foundations of some future influence were perhaps being laid. It is at least worth noting that Eugene McCarthy was by far the most intellectual political figure the Democrats had produced since Wilson.

2 The reformers' luck held in one respect. At the end of the decade De Sapio was convicted on a corruption charge of the kind repeatedly insinuated when he was in power.

21
City and Country: Marriage Proposals

SCOTT DONALDSON

For more than a century, urbanites having the money to choose their place of residence have moved away from the center of cities to the periphery. In the nineteenth and early twentieth centuries, most cities were able to annex these outlying settlements. In 1854 Philadelphia grew from two to fifty-four square miles, and in 1897 the New York state legislature created Greater New York by adding Brooklyn, Queens, Staten Island, and parts of the Bronx to the existing boundaries of New York City.

In the twentieth century, however, outside the South and Southwest, cities have found it increasingly difficult to annex new areas. Boston last added to its territory in the 1870s, because suburban settlements found it more to their advantage to remain independent than to join the city. Northeastern and midwestern cities now find themselves ringed by independent communities. These communities resist integration with the core city, try to use their powers of zoning and other forms of land-use control to attract the city's jobs while keeping out the poorer paid workers, and approach any form of cooperation with the core city with a wary eye as to possible costs. Major metropolitan areas now consist of hundreds, and in some cases more than a thousand, separate governmental units.

Only a few attempts to create integrated metropolitan governments have been successful. Most proposals in this direction run aground because of suburbanite fears of being saddled with the fiscal and the social problems of increasingly black central cities, and because black politicians and voters in the central city, achieving some power for the first time, do not want to be again rendered powerless by a white majority in the metropolitan area as a whole.

At present there seem to be two contrary trends in scholarly and popular thinking on the subject of the proper political organization of metropolitan areas. One school emphasizes the fiscal plight of the central cities, who have lost much of their economic base through the outmigration of industry, retail sales, and some forms of office activity, while having to continue to provide an expansive and expensive array of services as the core of the metropolitan area. Major medical, cultural, religious, and educational institutions remain in the central cities. The presence of these facilities does help to make urban life urbane, but they also mean considerable land off the tax rolls. And, as everybody knows, a disproportionate share of the poor live in the decayed portions of our central cities, so much so that inner city has become a code term for poverty. The answer according to many students is a better balance of needs and resources, requiring that the suburbs should pay their fair share of the costs of providing central city services through the creation of some form of revenue sharing. Advocates of governmental integration want to end political fragmentation of the metropolis and to increase centralization.

The opposite school of thought emphasizes community control, holding that our problems stem not from too little centralization but too much. Demands for local control of schools and police forces emphasize the feeling that for too long upper-class and bureaucratic elites have imposed their will upon the poor and the powerless, and that the time has come to confer power upon the people. Inner-city residents are now insisting upon what suburbanities have taken pride in: a government responsive to the needs and wishes of the people. The problem lies in reconciling the economic need for centralization with the legitimate demand for local involvement and responsibility.

In the following essay, Scott Donaldson deals with the attitudes of intellectuals and planners toward country, city, and suburb. Before World War II, most observers looked to the suburb as the answer to urban problems, although Lewis Mumford eloquently warned of the dangers of unplanned sprawl as early as the 1920s. After World War II, with the vast expansion of profit-oriented and unplanned bedroom communities, suburb became a pejorative term. Rather than representing the harmonious intermingling of city and country, the suburb was now viewed as the stronghold of Middle America, with its parochialism, its privatism, its indifference to the plight of the black poor, and its conventionality and conformity. Donaldson vividly reminds us that the solutions of yesterday often become the problems of today.

■ ■ ■ ■ **For Further Reading**

Frederic Howe, *The City: The Hope of Democracy* (Seattle: University of Washington Press, 1969) shows how a typical progressive of the early twentieth century looked to suburban decentralization as the answer to urban problems. Sam Warner, *Streetcar Suburbs: The Process of Growth in Boston 1870–1900* (New York: Atheneum, 1969) discusses suburbanization in the nineteenth century. Harold M. Mayer and Richard C. Wade, *Chicago: Growth of a Metropolis* (Chicago: University of Chicago Press, 1969) has important textual and photographic material on suburbanization in Chicago, a process which began very early in the city's history and continues to the present. Several of the essays in James Q. Wilson, ed., *The Metropolitan Enigma: Inquiries into the Nature and Dimensions of America's "Urban Crisis"* (New York: Doubleday Anchor Books, 1970) assess the contemporary impact of the central city–suburban dichotomy. Robert C. Wood, *Suburbia: Its People and Their Politics* (Boston: Houghton Mifflin Co., 1958) demonstrates the ambivalence of some American intellectuals toward suburbs in the late 1950s. Scott Donaldson, *The Suburban Myth* (New York: Columbia University Press, 1969) is a full-scale history of attitudes toward suburbanization and suburbs.

■ David Riesman, in his essay on "The Suburban Sadness," acknowledges that he writes as "one who loves city and country, but not the suburbs."[1] Riesman's position is not at all unusual. Most social commentators regard today's suburbs more with loathing than with love, finding them homogeneous, conformist, adjustment-oriented, conservative, dull, child centered, female dominated, anti-individualist—in a word, impossible —places to live. It was not always thus, with intellectuals.

For one thing, the American intellectual has not, until recently—until, in fact, the suburb came along as a scapegoat to replace the city—been willing to confess any affection for the city. For another, as Ebenezer Howard suggested in 1898, there was a time when the suburb was thought of as the hope of civilization, as the happy, healthy offspring of the marriage of town and country: "Town and country *must be married,* and out of this joyous union will spring a new hope, a new life, a new civilization."[2] Howard's Garden Cities represented the apotheosis of the suburban dream —places which were at once *real* communities, collections of people who would work and live together in civic and social harmony, and at the same time totally self-sufficient units, made up of discrete individuals able and willing to pursue their own private goals. Indeed, if hopes had not once been so high for suburbia, it surely would not have fallen so low in critical estimation at the midpoint of the twentieth century. For Howard was by no means the only theorist to envision the suburb as the product of a happy marriage between town and country, a union designed to resolve one of the most troublesome paradoxes of American civilization.

The paradox is, of course, the continuing worship of rural, countrified life in a nation where the pull of progress has created an unmistakably urban civilization. The roots of the agrarian myth stretch back to the beginnings of western culture and the paradisiacal garden. But the most powerful expressions of the myth came with the new nation and the Enlightenment, in the voices of such men as Hector St. John de Crèvecoeur and Thomas Jefferson. Jefferson's fondness for the farm and dislike of the city are legendary, and Crèvecoeur located his ideal Americans on the farms of the "middle settlements," midway between sea and wilderness, where the simple cultivation of the earth would purify them. These men expressed beliefs which have demonstrated amazing staying power. Their persistence can hardly be denied in a land where the Supreme Court must step in to assure city and suburb dwellers something like fair legislative representation, where farmers are subsidized not to grow crops, where it is still expedient for a politician to claim a rural heritage. And the beliefs persist despite their obvious lack of relevance to reality. Men mouth agrarian sentiments, but go to the cities, where the money is to be made. The American thinker, almost since the first days of the Republic, has been confronted with this paradox, and as time proceeded American thought arrived at a potential solution. It would be the suburb which would represent the best of both worlds, which would preserve rural values in an urbanizing world, which would enable the individual to pursue wealth while retaining the amenities of country life.

After the Civil War and owing to the development of the railroads, the first American suburbs were developed around New York, Boston and Philadelphia. From the beginning, these suburbs were regarded as ideal places to live, representing a rather wealthy middle landscape between crowded, unhealthy city life and the "coarse and brutal" frontier.[3] "So long as men are forced to dwell in log huts and follow the hunter's life," Alexander Jackson Downing wrote, "we must not be surprised at lynch law and the use of the bowie knife. But, when smiling lawns and tasteful cottages begin to embellish a country, we know that order and culture are established."[4] Downing had in mind rural villages full of tasteful "cottages" of real elegance, like those going up at Newport, Rhode Island.

Efforts soon began to scale down the lavish Newport cottage to the pocketbooks of the middle classes. Suburban homes and lots served as promotional bait in an 1876 *Harper's Weekly* advertisement aimed at attracting readers to "the Fourth of July Centennial Demonstration at the Third Avenue Theater." Two two-story cottages and ten $100 lots in Garden City Park, on Long Island, would be raffled off at the demonstration, the advertisement announced, as well as 100 silver watches and 388 one-dollar greenbacks.[5] Later in the same year, this magazine celebrated the joys of suburban life with a cover picture and article on "Summer in the Country." The picture, which shows a young boy and girl "walking side by side in the sweet summer fields," was designed to remind readers, "by contrast, of the sad lot of poor city children, who rarely have the opportunity to breathe the pure air of the country, and refresh their eyes with the sight of flowers and grass."[6] The "flowers and grass" make it clear that the "country" *Harper's Weekly* finds so desirable is somewhat nearer at hand than the Iowa corn fields, say. If such a stretch of country was inaccessible to most readers of the magazine, as it probably was in 1876, it still represented a popular goal. Then as now, the place to bring up children was out in the open air, far from noise and smoke. Three years later, in 1879, the radical Henry George proposed in *Progress and Poverty* that his single tax on land would have the effect of creating a sort of ideal middle landscape. Such a single tax, George maintained, would do away with wholesale speculation in real estate, and

> The destruction of speculative land values would tend to diffuse population where it is too dense and to concentrate it where it is too sparse; to substitute for the tenement house, homes surrounded by gardens, and to fully settle agricultural districts before people were driven far from neighbors to look for land. The people of the cities would thus get more of the pure air and sunshine of the country, the people of the country more of the economics and social life of the city. . . .[7]

Certainly most Americans agreed with this urban politician in an emotional preference for country over city; certainly most desired above all that union of country and city, sunshine and social life, he envisioned as a consequence of the single tax.

It remained for Ebenezer Howard, the London court reporter, to propose specific arrangements for this marriage of city and country in his influential 1898 book, *Garden Cities of Tomorrow*. Howard's proposals were welcomed on both sides of the Atlantic, and they remain today the guiding principles of so important an American critic and theorist as Lewis Mumford. Clearly, they are motivated by agrarian sentiments:

> It is well-nigh universally agreed by men of all parties, not only in England, but all over Europe and America and our colonies, that it is deeply to be deplored that the people should continue to stream into the already overcrowded cities, and should thus further deplete the country districts. . . .

How should we go about restoring people to the garden—"that beautiful land of ours, with its canopy of sky, the air that blows upon it, the sun that warms it, and rain and dew that moisten it—the very embodiment of Divine love for man?"[8] The restoration can be accomplished, Howard wrote, only if we reject two-valued, black and white thinking, and consider instead a third alternative.

"There are in reality not only . . . two alternatives—town life and country life—but a third alternative, in which all the advantages of the most energetic and active town life, with all the beauty and delight of the country, may be secured in perfect combination. . . ." To illustrate the point, Howard constructed the metaphor of the magnets. Each person may be regarded as a needle, attracted by magnets. Until now, he wrote, the town has had the most powerful magnet, and so it has pulled citizen-needles from the no longer all powerfully magnetic "bosom of our kindly mother earth." To remedy the situation, "nothing short of the discovery of a method of constructing magnets of yet greater power than our cities possess can be effective for redistributing the population in a spontaneous and healthy manner. . . ." Howard set about to construct this magnet "of yet greater power," the magnet which combined the best of both town and country. There was social opportunity in town, but it was balanced by a "closing out of nature"; there was beauty of nature in the country, but it was measured against "lack of society." The town-country magnet would merge the country's beauty of nature with the town's social opportunity. In economic terms, the town's magnetism resulted at least partly from the high wages paid, but rents were high in town as well. In the country, rents were low, but so were wages. In the new town-country land, however, the citizen would make high wages and pay low rents—he would have his cake and eat it, too.

What the town-country magnet boiled down to, in Howard's theory, was the Garden City, which was to be economically self-sufficient while still at peace with nature. Population would be restricted to a workable size in the Garden City, and jobs, including industrial jobs, provided for all inhabitants. But the homes would be surrounded with greenery; the presence of nature was never to be lost sight of in a pell-mell drive for the dollar. In his conception of the Garden City, Howard had constructed a new version of the middle landscape, closer to town than Crèvecoeur's. In Crèvecoeur's version, the middle settlements were located halfway between the city seaports and the wild woods; Howard had moved his middle landscape (in conception if not in fact) so that it was now placed between the city and those rural settlements which had served as Crèvecoeur's ideal. The ideal middle landscape, in short, was coming closer and closer to suburbia. It would be more explicitly located there by intellectuals in the early decades of the twentieth century.

This movement of the middle landscape closer to the city reflected a growing awareness, already obvious in the negative features of Howard's country magnet, that rural life left something to be desired. The farm could never be subject to the vilification the muckrakers brought to bear on the American city, but the agrarian life was not all milk and honey, either. The Country Life Commission appointed by President Theodore Roosevelt in 1908 reported that drudgery, barrenness and heavy drinking characterized rural regions.[9] The town boy did not have to visit Paree to pack up and leave; the question was rather, "how you gonna keep 'em down on the farm," after they've seen the farm? Young people continued to desert farming for the city, but the standard operating rhetoric of all Americans, whether they were urban or rural by birth, continued to hymn the praises and celebrate the virtues of life on the land. In their hearts, Americans knew that the good life was agrarian; but they listened to their heads, which told them to seek their future in the city.

Somewhat in the manner of Al Smith, who believed that the ills of democracy could be cured by more democracy, Teddy Roosevelt's Country Life Commission recommended a revival of rural civilization as a solution to its apparent degeneration. This revived rural life was to be different, however. In the words of the Commission chairman, Dean Liberty Hyde Bailey of the Cornell Agricultural School, it would be a "working out of the desire to make rural civilization . . . a world-motive to even up society as between country and city."[10] The scales were overbalanced in favor of the city. Something was needed to give more weight to the country's side of the contest. That something, several turn-of-the-century observers were convinced, was represented by the suburb.

Adna Weber, writing in 1900, surveyed suburban growth, then scarcely beginning, and pronounced it the happiest of social movements:

> The "rise of the suburbs" it is, which furnishes the solid basis of a hope that the evils of city life, so far as they result from overcrowding, may be in large part removed. . . . It will realize the wish and prediction of Kingsley, "a

complete interpenetration of city and country, a complete fusion of their different modes of life and a combination of the advantages of both, such as no country in the world has even seen."[11]

Court reporter Howard had located his town-country magnet in carefully planned Garden Cities of the future. Weber was more optimistic: mere dispersal of population to the suburbs, a trend already going its own merry, unplanned way, would accomplish the modern utopia.

Frederic C. Howe, in his 1905 book, *The City: The Hope of Democracy,* qualified the title's message by suggesting that suburbanization, not urbanization, represented the democratic hope of the future:

> The open fields about the city are inviting occupancy, and there the homes of the future will surely be. The city proper will not remain the permanent home of the people. Population must be dispersed. The great cities of Australia are spread out into the suburbs in a splendid way. For miles about are broad roads, with small houses, gardens, and an opportunity for touch with the freer, sweeter life which the country offers.[12]

Avowedly pro-urbanite, Howe could not resist, at least rhetorically, the charms of the countryside. These, he thought, could be made available to every man, living in "small houses" with gardens, in the suburbs of the future.

Two eminent Harvard philosophers took much the same view as Weber and Howe, though they did not advocate suburbanization by name. Josiah Royce, who deplored the excessive mobility, the homogenizing tendencies, and the "mob spirit" of city life, maintained that the individual was swallowed up by the city, and could avoid this fate only by fleeing to the provinces. In the "provinces" (what he seems to have meant by this term might be designated "rural villages") were located the small social groups in which freedom was now to be found. The individual could best exercise his individualism in a socio-economic-political community of limited size: the message, basically, of Thomas Jefferson, restated in twentieth-century terms by the leading idealist of the age. George Santayana blended a strong strain of the bucolic with his urbane philosophy. Describing his boyhood town of Avila, Spain, he "expressed his admiration of situations that he described by the phrases *rus in urbs, oppidum in agris,* or *urbs ruri,* some combination of city and country."[13] The search for the ideal middle landscape persisted along with the belief that city life was stifling to the soul. Louis Sullivan, in his *Autobiography of an Idea,* tells the sinister effects of being taken to Boston as a young lad. "As one might move a flourishing plant from the open to a dark cellar, and imprison it there, so the miasma of the big city poisoned a small boy acutely sensitive to his surroundings. He mildewed; and the leaves and buds of ambition fell from him." He would surely have run away, the architect recollects without tranquility, had it not been for his father's wise excursions with him to the suburbs, "on long walks to Roxbury, to Dorchester, even to Brookline, where the boy might see a bit of green and an opening-up of things. . . ."[14]

Perhaps the worst thing about the twentieth-century city, as such observers as Robert Park and John Dewey examined it, was its very bigness. In the urban maelstrom, the individual lost the identity that had been so assuredly his on the farm, in the village. The primary group tended to dissolve in the city, Park wrote in 1916, and people lost sight of the values of the local community in a search for excitement. "Cities," he wrote, "have been proverbially and very properly described as 'wicked.' " It is both ironic and appropriate that Park, the nation's first great urban sociologist, should have revealed a nostalgic preference for the secure values of an agrarian civilization, of the family on the farm.[15] Dewey, like Park, noted the frenetic quest for excitement in cities and suggested that it might be simply "the expression of [a] frantic search for something to fill the void caused by the loosening of the bonds which hold persons together in [an] immediate community of experience." As Morton and Lucia White point out in their valuable survey, *The Intellectual Versus the City,* Dewey and Park were both playing modern variants on an old theme of Jefferson's, "divide the counties into wards." Like Jefferson, these public philosophers of the twentieth century regarded the small local community as the fit habitation of democratic men.[16]

In 1917, John R. McMahon published a remarkable book entitled *Success in the Suburbs.* He agreed with Park and Dewey that the city failed to provide man with a healthy environment. By some mystical process, nature refused to function inside the city limits, as O. S. Morgan of Columbia's department of agriculture wrote in a foreword:

> Soil somehow has ceased here to function normally on root systems, has become dirt and dust. Tonic sunshine has ceased to function in chlorophyll bodies in the leaf, has become an unrevered model after which to pattern an enervating midnight glare.

The elect of the city, if they followed the good advice of author McMahon, would throw off this city spell. The advice was simplicity personified. Take yourself to the suburbs, he told his readers, where you can find true success. What was meant by success? Simply "an independent home establishment in a fairly countrified suburb; a household that is self-supporting as to fruits, vegetables, eggs, broilers, and such-like, produced for home use and chiefly by the efforts of the family itself. . . ." Such a successful life not only "means health and happiness"; it also means financial independence. There will be no *cash* dividends, but "in terms of edibles produced and economies effected above the cost of living in the city," suburban life "returns an annual profit on the investment of something like twenty-five percent." In the suburbs, then, a man and his family can enjoy the moral and physical benefits of contact with the soil, and they can make a pretty penny as well.[17]

McMahon's was a "how to" book, as the subtitle makes clear. To achieve *Success in the Suburbs,* one must know "How to Locate, Buy and Build; Garden and Grow Fruit; Keep Fowls and Animals." McMahon provides the answers. For him, clearly, "suburbs" seem to have little value connotation by themselves, until they are transformed into farms. But as the future site of a nation of subsistence farmers, providing economic as well as spiritual gain, the suburbs would come to represent the Jeffersonian paradise regained. This paradise is within your grasp, McMahon told his readers; simply follow my suggestions.

Every spring, he writes, "city folks yawn and have a hungry look in the eyes. They are restless and discontented, peeved and out of kilter." It is not love that troubles them, but nature: "they are bitten by the bacillicus countrycus," which "is beneficent to those who live in the country, but . . . torments those who are prisoned in offices and flats." Urbanites should divorce their city jobs and residents to form a more perfect union. Like Howard, McMahon adopts the marriage metaphor. "My argument is that all city folks who can, should marry nature and settle down with her." You don't have to be rich to escape to suburban wedlock, he counsels. All that is needed is "a snug little home in the nearby country and a piece of ground large enough to grow eggs, fruits, and vegetables."

It is amazing how the family will thrive in its new arrangement. Pale cheeks will grow rosy. Everyone will sleep like a log. Members of the family will get acquainted with one another, finding with relief that they are not "all monotonous Henry James characters" after all. There will be economic rewards as well. The family will raise its own crops for consumption, "thereby collar[ing] a string of middlemen's profits." In town, the family had lived up to its income and could save little or nothing; on the suburban farm, they "live better and are able to stow away a few hundred dollars annually without feeling it." In bestowing advice, McMahon seasons his overt agrarianism with good, hard, common, dollar sense. The first problem is to find a site, and beauty deserves some, but not final, consideration. "Scenery sticks around your habitation a long time and it is wise to pick out a brand that is pleasing and wears well," he writes. "At the same time scenery is not edible and *butters no parsnips.*"[18] The "dollar fiend" and the philosophical agrarian come together in the same paragraph; the author speaks at once with the voice of Thomas Jefferson, and with that of Benjamin Franklin. Like Franklin, McMahon keeps his eye on the main chance; he is nothing if not practical and up-to-date. It is the availability of modern tools and materials, in fact, which has made a utopian life on the suburban farm possible. You can achieve your individualism, and be comfortable about it as well. "On a country place you can attain much of the old frontiersman's independence while having comforts and a fullness of life of which he did not dream." There is not even any real risk involved. "Farming," he acknowledges, "is a gamble; suburban gardening should be a lead-pipe cinch." Marry nature and you live happily ever after; spurn her charms and you reject paradise. Attainment of health, happiness and wealth was ridiculously easy. All one had to do was to move out to the "real up-to-date suburbs, of uncrowded and unfettered Nature, [which] have become the promised land for the city man with limited means but a fair endowment of vim and enterprise. . . ."[19] The world of Thomas Jefferson was not lost. Every man could find agrarian peace and plenty, every man could achieve success on the suburban farm. A rural paradise waited for Americans, just around the corner.

Motivated by much this same kind of thinking, Franklin K. Lane, Secretary of the Interior at the end of World War I, backed legislation to return soldiers to health and prosperity on the farm. They would want "a man's life on returning, or a chance to make their way on the farm." But they would not tolerate the lack of society and the cultural barrenness unearthed by the Country Life Commission. The solution, once again, was a mixed marriage of town and country—"a new rural life with all the urban advantages." Each family should have enough land to provide for its own needs, Lane believes, but there should also be a central, John Dewey-style local "community, and that community having the telephone, and good roads, and the telegraph and the post office, and the good school, and the bank, and the good store all close together, so that the women can talk across the back fence and the man can meet his neighbors." Several soldier settlement bills designed to finance this latest version of the ideal middle landscape were introduced into Congress, but only one, appropriating $200,000 for a preliminary investigation of the public lands available for settlement, ever passed.[20]

The bills were opposed by the farm lobby, which figured there were enough of nature's noblemen already working the soil. Their position was understandable, especially when the depression of 1921 drove millions out of work and back to the land. By that time, Ralph Borsodi had moved his family out to a subsistence farm, and while others tramped city streets looking for work, the Borsodis cut hay, gathered fruit, made gallons of cider, and "began to enjoy the feeling of plenty which the city-dweller never experiences." Borsodi stressed the economic advantages of such a life, particularly if the family produced only for its own consumption. His wife, he concluded, could produce a can of tomatoes "between 20 percent and 30 percent" cheaper than the Campbell Soup Company by eliminating all middlemen. This kind of saving enabled them to be secure in times of economic stress. "The farmer at one time was self-sufficient," he wrote, producing his own food and clothing, building his own shelter, chopping wood for his own fuel. Borsodi's message was that those days were *not* gone forever; the farm family could still be self-sufficient.[21]

Like McMahon, Borsodi emphasized the part modern machinery played in making his "adventure in homesteading" a success. But Borsodi viewed "success" almost exclusively in economic terms. The healthfulness and virtue of country life he may have taken for granted; he did not make much of these beneficial effects in recounting his financial success story. For a century and more, the city had lured people with the promise of economic gain; the country suburb, its adherents now claimed, held even greater promise. An early advertisement for Waleswood, a 220-acre suburban tract outside Minneapolis, paid only token homage to the agrarian myth before hammering home its selling message:

> Instead of buying a quart of blue milk a day, take two gallons of rich milk a day from a cow for practically nothing.
> Instead of paying 19 to 90 cents or more of hardearned money for a dozen eggs only once in a while, pick up dozens of eggs every day laid for you for almost nothing by generous hens.
> Instead of buying potatoes by the peck, dig them by the bushel.
> Instead of buying dried apples or canned peaches at the store, gather all kinds of fruit from your own trees, vines and bushes.
> Instead of buying wilted vegetables once in a while, take young and crisp vegetables from your own garden.
> Instead of buying one golden egg, buy the goose that laid it for the same money.

Not only was the land fruitful and its creatures generous, but a lot purchased now would be a sound investment for the future. Quite accurately, prospective buyers were reminded that "as the city grows, the value of your property grows. Opportunity knocks but once at every man's door. This is your call."[22] Jefferson would hardly have recognized his agrarian utopia. Base motives threatened to sully the virgin land.

Most intellectuals, however, remained faithful to the Jeffersonian ideal. Twelve famous Southerners, for example, took their famous stand for agrarianism in 1930. The South, they wrote, could—and must—throw off the yoke of industrialism and restore men to cultivation of the soil, "the best and most sensitive of vocations." In a joint opening statement, John Crowe Ransom, Robert Penn Warren, Andrew Nelson Lytle, Allen Tate and the others agreed that to "think that this cannot be done is pusillanimous. And if the whole community, section, race, or age thinks it cannot be done, then it has simply lost its political genius and doomed itself to impotence." Lytle himself took a stand against emphasis on the economic advantages of rural life. Do not industrialize the farm, he advised; ignore those modern tools and methods urged on you by such preachers of the gospel of success as McMahon and Borsodi. "A farm is not a place to grow wealthy; it is a place to grow corn."[23]

The American public generally, despite the dollar appeal of "how to" books and advertisements about generous hens, and despite the inspiring rhetoric of the agrarian ideal, continued to flock to the cities. Then, in the 1920s, suburbanization became a demographic process of real magnitude for the first time. Compared to the flight from the cities after World War

II, the exodus of the 1920s represented only a minor trend. And few who migrated to the suburbs were industrious enough to "succeed," in McMahon's agrarian terms. There was nothing particularly visionary about these new suburbs; they were built to make money for developers, not to conform to anyone's idea of the perfect community. Still, the high hopes inherent in Howard's conception of the town-country magnet and in McMahon's successful suburb-farm refused to fade. In 1925, H. Paul Douglass concluded that a "crowded world must be either suburban or savage."[24] If they had their way, the planners would make sure that it turned out suburban. Clarence Stein and Henry Wright, under the financial sponsorship of Alexander Bing, started plans in 1927 for Radburn, New Jersey, before the greenbelt towns of the New Deal the nation's closest approximation of a Garden City. Other experiments were to follow.

The melodrama of American thought persisted, well into the twentieth century, in assigning the role of villain to the city slicker. Confronted with his scheming, legalistic ways, the poor farm girl faced Hobson's choice: either sign over the beloved farm or face a fate worse than death. It was the most natural thing in the world, of course, for the American intellectual of the 1920s and 1930s to regard the city with a jaundiced eye; urbanization was steadily destroying the agrarian ideal. In desperation, he turned to the suburbs as the hope of the future, just as the New Deal planners did. When that hope, too, came crashing to earth; when the suburbs turned out to be more citified than countrified, the intellectual of the 1950s relieved his frustrations with a spate of embittered attacks on suburbia, which had replaced the city as the villain in the rural-urban melodrama. In the mid-50s it was almost inconceivable to imagine that the suburb, in the dim days before World War II, had been regarded as the *hero* of the piece, the one who would rescue the farmer's daughter from the clutches of the city villain, and carry her off to a vine-covered cottage halfway between city and country. The record of New Deal legislation, however, makes it unmistakably clear that this was the case.

One of the more interesting and ambitious New Deal programs involved the construction of new communities. The 100 communities begun by the federal government in the 1930s, historian Paul K. Conkin points out, "remain vivid reminders of a time, not so long past, when Americans still could dream of a better, more perfect world and could so believe in that dream that they dared set forth to realize it, unashamed of their zeal."[25] Almost all of the 100 communities were made up of subsistence homesteads.

With the backing of President Roosevelt and Congress, $25,000,000 was appropriated in 1933 to establish and put into working order the Division of Subsistence Homesteads, under Harold L. Ickes and his Department of the Interior. Ickes chose M. L. Wilson, who "always had a sentimental, as well as a rationalized, love for agriculture," to take charge of the program

Wilson did not have his head buried in the land, however: he earnestly hoped to restore "certain moral and spiritual values . . . coming from . . . contact with the soil" by making use of more and more technology and efficiency. The public response to the subsistence homesteads appropriation was immediate and overwhelming. Wilson's division had $25 million to spend; by February 1934, requests for loans amounted to more than $4.5 *billion*. Wilson had a real problem in deciding how best to spend his appropriation, but he had made his basic decisions late in 1933. The typical community would contain "from 25 to 100 families living on individual homesteads of from one to five acres, which would accommodate an orchard, a vegetable garden, poultry, a pig, and, in some cases, a cow. Eventual ownership was promised for most colonists. . . ." Representative Ernest W. Marland, of Oklahoma, who was convinced that we must go back to the land "or we are lost," described the individual family's homestead somewhat more romantically:

> A small farm with a wood lot for fuel, a pasture for cows, an orchard with hives of bees, a dozen acres or so of plow land, and a garden for berries and annual vegetable crops.
> There is always plenty on a farm such as this.
> In winter a fat hog hangs in the smokehouse and from the cellar come jellies and jams and preserves, canned fruits, and dried vegetables. In the summer there is a succession of fresh fruits from the orchard and fresh vegetables from the garden.

Heaven, indeed, was to be the destination of subsistence farmers. But dissension within Wilson's division kept the program from growing, and as the economy turned upward, the back-to-the-land movement, which "had been motivated largely by the hopelessness and despair of the depression," began to lose its appeal.[26]

The subsistence homesteads program faded into insignificance, but the community building program of the New Deal was far from dead. Rexford Tugwell spearheaded the second, final and most significant phase of the program. Tugwell, whose enormous ability was matched by his self-confidence, set about "rearranging the physical face of America." He spurned the emotional attractions of the family homestead, and thought instead in terms of the planning process. For example, he saw that farmers trying—and failing—to eke out a living on submarginal land would have to be resettled on better land. But there was not enough good land to go around, and the surplus farm population would find its way to the cities, where millions were already trapped in slums. The solution to both problems, both "the inevitable movement from farm to city" and the barren poverty of urban slum dwellers, Tugwell found in the suburban town or garden city, in a middle landscape planned in hard, cold, pragmatic terms by the hardest, coldest, most pragmatic of planners. Surplus farm families could resettle in these suburban garden cities, and so could slum families. The federal government, in the person of Rexford Tugwell, set about in 1934 to plan and build these modern "middle settlements."

As boss of the Resettlement Administration, Tugwell had originally sketched out a program for 25 suburban communities. But the courts and the reluctance of Congress to finance projects the Republican National Committee soon characterized as "communist farms" limited the number of such communities actually constructed to three—Greenbelt, Maryland, near Washington, D. C., the most famous; Greenhills, Ohio, near Cincinnati; and Greendale, Wisconsin, outside Milwaukee. Consciously working on behalf of collectivist goals, Tugwell's Resettlement Administration was chewed up in the meat-grinder of American politics. By June 1937, the agency was no more.

In the greenbelt towns, however, Tugwell had created the "three largest, most ambitious, and most significant communities of the New Deal." As Conkin comments, they "represented, and still do represent, the most daring, original, and ambitious experiments in public housing in the history of the United States." The three communities relocated low-income families, both from farm and from city, in a suburban environment which combined the advantages of country and city life. The suburbs, clearly, were the hope of the future for Tugwell, who believed there should be three thousand greenbelt cities, not three. In suburbia, still a relatively unexploited frontier in the mid-1930s, was to be found "the best chance ever offered for the governmental planning of a favorable working and living environment. Past opportunities for federal planning had been ignored, with urban slums and rural poverty the results. This new area offered a last chance." The city had turned out badly, and so had the farm. The suburb was the last place to plan for a viable environment, and Tugwell, his idealism showing beneath the pragmatic exterior, was determined not to let the chance go by.

The greenbelt city, as he conceived it, was to be a complete community, with its area and population strictly limited in size, surrounded by a greenbelt of farms. There was to be plenty of light, air, and space, with safety assured for the children, plenty of gardens, and good schools and playgrounds. Jobs were either to be available within the community or close at hand, and the town and its utilities were to be owned collectively, not individually. Planning for the three greenbelt towns began in 1935, and construction was underway during the following three years. When completed the three projects contained 2,267 family units and complete community facilities. In many respects, the towns were successful: residents flocked to occupy the comfortable single-family and multiple dwellings in all three communities, and visitors from overseas were lavish in their praise But the greenbelt towns never worked out, economically. At the low rents charged, it would have taken over three hundred years for Greenbelt Maryland to pay for itself. In 1949, the Congress authorized the administra tion to sell the greenbelt cities at negotiated sale. By 1954, all three cities had been liquidated for $19.5 million, just over half the total cost to the federal government of $36 million, not taking interest or the devaluation of the dollar into account.[27]

However impractical they may have been in terms of dollars and cents, the greenbelt towns demonstrated what federal planning could accomplish in providing suburban housing for low-income families. Today, of course, the suburbs are full of people of all social classes, from the very wealthy to the nearly indigent. But the working-class suburb of the 1960s, conceived for profit and constructed in the same spirit, lacks many of the amenities of the greenbelt towns. Those who looked to the suburbs with stars in their eyes in the 1930s may be excused for disillusionment with the results of unplanned growth. Given enough money and time and the right political climate, Rexford Tugwell might have built a modern utopia in the suburbs of the United States. But there was not enough money or time, and the political climate, with its worship of individualism, was decidedly unfriendly. Tugwell's dream, like most, did not come true.

After the war, of course, came the deluge. The boys came marching home in 1945 and 1946, produced babies, and looked for homes to house their families. Instant suburbs, thrown up by developers with no professional planning or architectural assistance, supplied the homes, and the GI's moved out. To most of them, the new suburban homes, small and neat, seemed entirely adequate, but not to those intellectuals who, like Tugwell, saw in suburbia the last chance to create an ideal living environment. There were not enough playgrounds, not enough walkways, not enough trees— in short, not enough nature. In their disillusionment the intellectuals turned on the suburbs with a vengeance. Where once they had attacked the city for robbing America of its agrarian dream, now they zeroed in on the suburb, which had betrayed their fondest hopes for a twentieth-century restoration of the Jeffersonian ideal.

As the target of abuse shifted from downtown to the fringes of town, the city gained a respectability, a dignity, which it had never before enjoyed. Jane Jacobs, in her urban rhapsody, *The Death and Life of Great American Cities,* perceptively assesses the sentimentalization of nature as a major cause for "the bog of intellectual misconceptions about cities in which orthodox reformers and planners have mired themselves. . . ." Cities are just as natural as countryside, she maintains. Are not human beings part of nature? Are not cities the products of one form of nature, "as are the colonies of prairie dogs or the beds of oysters?" Of course they are, but Americans are not sentimental about cities. They are sentimental about the countryside, but they systematically destroy it in building an "insipid, standardized, suburbanized shadow of nature." Each day, the bulldozers flatten out the hills and tear up the trees; each day, acres of Grade I agricultural land are covered with pavement; each day, suburbanites kill "the thing they thought they came to find." Worst of all, it did not have to work out the way it has. There was no need for suburbs at all. Miss Jacobs would do away with the middle landscape, leaving only city and country:

> Big cities and countrysides can get along well together. Big cities need real countryside close by. And countryside—from man's point of view—needs big cities, with all their diverse opportunities and productivity, so human beings can be in a position to appreciate the rest of the natural world instead of to curse it.[28]

There is general critical agreement that suburbanization is systematically destroying America's priceless natural heritage. "These dormitory or bedroom communities displace the forests, the fruit orchards, and the fields of waving grain which up until a few years ago covered the countryside," a religious commentator writes, the echo of "My Country, 'Tis of Thee" sounding in his "fields of waving grain."[29] This accusation makes up only half of the indictment, though. For the suburbs are not only killing off the country; they are also doing away with the city. Nathan Glazer argues, for example, that suburbia is invading the city, not vice versa,[30] and political scientists complain that outlying communities are siphoning off the life blood of the city.

The suburbs, in short, have come to be regarded as combining the worst, not the best, of city and country. The dream of an ideal middle landscape has been transformed into the nightmare of a no man's land between two ideal extremes. In their suburbs, Americans have "succeeded in averaging down both the city and the [rural] village."[31] Nature only tantalizes the suburbanite:

> A fine spring or autumn morning in the city is nothing more than a 'nice day,' and in the country is something to drink to the deepest. But we suburbanites have to tear ourselves from such things and go climb a skyscraper. We'd like to stop and watch a brook run for a while and we don't feel too old to scuff autumn leaves. But no, the 8:19 is whistling around the bend and on we go.[32]

To some critics, the world of suburbia has become a dim, dull, basically *unreal* world. Children who live there, one commentator tells us, "need trips to both city and country to become acquainted with the world in which they live."[33] The implication is obvious. The suburbs, particularly the new postwar suburbs, are not meaningful places to live. They may exist, but they are not *real*. They represent a hazy half-world between the two real worlds of city and country.

But consigning the suburbs to a bland and opaque demimonde represents wishful thinking. The suburbs are highly visible and very much with us, as the census figures keep demonstrating; they are real places, and they have a meaning. The incredible speed with which the United States has become suburbanized testifies to this meaning. The flight from the city was entirely predictable in the light of the dominant mythology of American agrarianism. As two sociologists have remarked,

> what Suburbia means then, is a question that can be answered by viewing it more as a continuation of the older values that still exist rather than as a new phenomenon that has somehow taken the worst of all features of American life and encapsulated them within a split-level housing development. Perhaps the fact that Americans are moving in such numbers from the unplanned city to the poorly planned suburb is symbolic that really nothing much has changed except the time and the place.[34]

Nothing much, really, *has* changed. As much as ever, and despite the bitter lessons of history, America remains caught up in the Jeffersonian ideal, in the myth of the sturdy yeoman farmer plowing his own acres in self-sufficient independence, yet somehow part of a rural community. Conrad Knickerbocker has isolated the motivation which continues to produce the exodus to suburbia. The back-to-nature fixation, he writes, "has driven much . . . of the nation into street upon street of meaningless, tiny symbolic 'farms' stretching coast to coast." But these are farms with "60-foot frontages of crab grass," and no front porch on which to "set a spell" and fan yourself. "Rock-solid rural verities turn to sand in the treacherous climate of tract housing." Robert C. Wood, now Under Secretary of the Department of Housing and Urban Affairs, also blames "a rustic culture" for creating a decentralized governmental mess around our cities. "The need," he says, "is to develop a metropolitan conscience which demands something more than a rural shopkeeper's values."[35]

It would be reasonable to suppose, in the more heat than light of the tirade against the suburbs, that the concept of an ideal middle landscape might have disappeared from American thinking. But such a supposition underestimates the continuing pull of the country on the imagination of the urban intellectual. New Deal attempts to plan and construct the perfect community ended, if not in failure, at least in financial embarrassment. Now, the movers and shakers of the Great Society have determined to try once more, feeling again that there must be some way of happily marrying country and city. Following this goal, the administration has thrown its support behind the New Towns movement.

New Towns, of course, are really only another name for Garden Cities or greenbelt cities. But there are some differences. The New Towns of the Great Society are being constructed by private developers (often with government loans). And the New Towns will make a greater effort than was made in the cases of Greenbelt, Greendale and Greenhills to attract industry. As Wolf von Eckardt writes, the greenbelt program was abandoned "partly because . . . these towns could [not] attract sufficient employment so people could stay put." The success of the New Towns, he maintains, will depend largely on "whether they can actually attract employers."[36] For one goal of the New Towns, like that of Ebenezer Howard's Garden Cities, is to bring enough jobs out into the middle landscape between city and country so that the tedious commutation from suburb to city can be eliminated. To the extent that they realize this goal, the communities will be able to keep "closely accessible the recreative values of Nature." (The capitalization is not Ralph Waldo Emerson's, but that of the *Architectural Record,* April 1964.) It is Henry Ford's idea all over again: men can and should be industrial workers eight hours a day and nature's noblemen the rest of the time. The New Towns are not to have any standard population, which can vary from 50,000 to several hundred thousand, but the limit will be predetermined by planning. Surrounding land will be purchased and kept essentially open, to serve as a natural greenbelt.[37]

Perhaps the best known of some 75 American New Towns is Reston, Virginia, a 10-square-mile site 17 miles from Washington, D. C. which is planned for a community of 75,000 persons. Robert E. Simon Jr., the developer, is frankly enamored of outdoor life, and instructed his planners to be certain that the growth of Reston did not "destroy the very rural amenities that its residents would seek." As a consequence, apartments and town houses have been built to cluster population and preserve more open land.[38]

New Town planners hope that their middle landscape, once created, will be hospitable to all:

> We hope to create a community that is economically and racially integrated—i.e., contains a substantial range of income and occupation, and a substantial number of nonwhite families.

But they lack confidence that such heterogeneous towns can be built, so long as private developers stay in charge. The developer must not only be willing to admit minority families; he must actively seek them, since they are not likely to apply in serious numbers. Besides, if housing is not subsidized, it is unlikely that many minority families could afford to move. The solution, as Albert Mayer and Clarence Stein see it, is to put "the government back in the real estate business," a business it was supposed to have given up with the sale of the greenbelt cities 15 years ago. So long as there is a possibility of speculative profit, they state, "large-scale logically related development is not going to take place. . . ." What is needed is a philosophy of long-range disinterested planning by a powerful New Town Committee or Commission.[39]

Stein, one of the developers of Radburn, New Jersey, is back where he and Rexford Tugwell and the other planners of the 1920s and 1930s always were—on the side of centralized government direction and control of new American utopias. Ada Louise Huxtable, the architectural critic for the New York *Times,* is less insistent on federal control as well as less Panglossian. "Inevitably," she writes,

> New Towns may fall short of their objectives, and even share some of sub-

urbia's sins. But only through professional community planning can the chaos of the country's growth be turned into order. Concern with the total community is a heartening sign of sanity, order, rationality and realism in the American approach to the problem of urban expansion. There may still be hope for the suburban dream.[40]

Serious, intelligent planning; serious, intelligent concern with the total community bodes well for the future. Planning is not going to cure all the ills of our cities and suburbs, Huxtable realizes, whether it is done privately or through government channels. The intellectual must be prepared to realize, with Huxtable, that New Towns and other ideal utopias will inevitably "fall short of their objectives." It is not going to be possible to restore rural America:

> The wilderness, the isolated farm, the plantation, the self-contained New England town, the detached neighborhood are things of the American past. All the world's a city now and there is no escaping urbanization, not even in outer space.[41]

To the very considerable extent that the modern ideal of the middle landscape looks backward to the Jeffersonian ideal for direction, it is doomed to failure, and its adherents to disillusionment. In any marriage between city and country today the city is going to be the dominant partner. Ebenezer Howard in 1898, like American intellectuals of any period, wanted it the other way around.

■ ■ ■ ■ **Notes**

1 David Riesman, "The Suburban Sadness," in William M. Dobriner, ed., *The Suburban Community* (New York, 1958), p. 375.

2 Ebenezer Howard, *Garden Cities of Tomorrow* (London, 1965), p. 48. Italics his.

3 The term "middle landscape" is borrowed from Leo Marx, *The Machine in the Garden* (New York, 1964). Marx applied the concept of the middle landscape primarily to literature, not to intellectual history, but it has relevance to both disciplines. Note, for example, its application to Crèvecoeur's "middle settlements" in J. Hector St. John de Crèvecoeur, *Letters from an American Farmer* (London, 1926), pp. 44–45.

4 Alexander Jackson Downing, in John Burchard and Albert Bush-Brown, *The Architecture of America* (Boston, 1961), p. 101.

5 *Harper's Weekly,* XX (Apr. 8, 1876), 294.

6 *Harper's Weekly,* XX (Sept. 5, 1876), 709.

7 Henry George, *Progress and Poverty* (New York, 1884), p. 405.

8 Howard, pp. 50–57.

9 Carl N. Degler, *Out of Our Past* (New York and Evanston, 1959), p. 327.

10 In A. Whitney Griswold, *Farming and Democracy* (New Haven, 1952), pp. 179–80.

11 Adna F. Weber, *The Growth of Cities in the Nineteenth Century* (Ithaca, N.Y., 1963), p. 475.

12 Frederic C. Howe, *The City: The Hope of Democracy* (New York, 1905), p. 204.

13 Josiah Royce, *Race Questions, Provincialism and Other American Problems* (New

York, 1908), pp. 97–98; George Santayana, *The Background of My Life* (New York, 1944), p. 298.

14 Louis Sullivan, *The Autobiography of an Idea* (New York, 1922), pp. 98–99.

15 Robert Ezra Park, *Human Communities: The City and Human Ecology* (Glencoe, Ill., 1952), pp. 34, 140.

16 John Dewey, *The Public and Its Problems* (New York, 1927), pp. 211, 214. See also Morton and Lucia White, *The Intellectual Versus the City* (New York, 1964), pp. 177–79. The Whites maintain that the attitude of the intellectual toward the American city underwent a change in the late nineteenth century, from an attitude of basic hostility to one of belief in the potentiality of the city, once it was reformed. But the reformers seemed almost invariably to want to change the city back into the rural village.

17 John R. McMahon, *Success in the Suburbs* (New York and London, 1917), pp. x–xi.

18 McMahon, pp. 16, 24, 193–94. Italics added.

19 McMahon, pp. vii, 173, 201.

20 Paul K. Conkin, *Tomorrow a New World* (Ithaca, N.Y., 1959), pp. 51–53.

21 Ralph Borsodi, *Flight from the City: The Story of a New Way to Family Security* (New York, 1933), pp. 1–19.

22 Newspaper advertisement, undated, in files of Bloomington Historical Society, Bloomington, Minn.

23 Twelve Southerners, *I'll Take My Stand* (New York, 1930), in David R. Weimer, ed., *City and Country in America* (New York, 1962), pp. 121–22.

24 Harlan Paul Douglass, *The Suburban Trend* (New York, 1925), p. 327.

25 Conkin, pp. 6–7. In reviewing the community building programs of the New Deal, this essay relies heavily on Conkin's excellent book.

26 Conkin, pp. 87–130.

27 Conkin, pp. 153–325.

28 Jane Jacobs, *The Death and Life of Great American Cities* (New York, 1961), pp. 444–47.

29 Frederick A. Shippey, *Protestantism in Suburban Life* (New York and Nashville, 1964), p. 117.

30 Quoted in Anselm Strauss, "The Changing Imagery of American City and Suburb," *Sociological Quarterly,* I (Jan. 1960), 21.

31 Burchard and Bush-Brown, p. 121.

32 G. B. Palmer, *Slightly Cooler in the Suburbs* (Garden City, N.Y., 1950), pp. 214–15.

33 Sidonie Matsner Gruenberg, "The Challenge of the New Suburbs," *Marriage and Family Living,* XVII (May 1955), 136.

34 Thomas Ktsanes and Leonard Reissman, "Suburbia—New Homes for Old Values," *Social Problems,* VII (May 1955), 136.

35 *Life,* LIX (Dec. 24, 1965), 37, 139.

36 Wolf von Eckardt, "New Towns in America," *New Republic,* CXLIX (Oct. 26, 1963), 17.

37 Albert Mayer in consultation with Clarence Stein, "New Towns: and Fresh In-City Communities," *Architectural Record,* CXXXVI (Aug. 1964), 131–32.

38 "Reston," *Architectural Record,* CXXXVI (July 1964), 120. The community needed re-financing in 1967.

39 Mayer and Stein, 134–36.

40 Ada Louise Huxtable, " 'Clusters' Instead of 'Slurbs,' " *New York Times Magazine* (Feb. 9, 1964), 44.

41 Whites, p. 238.

22
Urbanism and Suburbanism as Ways of Life: A Re-evaluation of Definitions

HERBERT J. GANS

Herbert Gans's article attempts to modify the theory of urbanism advanced in Louis Wirth's famous essay "Urbanism as a Way of Life," published in the American Journal of Sociology *in 1938. Wirth was a member of the "Chicago School" of sociology along with such scholars as Robert Park, Ernest Burgess, Harvey Zorbaugh, and Frederick Thrasher. Park, the intellectual godfather of the group, was a former newspaperman who became interested in the scholarly study of cities and modern society. He developed the concept of "natural areas" to explain the processes by which the urban population divided itself and by which parts of cities developed into high-rent residential districts, rooming-house areas, bohemias, working-class neighborhoods, hotel and restaurant complexes, and commercial and industrial facilities. Park believed the division of the urban population to be "natural"—falling into a distinct pattern without any formal or external control as people sought others of similar background and interests, and looked for places having institutions that met their particular needs. Park, his colleagues, and their students borrowed from ecology—the science of the relationship between organism and environment—to explain the patterns of urban development.*

In "Urbanism as a Way of Life," Wirth defined a city "as a relatively large, dense, and permanent settlement of socially heterogeneous individuals," thereby emphasizing the variables of size, density, and heterogeneity in fashioning a theory of urbanism. These variables combined to produce secondary and tangential personal relationships among city dwellers. In his view, contacts between city dwellers were "impersonal, superficial, transitory, and segmental." Wirth did, however, define three perspectives from which to approach urbanism: "(1) as a physical structure comprising a population base, a technology, and an ecological order; (2) as a system of social organization involving a characteristic social structure, a series of social institutions, and a typical pattern of social relationships; and (3) as a set of attitudes and ideas, and a constellation of personalities engaging in typical forms of collective behavior and subject to characteristic mechanisms of social control." Although Wirth thus noted the influence of social class and personal attitudes, his emphasis was on ecology.

Herbert Gans finds this emphasis misplaced. He argues that the variables of social class and stage of life-cycle are more important in differentiating between the ways of life among, and often within, various segments of the metropolitan area such as the inner city, the outer city, and the suburbs.

Since many, but by no means all, urban and suburban dwellers can exercise some discretion in choosing residence and life-style, scholars must examine the factors accounting for those choices. Moreover, he finds that different people can use the same space for quite varying modes of life. Thus, the inner city can be the home of both the cosmopolites, urbane men and women who have either no children or a great deal of money or both; and the poor, the trapped, and the deprived. Size, density, and heterogeneity do not explain these facts as well as some other variables might, although ecological concepts have the attraction of being quantifiable. This may be a case where numbers offer misplaced precision, or more accurately, offer concrete answers to the wrong questions.

Gans finds much of Wirth's analysis derives from a contrast between folk society and modern industrial society. The German scholar, Ferdinand Tönnies used the terms Gemeinschaft *and* Gesellschaft *to differentiate between these "ideal types." The* Gemeinschaft *society is traditional, based on primary group (family and kinship) relationships, resists change, and is most likely to be found in isolated, self-contained groups. The* Gesellschaft *society is rationalistic, based on secondary relationships (associations formed to fulfill specific tasks among men who have no other contacts with one another), is receptive to change, and emphasizes achieved rather than ascribed status. The concept of* Gesellschaft *was meant to describe the modern industrial city.*

Since there are few folk societies left, Gans urges us to ignore this distinction between folk and industrial societies and to concentrate instead upon the different modes of life and types of settlement within the metropolitan area. He admits his formulations are time-bound—catching the city at one point in time, in this case the early 1960s. The student of history must be sensitive to variations in time and place, and must recognize that while Gans's model is useful, it may need substantial revision before being applied to an earlier or a later period.

■ ■ ■ ■ **For Further Reading**

Herbert J. Gans, *The Urban Villagers* (New York: The Free Press, 1962) is a participant–observer study of life among the Italians in Boston's West End just before it was demolished in an urban renewal project. Herbert J. Gans, *The Levittowners* (New York: Vintage Books, 1969) is a community study of a new suburb. Bennett Berger, *Working Class Suburb* (Berkeley and Los Angeles: University of California Press, 1959) destroys the myth that all suburbs are middle class and all suburbanites conform to the stereotyped images of suburbia. Maurice Stein, *The Eclipse of Community* (New York: Harper & Row Torchbooks, 1960) brings together some of the findings of previous community studies to assess the impact of urbanization, industrialization, and bureaucratization upon American communities. Lewis Mumford, *The Urban Prospect* (New York: Harvest Books, 1968) is only one of the many humane and perceptive books of this distinguished social philosopher. Mumford should be read and pondered.

■ The contemporary sociological conception of cities and of urban life is based largely on the work of the Chicago School, and its summary statement in Louis Wirth's essay, "Urbanism as a Way of Life" (40).[1] In that paper, Wirth developed a "minimum sociological definition of the city" as "a relatively large, dense and permanent settlement of socially heterogeneous individuals" (40, p. 50). From these prerequisites, he then deducted the major outlines of the urban way of life. As he saw it, number, density, and heterogeneity created a social structure in which primary-group relationships were inevitably replaced by secondary contacts that were impersonal, segmental, superficial, transitory, and often predatory in nature. As a result, the city dweller became anonymous, isolated, secular, relativistic, rational, and sophisticated. In order to function in the urban society, he was forced to combine with others to organize corporations, voluntary associations, representative forms of government, and the impersonal mass media of communications (40, pp. 54–60). These replaced the primary groups and the integrated way of life found in rural and other pre-industrial settlements.

Wirth's paper has become a classic in urban sociology, and most texts have followed his definition and description faithfully (5). In recent years, however, a considerable number of studies and essays have questioned his formulations (1, 5, 13, 15, 17, 19, 20, 23, 24, 27, 28, 30, 35, 38, 41).[2] In addition, a number of changes have taken place in cities since the article was published in 1938, notably the exodus of white residents to low- and medium-priced houses in the suburbs, and the decentralization of industry. The evidence from these studies and the changes in American cities suggest that Wirth's statement must be revised.

There is yet another, and more important reason for such a revision. Despite its title and intent, Wirth's paper deals with urban-industrial society, rather than with the city. This is evident from his approach. Like other urban sociologists, Wirth based his analysis on a comparison of settlement types, but unlike his colleagues, who pursued urban–rural comparisons, Wirth contrasted the city to the folk society. Thus, he compared settlement types of pre-industrial and industrial society. This allowed him to include in his theory of urbanism the entire range of modern institutions which are not found in the folk society, even though many such groups (e.g., voluntary associations) are by no means exclusively urban. Moreover, Wirth's conception of the city dweller as depersonalized, atomized, and susceptible to mass movements suggests that his paper is based on, and contributes to, the theory of the mass society.

Many of Wirth's conclusions may be relevant to the understanding of ways of life in modern society. However, since the theory argues that all of society is now urban, *his analysis does not distinguish ways of life in the city from those in other settlements within modern society.* In Wirth's time, the comparison of urban and pre-urban settlement types was still fruitful, but today, the primary task for urban (or community) sociology seems to me to be the analysis of the similarities and differences between contemporary settlement types.

This paper is an attempt at such an analysis; it limits itself to distinguishing ways of life in the modern city and the modern suburb. A re-analysis of Wirth's conclusions from this perspective suggests that his characterization of the urban way of life applies only—and not too accurately—to the residents of the inner city. The remaining city dwellers, as well as most suburbanites, pursue a different way of life, which I shall call "quasi-primary." This proposition raises some doubt about the mutual exclusiveness of the concepts of city and suburb and leads to a yet broader question: whether settlement concepts and other ecological concepts are useful for explaining ways of life.

The Inner City

Wirth argued that number, density, and heterogeneity had two social consequences which explain the major features of urban life. On the one hand, the crowding of diverse types of people into a small area led to the segregation of homogeneous types of people into separate neighborhoods (40, p. 56). On the other hand, the lack of physical distance between city dwellers resulted in social contact between them, which broke down existing social and cultural patterns and encouraged assimilation as well as acculturation—the melting pot effect (40, p. 52). Wirth implied that the melting pot effect was far more powerful than the tendency toward segregation and concluded that, sooner or later, the pressures engendered by the dominant social, economic, and political institutions of the city would destroy the remaining pockets of primary-group relationships (40, pp. 60–62). Eventually, the social system of the city would resemble Tönnies' *Gesellschaft*—a way of life which Wirth considered undesirable.

Because Wirth had come to see the city as the prototype of mass society, and because he examined the city from the distant vantage point of the folk society—from the wrong end of the telescope, so to speak—his view of urban life is not surprising. In addition, Wirth found support for his theory in the empirical work of his Chicago colleagues. As Greer and Kube (19, p. 112) and Wilensky (38, p. 121) have pointed out, the Chicago sociologists conducted their most intensive studies in the inner city.[3] At that time, these were slums recently invaded by new waves of European immigrants and rooming house and skid row districts, as well as the habitat of Bohemians and well-to-do Gold Coast apartment dwellers. Wirth himself studied the Maxwell Street Ghetto, an inner-city Jewish neighborhood then being dispersed by the acculturation and mobility of its inhabitants (39). Some of the characteristics of urbanism which Wirth stressed in his essay abounded in these areas.

Wirth's diagnosis of the city as *Gesellschaft* must be questioned on three counts. First, the conclusions derived from a study of the inner city cannot be generalized to the entire urban area. Second, there is as yet not enough evidence to prove—nor, admittedly, to deny—that number, density, and heterogeneity result in the social consequences which Wirth proposed. Finally, even if the causal relationship could be verified, it can be shown that a significant proportion of the city's inhabitants were, and are, isolated from these consequences by social structures and cultural patterns which they either brought to the city, or developed by living in it. Wirth conceived the urban population as consisting of heterogeneous individuals, torn from past social systems, unable to develop new ones, and therefore prey to social anarchy in the city. While it is true that a not insignificant proportion of the inner city population was, and still is, made up of unattached individuals (26), Wirth's formulation ignores the fact that this population consists mainly of relatively homogeneous groups, with social and cultural moorings that shield it fairly effectively from the suggested consequences of number, density, and heterogeneity. This applies even more to the residents of the outer city, who constitute a majority of the total city population.

The social and cultural moorings of the inner city population are best described by a brief analysis of the five types of inner city residents. These are:

1. the "cosmopolites";
2. the unmarried or childless;
3. the "ethnic villagers";
4. the "deprived"; and
5. the "trapped" and downward mobile.

The "cosmopolites" include students, artists, writers, musicians, and entertainers, as well as other intellectuals and professionals. They live in the city in order to be near the special "cultural" facilities that can only be located near the center of the city. Many cosmopolites are unmarried or childless. Others rear children in the city, especially if they have the income to afford the aid of servants and governesses. The less affluent ones may move to the suburbs to raise their children, continuing to live as cosmopolites under considerable handicaps, especially in the lower-middle-class suburbs. Many of the very rich and powerful are also cosmopolites, although they are likely to have at least two residences, one of which is suburban or exurban.

The unmarried or childless must be divided into two subtypes, depending on the permanence or transience of their status. The temporarily unmarried or childless live in the inner city for only a limited time. Young adults may team up to rent an apartment away from their parents and close to job or entertainment opportunities. When they marry, they may move first to an apartment in a transient neighborhood, but if they can afford to do so, they leave for the outer city or the suburbs with the arrival of the first or second child. The permanently unmarried may stay in the inner city for the remainder of their lives, their housing depending on their income.

The "ethnic villagers" are ethnic groups which are found in such inner city neighborhoods as New York's Lower East Side, living in some ways as they did when they were peasants in European or Puerto Rican villages (15). Although they reside in the city, they isolate themselves from significant contact with most city facilities, aside from workplaces. Their way of life differs sharply from Wirth's urbanism in its emphasis on kinship and the primary group, the lack of anonymity and secondary-group contacts, the weakness of formal organizations, and the suspicion of anything and anyone outside their neighborhood.

The first two types live in the inner city by choice; the third is there partly because of necessity, partly because of tradition. The final two types are in the inner city because they have no other choice. One is the "deprived" population: the very poor; the emotionally disturbed or otherwise handicapped; broken families; and, most important, the non-white population. These urban dwellers must take the dilapidated housing and blighted neighborhoods to which the housing market relegates them, although among them are some for whom the slum is a hiding place, or a temporary stop-over to save money for a house in the outer city or the suburbs (27).

The "trapped" are the people who stay behind when a neighborhood is invaded by non-residential land uses or lower-status immigrants, because they cannot afford to move, or are otherwise bound to their present location (27).[4] The "downward mobiles" are a related type; they may have started life in a higher class position, but have been forced down in the socioeconomic hierarchy and in the quality of their accommodations. Many of them are old people, living out their existence on small pensions.

These five types all live in dense and heterogeneous surroundings, yet they have such diverse ways of life that it is hard to see how density and heterogeneity could exert a common influence. Moreover, all but the last two types are isolated or detached from their neighborhood and thus from the social consequences which Wirth described.

When people who live together have social ties based on criteria other than mere common occupancy, they can set up social barriers regardless of the physical closeness or the heterogeneity of their neighbors. The ethnic villagers are the best illustration. While a number of ethnic groups are usually found living together in the same neighborhood, they are able to *isolate* themselves from each other through a variety of social devices. Wirth himself recognized this when he wrote that "two groups can occupy a given area without losing their separate identity because each side is permitted to live its own inner life and each somehow fears or idealizes the other" (39, p. 283). Although it is true that the children in these areas were often oblivious to the social barriers set up by their parents, at least until adolescence, it is doubtful whether their acculturation can be traced to the melting pot effect as much as to the pervasive influence of the American culture that flowed into these areas from the outside.[5]

The cosmopolites, the unmarried, and the childless are *detached* from neighborhood life. The cosmopolites possess a distinct subculture which causes them to be disinterested in all but the most superficial contacts with their neighbors, somewhat like the ethnic villagers. The unmarried and childless are detached from neighborhood because of their life-cycle stage, which frees them from the routine family responsibilities that entail some relationship to the local area. In their choice of residence, the two types are therefore not concerned about their neighbors, or the availability and quality of local community facilities. Even the well-to-do can choose expensive apartments in or near poor neighborhoods, because if they have children, these are sent to special schools and summer camps which effectively isolate them from neighbors. In addition, both types, but especially the childless and unmarried, are transient. Therefore, they tend to live in areas marked by high population turnover, where their own mobility and that of their neighbors creates a universal detachment from the neighborhood.[6]

The deprived and the trapped do seem to be affected by some of the consequences of number, density, and heterogeneity. The deprived population suffers considerably from overcrowding, but this is a consequence of low income, racial discrimination, and other handicaps, and cannot be considered an inevitable result of the ecological make-up of the city.[7] Because the deprived have no residential choice, they are also forced to live amid neighbors not of their own choosing, with ways of life different and even contradictory to their own. If familial defenses against the neighborhood climate are weak, as is the case among broken families and downward mobile people, parents may lose their children to the culture of "the street." The trapped are the unhappy people who remain behind when their more advantaged neighbors move on; they must endure the heterogeneity which results from neighborhood change.

Wirth's description of the urban way of life fits best the transient areas of the inner city. Such areas are typically heterogeneous in population, partly because they are inhabited by transient types who do not require homogeneous neighbors or by deprived people who have no choice, or may themselves be quite mobile. Under conditions of transience and heterogeneity, people interact only in terms of the segmental roles necessary for obtaining local services. Their social relationships thus display anonymity, impersonality, and superficiality.[8]

The social features of Wirth's concept of urbanism seem therefore to be a result of residential instability, rather than of number, density, or heterogeneity. In fact, heterogeneity is itself an effect of residential instability, resulting when the influx of transients causes landlords and realtors to stop acting as gatekeepers—that is, wardens of neighborhood homogeneity.[9] Residential instability is found in all types of settlements, and, presumably, its social consequences are everywhere similar. These consequences cannot therefore be identified with the ways of life of the city.

The Outer City and the Suburbs

The second effect which Wirth ascribed to number, density, and heterogeneity was the segregation of homogeneous people into distinct neighborhoods,[10] on the basis of "place and nature of work, income, racial and ethnic characteristics, social status, custom, habit, taste, preference and prejudice" (40, p. 56). This description fits the residential districts of the *outer city*.[11] Although these districts contain the majority of the city's inhabitants, Wirth went into little detail about them. He made it clear, however, that the socio-psychological aspects of urbanism were prevalent there as well (40, p. 56).

Because existing neighborhood studies deal primarily with the exotic sections of the inner city, very little is known about the more typical residential neighborhoods of the outer city. However, it is evident that the way of life in these areas bears little resemblance to Wirth's urbanism. Both the studies which question Wirth's formulation and my own observations suggest that the common element in the ways of life of these neighborhoods is best described as *quasi-primary*. I use this term to characterize relationships between neighbors. Whatever the intensity or frequency of these relationships, the interaction is more intimate than a secondary contact, but more guarded than a primary one.[12]

There are actually few secondary relationships, because of the isolation of residential neighborhoods from economic institutions and workplaces. Even shopkeepers, store managers, and other local functionaries who live in the area are treated as acquaintances or friends, unless they are of a vastly different social status or are forced by their corporate employers to treat their customers as economic units (30). Voluntary associations attract only a minority of the population. Moreover, much of the organizational activity is of a sociable nature, and it is often difficult to accomplish the association's "business" because of the members' preference for sociability. Thus, it would appear that interactions in organizations, or between neighbors generally, do not fit the secondary-relationship model of urban life. As anyone who has lived in these neighborhoods knows, there is little anonymity, impersonality, or privacy.[13] In fact, American cities have sometimes been described as collections of small towns.[14] There is some truth to this description, especially if the city is compared to the actual small town, rather than to the romantic construct of anti-urban critics (33).

Postwar suburbia represents the most contemporary version of the quasi primary way of life. Owing to increases in real income and the encouragement of home ownership provided by the FHA, families in the lower-middle class and upper working class can now live in modern single-family home in low-density subdivisions, an opportunity previously available only to the upper and upper-middle classes (34).

The popular literature describes the new suburbs as communities in which conformity, homogeneity, and other-direction are unusually rampant (4, 32). The implication is that the move from city to suburb initiates a new way of life which causes considerable behavior and personality change in previous urbanites. A preliminary analysis of data which I am now collecting in Levittown, New Jersey, suggests, however, that the move from the city to this predominantly lower-middle-class suburb does not result in any major behavioral changes for most people. Moreover, the changes which do occur reflect the move from the social isolation of a transient city or suburban apartment building to the quasi-primary life of a neighborhood of single-family homes. Also, many of the people whose life has changed reported that the changes were intended. They existed as aspirations before the move, or as reasons for it. In other words, the suburb itself creates few changes in ways of life. Similar conclusions have been reported by Berger in his excellent study of a working-class population newly moved to a suburban subdivision (4).

A Comparison of City and Suburb

If urban and suburban areas are similar in that the way of life in both is quasi-primary, and if urban residents who move out to the suburbs do not undergo any significant changes in behavior, it would be fair to argue that the differences in ways of life between the two types of settlements have been overestimated. Yet the fact remains that a variety of physical and demographic differences exists between the city and the suburb. However, upon closer examination, many of these differences turn out to be either spurious or of little significance for the way of life of the inhabitants (34).[15]

The differences between the residential areas of cities and suburbs which have been cited most frequently are:

1. Suburbs are more likely to be dormitories.
2. They are further away from the work and play facilities of the central business districts.
. They are newer and more modern than city residential areas and are designed for the automobile rather than for pedestrian and mass-transit forms of movement.
. They are built up with single-family rather than multi-family structures and are therefore less dense.
   Their populations are more homogeneous.
   Their populations differ demographically: they are younger; more of them are married; they have higher incomes; and they hold proportionately more white collar jobs (8, p. 131).

Most urban neighborhoods are as much dormitories as the suburbs. Only in a few older inner city areas are factories and offices still located in the middle of residential blocks, and even here many of the employees do not live in the neighborhood.

The fact that the suburbs are farther from the central business district is often true only in terms of distance, not travel time. Moreover, most people make relatively little use of downtown facilities, other than workplaces (12, 21). The downtown stores seem to hold their greatest attraction for the upper-middle class (21, pp. 91–92); the same is probably true of typically urban entertainment facilities. Teen-agers and young adults may take their dates to first-run movie theaters, but the museums, concert halls, and lecture rooms attract mainly upper-middle-class ticket-buyers, many of them suburban.[16]

The suburban reliance on the train and the automobile has given rise to an imaginative folklore about the consequences of commuting on alcohol consumption, sex life, and parental duties. Many of these conclusions are, however, drawn from selected high-income suburbs and exurbs, and reflect job tensions in such hectic occupations as advertising and show business more than the effects of residence (29). It is true that the upper-middle-class housewife must become a chauffeur in order to expose her children to the proper educational facilities, but such differences as walking to the corner drug store and driving to its suburban equivalent seem to me of little emotional, social, or cultural import.[17] In addition, the continuing shrinkage in the number of mass-transit users suggests that even in the city many younger people are now living a wholly auto-based way of life.

The fact that suburbs are smaller is primarily a function of political boundaries drawn long before the communities were suburban. This affects the kinds of political issues which develop and provides somewhat greater opportunity for citizen participation. Even so, in the suburbs as in the city, the minority who participate are the professional politicians, the economically concerned businessmen, lawyers and salesmen, and the ideologically motivated middle- and upper-middle-class people with better than average education.

The social consequences of differences in density and house type also seem overrated. Single-family houses on quiet streets facilitate the supervision of children; this is one reason why middle-class women who want to keep an eye on their children move to the suburbs. House type also has some effects on relationships between neighbors, insofar as there are more opportunities for visual contact between adjacent homeowners than between people on different floors of an apartment house. However, if occupants' characteristics are also held constant, the differences in actual social contact are less marked. Homogeneity of residents turns out to be more important as a determinant of sociability than proximity. If the population is heterogeneous, there is little social contact between neighbors, either on apartment-house floors or in single-family-house blocks; if people are homogeneous, there is likely to be considerable social contact in both house types. One need only contrast the apartment house located in a transient, heterogeneous neighborhood and exactly the same structure in a neighborhood occupied by a single ethnic group. The former is a lonely, anonymous building; the latter, a bustling micro-society. I have observed similar patterns in suburban areas; on blocks where people are homogeneous, they socialize; where they are heterogeneous, they do little more than exchange polite greetings (16).

Suburbs are usually described as being more homogeneous in house type than the city, but if they are compared to the outer city, the differences are small. Most inhabitants of the outer city, other than well-to-do homeowners, live on blocks of uniform structures as well—for example, the endless streets of rowhouses in Philadelphia and Baltimore or of two-story duplexes and six-flat apartment houses in Chicago. They differ from the new suburbs only in that they were erected through more primitive methods of mass production. Suburbs are of course more predominantly areas of owner-occupied single homes, though in the outer districts of most American cities homeownership is also extremely high.

Demographically, suburbs as a whole are clearly more homogeneous than cities as a whole, though probably not more so than outer cities. However, people do not live in cities or suburbs as a whole, but in specific neighborhoods. An analysis of ways of life would require a determination of the degree of population homogeneity within the boundaries of areas defined as neighborhoods by residents' social contacts. Such an analysis would no doubt indicate that many neighborhoods in the city as well as the suburbs are homogeneous. Neighborhood homogeneity is actually a result of factors having little or nothing to do with the house type, density, or location of the area relative to the city limits. Brand new neighborhoods are more homogeneous than older ones, because they have not yet experienced resident turnover, which frequently results in population heterogeneity. Neighborhoods of low- and medium-priced housing are usually less homogeneous than those with expensive dwellings because they attract families who have reached the peak of occupational and residential mobility, as well as young families who are just starting their climb and will eventually move to neighborhoods of higher status. The latter, being accessible only to high-income people, are therefore more homogeneous with respect to other resident characteristics as well. Moreover, such areas have the economic and political power to slow down or prevent invasion. Finally, neighborhoods located in the path of ethnic or religious group movement are likely to be extremely homogeneous.

The demographic differences between cities and suburbs cannot be questioned, especially since the suburbs have attracted a large number of middle-class child-rearing families. The differences are, however, much reduced if suburbs are compared only to the outer city. In addition, a detailed comparison of suburban and outer city residential areas would show that neighborhoods with the same kinds of people can be found in the city as well as the suburbs. Once again, the age of the area and the cost of housing are more important determinants of demographic characteristics than the location of the area with respect to the city limits.

Characteristics, Social Organization, and Ecology

The preceding sections of the paper may be summarized in three propositions:

1. As concerns ways of life, the inner city must be distinguished from the outer city and the suburbs; and the latter two exhibit a way of life bearing little resemblance to Wirth's urbanism.
2. Even in the inner city, ways of life resemble Wirth's description only to a limited extent. Moreover, economic condition, cultural characteristics, life-cycle stage, and residential instability explain ways of life more satisfactorily than number, density, or heterogeneity.
3. Physical and other differences between city and suburb are often spurious or without much meaning for ways of life.

These propositions suggest that the concepts urban and suburban are neither mutually exclusive, nor especially relevant for understanding ways of life. They—and number, density, and heterogeneity as well—are ecological concepts which describe human adaptation to the environment. However, they are not sufficient to explain social phenomena, because these phenomena cannot be understood solely as the consequences of ecological processes. Therefore, other explanations must be considered.

Ecological explanations of social life are most applicable if the subjects under study lack the ability to *make choices*, be they plants, animals, or human beings. Thus, if there is a housing shortage, people will live almost anywhere, and under extreme conditions of no choice, as in a disaster, married and single, old and young, middle and working class, stable and transient will be found side by side in whatever accommodations are available. At that time, their ways of life represent an almost direct adaptation to the environment. If the supply of housing and of neighborhoods is such that alternatives are available, however, people will make choices, and if the housing market is responsive, they can even make and satisfy explicit *demands*.

Choices and demands do not develop independently or at random; they are functions of the roles people play in the social system. These can best be understood in terms of the *characteristics* of the people involved; that is, characteristics can be used as indices to choices and demands made in the roles that constitute ways of life. Although many characteristics affect the choices and demands people make with respect to housing and neighborhoods, the most important ones seem to be *class*—in all its economic, social, and cultural ramifications—and *life-cycle stage*.[18] If people have an opportunity to choose, these two characteristics will go far in explaining the kinds of housing and neighborhoods they will occupy and the ways of life they will try to establish within them.

Many of the previous assertions about ways of life in cities and suburbs can be analyzed in terms of class and life-cycle characteristics. Thus, in the inner city, the unmarried and childless live as they do, detached from neighborhood, because of their life-cycle stage; the cosmopolites, because of a combination of life-cycle stage and a distinctive but class-based subculture. The way of life of the deprived and trapped can be explained by low socioeconomic level and related handicaps. The quasi-primary way of life is associated with the family stage of the life-cycle, and the norms of child-rearing and parental role found in the upper working class, the lower-middle class, and the non-cosmopolite portions of the upper-middle and upper classes.

The attributes of the so-called suburban way of life can also be understood largely in terms of these characteristics. The new suburbia is nothing more than a highly visible showcase for the ways of life of young, upper-working-class and lower-middle-class people. Ktsanes and Reissman have aptly described it as "new homes for old values" (22). Much of the descriptive and critical writing about suburbia assumes that as long as the new suburbanites lived in the city, they behaved like upper-middle-class cosmopolites and that suburban living has mysteriously transformed them (7; 14, pp. 154–162; 25; 36). The critics fail to see that the behavior and personality patterns ascribed to suburbia are in reality those of class and age (6). These patterns could have been found among the new suburbanites when they still lived in the city and could now be observed among their peers who still reside there—if the latter were as visible to critics and researchers as are the suburbanites.

Needless to say, the concept of "characteristics" cannot explain all aspects of ways of life, either among urban or suburban residents. Some aspects must be explained by concepts of social organization that are independent of characteristics. For example, some features of the quasi-primary way of life are independent of class and age, because they evolve from the roles and situations created by joint and adjacent occupancy of land and dwellings. Likewise, residential instability is a universal process which has a number of invariate consequences. In each case, however, the way in which people react varies with their characteristics. So it is with ecological processes. Thus, there are undoubtedly differences between ways of life in urban and suburban settlements which remain after behavior patterns based on residents' characteristics have been analyzed, and which must therefore be attributed to features of the settlement (11).

Characteristics do not explain the causes of behavior; rather, they are clues to socially created and culturally defined roles, choices, and demands. A causal analysis must trace them back to the larger social, economic, and political systems which determine the situations in which roles are played and the cultural content of choices and demands, as well as the opportunities for their achievement.[19] These systems determine income distributions, educational and occupational opportunities, and in turn, fertility patterns, child-rearing methods, as well as the entire range of consumer behavior. Thus, a complete analysis of the way of life of the deprived residents of the inner city cannot stop by indicating the influence of low income, lack of education, or family in-stability. These must be related to such conditions as the urban economy's "need" for low-wage workers, and the housing market practices which restrict residential choice. The urban economy is in turn shaped by national economic and social systems, as well as by local and regional ecological processes. Some phenomena can be explained exclusively by reference to these ecological pro-cesses. However, it must also be recognized that as man gains greater control over the natural environment, he has been able to free himself from many of the determining and limiting effects of that environment. Thus, changes in lo-cal transportation technology, the ability of industries to be footloose, and the relative affluence of American society have given ever larger numbers of people increasing amounts of residential choice. The greater the amount of choice available, the more important does the concept of characteristics be-come in understanding behavior.

Consequently, the study of ways of life in communities must begin with an analysis of characteristics. If characteristics are dealt with first and held constant, we may be able to discover which behavior patterns can be attributed to features of the settlement and its natural environment.[20] Only then will it be possible to discover to what extent city and suburb are independent—rather than dependent or intervening—variables in the explanation of ways of life.

This kind of analysis might help to reconcile the ecological point of view with the behavioral and cultural one, and possibly put an end to the conflict between conceptual positions which insist on one explanation or the other (9). Both explanations have some relevance, and future research and theory must clarify the role of each in the analysis of ways of life in various types of settlement (6, p. xxii). Another important rationale for this approach is its usefulness for applied sociology—for example, city planning. The planner can recommend changes in the spatial and physical arrangements of the city. Frequently, he seeks to achieve social goals or to change social conditions through physical solutions. He has been attracted to ecological explanations because these relate behavior to phenomena which he can affect. For example, most planners tend to agree with Wirth's formulations, because they stress number and density, over which the planner has some control. If the undesir-able social conditions of the inner city could be traced to these two factors, the planner could propose large-scale clearance projects which would reduce the size of the urban population, and lower residential densities. Experience with public housing projects has, however, made it apparent that low densities, new buildings, or modern site plans do not eliminate anti-social or self-destruc-tive behavior. The analysis of characteristics will call attention to the fact that this behavior is lodged in the deprivations of low socio-economic status and racial discrimination, and that it can be changed only through the removal of these deprivations. Conversely, if such an analysis suggests residues of be-havior that can be attributed to ecological processes or physical aspects of housing and neighborhoods, the planner can recommend physical changes that can really affect behavior.

A Re-evaluation of Definitions

The argument presented here has implications for the sociological definition of the city. Such a definition relates ways of life to environmental features of the city qua settlement type. But if ways of life do not coincide with settlement types, and if these ways are functions of class and life-cycle stage rather than of the ecological attributes of the settlement, a sociological definition of the city cannot be formulated.[21] Concepts such as city and suburb allow us to distinguish settlement types from each other physically and demographically, but the ecological processes and conditions which they synthesize have no direct or invariate consequences for ways of life. The sociologist cannot, therefore, speak of an urban or suburban way of life.

Conclusion

Many of the descriptive statements made here are as time-bound as Wirth's.[22] Twenty years ago, Wirth concluded that some form of urbanism would eventually predominate in all settlement types. He was, however, writing during a time of immigrant acculturation and at the end of a serious depression, an era of minimal choice. Today, it is apparent that high-density, heterogeneous surroundings are for most people a temporary place of residence; other than for the Park Avenue or Greenwich Village cosmopolites, they are a result of necessity rather than choice. As soon as they can afford to do so, most Americans head for the single-family house and the quasi-primary way of life of the low-density neighborhood, in the outer city or the suburbs.[23]

Changes in the national economy and in government housing policy can affect many of the variables that make up housing supply and demand. For example, urban sprawl may eventually outdistance the ability of present and proposed transportation systems to move workers into the city; further industrial decentralization can forestall it and alter the entire relationship between work and residence. The expansion of present urban renewal activities can perhaps lure a significant number of cosmopolites back from the suburbs, while a drastic change in renewal policy might begin to ameliorate the housing conditions of the deprived population. A serious depression could once again make America a nation of doubled-up tenants.

These events will affect housing supply and residential choice; they will frustrate but not suppress demands for the quasi-primary way of life. However, changes in the national economy, society, and culture can affect people's characteristics—family size, educational level, and various other concomitants of life-cycle stage and class. These in turn will stimulate changes in demands and choices. The rising number of college graduates, for example, is likely to increase the cosmopolite ranks. This might in turn create a new set of city dwellers, although it will probably do no more than encourage the development of cosmopolite facilities in some suburban areas.

The current revival of interest in urban sociology and in community studies, as well as the sociologist's increasing curiosity about city planning, suggest that data may soon be available to formulate a more adequate theory of the relationship between settlements and the ways of life within them. The speculations presented in this paper are intended to raise questions; they can only be answered by more systematic data collection and theorizing.

■ ■ ■ ■ **Notes**

1 I am indebted to Richard Dewey, John Dyckman, David Riesman, Melvin Webber, and Harold Wilensky for helpful comments on earlier drafts of this essay.

2 I shall not attempt to summarize these studies, for this task has already been performed by Dewey (5), Reiss (23), Wilensky (38), and others.

3 By the *inner city,* I mean the transient residential areas, the Gold Coasts, and the slums that generally surround the central business district, although in some communities they may continue for miles beyond that district. The *outer city* includes the stable residential areas that house the working- and middle-class tenant and owner. The *suburbs* I conceive as the latest and most modern ring of the outer city, distinguished from it only by yet lower densities, and by the often irrelevant fact of the ring's location outside the city limits.

4 The trapped are not very visible, but I suspect that they are a significant element in what Raymond Vernon has described as the "gray areas" of the city (32).

5 If the melting pot has resulted from propinquity and high density, one would have expected second-generation Italians, Irish, Jews, Greeks, Slavs, etc. to have developed a single "pan-ethnic culture," consisting of a synthesis of the cultural patterns of the propinquitous national groups.

6 The corporation transients (36, 38), who provide a new source of residential instability to the suburb, differ from city transients. Since they are raising families, they want to integrate themselves into neighborhood life, and are usually able to do so, mainly because they tend to move into similar types of communities wherever they go.

7 The negative social consequences of overcrowding are a result of high room and floor density, not of the land coverage of population density which Wirth discussed. Park Avenue residents live under conditions of high land density, but do not seem to suffer visibly from overcrowding.

8 Whether or not these social phenomena have the psychological consequences Wirth suggested depends on the people who live in the area. Those who are detached from the neighborhood by choice are probably immune, but those who depend on the neighborhood for their social relationships—the unattached individuals, for example —may suffer greatly from loneliness.

9 Needless to say, residential instability must ultimately be traced back to the fact that, as Wirth pointed out, the city and its economy attract transient—and, depending on the sources of outmigration, heterogeneous—people. However, this is a characteristic of urban-industrial society, not of the city specifically.

10 By neighborhoods or residential districts I mean areas demarcated from others by distinctive physical boundaries or by social characteristics, some of which may be perceived only by the residents. However, these areas are not necessarily socially self-sufficient or culturally distinctive.

11 For the definition of *outer city,* see note 3.

12 Because neighborly relations are not quite primary, and not quite secondary, they can also become *pseudo-primary;* that is, secondary ones disguised with false affect

to make them appear primary. Critics have often described suburban life in this fashion, although the actual prevalence of pseudo-primary relationships has not been studied systematically in cities or suburbs.

13 These neighborhoods cannot, however, be considered as urban folk societies. People go out of the area for many of their friendships, and their allegiance to the neighborhood is neither intense nor all-encompassing. Janowitz has aptly described the relationship between resident and neighborhood as one of "limited liability" (20, Chapter 7).

14 Were I not arguing that ecological concepts cannot double as sociological ones, this way of life might best be described as small-townish.

15 They may, of course, be significant for the welfare of the total metropolitan area.

16 A 1958 study of New York theater goers showed a median income of close to $10,000 and 35 per cent were reported as living in the suburbs (10).

17 I am thinking here of adults; teen-agers do suffer from the lack of informal meeting places within walking or bicycling distance.

18 These must be defined in dynamic terms. Thus, class includes also the process of social mobility, stage in the life-cycle, and the processes of socialization and aging.

19 This formulation may answer some of Duncan and Schnore's objections to sociopsychological and cultural explanations of community ways of life (9).

20 The ecologically oriented researchers who developed the Shevsky-Bell social area analysis scale have worked on the assumption that "social differences between the populations of urban neighborhoods can conveniently be summarized into differences of economic level, family characteristics and ethnicity" (3, p. 26). However, they have equated "urbanization" with a concept of life-cycle stage by using family characteristics to define the index of urbanization (3, 18, 19). In fact, Bell has identified suburbanism with familism (2).

21 Because of the distinctiveness of the ways of life found in the inner city, some writers propose definitions that refer only to these ways, ignoring those found in the outer city. For example, popular writers sometimes identify "urban" with "urbanity," i.e., "cosmopolitanism." However, such a definition ignores the other ways of life found in the inner city. Moreover, I have tried to show that these ways have few common elements, and that the ecological features of the inner city have little or no influence in shaping them.

22 Even more than Wirth's they are based on data and impressions gathered in the large Eastern and Midwestern cities of the United States.

23 Personal discussions with European planners and sociologists suggest that many European apartment dwellers have similar preferences, although economic conditions, high building costs, and the scarcity of land make it impossible for them to achieve their desires.

References for "Urbanism and Suburbanism"

1. Axelrod, Morris. "Urban Structure and Social Participation," *American Sociological Review,* Vol. 21 (February 1956), pp. 13–18.

2. Bell, Wendell. "Social Choice, Life Styles and Suburban Residence," in William M. Dobriner (ed.), *The Suburban Community.* New York: G. P. Putnam's Sons, 1958, pp. 225–247.

3. Bell, Wendell, and Maryanne T. Force. "Urban Neighborhood Types and Participation in Formal Associations," *American Sociological Review,* Vol. 21 (February 1956), pp. 25–34.

4. Berger, Bennett. *Working Class Suburb: A Study of Auto Workers in Suburbia.* Berkeley, Calif.: University of California Press, 1960.

5. Dewey, Richard. "The Rural–Urban Continuum: Real but Relatively Unimportant," *American Journal of Sociology*, Vol. 66 (July 1960), pp. 60–66.

6. Dobriner, William M. "Introduction: Theory and Research in the Sociology of the Suburbs," in William M. Dobriner (ed.), *The Suburban Community*. New York: G. P. Putnam's Sons, 1958, pp. xiii–xxviii.

7. Duhl, Leonard J. "Mental Health and Community Planning," in *Planning 1955*. Chicago: American Society of Planning Officials, 1956, pp. 31–39.

8. Duncan, Otis Dudley, and Albert J. Reiss, Jr. *Social Characteristics of Rural and Urban Communities, 1950*. New York: John Wiley & Sons, 1956.

9. Duncan, Otis Dudley, and Leo F. Schnore. "Cultural, Behavioral and Ecological Perspectives in the Study of Social Organization," *American Journal of Sociology*, Vol. 65 (September 1959), pp. 132–155.

10. Enders, John. *Profile of the Theater Market*. New York: Playbill, undated and unpaged.

11. Fava, Sylvia Fleis. "Contrasts in Neighboring: New York City and a Suburban Community," in William M. Dobriner (ed.), *The Suburban Community*. New York: G. P. Putnam's Sons, 1958, pp. 122–131.

12. Foley, Donald L. "The Use of Local Facilities in a Metropolis," in Paul Hatt and Albert J. Reiss, Jr. (eds.), *Cities and Society*. Glencoe, Ill.: The Free Press, 1957, pp. 237–247.

13. Form, William H., *et al.* "The Compatibility of Alternative Approaches to the Delimitation of Urban Sub-areas," *American Sociological Review*, Vol. 19 (August 1954), pp. 434–440.

14. Fromm, Erich. *The Sane Society*. New York: Rinehart & Co., Inc., 1955.

15. Gans, Herbert J. *The Urban Villagers: A Study of the Second Generation Italians in the West End of Boston*. Boston: Center for Community Studies, December 1959 (mimeographed).

16. Gans, Herbert J. "Planning and Social Life: An Evaluation of Friendship and Neighbor Relations in Suburban Communities," *Journal of the American Institute of Planners*, Vol. 27 (May 1961), pp. 134–140.

17. Greer, Scott. "Urbanism Reconsidered: A Comparative Study of Local Areas in a Metropolis," *American Sociological Review*, Vol. 21 (February 1956), pp. 19–25.

18. Greer, Scott. "The Social Structure and Political Process of Suburbia," *American Sociological Review*, Vol. 25 (August 1960), pp. 514–526.

19. Greer, Scott, and Ella Kube. "Urbanism and Social Structure: A Los Angeles Study," in Marvin B. Sussman (ed.), *Community Structure and Analysis*. New York: Thomas Y. Crowell Company, 1959, pp. 93–112.

20. Janowitz, Morris. *The Community Press in an Urban Setting*. Glencoe, Ill.: The Free Press, 1952.

21. Jonassen, Christen T. *The Shopping Center Versus Downtown*. Columbus, Ohio: Bureau of Business Research, Ohio State University, 1955.

22. Ktsanes, Thomas, and Leonard Reissman. "Suburbia: New Homes for Old Values," *Social Problems*, Vol. 7 (Winter 1959–60), pp. 187–194.

23. Reiss, Albert J., Jr. "An Analysis of Urban Phenomena," in Robert M. Fisher (ed.), *The Metropolis in Modern Life*. Garden City, N.Y.: Doubleday & Company, Inc., 1955, pp. 41–49.

24. Reiss, Albert J., Jr. "Rural–Urban and Status Differences in Interpersonal Contacts," *American Journal of Sociology,* Vol. 65 (September 1959), pp. 182–195.

25. Riesman, David. "The Suburban Sadness," in William M. Dobriner (ed.), *The Suburban Community.* New York: G. P. Putnam's Sons, 1958, pp. 375–408.

26. Rose, Arnold M. "Living Arrangements of Unattached Persons," *American Sociological Review,* Vol. 12 (August 1947), pp. 429–435.

27. Seeley, John R. "The Slum: Its Nature, Use and Users," *Journal of the American Institute of Planners,* Vol. 25 (February 1959), pp. 7–14.

28. Smith, Joel, William Form, and Gregory Stone. "Local Intimacy in a Middle-Sized City," *American Journal of Sociology,* Vol. 60 (November 1954), pp. 276–284.

29. Spectorsky, A. C. *The Exurbanites.* Philadelphia: J. B. Lippincott Co., 1955.

30. Stone, Gregory P. "City Shoppers and Urban Identification: Observations on the Social Psychology of City Life," *American Journal of Sociology,* Vol. 60 (July 1954), pp. 36–45.

31. Strauss, Anselm. "The Changing Imagery of American City and Suburb," *Sociological Quarterly,* Vol. 1 (January 1960), pp. 15–24.

32. Vernon, Raymond. *The Changing Economic Function of the Central City.* New York: Committee on Economic Development, Supplementary Paper No. 1, January 1959.

33. Vidich, Arthur J., and Joseph Bensman. *Small Town in Mass Society: Class, Power and Religion in a Rural Community.* Princeton, N.J.: Princeton University Press, 1958.

34. Wattell, Harold. "Levittown: A Suburban Community," in William M. Dobriner (ed.), *The Suburban Community.* New York: G. P. Putnam's Sons, 1958, pp. 287–313.

35. Whyte, William F., Jr. *Street Corner Society.* Chicago: The University of Chicago Press, 1955.

36. Whyte, William F., Jr. *The Organization Man.* New York: Simon & Schuster, 1956.

37. Wilensky, Harold L. "Life Cycle, Work, Situation and Participation in Formal Associations," in Robert W. Kleemeier, *et al.* (eds.), *Aging and Leisure: Research Perspectives on the Meaningful Use of Time.* New York: Oxford University Press, 1961, Chapter 8.

38. Wilensky, Harold L., and Charles Lebeaux. *Industrial Society and Social Welfare.* New York: Russell Sage Foundation, 1958.

39. Wirth, Louis. *The Ghetto.* Chicago: The University of Chicago Press, 1928.

40. Wirth, Louis. "Urbanism as a Way of Life," *American Journal of Sociology,* Vol. 44 (July 1938), pp. 1–24. Reprinted in Paul Hatt and Albert J. Reiss, Jr. (eds.), *Cities and Society.* Glencoe, Ill.: The Free Press, 1957, pp. 46–64. [All page references are to this reprinting of the article.]

41. Young, Michael, and Peter Willmott. *Family and Kinship in East London.* London: Routledge & Kegan Paul, Ltd., 1957.

A B C D E F G H I J   9 8 7 6 5 4 3 2 1